Wightman
Eastgate
Elsom
Fitzgerald
Hotop
Irvine
McLaren
Meates
Bowden
Bremner
Davis
Skeen
Bagley
Clark
Loader
Woods
Clarke
Dalzell
Freebairn
Hemi
Jones
Oliver
White
Wilson
Bowers
Dixon
O'Dea
Archer
Irwin
Smith
Stuart
Townsend
Vodanovich
Walsh
Gray
Katene
Brown
Buxton
Gill
McIntosh
Vincent
McAramney
MacEwan
Young
Clarke
Lineen
McMullen
Meads
Watt
Whineray
Gillespie
Levien
Molloy
Pickering
Soper
Cossey
Coughlan
Graham
Ashby
Clarke
Finlay
McPhail
Urbahn
Briscoe
Caulton
Conway
Diack
McCullough
Jermain
Cobb
Anderson
Curry
Davies
Graham
Horsley
Laidlaw
Sullivan
Stapleton
Cameron
Nesbit
Moon
Manor
Kay
Leadbeater
Wolfe
le
Barry
Leighton

- 625: Rod Heeps
- 626: Jules Le Lievre
- 627: Waka Nathan
- 628: Bruce Watt
- 629: Raymond Moreton
- 630: John Morrissey
- 631: Keith Nelson
- 632: Mack Herewini
- 633: Barry Thomas
- 634: Ian Uttley
- 635: Malcolm Dick
- 636: Ken Gray
- 637: Brian Lochore
- 638: Allan Stewart
- 639: Derek Arnold
- 640: Bill Davis
- 641: Chris Laidlaw
- 642: Ian MacRae
- 643: John Major
- 644: Ian Smith
- 645: Earle Kirton
- 646: Donald Clark
- 647: John Collins
- 648: Bruce McLeod
- 649: Mick Williment
- 650: Peter Murdoch
- 651: Ron Rangi
- 652: Bill Birtwistle
- 653: Fergie McCormick
- 654: Jack Hazlett
- 655: Sid Going
- 656: Brian Muller
- 657: Sam Strahan
- 658: Wayne Cottrell
- 659: Arthur Jennings
- 660: Grahame Thorne
- 661: Murray Wills
- 662: Phil Clarke
- 663: Alister Hopkinson
- 664: Tony Steel
- 665: Gerald Kember
- 666: Ian Kirkpatrick
- 667: Alan Smith
- 668: Graham Williams
- 669: Michael Knight
- 670: Alan Sutherland
- 671: Bill Currey
- 672: Peter Johns
- 673: Tom Lister
- 674: Terry McCashin
- 675: Tony Kreft
- 676: Mick O'Callaghan
- 677: Owen Stephens
- 678: George Skudder
- 679: Jake Burns
- 680: James Hendrie
- 681: Bevan Holmes
- 682: Bruce Hunter
- 683: Buff Milner
- 684: Neil Thimbleby
- 685: Blair Furlong
- 686: Keith Murdoch
- 687: Ron Urlich
- 688: Alex Wyllie
- 689: Bryan Williams
- 690: Bob Burgess
- 691: Ken Carrington
- 692: Richie Guy
- 693: Alan McNaughton
- 694: Tane Norton
- 695: Peter Whiting
- 696: Howard Joseph
- 697: Laurie Mains
- 698: Mick Duncan
- 699: Phil Gard
- 700: Hamish Macdonald
- 701: Trevor Morris
- 702: Bruce Robertson
- 703: Graham Whiting
- 704: Lin Colling
- 705: John Dougan
- 706: Ian Eliason
- 707: Duncan Hales
- 708: Jeff Matheson
- 709: Mike Parkinson
- 710: Alistair Scown
- 711: Lyn Jaffray
- 712: Graham Sims
- 713: Joe Karam

- 714: Mark Sayers
- 715: Grant Batty
- 716: Andy Haden
- 717: Ian Hurst
- 718: Kent Lambert
- 719: Ian Stevens
- 720: Ken Stewart
- 721: Lindsay Clark
- 722: Sandy McNicol
- 723: Murray Jones
- 724: Terry Morrison
- 725: Bob Lendrum
- 726: Peter Sloane
- 727: John Callesen
- 728: Ash Gardiner
- 729: Bruce Gemmell
- 730: Lawrie Knight
- 731: Andy Leslie
- 732: Jon McLachlan
- 733: Joe Morgan
- 734: Duncan Robertson
- 735: Kerry Tanner
- 736: Bob Barber
- 737: Doug Bruce
- 738: Bill Bush
- 739: Graeme Crossman
- 740: Kevin Eveleigh
- 741: Greg Kane
- 742: Ken Going
- 743: Terry Mitchell
- 744: Bill Osborne
- 745: Lyn Davis
- 746: Neil Purvis
- 747: Kit Fawcett
- 748: Gary Seear
- 749: Brad Johnstone
- 750: Frank Oliver
- 751: Perry Harris
- 752: John Brake
- 753: Scott Cartwright
- 754: Stewart Cron
- 755: Kenneth Granger
- 756: Kevin Greene
- 757: Graham Mourie
- 758: Doug Rollerson
- 759: Pat Ryan
- 760: Paul Sapsford
- 761: John Spiers
- 762: Vance Stewart
- 763: Eddie Stokes
- 764: Richard Wilson
- 765: John Black
- 766: Stuart Conn
- 767: Merv Jaffray
- 768: John McEldowney
- 769: Greg Rowlands
- 770: Murray Taylor
- 771: Mark Taylor
- 772: Stu Wilson
- 773: Colin Farrell
- 774: Brian Ford
- 775: Bevan Wilson
- 776: John Ashworth
- 777: Andy Dalton
- 778: Brian McKechnie
- 779: Dick Myers
- 780: Robbie Stuart
- 781: Mark Donaldson
- 782: Gary Knight
- 783: Barry Ashworth
- 784: Leicester Rutledge
- 785: John Fleming
- 786: Robert Kururangi
- 787: John Loveday
- 788: Ash McGregor
- 789: Clive Currie
- 790: Eddie Dunn
- 791: Dave Loveridge
- 792: Wayne Graham
- 793: Murray Watts
- 794: Gary Cunningham
- 795: Mike McCool
- 796: Lachie Cameron
- 797: Bernie Fraser
- 798: Murray Mexted
- 799: Barry Thompson
- 800: Mike Burgoyne
- 801: Kieran Keane
- 802: Rod Ketels

- 803: Tim Twigden
- 804: Allan Hewson
- 805: Geoff Hines
- 806: Wayne Smith
- 807: Brett Codlin
- 808: Graeme Higginson
- 809: Hika Reid
- 810: Mark Shaw
- 811: Stephen Scott
- 812: Nicky Allen
- 813: Grant Perry
- 814: Ken Bloxham
- 815: Andy Jefferd
- 816: Greg Burgess
- 817: Geoff Old
- 818: Jamie Salmon
- 819: Ken Taylor
- 820: Geoff Valli
- 821: Craig Wickes
- 822: Fred Woodman
- 823: Tu Wyllie
- 824: Hud Rickit
- 825: Steven Pokere
- 826: Frank Shelford
- 827: Gary Whetton
- 828: Andrew Donald
- 829: Wayne Neville
- 830: Jock Ross
- 831: Paul Koteka
- 832: Arthur Stone
- 833: Brian Morrissey
- 834: John Boe
- 835: Ian Dunn
- 836: Jock Hobbs
- 837: Warwick Taylor
- 838: Kevin Boroevich
- 839: Gary Braid
- 840: Scott Crichton
- 841: Robbie Deans
- 842: Craig Green
- 843: David Kirk
- 844: Alastair Robinson
- 845: Bruce Smith
- 846: Brett Wilson
- 847: Albert Anderson
- 848: Kieran Crowley
- 849: Murray Davie
- 850: Brian McGrattan
- 851: Mike Clamp
- 852: Murray Pierce
- 853: Alan Whetton
- 854: John Kirwan
- 855: Kawhena Woodman
- 856: Mark Finlay
- 857: Grant Fox
- 858: John Mills
- 859: Bruce Hemara
- 860: Wayne Shelford
- 861: Kurt Sherlock
- 862: Steve McDowall
- 863: Bryce Robins
- 864: Victor Simpson
- 865: John Drake
- 866: Frano Botica
- 867: Mike Brewer
- 868: Mark Brooke-Cowden
- 869: Greg Cooper
- 870: Andy Earl
- 871: Sean Fitzpatrick
- 872: Brett Harvey
- 873: Gordon Macpherson
- 874: Joe Stanley
- 875: Terry Wright
- 876: Brent Anderson
- 877: Michael Speight
- 878: Marty Berry
- 879: John Gallagher
- 880: Dean Kenny
- 881: Richard Loe
- 882: Michael Jones
- 883: Zinzan Brooke
- 884: Bernie McCahill
- 885: Graeme Bachop
- 886: John Buchan
- 887: Matthew Cooper
- 888: Robbie McLean
- 889: John Schuster
- 890: Paul Simonsson
- 891: Bruce Deans

- 902: Ian Jones
- 903: Matthew Ridge
- 904: Kevin Schuler
- 905: John Timu
- 906: Rob Gordon
- 907: Laurence Hullena
- 908: Simon Mannix
- 909: Paul McGahan
- 910: Olo Brown
- 911: Chris Tregaskis
- 912: Mark Carter
- 913: Jon Preston
- 914: Jason Hewett
- 915: Frank Bunce
- 916: Mark Cooksley
- 917: Richard Turner
- 918: Arran Pene
- 919: Eroni Clarke
- 920: Jamie Joseph
- 921: Blair Larsen
- 922: Ant Strachan
- 923: Graham Dowd
- 924: Robin Brooke
- 925: Stephen Bachop
- 926: Marc Ellis
- 927: Eric Rush
- 928: Pat Lam
- 929: Dallas Seymour
- 930: Glenn Taylor
- 931: Craig Dowd
- 932: Lee Stensness
- 933: Mark Allen
- 934: Stu Forster
- 935: Jeff Wilson
- 936: Liam Barry
- 937: Richard Fromont
- 938: Norm Hewitt
- 939: Shane Howarth
- 940: John Mitchell
- 941: Jonah Lomu
- 942: Alama Ieremia
- 943: Josh Kronfeld
- 944: Andrew Mehrtens
- 945: Glen Osborne
- 946: Simon Culhane
- 947: Todd Blackadder
- 948: Justin Marshall
- 949: Taine Randell
- 950: Tabai Matson
- 951: Carlos Spencer
- 952: Christian Cullen
- 953: Scott McLeod
- 954: Adrian Cashmore
- 955: Con Barrell
- 956: Andrew Blowers
- 957: Ofisa Tonu'u
- 958: Chresten Davis
- 959: Phil Coffin
- 960: Anton Oliver
- 961: Tana Umaga
- 962: Charles Riechelmann
- 963: Jeremy Stanley
- 964: Todd Miller
- 965: Mark Robinson
- 966: Steve Surridge
- 967: Aaron Hopa
- 968: Gordon Slater
- 969: Mark Mayerhofler
- 970: Caleb Ralph
- 971: Carl Hoeft
- 972: Isitolo Maka
- 973: Jodi Vidiri
- 974: Scott Robertson
- 975: Royce Willis
- 976: Norm Berryman
- 977: Kees Meeuws
- 978: Xavier Rush
- 979: Pita Alatini
- 980: Tony Brown

- Troy Flavell
- 991: Greg Somerville
- 992: Doug Howlett
- 993: Filo Tiatia
- 994: Ron Cribb
- 995: Leon MacDonald
- 996: Mark Robinson
- 997: Bruce Reihana
- 998: Jason O'Halloran
- 999: Marty Holah
- 1000: Carl Hayman
- 1001: Mark Ranby
- 1002: Jerry Collins
- 1003: Chris Jack
- 1004: Ben Blair
- 1005: Dave Hewett
- 1006: David Hill
- 1007: Simon Maling
- 1008: Nathan Mauger
- 1009: Paul Miller
- 1010: Roger Randle
- 1011: Dion Waller
- 1012: Tom Willis
- 1013: Aaron Mauger
- 1014: Richie McCaw
- 1015: Joe McDonnell
- 1016: Sam Harding
- 1017: Sam Broomhall
- 1018: Steve Devine
- 1019: Andrew Hore
- 1020: Keith Lowen
- 1021: Keith Robinson
- 1022: Ali Williams
- 1023: Danny Lee
- 1024: Brad Mika
- 1025: Tony Woodcock
- 1026: Keven Mealamu
- 1027: Daniel Braid
- 1028: Rodney So'oialo
- 1029: Regan King
- 1030: Paul Steinmetz
- 1031: Ma'a Nonu
- 1032: Joe Rokocoko
- 1033: Mils Muliaina
- 1034: Dan Carter
- 1035: Brad Thorn
- 1036: Corey Flynn
- 1037: Ben Atiga
- 1038: Jono Gibbes
- 1039: Nick Evans
- 1040: Sam Tuitupou
- 1041: Craig Newby
- 1042: Mose Tuiali'i
- 1043: Rico Gear
- 1044: Conrad Smith
- 1045: Saimone Taumoepeau
- 1046: Jimmy Cowan
- 1047: Steven Bates
- 1048: Casey Laulala
- 1049: Piri Weepu
- 1050: Jerome Kaino
- 1051: James Ryan
- 1052: Sitiveni Sivivatu
- 1053: Derren Witcombe
- 1054: Sosene Anesi
- 1055: Sione Lauaki
- 1056: Campbell Johnstone
- 1057: Luke McAlister
- 1058: Kevin Senio
- 1059: Chris Masoe
- 1060: Neemia Tialata
- 1061: Angus Macdonald
- 1062: John Afoa
- 1063: Jason Eaton
- 1064: Isaia Toeava
- 1065: Clarke Dermody
- 1066: Greg Rawlinson
- 1067: Scott Hamilton
- 1068: Andrew Ellis
- 1069: Brendon Leonard

- Filipo
- Schwalger
- Anthony Tuitavake
- Thomson
- Anthony Boric
- en Donald
- rd Kahui
- Wulf
- 1078: Kevin O'Neill
- 1079: Hosea Gear
- 1080: Cory Jane
- 1081: Jamie Mackintosh
- 1082: Liam Messam
- 1083: Kieran Read
- 1084: Ben Franks
- 1085: Scott Waldrom
- 1086: Hikawera Elliot
- 1087: Alby Mathewson
- 1088: Isaac Ross
- 1089: Tanerau Latimer
- 1090: Bryn Evans
- 1091: Wyatt Crockett
- 1092: Lelia Masaga
- 1093: George Whitelock
- 1094: Owen Franks
- 1095: Aled de Malmanche
- 1096: Tom Donnelly
- 1097: Zac Guildford
- 1098: Mike Delany
- 1099: Tamati Ellison
- 1100: Ben Smith
- 1101: Israel Dagg
- 1102: Benson Stanley
- 1103: Victor Vito
- 1104: Sam Whitelock
- 1105: Aaron Cruden
- 1106: Rene Ranger
- 1107: Colin Slade
- 1108: Sonny Bill Williams
- 1109: Jarrad Hoeata
- 1110: Brodie Retallick
- 1111: Julian Savea
- 1112: Aaron Smith
- 1113: Sam Cane
- 1114: Luke Romano
- 1115: Beauden Barrett
- 1116: Charlie Faumuina
- 1117: Dane Coles
- 1118: Tawera Kerr-Barlow
- 1119: Ben Afeaki
- 1120: Jeremy Thrush
- 1121: Steve Luatua
- 1122: Charles Piutau
- 1123: Matt Todd
- 1124: Ryan Crotty
- 1125: Tom Taylor
- 1126: Francis Saili
- 1127: Dominic Bird
- 1128: Frank Halai
- 1129: Luke Whitelock
- 1130: Jeffery Toomaga-Allen
- 1131: Malakai Fekitoa
- 1132: TJ Perenara
- 1133: Patrick Tuipulotu
- 1134: Joe Moody
- 1135: Nathan Harris
- 1136: Augustine Pulu
- 1137: James Parsons
- 1138: George Moala
- 1139: Nepo Laulala
- 1140: Brad Weber
- 1141: Charlie Ngatai
- 1142: Waisake Naholo
- 1143: Codie Taylor
- 1144: James Broadhurst,
- 1145: Lima Sopoaga
- 1146: Nehe Milner-Skudder
- 1147: Ardie Savea
- 1148: Seta Tamanivalu
- 1149: Elliot Dixon
- 1150: Ofa Tu'ungafasi
- 1151: Liam Squire

BEHIND THE SILVER FERN

TONY JOHNSON

LYNN McCONNELL

POLAR:S
PUBLISHING

ARENA
SPORT

mower

First published in 2016 by
POLARIS PUBLISHING LTD
c/o Turcan Connell
Princes Exchange
1 Earl Grey Street
Edinburgh
EH3 9EE

in association with

ARENA SPORT
An imprint of Birlinn Limited
West Newington House
10 Newington Road
Edinburgh
EH9 1QS

and

MOWER BOOKS, A DIVISION OF UPSTART PRESS LTD
B3, 72 Apollo Drive, Rosedale,
Auckland 0632, P.O. Box 302-749,
North Harbour, Auckland 0751,
New Zealand

www.polarispublishing.com
www.arenasportbooks.co.uk
www.upstartpress.co.nz

ARENA SPORT/ POLARIS PUBLISHING HARDBACK ISBN: 9781909715424
MOWER BOOKS TRADE PAPERBACK ISBN: 9781927262863
EBOOK ISBN: 9780857903334

British Library Cataloguing-in-Publication Data
A catalogue record for this book is available from the British Library

Designed and typeset by Polaris Publishing, Edinburgh

Printed and bound by arrangement with Asia Pacific Offset

CONTENTS

ACKNOWLEDGEMENTS

Firstly thanks to my colleague Lynn McConnell for being calm and organised through the whole process . . . one of us needed to be.

To Peter Burns at Polaris Publishing and Arena Sport, thank you for this wonderful opportunity. To my wife Sarah and daughter Lily for their love, encouragement and patience.

To Sarah Johnstone at Taonga, a special acknowledgement of your help in accessing the treasure trove that is New Zealand's sound archive. Likewise to SKY TV (NZ) for access to their library, and to my friends Charlie Stone and Paul Neazor for their help.

Thank you to the players who recognised the scope of this project and so willingly shared their experiences.

For my part, this book is dedicated to everyone who pulled on the black jersey with the silver fern, but to three in particular. To my late and much missed friend John Drake, and to two great figures of New Zealand rugby who passed away during the time of writing, Jerry Collins and Jonah Lomu.

TJ

With thanks to my wife Barbara, to Gregor Paul, Tony Johnson, Ron Palenski, John Griffiths and to all those All Blacks who made themselves available for an hour or two to revisit past campaigns and to share their thoughts.

LM

INTRODUCTION

PUT SIMPLY, THE question is how?

How has a country so isolated, so sparsely populated, been able, for so long, to achieve such ascendancy in a sport, over rivals with far greater population bases, and far superior financial, social and scientific resources?

It is often said that rugby suits New Zealanders. It appealed not only to British and Irish immigrants but also to the Maori who arrived before the great European migration. Rugby was a unifying factor between races. It also has massive appeal with those of Pacific Island origins who now make up around seven per cent of the New Zealand population. New Zealand's Chief Justice Sir Richard Wild, himself a New Zealand Universities representative, said at the New Zealand Rugby Union seventy-fifth Jubilee dinner: 'Our young men of that time [rugby's earliest days in NZ] not far removed from pioneering, needed a game that sharpened their senses and challenged their will; that demanded all their energy and exhausted all their vigour. Rugby exactly suited our climate and our soil. It matched the temperament of the New Zealander and in large measure it has moulded our national character. It is the team element that provides a spur for the weaker spirit, a curb for the selfish – and a discipline for all. It treats every man as an equal from whatever background he comes. There is no yielding to status in a rugby tackle, no privilege in a scrum. It is just because rugby means what it does to New Zealanders that the All Black shines in the spotlight of public adulation – at least till he bumbles a pass . . . But fame brings responsibility and the All Black at the top does well to remember that he carries in his hands tremendous power for good or ill. He owes it to the game that gives him fame to set a standard of sensible, disciplined living.'

A member of what is regarded as the first New Zealand team, the 1884 side, Harry (later Sir Henry) Braddon had been schooled in rugby at Dulwich, emigrated to Tasmania where he became an Australian Rules player before moving to Invercargill in New Zealand to play rugby. He wrote presciently of the qualities that characterised rugby's hold on New Zealand. 'As a game it rewards accuracy far more than onlookers realise. The slightest fumble or stumble makes all the difference: and the split second often differentiates a score from a missed opportunity. There is much store for skilled generalship: and, in the matter of tactics, a novel method of attack, carefully rehearsed, easily may turn the scale. Sound teamwork is perhaps the best feature of all – when the players are mainly concerned that the side shall score. Spectators instantly appreciate unselfish play: and as instantly denounce overdone individualism. After all, the game is a good school for later life – where sound teamwork may seem so much in so many directions. The readiness to sacrifice self for the side is of the very essence of loyalty and patriotism. Many lasting friendships trace back to that football era.'

It might have been Steve Hansen or Richie McCaw making the comments – some things about New Zealand's approach have never changed.

As one of the youngest societies to embrace professional sports culture, New Zealand was expected to be at a disadvantage to nations for whom professional sport was more than one hundred years old, such as England, Scotland, Wales, Ireland, France and Australia.

Amateurism was ingrained in New Zealand society and maintained by zealous administrators. No one was immune as one of the great captains of the All Blacks, Graham Mourie, found out when forced to forego his amateur status in order to profit from his biography. Yet, it was the ultimate compliment to the All Blacks that they were described as 'the most professional amateur team' in the world. When the game went professional in 1995 New Zealand not only defied predictions they would suffer, they improved their winning percentage.

New Zealanders have always seen sport as a means to stand up and be counted. For so long acquiescent in its colonial relationship with Britain, New Zealand even allowed the myth of the origin of the label 'All Blacks' to be attributed to an English newspaper when modern research has shown the term had already been used for some years before the famous 1905-06 tour. It was British history, therefore it had to be New Zealand's history. It didn't have its own seat on the International Rugby Board until 1948. There was both a wariness of Britain, yet an aversion to letting go the colonial apron strings – a situation eventually forced upon New Zealand in the 1970s when Britain joined the European Common Market.

The distance from the game's lawmakers allowed scope for innovation, as settlers felt the distant authorities ruled paternally on matters of the law and its application. One such innovation was the 2-3-2 scrum and the wing forward. This tactic allowed quick clearance of scrum ball while the wing forward roved freely instead of being bound to the scrum. It gave New Zealand an advantage until it was undone by the power of South African scrummaging in 1928 and while rulings were invoked to pressure New Zealand to abandon the method, much of the opposition already came from within New Zealand, and it was this paternalistic interference from Britain, that fuelled the sense of subservience to the rulers of the game. While the 2-3-2 scrum, and rucking as practised until the 1960s, were eventually lost to the game, the innovation gene persisted. There was also the attitude to winning which, as the population grew, became an extra incentive to succeed. That attitude was personified by the vice-captain of the 1905-06 All Blacks Billy Stead who said at the side's fiftieth Jubilee dinner: 'I reckon there's no game if you haven't got the desire to win, it's not a game. It's that desire to win that nerves up your spectators to urge you on. It nerves you yourself to give of your best. You can't play a game of cards if you don't want to win. There's nothing in any game if you haven't got the desire to beat your opponent.'

A natural pyramid coaching structure based around graduated improvement at club, sub-union, provincial and inter-island level became the basis of development in New Zealand rugby long before it was employed in other countries. It wasn't always successful. Administrators were appointed on a platform of parochialism, expected to look out for the 'interests' of their region. This self-interest, coupled with the egotism that often clogged the system, resulted in travesties such as the failure to select Otago man Vic Cavanagh as coach of the 1949 team to South Africa and the constant interference that forced Fred Allen to walk away from the job in 1968 in spite of having the best record of any New Zealand coach. The first may have cost New Zealand a series in South Africa in 1949, the latter quite probably the 1970 series in South Africa.

In having coach John Hart, with his background in industrial workplace management, New Zealand was ideally equipped to make a rapid transformation when the amateur laws were eased for the 1996 season. Public attitudes were slow to catch up by comparison and it was nearly twenty years before the demands of professionalism were fully obvious to the New Zealand public. The public demand for success only increased with professionalism, and failure, particularly at the World Cup, provoked some bitter recriminations, most notably affecting Hart. But by making a stand against the 'sack the coach mentality' in 2007 when New Zealand experienced their worst Cup campaign, the administrators forced a change of attitude on a public that had to be pulled screaming and shouting, usually through talkback radio, into the modern world. That stance was vindicated during the 2011 Cup campaign when New Zealand held out France 8-7 to win their second Cup, a success that allowed the coaching structure a breadth of vision and tactics to carry New Zealand in triumph through the 2015 World Cup campaign where victory was achieved by a quality of rugby that no winning World Cup team had hitherto managed. This time, no one quibbled with New Zealand's right to be world champions, to be the first to win the World Cup three times and to be the first team to win consecutive World Cups. The campaign may have achieved different results than envisioned by those coaches of earlier years, but were the end result of all that had gone before.

As successful as the All Blacks have been internationally, they have sometimes achieved this success in spite of themselves. At other times defeat has occurred when it might otherwise have been avoided. Selection debacles have denied players their rightful places, again a reflection of the parochialism that can clog the game's arteries. There has been a natural but often damaging rivalry with colonial cousins South Africa, one having acknowledged the role of her native race in her constitutional creation as a nation, the other subjugating her several native peoples by unofficial means before enshrining the attitude in apartheid law. New Zealand's tacit role was shameful, and something that could have been eliminated at the first instance of contention – in 1919, and not two years later as many aver. In time the relationship would divide New Zealanders like no other issue. Not only were lessons unheeded, an unprecedented rebel tour took place, further antagonising a growing anti-rugby element in New Zealand society. Only the advent of a World Cup, an event vigorously pursued by the Anzac partners in the face of Home Nations inertia, eased the assault on the game's image. The result is there for all to see in the modern rugby game.

In compiling this book, and the countless interviews involved in telling the story of the All Blacks through their own words, it is clear that New Zealand has not always been the beneficiary of enlightened coaching. Many All Blacks complained of a lack of any meaningful coaching from 'assistant managers' who were given a tour by the game's administrative masters as reward for a job well done around the board table, or in other areas of the game. Change first occurred when Fred Allen had the side in 1966-68, and through the reigns of JJ Stewart, Jack Gleeson and Eric Watson. But it wasn't until the mid-1980s when Sir Brian Lochore took over that coaching as it is now known occurred. What this highlights is that the All Blacks' success was achieved in spite of these impediments. That speaks more of the attitude of the participants toward the game, of their failure to bow down to the great names and institutions they were up against, and of a fierce desire to do well by their country. What the players learned was the ability to work together to sort out issues. That was the element taken back to clubs. Just as Sir Peter Blake and Sir Russell Coutts overcame all the know-how of NASA's computers in their 1995 America's Cup success, just as Arthur Lydiard master-minded an athletics formula that saw New Zealand dominate world middle-distance running in the 1960s, so the All Blacks reflected the attitude of their countrymen. The All Blacks were the sporting equivalent of the largely volunteer armies of two World Wars described by esteemed British military historian Sir John Keegan as the troops of the twentieth century – the difference being the All Blacks achieved their greatness by virtue of an unprecedented level of consistency which expanded as the needs, and laws, of the game required.

It has almost become a cliché for modern players to talk about the 'legacy of the jersey', of the impermanence of the number they wear on their back before it is passed on and of the desire to leave the game in better shape than when they were introduced to it. As big a driving factor is public expectation. New Zealand demands success of the All Blacks, and as long as that demand is there, they will strive to maintain that success, and to continue to evolve their game. This is their story.

Tony Johnston
Lynn McConnell
Auckland 2016

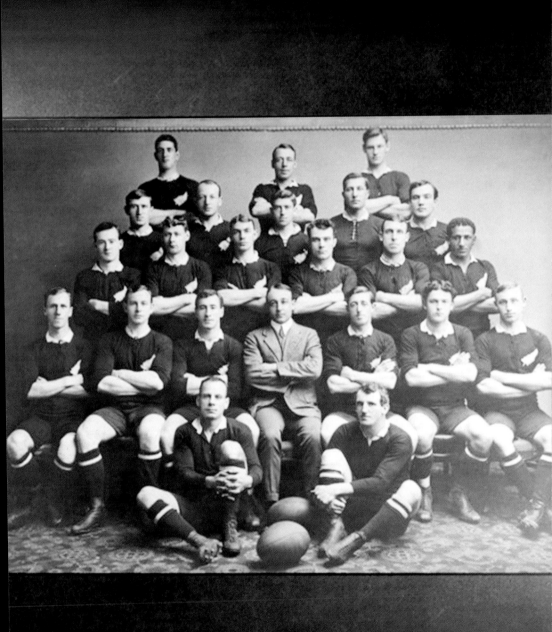

ONE

BEGINNINGS

'The visit of the Native team gave a great fillip to
rugby football throughout Great Britain'

NO PRECISE DATE on which rugby took root in New Zealand has been identified and there is evidence in various quarters of footballing games of different sorts being played around the country during the 1860s with gold miners playing Australian Rules on the Otago goldfields and of Auckland-based Irishmen playing a type of football, without goalposts or records kept, in the late-1860s. What is accepted as an agreed starting point is a game between Nelson College and a Town team in Nelson on 14 May 1870. This resulted from a return to the region from Christ's College in London of Charles Monro who had played rugby. According to rugby historian Dr Ron Palenski in *Rugby, a New Zealand History*, Monro, and a Rugby School old boy Robert Tennent, made a suggestion to the headmaster of Nelson College, Frank Simmons that a shift to rugby rules should be made. The 14 May game resulted and then on 12 September that year, Nelson sent a team to Wellington to play a Petone side giving evidence of the first inter-district game. As communities grew, so did competition between them and rugby became a popular outlet. Auckland and Christchurch were early rivals playing a game in 1875. It wasn't long before entrepreneurs became involved. A team from New South Wales toured and played eight games in 1882 and then a first New Zealand side was mustered. Otago, Wellington and Auckland were asked to provide five players each while four were to be from Canterbury. One of the team members Harry Braddon, later Sir Henry, said: 'Early in 1884 the New Zealand Rugby Union [sic – it wasn't formed until 1892] decided to despatch to New South Wales – for a tour of eight matches – the first great "All Black" team to leave New Zealand. I sent in my name – was selected – and resigned at once from the bank[he was a bank clerk].

'The New Zealand "reps" played eight matches in New South Wales within two and a half weeks – and won them all. It was really rather too strenuous a campaign. We played the day after we arrived, in Parramatta, and three days later against New South Wales on the Saturday. Three matches the next week, including one at Newcastle, and the renewed "Test" at the weekend. Again, three matches in the succeeding week, with one at Bathurst, and the third and final NZ v NSW on the Saturday,' Braddon said. He did not return to New Zealand after the tour.

Harry Braddon (1884, 7 games): In Newcastle the [1884] team was banqueted after the match; and the chairman, a banker with New Zealand experience, rather boasted his knowledge of the Maori language. One of our 'reps' was Jack Taiaroa – a native prince in his full rights – an undergraduate of Dunedin University [Otago] – a very likeable young man, and a fine footballer. The banker rather too persistently pressed Jack to speak

Opposite: The New Zealand team of 1894.

New Zealand's first rugby union representatives.
Back row: J. O'Donnell, H. Udy, G.S. Robertson, J. Allan, E.B. Millton, T. Ryan, J.R. Wilson
Middle row: J.G. Taiaroa, G. Carter, J.T. Dumbell, W.V. Millton (captain), H.Y. Braddon,
G.H.N. Helmore, P.P. Webb, S. Sleigh (manager)
Front row: E. Davy, J.G. Lecky, J.A. Warbrick, H. Roberts
Absent: T.B. O'Connor

in Maori, and very reluctantly the latter finally consented. He addressed us very quietly for about three minutes: and the only other member of our team who understood the language was convulsed with suppressed laughter. The banker warmly thanked 'Prince Taiaroa' for all the nice things he said about Newcastle hospitality, and about the match: and again the lingual expert nearly suffocated. Then the murder leaked out. Jack had said the Lord's Prayer in Maori! The New Zealand team of 1884 – the first of the great 'All Black' combinations – stands out in my recollections like a peak above the foothills. A fine team – good sportsmen – and no needless roughness . . . Long passing was in its infancy in those days: and our team was credited with teaching New South Wales something of the novelty. We played three 'three-quarters', and therefore one more forward in the 'scrum': otherwise the game was very much as it is now – conceding some improvements in 'passing' and tactics.

Another New South Wales (NSW) team toured in 1886 while a British team toured in 1888, in two sections, the first in April-May and the second in September but no game was played against a national selection. A New Zealand Native team, of twenty-six players – five of them European – toured Australia and Britain in 1888-89. Before reaching Britain they played eleven games, and then on their way home they played another thirty-three games – including eleven games of Australian Rules, all over the space of fourteen months away from home. Games were not regarded as New Zealand appearances.

Joe Warbrick (1884, 7 games): Auckland contains a population of 35,000. Out of that number 16,000 assemble on the football field when fixtures are played. That, of course, is the Rugby game. Hardly anybody goes to see it [soccer]. Don't think me biased or selfish, but I can assure you that the only men who play the Association game are fellows who can't make their way with the other code – in fact, broken-down Rugbyites. Our original intention was to keep it a purely Native team. But my 'smash' altered affairs. The [four] Englishmen, however, really belong to us, for they were all born in New Zealand. Our proper title is: 'The New Zealand Native Football Team'. But we don't object to 'Maori'.

Tom Ellison (1893, 7 games): I was not very deeply impressed with the play of the Britishers; for, with all the players they had available, I saw no one to compare with Jack Taiaroa, J. Warbrick, Whiteside, Keogh and Co., except Lockwood, Stoddart, Valentine, Bonsor, and a very few others. Their play generally was of the one style and description, from start to finish – hooking, heeling out, and passing all day long, whether successful at it or not. I never played against a team that made any radical change of tactics, during the course of a game . . . We met the best forwards in Yorkshire, where they could pick, I suppose, one hundred to our one. They were generally big, strong fellows, but they never struck me as being clever players. On the lineout they were generally inferior to our men, who were not particularly good. In the scrum we invariably beat the best English packs, not through having better men, but through our more scientific system of packing the scrum, and having specialists in each position, instead of merely fine all-round men; the result being that our two front-rankers, for instance, simply buried the two Jacks-of-all-trades who happened to be pitted against them in the different scrums. Their backs were generally no better than ours, except the Yorkshire County, and All-England Teams, but, it must be remembered, that after our first few matches, we were never able to put our best team in the field; somebody or other inevitably being either on the sick or injured list.

The 1888 team before their tour to England.

George Williams (NZ Natives team): Although it may be thought that England had nothing to learn from us at Rugby in 1888, it is a fact that the tactics of the Native team in playing three halfbacks and only eight forwards were not adopted until witnessing our play, and that they approved such tactics is apparent, as they were adopted by some of the best clubs. The visit of the Native team and the reputation it gained gave a great fillip to Rugby football throughout Great Britain during our stay there . . . In certain parts of the North of England the public expected to see a tribe of black fellows. As a genuine nigger could not be numbered in the team it looked almost like a fraud to expect the British public to believe that these were typical specimens of the New Zealand aboriginal. In order to try to keep faith the team, on one occasion, purchased a number of black masks. Whenever the train on which they were travelling pulled up at a station the players donned these Guy Fawkes masks and peered out of the carriage windows on the expectant crowds who had assembled to see the black fellows from New Zealand. In the first match on the tour the Native team appeared in their flax mats and armed with meres, and gave their war cry: 'Ake, Ake! Kia Kaha!' which, being interpreted, means 'Be strong.' This pantomime was ridiculed by a section of the English press, and the mats and meres were afterwards discarded.

Tom Ellison: The best team we met in England was undoubtedly the Yorkshire County team, who gave us a big beating, and who could have beaten our best team in its best form, owing to the all-round superiority of their backs. The All-England team of that year was inferior, in my opinion, to the Yorkists, and should never have won the game against us so easily, but for three early and distinctly erroneous and depressing decisions of the referee, Mr. G. Rowland Hill.

The first was awarding a try to England after the ball had been made dead by W. Warbrick; the second, awarding another try to England after they had deliberately ceased mauling with H. Lee, and Lee had forced down . . . In the first instance Warbrick started to run the ball out, but, finding that some of the English forwards were within his goal-line, altered his mind and forced down, but immediately lost possession of the ball, upon which the Englishmen dropped, and claimed a try, which the referee immediately allowed. In the second, Lee failed to take the ball cleanly, and put a number of offside Britishers onside who immediately pounced on him, and three of them began a maul in goal. Lee quickly shook two of his opponents off, and the betting was certainly a sovereign to a crumb on Lee, when his opponent was advised to give up, which he gladly did, leaving Lee victor. As we strode out to restart the game – Great Heavens! the word came out that Lee's force-down had been awarded a try to England.

But both these were as nothing compared with what followed. Mr Stoddart made a fine dodgy run, and, after beating several of our men, I lured him into my arms by applying the feign dodge. By a quick wriggle, however, he escaped, but left a portion of his knickers in my possession. He dashed along, and the crowd roared; then, suddenly discovering what was the matter, he stopped, threw down the ball, and in an instant we had the vulgar gaze shut off by forming the usual ring around him; stopping play, of course, for the purpose. While we were thus engaged, Evershed, probably seeing an opening for a try, seized the opportunity and the ball, and flew for the goal-line, where Madigan put him down near the corner flag. We, of course, disputed the try, and, while the discussion was proceeding, Mr Evershed very boldly picked the ball up from the corner, and carried it between the goalposts and claimed a try there, which the referee very happily granted. It was at this juncture that three of our men, thoroughly disgusted at the treatment we were receiving, marched off the field. As to the alleged defect in our sportsmanlike qualities, I need only say that we played in all seventy-nine matches in England, of which we lost nineteen besides the All-England match, and, notwithstanding the inferiority of most of our opponents to the All-England team, we took all those beats with the utmost good spirit; and that a few weeks prior to the All-England match we met the Yorkshire County team, and took, without a murmur, the biggest beating we received in our whole tour (26 points to 6). Surely, such a record for seventy-nine matches is unique, and requires more than an attack based on one match, wherein there was abundant mitigating circumstances, to smudge!

With the formation of the New Zealand Rugby Football Union in 1892, the first official team left to tour Australia in 1893. Other tours followed in 1897 and 1901 while the first Test match was played, against Australia, at the Sydney Cricket Ground on 15 August 1903. A year later New Zealand hosted Great Britain at Athletic Park in Wellington.

Tom Ellison: The next very enjoyable part of my career was my trip to Australia in 1893, as captain of the first New Zealand team under the auspices of the New Zealand Rugby Union. The team chosen on that occasion was a fairly strong one, but not the strongest available in New Zealand, owing to the Southern Unions, except the South Canterbury Union, not being within the pale of the New Zealand Rugby Union. The game adopted, and recommended by the selectors of the team, was the wing-forward game.

After that tour contact between Australia and New Zealand became more common with Queensland touring New Zealand in 1896, playing six games, including an international won 9-0 by New Zealand, but it was not a fully representative team as Otago was in dispute with the NZRFU over the terms of their game with Queensland, and it was cancelled with a second game being organised with Canterbury. Otago's players were barred from playing for New Zealand. An eleven-match tour of NSW and Queensland by a New Zealand side was made in 1897. NSW were hosted in 1901. And in 1903 a full New Zealand tour of Australia was the forerunner to the first of the great tours.

Billy Wallace (1903-08, 11 Tests, 51 games): In 1903 I won my All Black cap and was selected to go to Australia. That team was, in my opinion, one of the best that has ever represented New Zealand. I remember that before we left New Zealand, we had been subjected to very severe criticism and were told that our defence was weak. Nevertheless, we played ten games, won them all and scored 276 points, while only 13 points were registered against us. Those of us who took part in the match against the New South Wales team that year are not likely to forget it for the game was played with the ground covered with a vast lake of water. The water was over our boot-tops and if we tried to kick the ball it would slither along the top of the water or perhaps spin around like a top.

I kicked the penalty goal that won the match but my luck was in because I was just able to strike a little mound in the ground where the water couldn't reach the ball. On the other hand, when we went to Brisbane, the ground was so hard that when a sweeping forward rush was in progress, we couldn't see the ball for dust. Buckets of water had been placed all round the ground, where the players could sponge their faces or moisten their lips. It was a memorable tour and laid the foundation for the success of the famous 1905 team which made such a reputation in the United Kingdom.

Billy Stead (1903-08, 7 Tests, 42 games): I think the 1903 team was the best team. Australia was very strong. They weren't easy, those matches. We had a magnificent team. We had Billy Wallace fullback, Opai Asher – I've never seen a better three-quarter myself. We had Duncan McGregor who made a name for himself a year later against Sivright's team, Morrie Wood, Jimmy Duncan and myself five-eighths. I was only a young lad, I had to work my way into that combination. Two halfbacks, Kiernan and Skinny Humphries of Taranaki, and a magnificent set of forwards and just as good a set as we picked from the best in 1905.

Billy Wallace: While we were in Sydney, two Victorian teams came across from Melbourne to try to start the Victorian (Australian Rules] game going in Sydney. They stayed at the same hotel as we did and, of course, we got into arguments, especially Jimmy Duncan. They reckoned we couldn't kick. 'Can't we?' said Jimmy. 'Well, you come out to the match tomorrow and we'll show you a kid who can kick.' The 'kid' Jimmy referred to was myself. They came out to the match and during the game, 'Skinny' Humphries took a mark on the halfway line. In those days, anybody in the team could take the kick and Jimmy called me up to take the shot at goal. I protested that the distance was too great, but Jimmy insisted and told me to show the Victorians what New Zealanders could do. There was no escape and so I came back about 11 yards behind the halfway line and placed the ball. The ball sailed straight and true, clean between the posts, at a great height, right over the dead ball line, over the heads of the crowd and landed behind them. It was the finest goal I have ever kicked. The crowd gasped and I think that the Victorians were satisfied. A very faint breeze was blowing at the time but it was practically of no assistance.

Billy Stead: I was honoured to be captain of the first New Zealand side to play Britain in a Test match [1904]. The result of that match I think really clinched a desire the [New Zealand Rugby Union] executive had in mind that our football had got to the degree where we should try out some of these great international sides.

Billy Wallace: We were on the ground about quarter to one to find one of the biggest crowds Athletic Park had ever held. The gate takings for the match were £2,114. Our team that day was: – Fullback: R. McGregor. Three-quarters: W.J. Wallace, E.T. Harper, D. McGregor. Five-eighths: M.E. Wood, J.W. Stead. Halfback: P. Harvey. Wing forward: D. Gallaher. Hookers: A. ('Paddy') McMinn and G.A. Tyler. Lock: B.J. Fanning. Side row: T. Cross and W.S. Glenn. Back row: C.E. Seeling and G.W. Nicholson.

Billy Stead: Having the wind against us, and anticipating an attack by the British backs, we went for a forward game, especially as our forwards were as fit as a fiddle, and, knowing that the Britishers, having had a pretty rough routine, were slightly stale at half-time. I was in fear of goals, but had no fear of their crossing our line. Our forwards went eyes out all through, and they are the finest forward team I have ever played behind. In the second spell they heeled out on only three occasions, from one of which we scored. Our plan was not to heel till we got right to the twenty-five, or in a good striking position. We made more ground by taking the ball and screwing the scrums.

Billy Wallace: In the first spell I kicked a penalty goal and, as Harding did likewise, we finished up at half-time three-all. Harding's was a wonderful kick, being against the wind . . . In the second spell we had to face the wind but by this time we were settling down and were playing better. About halfway through the spell, from some loose play, the ball was sent out to our backs who all handled it faultlessly until it came to Duncan McGregor, who, with a brilliant burst of speed, dashed down the touchline and dived over for a try about six inches in from the corner flag. The excitement was intense – hats, caps and umbrellas flying into the air, and I don't think that any of their owners regretted it if they did not see their headgear again. The same scene was renewed a few minutes later when Duncan, with another characteristic dash, scored another try in almost identically the same spot. And so we came off winners by 9 points to 3.

Billy Stead: I do not hold with their method of attack. They take too much risk in flinging the ball about anywhere. The only redeeming feature of their tactics is that they are fleet of foot enough to back up. We are taught to pass to a man, not to fling the ball away, but they don't look where they pass. They are not particular whether it goes back or forward.

Billy Wallace: At the dinner I sat next to Llewellyn, my opponent, whom I had to mark during the match and in our friendly chat I sympathised with him at the only defeat the team had sustained on tour. (They were afterward beaten by Auckland.) He told me he hoped I would be chosen to come over with the 1905 team and promised to give me a jolly good time. He kept his word too, and, strange to say, we sat together after the defeat in Wales, when he returned the compliment by sympathising with me in the only defeat we had suffered.

Not long after the British Test, on 2 October, Tom Ellison died. He played a significant role in the creation of New Zealand rugby's identity, he developed the highly-contentious wing-forward position and as a delegate to the first annual meeting of the NZRFU moved that the jersey for the national team be all black. His book *The Art of Rugby Football* was an early classic detailing the tour of Britain and Australia by the Native team.

TWO

THE ORIGINALS

'the cheering was renewed, in almost sufficient volume
to lift the roof off the universe'

THE LEGEND OF the All Blacks really begins with the great tour of 1905-06.

The 'Originals' left New Zealand unheralded in July of 1905, returning seven months later to heroes' welcomes, having taken the rugby world by storm.

They racked up an astonishing record, establishing the founding principles of the New Zealand game: skill, innovation, tactical acumen, athleticism and absolute physical commitment. The quest for a tour to the Home Unions gathered momentum early in the new century, as New Zealand began to play regularly against Australian state teams. Prohibiting factors were the costs, both logistical and personal, and doubts over the ability of a team from the sparsely-populated colony to provide worthy competition for the club and county teams of Britain, let alone their national sides. But the victory over Australia in 1903 strengthened the case, and by the time Great Britain arrived for a tour in 1904, the RFU had finally relented to the NZRFU requests.

The New Zealanders were given a financial guarantee from each match to cover a total tour cost expected to exceed £5,000. This included a three shilling per day allowance to each player. Three of the four Home Unions agreed to this arrangement, the dissenting voice being Scotland, who considered the per diem contravened rugby's amateur laws, whilst their reluctance to offer a cut of the gate reflected the views of the Scottish captain of the 1904 Great Britain team. 'Darkie' Bedell-Sivright suggested the New Zealanders would stand little chance in the internationals, although they 'would probably win most of the county matches.'

A six-match warm-up tour of New Zealand and Australia offered little idea of the success that would be achieved. Three players, including Dave Gallaher, were added to the squad. Patrick Harvey of Christchurch was a late withdrawal. He was one of a limited number of people in New Zealand proficient in the teaching of deaf children, and the Ministry of Education decided, with Prime Ministerial backing, that he could not be spared for the tour. Harvey became known as 'the unlucky one' and the team left with only one specialist scrum-half. The twenty-six players were managed by the Huddersfield-born George Dixon, with former captain Jimmy Duncan appointed coach. The captaincy fell to Gallaher. Gallaher was born in Ramelton in County Donegal. His family had endured hardship and tragedy since arriving in New Zealand but from those setbacks a strong leader of men had emerged. A capable horseman and a good shot, he had distinguished himself as a Sergeant-Major of the New Zealand Mounted Rifles during the Anglo-Boer War, and while not a great player, he was regarded by the NZRFU as the ideal captain. He was officially thirty-one years of age, although it's suspected he had 'shed' a couple of years following his tour of duty in South Africa.

Opposite: Dave Gallaher, captain of the 1905 'Originals'.

Only a few days into the voyage Gallaher became aware of a disgruntled faction, mainly Southerners, who disapproved of having a captain 'foisted' upon them by the NZRFU. They also believed their 'Old Man', Duncan, was being marginalised as coach by the Aucklanders in the team. Gallaher moved quickly, calling a meeting and offering to resign, as did his vice-captain Billy Stead. Stead was a Southlander, and the support of he and the team manager Dixon were telling factors in a hardly overwhelming 17-12 vote in favour of Gallaher.

From there on, Gallaher's leadership was never questioned, Stead became the strategist, coaching duties were shared amongst senior players and Duncan took residence in the shadows. Stead and Gallaher's post-tour book, *The Complete Rugby Footballer On The New Zealand System* would become a classic of its type, with many of its observations applicable even now.

The journey to England took forty-two days, arriving in Plymouth on 8 September. Hours were spent on maintaining fitness, and framing a tactical approach based on speed of movement and quick passing, complemented by a catalogue of set moves with code names, often in the Maori language.

Billy Stead: On Saturday [the sixth day out] at mid-day the glass went down with a thump, and within two hours the wind shifted around to north-west catching us on the larboard quarter, and then I realised the difference between a gale and a hurricane. The seas came up with a terrific roar . . . accompanying the hurricane were some terrific hail showers and the crew had great difficulty getting about, although lifelines were stretched all round the ship. Precisely at 9pm the wind chopped round to south-west and a tremendous sea, the first she had shipped so far, struck her on the starboard quarter (right on our cabins). It was a terrible shock. Portholes were smashed, all our cabins

The 1905 'Originals'.

flooded, people were knocked down, and we were wading about almost knee deep in the saloon which is on the hurricane deck.

Alex McDonald (1905-13, 8 Tests, 41 games): It was a pleasant tour, I enjoyed every minute of it. We were a happy band right through otherwise we couldn't have gone on the way we did . . . of course, the forwards and the backs would naturally take a bite at each other. We had one or two great wags in the team. Steve Casey [for] one, he was the life of the party. Jimmy Hunter never said much. If ever there was a second-five, you could give me Jimmy Hunter.

The All Blacks had an immediate test in Exeter against Devon, runners-up in the previous year's County Championship. What happened was greeted with disbelief. Playing under a scorching sun two players, George Gillett and Billy Wallace, wore hats, as the New Zealanders ran the county side ragged scoring twelve tries in a 55-4 thumping. Wallace, nicknamed 'Carbine' after the Melbourne Cup-winning racehorse, scored three tries while centre George Smith, a former champion athlete, netted four. They cut a swathe through Southern and Midland England.

Billy Wallace: From what we had seen the previous Saturday, we were quietly confident; but the Devon team had been well cracked up in the papers. It was our first game and much depended on it. We were feeling a bit jumpy, but were in good nick, and, as soon as the ball was properly in play, we lost our nervousness. That result was as great a sensation in England as I believe it was in New Zealand. Some papers, when they got the results, assumed that a mistake had been made in transmitting the scores and put them the other way round!

George Gillett (1905-08, 8 Tests, 39 games): We improved a bit as we went on our way, it just flowed along like a river. They could have just eased the teams a bit and found out exactly what talent they had in the team instead of wearing out those they already knew of. The injuries and sicknesses didn't help us in the harder matches towards the finish.

Billy Wallace: We worked out a scheme whereby we changed the team by three, and we worked that way where that three would stay in the team for six or seven games and as they came around they automatically followed one another, although we always had the right to pick our best team for the Tests. It was going lovely until we started to get men on the injured list. Bunny Abbott got a poisoned knee and had to lay-up, Jimmy O'Sullivan broke his collarbone, [George] Smith broke his collarbone. Several had pulled muscles and by the time we got to the end of the tour we had too many cripples just when we needed them most and we could never pick our best side.

George Tyler (1903-06, 7 Tests, 36 games): At first they [British referees] did not understand the inside foot hooking in the scrum, and penalised us; but when they dropped to our style and saw it was fair they were all right. We really enjoyed the trip, but found the continuous travelling monotonous. It meant packing and unpacking all the time.

Billy Wallace: There is just one more incident in connection with this [our] visit to Leicester which deserves mention. It concerns a joke which misfired. Bob Deans had slipped down to the bathroom one morning and left his door open. On the dressing table was a valuable gold watch and chain and a sovereign case belonging to him and as Billy Stead passed, he thought he would play a joke and expected Bob would raise a hue and cry. But not a word was said. After keeping it for a few days, Billy Stead said to him, 'Didn't you lose something at Leicester, Bob?' 'Yes, I did,' he replied. 'I lost my watch and chain and sovereign case.'

'Here it is,' said Billy, 'we were playing a joke on you. Why didn't you complain before?' 'Well,' said Bob, 'when I looked at the two housemaids I could see by their faces that they were honest girls and I knew no member of the team would take it so I just thought I would shut up and say nothing about it.' It is a small incident, but it will perhaps show the generous nature of the great-hearted Bob.

Bob Deans (1905-08, 5 Tests, 24 games): English football is not so good as we expected to find it. There are some good teams, notably Devonport Albion and Leicester, but the average team is not up to the standard of the best club teams in New Zealand. One reason for that may be that the season there is very much longer than it is here. It lasts nearly eight months, and naturally players lose their keenness.

Billy Wallace: George Nicholson was our line umpire that day [against Middlesex] and, as he took up his position at the goalposts for the kick at goal [after a Massa Johnston try], he overheard the Middlesex captain remark to his men, 'What a fluke! Stick to them, boys!' I converted and the game started again. Nine minutes later Deans and Hunter got away and Jimmy ran right round the fullback to score a nice try, which I also converted. Again, as George Nicholson took up his position, he heard the captain say, 'Another darned fluke! What a lucky team! Keep it up, boys!' We were having much the better of the game and both backs and forwards were going well. Twenty minutes later George Smith brought off another of his brilliant runs through the opposing team and scored between the posts. I converted again. This time the Middlesex captain had altered his opinion somewhat for George Nicholson overheard him say: 'What a wonderful team they are, boys.' And after that he sang our praises after every try.

By the time the first Test arrived, against Scotland, nineteen English teams had been put to the sword, 612 points scored and only 15 conceded. Their play was a potent mix of fitness, skill and speed. They were better organised than their opponents with their team tactics and planned moves and, something quite uncommon in the Home Unions, dedicated positions in the forward pack. They also gave rein to some startling individual talent. Wallace with his electrifying forays from the back or the wing, the strength and pace of Deans and Smith in the centre, the guile of Stead, and the corkscrewing runs of Hunter, who scored an incredible forty-four tries in twenty-four appearances. The adulation and warm hospitality of the first two months gave way to a frosty reception from the Scotland Union. They tried to have the Test match on the frozen Inverleith pitch called off, but the All Blacks, on seeing the size of the crowd, insisted it be played rather than disappoint the fans. The Scots had not foreseen the All Blacks' popularity and refused to pay the £300 guarantee. They told the New Zealanders they could have whatever gate takings were raised, a decision that resulted in a windfall for the touring team, and a loss of almost £1,400 in potential earnings for the host union.

Billy Wallace: Edinburgh was the only place on the whole tour where we did not receive a warm official welcome as we stepped off the train. It was a great pity that there should have been this jarring note, and that there should have been such a glaring display of lack of sportsmanship on the part of the Scottish Union towards us. Several of us (myself included) were of Scottish descent and were proud of it. During our stay in Edinburgh, the Scotch [sic] officials did not come near us, or recognise us in any way. Indeed they did everything to make the match a 'wash out'. They refused to protect the ground against frost, as is always done by covering it with straw the night before, and so when we stepped out for the match, the ground was positively dangerous. It was as hard as concrete and we slipped round as if we were running on ice, as, indeed we actually were. For the first ten minutes it looked as though we might win comfortably, for, though we were slipping and sliding about all over the place, our backs were going well. Freddy Roberts worked the blind side of the scrum and I dashed across for a try in the corner but the referee called us back, as he reckoned the pass was forward. But it was as fair a pass as had ever been given on a football field. Shortly afterwards, George Smith was also well under way, with an open field and a certain try, when once more the whistle went for an alleged forward pass. After about ten minutes' play, the Scottish forwards started off with a loose rush from about halfway. It was offside in the first place, but the referee did not see it and the rush was not pulled up until it was almost on our goal-line. Then a scrum was formed. The Scottish forwards hooked the ball and the half-back sent a neat pass to Simpson, who potted a goal from right in front of the posts. The ball just dropped over the bar and Scotland were four points up. This was the first occasion on the tour so far when we had been behind in points. Shortly after this score I was laid out by a foul charge. I was in midfield at the time and had just made one of my long kicks for touch near the corner flag. The ball was travelling nicely and I was watching it bounce into touch when all of a sudden I felt a bump. My feet flew up from under me and I landed with a crack on the back of my head. I was, of course, rendered unconscious.

Billy Stead: The game itself was one of the most exciting I ever played in. Our backs were not on their best behaviour, though the frozen field, which rendered swerving, cutting or recovering an almost absolute impossibility, had much to do with it. At the same time there was a noticeable nervous excitement which had its effect on our play. The referee, an Irishman, appointed without our approval, in direct opposition to one of the rugby rules, came on in ordinary dress and had only one eye. At times twenty yards behind the play, he disallowed two fair tries for us, and it was entirely his one-eyedness that made us, six minutes from time, look a beaten team. Shall I ever forget the look of my captain when (during a temporary lull in the game) he said: 'Only six minutes Billy. Only six more minutes!' And here we were defending our own line. Seven points to six, and still we could not get the ball away from those lingering tight scrimmages. Four minutes from time the long-prayed-for chance came at our twenty-five flag. Out from the scrum came the ball, and with desperate accuracy we got it out to Smith who scored a splendid try in the corner. It had been chronicled that 'for once the New Zealanders lost their heads for they fairly hugged and kissed the hero' . . . Before time we scored another try, and I believed that we would have romped over them had we been playing another ten minutes. Thus ended our first international, one full of excitement and incident, and also a lot of roughness.

The bad feeling continued afterwards, when the Scots refused to invite the New Zealanders to a post-match dinner.

Billy Wallace: We went to Ireland. We were on our way to have a bit of practice and they announced the route in the papers. Everybody was at the gates to see these All Blacks go past, and they were actually expecting us to be 'all blacks', and as we went past they were saying, 'but they're as white as ourselves!'

The Test in Dublin was one of the best matches of the tour, the 15-nil scoreline not doing justice to a rousing Irish performance, and after a romp against Munster the team returned to England for the final, climactic phase of the tour. They had established a good bond with the Irish, and on the day of the Munster match the local newspaper in Limerick stated, 'The New Zealanders are the men of the moment. Their visit has shaken up the dry bones of Rugby Football and created a revival in the game that will be felt for years to come.'

Billy Stead: The Irish fifteen played good, honest, dashing football, which gave us a great deal of trouble, but which we were very glad to have played against us. There was no half-heartedness in the Irish attacks. There was any amount of devil in the Irish forwards, who put more 'go' into their game than any other forward division we had encountered. They made the pace very hot indeed for the early part of the game. In the circumstances we thought that the best thing to do would be to let them run about as much as they wanted and tire themselves out. We could bide our time . . . If the Irish forwards had been supported by a better back combination, the result of the match would have been very problematical.

The strain of twenty-three games in ten weeks was starting to show, with injuries, illness and fatigue weighing on the team. Smith had a busted collarbone, Gallaher missed the Irish Test, not well enough to leave his hotel room, others were ravaged by boils, and it wasn't until the twenty-third game that Mackrell was able to play. And there were still England and Wales to come. The England Test was played in front of a crowd of over 70,000 at Crystal Palace, the largest to attend a rugby match, and tickets valued at a guinea were fetching ten pounds.

Billy Wallace: We played [England] on the Crystal Palace ground and . . . unfortunately we'd had about three days' rain in London and it made the ground there sloppy and muddy. In those days you were only allowed to play with the one ball and we weren't allowed to clean the ball! Not on your jersey or anything so it was absolutely impossible to kick goals. It was very difficult. We'd only been going five minutes when McGregor scored the first try . . . McGregor had scored three tries by half-time. And to finish up the game he scored again on the short side. And they were all good tries.

Bob Deans: The English team suffered from lack of combination. Of the crowds before whom we played, the English were the best. It did get rather tiresome towards the end and the fellows were pretty sick of it before we finished up in England. It was the travelling, and the want of rest, and then the hard matches were left to last. We were very lucky in the weather for it was one of the mildest winters England has had for years – no rain to speak of, and no snow, with frost only in Scotland.

Throughout the tour the All Blacks had been told . . . 'Wait 'til you get to Wales'.

Sadly for them, by the time they got there, the All Blacks were in a degenerating state, and the champion Welsh were more than ready. They declared their intentions to fight fire with fire, by picking a wing forward, or 'Rover' of their own, and they had a surprise for the All Blacks in pre-match.

A poster showing portraits of team members in the 1905-06 tour, with a list of fixtures.

After standing up to the challenge of the haka, the Welsh players began to sing their national anthem in response. The crowd joined in, and so for the first time 'Land of My Fathers' swelled around the Arms Park, and a great tradition was born.

Billy Wallace: After lunch the selection committee got down to serious business. Billy Stead and Bill Cunningham were both suffering from heavy colds and were quite unfit for play. George Smith's shoulder was giving him a lot of trouble and though he tried to make light of it, we knew he was not fit. Here were three of our best men out for a start.

Billy Stead: Studying the condition and fitness of the men both physically and with regard to their playing abilities, we placed the best possible team, in our opinion, that we could get together. They were all in the very best of condition and keen as a knife-edge.

George Gillett: Eventually we end up with this match against Wales, which we were looking forward to. But again the situation arose where men were not spelled and given the opportunity to see the end of the tour right out. By the time we met Wales and the harder matches, there were already four or five of our recognised Test team on the sideline. And that was rather fatal on the day. There were another half dozen that would have gladly stood aside for a rest if they'd had the opportunity.

Billy Stead: We just played the very game that Wales expected us to play and our forwards, a magnificent set of forwards that were never bettered, the Welshmen never bettered them, they really were short of a gallop at the finish, they never got a chance to go. They kept hoofing the ball, hoofing it out. The Welsh were playing off against our fellows, right onto them and the referee was not too fast and every time we put the ball in the scrum it would be a free kick because Gallaher would be penalised. I'm not talking eyewash, that's a fact.

Nothing could be taken away from the Welsh try, a superb set move involving a clever switch of play to put the flying winger Ted Morgan in at the corner.

A short time later, Wales had a second try disallowed.

Billy Wallace: A lineout had been formed a little on our side of halfway and from a long throw-in, the Welsh forwards gained possession. Freddy Roberts was just in front of them and in order to beat him they made a diagonal kick, but just a little too hard. I was on the wing on the touchline side and I dashed in, scooped up the ball in my stride and cut across in front of the forwards before they could lay their hands on me. I then made diagonally across the field until I came in front of Nicholls. In order to beat him, I turned and straightened up and when he came at me I sidestepped him and slipped through between him and Gabe so that I had a clear run through to Winfield, the fullback who was standing about the twenty-five yards line. Meanwhile, Bob Deans had run his hardest to come up in support. As I neared Winfield, I was undecided whether to kick over his head or sell him the dummy and then I heard Bob calling out, 'Bill! Bill!' I feinted to pass and could have gone through on my own, for Winfield took the dummy, but he quickly recovered himself and came at me again. Rather than risk any mishap at this critical stage, I threw Bob Deans out a long pass which he took perfectly and raced ahead.

But he made a slight mistake here, for instead of going straight ahead he veered in towards the goalposts. Teddy Morgan, the Welsh wing three-quarter, was coming across fast from the other wing and Bob was becoming a little exhausted. Bob saw Teddy Morgan in time and altered his course to straight ahead and just grounded the ball six inches over the line and about eight yards from the goalposts as Teddy dived at him and got him round the legs. But the try had been scored. Our chaps all came racing up and shook Bob warmly by the hand, congratulating him and patting him on the back, for the position was a very easy one for me to convert. But here again Bob made another mistake. He got up off the ball and Owen, the Welsh half, picked it up and put it back about six inches in front of the line. The referee had been left standing by the movement and when he came slipping and sliding up from about thirty yards back, Owen said: 'He forced the ball here' and pointed to a place where the ball was. We, of course, were amazed and protested strongly against this unsportsmanlike statement, and in the end the referee awarded a five yards scrum. Had Bob not got up off the ball, the referee could not have done anything else but award the try. There was a dead silence among the crowd and this in itself is evidence that the try was scored. Had Teddy Morgan's tackle saved the try, what a roar of applause there would have been! He certainly made a very gallant effort to save the score but he himself has always admitted that Deans got the try. But the referee ruled the scrum and after a very tight struggle under the Welsh goalposts, Bush found touch and brought relief and a hurricane of applause. The Welsh crowd were not impartial in their applause and in particular heckled Dave Gallaher very unfairly. We kept up the attack and, on another occasion, Simon Mynott was almost across, being held up before he could ground the ball. Still our forwards battled gamely away and penned the Welshmen in their own quarters. Bob Deans made another dash but was brought down by Gwyn Nicholls.

Billy Stead: Deans had a peculiar way of scoring tries. He seldom fell over the line with the ball, but preferred to press it down with his hands and leave it there. He objected to having a mass of humanity fall on him, but he certainly got it that day. The spectators knew it was a try. All through the game, they had cheered on their men, but when Deans went over, once could almost have heard a pin drop in that vast gathering. Then when it was seen that the referee had not given a try, the cheering was renewed, in almost sufficient volume to lift the roof off the universe.

Bob Deans: It was as fair a try as ever was scored.

Jimmy Duncan (1897-1903, 1 Test, 10 games): I can't see how the referee could not see it as we could see it from the far end.

George Smith (1897-1905, 2 Tests, 39 games): I was alongside Dave Gallaher when he congratulated the Welsh captain, Gwyn Nicholls (who, by the way, is a fine fellow – one of the best), and in reply to Dave's congratulations he said, 'We are pleased at defeating you, and are proud of our victory; morally, however, it was a draw.'

Bob Deans: As far as the Welsh team was concerned, one of their supporters told me afterwards that they played against us thirty per cent above form, while our backs seemed unable to do anything right.

George Smith: We were beaten [by Wales], but there was no doubt the team were feeling the effects of the travelling and playing. The extra little bit that means everything was missing.

A lot of controversy centred on the wing-forward position, and in particular, Gallaher. The New Zealanders packed a 2-3-2 scrum, with two hookers in the front row, a single lock, two side row, and two back row forwards.

This left one spare, the wing-forward. As the name suggests, this peculiar Kiwi innovation claimed the privileges of both forward and back, its legal boundaries somewhat cloudy. The wing forward was free to play a destructive role, targeting the opposition inside-backs, especially from the set piece. As with the lineout, the wing forward fed the ball into the scrum, where it was quickly heeled through to the halfback stationed at the base to collect and clear the ball. Rather than retreat Gallaher would stand his ground, effectively blocking the opposition scrum-half from pressurising his opposite. The New Zealanders considered this acceptable under the laws of the game, and many referees concurred, but criticism in the press and in the stands gained momentum. The New Zealand captain became a pantomime villain, to the point when in one county game one fan kept calling loudly for the 'cheat' Gallaher to be sent off, much to the amusement of the man himself who was sitting nearby in the grandstand, prompting Gallaher to joke to his team-mates 'I didn't realise I was so popular.'

George Tyler: Had the wing forward been called a halfback, no objection would have been raised. It was purely due to the fact that he was called a wing forward, which was new to the Home players, that made them criticise it. For instance, when Sullivan was hurt in the Cardiff match, Gallagher went into the front row, and the Cardiff men put the ball into the scrum. We still got the ball out as often, and perhaps more often, than we had done when Gallagher put it in.

Bunny Abbott (1905-06, 1 Test, 11 games): The 2-3-2 had everything in its favour . . . this mongrel scrum they have nowadays has nothing in its favour.

Billy Wallace: Dave [Gallaher] was a wonderful captain. As a player he was outstanding and it was most unfortunate, as well as unjust, that he should have been falsely accused of unfair tactics by a number of English and Welsh writers. To those who knew Dave well, such tactics were quite foreign to his nature. He was immensely popular with the team and also with the officials wherever we went. Always the welfare of the team and the honour of the country he represented were the first considerations. I was on the selection committee with him right through the tour and so I am in a position to speak concerning the immense amount of time and thought he put into all his work.

Jimmy Duncan: Dave never turned a hair and as to his unfairness in putting the ball in the scrum, look at the Cardiff match. Gallaher had to go in the scrum, and yet we got the ball pretty well all the time. The people who attended the matches were very good sports, but the Welsh have only one eye – an eye for their own men.

Billy Wallace: He [Gallaher] played very well indeed. He never played the real wing forward position as we knew it on account of the dislike they had for it over there. Then he got a knee injury and Gillett took over the wing forward and turned out one of the finest wing forwards we ever had.

Bob Deans: Generally speaking, the refereeing was not up to the New Zealand standard. Though generally acting strictly up to the letter of the law, the officials' rulings, especially in regard to offside play, were not consistent.

Deans' non-try sparked one of the greatest rivalries in the game between two small nations in which rugby is something akin to a religion. But the defeat left the 1905 All Blacks shattered and demoralised. Somehow they managed to snatch wins against Glamorgan, Newport, Cardiff and Swansea, the latter a 4-3 win courtesy of a remarkable 40-yard dropped goal by Wallace in a troublesome wind, but the fire had somewhat died. A trip to France provided some light relief.

Billy Wallace: Of course we played the 2-3-2 scrum and the first scrum we had against France the French wouldn't go down. It was very amusing. We had to tell them how to pack it. Our back play was too superior for them.

Bunny Abbott: I was the fastest in the team. I scored two tries [against France], including the last one. They were right on our line with three minutes to go and it looked as though they were going to go over, but Roberts stripped the ball away from their feet, gave it to Wallace, and he would then be about five feet in front of the line . . . he gave it to Jimmy Hunter who was about eighteen inches behind the line and he gave it to me, I was about a foot behind the line. I got past the French three-quarter and the fullback . . . well he didn't understand the swerve so I went past him and when I put the ball down between the posts the two teams were still back at the other goal-line where we'd left them. The French forwards made it hard the whole time . . . they made it hard right til near the end of the game. Really our forwards just fed the backs all day.

Billy Stead: I would say that of all the outstanding players perhaps the best player of the lot, in my humble opinion, would be Billy Wallace. You could play him anywhere in the backs but he was such a good fullback that he mostly played fullback and, of course, he was always in the team when he was available. He was a wonderful place-kicker.

Billy Wallace: Freddy Roberts had not been able to play in the last game [in San Francisco], for, on my rejoining the team, I found that he was not at all well, and was apparently sickening for something. This turned out to be tonsillitis and we were all very sorry when the next morning, the day we were to leave for New Zealand, the doctor refused to allow him to travel. I felt that I could not leave him at this stage. So I volunteered to stay and follow with him on the next boat. It was about ten days before he was well enough to leave his bed. When Fred could get about once more we went along to see the doctor – Dr Stinson – at his surgery and after examining Fred's throat, he advised him strongly to have his tonsils removed. He took them out there and then without an anaesthetic, and I had to sit there and see the business through. It was a lucky thing for us that we left by this boat [the *Ventura*]. Had we been compelled to wait for the following boat we would have been right in the middle of the big San Francisco earthquake. The Californian Hotel, in which we had stayed, was totally wrecked in that big shake and Dr Stinson was killed. At each end of the hotel was a fancy turret, which collapsed. One of these fell on him and killed him instantly.

Seven months and six days after leaving Wellington, the Original All Blacks returned to a rapturous welcome in Auckland. In contrast to the ten people who'd been prepared to buy tickets to a function on the eve of their departure, thousands lined the streets to pay homage to New Zealand's sporting heroes. Dixon and Gallaher thanked the crowd, and Gallaher suggested that future All Black teams should face Wales earlier in the tour!

The Originals had established, once and forever, rugby's position as the game for New Zealand. Ever after, young Kiwis would aspire to wear the black jersey with the silver fern, and when that was achieved, aspire to enhance the legacy established by this pioneering team.

THREE

SURVIVING THE SPLIT

'Give nothing away; take no chances'

UNTIL 1907 NEW Zealand had not had to face any issues associated with the professional game of rugby league. However, the success of the Originals proved an asset when Wellington club rugby player A.H. 'Bert' Baskerville mounted a side to tour Britain to play rugby league. He set about assembling a team which included four of the Originals, Duncan McGregor, Bill Mackrell, George Smith and Billy Johnston. Four other All Blacks were Hubert Turtill, Edgar Wrigley, Tom Cross and Eric Watkins. Known as the All Golds they had less success than the Originals, fashioning a record of nineteen wins, two draws and fourteen losses.

Before the details of the rugby league venture were known, an inter-island game was set for Christchurch in June, but before they could play all players were required to sign declarations they would not play league. Twelve of the Auckland players in the North Island side refused to sign. After negotiations they agreed to sign and five of them were included in the New Zealand team named to tour Australia. One of the stars of the Originals Jimmy Hunter captained the side to a 3-0 series victory over an Australian side which included in the second and third Tests an impressive wing named Dally Messenger. He would become one of the great figures in Australian rugby league and started in league as a member of the All Golds team which toured in 1907.

New Zealand had offered South Africa an invitation to tour, after the South Africans had followed the Originals with a tour to Britain in 1906-07, however this was declined. Another invitation would be extended late in 1911 for a tour in 1912 but the South African Rugby Board declined saying it would take too long to raise funds. A similar invitation in 1913 for 1914 was also declined.

A tour of New Zealand by the Anglo-Welsh side in 1908 proved a fillip for the game after the ructions over league the year before. Captain Arthur F. Harding would note that while the Welsh were accused of 'giving too much attention to the game' they could not be compared with New Zealanders. Writing in R.W. Barr's *British Rugby Team in Maoriland*, Harding said: 'This indicates the keenness of the public, which to us seems to be practically a religion – whether this is beneficial to the sport or not is open to doubt.' Harding also continued the criticism that had attended Gallaher on the 1905-06 tour by stating, 'We have also repeatedly had our attack nipped in the bud by the wing-forward getting on our scrum-half before he received the ball, and have been astonished by the latitude allowed this player in almost every game.'

Team manager George Harnett in the same book produced a line that has lived through the ages when asked of the opinion of New Zealand's play? 'To be frank, there is a tendency to roughness.'

Opposite: Billy Wallace.

The touring side was weak in terms of experience with only ten players of the twenty-eight having played Test rugby. The New Zealand selectors recalled several members of the Originals, including Billy Stead to captain the team. He was reunited with halfback Freddie Roberts and second five-eighths Jimmy Hunter, the unit which had so impressed in Britain in 1905-06. They were too strong for the visitors and wholesale changes were made for the second Test to blood new players. However, the match was drawn 3-3, and the side was returned to full strength for the third Test in which the All Blacks ran in nine tries, only one of which was converted in the 29-0 victory. While it was the last outing for several players it was especially poignant when a month or two later centre Bob Deans died.

A feature of the series was the debut of N.A. 'Ranji' Wilson in the forwards. A decade later he would feature in a significant event in New Zealand rugby history. However, that was well in the future when the All Blacks toured Australia in 1910. Three Tests were played within eight days, all in Sydney. New Zealand won the first 6-0 but then two days later lost the second 0-11 before coming back strongly to win the third 28-13 and with it the series.

Billy Stead: They came out at just the right time. There was a slump in 'big' football, and the game was in a kind of dormant state. Personally, though keen to play for my province, I thought three seasons' absence from strenuous football had undoubtedly lowered my standard of play, and my inclusion in the New Zealand team for the first Test surprised myself, as it did many others. This all the more emphasises my contention that football was not too strong.

Billy Wallace: I had been chosen to represent New Zealand in the first Test, but on the Saturday after the Wellington match I received a knock on the knee in a club game. I

A souvenir programme from the 1908 Anglo-Welsh tour. *John Griffiths*

managed to finish the game, but next day my knee was very much swollen. This was the beginning of the end of my career. I rang 'Hen' Kelly, who was one of the selectors, and he came up to see me. As soon as he saw it, he said, 'Oh, you can't play with that knee' so very reluctantly I had to pull out.

Billy Stead: Their forwards were not so formidable as constant scrumming and vigorous training might have made them. As scrummers they were excellent, on the lineout they were good, as dribblers they were incomparable (although their rushes are of a different stamp from the bustling, strenuous New Zealand forward rush), and, from a British standpoint, one might well ask, 'What more do you want?' That is just the point they do not grasp and wherein they fail. We in New Zealand expect more than these qualities in a first grade forward, and until Britain can train and develop a stamp of forward who can take, kick, tackle and pass also, the vanguard must suffer by competitions. Their forwards seldom 'worried' or hampered our backs. Can the British rearguard say that that was their experience?

Billy Wallace: The Britishers had a week's spell before the second Test which was played at Wellington on Saturday, June 27. On the Thursday prior to the Test a bombshell was sprung on the team in the shape of a cable from the English Rugby Union, recalling Jackson, one of their best forwards, for an alleged breach of the laws regarding professionalism. He left for Sydney on the Friday and several of the team were very much upset at the incident. Wet weather prevailed for most of that week in Wellington, nor did it clear up for the day of the match. My knee seemed to be very much better and I was selected at fullback. This was the last game of football that I played. The knee gave no trouble during the game but about an hour afterwards it began to swell and it was bad for a couple of months. I had, therefore, no option but to give up the game.

Billy Stead: They played [the third Test] as if they were subordinate parts in a machine, only the connecting links between the scrum and that brilliant three-quarter line. There was absolutely no variation in their attack, no deviation from a given rule, not even a swerve from an orthodox course – nothing at all to mystify or 'bluff' the opposing halves.

There was no more international play until 1913 when Australia visited for three Tests, losing the first two 5-30 and 13-25 before taking the third 16-5. The New Zealand team was made up of players selected to tour the west coast of the United States and Canada. The tour came a year after Australia had toured the same area, suffering two losses and being pushed hard by All-America in the tour's Test match.

It has been something of a forgotten tour in All Blacks history, possibly because of the fact that in sixteen games only six points were scored against them while they scored 610. A tour to Australia was held under the shadow of developing war in Europe. It started on 1 July with a game they lost to Wellington before the side travelled to Sydney where they played on 11 July. That proved the only loss with the Test series won 3-0.

War was declared with three games remaining. Three members of the team died during the war. AJ 'Doolan' Downing died in a bayonet charge at Gallipoli, R.S. 'Bobby' Black was believed killed in action during the Battle of the Somme and Jim McNeece died of injuries sustained at Messines. Two members of the 1913 side to the United States and Canada, Henry Dewar (Chunuk Bair, Gallipoli) and George Sellars (Messines) also died in action. They were joined by earlier All Blacks Jim Baird (Messines), Ernie Dodd (Havrincourt), Dave Gallaher (Gravenstafel Spur), Eric Harper (Palestine), Jimmy Ridland (Le Quesnoy), Reg Taylor (Messines), H.S. 'Jum' Turtill (Givenchy), and Frank Wilson (Somme).

Lt E.E. Booth (1905-07, 3 Tests, 24 games): The news of the sad and sudden death of my old skipper 'Dave' has distressed me beyond measure . . . Dave was a man of sterling worth, slow to promise, but always sure to fulfil. Girded by great determination and self-control, he was a valuable friend and could be, I think, a remorseless foe . . . as an opponent he was simply merciless, wanted everything and all; but I honestly think he ever meant to be nothing but legitimate and fair. To us 'All Blacks' his words would often be, 'Give nothing away; take no chances.' As a skipper he was something of a disciplinarian, doubtless imbibed from his previous military experience in South Africa. Still he treated us all as men, not kids, who were out to play the game for good old New Zealand . . . His greatest regret on the tour was the lateness of the Welsh fixtures. He foresaw the likelihood of staleness.

Somehow, time was found for rugby during the war years, especially after the New Zealanders moved to France. In 1917 a New Zealand Army XV, regarded as near Test strength, became known as the Trench Blacks and made a nine-game tour meeting British, Welsh, Irish and French sides with the penultimate game, with France, resulting in a 40-0 win and the presentation of the Coupe de Somme. The game was played at Vincennes Velodrome.

In 1919, after the war was over but with thousands of men waiting for suitable shipping to take them home, the King's Cup was one of several sporting tournaments devised to fill in time. New Zealand beat Canada 11-0, South Africa 14-5 and England 6-3. They lost to Australia 5-6 but had done enough to qualify for the final against England, which they won 9-3.

Jim Ryan (1910-14, 4 Tests, 15 games): We certainly had to do our best to win that cup [Inter-Services Cup], and at one time I feared the team were sinking into a state of staleness. I think we were at the top of our form in the South African engagement. At Inverleith [against the England side] I never doubted our forwards' ability to win, but the gale made things very tricky. The offside rulings here puzzled us at first, but we soon got into the way of things. Several small improvements we have tried in New Zealand would open out the game more and improve it from a spectator's view. I think comparisons [in the press] between the Original All Blacks and our team rather unfair. The All Blacks of 1905 were the result of years of experience and training, being, in fact, a team of captains, while we are all (except Wilson, Cain, and myself) newly developed players since coming over to Europe.

Arthur 'Ranji' Wilson (1908-14, 10 Tests, 21 games): Our two hardest games were against the Mother Country fifteen and South Africa. We really played our best against the latter. The Army Rugby Union performed almost a miracle in instituting the competition, and we had some degree of luck in winning.

Dick Fogarty (1921, 2 Tests): The referees here order far too many scrums, which tend to slow down the game very considerably. When a British team again visit New Zealand we will give them a great time.

William Fea (1921, 1 Test): The majority of the backs here run too much across-field and seem to fail as straight runners. I think the referees are a bit too exacting in such small matters as unintentional offside and petty knock-ons. I quite failed to follow some of their rulings for some time, but latterly got used to them. The game here, if properly handled and controlled, should have a greater future than ever. The Welsh are hard players and fearfully keen on winning. Their back play resembles our style very much.

Lt E.E. Booth: By his presentation of the [King's] Cup the All Blacks consider the King the greatest of sportsmen, and the cup itself is jealously guarded by Major Cameron, our sports representative . . . In New Zealand it will be valued more than any guns, medals, flags or other souvenirs of the war, and will probably find a resting-place in the Houses of Parliament in Wellington. By winning the Army competition and then beating Wales on her own ground, thus revenging [sic] the defeat of 1906 [sic], the team are really carrying back in the King's Cup the ashes of British rugby.

King George V shakes hands with the New Zealand players at the inter-services championship final at Twickenham, London in April 1919. *Getty Images*

FOUR

AN UNFORTUNATE PRECEDENT

'he thought he could catch him, but it didn't come off'

NINETEEN PAST OR present All Blacks were included in the New Zealand Army team which toured Britain and France playing thirty-eight games after World War One. They played another twelve games in South Africa on their way home, a visit that proved a precursor to troubled times that lay ahead.

On 1 April 1919, the South Africa Rugby Board telegraphed their High Commissioner in London asking if it would be possible for him to arrange either the Australian or New Zealand Army teams to break their journey home in order to make an all-expenses-paid six-week tour of South Africa. The High Commissioner was the former Prime Minister of the Cape Colony, and former president of the SARB, William Philip Schreiner. Schreiner replied on 19 May that the New Zealand Services team of twenty-nine players would be available to tour.

Arrangements were completed but on 2 June the SARB met and it was discussed that the team might include Maori. By a vote of 8-6 it was decided to cable the High Commissioner: 'Confidential if visitors include Maoris [sic] tour would be wrecked and immense harm politically and otherwise would follow. Please explain position fully and try arrange exclusion.'

That this was agreed to by the New Zealand officials, albeit without the knowledge of the New Zealand Rugby Football Union, remains a blight on New Zealand history. Two fine players, Arthur 'Ranji' Wilson and Parekura Tureia were prevented from touring. It was put about that Tureia had missed the boat taking the steamer to South Africa, according to the *Poverty Bay Herald*, printed in Tureia's home town of Gisborne. How Wilson's exclusion was explained is not so clear. He had been born in Christchurch of a West Indian father and British mother. Wilson met up with the team when the ship he was returning home on called into Durban. He did not play rugby for New Zealand again but was a selector of the 1924-25 team to Britain and France. Tureia played for New Zealand Maori in 1921 and 1923.

While South Africa did not enshrine their racial policy of apartheid in law until 1948 the New Zealand team of 1928 was asked not to include Maori players and while four players, three Maori and a Samoan, were included as honorary whites in the 1970 All Blacks team to South Africa, it wouldn't be until 1992 when the racist policies were discarded that New Zealand teams could tour unencumbered by South African 'favours'.

When the All Blacks toured Australia in 1920 six pre-war All Blacks were included. A surprise in the choice of captain occurred when Jim Tilyard was named ahead of Charlie Brown, who had led the New Zealand Army side on their South African tour.

Opposite: Vice-captain Jock Richardson, September 1924. *Getty Images*

As rugby had not regained a footing in Queensland, the tour involved seven games in New South Wales and three in New Zealand.

But the tour that rugby fans had been awaiting was that by a South African side in 1921. It was to prove inconclusive as New Zealand won the first Test in Dunedin 13-5 with the most memorable feature being a superb try scored by wing Jack Steel who caught a cross-kick from five-eighths Ces Badeley before racing forty-five metres to score. South Africa won the second Test played at Eden Park 9-5. Before the third Test was played a New Zealand side, including three players from the South African series, played the touring New South Wales Waratahs only to be beaten 0-17. The final Test of the South Africa series was played in heavy rain in Wellington and resulted in a 0-0 draw.

Ginger Nicholls (1921-23, 1 Test, 7 games): It was a beautiful fine day in Dunedin, as good a day as you could wish to play, there wasn't a semblance of wind and it was a fast, open game. We made it fast because we got the ball and our backs combined well and attacked by high punting and by passing. The Springboks tried to open it up and one rush they had which I remember where van Heerden looked like he might score and he had to pass infield. But he gave such a bad pass it went along the ground. As I remember the [Jack Steel] try came from a scrum. We got the ball and it was passed to Badeley the first five-eighths and he high punted and the ball went between their backline and their fullback and bounced back very high towards the centre of the field and out to the right, and Steel, following up very fast, caught the ball with one hand high in the air and brought it down in his stride and carried on. There was a South African back du Meyer about three yards from him at the time and it looked like he was going to catch him, but Steel

veered away and bore off the fullback and ran about another forty-five yards right round behind the posts, a most magnificent try.

Percy Storey (1920-21, 2 Tests, 12 games): I think it was Morkel, tried to chase him . . . well it was almost ridiculous to watch it . . . he was only about four or five feet behind Jack all the time and he only had to dive at him and he'd have caught him, he was close enough, but he thought he could catch him, but it didn't come off . . . Jack just went on and scored. In the first twenty-five minutes I had my shoulder injured, and I couldn't do much. I couldn't raise my right

All Blacks captain George Aitken, referee Ted McKenzie and Springbok captain 'Boy' Morkel before the first Test.

Halfback EJ Roberts leads out the home side for the third Test against the Springboks.

arm, but nevertheless managed to play my part in the game. George Aitken, our centre and captain, happened to get the ball and it came out to me and I had enough pace on to barge over and get the final try.

Ginger Nicholls: The selectors were that thrilled after us winning the first Test. I think in view of the outcry of the football fans in New Zealand about [Teddy] Roberts being left out of the team and me replacing him, they thought, 'Oh well, we'll give Roberts a go' and Teddy was put in. He was a great friend of mine and he was put in the team to play in Auckland.

Mark Nicholls (1921-30, 10 Tests, 51 games): I'm fairly certain the All Black selectors did a bad job of selecting the team for that series. I felt that if they couldn't pick me for my right position I shouldn't be in the team. To play me at centre in the last Test and to play a fullback [Siddells] at wing three-quarters was an experiment that was beyond comprehension.

Jock Richardson (1921-25, 7 Tests, 42 games): I played all three Tests and for Otago against them. They were bigger in the forwards than we were and were very good players. They were mobile as well while their backs were all big players. I liked them, they were the best team that I have ever seen.

FIVE

THE FIRST GOLDEN ERA

'I was bowled over and knocked out as if I had been sandbagged'

'THE WEAKEST TEAM New Zealand has ever had – weak in the scrums, weak on defence, and lacking in pace – sums up the present All Black team after the match at Eden Park yesterday.' By these words describing the 1924-25 All Blacks team who became known as 'The Invincibles', George Tyler of the 1905-06 team provided the grist to the mill that would serve the side all the way through their unbeaten tour of Britain and France. To compound his forthcoming ignominy Tyler said it was a shame that men like Paewai, Nepia, Mill and McGregor should be chosen.

The record speaks for itself. The team were unbeaten, although they did not play Scotland who were still smarting from the 1905-06 experience when they didn't take a share of the gate. They were also upset by England's choosing to offer the invitation to the All Blacks rather than having the four Home Unions issue it as had been agreed. In all respects the side was too good and achieved the main goal of the tour in beating Wales, not in Cardiff, but in Swansea. Along the way some great names were carved into the game's history. Leading the way among a forward pack still playing the 2-3-2 scrum formation and succeeding in spite of only winning thirty per cent of possession on average during the tour, according to Carwyn James and John Reason in *The World of Rugby*, were locks Maurice Brownlie and Jock Richardson. They were war-hardened men who thrived in the heavy going while in the loose Andrew 'Son' White would emerge as one of the leading loose forwards of the day, completing a remarkable recovery from his own war experiences which saw him invalided home with shell shock. Team captain Cliff Porter stood himself down in the Tests against Ireland, Wales and England with Jim Parker taking his place and Richardson the captaincy.

One of Tyler's undeserving players George Nepia would play every game on tour and win a reputation as one of the greatest fullbacks to grace the game. Second five-eighths Bert Cooke would set a standard in running back play that would last for generations while Mark Nicholls would establish himself as one of the great thinkers of the game. After the first Test of the tour against Ireland, it was decided to play Neil McGregor at first five-eighths, Nicholls at second and Cooke at centre against Wales and England. Wings Jack Steel and K.S. 'Snowy' Svenson and Nepia completed the line-up.

Nepia especially left an indelible impression and one description of his tour was provided by English journalist Dai Gent. 'There may have been better fullbacks than the swarthy Nepia. So far as I can judge, and confining my experience to those I saw play when I had any football sense at all, I have never seen a better . . . But fullback armed at all points, has there been a better than Nepia? Kick, tackle, stop a rush, start a passing movement, kick goals, score a try – here was the complete fullback, I suggest, and all done with the full-blooded vigour of superb physique.'

Opposite: George Nepia.

Bert Cooke (1924-30, 8 Tests, 44 games): The first Test against New South Wales [in 1924] was our first game together, and Otto Nothling, Jack Blackwood, 'Wakka' Walker and Co. were too good for us, winning by 20-16. [Ces] Badeley and I were five-eighths in the first Test. In the second and third Mark Nicholls was my partner. We won the second Test by 21 to 5, and the third by 38 to 8.

George Nepia (1924-30, 9 Tests, 46 games): I was far from my best in Australia. I knew it myself but the Australian critics proceeded to tell the rugby world that I was a hopeless case. They slammed me up hill and down dale and in no uncertain terms wrote me down.

Bert Cooke: Badeley had been appointed captain for the Australian tour, but Cliff Porter was appointed later for the English tour. As far as I know there was no mystery about this, and there was no question of any lack of confidence in Badeley. It was simply that Porter was playing exceedingly well, and showed himself to be an astute tactician. Also, he showed later when he stood down from international matches in Britain that in addition to being a good player he was prepared to put the welfare of his side above personal ambition.

George Nepia: All this adverse criticism reached New Zealand in a matter of minutes and when we lost one of the Tests to New South Wales, my native country began to say all manner of unkind things about the team in general and myself in particular. The result was that we were 'for it' when we returned to New Zealand for our last two matches there before setting sail for England.

Bert Cooke: Returning from Sydney on the old *Manuka* we had a shocking trip, no one being allowed on deck for two days. In the middle of this tossing we got a wireless message that we were to play Auckland the day after our arrival. Imagine our feelings! Some pretty terse comments on the New Zealand Union were made. The boat got into Auckland on Tuesday night, and our cot-cases staggered ashore.

George Nepia: We arrived back at Auckland after midnight, hours late and went straight to bed. For several of us there was little sleep, a none too comforting thought considering that, in about twelve hours we were to play the Auckland reps. Some of us got into our rooms only to find that the seasickness was still with us with the bedroom rolling and pitching. We were still in this condition when we took the field at Eden Park for the match. I was one of the worst, and when I tried to run for the ball the field would rise and fall after the motion of the *Manuka*. Every time I did this I would miss the ball completely and go sprawling all over the field. I remember Cyril Brownlie doing the same just as Auckland scored. I staggered round helplessly throughout that match – a never-to-be-forgotten game.

Bert Cooke: The veterans who promptly burst into print to allege that we were the worst side ever chosen for New Zealand probably did not know, and did not take the trouble to find out, that some of our crowd had not yet got their land legs and were actually vomiting at half-time. From Auckland we went to Palmerston North and beat Manawatu-Horowhenua by 27 to 12.

Jock Richardson: The majority of the team were young. They were just coming into their skills and the continuous games [on tour] allowed them to develop. Not many fellows had represented New Zealand before and we were sent to Australia before we left. When we returned from Australia we played Auckland. None of us wanted to be injured in the game because our trip was virtually assured. Afterwards the 1905 All Black George Tyler wrote we were the worst team that had ever been assembled in New Zealand. After each match we won in Britain we would always say: 'That's another nail in bloody Tyler's coffin.'

Read Masters (1923-25, 4 Tests, 31 games): The four Home Unions had agreed previously to have any invitations to overseas teams decided and issued by the Home Unions. England, for some reason, didn't comply with that arrangement and they issued the invitation to the 1924 All Blacks to visit the British Isles. That invoked the displeasure of the Scots, who decided they should protest and the result was they refused participation in the tour arrangements and finances. England paid all expenses and sold games to Wales, Ireland and France and as it was not in keeping with the previous agreement Scotland stood on their dignity and decided that they would positively not meet our team.

George Nepia: We were glad when finally we did set sail from Wellington on the *Remuera* and were out of sight and sound of the unkind things that had been said and written about us. Our manager S.S. Dean called us into the lounge and said, in effect, 'Well, boys, we're going over to play football. You'll have plenty of time for other fun on the tour as well, but the consideration of football will come first. Agreed?' We put in an hour and a half hard tackling and scrum practice every day, and every afternoon we had an hour's team talk on tactics and strategy. Those talks were so thorough, so detailed and so critically analysed that they made our record success assured before we ever sighted the shores of England!

Neil McGregor (1924-28, 2 Tests, 27 games): He [Cliff Porter] had a very sound knowledge of both forward and back play. He played great rugby in the trials and when the team went to Australia ahead of the British tour he played such great football there that the captaincy was given to him when we came back to New Zealand.

George Nepia: It took us a few weeks and a few matches to get our land legs in England and get acclimatised, but we had no sooner got into our stride, and beaten Swansea by 38 points to 3, than we ran into Newport and came perilously near to being defeated.

Bert Cooke: Welsh football has never been renowned for gentleness, and I had painful evidence of this in the Newport match, which was about our narrowest escape on the 1924 tour. It was hectic from the kick-off. Newport led 5 to 0 at half-time. Just afterwards I had kicked for touch, and was actually watching the ball bounce over the touchline when I was bowled over and knocked out as if I had been sandbagged. Well I didn't remember anything more until I 'came to' as I was being carried up the steps under the stand. I had

The 'Invincibles'.
Back row: L M Paewai, J H Parker, M J Brownlie, C J Brownlie, A White, Q Donald, G M Nepia.
Second row: W R Irvine, I H Harvey, A H West, L F Cupples, R T Stewart, R R Masters,
A C Robilliard, J Steel.
Sitting: A H Hart, B McCleary, H G Munro, C Badeley, S S Dean (manager), J Richardson (vice-
captain), C J Porter (captain), J Mill, M F Nicholls.
In front: N P McGregor, W C Dalley, A E Cooke, F W Lucas, K S Svenson, H W Brown.

seven stitches put in the back of my head there and then, and in view of the critical state of
the game I then tottered back on to the field. We were still 'down the well' with a minute
to go, when Maurice Brownlie fielded a loose ball and put Snowy Svenson in for a try.
Mark Nicholls converted and we won by 13 to 10.

George Nepia: I didn't know I was going to play every game on tour until after the
Newport game [sixth game]. During the game against Newport I had a thumb put out of
joint. It was kicked and I was in bandages. On the Thursday morning the manager and
captain told me I was going to be spelled on the Saturday so of course I relaxed. But on
the Saturday morning they decided to play me again, and it was then they told me I was
to play in every game on tour.

Read Masters: Ireland had a magnificent pack of forwards, a wonderful pack of forwards,
and an amazing backline. Their defence was just phenomenal. Their fullback, Crawford, I

would feel was one of the best I ever played against. He was quite a smallish man, but his defence in rush stopping, tackling, and line kicking was just phenomenal.

George Nepia: I had a terrific duel with Ireland's fullback, and, let me say, I got no change out of him. Ernie Crawford was a truly grand player. When the tour was over, and we were homeward bound, we fell to picking out a No.1 of opponents. We were unanimous that Crawford was the best of the lot. Had it not been for the fullback Ireland must surely have been beaten more heavily than by 6 points to 0. His fielding and kicking, too, were out of the copybook, so to speak, and I learned much from him. To me the amazing thing about Crawford was that there seemed to be so little of him. George Stephenson got away on his own and came racing towards me with nothing but mud and me between him and the goal-line. He was surely going to get away from me but which way I could not, for the life of me, decide. I concluded he would get to the right of me, and in that very second, he cut away to the left of me. I was beaten. Then something happened. Providentially, George Stephenson slipped and fell, and for once in a while Clinch was in the immediate background to take the ball at his feet. I just had time to get to the ball before the Irish pack tore down on it . . . It was a pity it was such a wretched day, for I should have enjoyed seeing the brothers Stephenson (George and Harry) and the brothers Hewitt handling a dry ball against our backs. There would have been one of the finest and most open games ever seen.

Jim Parker (1924-25, 3 Tests, 21 games): Critics in this country write and talk about our forward play, but that's not our strength. Our strength is forwards and backs combining, throwing the ball to each other.

George Nepia: The next two outstanding occasions of our tour were our games with Cambridge and Oxford, particularly the latter. We managed to pull through against Cambridge by a goal to nothing. The other outstanding feature of the match was the fine stamina of the University men. It was the same against Oxford, though the Dark Blues gave us a much harder game. Oxford had several Colonials in their side, and they came at us with their – and our – strongest suit, which was attack. Right from the kick-off they assumed the offensive, beating our attack with counter-attack, till towards the closing stages our fitness turned the scale, our greater weight in the scrum and heavier backs told their tale, and we won. The score of 33 points to 16 in no sense represents the run of the game territorially . . . I had more tackling to do that match than in any other of the tour . . . simply because the Oxford three-quarter-line was always contriving to outwit them and by speedy combination get through.

Mark Nicholls: For sheer good football this match [Oxford University] had everything. Both teams passed from the halfback to the wing continuously with no mistakes. There were eight tries, five by us, three by them, and all were converted. There were two attempts at dropped goals and both succeeded and the score see-sawed till we spurted ahead from 19-15 with fifteen minutes to go to win 33-16.

George Nepia: Cardiff was a hard game but they never looked like beating us.

Mark Nicholls: We were undefeated going into the Wales game . . . we'd already beaten three of their club sides and we didn't expect to have any great difficulty beating Wales. I sometimes thought the club games, where the players have combinations, are harder to beat and in that case it's how it turned out. When the Welsh had their trials down in Cardiff, Cliff Porter and I went down from London to watch and we came away fairly well convinced that we would beat them quite easily, and so we did. We had a confidence in our ability. We knew we wouldn't go out there and make mistakes, drop the ball at critical moments. We won the toss and Wales had to kick off, and Hiddlestone, one of their forwards was about to kick off when their captain Wetter rushed up to him and stopped him. He picked up the ball, threw it on the ground and it bounced up about 15 feet in the air. The referee ran over and asked what was the matter. Wetter said that ball is no good, we're not going to play with it. Now, prior to the game they'd brought four balls in for me to examine. Because I was the place-kicker in the team and the kicker always examined the balls to see if they were too tightly blown up, and so on. Now, if the other team knew you had a good kicker they'd blow the balls up like concrete so you can't kick goals with them. I picked out two balls I thought were good enough, and the Welsh accepted them, but when we got out onto the field Wetter refused to play with them. Well this held the game up for about five minutes while they took the balls to the sideline. In the end Wetter chose two balls, I don't know if they were the same ones . . . he just did it to upset us.

George Nepia: There was, we in 1924 well remembered, the blot on Dave Gallaher's 1905 team's record, of a defeat by the Principality, and we were out to get revenge for it. New Zealand was expecting us to get her own back for her, and the morning of the match we received a special message from our Prime Minister expecting us to win. I sat in a corner of the dressing room, as soon as I had changed into my togs, too keyed up for words. I was a bundle of nerves. Then the Welsh crowd started their amazing singing, and, though I love music second to none, their splendid chorus work only made me feel worse . . . Then we took the field. We gave our haka, the whistle went, and in that second I didn't care if all the giants of Welsh rugby's past glory had come to life and were opposed to us.

Mark Nicholls: When they kicked off we got right into it. We never gave them a moment's peace. We belted into them in the forwards, Morrie Brownlie and Co., tore right into them. We attacked in the backs whenever we got the ball. We got a penalty which I kicked quite easily and then from a lineout close to the line, Brownlie bashed his way through and gave the ball to Irvine and he scored. Morrie Brownlie was a terrific man. Jack Steel made a terrific run down the touchline . . . a press photographer came onto the field to take a photo of Steel coming down the line and Jack didn't see him and he hit this fellow and his camera went about twenty-five yards. The photographer turned a somersault but it never impeded Steel. He went on and scored but the line umpire put his flag up and said that Steel was out. The referee had awarded the try but looked back and saw the flag up. The referee said to me 'if that was the deciding try in the game I would have given it.'

George Nepia: I figured in three incidents in that game. Two of them were freak happenings. One was of my own making. In the first I had to get the ball from the feet of three Welsh forwards, one of whom was Wetter – the names of the other two have slipped my memory. They were rushing the ball downfield, passing it one to the other in close-in soccer fashion – and I stood alone between them and a try for they were on our twenty-five line. I was barely in front of them and to their right as I made to get the ball. I simply had to get it – and what is more – get it into my own hands and find touch to give our forwards relief for a few moments, as they had been particularly hard-pressed for a while. I made up my mind to dive for the ball. I knew I had to time my dive so that I would reach the ball the very second it was kicked from one forward's feet to the other's. So I dived for the feet of the man furthest from one of the three. I got the ball, brushed through them and found touch back on the Welsh twenty-five. Then the whistle went. I turned round and there was Wetter and another of the trio of forwards lying flat out. To this day I have no recollection of colliding with any of them. I felt nothing as I brushed through them, if 'brushing' through is the correct word to use in view of what happened. The second incident was when I described a complete double somersault after being trip-tackled. I had dashed upfield after eluding several forwards charging down on me and was making ground rapidly when one of the Welsh speed merchants, realising he could not grass me by tackling me, dived, and with one hand knocked my two knees together. He had come at me from the side, and the immediate effect was to send me somersaulting as I leaped to avoid him. I turned over twice before I was able to steady myself, but before anyone laid a hand on me I had contrived to make good my kick into touch. The final score was 19 points to nil, and the fact the Principality failed to score one try was due to the perfect working of a little plot of mine when Wales had her best chance of scoring. The player who fell into the trap was none other than that great back Rowe Harding. He was tearing along the wing at a tremendous lick and, as usual when faced with the problem of saving a try, I looked to see what other opponents were thereabouts. I saw another of the red-jerseyed men running at breakneck speed through the centre, and making to close with Rowe Harding. Needing to work quick, I staged a bit of make-believe by walking a few feet from the touchline towards the centre of the field, thus leaving a fairly wide gap between myself and the touchline, and one which Harding promptly thought wide enough for him to get through. I knew my limitations, however, and I knew just how much rope I could give that famous Welsh flyer. He made straight for the gap, and I turned and made straight for him. I threw him yards over the touchline with the ball.

Mark Nicholls: [George] Nepia played a remarkable game. They had quite a few dribbling rushes, and two or three times they managed to get through our defence and George stopped them every time.

Bert Cooke: Nobody in New Zealand has ever seen George Nepia play as he played on this tour, and I have never seen a fullback who could touch him in this period when he put up a remarkable record of playing in every game. He touched his greatest heights in the Welsh match, the game we were most anxious of all to win. We felt that the eyes of New Zealand were on us. In that game George would repeatedly sweep the ball up from the toes of the Welsh forwards and charge backwards through them, and in one of these daring and spectacular exploits he skittled no less than three of them, including the Welsh skipper Jack Wetter.

Neil McGregor: I'll always remember George [Nepia] for his wonderful game that day. One thing I'll always remember was the moment when three Welsh forwards were dribbling the ball towards Nepia, a matter of only ten yards from our goal-line with only Nepia to beat. And he, travelling at full speed, threw himself through the air at the ball, bashed into the forwards, turned a couple of somersaults, regained his feet, had the ball in his hands, ran some twenty or thirty yards and then found touch within about five yards of the corner flag at the other end of the field – an amazing effort – an individual effort that I've not seen the like of since.

Jock Richardson: Many a time we were going to spell George on that tour but he assured us that he was all right. We told him that if his play deteriorated we would give him a spell. But he just got better and better. He had a good long kick and was safe.

George Nepia: We played Wales on a Saturday. We had a few injuries, and on the Tuesday following we were to play Llanelli. And what a match! I felt the injuries I suffered against Wales very much but I had to play again. Bert Cooke had to play against doctor's orders, but of course had Welsh blood and, coming from Llanelli years before, it was only right that he should play. Rumours have been circling round that when Ernie Finch scored his try he was so scared that he stopped dead in his tracks and that, when I went through with my tackle, I missed him and that this was how he scored his try. The truth is that Ernie Finch broke through and that, when I was getting across to crash tackle him, he showed what a brilliant winger he was. At the critical moment, and just a second or two before I launched the tackle, Ernie swerved into me, breaking my speed and my timing, and then swung outwards again. By the time I regathered speed, Ernie had score a lovely try. I can count on the fingers of one hand the number of times I was beaten by a player in that kind of situation, and Ernie Finch was one of that small number.

Bert Cooke: The match against England started off at high tension and this produced the unfortunate Brownlie incident, in which there were certainly two parties to blame. Reg Edwards, the Newport forward, was not again invited to play for England. I will say no more on that point. We also thought the tactics of A F Blakiston, a well-known English forward and a great chap off the field, were to some extent provocative. But for all this it was a magnificent match and the English forwards, led by Wakefield, rose wonderfully to the occasion, while Young played a superb game behind the scrum.

Mark Nicholls: Three times in the first ten minutes Mr Freethy stopped the game and cautioned both sets of forwards. This is something that should be remembered, especially by English critics who are prone to explain away the English defeats by reference to the All Blacks' rough tactics.

George Nepia kicks for goal. *Getty Images*

George Nepia: I have never been able to think of the 1924 tour without thinking of Twickenham. I never shall . . . There was the thrill of shaking hands, before the kick-off, with our present King, and the impatience for the kick-off; there was the deafening roar that went up from 70,000 throats when the game did start, and which continued like some non-stop thunderstorm till that tragic moment when the referee blew the whistle and a lone All Black walked to the dressing room – dismissed from the game. That silence was ghastly. To everyone, the sight of such a fine forward as Cyril Brownlie ordered off the field was more ghastly still.

Edward, Prince of Wales, meets the All Blacks before
the Test match against England at Twickenham. *Scran*

Read Masters: Through the over-keenness of one of England's forwards – who had also adopted illegal tactics in a previous game – heated play was in evidence in the first scrum and many subsequent scrums, while in the tight play arms were freely swung . . . Never in all my life have I experienced anything like the weird silence that fell over Twickenham as [Cyril] Brownlie walked away. If England had any chance of winning, and up to this stage it certainly appeared as though they had, it was reduced to a minimum now.

Mark Nicholls: Both packs had been going 'all out', and most of the 'hard stuff' that is supposed to be barred in the game was in evidence. All were equally to blame – not just the New Zealanders. The Rugby Union's own players were in it up to their necks. After five minutes of play Tom Voyce, who was having his first game against us, said, 'Gee, I never knew they went as hard as this. Come on chaps.'

Jock Richardson: It was a terrible incident but I didn't see it. There had been a lineout from which a ruck formed. I was on the ground and when I got to my feet Freethy was ordering Cyril from the field. I asked the referee what had happened. He told me that Cyril kicked a player on the ground. I spoke immediately to Wavell Wakefield, the England captain. He either ignored me, or didn't hear me. I gave him the benefit of the doubt. The referee insisted that Cyril be sent from the field. I then had to tell him to go. We had to bring Jim Parker in from the wing forward position and into the scrum while Jimmy Mill, the halfback, then put the ball into the scrum. That left us with no one on the fringe but we decided amongst ourselves to score as many points as we could and sit on England.

George Nepia: I could see clearly the faces of my team-mates when they realised what had happened. Had all the spectators been able to appreciate the expressions of the All Blacks' faces as I did, they would have known that we were out to win – with all the added fire of avenging the slur on a great All Black's good name. Revenge is more than a terrific urge. It is a power as such moments to be experienced to be believed.

Jim Parker: He [Cyril Brownlie] was the victim of an incorrect and unjust decision. That is the truth and no one was in a better position than I to know it.

Mark Nicholls: I have a photograph of the scene as Cyril is walking off, and if any proof is wanted as to the number of guilty English forwards, this photograph supplies it. Three of the English forwards are 'smothering up', apparently apprehensive that they might be sent off too. I am not going to be so unwise to say that everything was fair and above board, because I know it wasn't, but to single out one man from sixteen guilty ones was, to my mind, unfair, and showed discrimination. Mr Freethy was a wonderful referee, but in what should have been his greatest triumph, the greatest match of his career, he made a scapegoat of a great footballer and gentleman, when he himself was at fault.

Bert Cooke: Maurice Brownlie's try in the closing stages of this game was among the greatest I have ever seen. He was playing like a demon and the way he tore for the line with that grim expression on his face he would have gone through a brick wall . . . We were determined to avenge the unjust charge made against Brownlie . . . and a new spirit seemed to obsess us. Play had been resumed for twelve minutes [after half-time] when M. Brownlie, almost on the spot where his brother had been ordered off, picked up from the loose following a lineout and looking neither to right nor left for support, put his head down and charged for the line. He smashed his way through a bunch of opponents and got across, with Gibbs hanging to him like a terrier, to score the most determined try I have ever seen.

Mark Nicholls: 'Moory' Brownlie secured possession and, brushing off his nearest opponents, and ignoring Young's efforts to tackle him, he sprinted for the line, beating Kittermaster and the fullback, Brough, to score in the corner. This was a great try, and no words of mine could do justice to it.

George Nepia: The heroes on our side were the forwards left to battle with England's eight. We had lost Cyril Brownlie; Parker had to be on hand to keep wing three-quarter Gibbs in check, and 'Son' White wasn't allowed to shove in the scrums in case the balance was upset. The five left did all the work, and watching their struggle for possession of the ball in the scrum was a sight for the gods. I watched their legs take a strain that would have broken limbs less stout than theirs, and it was little for wonder that they left the field at the end of the match utterly spent, able to get to their dressing rooms and no more. If there was one thrill greater than all others in that match it was the sight of

Cyril Brownlie is dismissed at Twickenham. *Scran*

Maurice Brownlie crashing his way over the English line to score a try. He had gathered the ball almost on the exact spot his brother had started his walk to the dressing room, 'in disgrace', and, though Gibbs was holding on to him, Maurice was not to be baulked of his full share of upholding the grand name of Brownlie.

Cyril Brownlie: It was a piece of sheer ill-luck on my part. I found myself involved in a series of minor retaliations and was unfortunate to be dropped upon as the second man in the affair. I am most sorry this has happened in the last match, but I do think another man should have gone off the field beside myself. Nevertheless, there is no ill-feeling.

George Nepia: Wakefield and Voyce alone showed a sense of humour now and again to relieve matters. Both were fine sportsmen, as indeed, were the whole English team – with one possible exception. He seemed to have lost his head completely in that match, as he did in a previous game against us. But for him the game would, I am sure, have been played under far happier circumstances. That whole English backline was distinctly useful . . . England's forwards were, however, too stodgy to be of much scoring efficiency against our fast-moving pack.

Cliff Porter (1923-30, 7 Tests, 41 games): At Toulouse the crowd were marvellous . . . about 35,000 on a very hot day. It was very much to our liking, although we had a little bit of trouble there. It took us about a quarter of an hour to get to our dressing room after we arrived. The game started off at a hot pace and after twenty minutes things looked pretty serious for us, but we settled down and we got into our stride. We believed in open play, we tossed the ball around a lot, we'd worked into a combination by then. We won that match by 30 points to 6.

George Nepia: I enjoyed every minute of every game. What a pity, we all thought, that we hadn't had a chance to try conclusions with Scotland. As a matter of fact, the Scottish players themselves took the initiative in the matter and approached Stan Dean to try to get a match fixed. Stan tried, but as everyone knows, nothing came of it.

Bert Cooke: Poor Dumanoir, the player I marked in the international, was killed a few days later in an air crash. He was a pilot in the French Air Force.

Tours with NSW were exchanged in 1925-26 while 1927 was free of international contests as selection began for the first great trek to South Africa.

New Zealand's acquiescence to South African demands that no Maori be included meant that two key players, Nepia and halfback Jimmy Mill, were excluded, while a third, Cooke, was unavailable. Compounding matters was the strange refusal to select Nicholls, despite his ranking among the great five-eighths, for the first three Test matches. He played the fourth and duly won the game for New Zealand in what South African legend and rival five-eighths Bennie Osler said was the greatest display he ever saw. Apart from anything else the tour was the beginning of the end for New Zealand's 2-3-2 scrum. The South Africans were too strong and were able to call for scrums instead of lineouts to extend their advantage and Nicholls was one who became a critic of the strategy. It would take a few more years but the end was nigh.

Above all other considerations the era from 1924-28 was a great one for the All Blacks, a period in which they played eight official Tests with the only two losses being against South Africa in the drawn series. As well, ten internationals were played against New South Wales for eight wins and two losses, however these were not accorded Test status, as New South Wales, despite featuring the cream of Australian talent in Queensland's absence, were not regarded as fully representative of the country.

Interestingly Jim Ryan, based on his experience of South Africa in 1919, had observed before the 1928 tour, 'Two matches per week and long railway journeys and hard games on sun-baked surfaces in a programme of twenty-two matches, of which four are Tests, will be a hard pill to swallow. Many casualties will result before the players adapt themselves to the hard grounds and a judicious selection will have to be made in order that the best players will be fit and available for the all-important Test games . . . I consider that we have sufficient pace, weight and experience in the team to win the Tests, provided our best inside men are available all the time.'

George Nepia: It was known that a team would be chosen [to tour South Africa] at the beginning of the [1927] season, and that trials would be held just as they had been in 1924. I never got so much as an invitation to play in a real trial and I did not play in even a semblance of a trial! Nor did any other Maori. You might well ask the reason. It had been made plain, it appears, to the New Zealand Union that, in view of the difficulties of the 'colour' question in South Africa, 'it would not be desirable to have Maori players in the team to represent New Zealand'. Yet, seven years previously, South African players had played against Maoris in New Zealand – and were nearly beaten. More unutterable nonsense was never advanced as a reason for anything than that stipulation about Maoris. I need hardly say the whole of New Zealand was highly indignant, not only at my exclusion from the team but also at the slur on her Maori citizens.

Jim Burrows (1928, 9 games): Our first discovery was that in South Africa there was a dedication to rugby and a knowledge of play and players that matched anything we knew in New Zealand. Not surprisingly we also found, as part of this dedication, a scientific approach to the game that quickly jolted us out of any complacency we may have felt on arrival. As an example, the Springboks during their 1921 tour of New Zealand had obviously appreciated that the weakness in New Zealand play lay in the two-fronted scrum and this weakness they intended to exploit to the full. This was shrewd thinking.

Mark Nicholls: We met Western Province country team in the first match, and won. Then we opposed Western Province town, one of the hardest teams in South Africa to overcome. We played our next match 4,500 feet above sea level. Then we rose another 2,000 feet for the following match. The air was so rarefied that we could hardly breathe. In the first six matches we played were five of the hardest of the tour. At Kimberley there wasn't a blade of grass on the ground. Every time we fell over it took lumps of skin off. We didn't fall over often.

Jim Burrows: Transvaal fielded heavy forwards with the usual trio of big men in the front row. They had a formidable pack and, following a line now familiar to us, they called for scrums instead of lineouts when it was their ball. By contrast we were not a good pack at all. How could we be? Not only were we unfamiliar with the techniques of the South African scrum, but we made the fatal mistake of failing to recognise the importance of lock forwards in this new formation. Our two locks were Geoff Alley and Ian Harvey and neither was picked to play in this game.

Mark Nicholls: The tremendous amount of travelling from high to low altitudes and vice versa, resulted in a succession of colds and influenza, while the hard grounds certainly caused minor injuries. We also found the eight-seamed balls as used here, difficult of handling and kicking, but now we are getting accustomed to them. We found the train journeys rather arduous and irksome. Some of the boys slept like tops all through, but the majority did not sleep at all well. Train travelling for hours at a time – and in some cases days – is hard on athletes when suffering from injuries and sickness.

Frank Kilby (1928-34, 4 Tests, 18 games): The travelling is most strenuous, long journeys being a trying feature. The trains are most comfortable, but there is no opportunity to exercise, and players are inclined to eat too much. The New Zealand team travelled from Durban to Capetown [sic] on arrival – three solid days – and then had only two days before meeting a strong Western Province side.

Jim Burrows: The outstanding feature of the 2-3-2 scrum was its ability to get the ball quickly; the outstanding weakness of the 2-3-2 scrum was its inability to get its fair share of the ball. You cannot give away the loosehead in every scrum and expect to remain on equal terms with the other side, particularly when that side is South Africa. We learnt much from the play of the Springboks, particularly from their scrummaging techniques, though I must admit that it was typical of our conservative way of doing things that another four years elapsed before we adopted the three-fronted scrum and, in my opinion, about another twenty years before we could begin to say that we had mastered the techniques of this scrum.

Mark Nicholls: Mr George Devenish, one of the 'big five', a South African selector, told me that when he first saw them line out on the field at Cape Town to play, that they were, physically, the finest set of forwards he had ever seen, and that his heart went down to his boots for South Africa. After the first Transvaal match he said, 'They cannot scrummage and they will be beaten at forward everywhere.' The Springboks won the first Test by 17 points to nil. There was no question about their win. It was a most decisive one. As was expected, they dominated the game forward, winning the scrums by 36 to 15. But that was not all, for they heeled from fully ninety-five per cent of the loose rucks. In fact we were on the defensive right through the game.

Maurice Brownlie (1922-28, 8 Tests, 61 games): The result was overwhelming, but we can still smile and say bravo. We are not downhearted . . . We have appreciated our matches and we look forward to those to come.

Mark Nicholls: In spite of the fact that we had been consistently beaten for possession from set scrums by every other country, we had clung slavishly to our scrum formation. For six years we had been slowly but surely sacrificing the very heart and foundation of our game. Our men were as heavy, and it is reasonable to suppose, as powerful as the Springboks, yet with numbers equal in the scrummage all through the second spell, and with one of their forwards not infrequently out of the scrum during the first half, we were more and more clearly and completely mastered the longer the game proceeded.

Sid Carleton (1928-29, 6 Tests, 21 games): We were unable to get even fifteen per cent of the ball in this game. Bennie Osler was able to stand fifteen yards behind his forwards and he was able to find the line until he was on position to get in a drop at goal. We had two of our three-quarter line injured in the first twenty minutes . . . one of them, Alan Robilliard, couldn't even throw the ball into the lineout.

Mark Nicholls: They pushed our pack all over the field, they got possession from the set scrums at will, and during one period of the second spell they heeled from sixteen set scrums in succession. In the rucks they were always our masters, and behind it all, getting a royal feast of the ball, was the arch strategist and superb line-finder, Bennie Osler. Thus was shattered the 'Aura of Invincibility' which had sheltered and sustained the morale of the All Blacks. It was a far more serious-minded and more formidable All Black team which left Durban after the biggest defeat any New Zealand team had suffered in a Test match.

Alan Robilliard (1924-28, 4 Tests, 27 games): It was very hard going all the time particularly as I didn't get to play in many of the easy games. I found it very hard to get past the defence – you would beat a couple and then there would be another couple in front of you.

Frank Kilby: The spectacular forward is not encouraged in South Africa, whereas he is the man we go for in New Zealand. They play a real dour 'head-down-all-the-time' type of game.

Mark Nicholls: For almost a week prior to the second Test we trained seriously and hard. We evolved the loosehead and practised it secretly. Our idea was to have the loosehead on every possible occasion; for having the loosehead meant that we were certain to get a great deal more of the ball from set scrums than we did at Durban. This secret was carefully guarded . . . not a soul but the team knew of 'the stunt' until the first scrum went down in the second Test. We won the Test by 7 points to 6. As a spectacle, the game was a poor one, being decidedly dull and drab. That we deserved our victory there can be no gainsaying. Our play was the more enterprising.

Bill Dalley (1924-29, 5 Tests, 35 games): The team got their heads together and we thought, 'Well the only way we can get the ball from the scrums is to have three men in the front row', so we went out training at the Wanderers ground a few days before the second Test and locked the gates. What they did was that Ron Stewart, who was the wing forward, would come up onto the side of the scrum where the halfback was putting the ball in and play in the front row, and this enabled us to get the loosehead and we got our fair share of the ball in that Test.

Ron Stewart (1923-30, 5 Tests, 39 games): I was big enough and thought strong enough to take on the big Springbok front rowers. Also, by using me as a rover, a position I had played in on tour, and dropping the out-and-out rover Scrimshaw, we in effect had eight genuine forwards on the field – just like the South Africans.

Mark Nicholls: The most amazing feature of the game was the transformation of our scrummagers. They played with skills, method, cohesion and design. Our new tactics, and the determined scrummaging, was too much for the Springbok pack, which was exactly the same one that had wiped the floor with us at Durban. We had learned a lesson at Durban – that two men cannot beat three in the front row of the scrum . . . We also learned that the heart of the game is good, solid, intelligent scrumming.

Dave Lindsay (1928, 3 Tests, 14 games): I may be exaggerating but from my memory from where I was on the field was that there was a scrum about five yards from the sideline and five yards from the goal-line. Ron Stewart got the ball and tossed it to Strang and said, 'Have a pot', and it just flopped tiredly over the bar.

Mark Nicholls: The major part of the first half was in favour of South Africa, and at half-time, with the score 8-6 against us, it appeared to me that with a shade of luck we could win. The pace was a cracker from the start, and it was a question of which pack would crumple first. The Springboks showed signs early in the second spell, but Bennie Osler nursed them with judicious line-kicking to such effect that they came back like giants refreshed, and in the last twenty minutes gained the ascendancy. Our forwards performed with distinction, and it was only in the final quarter they wilted.

Dave Lindsay: I think in this game we could quite easily have won it, we missed about three tries.

Lance Johnson: (1925-30, 4 Tests, 25 games): Bennie Osler was a superb footballer, good hands, splendid punt and drop kick and he was also very solid in defence.

Mark Nicholls: We won this fourth Test match by 13 points to 5, and squared the rubber. We went on to the field with the knowledge that South Africa thought they could not lose. If we had failed, then New Zealand's great name in rugby would have been lowered to second place. Anyhow we won, and won without the shadow of a doubt. For the first time in thirty-seven years South Africa were beaten on their famous Newlands ground. It was a day for the good, honest and strong forward – the man who could scrum, push, dribble and possessed 'devil', and to that we owed our success.

Dave Lindsay: The difference between a good footballer and an average one is that a good footballer takes advantage of opportunities, and Mark certainly took his on that day. Our forwards certainly dominated the game.

Maurice Brownlie: We consider that rugby in South Africa is of a remarkably high standard. We found the South Africans worthy foemen, and we shall carry away to New Zealand most pleasant recollections of the many hard matches we've played. If we'd had Nepia and Cooke we wouldn't have lost a match.

Mark Nicholls: There have been many rumours about ill-feeling among members of the team, particularly between Morrie Brownlie and myself. I desire to give here a public denial. Morrie and I have been the best of friends at all times. We might differ, and have differed, on various matters in rugby, but in this team all put their shoulders to the wheel and did their best for New Zealand.

Alan Robilliard: There was a split – in the papers but there was nothing in it . . . Certainly they [Brownlie and Nicholls] didn't get very close to each other but they were different types.

SIX

A FUNDAMENTAL CHANGE

'I grassed him. The Test had been saved for New Zealand.'

IN THE WAKE of the South African experience, debate increased about how much longer New Zealand could continue to play the 2-3-2 scrum with its detached wing forward. Opinions were divided and the debate was fuelled when the manager of the 1930 Great Britain side, James 'Bim' Baxter, following the first game of the tour in Wanganui, called for the wing forward position to be abolished. After the second game against Taranaki he called the wing forward a cheat. Ironically, New Zealand had introduced a law variation which placed an offside line through the middle of the scrum and the wing forward was not permitted beyond that. However, the Home Nations administrators had demanded the tour be played under 'international' law which allowed the wing forward unlimited scope to go about his particular actions. If that unfortunate interference in the debate didn't help those who may have been wavering, there was a solid body of opinion for change including Mark Nicholls. But one prescient comment was made by a wing forward, the All Blacks captain of the day, Cliff Porter. He remarked some years later, 'So long as the game of Rugby is played, there will be wing-forwards. Scrum formations will make no difference, for it matters not whether a 2-3-2, a 3-3-2 or a 3-4-1 scrum is packed, there will always be wing-forwards. Perhaps his name may be changed or his duties lightened, but that is all. In England they are called winging forwards and in Australia breakaways,' he said.

But before the issue dominated the Great Britain tour, New Zealand sent a team to Australia in 1929. It included many new players from that which toured South Africa and it was beaten 0-3 by the reformed Australian side. Nepia had returned to the side but was injured in the third game and did not play again. By the time the British arrived for their tour Nepia was restored to health, Bert Cooke was available for selection again and Porter, who had not been chosen for South Africa, and who had captained the 1929 side, was restored as captain.

Great Britain beat New Zealand 6-3 with snow falling, in the first Test, played at Carisbrook in Dunedin. Nicholls was brought back for the second Test and had a significant bearing on the 13-10 win in Christchurch, although his individual effort was eclipsed by the two superb tries by the Great Britain centre Carl Aarvold, who later presided as a High Court Judge in the trial of the Kray brothers in 1965. New Zealand won the third Test in Auckland 15-10 and wrapped the series up 22-8. It was the end of an era for New Zealand with the subsequent retirement of a clutch of great players including Bert Cooke and Cliff Porter who scored two tries each as well as Nepia, Fred Lucas, Nicholls, 'Bull' Irvine, Ron Stewart, Ian Finlayson and Bill Hazlett.

Opposite: Cliff Porter. *Alexander Turnbull Library, Wellington, New Zealand*

George Nepia: In 1929, I went with the All Black team to Australia. The Australian teams included most of the Waratahs who had been touring England in 1927, and as this made a formidable opposition, I was keen to be at my best. I had a special reason for wanting to be at my best. Five years previously, the Australian critics had said everything bad about me they could think of and I had deserved it. Now, I wanted to show them that I had not been in form in 1924, and that I could do a great deal better. The best of plans and hopes go wrong sometimes, and against New South Wales, I got crocked and was unable to play again during the tour. Porter also got crocked and he too, was just a passenger for the rest of the trip.

Bert Cooke: The 1930 British team was as fine a team as we have seen in New Zealand to my knowledge, and they certainly played attractive football. Their backs were so fast that we could never feel safe, and both the second and third Tests might quite easily have gone the other way. Spong was the king-pin of their backs. He was a chap who took a lot of stopping on account of his nuggety build and great determination. Aarvold, Bowcott, Murray, Novis and Morley were players of real class, and Bassett, the fullback, was very steady.

Cliff Porter: They're good to watch but they seem to lack that fire and one or two crash tacklers. At that time perhaps our backs were just as speedy as the British backs. Spong was the starting point, similar to a stand-off or five-eighths. When the British got the ball my job was to run outside Spong, even attempting to catch him. Nine times out of ten he attempted to cut back in and there was our five-eighths waiting to catch him.

Bert Cooke: The first Test at Dunedin was played on an unforgettable day, with a blinding snowstorm which continued right through the curtain-raiser, and did not let up until well on in the big match . . . The most remarkable feature of this match was the great try scored in the last minute of the game by Jack Morley. This was the greatest try I

Lions fullback Jack Bassett looks to evade Don Oliver during the first Test in Dunedin.

A souvenir poster from the Lions series. *Alexander Turnbull Library, Wellington, New Zealand*

ever saw. A scrum had gone down in the British twenty-five quite close to the goal-line, and near the touchline. New Zealand hooked the ball, and Mill set out to go round the blindside, but found himself blocked, and threw a long high pass back infield to Lilburn, the first five-eighth. That split second of delay caused by going round the blind was fatal. The alert Ivor Jones intercepted in a flash, and with a great sense of positional play he ran out towards the touchline to bring Morley into position. At the same time he dummied to the open side and threw most of our backs on to the wrong foot. It was a great piece of quick thinking. As he approached Nepia, Morley was up with him. I yelled out to George as I raced after Ivor Jones to watch Morley, as I could cover Jones. Nepia said afterwards that he did not hear me. He was faced by two men and thought he should go for the man with the ball. Jones delayed his pass till the last fraction of a second, and as he sent the ball out, he ran on into Nepia, and they both went down together. That left Morley and me racing together from halfway, but he had just too much start, and coming from infield I had a shade further to go, and all I could do was touch him as he went over at the corner.

George Nepia: It came to the second Test, at Christchurch. New Zealand was leading by 13 points to 10 when there happened one of those things which settle the fates of so many Tests and the morale of many teams. Aarvold had the ball. He was making for the line 'full steam ahead'. Right down the centre of the field he came towards me, and – as I saw to my horror – with Novis in attendance on him. Aarvold I could grass: Novis was a very different problem, for his speed was too much for me. I knew that if he got the ball, it was 'all up' for New Zealand in that Test and England [sic] would be two to the good. Novis was one of the fastest and strongest running three-quarters I have ever encountered. To my utter amazement and intense relief, may I add, Aarvold held the ball and gratefully, I grassed him. The Test had been saved for New Zealand.

Bert Cooke: It is hard to say how the match [second Test] would have gone had [Paul] Murray not gone off, but there is every chance they would have beaten us. As it was, both sides scored two converted tries, but a goal from a mark by Mark Nicholls, who played as well in this match as I have ever seen him play, enabled us to win by 13 to 10 . . . Mark Nicholls initiated a great try in this match by starting to run to the open side, then 'propping' to go round the blind and put Don Oliver in at the corner. Mark also did a tremendous lot of work in covering Corner, who was having his first international game. Corner, however, showed that he could stand on his own feet, and he made a great entry into Test rugby.

For the third Test, at Auckland, Oliver was dropped and Lucas went out from centre to wing. Strang came in at first five-eighth, Mark Nicholls went to second, and I to centre. We won at Auckland by 15 to 10, and undoubtedly had a shade the better of things. This game, too, produced some controversies. Towards the end, the ball was kicked over my head and Spong and I both went after it. I had to turn round, of course, and when the ball was still half a yard in front of me Spong tackled me, Ivor Jones picked up the ball, and raced clear to put Aarvold in from halfway, the latter absolutely leaving Nepia standing flat-footed with one of his paralysing swerves. Thus a try was given against us, under the posts, instead of the penalty in our favour which we expected and were entitled to. My main recollection of that match is the amount of backing up I did, as George Nepia was very casual and used to nearly give us heart failure by strolling about with those British speedsters coming down on him.

All Black halfback Merv Corner prepares to launch a box kick over the on-rushing Lions forwards during the second Test, 1930. *Alexander Turnbull Library, Wellington, New Zealand*

The fourth Test we won easily 22-8, though there was hardly that much between the teams. However, they were a very stale side. We scored six tries, but there was an element of luck in one or two of them, and I know in one that I scored, the ball rolled for me perfectly as I dribbled over from about fifteen yards out.

In 1932 New Zealand finally decided it would no longer play the 2-3-2 scrum. New Zealand struggled to adjust and played the last Test under the system with Frank Solomon the last player in the wing forward position, against Australia in 1931. A new broom swept through the game in 1932 for a tour of Australia which was one of the most successful with a record number of points being scored and while the first Test was lost 17-22, the series was won with victories in the second and third Tests 21-3 and 21-13 respectively. Another tour followed in 1934, a year after Australia had won two Tests in a five-Test series in South Africa and buoyed by that experience the Australians won the Bledisloe Cup for the first time, beating the All Blacks 25-11 in the first Test and drawing the second 3-3.

Beau Cottrell (1929-32, 11 Tests, 22 games): We gradually worked out what we had to do [with the 3-4-1 scrum]. We were pretty loose at first, but we started to get the hang of it. The functions of a hooker in the old scrum were not too different from those of a prop in the three-fronted scrum, as the old hookers had to do their share of pushing as well as doing a bit of hooking.

SEVEN

COMING TO GRIPS WITH THE SCRUM

'they went about their rugby in a ruthless way'

THE BRITISH AND Irish tour of 1935-36 was the first real test of the new scrummaging demands. While packing a three-fronted scrum the All Blacks persisted with their eighth man, Hugh McLean more often than not feeding the ball to the scrum and then racing back to play in the wing forward mode. However, the greater weight enjoyed by opposing sides denied New Zealand scrum ball too frequently and McLean was eventually forced to contribute his weight to the effort at No.8. The best New Zealand pack was able to hold its own against the British sides. The weak link in this side, captained by Jack Manchester, was at first five-eighths. It had been intended that a running style would be led by playing J.R. 'Rusty' Page with Pat Caughey and Charlie Oliver at centre but in his second outing Page did his knee and played only once more, in the twenty-first game, the load being transferred to the two Wellingtonians Jack Griffiths and Eric Tindill, a specialist halfback. Their hopes were undone by the pack's inability to dominate scrums. When they did get sufficient ball it was too often kicked away. New Zealand lacked the specialists for the new scrum – an issue that wasn't resolved for another fifteen years.

Charlie Oliver (1929-36, 7 Tests, 33 games): The 1935 team was not recognised in New Zealand as a good one, but after all, after twenty-nine games we only lost three of them and two of those were internationals. The other of course was Swansea.

Eric Tindill (1935-38, 1 Test, 17 games): Everyone agreed the British standards had improved and we were a younger team than the 1905-06 and 1924-25 teams. I was lucky. I played a trial when coming on as a first five-eighths for the last quarter of an hour. When I got on things just seemed to start happening and I potted a goal at the end to give us a win 23-22. That saw me get a place in the final trial where I dropped another goal and I was named.

Mike Gilbert (1935-36, 4 Tests, 27 games): We had a long trip over on the boat and needed to stay fit. The bosun made up this scrum machine for us to practice on. It was made up of piping and he was very proud of it, but it hurt our forwards' shoulders a lot and they weren't so keen on it. One night there was a bit of a party on the boat and the thing ended up going over the side.

Hugh McLean (1930-36, 9 Tests, 29 games): We hadn't been long in England before we realised that we were up against more than some of us, at least, had bargained for. I think the first unpleasant shock came in the first match, when, although we won comfortably,

Opposite: A Springbok player risks life and limb as he dives on a loose ball during the third Test of the 1937 series. *Alexander Turnbull Library, Wellington, New Zealand*

the Cornwall and Devon forwards sometimes gained yards in the scrum by pushing before the ball went in. Frequently in this game our front row would be standing up waiting for the remaining forwards to pack in behind them, and the Devon and Cornwall forwards would crash in against our chaps' hips. Naturally, accustomed to New Zealand rulings, we would expect them to be brought back and the two front rows packed down properly. Instead, the ball would go in as soon as their halfback could get his hands on it.

Artie Lambourn (1934-38, 10 Tests, 40 games): I was probably the first of the 1935 side's front row forwards to have the experience of packing against a three-fronted scrum. When Mark Nicholls came back from South Africa in 1928 he was absolutely convinced of the merits of the 3-4-1 scrum, and introduced it to Petone. I used to pack down in the front row against the club's senior team, which started using the 3-4-1 scrum. By the end of the 1935 tour we really had quite a competent scrum. After the two-thirds mark, I think we out-scrummed every team we played against, internationals included. Although practically every team we played against used the 3-2-3 scrum, Britain was on the verge of change.

Hugh McLean: We lost Bill Hadley in the first game . . . As a specialist hooker we met no one on the tour who could hold a candle to him. Without Hadley we were faced with the position of not being able to get the ball, and this was undoubtedly the cause of our troubles in the early part of the tour, when we were beaten by Swansea and had close calls in two matches in Scotland.

George Adkins (1935-36, 10 games): Bill Hadley was a very fast striker of the ball and had the advantage in every match he played. In the games where he didn't play the opposition would take scrums instead of lineouts.

Hugh McLean: The Swansea match was, of course, a blow at that stage of the tour. Beaten in the fifth match! It was not very pleasant. This was where we encountered the famous 'schoolboy halfbacks', Tanner and Davies. I might say in passing that if they were in New Zealand it is highly improbable that they would still be at school, as they are well past what we would recognise as secondary school age.

Jack Manchester (1932-36, 9 Tests, 36 games): Tell them in New Zealand the better team won [Swansea]; but don't tell them we were beaten by schoolboys.

Joey Sadler (1935-36, 5 Tests, 19 games): At Swansea it was one of those days when things do not go right. They started well and we struggled to get under way. But once a team gets the upper hand early it is hard to win back mastery. We beat Llanelli, Cardiff and Newport in successive games, matches we won fairly comfortably, but the Swansea match was the one the Welsh remembered.

Hugh McLean: Eddie Long, the Swansea captain playing loose forward, practically camped on Eric Tindill all day. At this time we were taking our scrumming so seriously that we had gone to the opposite extreme and were not breaking fast enough, so that any advantages in spoiling were definitely with the Welsh loose forwards. Long was frequently offside and was cautioned by the referee several times. In this match [Swansea] we had our first experience of the red-blooded Welsh forward play. I've seen some tough football in New Zealand, but those Welshmen have developed an 'all-in' style of rugby which makes our most hectic encounters seem insipid by comparison.

After the loss to Swansea, the side was unbeaten until the Wales Test, still the key game on a tour of Britain, in the twenty-sixth game when they went down 12-13 after the Welsh scored with five minutes left.

Hugh McLean: The backs had a series of tactical moves, known by various names. One of the most successful was the 'PK' in which the wing came inside between the half and first five-eighth. George Hart scored two brilliant tries from this movement against East Midlands at Leicester. One of these was his memorable solo dribble, one of the most remarkable tries I have ever seen, in which he darted diagonally across the ground for about seventy yards, playing the ball past various opponents with his foot, eventually lofting it over the fullback's head, and racing up to catch it on the full over the goal-line.

Joey Sadler: It was my first international, Scotland, something one never forgets. It was a beautiful day and we were at peak form . . . Conditions were ideal, sunshine but no wind. When we started off Scotland got a try quite early in the piece and that cheered up their supporters, but we gradually got on top. Our first try came from a beautiful cut-in by Jack Griffiths who beat his man, passed to Pat Caughey who scored near the posts and that was converted. Later Bill Hadley, from a ruck near the line, snapped the ball up and went over. Towards the end of the first spell Pat Caughey went over again and at half-time it was 13-3, but Scotland came again with a rush in the second half and they scored and things started to move a bit, but gradually we got on top and towards the finish I went round the blindside, passed it to Brushy Mitchell who went up to their fullback, drew him, and passed to Pat Caughey who got his third try.

Hugh McLean: We stood in considerable awe of those Scottish forwards, and the Scots themselves were confident that they could beat us. Hadley was back, and we aimed specially at getting possession and getting the ball to the wings.

This was Pat Caughey's great day, as he scored three tries. The last was a magnificent effort in which he, Mitchell, and Sadler all did brilliant work. At Aberdeen 'Mike' Gilbert got into three figures, scoring his hundred points for the tour, and running up into the three-quarter line all day. On one occasion he nearly went clean through from fullback. People in New Zealand probably do not realise what a versatile player he is. He would make a really high-class centre.

Charlie Oliver: We won the Test [Ireland] by 17-9 but really only played on half of the ground because of the bad conditions. Jack Griffiths our first five would kick for the line until we were inside their twenty-five and then we'd attack. We had a good backline, but the conditions we had to play in, they were pretty useless.

Hugh McLean: The Irish forwards made things pretty hectic in the second spell, but one of the Dublin papers condemned their destructive tactics and was pretty candid in appraising the respective merits of the two teams. Oliver in this match scored an absolute gift try. Ireland were in difficulties and one of the backs passed back to Morris, the full-back, under the posts. Morris attempted to kick but missed the ball altogether, and Oliver simply picked up the ball and scored.

Joey Sadler: [Wales] No decision was made on who would play halfback – Merv Corner or me – and till the actual morning of the match we did not know. I suppose I should have been nervous about it but being young it simply did not affect me in any way at all. It is not that I was casual about it, but even when I knew I would be playing it was just something I accepted. As we prepared for the Test, the main thing we realised was that we would have to get mastery in the forwards. We thought we had the backs – George Hart on the wing and so on – to get us a few points up if we could give them room to move. Normally before a game I was conscious of the crowd, its size and its noise. But here, with the singing audible in the dressing room, I was more conscious of the crowd than ever before.

Hugh McLean: One must give every credit to the Welsh backs, among whom I think that, despite the praise accorded to Wooller, Cliff Jones was the best. I can describe him as a sort of 'super Spong'. New Zealanders will remember the elusiveness of Spong. Jones is Spong and a bit more added. He sidesteps like a dancing master. The remarkable thing about the Welsh tries was that they were all scored from the bounce of the ball, and it will probably be a long time before the ball rolls so nicely for Wooller and Rees-Jones as it did that day. Rees-Jones touched down twice from short punts by Wooller. He also fumbled and let Kelly Ball in for the try that gave us the lead after Mike Gilbert's great potted goal. I remember hearing Rees-Jones, at the dinner that night, claiming modestly that he had scored three tries – two for Wales and one for New Zealand.

Joey Sadler: The Welsh recognised our need to get the ball through quickly, too. We had our advantage in the forwards but the Welsh were getting through on to us very quickly. They employed Haydn Tanner as a halfback-cum-wing-forward. He was getting round on to me and others were on to Jack Griffiths. They knew they had to bottle us up inside so that we could not get the ball through to the wings.

Hugh McLean: Up till half-time I thought we had this game safely in hand. We had a lead of 3-nil, had had a good try [Hadley's] disallowed, and had definitely had the edge on the Welsh forwards. Had we managed to add another try immediately after half-time I believe we should have won comfortably. Unfortunately for us, this was the time when Wooller, having come into the centre, 'went mad', and in a few minutes we were seven points down. The scenes of enthusiasm at this reversal of fortune in favour of Wales were simply incredible, and Wooller became a national hero.

Joey Sadler: Then Wilf Wooller made his break, and kicked ahead, for Rees-Jones who took the ball as it bounced backwards. Poor Mike Gilbert. The ground was slippery here and there and in other places the frost was still hard. It was terribly difficult for him to stop in full stride and turn. In the very last minute we broke through and charged after a high kick to their fullback, Vivian Jenkins. He took it and found touch and that was it.

A fortnight later the final Test against England resulted in some strange selections. Tindill was given the Test ahead of Griffiths while Merv Corner replaced Joey Sadler who had performed well throughout at halfback. George Hart was dropped as wing in spite of being recognised as one of the fastest players. He and fellow wing Brushy Mitchell scored twelve tries each on tour, second only to Pat Caughey who scored eighteen.

Merv Corner (1930-36, 6 Tests, 25 games): I did have the honour of playing in that game [England]. Joey Sadler played the other three. I envied him. As it turned out I was to play in the game when New Zealand suffered its most severe loss. I think in terms of territory we had the equal of the opposition, but the running of the English backs was the deciding factor and in particular the running of Obolensky. I will never forget covering behind our backline watching Obolensky score his first try. He fooled Ball by coming in and then running around him and he did the same to Gilbert, who made sure he wasn't going to come infield and beat him. But then with a terrific burst Obolensky went around outside Gilbert to score. Later on Obolensky was to put the seal on the victory as far as England was concerned by instead of running around Ball suddenly propping and then coming across field in the opposite direction. Then finally despite the terrific effort of Brushy Mitchell, who dived and actually did touch his ankle, he was able to score in the other corner.

Jack Hore (1928-36, 10 Tests, 45 games): I felt that we were outplayed in the whole game. Irrespective of who was behind the scrum or in the forwards we simply weren't good enough. Perhaps if things had gone our way earlier in the piece we might have capitalised with one or two tries.

Eric Tindill: We lost the Welsh Test in the last minute 12-13 but we were well beaten against England, it was just like playing against a brick wall.

Hugh McLean: After the Twickenham match Obolensky was the hero of the hour, and he certainly had every right to celebrate the occasion. But to my mind the honours definitely belong to Peter Cranmer, who was prevented from playing against us earlier by an injured knee . . . Cranmer would walk into any All Black side. He has not only got a beautiful sidestep, but he is a big chap, and runs hard, with a strong fend. He is not as big as Wooller, but is more resourceful, and he was the king-pin of the English attack at Twickenham. Sever, on the opposite wing to Obolensky, was one of the soundest wings we met, and his try from an opening by Cranmer was a perfect piece of orthodox rugby, and as such quite as meritorious as either of Obolensky's tries. Probably Obolensky will never again tread the heights as he did that day. Everything went right for him. His second try, when he turned infield, might not come off again in a hundred years. Candler had thrown a pass into the blue, a despairing effort – and there was Obolensky, running infield because he had nowhere else to go, and miraculously finding the way open to him.

A home series with Australia in 1936 resulted in two Test wins and the stage was set for the tour by South Africa in 1937. From the outset the big side dominated New Zealand combinations and it was a surprise, not only to the South Africans, when they lost the first Test 7-13. In a tough second Test the Springboks levelled the series 13-6. The New Zealand selectors panicked and moved their best back, and future New Zealand Rugby Union chairman, Jack Sullivan from centre to wing. The injured Brushy Mitchell, who had hardly played for Southland that year due to a leg injury, was deemed to have passed a fitness test in Auckland and was selected at centre where he had played in the third Test against Australia a year earlier, his previous Tests being on the wing. Pat Caughey, who had played only one game for Auckland due to being overseas, was named ahead of John Dick on the wing. Mitchell's injured leg went early in the game and he moved to Caughey's wing. Not that it mattered too much, as the Springboks tied the ball up in the scrum. Rather than opt for lineouts, captain Phil Nel, as he was entitled to do under the laws of the day, called for a scrum. This was in response to a message he'd received during the week before from South Africa's captain to Britain in 1906-07 Paul Roos which said simply, 'Skrum, skrum, skrum'. New Zealand suffered one of its heaviest defeats 6-17 conceding five tries without reply.

Jim Burrows: They were the best team to visit New Zealand. For their all-round good football they deserved all the praise showered on them. They left us with a message that rang loud and clear throughout the land – you cannot score points in rugby unless you have possession of the ball. We knew what we were up against in the scrums, but we didn't have the Springbok technique, nor did we have any front row men the size of the Springboks. We played the best front row available, and they were all excellent forwards, but they were much smaller than their opponents.

Artie Lambourn: The Springbok pack was different to any other the All Blacks of that era had played against. Its whole game was centred around the scrum, and the forwards were a scrumming machine. They were all big men, and very strong. We had never come up against such big props before. Even in Britain the props were all around our size. Their main technique in 1937 was their tightness and togetherness. They were as tight as a drum. Jan Lotz was a tremendous hooker, but he had the advantage of a massive shove from behind.

Doug Dalton (1935-38, 9 Tests, 21 games): The Springbok props were so much harder than anyone we had come up against before, and they knew what they were doing.

Artie Lambourn: The Boks were also technically ahead of us in another way. By getting their front row to keep their feet well back, they moved the centre of the channel closer to their side, and were thus closer to the ball and in a better position to hook. According to the laws in those days the centre of the scrum was the point halfway between the feet of the opposing front rows. Having their feet so far back, which they could do fairly easily anyhow as they were bigger than us, meant that the ball was being put in at a spot somewhere below their chests, and further away from us. In the third Test they just wore us down in the scrums. At one stage Doug Dalton and I switched places to see if we could get more ball, but we didn't do any better.

Ron Ward (1936-37, 3 Tests, 4 games): They were complete footballers. They had big forwards who were fast and who knew what to do, while they had a fine backline and they went about their rugby in a ruthless way.

Jim Burrows: The sports writers were concentrating on the Springboks, and few were rating our chances very highly. This was so unusual in New Zealand that I think every one of us, in our isolation at Otaki, said, 'We'll show them.' We won the first Test 13-6 and, because there had been apprehension in New Zealand before the match, the celebrations afterwards shook the whole rugby world.

Ron Ward: I was named as the forward to go out into the backs if anyone should be injured. Sure enough, twenty-five minutes into the game wing Don Cobden was tackled heavily and forced to leave the field. I went out to the wing. I was given great encouragement by centre Jack Sullivan, fullback Jack Taylor and second five-eighths Jack Hooper. You would have thought I was a star player the way they looked after me, even if I did something wrong. I was disappointed about having to leave the pack. The South Africans had named Danie Craven at first five-eighths and had Pierre de Villiers at halfback. I felt the way I was playing at that time that I could have handled Craven. The difference between de Villiers' passing and Craven's was like chalk and cheese.

Artie Lambourn: I cannot look back on this without first thinking of Ron Ward and the great game that he played for New Zealand, by looking after Williams, the South African winger who was their fastest and certainly most dangerous runner.

Jim Burrows: We lost the second Test 6-13. Both sides scored two tries, in our case both by J.L. Sullivan, the centre three-quarter, but the Springboks converted their tries and kicked a penalty. Though the game was close and at one stage could have gone our way, the Springboks were a better team. The power of their scrums was frightening.

Ron Ward: We should have won that game. Jack Sullivan scored two tries in the first half and the South Africans went back to their dressing rooms at half-time a beaten team. But when I talked with Springbok prop Boy Louw after the third Test he told me what happened. This is how he put it to me: 'Everyone had their tails down. I spoke up and said we can still win this game. Skipper Phil Nel said to me: "If you think you're so bloody clever, tell us how." I said, "You fourteen continue to play rugby and I'll look after things." I said I would crack my opposite prop Doug Dalton because I knew after playing him earlier that if I could upset him he would do his block. I hit Doug and he did his block. I had also told our guys that if he tries to cool down I would hit him again, and I

Springbok fly-half Tony Harris slices through the home defence at Eden Park
during the third Test of the 1937 series. *Weekly News*

did. That was when we got on top and won the game.' It was interesting that former All
Black Billy Stead wrote several times in the *New Zealand Truth* that he thought centre
Tony Harris should switch to first five-eighths. He said Harris' blistering speed would be
ideal for a first five-eighths and he became a highly-rated player in the position. He always
acknowledged that Stead played a role in him being named in the five-eighths.

Jim Burrows: At the third Test, when their captain called for a scrum instead of a lineout
the first time the ball was kicked out by New Zealand, I feared the worst. They defeated
us 17-6 and for the first time in rugby history the All Blacks had been beaten in a Test
series. Throughout the country there was consternation and dismay . . . This was the best
touring team yet to visit New Zealand. Nothing like its scrum work had been seen before
in this or any other country, and for its all-round good football it deserved all the praise
that had been showered upon it.

Ron Ward: In the third Test Brushy Mitchell should never have played. He and Pat
Caughey had both been injured. Good footballer as Brushy was he should not have
been picked. But the real problem was we kept kicking the ball out and they, as they
could do under the laws of the time, kept calling for scrums. They were so decisive.

They couldn't do anything wrong, whether it was kick, run or pass and at times they were just unstoppable.

A year later it was back to Australia and ten new All Blacks were named as the rebuilding began with a view to South Africa in 1940. The tour was a great success with all nine games won and a new inside-back combination of Charlie Saxton and Trevor Berghan setting a talented backline alight. Hopes they would carry New Zealand's banner in restoring honour against South Africa were denied them by the outbreak of the Second World War a year later. Trials were held to select a team for the 1940 tour but it was never announced by sole selector Ted McKenzie.

Brushy Mitchell (1935-38, 8 Tests, 32 games): [In a letter to the NZRFU] I think you will agree with me that the South Africans in 1937 taught us the value of the long pass from the base of the scrum. We in Australia this year employed the same long pass and, I think, proved to 'Doubting Thomases' that for three-quarter play this long pass was essential. Yet, on returning to Dunedin, and having witnessed Otago play four Ranfurly Shield games, I was amazed to see that the only side employing this method was South Canterbury with Saxton as halfback. To my mind it is absolutely essential to employ this long pass, otherwise three-quarter play in New Zealand will not advance. If I remember correctly, I think this recommendation came from the committee set up for the purpose of going into the lessons learned from the Springboks, and yet we find that the only ones using it in their clubs are those who have had actual playing experience against this longer pass. It therefore seems that, until the present generation of players grows up and begins coaching, these lessons will not be heeded, for, speaking from my own experiences, the greater number of the older generation seem loth [sic] to scrap the formation which was so successful in their day but which was behind a 2-3-2 scrum. With the South African tour [1940] so close, and so much at stake, something should be done to give our players every chance against such formidable opponents.

Charlie Saxton (1938, 3 Tests, 7 games): Most of the boys in the South team [in the annual inter-island match of 1939, won by the South 25-19] would have gone to South Africa with the All Blacks the next year. The team that never was. Selected but never publicised. A pity. The length of the war was a big slice out of a lifetime, let alone a rugby career. None of the boys played for New Zealand after the war.

EIGHT

RECOVERING FOR ANOTHER TREK

'we were losing because I wasn't good enough'

WAR ONCE AGAIN cast its shadow over the world between 1939-45. New Zealand was involved from the outset and while some first-class rugby was played it was piecemeal rather than at the competitive level associated with peacetime. There were no Ranfurly Shield challenges and no inter-island games. Overseas there were games played, especially during the North African campaign with a notable contest played in November 1941 between a 2nd NZEF selection and a South African side which the New Zealanders won 8-0. Other rugby was played regularly and as soon as the war ended in 1945 the Commander 2nd New Zealand Expeditionary Force, General Bernard Freyberg VC, issued an order for the preparation of a tour of Britain by a New Zealand Army side. He had discussed this prospect with Alan Andrews, who would be appointed manager, as early as 1940. Trials were staged in Austria and England and twenty-nine players were named in a side that became known as the Kiwis and who would win a special place in New Zealand rugby history for their contribution not only to morale in the post-war era but to rugby development courtesy of their running style of play under the captaincy of halfback Charlie Saxton. Seventeen members of the side became All Blacks.

But the war had taken its toll and again several All Blacks were lost. Bill Carson, also a New Zealand cricket representative, who had toured Australia in 1938 and who had been regarded as a certainty for the 1940 side, died of wounds suffered in a mortar attack on a vehicle he was in in Italy in 1943. He was on a hospital ship on the Mediterranean returning to New Zealand when he died. Don Cobden, the West Coaster who was injured in the first Test against South Africa in 1937, joined the RAF and died during the Battle of Britain when his plane was downed over the English Channel. Jack Harris, who played fullback for the All Blacks in 1925, died at Cassino in 1944. Wing George Hart who played 11 Tests between 1930 and 1935 and who was also a national sprint champion, died when his tank was hit in Italy in June 1944. Cyril Pepper, a tourist to Britain in 1935-36, died when back in Wellington after winning the Military Cross in North Africa in 1941. He had recovered after being invalided home and was undertaking a jungle warfare course when he suffered a fall and died in May 1943. Southland midfield back Arthur Wesney, who toured Australia in 1938 and was considered another certainty to have toured South Africa in 1940, died at Sidi Rezegh a few days after playing for the 2nd NZEF side against South Africa in 1941. Another 1935-36 tourist, loose forward Jim Wynyard, who served as a tank commander, was killed during the second Battle of Alamein in November 1942.

Bob Scott (1946-54, 17 Tests, 52 games): The most enjoyable football I have ever played was with the New Zealand Army team, the Kiwis, in the British Isles and on the

Opposite: Ron Elvidge breaks through the tackle of Jim Stone to score against the Wallabies at Eden Park in 1946. *RR Elvidge Collection*

Continent in 1945-46, and in a great many respects this was the best team of my era. The discipline in this team was natural, unaffected and magnificent and will always remain my ideal of the kind of spirit which should be developed in a rugby team.

Fred Allen (1946-49, 6 Tests, 21 games): Charlie [Saxton] was in pain for most of the time on that tour but he still played some great rugby. He did a great job [as captain and coach]. He taught us young fellows a lot – gave us a good grounding.

Charlie Saxton: It was an extremely fit team and there was a marvellous spirit. From the team came sixteen post-war All Blacks. Just about everyone played for their union on their return home. In doing so, they helped to revive the game in New Zealand after World War Two. I like to think that we also left rugby in Britain and France in a better state.

Johnny Simpson (1947-50, 9 Tests, 30 games): Bob Scott and I were taken in to see the manager of the team individually. Bob went in before me and came out and just said, 'Sign it.' 'It' happened to be a declaration that we would never play league again. But I always enjoyed rugby much more anyway. There was far more to the forward play and a greater degree of skill in the moves. The Kiwis tour was a marvellous tour. The game we played was a beautiful flowing game. Players like J.B. Smith were in their element. He could walk on water, J.B. If he didn't beat you one way, he would do it twelve others. The tour helped put rugby back on the map in the UK. And I learnt a terrible lot.

Ron Dobson (1949, 1 Test, 1 game): For a while we weren't known too well and we were travelling in 'third class' on the back of army trucks, three-tonners, until we started to win

Players from the New Zealand Army team get ready for kick-off before facing Scotland at Murrayfield in 1946. Charlie Saxon is on the right. *Scran*

a few games and one of the writers got on the case and said it was a pretty poor show that these chaps were being treated like this. From there on, the whole thing changed and we struck the limelight with the press and the accommodation and the facilities we received were altogether different.

Jim Kearney (1947-49, 4 Tests, 22 games): There hadn't been a touring team there since 1935. We were all a band of inexperienced players, few of us had played any big rugby at all, except for Charlie, and there is no doubt about it Charlie knew the ins and outs of rugby. And his idea was to keep the ball moving, in other words the 'three Ps': possession, position, pace – and to handle the ball and try and play enterprising rugby, not so much dour, but enterprising to entertain the people.

Charlie Saxton: The singing of the crowd [Wales] is something to be seen and to be remembered. It really is awe-inspiring and almost frightens one for a moment, but then the game starts. Now when we were there, no New Zealand team had ever beaten Wales in Cardiff – the 1924 team had won in Swansea – and we were under a bit of a strain. That game was played in fine weather and on a firm ground. Our forwards put up a particularly fine fight that day. The Welsh loose forwards were quite a thorn in our side. The greatest memory of that game is [Jim] Sherratt's try. It was a glorious try and Sherratt got a glorious hand from the crowd – perhaps one of the greatest ever scored on Cardiff Arms Park. You can imagine as we saw Sherratt stride ahead, it was as if he was carrying every member of the side on his back.

Jim Kearney: Going to Murrayfield, especially after Gloucester . . . we'd had quite a big win there . . . we felt as if we were coming into reasonably good form and the Scottish people were convinced that we'd put up a good score against them. There'd been a very hard frost and they had to put straw on the ground. Instead of finding Scotland the weak international team it was supposed to be, we found them a bit tougher opposition than what we expected. Things just didn't go very well at all. The Scots forwards, they got at us and we were on our back haunches for a fair bit of the game. Then they brought their backs into play and we found out that they had a lot of pace in their backs, more than what we expected and it was certainly very tough going.

Charlie Saxton: We had a good team opposing us, we had a good referee, we had no complaints, no excuses, we were beaten on the day's play by the better team and we congratulated them on the victory.

Ron Dobson: We played a strong British Army team and General Freyberg had had a bet . . . a five pound bet with a British general that we'd beat them. During the game Johnny Smith said to me, 'Would you mind moving out to centre for a moment Dobby, I think I can score a try here.' Well the ball was shot along the backline to Johnny and he crashed through Risman, past their fullback and scored by the posts right on half-time. Freyberg came to the dressing room at half-time, and in that peculiar voice of his said, 'These chaps are pretty tough, how do you think it'll go?' Johnny patted him on the back and said, 'She's right Tiny, we've got 'em now.' We ended up 25-5 and Freyberg threw his five pound note into the dressing room after the game and said, 'Cut it out boys, it's on me!'

Jim Kearney: We went to Paris not knowing very much about them or what type of football they played. Our boys weren't too sure what we'd come up against. We got underway in Paris – a lovely ground they had there. They'd taken snow off the ground the day before but the conditions were very good. They had a packed grandstand, in fact a lot of people couldn't get into the match. France was pretty keen on its rugby then. The French players reminded me very much of some of our very good Maori teams. They played very open rugby and were very hard to stop, short nuggety chaps. I can assure you they hurried our boys along a bit. They called Jim Sherratt, Le Grand Cheval, and when he got underway he did remind you a bit of a galloping horse. The French crowd really fell in love with Jim and he felt very embarrassed about it when they gave him an ovation.

Had they had a decent goal-kicker, which the French had been lacking for quite a while, it could have got them a lot more points and we were quite grateful they didn't. The French were pretty keen on their rugby and our team, having just come out of the Army, still in uniform, they thought quite a bit of us.

New Zealand resumed international play late in 1946 with a two-Test home series against Australia, winning 31-8 and 14-10. A return tour occurred the following year with nine of the Kiwis team included and nine others who had played for the All Blacks before. In the ten games, including one against Auckland on their return, the side won eight, losing to NSW 9-12 and Auckland 3-14. But both Tests against Australia were won, 13-5 and 27-14. No international games were played in 1948 as the country prepared for a return tour to South Africa.

Bob Scott: Playing against Australian teams straight after the Second World War in 1946 was an uncertain area. But you had confidence in your ability. You'd been picked for the All Blacks and it meant that you were top of the list. Consequently, you anticipated that you were going to be better, or hoped you were going to be better, than them. I was always a bit wary of the Australian backs, who were generally so brilliant, and as a fullback you're trying to cover everything.

I took the field for the first Test at Dunedin in a state of mind that I have never otherwise experienced. I was nervous as well as proud . . . I was so determined not to let New Zealand down that if the Wallabies had thrown a kangaroo at me I would have made some sort of stab at anticipating his hop. After the first international, you never again experience quite such a confused state of mind, even in the heart of South Africa or Wales. The Australians of 1946 were a lively side, with paralysing pace in the backs.

Johnny Simpson: This [1947] was the first series against Australia since the end of the war. We played nine matches and were defeated only once, which was by NSW.

Bob Scott: We played at the Sydney Cricket Ground in 1947 and I know that next door, I think it was at the Showground, they had a league game on. It wasn't a Test, but they had a bigger crowd there than what we had at the Sydney Cricket Ground playing against Australia. To me it didn't matter whether I was playing against somebody in Timbuktu. I was playing for the All Blacks and it was important to win. I struck an amazing streak of goal-kicking, easily the best I have ever had. In two matches on the Sydney Cricket Ground, I kicked fourteen goals in fifteen attempts . . . I played in six of the nine matches and scored 72 points from twenty-one conversions and ten penalty goals. Later on, in South Africa in 1949, I played in seventeen of the twenty-four matches and the best I could do was score one try and place nine conversions, eleven penalty goals and two dropped goals. Without disparagement to the Australians, I'd have willingly chucked away the triumphs of 1947 for half as much luck in South Africa.

Johnny Simpson: The Wallabies at the time were a pretty good team. We had a little bit more experience and our forwards were stronger and one or two of our backs were outstanding. But they also had some wonderful backs. The chap [Charlie] Eastes that played on the wing, he was a very good player. There were the Windon brothers, and there was Phil Hardcastle, the captain and forward, who I had one or two run-ins with. In one of the games he pulled me down a few times when I jumped for the ball in the lineouts. As a matter of fact, I had a bit of bad luck because our lock forward Charlie Willocks put his head up at the wrong time and copped one from me when I had a swing at Hardcastle. He'd just put his head up to see what was going on and wasn't very happy about that.

Bob Scott: J.B. Smith was my first example of the thinking footballer. He toured the British Isles with the NZ Army team immediately after the war. Then he went to Australia with the All Blacks in 1947. Subsequently, he could not win a place in a full-scale New Zealand team though, at about his finest, he was debarred from joining the All Black team which toured South Africa in 1949. Smith was a cunning, crafty old fox from his earliest days. He plodded about the field like a ploughman wandering o'er the lea. His hands seemed to dangle below his knees, his shoulders were hunched, his face, though impassive, was drawn in melancholy. He looked the saddest, most incongruous spectacle ever thrown on to a field. There never was a finer disguise. Actually, he had an ice-cold, analytical brain which was incessantly studying every situation and which was particularly concerned with his immediate opponent. He could be the most patient dissembler, carefully biding his time and giving no indication of his intentions. And then would come the moment when his eye would flash, his fend would dart out, his hips would shift sideways and his legs would start moving at their fastest. That was the moment when the tackler himself went down – alone. That was the moment when Smith, the thinking footballer, outguessed his man . . . J.B. Smith says that he can tell from the way his opponent handles the ball in the first rush of the game what sort of player he is.

Johnny Simpson: The Australian selectors were concerned about their locks and asked me to have a look at any players who I thought might play for Australia. We played New South Wales B and Nick Shehadie did very well against us. He hit the rucks hard and wasn't afraid to get stuck in, so I mentioned him to the selectors. He was picked for the first Test. Both those Tests were very hard and I remember the wonderful efforts of Bob Scott who did not miss a penalty kick or conversion on the entire tour. The other great effort was from Neville Thornton and the kick he had from halfway in the Sydney Test. We had a penalty right on halfway, but Bob Scott had tweaked a groin injury in a tackle. So our captain Fred Allen said to Neville, 'Here, have a kick.' He placed the ball on halfway and Fred looked around and said, 'What are you doing? I want you to kick for the sideline.' He said: 'No Fred, I'm going to kick the goal.' All the people were laughing at the start and then there was dead silence. Then he kicked it and it went up and up and up and over the top of the posts between the middle. The whole crowd at the Sydney Cricket Ground got up and cheered. It was a wonderful kick by a forward and we won that game 27-14.

In those days we concentrated on good scrumming, good lineouts, good rucking and quick ball. And the old three Ps came into it – possession, position and pace. And in those days the forwards weren't out in the backline getting in the way. The No.8 was taught to go to the corner flag. He went straight to the corner flag as fast as he could so that he could be there in defence or join in the attack.

As was the custom in that era, trials were held in 1948 with no stone left unturned as games were played between July and September. Excluded from consideration because Maoris were still not welcome, this a year after the National Party had won the South African election in 1948 and were to enact the apartheid laws, were Vince Bevan, Johnny Smith, Peter Smith, Ben Couch, Alan 'Kiwi' Blake, Brownie Cherrington, Mick Kenny, who had achieved a remarkable recovery after sustaining machine-gun wounds in Italy, and Ron Bryers. Bevan's omission was unfortunate as halfback became a vital weakness. The selectors wanted only forwards over 14 stone and players were subjected to weigh-ins to prove the fact. Yet upon arrival in South Africa, the captain of the 1921 Springboks in the Tests against New Zealand Boy Morkel said, 'Your forwards. They are too big. For every pound over 14 stone they will lose a yard of mobility. They are too big.' The scrum was again to be the issue although confidence was high before the tour that New Zealand had sorted their scrum. Selection convener and 'coach' Alex McDonald commented: 'We will no longer be at a disadvantage in respect to the 3-4-1 scrum, which has handicapped us against the Springboks in the past. We can now use it just as well as they can.' By the sixth game of the tour, against Natal, Simpson would thump the table in the dressing room and say, 'Whether we like it or not we have got to learn to scrum the South African way.' He said the next day, Sunday, they would work on the technique with their South African liaison manager on the tour, the former Western Province player Bo Wintle, showing them how it was done. Later South Africa's coach Danie Craven would lecture the All Blacks on scrummaging. So quickly did they adapt that Craven would later rate Simpson and fellow prop Kevin Skinner among the great props in world rugby.

Yet New Zealand would suffer even more than they had in 1937. They lost the series 0-4 and to add to the injury Australia toured New Zealand and won both Tests to reclaim the Bledisloe Cup. On 3 September, New Zealand lost two Tests on the same day! It was a miserable tour, the South Africans spent their time trying to shut down the All Blacks backs and Bob Scott had a dreadful time with his goal-kicking. To cap it off, tour commentator Winston McCarthy would write, 'Biased refereeing there most certainly was; in fact two Tests were probably lost on those grounds, as was at least one other match.

Bitter to take, but nothing unique.' The consequences of New Zealand's loss would be seen in 1956 when rugby entered a dark age.

Bob Scott: The 1949 tour of South Africa was a terrible shock to New Zealand, the worst we have ever had. We began the trials and tribulations of 1948 with the belief that the surest way to beat the Springboks was by size. We were not going to be out-scrummed a second time. Forwards under 14 stone need not apply. Because of the demand for size, every player in the trials had to be weighed in his football togs in the presence of the three selectors. Weight is a great quality, especially in forward play, but it is not of the first importance. Playing for Auckland against Waikato in the first representative match of the season, in June, [Fred] Allen had somehow torn the muscles at the back of his neck. The injury never ceased to trouble him and though he remained a great attacking back he never again reached the standard of the Kiwi tour.

Kevin Skinner (1949-56, 20 Tests, 63 games): They allocated us a little bit of the deck, every morning, and we got up early and did what we could on the deck, anything really, to keep physically fit. It was exercise, that was all you could say it was. We did have three weeks in Africa before playing a game. We were at Hermanus and trained there for three weeks pretty solidly. Some of us put on a wee bit of weight on the boat, it was good tucker on board.

Jack McNab (1949-50, 6 Tests, 17 games): It's silly but there appeared to be a lot of jealousy in the Rugby Union. In the build-up to the tour there was a lot of haggling for the coaching position. The NZ Rugby Union made a mistake. They appointed a man as coach [Alex McDonald] on the 1949 tour of South Africa who was far too old for the job, and we had one of the greatest coaches New Zealand has ever had in the Otago man, Vic Cavanagh. If he had been with us, it's my belief we would have lost very few games and have questioned the South African organisation of the tour. It was nothing to do with him [McDonald] as a person – he was a good bloke actually – very fair – the problem was within the Rugby Union. The coach Alex McDonald, while a good man, was sixty-seven and near the end of his career. He was heard to say that he wasn't much up to coaching any more and at one point invited Fred Allen to take an active role.

Vic Cavanagh believed in a good diet and plenty of physical exercise. He would have questioned the amount of junk food and sweet desserts that were put in front of us and he would have kept up with us at practices ... There was no structure to the tour either. The long distances of up to twenty-four hours on a train, from Johannesburg to Cape Town for the first Test and the following day, twenty-four hours back to Johannesburg was outrageous. Vic would never have allowed it to happen. But what was wrong with the New Zealand Rugby Union? They must have approved the tour – they must have known.

Bob Scott: We played a game in Johannesburg on the Saturday, and then got on the train, travelled all Saturday night all day Sunday.

Kevin Skinner: We were away nine nights and spent eight of them on the train. We got on the train on a Monday afternoon, went all the way to the Victoria Falls, had a day at the falls, got back on the train Tuesday night, back to Bulawayo on the Wednesday morning, went to bed and then got up and played at half past two. The night after we played at Bulawayo, after the reception, we went down and caught the train again, then we had a head-on collision with another train, which didn't help much.

Fred Allen: We used to get off at night when they were filling up with water and coal, and try to train.

Jack McNab: We had our meals on the trains. We could eat what we liked. There were huge amounts of everything, especially fruit, pineapple, oranges, bananas. But also high calorie foods like cream, desserts and dressings. We believed the South African Rugby Union made lavish food available on purpose. We ate out of boredom as the train chugged along the long straight tracks. We were fattened for the kill – lambs to the slaughter.

Johnny Simpson: Packing down against some of the Springbok front rows in 1949, especially against men like Jaap Bekker, was more demanding and exhausting than sprinting around the field. You came up from a scrum knowing you had really worked. We more than held the Springboks in '49 after learning their style.

Jack McNab: When we got to Africa we found the South African scrum rulings were different to ours and they hooked the ball a bit differently to us. It took us a while to come to terms with it. In the front row, New Zealand always hooked with the opposite foot but in South Africa they hooked with the foot nearest to the ball. We had to develop our footwork immediately to suit their rules or we knew we would be sunk.

Kevin Skinner: We never had a coach. Alex McDonald, this old soul, he was thinking 1905 and it was 1949. You've got to be able to get the guys to put your body on the line for them and we didn't have that. Those South Africans were big and heck, every game was like a Test. The war was over but we were all saying it, we had a hell of a fight on our hands.

Neville Thornton (1947-49, 3 Tests, 19 games): Their forward play was very much suited to the game the way they saw it. They had the great tactician Danie Craven on their side. Our backs were superior to theirs, that was evident from the first game against Western Province Universities. [They saw] just how effective our backs could be if they weren't stopped and Craven found the answer in the No.8 player . . . the writing was on the wall and he produced this No.8 forward [Hennie Muller] plus the No.7 who was very effective most of the time. In the forwards we obtained a lot of ball, our forwards were very, very effective in rucking, in particular, we might have even obtained too much. In scrummaging after we'd caught the technique used by the South Africans in the early games, we obtained as much ball as they did. But where they scored was in this direction . . . they were prepared to leave two or three forwards out of it and hold us in the pack with the rest. You might imagine they were leaving a lot of weight out but in the scrums it didn't matter. It was in the lineouts where the most damage was done. In the lineouts, on any occasion where we started to move them, their remaining five or six strongmen were able to collapse things.

Bob Scott: One could offer not criticism of Geffin's first penalty, for Grant was plainly offside, but the second, occurring when we were leading 11-3 was against Grant for swinging around, while retaining a hold on the scrum, to assist in the heeling; and this was unfair. Then came a penalty for an infringement in a ruck which followed a lineout after Thornton had caught Wahl just short of our goal-line. I do not know what the infringement was, but Mr Hofmeyr was entitled to his opinion. Then came the second disputed penalty, which Mr Hofmeyr awarded when he 'thought', as he told Winston McCarthy, that Savage had touched the ball while it was still in the scrum. South Africa was now leading 12-11 and when Boggs put his hand on Moss's back while he and the latter were racing for a loose ball, it was 15-11 and we were done for. We all left the field in a fury and it took a long time for the emotion to subside.

Jack McNab: They beat us on penalty goals and we all thought the referee was wrong. Bob Scott had fielded a ball and Bill Meates was running back to help him when the referee blew the whistle. He said Bill was shepherding – but it was just ridiculous – impossible actually. Another was when a scrum went down. In those days you got penalised if you lifted your foot before the ball went in to the scrum. We all decided to keep our feet firmly on the ground, which we did, but the referee penalised us for lifting our feet just the same.

Fred Allen: Each time, or the very few times, they got into our territory there was a penalty, which Geffin kicked.

Johnny Simpson: Halfway through the tour we were getting stuffed in the front row. We were not used to the three-fronted scrum. I kept harping on about it and one Sunday we decided to sort it out, even though that was frowned upon on a Sunday. We had hours of scrummaging, we got into it and stayed until we got it right. By the end of the tour we had the better of them in scrummaging. Craven called [Has] Catley a cheat, and someone said Has would get kicked one day. On one occasion he was kicked and I hit my opponent, Okey Geffin. He said to me, 'It wasn't me.' But I told him: 'You're the nearest one Okey.' It didn't happen again.

Bob Scott: I should put the front row of Simpson, Catley and Skinner against the world with absolute confidence in its ability to prove superior. Simpson was a veritable rock. He stood six feet or thereabouts and had a trunk like a kauri tree. He was also extraordinarily powerful in the thigh and calf. Catley was more complex. He saw life as a series of symbols – scrums won and scrums lost . . . he was 15 stone of battle-scarred farmer, very strong in build, and technically extremely fast. [Skinner] was our greatest forward; and though, in later years, he was always outstanding and in 1952 gave one of the greatest of post-war forward displays against Australia in Wellington, I do not myself believe that he ever afterwards gave such a sustained exhibition of forward play as in 1949. I am quite sure I reached my finest form in South Africa.

Neville Thornton: There's no doubting about it that Hennie Muller was a really great player. He ran well, he tackled magnificently, his handling was beautiful and he ran as well as a back. He could have played equally well in the backs. When the ball was obtained by us he was prepared to stay right out of it. That's not to say that he didn't give his share in the scrums and rucking. But when it was the lineout he was prepared to stay right out of it and concentrate on our inside backs, leaving his core men to do what they could to get the ball. And if they didn't, there he was right in amongst our backs. He didn't usually go for the first five-eighths. He stood very much further out on many occasions. We frequently won the ball and looked up and there was Muller right in the middle of our backs and we were losing ground. We appeared to have no answer to him. We talked about various ideas but we didn't think of the Ponty Reid-Des Connor technique of kicking over the lineout, it was never tried. We tried bringing in the wing, we tried running the blindside but generally speaking we remained faithful to the tradition of spinning the ball along that backline, getting out quickly to the backs and winning the ball from there. It didn't work. We were playing the same game at the end of the tour as when we started and I think that was our downfall.

Bob Scott: Our one real comfort before the end of the game [second Test] was a cut by Allen which led to a pass to Elvidge and a further pass to Meates and a ninety-yard run to within three yards of the Springbok line. The man who bowled Meates into touch was the wonderful Muller. How he must have run! It was a great movement, in thought and execution, and gave us something to think about for the next Test.

Fred Allen: Brewis was playing first-five for them. He went to go one way on the open side – he paused as though he was going to drop kick for goal, and then he shot back when he saw he was covered, completely bamboozling all our players on defence. Brewis, I'm sure, was amazed to see the gap open up on the blindside and the line in front of him. Bob Scott came haring across right on the goal-line, and he arrived at the same time as Brewis, but too late to stop him from scoring.

Neville Thornton: We found the grounds very severe on us, they were as hard as steel, like playing on a tar-sealed road, and I can well remember our inside backs having very badly scarred hips. I remember Fred Allen with blood running down his legs after he'd knocked the top off a scab that had formed. They did try rubber pads. That didn't seem to help – it slowed them down, and we were very sore under foot.

Fred Allen: Okey Geffin was a very fine goal-kicker. As a front row forward, I think he was just average and I think the fact that he was such an accurate kicker helped him maintain his place in the South African side.

Morrie Goddard (1946-49, 5 Tests, 20 games): In the 24 games we played in South Africa our line was only crossed eight times . . . yet we lost four Tests. All the penalties against us over there – well, after that I thought neutral referees should control these games.

Bob Scott: The third Test was about the lowest point of our tour. By now we were receiving the full spate of criticism from New Zealand and the obvious failure to work out a counter to Muller had increased our state of depression.

Fred Allen: Local referees like Burmeister missed the odd vital infringement when the pressure was on, possibly through one-sidedness. As far as Mr Hofmeyer was concerned, he was much more severe in lineouts and scrums and appeared to be paying a lot more attention to the visitors. However, I'm sure it was unintentional and he was doing his very best as all referees do.

Bob Scott: I shall always remember the feeling of dread I experienced in the first few minutes of the fourth Test. South Africa was penalised about forty-five yards from the goal and Elvidge, our captain, tossed the ball to me. 'No, no,' I said. 'Give it to someone else, Ron.' By that stage of the tour, my inability to kick goals at vital moments, especially in the Tests, had practically given me nightmares. I had lost that confidence which is so essential, and genuinely dreaded the thought of making a fool of myself and the team. As I remember it, I left the field more profoundly depressed than I have ever otherwise been in my life . . . no matter how much I tried to rationalise, all our failures seemed to be my fault. We were losing because we could not kick goals. I was taking the kicks at goal. Therefore, we were losing because I wasn't good enough. It seems a little ludicrous to say now that I left the field in so total a state of dejection that, when I had sat down on the hard bench in the dressing room, something impelled me to say, 'I'm sorry fellows,' and all at once I was having the biggest howl of my life since childhood.

Fred Allen: We had a wonderful team spirit despite many reports to the contrary during our tour. That proved itself when we got back to New Zealand and not one player made any excuses publicly or press wise. I must say as skipper I admired their loyalty and team spirit . . . Bob Scott was tragically unlucky and I cannot recall any kicker hitting and shaving uprights as much as he did during that tour, and I can't help but think back to the 1947 Australian tour when he kicked goals from every conceivable angle and distance, as if there was a magnet between the uprights.

NINE

RESTORING HONOUR

'the kind of rugby he dreamed about in boyhood, wanted to play
when he was a man, and lingeringly thinks about now'

RETIREMENTS AFTER THE South African tour meant a rebuilding exercise was required in 1950 but there was little time to scour the country as the British Isles side was due. Two trials and an inter-island match, as well as the early games by the tourists, were played before the first Test. Losses to Otago and Southland just before the first Test caused visiting captain Karl Mullen to tell his side they would prepare with their limitations in mind. He believed the losses would ensure the All Blacks' complacency and that the Lions had a chance. With Jackie Kyle, one of the greatest of five-eighths, Bleddyn Williams, Jack Matthews and Ken Jones, their backs were a genuine force and they had New Zealand on the ropes before they came back to draw the first Test 9-9. They lost the second and third Tests but were unbeaten in their remaining provincial games. The third Test is one of the classics of NZ rugby history with the winning try scored by Ron Elvidge who had returned to the field after suffering a severe shoulder injury and who was little other than a passenger for the game. With Johnny Simpson suffering a career-ending knee injury, New Zealand's pack was reduced to six men for three-quarters of the game, yet they held the Lions to claim a 6-3 win. Down 3-11 in the fourth Test the Lions ran the ball from their own in-goal and the flying Ken Jones scored to set up a thrilling finale to the game before the All Blacks held on to win. Little wonder the crowd refused to leave the ground at the end of the game.

Bob Scott: Despite the losses, the tour was truly memorable. No finer pride of Lions has ever assembled. The players were cheerful, gregarious and extraordinarily popular. As a team, they fell down on forward play . . . Had their forwards done better than hold ours, they would have beaten us in each of the four Tests. The rugby personality of the tour was, I suppose, [Jackie] Kyle. He had been written up as a great player before the tour began and I think the tour itself amplified this opinion. For myself, I would be quite prepared to say that he was a genius . . . He had the true quality of greatness, the ability to produce memorable rugby when it was most needed. By ordinary standards he was incalculable. He was an instinctive rather than a manufactured player and reacted to situations in a flashing fraction of time ahead of anyone else.

Peter Johnstone (1949-51, 9 Tests, 26 games): It was a great shock to all of us who were playing [the first Test]. Admittedly we were together as a team for the first time but to realise that the British Isles were a team of that quality was a shock to all of us and we had quite a job in holding them to a draw. I think the highlight would be Ron Elvidge's try which allowed us to draw 9-all. Up to that time we were a very poor second with the score being at 9-6 with a few minutes of play left.

Opposite: Richard 'Tiny' White looks on as running repairs are carried out during the third Test against the Lions, Athletic Park, 1950. *Alexander Turnbull Library, Wellington, New Zealand*

Bob Scott: Someone had once told me, I think it must have been Vic Cavanagh, that Otago had found that Elvidge, going to the right and using his left arm to fend, was unstoppable. We were 6-9, only seven minutes remained and then Bevan gave Elvidge the ball from a quick heel. Away he went toward the right-hand corner flag. It was like a human tank . . . At least three men succumbed to that mighty fend; and then he was diving, triumph all over his face . . . I missed the kick. I desperately wanted to get it, but in afterthought I am glad that I didn't. The British Isles deserved the game. Out of the draw, they got much greater honour than we did.

I think it is fair to say of the second Test that the All Blacks were decidedly the better team . . . Our forwards approached their South African standard much more closely than they had managed in the first Test.

Peter Johnstone: Ron Elvidge was a very popular captain. We liked his style of play and the way he handled the team on the field and it was a big disappointment to the New Zealand side when he had to leave the field [in the third Test]. Johnny Simpson also had to leave the field. We had our backs to the wall. Later on in the second half Ron Elvidge came back onto the field and received the ovation he deserved because he was badly injured. He had a cut eye and I think a cracked chest bone and he was grievously sick. I don't think he played another game of football after that match. I had to go on the wing to fill the backline when he left the field. When he came back on he came up to me and said, 'Look Peter, any time you get the ball, be on your guard, I might try and get outside you.' That was his only remark to me. I can tell you I was looking for him every time I got my hand on the ball because being unaccustomed to wing three-quarter play I was ready to let somebody else have it. This try that Ron scored that won us the match 6-3 – it came from a passing movement that went through the backline. Roy Roper made a break, threw out a long pass to me on the wing and cut out the centre altogether. The moment I touched the ball Ron Elvidge called for it outside me and I gave it to him and Ron went on and scored a beautiful try.

Bob Scott: In my experience, this [third Test] was the game of a lifetime. We should never have won it. Simpson went off injured after twenty minutes – he was tackled by Evans in a movement which began from a forward pass – and after thirty-three minutes Elvidge retired looking, except for uniform, exactly as if he were a walking-wounded casualty of the battlefield. When he returned a minute after half-time – and what a cheer there was, a personal tribute as moving as I have heard in a game – he looked like a ghost. Thus we were reduced to thirteen effectives and though Rimmer had been hurt in the Simpson tackle, and Matthews late in the game suffered double vision from the violent clash of the tackle he had made of Elvidge, the Lions palpably had the physical advantage of us. To my mind, we won because our tactical thinking was superior. Matthews struck Elvidge with shattering violence round about the short ribs, and what had been a moment before a figure of superb physical elegance was violently turned into a bleeding hulk.

Ron Elvidge (1946-50, 9 Tests, 19 games): If it had not been for the rules I'd have not gone back. I'd have to say the rules of the time were absolutely stupid and dangerous. I was still shaky and groggy and it was because of that I decided to have a go at Cleaver myself. I was scared that had I passed to Peter, my handicap might not have meant the ball reaching him.

Eric Boggs (1946-49, 2 Tests, 9 games): A scrummage on the line, the ball is hooked by the defenders and – not, it is not kicked for touch, it is spun out along the backline towards their own goalposts . . . 'Lewis Jones!' scream 60,000 stirred voices . . . On he speeds toward the halfway line. Black jerseys turn in hot pursuit but there is only one in front of him . . . Bob [Scott] manoeuvres himself into position to cut down the flying Lion . . . A quick transfer from Lewis to Ken [Jones], expertly achieved, a feint at Scott and then in the clear. Amid the wildest acclamation he dots down between the posts. The score now: 11-8 to the All Blacks. Back for the kick-off. It's Roy John's ball and in a flash the lanky lock weaves his way right through the wall of All Blacks seeking that ball. Thirty yards to go, a perfect pass to Bleddyn Williams . . . the ball hasn't touched the ground since that great try. This time however the boot is on the other foot and Peter Henderson executes one of his famous dives . . . Back on attack come the All Blacks with the Lions in their own twenty-five. Referee George Sullivan is looking at his watch and as he does, Jackie Kyle gets the ball. The little Irishman dances his way out of trouble, moves upfield along the stand touchline and left-foot centre kicks. 'Ken Jones!' There's the great Welshman haring after the ball, anticipating its point of contact with the ground. If he gets it he's in and the Lions will equalise! Thud. The ball hits the ground and as the wizard of Wales stretches his hands out to cradle it home for that final try somehow it twists away from him and is smothered in black jerseys. Referee Sullivan blows loud, long and clear.

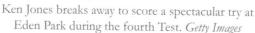

Ken Jones breaks away to score a spectacular try at
Eden Park during the fourth Test. *Getty Images*

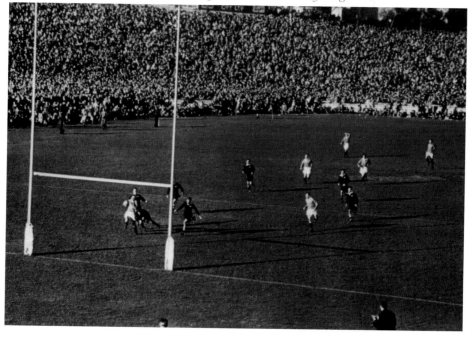

Bob Scott: Of a great many people I have met in the years since [the fourth Test], not one does not seem to feel, passionately, that this Test represented the kind of rugby he dreamed about in boyhood, wanted to play when he was a man, and lingeringly thinks about now in moments of reverie when he is recalling his fondest memories of sport. Only one team was in the game for the last five minutes – and it wasn't us.

Further retirements left New Zealand sending a new team to Australia in 1951. Players like Kevin Skinner, Bob Duff, Richard 'Tiny' White, Ponty Reid and Ron Jarden were to be the cornerstone of the side that would meet South Africa in 1956. Jarden was a revelation and in one game scored 38 points. Australia toured New Zealand a year later and won the first Test 14-9. In the second Test injury, when Ray Bell suffered a knee dislocation, again visited the All Blacks in Wellington and flanker Eddie Robinson was moved to the wing. Robinson set up the first try for the All Blacks and scored the second in the 15-8 win. He was never chosen again.

Bill McCaw (1951-54, 5 Tests, 32 games): We played the first Test at the Sydney Cricket Ground. There was a lot of rain around that time and the ground was just a quagmire. You couldn't see a blade of grass from twenty-five to twenty-five. You only knew who your opponents were by the way they were travelling. I saw the Bledisloe Cup afterwards but it was no big deal and there had been no talk about it beforehand. It was a nice introduction to the All Blacks.

Ron Jarden and John Tanner were both members of the NZ Universities team and they'd been touring Australia before our arrival so they stayed on and joined us when we arrived. Jarden was in tremendous form. He had terrific acceleration and he just ran around his marker, they couldn't compete with him and he was also a good goal-kicker so in several of those games he scored up to 20 or 30 points. I think that was the best form I ever remember him in. On the 1953-54 he had just been married and I think he was lovesick on that tour, he wasn't quite himself. And of course, Morrie Dixon and Alan Elsom gave him what-oh. They weren't kindly disposed to him. Dixon always hounded Jarden on the field and never gave him any room to move. The thing that came out of that tour was the second five-eighths Tom Lynch was a very strong player, that was the biggest regret we had in the 1953 side. We didn't have a good second five-eighths. If we'd had Tom Lynch . . . but at that time he had decided he was going to league and he wasn't available. We needed a penetrative back like him.

Bob Scott: In many respects, the most striking feature of the tour of the British Isles by the Fourth All Blacks was the emergence of R.C. Stuart as a great captain, universally admired and praised.

Bob Stuart (1949-54, 7 Tests, 27 games): We had a good team – a forward pack which was never mastered – and slick backs. It was so good we could make about thirteen changes between a Saturday and midweek team and not notice the difference. Because of the laws and interpretations, we were never allowed to play the type of game we wanted, and were accused of being dull and boring.

By the time the All Blacks met Wales they had already lost 3-8 to Cardiff and drawn 6-6 with Swansea. They had their chances to win the Test, spending much of the second half in Welsh territory but unable to get through and a piece of opportunism by flanker Clem Thomas saw a cross-kick lobbed into the All Blacks' goalmouth where the bounce of the ball beat wing Ron Jarden and fell to Wales' wing Ken Jones and he scored. Ireland were beaten 14-3, England 5-0 and Scotland 3-0. They went into the French Test match on the back of an 8-11 loss to South-West France. In the Test Jean Prat scored the only try as France won 3-0.

Bill McCaw: Bob Stuart missed several games at the start of the tour because he got an infection and was allergic to penicillin. So that allowed me to come into my own as I was the other No.8. It meant I got quite a few games until he came right again.

Bob Stuart: Rugby in the British Isles and France was generally of a high standard. If it suffered from one thing more than another it was indifferent teamwork. The backs in the British Isles, individually were extremely accomplished. They had speed, they could definitely teach New Zealand a lesson in accurate catching and safe and swift passing, and they had a venturesome spirit which was probably superior to the like spirit in the New Zealand game. From the beginning of the tour the All Blacks perforce had to accept the standard practice of referees quite often causing the ball to be put in six or eight times into the scrummage before allowing play to proceed. The pushing and shoving during these encounters was exhausting.

Ron Jarden (1951-56, 16 Tests, 37 games): Observations of a local English game before our first match convinced the selection panel that it was not possible to effect back passing movements from set play, particularly from lineouts. This attitude, once adopted, was adhered to throughout the tour. We endeavoured to control the game by forward domination and by playing the ball up the sideline, hoping to eventually reach a position where combined forward strength and close play round the side of the scrum could result in tries . . . limitations, however, obviously existed. The New Zealand team not only lost games it might have won, but throughout the tour won games by far smaller margins than it should have done.

Bill McCaw: I was made captain against the North of Scotland. Bob Stuart wasn't fit at that time, and they must have given Kevin Skinner a rest so I was next in line. It was always an honour to captain your country. Bob was an essential person on the tour, not so much for his playing ability but for his leadership because in that [social] climate in Britain when there were so many of these dinners you would have a professional toastmaster saying, 'My lords and ladies, pray silence for Mr R.C. Stuart, the captain and so on', they were quite toney. I think Skinner probably told the selectors he would prefer not to be captain because he had the feeling there was going to be a lot of attention for a captain. Bob was great, he made you proud of being an All Black when he got up to speak because he handled it so well.

Richard 'Tiny' White (1949-56, 23 Tests, 55 games): We had a running first-five in Guy [Bowers] as opposed to a flat-footed one in Laurie [Haig]. But we had to put up with the offside play of the British sides that was allowed to go unchecked so we had little choice but to go for Laurie. It was a style that was forced upon us.

Bill McCaw: The loss to Wales was a big blow. We dominated them more in the forwards but we just didn't have the penetration in the backs. I can still remember the try that swung it. Clem Thomas received the ball right on the touchline. He looked a bit startled and so just kicked it out into the middle of the field. Jarden came from one end and Ken Jones was coming the other way and Jones got the bounce and took the ball under the posts and that cooked us. The Welsh were so fanatical about their rugby. I remember the first game of the tour we played down in Hove against Southern Counties and in a ruck a red-headed Welsh guy said: 'Wait till you get to Wales.'

Bob Stuart: It's almost unbelievable how much ball we won, how much bad luck we had, and how much we lost by [against Wales]. I would have been happy though, to have settled for the 8-all draw the game was heading for. Ron Jarden had it [Clem Thomas' cross-kick] covered and I thought 'all it has to do is sit up all right'. It did – but for the flying Olympic sprinter Ken Jones.

Bill Clark (1953-56, 9 Tests, 24 games): Coming in on the bus from Porthcawl, our headquarters about twenty or thirty miles away, the tension was really on. Above all, we wanted to beat Wales, not just because it was Wales, but because earlier in the tour we had played Cardiff and had been beaten 8-3. That was a sore point. We didn't play at all well and we desperately wanted to make up for it. Bob Scott had caught the ball and Brian Fitzpatrick called for the pass, but it went astray. Sid Judd picked it up and scored. It was all very simple. They converted and led 5-nil. Ron Jarden kicked a penalty for us and then there was this forward rush up the right-hand side. There was a bit of fumbling and I was following through and just managed to force it. It was a great thrill and when Ron converted it we had the lead, 8-5. That was the way it stayed till about ten minutes from the end. We stayed camped inside their twenty-five all that time. And did everything but score. Fitzpatrick missed scoring by what must have been an inch and Bob Stuart almost got over, too. Then with about ten minutes to go Gareth Griffiths, their centre, who had been off the field injured, came back and that seemed to lift their game, for they broke upfield for about the only time in the spell. We held them up, but I got penalised right in front of the posts for holding the ball on the ground and that made it 8-all. I didn't feel very good about it, but certainly didn't despair. With the score 8-all the crowd was going mad and the Welsh must have been encouraged for they got back into the twenty-five. Clem Thomas was right on the sideline, players were all round him, and for some unknown reason he kicked it infield instead of out.

Ron Jarden: Never have I experienced such a silence from so many people as 65,000 patriots saw their team being hammered into the ground for sixty-nine minutes and down 8 points to 5. A penalty and 8-all! The transformation was fantastic and almost ear-shattering as Ken Jones scored his try to give Wales the game.

Kevin Skinner: You'd think it was the first win they'd ever had the way they carried on. They knew they'd beaten the better side!

Morrie Dixon (1953-57, 10 Tests, 28 games): It was a big thrill to play in that [Irish] Test because it was my first. I'd expected something really hard and I suppose it was hard, but being so tensed up and thrilled it just seemed to be quite another game really. In the first half we were 9-0 up and the points came quite easily, even though the Irish are traditionally a very competitive team. I had to play both wings and centre because we lost both Ron Jarden and Guy Bowers.

Ron Jarden: Prior to the Test against England, there had been some hard frosts and the ground had been covered with straw for a week to prevent the turf freezing. Unfortunately, the straw had been laid only to the sidelines and the ground outside was frozen solid. Every time Ted Woodward and I tackled each other we landed on the frozen patches outside the sidelines, with me underneath, it seemed. By the end of the game I was more All Blue than All Black.

Bob Stuart: I was so cold that day [against Scotland] I didn't hear much of the crowd but I can remember the bagpipes. Some say we got a shock there . . . We'd played the three Scottish teams and had fairly easy wins . . . the Borders, they were tough . . . the game broke our way and points piled up . . . but internationals are a different kettle of fish. Any international team can pull itself up by the bootlaces, no matter what it's got and no international can be taken easily. The man who made the difference, the man who made the game tough for us was their captain Doug Elliot. He had been out of the game a couple of years more or less retired and there was a tremendous hue and cry about

Bob Stuart dives to score against Ireland at Lansdowne Road in 1954. *Getty Images*

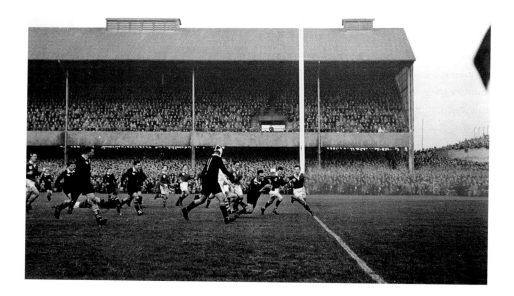

bringing him back in but he was one of the finest forwards I ever played against. He was a Border farmer, a magnificent build of a man, and he absolutely gave them the fire and fury that day. He and his pack gave a magnificent exhibition. We had one unfortunate experience, Haig was injured early, took a nasty knock but came back and didn't drop the ball all day, played an extra good tactical game. We pulled a move, it didn't come off so we tried it again and Haig went over for a very nice try . . . but the ref ruled it out. I felt sorry for Haig. He was born in Scotland and a lot of his relations had come to see him play and were sitting close to where he went over.

Ron Jarden: The game was played in appalling conditions and it was difficult to sort out any movements largely because of that . . . however I will always remember the magnificent penalty kicked by Bob Scott to give us victory. It was kicked over from my side of the field, about ten yards in from touch and he hoisted the ball out of about six inches of mud for a very long goal under the greatest of strain.

Bill McCaw: The Barbarians game, besides the win, was good. It was a very strong side, like a British Isles side. One of the great memories of that tour was at the end of the game both the Barbarians team and the All Blacks formed a big circle in the middle of the ground with the referee as well and the crowd sang Auld Lang Syne, it was a great occasion.

Morrie Dixon: The pattern of our play was to get control of the ball in the forwards . . . but we had perhaps too much control in some ways. We got seventy-five per cent of the ball [against France] and all Ron Jarden and I did was chase the ball all day. The ball didn't go past our second five once. We were very lucky in a sense not to be beaten by more. We had Guy Bowers at first five and with their concentration of quick fast loose forwards he couldn't overcome it . . . he was quick himself, but he was just a bit lost.

Ron Jarden: The Test we played at the Colombes Stadium in Paris in 1954 was a completely novel experience for me . . . At the end of the game, which we lost 0-3, I could not have told whether I was marking the same fellow as I was at the start, or to what extent their back positions had changed, if at all . . . French rugby will be a revelation also to every New Zealander. They bring a fresh tactical approach to the game and are unconditioned by years of stolid 'Teutonic' rugby and the patterns of play which have stemmed from it.

Bill McCaw: France were strong in the backs, again our forwards out-powered them. We won that much ball but we didn't have that many polished backs except for Bob Scott, Jack Kelly and Ron Jarden. And the 0-3 loss to France was just one slip-up and we were gone.

Arthur Woods (1953-54, 14 games): We played in Bordeaux against what was supposed to be a Juniors side. Well they weren't juniors and we lost. I feel if we had been playing good football we would have overcome the refereeing, which to be blunt wasn't good. I'm sure we scored two tries. I remember one occasion I came around the side of a scrum and charged down a kick. The ball went over the line, I forced it and the referee took it back for a five-yard scrum. One game Bevan went to put the ball into the scrum . . . he baulked it, and the referee penalised him for not putting the ball in straight, and Bevan said, 'But I've still got it in my hands!'

Bill McCaw: It's a new game nowadays, a different game altogether. There's no rucking, you can retain the ball by going to ground, as long as you get support you can retain possession. In our day we didn't have the skill, or fitness. We didn't have coaches. Len Clode coached us in 1951 – well I don't know if Len had ever coached a team. He was just an administrator. Look at 1949 when they took old Alex McDonald who was well into his sixties. He was no use to them as far as coaching went. Vic Cavanagh in 1949 was a proven coach yet they wouldn't take him, he would have made all the difference. The same happened in 1953-54 with Art Marslin, I don't know if he had ever coached a side much and it was mainly up to Bob Stuart to do the coaching. I always felt very sad that you didn't learn. I thought going away with the All Blacks I would learn so much about new ways of playing but I don't think I ever learnt much at all. I feel a wee bit cheated in a way. There was so much you could have learned under a really good coach.

With the Springboks on the horizon in 1956, a home series was played against Australia in 1955. Eight new caps were included for the first Test, won 16-8 by New Zealand, but that wasn't enough for the selectors and another four changes were made for the second Test which New Zealand won 8-0. Then for the third Test seven more changes were made and, not surprisingly, Australia won 8-3. By the time the series was completed the selectors had had a fair look at their resources for 1956 and fourteen players who appeared in the 1955 series would be selected.

Ron Jarden: The [Australian] team which defeated New Zealand at Eden Park that year [1955] was as good an international side as had ever graced Eden Park, and it was not only an insult to the Australians, but also to the New Zealanders who played against them, that their ability was universally underestimated.

Bill Clark: That series [1955] was regarded as a trial for 1956 and they used a whole lot of players (twenty-four) in the three Tests. They then sent letters to everyone who was a possible player against the Springboks in the summer urging them to ensure they got fit and, what was unusual for those times, telling us to stop smoking.

TEN

A NATION UNITED

'there were sixty thousand people out there at the park
waiting and hoping for the first victory in sixty-two years'

IT IS DOUBTFUL any rugby nation had ever been so wound up about a rugby tour as New Zealand in 1956. The humiliation of 1949 was embedded in the public psyche, and the defeat of 1937 in the third Test still lingered in the minds of older fans. This was the year when revenge had to be taken. In the years since 1949 the Springboks had lost only three Tests of fifteen played while their 1951-52 tour of Britain and France was regarded as one of the great rugby expeditions. They had also, a year earlier, played a monumental series with the British and Irish Lions. But the visitors were literally hamstrung throughout the tour, as several succumbed to hamstring injuries on the cloying, muddy fields of New Zealand.

Ron Jarden: By 1956 the New Zealand selectors, benefiting from the experiences of 1953-54 and 1955, had developed tactics which they felt would succeed against South Africa, and throughout that series applied a basic strategy designed to counter the 'offensive defence' of the Springbok team . . . New Zealand not only countered the Springbok offence, but also proved that intelligent strategy, correctly employed against a team no matter how great, will win matches. We did not attempt passing movements from set scrums or lineouts. Instead of making play from these first 'phases', i.e. set scrums and lineouts, we created instead a second phase, i.e. a ruck which took place behind the opponents' advantage line. It was from this ruck that possession was to be obtained and back play initiated.

Pat Walsh (1955-64, 13 Tests, 27 games): What I remember most is the intensity of the preparation. There was a fervour throughout the country to beat the Boks for the first time in a series. It was almost a win-at-all-cost mentality. The pressure was so great when Jeremy Nel kicked off for South Africa, his toe hit the ground a couple of inches in front of the ball, and it just trickled in front of his feet. It was a scrum back and New Zealand's ball. That to me signified the pressure of it all.

Kevin Skinner: Afrikaners are hard men, they don't get much. I made some nice friends with them. I had corresponded with Chris Koch before he died, and Okey Geffin. I think he's aware the referees in South Africa should have been wearing glasses in '49. They thought they saw things they didn't see, and Okey would turn and say, 'Sorry fellers but I'm going to put this one over too.'

The first Test was a torrid affair, seven players leaving the field to have injuries attended to at one stage or another but the home team won 10-6.

Opposite: Ron Jarden throws into a lineout during the Test at Eden Park against the Springboks in 1956. *RA White*

Ron Jarden: I had centre-kicked earlier on from halfway, and the ruck formed a few yards from the South African goal-line. The South Africans won the ball and Ackermann came around on the blindside on my side of the field and the swing of the play was such that he and the wing on the outside were virtually in the clear and I had no one behind me. Ackermann was very difficult man to tackle and I was concerned whether he was going to pass or run. Fortunately for me, he gave every indication he was going to pass and did so. I hopped in between and collected the ball and I was probably over the line before they'd realised what had happened, and indeed before I realised what had happened. It was a very lucky eventuality and a very happy five points.

Pat Walsh: I felt totally deflated. There was a lot of physical and mental pressure on us for the last couple of weeks. It intensified as you got closer to the game. Everyone was patting you on the back. You don't know half the people, but they adopt you. You've given it your total effort, and when you go back to the dressing sheds you just sit there mentally exhausted.

Ron Jarden: The South African team of 1956 was rather disappointing in the singular lack of variety in its attack, apart from the standard stereotyped attacking plays which characterise any rugby team. The Springboks resorted only to two specific tactics on attack. The first was the use of the redoutable trio of loose forwards, and the second was a most effective combination of the running halfback with loose forwards.

In the second Test, strangely, South Africa showed a far better appreciation of how to play in Wellington's wind and took an 8-3 win.

Bill Clark: They had some outstanding players and were extremely difficult to beat. They were not a very happy side though, and the only time I recall them smiling was after they had beaten us in the second Test at Athletic Park. The smiles never left their faces and frankly with some of their behaviour after that game they acted like children.

Pat Vincent (1956, 2 Tests): It was a day of missed chances, missed goal kicks, up-and-unders that finished over the dead-ball line, back play that ran into a flat defence and fizzled before it started, rugged forward play and incidents and so on. It was, in a way, the watershed of New Zealand rugby. Just think of this, Don Clarke had been playing provincial rugby for six seasons and that was the last Test that he did not play in when available for a very long time. The team, too, had many changes. [Robin] Archer and [Mark] Irwin had both been injured, but altogether, four forward changes seemed inexplicable, three of them, [Dennis] Young, [Frank] McAtamney and [Don] McIntosh were playing their first game. I often think that coaching is comparatively easy . . . selecting is what is difficult.

Ron Jarden: The problem [in the second Test] was largely inaccurate kicking. Kicking was the right tactic for the occasion because it was almost impossible to move the ball through routine passing movements in the way we were accustomed to. We chose what

Don Clarke. *Getty Images*

we thought were the right tactics and possibly they could have been if we'd been able to control the ball in this ferocious wind. It took us most of the first half to realise it was almost impossible to do this and thus we frittered away our advantage in this spell. The Africans used the wind to much greater advantage, and possibly learned from our mistakes, but certainly they came out in the second half and played it in the scrum and any possession they won was used by close running round the scrums and in-passing to loose forwards breaking from the scrum.

Pat Walsh: The scrum was always full of tension. It was interesting to have Ian Clarke at prop in all four Tests. Against the Wallabies the year before he played at No.8.

The reaction to the Wellington defeat was drastic. Captain Pat Vincent was replaced at halfback by Ponty Reid, in came Don Clarke at fullback and, significantly, as rugby legend has noted, prop Kevin Skinner, the former national amateur heavyweight boxing champion, was persuaded to return. New Zealand gained some parity in the scrums with much talk of the job Skinner did on the South Africans but the more significant factor was the boot of Clarke kicking the ball prodigious distances at the start of an eight-year tenure of the fullback's jersey. New Zealand won the third Test 17-10 and couldn't lose the series.

Kevin Skinner: The series wasn't going very well for New Zealand, and there was a lot of agitation among rugby people to get Peter Jones, Don Clarke, Ponty Reid and myself into

The All Blacks and Springboks run onto the field for the fourth Test
at Eden Park in 1956. *Peter Bush*

the team. But when Frank McAtamney was crocked in the second Test – and after what
he had put up with – I made myself available.

Johnny Simpson: The selectors asked me to go and see Kevin at Waiuku. He had been
available for the first two Tests but wasn't wanted. Because of that he didn't want to play.
Finally, I said to him that was great, when his Otago team-mate Frank McAtamney had
been bitten on the hand, which he had, while propping in the second Test. He said, 'Is
that right?' and agreed there and then to play.

Kevin Skinner: There were no instructions whatsoever. I went out to play rugby and
I hoped they were of the same mind. What I did in 1956 was simply to stick up for
my rights. The Boks thought they could get away with some illegalities and, had we
continued to let them, they were halfway home. We decided we wouldn't stand for any
intimidation by the Boks, which they were trying on us. They [the All Blacks] had lost
confidence in themselves and I think we just decided it was time to get it back on track
again. Remember, I had the advantage of playing against them in 1949. I knew the tactics
they were using and I wasn't going to put up with them. That was all there was to it.
I took umbrage at Chris Koch in the lineouts. He was getting over into our side and
slowing down our ball there. I warned him not to do it again, he persisted, and I gave him
a cuff around the ear. That was all there was to it. If you clout someone right in front of
the referee he had to do something about it, doesn't he? The main problems were in the
lineouts but they were also pushing at an angle and pinning us in the scrums. It's pretty
difficult for a referee to pick up but, if it's highlighted to him, he has to keep an eye on it.
Bekker was a big man who could wear you down and, at half-time, I asked Ian Clarke how
he was making out. Ian said he could do with a spell, so I said I would change sides and
look after Bekker. Bekker tried to 'pop' me and I said: 'Lay off that – we won't have any of

that.' There was a bit of a scuffle but it was soon sorted out . . . I like to think I was always in full control of myself. I was coached that if I put the boot into anyone I wouldn't play again. That became my rugby philosophy . . . I was there to play rugby, and they realised that. After that, after a while, there was no more funny business going on and we got down and played the game as it should be played. The folklore is out of line. I blame the reporters. They saw things that didn't happen. People believe what they read. At that time I was annoyed because I didn't want to think I was out there just because I could throw a punch, there's a lot of other guys can throw punches and I've had my fair share of them on the receiving end I can tell you.

Richard 'Tiny' White: It was extremely hard rugby, no question about that, but there have been a few myths about it, particularly the one about Kevin Skinner being recalled and acting as if he was Muhammad Ali to help us win. The reality is that we did not have to resort to punching anyone to win. We beat the Springboks in the series through a combination of power, strength and rugby knowledge. We ground them out of the series. We had a front row in Skinner, Ron Hemi and Ian Clarke that would never buckle and could withstand the power which came from two near 17-stone locks like myself and Bob Duff.

Don Clarke (1956-64, 31 Tests, 89 games): My first Test, against the Springboks at Lancaster Park in 1956, was a magical occasion, especially as I'd damaged my knee playing for Waikato the previous weekend. That injury became one of the best-kept secrets in New Zealand rugby. I received treatment all week and was only cleared to play twenty-four hours before kick-off.

Ron Jarden: The result of the series was an enjoyment. The games were hard, the hardest I've ever played in and, because of that, most satisfying. I certainly rank them the most memorable games of my career.

There was history riding on the final Test at Eden Park. New Zealand could claim their first series win over South Africa, while the Springboks stood to lose the first in their sixty-year history. It was a tense time, but the All Blacks enjoyed a large measure of control courtesy of Clarke's goal-kicking and when midway through the second half No.8 Peter Jones latched onto a ball toed ahead by hooker Ron Hemi the match was all but won. He raced thirty metres to score what would stand for some time as the most celebrated try in New Zealand history. South Africa did score the final try but the win was New Zealand's and honour for 1949 was restored. Sadly, 'Tiny' White's career was ended by a kick intended for Kevin Skinner. Springbok prop Jaap Bekker later owned up to it in a tearful interview during a New Zealand television documentary. It was the final act of a brutal, but famous series.

Peter Jones (1953-60, 11 Tests, 37 games): The team-talk [before the fourth Test] was given in the commercial room of the Station Hotel. It was the greatest team-talk imaginable. Tom Morrison told us that there were 'sixty thousand people out there at the park waiting and hoping' for the first victory in sixty-two years, and that we must never let them down. That was about all he had to say. A man's nerves were at a high pitch, the countdown was starting.

Kevin Skinner: Apparently there was a consortium of Springboks who got together and were going to see if they could line me up, get me off the paddock. I didn't know, thank God, I wouldn't have been keen to get out there. It was a bit late in the day, wasn't it, to have a shot at Tiny White with three minutes to go, you know the game was lost by then. I felt sorry for Jappie, he was upset when they asked him about it recently, he had a tear in his eye.

Peter Jones: Then came a lineout just inside the Springbok half, in front of the grandstand. Standing at Number 6 or 7 I saw Hemi come through the front of the lineout with the ball at his toe, then kicking it about ten yards ahead. Already I'd started to move hard. It flashed through my mind that this was an excellent position, between the twenty-five and halfway and not too close to the touchline. A hole had suddenly appeared. I got my foot to the ball, trying to toe it ahead. The effect was more that of a little kick. The ball pitched about five or ten yards ahead and bounced gently up into the air. On the other side of it I could see Viviers, waiting with his hands up. It was a very long second . . . Viviers' eyes were bulging. He knew he had to take the ball, and that as soon as he did he was going to be bowled, ball and all. I could have let him take it and bowled him for a row of ashcans – or taken it myself. In all my life I had never been attracted to mauling the man; I'd always liked to get hold of the ball and run . . . I started moving to the left, stretched out my right arm and, as Viviers reached up for the ball and had just touched it, I plucked it down and swung it under my right arm. I dropped my body away to the left. There was an open field. I stoked up everything. After about five yards I could see or sense two men coming after me from the left. I ran harder than I'd ever run in my life . . . I wouldn't have known if I was wearing track spikes or hob-nailed boots; I couldn't feel a thing. I knew after fifteen yards that it was mine. I knew I had six yards on them and that even if they were fast I could hold them to the line. Then I found myself veering towards the posts, acting automatically. I dived into the ground, burying the ball underneath me.

Kevin Skinner: I thought, 'That's it.' I thought they wouldn't be able to come back after that – and they couldn't. There was another official dinner after the fourth Test. The Springboks were disappointed. They had lost the series. I knew how they felt. I had played in six Test matches before I was on a winning side. We lost all four Tests in South Africa in 1949 and drew the first Test against the Lions at Carisbrook in 1950 before we won the second.

Don Clarke: It was satisfying to think I had been able to take revenge for what Okey Geffin had done to our team in South Africa in 1949.

Kevin Skinner: The '56 series was as intense as anything else I've gone through in my life.

I wouldn't want to go through it again. We were expected to do the Boks in that series, because we had gone through '37 and '49, and the public expected better things from us. It was something the modern rugby player knows little about.

"I DON'T KNOW ABOUT YOU BUT I'M ABSOLUTELY BUGGERED!"

Caricature of Peter Jones, the All Black made famous for saying, "I'm absolutely buggered" when interviewed after the fourth Test win over the Springboks at Eden Park in 1956. *Murray Webb*

ELEVEN

ANOTHER START

'These guys are in the team, they're part of the side,
and they should have the silver fern'

IT WAS INEVITABLE that such a demanding series would result in retirements, especially among older players. The next great contest was the British and Irish Lions tour of 1959 followed a year later by another tour to South Africa. New blood was needed and the 1957 tour of Australia offered the chance for changes. Ten new All Blacks were selected in the squad of twenty-five, and they included names that would feature highly in the immediate future: Wilson Whineray, Colin Meads, Terry Lineen and Frank McMullen especially. In a rare break from the rugby-playing style of the time tries aplenty were scored as New Zealand won all thirteen matches including the two Tests 25-11 and 22-9. The Australians returned the favour in 1958 and as so often happens after increased exposure to the All Blacks they took the second Test 6-3, after New Zealand won the first comfortably 25-3. That set up a Bledisloe Cup decider which New Zealand won 17-8.

Wilson Whineray (1957-65, 32 Tests, 77 games): The first Test in Australia was my first Test and it was Colin Meads' first Test as well. I wanted to get out on the field in a jersey in the Test match and I just didn't want to fall down the steps from the hotel or trip over something in the car park getting on the bus, or whatever, just get out on to the ground and get the thing underway. What nerves you have tend to vanish immediately the whistle goes. The worst nerves you have are the ten minutes or quarter of an hour before kick-off. What you're really nervous about is not of the game or getting bumped around, it's not letting the team down.

Colin Meads (1957-71, 55 Tests, 133 games): Being an All Black was something out of this world. It was something we had been brought up with as kids. And once you got there you always worried about staying there.

Terry Lineen (1957-60, 12 Tests, 35 games): It was a hell of a thrill to be selected for the tour of Australia. I had a good tour and it was a bit of a shock to be selected for the first Test. Bill Gray had been there through the 1956 Springbok series but I think he got knocked around a lot by the Boks. Dick Everest [coach] did a great job with the team. He had been so good with Waikato and he liked to let the backs have a go and we had a bit of structure to our game.

Colin Meads: We got over to Australia and Dick Everest, who was in his first year as coach, wanted another game so they took us down to Woollongong and we played some XV down there but it wasn't a first-class game. We were in our All Blacks gear and that

Opposite: Lions captain Ronnie Dawson and All Black captain Wilson Whineray lead out their teams before the first Test in the 1959 Lions series. *Getty Images*

was our first game as far as we were concerned. I remember sitting next to Whineray, and I said I was scared I was going to break my ankle and be one of those poor buggers you've read about who were All Blacks but who never played a game.

Wilson Whineray: In early 1958 I'd captained a New Zealand Junior team to Japan and Hong Kong and so obviously someone thought I had possibilities as the captain at that stage and when the team was picked to play Australia later in the year Ponty Reid, our skipper in 1957, had retired so there was a vacancy there. They had to put someone in, and I guess they thought I could handle it. So there I was, thrilled of course, but it's a game that just throws another little responsibility on you. The thing I wanted to do was be in the team, captaincy was an add-on.

Colin Meads: In my second Test our centre Frank McMullen got hurt and Pat Walsh came into centre and I went to wing. I was marking a chap Morton who was a sprint champion who had run in the Empire Games. Pat was brilliant and said to me not to let him come inside me, to force him outside and Pat caught him every time in cover. And he said, 'When you get the ball run straight at him. Don't try and run round him, go straight at him.' I met him a few years ago in Perth, he had moved there, and he said he had been all right marking Pat, but when I came out he was just hanging onto me on the three or four occasions I did get the ball.

Terry Lineen: The Aussies played well when they came here in 1958. We won the first Test easily but everything went to crap in the second Test. Nothing went right. We played the third Test at the Epsom Showgrounds but that was nothing unusual as we played club rugby there most Saturdays. It was a good ground.

Ralph Caulton (1959-64, 16 Tests, 50 games): I think it was fortuitous I played my rugby in Wellington. They played a free-flowing game and there were a lot of opportunities to get the ball. I learnt to centre kick with my left foot as a result of watching Ron Jarden and Bill Clark play. Often Jarden would be running down the left wing and when blocked he would put in a centre kick and there would be Bill Clark waiting for the ball. When I was called in as a reserve for the third Test in Auckland against Australia in 1958 I felt it was all paying off. It was interesting when we got our team photograph taken on the Friday before the game that Tom Pearce, the manager, changed the policy regarding the reserves in the photo. Up until then reserves just wore a black jersey with no silver fern on it. But Pearce said, 'These guys are in the team, they're part of the side, and they should have the silver fern', so that was the first time that happened.

A stupendously talented British and Irish Lions team toured in 1959 sporting players who influenced a generation of New Zealand rugby fans: Ken Scotland, Tony O'Reilly, Peter Jackson, David Hewitt, Malcolm Price, Bev Risman, Dickie Jeeps and Andy Mulligan, all dazzled with their play but they came up against an emerging juggernaut forward pack and the booming boot of Don Clarke. It is little wonder the British back play was recalled with such fondness, as there was not a lot from the All Blacks to inspire. The first

Ralph Caulton scores in the second Test. *Getty Images*

Test in Dunedin has a notorious place in All Blacks' history, as a game most fans believed the Lions deserved to win. There was a lot of embarrassment about the six penalty goals Clarke landed in the 18-17 win, but to the players there were no such qualms. They were firm in their belief the Lions had been punished for their transgressions. Clarke wasn't only a goal-kicking match-winner as he showed when thundering over for the winning try in the second Test in Wellington. New Zealand were much more positive in the third Test and had their best win, 22-8. But in a final statement that summed up the different playing attitudes between the sides the Lions won the fourth Test 9-6, three tries to none.

The All Blacks had won the series but, more importantly, they had blooded some new talent in their quest to return to South Africa in 1960 to take on the Springboks. Wing Ralph Caulton, halfbacks Kevin Briscoe and Roger Urbahn, flanker Red Conway and flanker Kel Tremain were introduced while Don Clarke, Wilson Whineray, Colin Meads, Terry Lineen, John Graham and Dennis Young had all acquired experience to set them up for the task ahead.

Wilson Whineray: That was a great series [1959] and they were a good side. I think overall they were one of the best sides I ever played, potentially, but they never quite gelled . . . they had no coach and that was left largely to Ron Dawson who was the captain. He coached the team, helped select it, and the minor disciplinary stuff Ron had to deal with. So it was a real burden, but the talent in that team was absolutely outstanding. The backline? We used to lie in bed at night thinking 'Good Lord, how are we going to pull these guys back?' They had four guys in that team with track times of 9.8 which for rugby players is pretty damned fast. O'Reilly and Jackson, John Young, and David Hewitt, the Irish centre, and we knew if they got clear we would have had trouble pulling them back.

The Test in Dunedin turned into the muddle it did largely because we effectively lost two of our loose forwards [Brian Finlay and Peter Jones] in the opening minutes with groin and hamstring injuries. Of course, those were the no-replacement days, so they stumbled on but Rex Pickering was basically the only loosie we had who could still run

Don Clarke dives over to score in the Second Test. Fairfax Media

and he exhausted himself. Almost every loose ball the Lions were able to grab. It was a fantastic kicking performance [by Don Clarke] with a greasy ball. The best exhibition I ever saw – four of them were quite big and difficult kicks and every penalty I have to say was thoroughly deserved . . . They just weren't disciplined on that day. But we weren't keen to come off after that one and face the music.

Terry Lineen: They really deserved to win the first Test, they played a lot better than us. The only real training run we had was on the Thursday because you couldn't have a hard run on the Friday. We were completely outplayed but we never liked to lose. We weren't satisfied with our effort.

Colin Meads: I never forgot after that first Test at the dinner the Lions misbehaved, they were throwing things around and Tony O'Reilly was the worst bastard of the lot, him and the little halfback Andy Mulligan. I know something hit Tom Pearce at the top table and there was hell to pay.

Ralph Caulton: You never knew where you were with the selectors. I wasn't in the Dunedin Test against the Lions. They had a penchant for picking guys out of position. Dick Everest, Jack Sullivan, and Ron King picked Pat Walsh on the wing and he hadn't played well, people were saying I might be in with a chance. I was named in the side. And Tuppy Diack, who had to withdraw before the first Test for what would have been a debut on his home ground, came back in. Somebody asked me what wing I would be playing on because both Tuppy and I were left wings. So I thought I had better go and talk to Jack Sullivan and ask him what wing I was playing on? He asked me why? And I replied that we were both left wings. He said, 'He's had more experience than you so he can play on the right.'

Colin Meads: The 1959 Lions tour was an eye-opener for me because they were still playing me as a loose forward. I had a bit of a bad run and I didn't make the first Test. I was sour. I was in the nineteen but took no part in things. There was Peter Jones, Rex Pickering and a chap Findlay in the loose forwards. I told them at training they were leaving holes and the Lions could have a feast. But then I just shut up. After we lost that Test Kel Tremain, Red Conway and myself were the loose forwards from then on. I got down to Wellington and I got the 'flu but I was still determined to play although I was as crook as a bastard. I got them to put me in another room because they were having to change the sheets I was sweating so much. Next morning they checked to see if I would be playing because Dave Gillespie had been warned that I mightn't be right to play. I said I was and Jack Sullivan said, 'You know if you play poorly what will happen? You won't be picked again.' I was so determined to play well that I marked a fellow called Roddy Evans in the lineout. I pushed and shoved and belted him in the first or second lineout and Tremain, who was in his first game said to me, 'Is this how it always is?' I explained afterwards that I'd had a bit of a warning and I was worried and I didn't want that bugger to play well. It was the start of a great relationship with Kel Tremain, he became my greatest friend.

Terry Lineen: In the second Test I put a step in and went right through. Then I kicked for the wing and it sat up for Ralph Caulton. I kicked quite often. I practised kicking with my left foot. I set up another chance for Ralph and then passed the ball to Don Clarke when he scored his try. We loved that win, it was a really good feeling afterwards. I always enjoyed playing on Athletic Park. On a good day you couldn't beat it, it was my favourite ground.

Ralph Caulton: I ended up with two tries in the first quarter-hour of the game. The ball came out and Terry Lineen stabbed a kick through to the corner. Ken Scotland, their fullback, was injured and didn't play in the Test and Terry Davies was playing there. It was one of those kicks that bounced along the ground and then all of a sudden popped up for me, instead of Davies, and I just fell over the goal-line. If the bounce had been a fraction different he would have got it. We had talked before the game that we would put a few kicks through and then next thing we won a lineout and Kevin Briscoe threw an awful pass, I don't know whether somebody may have grabbed his arm but John McCullough came flying around the blindside and passed to me and I ran in and I can remember as I looked to be getting close to the dead-ball line Wilson Whineray yelling: 'Put it down, put it down!' Then my winger John Young scored for the Lions. We had agreed that when the opposition had created an overlap each back would move in one position and leave the overlap player isolated, to be taken by Don Clarke, who was covering across the field. However, when we were in our twenty-five there wasn't enough field left for him to get across so we talked about it and we decided that flanker John Graham would provide cover to take that player out. The Lions were leading 8-6 and then Clarkey scored. I was free outside him and might have scored a third, but he threw a dummy and scored.

Kevin Briscoe (1959-64, 9 Tests, 43 games): I was pushed into the ground as I passed and the ball rolled along the ground. The ball bounced past my first five-eighth McCullough, for [Terry] Lineen at second five-eighth to pick it up. Roaring into the backline was D.B. Clarke and Lineen gave him the ball to score the winning try. The mere fact that the pass had been a poor one caused the Lions' backs to overshoot the ball somehow.

Wilson Whineray: We won in Wellington reasonably narrowly, but I think we deserved to win that game. In the third Test in Christchurch we had a good win. Games often pivot a bit. There comes some point in the game where it flops one way or the other. They scored a cracking try ten minutes or so before half-time where David Hewitt, who was in the track team for Ireland and ran one of the relays at the Commonwealth Games, that's how quick he was, was outside-centre and he broke and he whizzed past Don. I thought this is going to be painful if we can't close him down. Then we were about even going into half-time and I didn't want to be behind at the half and from about their own twenty-five they broke, and there's Hewitt, roaring along up midfield, he got towards the cricket pitch, and then ranging up outside him came O'Reilly, another 9.8 man and only Don standing there. I thought, 'There's another one under the posts' and Hewitt surprisingly threw a dummy and cut back on the inside and Don put out a big loopy right hand and knocked him over. Some people cried 'Penalty, high tackle', and I think with some justice, but it looked like a pretty damned good tackle from where I was standing. Anyway, we scrambled out of it.

Tiny Jill tackles Lions player Dickie Jeeps during the third Test. *Photosport NZ*

Don Clarke: I faced the two fastest guys on the paddock [in the third Test]. There was no way I was going to stop [Tony] O'Reilly once he got the ball. Now I knew Hewitt loved the inside break, so I played a desperate hunch. As they neared me, I feinted to move towards O'Reilly. Hewitt took the bait. He tried to cut inside me. As he did so, I put up my left arm and he ran straight into it, almost knocking him out. O'Reilly went berserk because he hadn't got the pass.

Terry Lineen: The third Test against the Lions was the best for us. It was the only game the forwards really got on top and we got some good ball.

Colin Meads: They were a good team to play against. They had brilliant backs. That 1959 backline was as good as any we've had tour this country. People used to say if they get forty per cent of the ball we'll get beaten.

Ralph Caulton: In the third Test, the game opened up a lot more. Phil Horrocks-Taylor was at first five-eighths and he would slip the ball in behind us. The wing had to hang back and collect the ball. I would swoop on the ball, take it at full speed and cut through with only one wing or their fullback to beat. It was quite a tactic for us. I would stop the ball rolling by pushing down on it before I picked it up which prevented knock-ons occurring.

Wilson Whineray: Then we lost narrowly in Auckland. They had a very good fly-half back in the team after being injured early, Risman, and he sharpened the whole thing up, we never quite fired properly, and they deserved to win that game.

Terry Lineen: The fourth Test was a very scrappy game and the Lions were happy to get a win. Tony O'Reilly and I got on well through my Irish connection. He was a good man and a good player. He was big for a wing but very quick. They were a good team and deserved to win the Test. I think some funny decisions at selection time didn't help them.

Wilson Whineray: They were a great side, one of the best I ever played. Had they the forward power of later Lions teams they would have donkeyed us, to be honest. The backline was the finest I've played against. We were very lucky to get out with a 3-1 victory, 2-2 would have been a better reflection.

Ralph Caulton: The downfall of the Lions was that they all came from different societies and their lack of success often had a lot to do with their management. And in 1959 the management were here to enjoy the trip. The players were pretty good guys.

Wilson Whineray: A captain usually gets better as he goes along – as he develops his experience of match situations, weather and getting along with people. I think that I probably finished up a better captain than when I started. One of the first essentials is that the captain plays well enough to hold his place.

TWELVE

ON TREK AGAIN

'In those days players would plan for the big tour then a lot of them would retire afterwards. The Springboks were the pinnacle.'

OPPOSITION TO SOUTH Africa's insistence of an all-white team was on the rise and while they didn't know it at the time, Wilson Whineray's tourists of 1960 were the last All Blacks to South Africa selected without Maori or Pacific Island players. It also included flanker Dick 'Red' Conway who had a troublesome finger amputated in order to make the tour. Hopes were high as the team flew out for their tour, stopping off for five games in Australia and then carrying all before them in their first seven games in South Africa. However, the South African media were not impressed with the play of the side and there were claims the All Blacks were too stodgy and relied too much on Don Clarke's goal-kicking. It was hard to complain because they did play to their strengths, their forwards and Clarke's boot. But in the first Test they suffered a significant setback, beaten 0-13. Playing at altitude was no excuse for the All Blacks as they were outplayed. The second Test was back at sea level in Cape Town and while it was only seven minutes from the end before the All Blacks scored their only try, they had been much more combative in dealing with the Springboks' physical play and won 8-3. The All Blacks produced a thrilling comeback in the third Test to keep their hopes of winning the series alive. Down 6-11 with six minutes of the Test left, Clarke landed a penalty goal and then just before full-time wing Frank McMullen scored out wide and Clarke landed a superb conversion to draw the Test 11-11. Injury denied Terry Lineen his place in the fourth Test and centre Laidlaw was moved in to second five-eighths while Tony Davies, who had played only two games at first five-eighths on the tour, was preferred to specialist Steve Nesbit. In the forwards John Graham was dropped to allow Colin Meads to play on the side of the scrum. It was all to no avail as the Springboks claimed the win 8-3. A seemingly fair try scored by McMullen but not awarded did nothing to allay the criticism of South African refereeing.

Wilson Whineray: Throughout the era I played, which was fairly much all of Don's All Blacks rugby, he and Colin Meads were the kings of the game. The All Blacks' on-field presence was always enhanced if those two were playing and, in a way, perhaps even more in Don's case at the time. Being a back and isolated as you are at fullback, you attract a lot of attention whereas Colin was buried in the forward play. Don was such a force for us. He was unparalleled in the world of rugby really. If he had been playing in the media era we now know he would have been a superstar, as big or even bigger than anyone we've had. He'll always be renowned for his kicking ability through punting, place kicks and drop kicks, but he was a hell of a good fullback as well, particularly on the harder grounds. As he got a little older and the grounds got softer, as they were in Britain, then it was more difficult for him. In South Africa, especially in elevated places like Pretoria, Johannesburg

Opposite: The 1960 All Blacks. *lexander Turnbull Library, Wellington, New Zealand*

and Bloemfontein, Don would get an extra seven, eight yards or more on his kicks. If we were inside our own twenty-five and won a nice tidy ball, Don would end up with it about ten or fifteen yards from the goal-line and next thing it was halfway towards the opposition's twenty-five-yard line.

Colin Meads: We always wanted to go to South Africa. In those days players would plan for the big tour then a lot of them would retire afterwards. The Springboks were the pinnacle. We used to get up at all hours of the morning and listen to them in South Africa in 1949. Sometimes we only had a battery radio. There'd be static during the commentary and the old man knew where to smack the radio on one side. He was the only one who knew where to hit it.

Kevin Laidlaw (1960, 3 Tests, 17 games): I worked my way through the various trials before the tour. I may not have been in the more likely team, the Probables, in the final trial but I was in the winning team and that helps. I didn't view the trials as an individual thing and my focus was on setting others up.

Colin Meads: We knew from history that they were rugby mad and they were big buggers. I loved South Africa, we were there four months and saw rain twice in 1960, which was an unusual year, and one of those was just a cloudburst in Durban. And the other one was in Cape Town, but it often rains in Cape Town.

Kevin Laidlaw: We had five games in Australia, including a couple of double-headers. It was a good chance to get to know one another and it was starting to look like there was a definite A and B team but different injuries came into the picture. We left from Perth and went via the Cocos Islands and Mauritius before arriving in Johannesburg. Early on the South African media were critical of our style. They thought we were relying on our forwards to win games. At times I felt we didn't move the ball enough. We could have been a bit more adventurous. We hadn't done a lot of work on our back play. In rugby you have to take your opportunities and if you want to play running rugby you have to have certain moves. Don Clarke did have some goal-kicking issues early on but he was probably trying kicks that nobody else would try. Apart from that he was a tremendous fullback. It was seldom that he was ever out of position.

Wilson Whineray: We were playing Western Province at Newlands, and staying at a hotel that was twenty or thirty minutes away from the ground by bus. Don used to hide his boots because they were stolen quite frequently. He came to the ground and we were changing in the room about twenty minutes from kick-off and he said, 'God I've left my boots behind.' Well, of course, we knew they were at least half an hour away, so we sent off a traffic cop, and telephoned the hotel, to find where they were hidden, and we knew even with sirens going we were going to be quarter of an hour into the game before they got there. What do we do? Kel Tremain said, 'I've got two pairs of boots, I always bring a second pair.' The second pair weren't very good but he said to Don he was welcome to try them. Well, they were a bit tight on Don – they were an old training pair with sprigs pointing in all directions, the stitching was all soft and broken. So out we go on to the field and we're playing for a while and the ball came back to Don on about the halfway mark. I was right in front of him and I saw him shape up for a dropped goal and, bang, I had to duck out of the way. It came at me like an Exocet missile, and kept going and over it went, but the boot disintegrated. The sole came off, sprigs and all, so he had to play about ten minutes in his stockinged foot before the replacement boots arrived.

Colin Meads: There was a tendency to disregard Clarke's ability as a player and to regard him as merely a kicking machine, but he was a fine field player with good positional sense, unworldly hands and he was a very difficult man to beat.

Kevin Laidlaw: Nev MacEwan had a great tour and Ron Horsley was another who probably wasn't regarded as a Test lock but he proved himself and John Graham came through strongly. I liked it when he was at No.8 or off the back of the lineout because I knew he could look after the inside channel and I could concentrate on what I was trying to do. He was a good No.7. We were confident going into the first Test. We had beaten Northern Transvaal the week before and they were meant to be one of the strongest provincial teams. But in the Test I remember thinking when they scored a try, 'How the hell did that fellow get through?' They worked a couple of moves to get their two tries and that was the difference.

Terry Lineen: South Africa in the first Test at Ellis Park was a really hard game. It really mystified me. We had no energy and no one could understand why. It was the altitude and when they made breaks we couldn't even chase them.

Kel Tremain scores the winning try against Eastern Transvaal. *NZ Herald*

Wilson Whineray: I'm convinced the altitude affected us in the first Test in Johannesburg. I personally played poorly. As a captain I had no sense of urgency when we were down or any bright ideas. In fact, it was a sort of mental blockage. It's never happened before or since.

Colin Meads: In the first Test in 1960 they put one over us by sending us up to Johannesburg. Their big wing Hennie van Zyl scored a couple of tries, jeez he could run. We always found the referees would fall over backwards to help you in the provincial games when they were trying to get a Test match. Then when you'd picked out one you thought would be a good one it turned around completely in the Test match. But that would be Danie Craven. He used to go in and have a word with them before games. He was a great man. A lot of New Zealanders hated Danie Craven but every country needs a Danie Craven. He was a student of the game and he did a lot of things in training that had never been heard of before down at Stellenbosch. I marked Johan Claassen, he was one of the better players I played against. He wasn't that mobile at that stage but you couldn't put him off his game. A dour bugger, you couldn't have too many beers with Johan.

Ian Clarke (1953-64, 24 Tests, 83 games): We were beaten convincingly, 13-0. That's a big loss in any Test against anyone. I'm not laying the blame altogether at the altitude but I definitely think it had a bit to do with it, especially in the second half as things got on a bit our players began to tire. Some of our chaps were hardly out of a walk. It did have a big effect on the game.

Ralph Caulton: In the first Test in South Africa we analysed what we were doing afterwards. We were not even in the game. We had to be cleverer than that. They were bringing an extra man in from the wing, and we decided we would let them continue that but someone would watch him and pick him up. It was difficult to make any ground against them because the backs lined out from the middle of the scrum.

Frank McMullen (1957-60, 11 Tests, 29 games): There's no point in going away and trying to maintain an unbeaten record which interfered with us definitely. The focus must be on winning the Tests, not going away trying to be unbeaten.

Terry Lineen: We didn't really have any coaching and while Jack Sullivan was a good guy, and a good coach, it was the forwards who had to get the job done. We didn't have big enough men up front. Hugh Burry should have been picked, he was playing really well at No.8 and Mark Irwin was missed in the front row. They even played Nev MacEwan in the front row but none us could understand that. He wasn't a prop, but a great lineout forward.

Kevin Laidlaw: Wilson Whineray was a terribly good captain but I am not so sure on the tactical side. It probably started with Jack Sullivan. We hardly got any coaching in the backs, he spent bugger all time with us which was a surprise because he was a back. There was some trouble at Port Elizabeth in what became known as the Battle of Boet Erasmus. I did suffer a broken nose but that was because one of our own fellows copped me. The

East London game was a dirtier game, it was an absolutely terrible game but we got a win. We tended to find that the backs of the two sides would get together after games but the forwards, especially up on the veldt, were a bit more stand-offish.

Terry Lineen: The second Test was one of our best, we really turned it completely around.

Wilson Whineray: At sea level in Cape Town we won the second where we could breathe the salt laden air that New Zealanders seem to need.

Kevin Laidlaw: I was happy with how I played in the second Test. Don kicked the conversion to win the game for us. Kevin Briscoe threw a pass which no one took but I got it and made a bit of a break and I passed it to Colin Meads. It was a metre forward but it wasn't called and he scored. It was great to come off knowing I had contributed to his try. I loved playing alongside Terry [Lineen], I wished he had been there for the fourth Test.

Wilson Whineray: Clarke was a great morale booster. You felt you were never beaten while you had him back there. We were down 3-11 with about eight minutes to go [in the third Test]. We took a tap penalty near our own twenty-five and rushed straight at the nearest Bok. He wasn't the regulation ten yards away so when he tried to stop us we had the penalty advanced. We repeated the performance and again the referee marched ten yards upfield. This time we were about five yards inside our own half, so I called Don up. He kicked an enormous goal, a good sixty-yarder, and that put us within reach of them at 6-11. We threw everything into the game and right on time Frank McMullen managed to rake in a cross-kick and score out near the corner flag. I'm sure most of the All Blacks couldn't bear to look at the kick, but Don coolly lined up the shot and banged it over to tie the Test 11-11. Don's percentage wouldn't be as good as Dan Carter's and other kickers from the modern era but the balls were so different then. It needed a big man to kick a leather ball fifty-five yards.

Kevin Briscoe: I received the ball under similar circumstances as in the Lions match, and as happened then, my pass went bouncing along the ground past Nesbit at first five-eighth. Coincidentally, it was Lineen who was first to the ball, but instead of trying to pick it up and pass it, he more or less knocked it across to Laidlaw at centre. Laidlaw ran, was blocked and put up a lobbing sort of kick towards the Bok goal-line. It bounced high and there leaping for it was McMullen, and over he dived for the try.

Kevin Laidlaw: I still remember Don Clarke's conversion to draw the third Test. The conversion wasn't a hard one for him. He didn't have any nerves but I was nervous watching him take it.

Don Clarke: If you're playing well and kicking well there's nothing that can't be accomplished and funny enough, when I went up to take that kick, that final kick, I felt as confident as anything, and I said to myself, 'I'll get this one' . . . quite simply.

Terry Lineen: I was walking back with Don Clarke and wished him luck and I can still hear him saying to me: 'Don't worry about luck Terry, I'm not going to miss this.' I didn't think the ball was ever going to come down after he kicked it.

Wilson Whineray: There was a lovely photo in the South African papers on the Monday morning of the ball sailing over the goalposts, the flags going up, and Don with his back to it all, walking back to the halfway line. I said, 'Good God Don', when we were looking at the photo. 'I couldn't look at it, I turned my back on it, but I thought you would have followed that.' And he said, 'Didn't need to, the moment it left my foot it was over.'

Colin Meads: Ian Clarke was the line umpire. Can you imagine it now, a player being a line umpire? He had the flag up before Don kicked it, I'm sure. Don Clarke would be a superstar. He'd be up there with Dan Carter. The ball they kick nowadays, he'd be kicking that from eighty yards away. He was a bit of a showman. In the second Test he dropped a goal from forty-five yards out and left one boot behind. He put a lot of work in at training in his kicking but he was a lazy bugger otherwise. He could have lost a lot more weight and he was a lot quicker than people thought. Because he was such a big man they thought he was slow but not many people ever beat Clarkey.

Terry Lineen: Against Boland I got the ball and made a bit of a run. I had the ball under one arm but the tackler grabbed my other arm and pulled it back and stretched me. That was where the damage was done. I couldn't tackle at all. I still can't lift my right arm any higher than my shoulder. I was told I was finished. I came home and met with my doctor who told me I might get one or two games a year but the shoulder could go again. So I ended my career.

Kevin Laidlaw: Before the fourth Test, Mick Bremner came to me and asked who I would prefer to have at first five-eighths. I was moved in to second five when Terry was injured. I said to Mick it was embarrassing but now that he had asked what I thought, I would prefer to play with Steve [Nesbit]. He was capable of beating anyone against him. But I knew that when they chose Tony [Davies] they were going to play the sidelines and rely on Tony and Don Clarke for that. I enjoyed playing with Terry Lineen inside me, he was a hell of a good tackler and the fact he wasn't playing cost us the fourth Test. Tony Davies was a great thinker, but not a quick thinker. We played a staid game, we should have won. Frank McMullen scored and was penalised for rabbiting but no one held him.

Colin Meads: Jack Sullivan didn't get on with Steve Nesbit. Nesbit wouldn't kick, he got a bit pig-headed at times. He was a good little fellow but wouldn't comply with Jack's wishes. He would have played the fourth Test but Jack got the pricker with him and Tony Davies played. Terry Lineen was a huge loss – he was a great player, one of the greatest. He was fast, and a deadly tackler.

Wilson Whineray: We were 8-3 behind and Frank broke, he was one of our very lively players, a very good runner with the ball, quite quick, and big sidesteps, and he broke right to clear. I suppose he was about twenty yards from the line and the last despairing tackle, a guy sort of clipped his heels, and Frank staggered on about three or four more steps, getting lower and lower, and fell over a couple of yards from the line, then got up and simply put the ball down under the posts. It was ruled that he hadn't released the ball in the tackle. A tackle is defined that you've got to be held . . . and what he did was no different from a fellow running and slipping over. You don't have to release the ball, you just carry on. So I think it was a clear error of judgment, but that was the ballgame. We could have tied it and that would have been about right for that series, we were pretty even. In saying that, however, South Africa played the slightly better rugby over the four-match series.

Frank McMullen: I sidestepped a couple of them. Their fullback came at me, and I stepped him too. The last of their defenders, Keith Oxlee, ankle-tapped me. I fell forward, and got up and went over the line. The ball didn't touch the ground and no one held me. It was a fair try. [Referee Ralph Burmeister] 'No try. You rabbited over the line.' I called him a cheating bastard. Wilson [Whineray] came over and there was another little chat. Burmeister started talking about sending people off, so we had to let it go. After the game I went over and apologised for swearing at him. When I asked him whether he thought it was a fair try or not he walked away without saying a word.

Ralph Caulton: We should have won the game. Don Clarke missed a lot of goals. A few of them were so high, and above the posts that they could have been regarded as posters. It wasn't cheating to say they weren't goals but any doubt would go the way of the South Africans.

Terry Lineen: Don [Clarke] was faster than he looked. He was a real good country boy and the heaviest player in the team. We did see some of his cricket skills. On the way back from South Africa we stopped over in the Cocos Islands. We couldn't go swimming because of some fish that were dangerous there. Some Aussie engineers working at the airport challenged us to a game of cricket. Don bowled and showed us why he played for Northern Districts with his fast stuff. I was wicket-keeping and the hands felt it.

THIRTEEN

THE STORMIEST TEST

'C'etait magnifique, mais ce n'etait pas le rugby'

FRANCE WAS THE first of the then Five Nations teams to make an individual tour to New Zealand in 1961 and after their memorable tour of South Africa in 1958 they were expected to offer tough opposition to the All Blacks. Their record of not being the happiest tourists was borne out with seven losses on the tour, and a clean sweep to the All Blacks in the Tests, 13-6, 5-3, and 32-3. The second Test was a famous contest played in a storm force southerly wind at Wellington's hilltop Athletic Park. It took an extraordinary conversion by Clarke, kicking with the wind at his back, to secure a win. And in the third Test All Blacks fans were treated to a rare display of running rugby as five tries were run in to secure a big win.

Don McKay (1961-63, 5 Tests, 12 games): We were looking forward to France's tour. We generally only had overseas tours from the Springboks and the Lions. They were a bit of an unknown factor and we weren't sure whether they would travel well. They proved an inventive team. They had a move which Auckland pinched off them and which became the Willie Away for Auckland and New Zealand. It involved Wilson Whineray coming around the back of the lineout after taking a tap down from the lineout and creating a ruck in order to get a quick heel. He wasn't the fastest man but it was all a matter of timing.

Wilson Whineray: The first Test at Eden Park stays in my mind for two reasons. In a sensational start to a Test Don McKay scored a well-constructed winger's try from a set play in the first minute of the game. Don Clarke converted from the sideline. I never played in any game for New Zealand where we were 5-0 up in the first minute . . . what a stunt in an international. Following this early setback the French worked steadily like a machine, employing such tactics as pulling away from the back of the lineout and using the strength and guile of their loose forward trio to give Albaladejo the platform he needed for two fine drop-kicks. At half-time France was leading 6-5 and looked set to win the Test. Albaladejo looked like the rock we would founder on, and the forward struggle was poised to go either way. Within six minutes of the resumption came the second memorable moment as Pinetree [Meads] led us away in a charge during which six forwards handled before Terry O'Sullivan scored, and I breathed more easily. Don Clarke slammed over another dropped goal to give us the second spell and the Test.

Don McKay: I got into the side after Ralph Caulton had an injury problem at training on the Thursday. We had all trained together because you never knew if someone might

Opposite: Wilson Whineray. *Alexander Turnbull Library, Wellington, New Zealand*

wake on the morning of the game with the 'flu. Having run with the team helped my preparation and I knew I was as fit as I could ever be. I was the fastest player in the team so I felt I would be able to cope.

Wilson Whineray: The French had an influence on our play. They didn't have a particularly successful tour here in 1961 but we learnt from them.

Don McKay: It was great to play my first Test on my home ground at Eden Park. I had played in front of big crowds in Ranfurly Shield games but I remember the intensity of the crowd when we ran out. The air was electric. I felt like I had a block of ice in my stomach. You were concentrating so much the halves seemed to be about ten minutes long. Don Clarke kicked the ball dead to start the game, which you were allowed to do then. The French brought the ball up to the twenty-five and a Frenchman was in front of the re-start. So we got the scrum feed in the middle of the field. Des Connor at halfback always looked for space. He got the ball from the scrum and Neil Wolfe, the first-five, came around my side with the ball and passed to me. The French fullback was standing on the goal-line so it was easy to run in and out at him to score. Des had his first touch of the ball in Test rugby when he fed the scrum, Neil had his first touch when passing to me for my first touch in Tests. Scoring the try so early in the game gave me a sense of relief.

Ralph Caulton: Having missed the first Test because of an ankle injury at training in Auckland, I was included in the second Test. Conditions were atrocious – it should never have been played. They had bamboo flags on the sidelines and they were blowing flat. It was quite a fine day, but just a bitterly cold southerly. The wind was so severe you couldn't drop the ball to make a kick because the wind would blow it away before you could kick it.

Don McKay: I was rooming with Ian and Don Clarke in the Midland Hotel in Wellington. When we woke up on the Saturday morning we could hear this noise. We thought they must have put extra trams on to get the people to the rugby but Ian opened the shades and we could see it was wind and rain.

Wilson Whineray: Organised orderly play was impossible in a wind which gusted to 79 mph where words of instruction were impossible and even kicking a ball or directing a pass was hopeless. I desperately wanted to win the toss in order to play into the wind, survive the first half, and take command of the second. I was certain the French captain would feel the same way. Moncla won the toss, pondered his decision for what seemed an age and finally decided to play with the wind. I couldn't believe our good luck and sped off before he could change his mind. France clearly paid for that decision. The next eighty minutes, though a travesty of rugby, were unbelievable in drama and were totally absorbing.

Ralph Caulton: We scored our try because Claude Lacaze wasn't strong enough to get the ball out of the dead ball area, and Kel Tremain charged it down. He kicked the ball

The ball goes loose against the French. *FotoSport/Photosport NZ*

as hard as he could but it would end up going up in the air and then behind him. Then they scored through Jean Dupuy, down the right-hand side and into the southerly gale. Unbelievable!

Don McKay: We had no option but to play. We were given woollen long johns which we cut the legs off to keep us warm. They weren't heavy. The tactics were pretty obvious, the forwards would get the ball and hang onto it.

Wilson Whineray: Nev MacEwan was magnificent for New Zealand, denying France most of the lineout ball and thus most of the initiative in the first half. We played entirely within our twenty-five-yard line for most of the half . . . a mile to touch from your midfield was no exaggeration. At the interval we turned 0-0 and I was certain we had the Test and would win by ten clear points. I knew that tries would be difficult as the ball couldn't be passed, but I thought we would reap a big harvest from Don Clarke's boot. But this was not to be. After twenty minutes or so we had fared no better than the French. The wind had made rugby impossible.

Don McKay: Throwing the ball into the lineouts wasn't too hard as they were short throws. Defending the French it was a case of each man moving in one and Don Clarke would take the player who got the overlap. But my one regret was when Jean Dupuy got the ball Don yelled at me to go inside and take the centre Jean Pique because he had Dupuy covered. Don was the senior guy so I did what he said but it always hacked me

Whineray scrabbles for the ball against France at Eden Park in July 1961. *Fotosport/Photosport* NZ

off that I did. I was faster than Dupuy and I should have stayed on him. Dupuy told me some years later when we met that he got the ball on the driest part of the paddock. And because of the wind Don wasn't able to get across and Dupuy ran away to score.

Wilson Whineray: In my view that try was one of the most stunning things I've witnessed in rugby . . . without being there, nobody could imagine the difficulty the French had in scoring it, and the effect it had on the game.

Ralph Caulton: Dick Everest said to me afterwards that I should have covered him [Dupuy] but that wasn't the way we did things. I was dropped as a result.

Don McKay: Then Kel Tremain scored his try when taking the ball as Claude Lacaze tried to kick it. Kel was one of the slower players in the team over 100 yards but his power-to-weight ratio in the first few yards was good. And then Don had that unbelievable kick where he aimed along the twenty-five line and it curved like one of those putts you see in golf and went between the posts. In those conditions luck came into the final outcome.

Des Connor (1961-64, 12 Tests, 15 games): Don Clarke behind a team meant more than just a bloke who could kick sixty-yard goals. He was a terrific inspiration because of his superb general play and experience.

Wilson Whineray: What went on that day at Athletic Park would best be summarised by amending the international quote, 'C'etait magnifique, mais ce n'etait pas le rugby.' (It was magnificent but it wasn't rugby.) What was certain was that we never won the second Test . . . the French lost it.

Don McKay: When we went to Christchurch we had won the series and psychologically that showed. The French were probably keen to get a few plaudits and they ran it a lot. They got a bit stroppy at one stage but it was great conditions to play in. Lancaster Park was an open, free sort of ground. It seemed bigger than most other fields and we were able to run on top of the ground.

Wilson Whineray: The great French era of 1958-61 ended at Lancaster Park with the third and final Test. Time catches up with every sportsman eventually and any footballer who can't accept this is a fool to himself, and time had run out for several of these great French rugby players. New Zealand won 32-3 with tries to Graham, Little, Meads, Tremain and Yates backed up by magnificent kicking from Clarke. I remember saying to the French team when speaking at the dinner that evening that 'great teams never die – they simply rest for a while'. Some of the looks of despair relaxed, the red wine flowed and life went on again in true rugby style, as it always does.

New Zealand toured Australia in May-June 1962 playing ten games and losing one, their second of the tour against New South Wales 11-12. But the Test matches were won 20-6 and 14-5. Along the way at the small town of Quirindi the Northern New South Wales team was beaten 103-0, the All Blacks scoring twenty-two tries, eight of them to wing Rod Heeps, and five to fellow wing Don McKay. Australia then toured New Zealand in August-September of the same year and demonstrated yet again the value of contact with the All Blacks by drawing the first Test 9-9 in Wellington. A solitary penalty goal to Clarke decided the second Test in Dunedin while in the third the All Blacks won 16-8.

Don McKay: On the Australian tour in 1962, in the opening game, up in the Blue Mountains at Bathurst, we played Central West on a rock hard ground and only a few minutes into the game I was tackled and landed on my head and I appreciate now that I suffered concussion. We won 41-6. It took me a week to ten days to feel fully fit again and I think that was what cost me my Test place. I did play at Quirindi against Northern New South Wales after the first Test. I hadn't scored a try by half-time but I finished up with five. I ran into the backline from my wing and the gaps kept opening up. Rod Heeps got eight. [The 103-0 scoreline was a world record, the first time more than 100 points had been scored.] Rod and I had grown up together on the North Shore. I scored sixteen tries on the tour.

England toured New Zealand and played five games in May and June in 1963. The home team won the first Test in Auckland 21-11 while Clarke's goal from a mark decided the second Test 9-6 in Christchurch.

Don McKay: England came out in 1963. They hadn't played the All Blacks since 1953-54 and all we knew about them was what we had seen in newsreel footage and read in the newspapers. We would head off into town to a cinema at lunchtime and watch these newsreel films to see what we could learn. We knew the English were very good scrummagers but really they were an unknown quantity with no household names in their side.

Ralph Caulton: I was called in when Rod Heeps pulled out. This was on Friday afternoon, and I was on a flight out of Rongotai [Wellington] that night. I rushed home and got some things together and got on a DC3 to Auckland. But there was bad fog in Auckland and we had to go back to Palmerston North. We went out to the airport next morning. I had my blazer on and someone asked me why I needed to be in Auckland and I said I was supposed to be playing in the Test. We flew to Auckland and landed at Whenuapai. I knew the drill pretty well so got in a cab and went to the Station Hotel where we always stayed. I got there about 11.45am. The liaison officers were still out at the airport looking for me.

We were losing 0-6 at half-time, and while Don Clarke kicked a penalty goal to make it 3-6 an English try took it to 3-11 early in the second half. I was absolutely exhausted by half-time, with all the nervous energy I had been releasing before the game. After we scored through Don Clarke we got to 8-11 and then halfway through the second half, Neil Wolfe kicked into the English twenty-five and Ian Uttley, who was at centre, picked it up and passed to me and I scored running around under the crossbar. Don converted

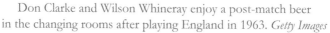

Don Clarke and Wilson Whineray enjoy a post-match beer in the changing rooms after playing England in 1963. *Getty Images*

it and we led 13-11. Five minutes from the end, Bruce Watt broke down the blindside and passed to me and I scored for Don to add another conversion and then kicked a late dropped goal. I remember selector Neil McPhail said to me that he liked the way I ran around behind the posts. He said it showed I knew we had to get in front.

Don McKay: We won the first Test reasonably comfortably but the second Test was much closer. I ran into the backline and got a good, flat pass from Ian Uttley and scored. Then, Don Clarke landed a goal from a mark to win the game. It was a mighty kick from around sixty-five yards. After he placed the ball the English charged early and they were not allowed to run in when he kicked.

Don Clarke: It was said by the pressmen that I intimidated the English but, in those days, the ball had to be held [by a team-mate] from a mark and the ball had to hit the ground before they could charge. My brother Ian and I could hear the English talking and, as I placed the ball, Ian made the comment: 'This should be fairly easy, shouldn't it?' He wasn't going to put the ball down until I had taken my step forward but they started to charge as I started to move in, and before Ian had put it down. That was completely against the law as it was and I immediately asked the ref if I could have a free go. He gave it to me, Ian then placed the ball and fortunately I hit it pretty well and it sailed true and clear to give us a 9-6 win.

Ralph Caulton: I told Don to mark that ball. I was standing just inside halfway and I yelled at him to 'mark it'. He did and he and Ian had such a good combination going in placing the ball that they could have a shot at goal from a mark [no longer allowed]. The English were entitled to charge, but they charged before Don ran in and a penalty was awarded. That was a catalyst for them changing that law because we never played under it on our tour of Britain and France later in the year.

FOURTEEN

A TOUR FOR THE FUTURE

'If you want to play for the All Blacks, you cope, you sort your head out'

WILSON WHINERAY'S TEAM to Britain and France was notable for the number of experienced players left behind for a crop of untried young players. In the longer term, and just about to a man, those younger players were to guide the All Blacks through one of their greatest eras. BJ Lochore, Chris Laidlaw, Ken Gray, Ian MacRae, Bill Davis and Earle Kirton were to advance by varying routes but be the cornerstone of the side of the future. However, under coach Neil McPhail, Whineray's men continued, with only occasional outbreaks, to play the game tight, relying on forward power and the boot of Don Clarke, in his final overseas tour. A shock early 3-nil loss to Newport, courtesy of a dropped goal to Dick Uzzell, contributed to this pragmatic approach, although there were signs of what might have been achieved with a more positive attitude, when London Counties were beaten 27-0, with seven tries scored.

There were many tight games, although there was a tendency to close up shop once a lead had been secured. Cardiff were beaten 6-5, Munster 6-3, South of Scotland 8-0, Swansea 16-9, Leinster 11-8, South-Eastern Counties 9-6 and South-East France 8-5. Clarke bore a heavy load. Despite constant injury issues, he played in twenty-six of the thirty-six games although his goal-kicking was not as dominant.

The results were more in keeping with New Zealand public expectation, with only that one loss, and a 0-0 draw with Scotland that denied them a first All Black Grand Slam. Whineray's leadership was a significant factor and helped ensure the side was remembered affectionately. A Test win over Wales, the first by an All Blacks team on Cardiff Arms Park, was most satisfying even if it was a tryless encounter. Ireland were a tough proposition when playing beyond their expected capabilities to hold the All Blacks to 6-5. England were expected to be tough but were unable to break New Zealand's defences and the 14-0 margin was the widest of all the Test matches. France were beaten 12-3. In their final game in Britain, against the Barbarians at Cardiff, the potential of the side was unleashed as the All Blacks ran rampant to score eight tries, the last, memorably, to Whineray.

He sold a superb dummy to score his only try of the tour, and as the team acknowledged their skipper's effort, the crowd broke into 'For He's a Jolly Good Fellow', a rare tribute to a New Zealand player from the Welsh faithful. While he would go on to play the 1965 series against South Africa, the occasion was a fitting farewell from the British public to one of the great leaders of the game.

Wilson Whineray: A British tour! For most New Zealand rugby players, the greatest event of their playing career . . . I know some who preferred South Africa where the formality was less, with more chances to relax. In Britain there are many formal dinners, with

Opposite: Wilson Whineray leads a musical interlude while on tour to Britain and France in 1963-64. *Fotosport/Photosport NZ*

speeches, dinner-suits, even bow-ties to be worn – but it was all part of the British rugby atmosphere . . . Certainly I went later in my career – in 1963-64, already twenty-eight and seven years an All Black captain – but I loved the atmosphere. That four-month tour, the thirty-two games we played and the dinners and meetings with royalty and the British rugby fraternity stands in my memory as the happiest and most enjoyable time I ever spent in rugby. Encounters with British sporting heroes, film stars, diplomats, military people and so forth occurred frequently, but I particularly remember one afternoon in the changing rooms at Twickenham. It was just half an hour to kick-off in the Test against England, and a nose like a fox terrier came around the door, followed by a face I thought I knew. 'I'd like to say hello to the New Zealand team,' said the face. 'Montgomery is my name.' He'd popped down to pay his respects because, he said, of his deep regard for New Zealanders who'd served with him in the desert campaigns of World War Two in North Africa. As for Twickenham itself – it is the headquarters of English rugby, and so, in a very real sense, the headquarters of world rugby . . . It's difficult to describe but I think it is like this: if you're a mountaineer, you probably want to set foot on Everest before you hang up your crampons; if you're a tennis player, it's Wimbledon; if you're a cricketer it's Lord's. For me, it was Twickenham. I played there twice, and there is no doubt of this powerful effect.

Ralph Caulton: I went to South Africa as a new guy but by Britain in 1963-64 I knew how it worked. There was quite a routine to touring and some guys could cope with that while others couldn't. It never worried me. I guess it was the disposition I had. Test matches didn't faze me either. I was able to handle them but some guys got very nervous and unfortunately never played their best rugby.

Brian Lochore (1963-71, 25 Tests, 68 games): I had played everywhere else except hooker during my career. I had never played No.8 and was so pleased they took me as a No.8. I never found out why or how I got there. I know I was the last one out when they announced the team. They went through the locks where I had played a little bit, flankers where I had played in the trials and I thought, 'Well, I'm home on the farm' then at number thirty I got announced as a No.8. It was a bit of a shock. It suited my game absolutely perfectly. I was reasonably good in the lineout I suppose and reasonably tall for a No.8.

Colin Meads: You got a wee bit more confidence once you had been in a while. No one beats you and you can throw a bit of authority around. But you did always worry about getting in. Once Stan [Meads' brother] came along I never knew why, whenever there were trials we never played in the same team. Unless it was New Zealand v the Rest we were never on the same side. Well the dumb selectors didn't realise, and I don't know how they couldn't work it out, that we would ring up the night before and tell each other our lineout calls. We would only say what our call was, not the other players. Stan always played five and I played three. He had to tell me what their three call was and I would tell him our five. I remember marking Nev MacEwan. He was easy to mark because he displayed when he was going to be the target of the throw. I knew the call and could get in front of him, or push him out, and he would get wilder and wilder, and he was a good forward in those days, but he couldn't work out how he was getting cleaned out.

Ian MacRae (1963-70, 17 Tests, 45 games): I was pretty hopeful. A lot of people were talking and I did have aspirations of going all the way. I was picked for the North Island side but pulled my hamstring in training and was concerned that could cost me. I was a bit concerned in the final trial as I burst a blood vessel in my arm when tackling Don Clarke and it swelled up. In those days if you didn't pass fitness inspection there was an IRB rule that if you were not 100 per cent fit you couldn't tour. It was incredible when you look back on it how many of us young players were selected for the tour. There was very much a Wednesday side and a Saturday side, and the tour was forward-dominated. We didn't get a lot of ball to play with but we were young and happy to be there.

Earle Kirton (1963-70, 13 Tests, 49 games): My father said when he gave me the last handshake before I went away, 'You are incredibly lucky to make this side, it's not that I don't feel wonderful but they'll never be able to take it away from you. You'll at least have made the All Blacks once. You've got halfway there but you won't get the full way there. The game they are going to play is not going to suit you. They don't want to run it, they want to kick it, that's the style they've played and that's the way McPhail and the Canterbury team play it.' And he said, 'Don't bitch, you're so young, you'll get another whack if you keep playing well.'

Ralph Caulton: A lot of the players who went on that tour were second-string players who developed as a result of their experience. I didn't understand at the time why some more experienced players were left at home but looking back I can see why. As a selector if you are faced with older and younger players vying for the same position you would take the younger guy and that is now very evident in the selection made for that tour. When we flew to Britain in 1963 there was a group of us, Wilson Whineray, John Graham, myself, Dennis Young and Neil McPhail and we asked ourselves what we wanted to do on the tour? We wanted to win the Test matches and we wanted to win the Barbarians game. You would try and win all the games but it was important to win the games people would remember. We would try and rotate the teams as much as we could and the Tests would be played by players who were in the best form. Test players would have the inside running, and injuries would play a big part.

Wilson Whineray: Our troubles started [against Newport] – as they invariably do in rugby – up front and at no stage did we establish any sustained superiority with our pack. True, we had had our moments but for much of the game, the fire and skill of the Newport pack, and the mud, forced all of our forwards to commit themselves, and did not allow loose forwards to range freely as Tremain, Nathan and Lochore did so well and so often on the tour. Price and Ford held their own in lineout, hooker Bevan had a decided edge in the scrums and with the tight core going so well the loose trio of Poole, Davidge and Thomas made life pretty miserable for Briscoe, Kirton and Walsh.

Ralph Caulton: Losing the third game at Newport was probably a good thing in the end. It was an ugly old dropped goal and while it was disappointing it meant we didn't have to worry about an unbeaten record.

Brian Lochore: Newport didn't help me a lot. I was lucky enough to get the first game on the tour then the third game was Newport and it was a very poor team performance. I guess the young guys in that particular match suffered a little bit afterwards in terms of getting major games. It wasn't an ideal start to the tour but it taught me a hell of a lot.

Earle Kirton: After the Newport game it was very, very sad because I had played like a dick and I knew that was probably it. I think I must have dropped damned near ten or twelve balls. Now when I look back on it and I got into coaching myself, I don't reckon I saw the balls coming. Not even coming, let alone catching. I never slept for four nights [before]. I couldn't believe I was going to put on the black jersey. All I had were dreams, and nightmares before playing, because I could see David Hewitt of the 1959 Lions, he was still playing in Ireland, and all I had were these images of guys who were just carving up New Zealand and brilliant fast backs like [Tony] O'Reilly and Co., and I found I was chasing them in my dreams . . . nightmares. They were 'mares, they weren't dreams.

Wilson Whineray: Behind the scrum, Prosser and Watkins were never under pressure and Watkins in particular skimmed over the mud and kept us moving backwards. We changed our defensive pattern after this game, playing more pressure on the opposing fly-half, but our efforts this day were too little/too late. In the final analysis we were beaten by a side of dedicated individuals, wonderfully prepared for the game by Bryn Meredith, each man knowing his part in the team pattern and playing for victory with unanswering resolution. These are the very qualities that we recognised, admired and sought ourselves.

Ian MacRae: Newport saw us get off to a bad start. We drove to Newport and had to stop in Cardiff to pick up Wilson Whineray who had just sat an exam. The conditions were bad, it was cold, raining and dark. I went back there for their fiftieth Jubilee celebrations and only three of the team had not survived. I was concerned it would be hard work but they were so sportsmanlike and it was clear the reverence in which they held NZ rugby. Brian Price, the captain, revealed their game plan. It was about denying us the ball, slowing the ball down and pinning us in our own half. It was pretty much the recipe you always need to beat the All Blacks and they put it into good effect. Don Clarke also had an off day with his boot. I was quite proud of the way we took that defeat but back at training you realised you wouldn't want to be on the end of too many losses. It was tough.

Wilson Whineray: I somehow found my way through the milling masses back to our room and spent a few minutes with the team. It wasn't hard to find the Newport rooms for the noise was like a radio beacon to a bomber pilot and in stockinged feet I slipped quietly into the room. I waited momentarily wondering how I could get a word in, when, almost magically, I was noticed by several people at the same time and an immediate and rather unnerving hush settled over the whole room. The time wasn't appropriate for many

The All Blacks huddle together during the Test
match against Wales in 1963. *FotoSport/Photosport NZ*

words, least of all by me, but I wished to acknowledge their clear and decisive victory, won
by a team that outplayed us, in virtually every department on the day. Indeed, I spoke for
the whole New Zealand team in saying that in fairness, Newport should have won by a
further three points, had fullback Cheney's kick not hit the crossbar and bounced away.

Brian Lochore: I started to wonder if I had done something wrong because I was getting
about one game in every five and when you are training all the time you need games,
particularly when you are on tour. Late one night when we had had a few beers I said
to John [Graham], 'Have I done something wrong or is my form bad?' And he said,
'No, you're going well. I only had two games in the first eight in South Africa in 1960.'
I couldn't believe that because when you're a young guy looking at the hierarchy he was
definitely one of the senior players and I could never believe that he had gone through
the same period like I had. And you wouldn't believe it, a week later I was playing a Test
match.

Earle Kirton: The funny thing was my other partner in crime was BJ Lochore. We called
one another 'Wednesday' because we could only ever get a Wednesday game. And I think
after Newport I had to wait five or six games. They weren't prepared to risk me. Then
the first game after that was against Cambridge University and a chap who looked pretty
good. They thought, 'University, the same ilk, he'll be all right there, he won't cause too
much trouble.' I got beaten twice by [Mike] Gibson till I went miles outside him and
drove him back and if we hadn't had Don Clarke at fullback we'd have damned near got

beaten by Cambridge University. I knew it would be a long gap before another game and it was shaping like nine games on a thirty-six-game tour. But it was the way they did psycho then, 'If you want to play for the All Blacks, you cope, you sort your head out.' Their way of showing me was brutal but it was still reasonably fair because they weren't interested in killing me. But they showed me if I wanted to play for the country I had to get my head sorted out. The only guy who came near me or gave me a bit of psych talk, was Pat Walsh. He was tremendous.

Ian MacRae: Paul Little and I played centre in every match on tour. There was some debate that I should probably have been given some Saturday games but I guess it was a very comfortable situation for the selectors to have two centres playing well. What was disappointing was that both our second fives, Pat Walsh and Derek Arnold, got injured and had legs in plaster. They tried everyone else at second five-eighths, Earle Kirton, Bruce Watt, Malcolm Dick, except me.

Pat Walsh: I was rather outspoken on the subject [of weakness at second five-eighths] after I got injured on the tour. I say this that the forwards played so well, too well in fact, that too often the backs were used only as a last resort. You see with men like Wilson Whineray, Waka Nathan, Kel Tremain, Colin and Stan Meads and Ken Gray there, who could all run and handle as good as backs, we were neglected. The backs used to operate a damn [sic] sight better behind the mid-week pack when guys like Jules Le Lievre, Ron Horsley, Kevin Barry and Brian Lochore – the real work horses – were content just to win the ball and get it back to us. What our backline needed was a second five-eighth who could set the line alight or kick for touch as required.

Wilson Whineray: Does he [the captain] give orders to spin the ball in the hope it will produce a try and put the issue beyond doubt, or does he make his team play it safe? . . . I was in this predicament against Cardiff. We hit the front at 6-5 with twenty minutes to go. Another try may have meant an easy win, but it was a match New Zealand had waited ten years to win – and I told the boys to play it safe. We did, and we won 6-5.

Ireland were the first international we had, they hadn't done too well the year before and the media had us winning by about 40 points. But the trouble is the Irish are different, they don't read the media to the same extent, but we gave them a hell of a thumping anyway, 6-5! They gave us no room at all. I can remember the Irish guy scoring the try, Fortune his name was. They got good ball and an overlap and suddenly the team we were supposed to beat by 40 points was leading us 5-0. It was a pretty good try. We clawed our way back and Kelvin Tremain scored and we got another three and got in front . . . Late in the game, with time running out, we were holding our 6-5 lead. I think Fortune again, broke up the right-hand wing and I was thirty yards back and he centre-kicked and it was a beautiful kick. It dropped right in front of our goal, and there were about three big Irish forwards charging in on it, and I think one of our lone backs Mac Herewini came from somewhere, about 5ft nothing, and the ball bounced, with everyone trying to get ready for which way it would bounce, and it went straight up in the air and the eyes of these three Irish forwards lit up like plates, immortality beckoning, they all leapt for the ball at

Derek Arnold sends Tom Kiernan off balance as he takes an inside line through the Irish defence at Lansdowne Road in December 1963. *InphoSport*

once and knocked it on. If it had stuck we would have been rueing another loss.

Ralph Caulton: It was a miserable day in Dublin. We wanted to control the ball in all facets, lineouts and scrums. The game plan was pretty basic, based on our defence. My role was to cover kicks behind us and we would back up Don. If we got the ball we had to make sure it went out. The main requirement was to make no mistakes. It was wet so the ball was kept close to the forwards.

Wilson Whineray: [The Wales Test]I always thought it was best to let a team know early that you had a kicker who could kick big distances. It's one thing to read about it, but seeing is believing. And we got a penalty on about the halfway line right out by the sideline, maybe one yard in, and Don came up and I said, 'How's it look?' and he said, 'I think I can handle it.' So I said, 'Off you go.' Well he kicked and it hit the post two-thirds of the way up! We rushed forward and they scrambled and kicked for touch on the other side of the field and Don was already across there and caught it, at about the same position on the other side of the field. He stepped in, took two or three steps and banged a left-foot drop-kick and it hit the other post also about two-thirds of the way up and well, that was the end of any pranks or rule-breaking from the other party.

Ken Gray (1963-69, 24 Tests, 50 games): We were never in any doubt that this was the most important of the thirty-six matches on the tour – and this was made even more intense by the fact that we had been beaten by Newport. A day before the Scotland Test

I couldn't have told you who the fifteen opposition players were. But with the Welsh we analysed every player – and I can remember feeling a bit delighted with the front row they selected – Cunningham, Jones and Gale.

Malcolm Dick (1963-70, 15 Tests, 55 games): He [coach Neil McPhail] rammed home to us the supreme effort the runner with the withered arm [New Zealander Murray Halberg] had made to win the gold medal in the three-mile race [at the Cardiff Empire Games in 1958]. On top of that, we all knew the All Blacks had never won a Test on the Arms Park and we had to overcome the hoodoo.

Dennis Young (1956-64, 22 Tests, 61 games): We all know the stories about New Zealand's efforts to win on Cardiff Arms Park. We all know about the try that Deans did or didn't score, so does every Welshman of course know about it, and they would point with pride to the spot where he didn't score the try. The game itself we played to win. This historic match wasn't one that will live in my memory. I have regrets that we didn't win by scoring tries, there was no doubt about it that we were the better side. We were 15 points better than they were but we just couldn't get across. We had to rely on the boot of Don Clarke and the drop-kick of Bruce Watt to win the game.

Ken Gray: I'll never forget them [Clarke's missed kicks]. Nor will I forget the one he put over, a much easier one, to give us a 3-0 lead at half-time. The Welsh failed to recognise that for a large part of the game Clarke was one-legged. He suffered an injury and could kick only with his left foot.

Ralph Caulton: We could have won a lot easier than we did. Once we scored we closed it up. Don Clarke kicked a penalty early and we made sure we tackled anything that moved. They didn't really have any attacking moves.

Ken Gray: The tackling of Paul Little, our centre, played a big part in our fortunes – magnificent, aggressive tackling. We had been apprehensive about David Watkins, the Welsh fly-half. We saw him as the danger man with the ball he could have received through Brian Price. However, Price was well contained and Waka Nathan hounded Watkins unmercifully. Wilson Whineray had kept at Nathan for days about Watkins till I'm sure Waka was dreaming about him . . . Alun Pask got a lot of ball at the back of the lineout and played a fine game but the tactic of Pask picking up at the back of the scrum recoiled on them because we were pushing the Welsh forwards back. We had a lot of control in this game and even though there were still about thirty minutes to go when Bruce Watt drop-kicked his goal – a good one – I knew we'd won. It was only 6-0 yet I was sure the Welsh could not beat or draw with us. This team had control and, as a touring team, it had better control on the field than any All Black side I've played with. This was one of the hardest games I have ever played in. Though I seldom touched the ball in the loose I felt I had played my guts out. It was a tight game with few frills and for days I felt tired mentally as well as physically – probably it was a result of the weeks of tension leading to the game.

John Major grapples for possession against Cambridge University. *Getty Images*

Brian Lochore: [On the day of the England game] I was going to go and have a game of squash with a friend of mine in London. It was ten o'clock in the morning and I was just outside the lift as Whineray went past and he said, 'Where are you going?' and I said, 'I'm just going to have a game of squash.' He said, 'You had better go back to your room, we might need you.' I was rooming with Keith Nelson who had trained in that position during the week and his parents rang up because they knew Waka Nathan wasn't playing and I could hear him on the phone talking to his parents and saying, 'Yeah I think I probably will be playing because Waka has been ruled out.' He put the phone down and looked at me and said, 'Why are you here?' I told him exactly what had happened then the phone rang and it was Frank Kilby, our manager, and he said, 'You'll be playing.' I said, 'I've got a bit of a cold' and he said, 'You'll rise above that' and 'Bam' down went the phone. So from ten o'clock until two o'clock, that's how much time I had to get ready. I had confidence in the blokes around me. I was well looked after by Kel Tremain and John Graham, both of them very experienced players. You couldn't be more excited about having your first Test at Twickenham.

Ralph Caulton: They played a lot of players who had played out here earlier in the year, so we knew them. We started to move the ball about. Horrocks-Taylor put kicks through but John Graham covered them and we were well on top.

Wilson Whineray: I had a talk over a beer with Ian MacRae halfway through the tour and said to him that I couldn't recall him making a break. I said to him you're a big, strong boy who is being seen as a fine prospect so what was the problem? He confessed he was simply too scared to try anything for fear of cocking it up. So I told him the next time he was playing, and if we were eight or ten points up, just to give it a crack and if he was held up to stay on his feet long enough for our loosies to get there and help him out.

Dennis Young: We were certainly lucky to get through with a nil-all draw with Scotland. We had one chance to pull the game out late in the piece when Don Clarke came into the backline . . . one of the few times he did on the tour . . . he came in very well on that occasion and broke but he lost his support and kicked ahead and the ball went out.

Wilson Whineray: It was a flat game, but having said that, the Scotties took it to us pretty well. They were proud of themselves and they deserved to be that day.

Ralph Caulton: They were a bit of a surprise. We underestimated them a wee bit. They denied us a lot of ball but we had several close shaves and close calls. We were very disappointed we didn't win. It wasn't a nice day, they had the electric blanket on under the ground the night before to stop it freezing, and it was a bit of a nothing game. Clarky missed a few kicks too.

Earle Kirton: I went and had a chat with Willie. He was a great man. He used to make you so proud the way he spoke and handled himself. He was a good bugger and a good player. He was really a No.8 rather than a prop but he fitted in to go with the plan. And a grand captain. You'd go over the hill with him in wartime. But I went to him and said, 'What have I got to do to get any better?' I can still see the brown carpet at the British Caledonian Hotel in Edinburgh and we were twenty-two games into the tour. They had the idea I wasn't training hard enough because that was what they all did. They just trained harder and smashed into it more. It wasn't fitness, I was so young I could run all day if I had to. And he said, 'You'll have to lift your game thirty per cent.' I thought, 'What's thirty per cent? Give me something Willy.' I should have asked him for more but Dad had said, 'Don't bitch' so I didn't go back to him because he would have had something. But I got angrier and angrier about my performance, not with anyone else, because I reckoned I should have improved therefore I was a failure. Coming back on the plane I sat with Billy Davis, BJ Lochore and IR MacRae was on the other side, the youngies. And I said to BJ, 'There's one thing I'm going to do. I'm going to get back into this bloody side even if it takes me five, six, seven, eight, nine or ten years. And I said, 'I know how to do it.' I had spent so much time thinking about it. And Billy Davis said, 'I reckon I can play too, I'm going to have a real crack.' IR was going all right, he was good and steady and he played pretty well anyway and he always looked as if he was going to shore up midfield. BJ didn't say anything but he came up afterwards, when I got back [in the team], and said, 'I remember you saying to me, you and Billy Davis,' and he said, 'Ernie, I thought you were going to have a hell of a struggle.' That was it, he never said any more about it.

Ralph Caulton: I enjoyed playing in France. Their rugby was a bit more expansive. We played France B and someone said if they beat us they would be the France A side for the Test. We were struggling in the backs against them although we had plenty of ball. At one stage Whineray came out to us at a lineout or a break in the game and said, 'For heaven's sake would you guys please score some points.' We ended up scoring two tries in two minutes which was a relief. In the Test we got our noses in front and shut the game down. We had too much riding on it to fall at the last fence.

Wilson Whineray: One of my most difficult rugby days was the Test in France. Don certainly wasn't up to his best form on that trip, not the form we'd become accustomed to. There was even a bit of a selection debate about Don. The question was raised whether we should play him against France and everyone looked down at each other and said: 'When has he ever let us down? No, he never has.' So he played that match and he didn't kick well but on defence he was as solid as a rock. They popped high balls at him but he was flawless. Playing France over there is a hard day at the office. It's very important to get in front and then get a bit more in front. Don missed two moderately easy attempts by his standards . . . Then we had another penalty and I called Mac Herewini up to have the shot and that was close to the only time I ever asked anyone to kick when Don was playing. Anyway, Herewini kicked that one against France.

Dennis Young: The match I remember best of all was the Barbarians match which was the last of my career . . . and this is the game I would want to be the last game of my career. It had everything. It had drama, humour and had the most wonderful rugby you would ever wish to see. I've got a tape of the crowd singing after Wilson Whineray was walking back after his try . . . it was the first try he scored on the tour and it was a tribute to WW as a man, as a player . . . as I listen to this tape the hairs on the back of my neck stand straight up on end.

Wilson Whineray: It was a very moving moment. After I scored that try I was like a cork bobbling along in the waves. I don't remember anything clearly. I was pushed up on to somebody's shoulder, I slipped down, I went up again. That crowd was yelling. Finally, I fought my way through the tunnel and into the dressing room where it was suddenly quiet. I've watched my try on television since then and the thing that touches me most is the obvious pleasure my fellow All Blacks got out of me scoring.

Ralph Caulton: This was the best game I ever played in. There was some relief that it was our last game, apart from a couple of games in Canada, but they were a strong team. Phil Sharpe hadn't been able to play against us earlier but he was fit again and they picked their best guys for each position. They invited Ian Clarke to play for them. We were a pretty well-drilled unit and we said to ourselves we were going to throw the ball around. The ball was all over the place. Guys were running from everywhere. It was a style every boy wanted to play. Their only points were a dropped goal kicked by Ian Clarke.

Ian MacRae: Wilson Whineray was the best off-field captain. He had mana, the gift of speech-making and he knew how to handle himself in the hoitey-toitey world of the British administrators. But the tour itself was a very forward-dominated tour and there was not a lot of discussion with the backs.

FIFTEEN

GETTING READY FOR THE SPRINGBOKS AND LIONS

'Go and talk to them and tell them how good Mike is,
we've got to keep him in the team'

THE DEMANDS OF such a long tour were felt when New Zealand hosted Australia in 1964. The side featured several newcomers and while the first two Tests were comfortably won by the All Blacks 14-9 and 18-3, the third was lost 5-20 and was one of the fine Australian efforts in trans-Tasman Tests. That loss marked the end of Don Clarke's career. Since 1956 he had played 31 Test matches and scored 207 points. In all first-class rugby for New Zealand he scored 781 points – only Dan Carter (1,598), Grant Fox (1,067) and Andrew Mehrtens (994) have scored more points for the country. John Graham and Des Connor also retired while Ralph Caulton was named to play the first Test against South Africa only to withdraw due to injury and he retired.

Ralph Caulton: We weren't long home and we played a series against the Australians. We won in Dunedin and Christchurch to take the series. We lost the third Test in Wellington but I think by then we'd had enough rugby. The Aussies did as they do sometimes, played one out of the box. There was no way we had the tenacity to come back. The nucleus of the team was from the team that went away and we were happy we had won the series.

Brian Lochore: We only played Australia in the year we came back and it wasn't a successful tour from a New Zealand point of view, and it didn't worry me unduly that I wasn't selected.

With South Africa due to tour in 1965, the loss to Australia was a reminder that the All Blacks needed to be at their best. The South Africans were a strong side, fielding a typically big forward pack and a talented, if restrained, backline featuring such familiar players as captain and halfback Dawie de Villiers, first five-eighths Keith Oxlee, second five-eighths John Gainsford and fullback Lionel Wilson. Wilson Whineray returned to lead the side after having 1964 out of international play while Wellington's fullback Mick Williment, who had played in the first two Tests against Australia, won the race to replace Clarke, although Fergie McCormick played the fourth Test as a result of injury to Williment. Three-quarters Bill Birtwistle and Ron Rangi were introduced along with five-eighths John Collins and Peter Murdoch while recalled to service during the series were five-eighths Ray Moreton and Mac Herewini. Only eight forwards were used during the four Test matches with Red Conway playing the openside flanker role for the first time since the 1960 tour of South Africa. New Zealand won the first two Tests 6-3 and 13-0 but suffered one of their most ignominious losses in the third in Christchurch when having led 16-5 at half-time as the result of some fine rugby. However, South Africa let

Opposite: Brian Lochore and Lions captain Mike Campbell-Lamerton lead out their sides ahead of the first Test of the 1966 series. *Ron Palenski Collection*

loose in the second half and eliminated the deficit to claim victory when lock Tiny Naude kicked the winning penalty goal just before full-time. South Africa had hopes of winning the fourth Test to level the series, but the All Blacks responded with a powerful display to score five tries in a 20-3 win.

Wilson Whineray: We had a build-up in strength in the quality of the All Black team from the early 60s on, I think, and it seemed to culminate a bit in the British tour of '63-64. Most of the '65 side came from that touring squad so it was a very good patch for us really, a strong team and it wasn't ever going to be easy for the Africans to win. They brought, as always, a very big, strong, physical pack and some lively backs. We played the first two Tests at Athletic Park and Carisbrook – both heavy grounds, difficult conditions and we won narrowly both times. Then, in the third Test at Lancaster Park, we had a handsome lead at half-time . . . Having said that we didn't quite deserve to be as far in front as we were, there were a couple of chance factors and a try or two were scored that shouldn't have been. But they scored, their backs played very well, made some good breaks, there were a couple of crucial missed tackles and suddenly there was a great big forward, [Tiny] Naude, about forty yards out on the sideline having a shot at goal at the end of the game when we were tied up, and, of course, he kicked it. So they won the third and the media, the African media, took a new line. 'Well you beat us in the mud and you're better at that than us, but we beat you in reasonable conditions. If the ground's good at Eden Park, watch out!' In fact, we won that handsomely, scoring four or five tries, a big score in those days. Ian Smith got a couple and Bill Birtwhistle, I think even Ken Gray. That was my last Test, so I was very pleased with the boys for sending me off in style.

Colin Meads: Four or five of us in 1964 went to South Africa for their seventy-fifth Jubilee so we got to know the South Africans very well during three games. I don't know who came up with the idea but in the first game they played the World forwards with the South African backs. They had Dawie de Villiers, Keith Oxlee, John Gainsford, Lionel Wilson and others, and we got to know them well because we were living with them. The second game was all mixed up higgledy-piggledy and it was a shocker so the third game they went back to how it was in the first game. As we were leaving the ground in Dunedin he [Gainsford] came up behind me with the mud and then took off, I chased him all the way to their dressing room and had a beer with him. He was laughing his head off.

Brian Lochore: We were a bit slack in Christchurch. We got 16 points up in about that many minutes and we were cruising, and we should never have cruised. They came back and whipped us. We were never going to let that happen in Auckland. What was great about that pack, and probably for two or three years after that, was that we absolutely trusted one another. We knew how people were going to react in every given situation and people put themselves in a position to assist and you knew what people would do in a tight situation. Great packs are made of confidence in one another.

Colin Meads: [Referee] Murphy went off at half-time, we were winning 16-5 and Alan Taylor came on and blew us up. Tiny Naude kicked that penalty goal from a long way out in the mud. That was a trying time for Whineray. There was a lot of councillors, one or two of them didn't like Whineray and one of them said, 'Where's your great Whineray now?' I stayed with Wilson all night. We were great mates. We had the dinner and after that we went round and saw his Mum and Dad, who were down for the game. That fourth Test, well it was one of those days where things go right for you.

Stan [Meads] had an injury-plagued early career. He would probably have gone away in 1960 if he had been free of injuries. When we came back we played the Rest and he was in that team. Stan had to mark Frik du Preez in the 1965 series. Frik was a bit lazy and reminded me of Peter Jones quite a bit. Stan reminded me of Kirky [Ian Kirkpatrick] a lot. Ken Gray was the strongest man I ever put a shoulder on. His physique was great, he was 6ft 3in, nearly as tall as I was. He was my greatest ally. If I was

Kel Tremain on the break against South Africa, Athletic Park, 1965, with Chris Laidlaw in support. *Peter Bush*

having trouble in the lineout I would say to Whineray, 'Play Ken for God's sake.' I would look after my man on his ball. Ken was a great player. Waka Nathan and Red Conway were good players as well.

That success set the scene for the tour of the Lions a year later. Now under the coaching of Fred Allen, the All Blacks started to throw off the inhibitions that had marked the previous ten years and moved the ball. Second five-eighths Ian MacRae became a key man setting up second phase play for the side where quickly rucked ball could be used to spread the defences. The Lions had a hard time of it and lost their first three Saturday matches on the tour to Southland, Otago and Wellington.

In the Test matches they were unable to contain a pack which had only two changes from that of 1965. Jack Hazlett replaced Whineray while Waka Nathan was on the flank for Conway. Neither diminished the quality of the side and all eight forwards played in the four Test matches. The Lions lost the first Test 3-20, got closer in the second 12-16 but were soundly beaten 19-6 in the third and 24-11 in the fourth. Unable to win ball from the All Blacks forwards, the Lions couldn't unleash their quality backline where Mike Gibson was the king-pin in midfield.

Brian Lochore: They weren't a great side, but we were. I think 1966 was as good as we got.

The Springbok backs launch an attack during the third Test in 1965. *Scran*

Colin Meads: Fred Allen in 1966 was probably the first coach we had as such. Fred had been around and he'd been a selector. For the first year or so we never got on too well. We became great mates, more when he was a selector not the boss. He'd come straight from Auckland, and it was all about his Auckland boys. King Country were playing Thames Valley and Ned [Kevin] Barry had gone back to Thames Valley – he was captaining them and I was captaining King Country. We'd been All Blacks and we knew one another terribly well. Ned started pushing me and I said, 'Ned don't do it, you know what will happen.' And he never thought I'd do it. That morning in the *NZ Herald* Fred had said he was worried about the forwards who were not aggressive enough, not tough enough, were getting soft, and all this sort of stuff. I thought to myself I would wait until I was in front of Fred and I would get back at Ned. We knew where Fred was sitting, in that little grandstand they've got in Otorohonga. When the time came I sat old Ned on his arse. Fred came and saw me afterwards and really got stuck into me for doing that. I said to him, 'Bugger you, I read in the paper we're not tough enough, we're not this and we're not that, and I thought I'd show you.' He said, 'It's not you we're trying to get at, we're trying to get Tremain worked up.' And I thought, 'Why don't you just tell him?' We did become very good mates after that but we weren't speaking for a while. Making Brian Lochore captain was one of Fred's great achievements – him and Charlie Saxton. All the talk was about Tremain, there was Ken Gray, there was myself who were going to be captain. I never really wanted it. Tremain did and he was captain of Hawke's Bay and they were doing well. And then they named BJ. When the team got together we, Kel, Ken and myself, had a private little meeting and made a pact to support BJ. We had to speak up and let the rest know that he had our support. It was one of Tremain's great speeches to the team how we were right behind BJ. And Brian was such a good guy so there was no trouble over it.

Bruce McLeod scores the All Blacks' first try of the 1966 Lions Test series, with Brian Lochore and Kel Tremain in support. *Getty Images*

Ian MacRae: Fred gave me some incentives and a direct role in affecting the way the team played and I was quite happy to do that for him. It was the start of phase play. We had never heard of second-phase ball. He told me he wanted me to take the ball forward and tie up the opposing second five-eighths. It was designed to take the Lions' second-five Mike Gibson out of play. Mike was an outstanding player and it was aimed to reduce his effect. I ended up with two buggered shoulders by the end of the year, I did get one of them fixed, and during the summer they would come right again. That Lions team had some brilliant individuals but a poor captain. Their forward pack was not up to much and we dominated them and created plenty of opportunities for us backs. We never took them as easybeats but we won 4-0. I loved every minute of that series and it was good to be playing a major part in the team's game plan. The only frustration was that I got daubed with that style of play which annoyed me because it was only the team pattern for that series, although it did give me the ability later when things were looking a bit tough to turn the ball back to the forwards knowing they would be quickly there in support.

Colin Meads: Mike Campbell-Lamerton was a lovely guy but he shouldn't have been the captain. Fred Allen used to say 'Go and talk to them and tell them how good Mike is, we've got to keep him in the team.' Because otherwise Willie John McBride and Delme Thomas would be in. They had some good players in spite of their record.

SIXTEEN

RUNNING REVIVAL

'There's 60,000 screaming Welshmen out here and fifteen of us,
let's make it work.'

KNOWING THE ALL Blacks were capable of much better rugby, coach Fred Allen decided to take up the running game that had been the legacy of the Kiwis team he had been part of after World War Two. New Zealand's forwards were capable of highly-mobile rugby while backs of superior quality were emerging. Halfback Chris Laidlaw's outstanding passing ignited the backline and his efforts were supplemented by the challenge provided by a different type of halfback, but one equally able to serve the side, Sid Going. Earle Kirton, having regained his equilibrium at provincial level, was welcomed back by Allen to ensure the direction he wanted at first five-eighths. Ian MacRae and Bill Davis had been hardened by Ranfurly Shield rugby for their Hawke's Bay side while the solid Malcolm Dick had been joined by the national sprint champion Tony Steel on the wings. Add in the running fullback Fergie McCormick and the bones of an attacking side were in place.

New Zealanders were given an often forgotten prelude to what would happen on the tour playing a seventy-fifth Jubilee Test match against Australia in 1967. The Australians were beaten 29-9 in an outstanding display.

After the disappointments of the 1966 Lions, British rugby was ready for a shake-up and under captain Brian Lochore the All Blacks provided it in what was regarded as a revolution in the game. Only an outbreak of foot and mouth disease in England denied Lochore's men a Grand Slam that would have been the first by the All Blacks. Irish authorities would not allow contact between England and Ireland so the Test match was cancelled. However, they did allow referee Kevin Kelleher to travel to Scotland to control the All Blacks' contest and that provided the most controversial moment of the tour when Colin Meads became only the second man to be ordered from the field. But such was the regard in which Meads was held, and the stature of the 1967 team, that Meads suffered none of the anguish that was the lot of Cyril Brownlie in 1925 when he was sent off at Twickenham against England. The complete opposite was the case. Television coverage, now commonplace in New Zealand, showed that Meads' act in trying to kick the ball as Scots first five-eighths David Chisholm attempted to catch it was not wilful. Rather it was the quality of rugby that the All Blacks played that lived longest in the memory and won the side the accolade as one of the greatest touring teams in rugby's history.

Ian MacRae: The 1967 Jubilee Test saw Billy Davis make his debut and was the reason the replacement law finally got changed. The Aussies' wing Phil Smith broke his collarbone and then came back with his arm in a sling. It was a bit pathetic and we didn't want to tackle him – it was the catalyst in putting that rule to bed. It was also the game that saw the resurgence of the Bledisloe Cup. As a player I had never heard of the Bledisloe Cup. It

Opposite: Colin Meads in action during the 1967 tour. *Getty Images*

had actually been found in the office of NSW Rugby in Sydney. But it was a special day and they dusted it off for it.

Sid Going (1967-77, 29 Tests, 86 games): I hadn't actually seen a lot of the All Blacks until I played. We never got TV until I got into the All Blacks. I had never considered being an All Black but things happened when I got back off my [Mormon] mission. I got to play for the NZ Maoris against the Springboks and then got into the North Island team but I knew I had to get to play against Chris Laidlaw and that didn't happen in that first couple of years.

Brian Lochore: The cancellation of the 1967 tour to South Africa wasn't a big deal. I think we all agreed, 'No Maoris, no tour'. Most New Zealanders felt like that. The fact we were going to the British Isles and France was a reasonable compromise.

Colin Meads: Not going to South Africa in 1967 was a bigger disappointment for the likes of Stan, he'd have gone but once we were going to England he pulled out. He had such a disappointing tour with his health in 1963-64 he didn't want to go back.

Grahame Thorne (1967-70, 10 Tests, 39 games): When I first met Colin Meads, who was captaining the trial team I was in, his first words to me were: 'You'd better be the goods. We've heard a lot about you.' He told me I would never score between the posts because my head wouldn't fit. When I scored in the Wellington trial it was between the posts just to show Meads that I could do it. After the trial Winston McCarthy asked me what I thought after scoring the try and I said I thought it was a free ticket to England. I also said I would love to play cricket for New Zealand.

Ian Kirkpatrick (1967-77, 39 Tests, 113 games): We had the trial and then we stood around in that awful bloody place under Athletic Park for the team to be read out. It was all a whirlwind, and to be picked in that team was just . . . I knew I wasn't going to play many games; I was just happy to be there. I was picked as a No.8 but I only played one game there.

Brian Lochore: Fred indicated right at the beginning of the tour that he advocated a fifteen-man game which absolutely suited us all. Our greatest strength, and it still is in my view, is the forwards' ability to run with the ball. It suited us perfectly, we had great runners with the ball who had been a little restricted by the tactics previously. It was all about, 'Are you prepared to run to the wing and have a ruck out there?' We said, 'Yeah we'll run out there' and often we did but often we didn't have a ruck, we got an in-pass instead. It was great rugby to play in. It was a surprise that Mick Williment was dropped but Fergie McCormick was a magnificent running fullback.

Colin Meads: Fergie's selection didn't surprise us. He was a tough little bloke and he was a good tourist, the more they played him the better he loved it. It did surprise me that he was the only fullback named. The tragic part was Mick Williment missing out. Mick was the complete opposite to Fergie and I think when they realised they had picked 31 players if they had sat down and thought about it, it would probably have been Gerald Kember who missed out. Nothing against Gerald because he was a good guy too, and he played pretty well as a fullback.

Earle Kirton: I always hoped that some day, I might get another chance. I never completely gave up. It wasn't easy to maintain this front and there were times when I was almost ready to give in to my disappointment.

Brian Lochore: Ian Kirkpatrick was selected as a No.8 for the tour and after the first Test on that tour I deliberately gave him an English Test jersey because I felt a little bit sorry for him having to be second fiddle to me and knowing how good a player he was. But it didn't last long! He got a few caps on that tour as well so it was great really as it was the start of his great career.

Colin Meads: Fred told us what was going to happen. 'We're going to run the ball, it's going to get out to the wings and you big bastards are going to get there, there'll be no taking shortcuts,' he told us forwards. He used to get into us terribly which was good for us. And we took to his philosophy. It wasn't hard, we had good players and we were all fit. After 1967 we had a talk at the end of the tour and said we would go back and promote Fred's philosophy through our provinces. It was the start of running rugby. If you looked at the difference between 1960 and 1968 it would be phenomenal. We were lucky we had Charlie Saxton with Fred, because he could handle Fred. They went back to the Army. He was the boss. Fred used to play up something terrible but Charlie would give him the message whereas Duncan Ross, who managed the team the next year in Australia, couldn't handle him.

Ian MacRae: Fred had our complete respect. He was a disciplinarian and he probably took that to a bit of an extreme. He probably wouldn't get away with it now, but the harder it was, the better we liked it.

Colin Meads: A lot of sad things happened too. Ron Rangi could have been one of New Zealand's most brilliant centres. Fred picked him in Auckland from the Air Force team which was third division in Auckland. Ron Rangi never drank before he became an All Black and once he became an All Black he thought he had to drink. We were allowed a couple of beers after training and of course at the dinners and socially it was quite heavy. Tragically he became an alcoholic later in life. He was big, strong, a great tackler, he had everything going for him, then along came Grahame Thorne. He played in a North Island trial in Palmerston North and had a brilliant game, we didn't know him, nobody knew him. After about seventy minutes he went down injured and wanted to go off. Fred came onto the field and said, 'If you go off you won't go to England, we want tough men.' Well, Thorney got up as if there was nothing wrong with him. He would have been brilliant if Fred had taken us to South Africa.

Ian Kirkpatrick: Fred was about making good players play well all the time, that's why they called him 'The Needle' because of that gift he had. When we trained before the third game in France, I mean I guess the physicality was nothing like it is now, so the day after playing a game, you'd still train the next morning. And I thinking I'm really going for it, and he stops on halfway and he said, 'There's a bunch of slackers here at the moment', and I'm thinking some poor bastard's going to get it, and he looks at me and says, 'and you'd be the worst.' Well, did I find another gear?

Fergie McCormick (1965-71, 16 Tests, 44 games): I used to run and Fred liked to use the blindside a lot. Fred always liked the fifteen-man game and we were tremendously fit – it made training so much easier. Fred could also get inside the minds of quite a few players and get the best out of them.

Earle Kirton: I was very fit as a result of our early start with the NZ Universities team in Japan in February and March. With Chris Laidlaw inside me on that tour, and both the Christchurch and Wellington trials, I realised that if I was ever going to make it again, it had to be now, so I put all I had into 'firing' our backs in each case. It worked and I was away again. It was wonderful to hear 'Well done, Earle' from so many people. One of the most encouraging of all tributes came from Tom Morrison, the NZRU chairman. Immediately after I'd been chosen for the tour, he came over and shook my hand. 'Earle,' he said, 'my sincerest congratulations. They don't very often get back and you've done it.'

Sid Going: In 1967 Fred got stuck into trying to improve me and after trainings he would spend an extra twenty minutes working on getting my passing quicker and more accurate.

Ian MacRae: Fergie was unbelievably outstanding. He was the only fullback selected for the tour and was indestructible. His goal-kicking was spot on and he made some amazing defensive tackles. In the game against the Barbarians, Jones, the British sprint champion beat him and gave him a five- or six-yard start but Fergie dragged him down from behind. No one ever got past him. I remember him flattening me on Lancaster Park when I was playing for the West Coast as an 18-year-old. We could have won that game and I made a break with one man, Fergie, to beat. One minute I was making up my mind what to do, and the next I woke up in the showers.

Ian Kirkpatrick: He gave some magnificent team talks. If we played at 2.30pm, he'd give one at the hotel at 1.00pm just before you got on the bus and he used to get quite emotional. He certainly fired me up. Obviously he and Charlie Saxton were in that Kiwis team together so there was no clash of ideas, and the way they wanted to play suited me because it was about support play. It was pretty simple rugby when you think about it.

Ian MacRae: As soon as we got to England, Fred went on television and told them that he had instructed us that he didn't want us kicking the ball and said everyone should come along and watch us because we were going to play some spectacular rugby. We were a bit worried about that but really it was the most marvellous rugby to play. He and manager

Earle Kirton dives in to score one of his two tries against England at Twickenham.
Alexander Turnbull Library, Wellington, New Zealand

Charlie had a great affinity with the game and they gave us the confidence to move the ball. New Zealand has always felt the need to set the standards for entertainment and it is not so much about winning, but the way we win.

Brian Lochore: Earle Kirton had gone through a pretty low patch after 1963 and he said that if he ever got another chance he wasn't going to muck up again. And he didn't, he was absolutely superb on that tour. But so was Bill Davis. I think just about every time he went for a gap he made it. The reason Graham Williams was able to play so well was that we could handle most packs with seven players and we let him rove. That was a deliberate tactic on our part and Tremain and Kirkpatrick became the guys, who could sometimes go as well but if things were a bit tough up front they would come back and help us in the tight.

Ian MacRae: In the Midland, Home and Southern Counties game Danny Hearn, in the first tackle of the game, hit me on the hip and suffered his neck injury. I had a huge bruise, about half the size of a football. We later became very good friends. The management wouldn't let me visit him until the end of the tour. I kept wondering how he was and what was going on and I was determined to go and see him before we went home. There wasn't a lot of media about it back then. 'Don't blame yourself' were his first words to me and that made things a lot easier. He had wanted to put a peg in the ground for the England Test in which he would have played a week later. He was clever, had a great brain and carried on teaching and coaching the first XV from his wheelchair. The senior boys had turns looking after him. He came out to visit me a few years later when we were still playing for the Ranfurly Shield and brought one of the boys with him. They both stayed with us. He was rapt to experience a Shield challenge, he loves New Zealand rugby and follows it. He was keen on horses so we arranged for him to go out to Waimarama Beach where Ricky Allen trained trotters. I couldn't go but Marilyn my wife took him out there and all the locals gathered, gave him a Maori welcome and prepared a meal with plenty of seafood. Then they rigged up a sulky so he could take a ride down the beach with a horse. He loved it.

Brian Lochore: The Danny Hearn incident was a shocking thing. I have kept in touch with him and he has stayed at our place a couple of times. He has retired now and lives in the south of Ireland. I can see it as if it happened yesterday. We were going really well and then after he was injured we stood around for fifteen minutes. I saw the incident happen. He was a very competitive fellow and he had a chance to bowl his opposite and he just got his head in the wrong place. It destroyed everything about that game.

Grahame Thorne: After the England Test we went down to Wales and it was pretty much a second XV playing against West Wales. They hit us with everything. Pinetree, who was captain that day, said, 'When they start singing get up the other end because that's what stops them.' My try came in a mis-move from Mackie [Herewini] and I got through a gap. I could have passed at one stage but I kept on going and scored. Fred gave me a bollocking about not passing but deep down he was very proud I had done it. It vindicated my selection.

Ian Kirkpatrick: Kel Tremain had an Achilles problem so he wasn't a hundred. They say I put him out but that wasn't the case. It was a shortened tour, and we played teams we wouldn't normally play on a UK tour. We played West Wales in Swansea in the week before the Test . . . I played in that game.

Fergie McCormick: Fred was especially keen the All Blacks should beat Wales. Before the game I hurt myself in a big tackle and my right side wasn't right. I worked on the injury and had no doubt I would play but I don't think the team was aware of how badly hurt

I was. I took the view that if I could train I would play. I got through the game and was elated. To beat Wales on Cardiff Arms [13-6] was a highlight. I'll never forget Needle after we beat Wales. He was out on the ground in mud over his shoes congratulating the guys. He was the team's man. We were his boys and that was that. He didn't let you make mistakes – he was my best coach by a street.

Ian MacRae: I had experienced the Welsh fervour in 1963 sitting in the grandstand. It was like war in the trenches but we were the better team in 1967. Out on the field hearing the anthems was different and some of the young fellows in the team had tears in their eyes. BJ said to us, 'There's 60,000 screaming Welshmen out here and fifteen of us, let's make it work.'

Brian Lochore: Having Chris Laidlaw and Sid Going, two different types of halfback, gave us a massive point of difference. Don't worry, Laidlaw could run too, he was a beautiful passer and he had a good combination with Earle, of course, because they played together for a long time at club rugby, and provincially. But Sid was just a magnificent runner with the ball and while he didn't pass quite as well as Laidlaw, it was OK.

Ian MacRae: I was vice-captain on the tour and was involved in selections. One of the hardest things was the selection of the French Test team when Fred and Charlie were adamant that they wanted some attacking flair against France and that involved bringing in Sid Going and Ian Kirkpatrick and dropping Chris Laidlaw and Kel Tremain. They both had outstanding games, and scored tries, and Fred and Charlie were proved right.

The team gather for a photograph before the France Test. *NZ Herald*

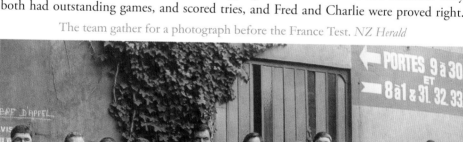

We had concurred in the final selection. It was obvious that Kirky was going to be a star player, although it probably happened sooner than he had expected. I always thought that French Test was the toughest in my time. They were gunning for us and scrapping the whole time. There was some pretty brutal stuff – Pinetree was dealt to on the ground and when they were running past you they would clip you around the head, from behind.

Colin Meads: The night before the French Test, Charlie and Fred had a meeting, Brian Lochore wasn't in on it. They reckoned the French lineout was going to clean us out. There was Benoit Dauga, Alain Plantefol and Walter Spanghero, and all these players. Charlie had this belief that we had to confuse the French. If you played the way they were used to playing you wouldn't cope. We were having our team talk when they came through and told us what we were going to do. They got it so that [hooker] Bruce McLeod would stand on the five-metre mark and the No.2 person went back five yards and you would have a huge gap there and just have your normal lineout from there. You just threw the ball to the middle of the lineout to Sam Strahan or we could all have a jump at it. We all looked at each other. Someone said, 'What about we only do it outside our twenty-five?' and we got that through. When we were right back on defence we went back to our normal lineout. We hadn't practised it or anything. It was shock tactics. The French didn't know what to do. They were arguing and squawking and going on. It worked. It took them more than halfway through the game to work it out. We would go back to marking them in their lineouts and give them hell and get a bit of their ball. Sam Strahan had a great game. It was harder for the wingers throwing it in but they still had the same lineout calls. But we were all prepared to jump if the ball wasn't quite right. Apparently the Kiwis had used it when they played in France. That was Charlie, he was a great thinker of the game. He was the first manager we had who took a big part in how you played.

Ian Kirkpatrick: It suited us in France where the grounds were better. Blokes kept telling me I was in with a chance of a Test, but I didn't want to believe it. I suppose I took my chances and I loved the rugby. I managed to score a few tries outside the wingers and I remember in the France B game that I got outside Bill Davis and scored in the corner. I mean there was no one to tackle me so I just went over and Tony Steel came up to me and said, 'You should have passed. I would have scored under the sticks.'

Sid Going: They were talented and you could never let up. If you relaxed at all they would score. It's funny, I played pretty well in that game and never got any more games. It was disappointing.

Brian Lochore: It was the best Test I played in. The toughest. It was the most physical and exhausting game I ever played. We were genuinely worried about various aspects of their game and they had a tough backline. Ten minutes afterwards, the others came down to the dressing room all delighted with the win only to see us all sitting there with our heads down, not having moved.

Ian MacRae: Ken Gray had a big game and he was the most valuable forward in any team in my time. He was athletic, a tremendous scrummager, had ability in the lineout and we could jump him at two or three, and he was never beaten, you could bank on him winning the ball.

Ian Kirkpatrick: It was fairly tough and we had to do a lot of work. I broke my nose early on but I thought there was no way I was going off. It was all quite an eye-opener for me. It was as hard a Test as any I played.

Brian Lochore: I couldn't believe it. I didn't see it at all. I was at the bottom of a ruck and I got up and here was the referee pointing to Pinetree to go off. Pinetree went a few steps and then I asked the ref what was going on and Pinetree came back, but he wasn't going to change his mind. I think Tremain and I caused that in a roundabout way. I was marking the Scottish captain and every time there was a lineout he would either push me, or pull me down, so I warned him. I said, 'I wouldn't do that' so we threw one to me and Tremain hit him in the breadbasket and he went down and couldn't breathe. The ref never saw it and Tremain was well away by the time the ref had a look around. So I went over and he knew what had happened and he knew why it had happened so I was being very sympathetic to him, as you did. I think the ref didn't know how it had happened and he got a little flustered and it was only about half a minute after that that Colin came through. I've seen many replays of it and he never went for that guy at all. He went for the ball and tried to kick it out of his hands which is totally legal. Chisholm came into our dressing room and said, 'Look you didn't do anything to me, I'm sorry that this has happened.' But the hearing just about destroyed Charlie Saxton. It wasn't a hearing, there was two of them and one of us and we had to send him away for a couple of days, he was just destroyed with the outcome of the whole thing – the process. I think they used Colin as a means of tidying up their own problems over there. It was sad, it was a very, very sad occasion.

Colin Meads: Charlie was very upset after the hearing for my ordering off. I never really heard the full story. I was on standby to appear but they wouldn't let me speak and I've never seen Charlie upset so much as he was that night. I thought that was the end of my career. But I came home to Te Kuiti to a huge welcome and it never affected me. I think ninety per cent of the people realised I had done bugger all. I still get a card from the referee Kevin Kelleher. I never got any abusive messages afterwards but I got cards from a lot of guys I had played against saying, 'Bad luck.'

Ian MacRae: The low point of the tour came just after we had beaten Scotland when we found out the Ireland Test had been cancelled due to the foot and mouth outbreak. We could have achieved a Grand Slam if we had gone there and that was a bit of a wet blanket for us, especially coming after Pinetree was ordered off in that Test. I had a pretty good view of what happened and when Pinetree went to kick the loose ball, the crowd just roared. He hadn't hit anything and had just tried to kick the ball. He was a pretty fearsome looking sight with his head all bandaged up from the French Test but nothing actually happened in the incident. Everyone saw what I saw. How he got ordered off I don't know. I blame the crowd reaction. It was a combination of the reaction and an inexperienced referee.

Brian Lochore: Not being able to go to Ireland was a shame from our point of view. A Grand Slam hadn't been done before and we had a great opportunity to do it but we missed out on that. It was a strange end to the tour. Our game against East Wales was cancelled due to the ground being covered in snow. It was an incredibly stupid day. Although there was no game, we had lunch at the time that had been arranged at 11am. We went to the after-match function and then to the match dinner. They decided to reschedule the Saturday game on the following Wednesday ahead of our final game against the Barbarians. Because we weren't booked in to play the game on the Wednesday, we had to train back to London and then come down to play the game on the Wednesday morning on the train. It was very frustrating and we could have got bowled. We drew 3-3 after Tony Steel scored a try. Tony didn't have a large skill-set but he knew his strengths and he probably saved us in the last two games from defeat and was one of the great success stories of the tour.

Colin Meads trudges disconsolately to the changing rooms after being sent off against Scotland. *Getty Images*

Fergie McCormick: It's great to kick goals, particularly when they're match-winners, but it is also a tremendous help to a side if its fullback can save tries with crunching tackles.

Brian Lochore: I can still remember the Welsh sprinter Keri Jones getting in the clear. I was running across in cover and Fungus [McCormick] was screaming at me to 'go wide'. But I thought that was a bloody stupid thing to do because he would cut inside me. But I did what Fergie said and Jones did step inside me, but it was just at the same moment as Fungus launched himself at Jones and got him.

Ian MacRae: The Barbarians game was not one of my better games. I was struggling to get things going and at one stage Bill [Davis] said, 'Get out of there' and went in to second five and I went to centre. He was thinking a bit better than I was and then I was pleased to score a try to get a draw. I had my doubts that we could pull it off. But then BJ took to the kick-off and set it alight for Tony Steel to score the match-winning try.

Earle Kirton: Whineray was a great captain in terms of what he set out to do. But Brian Lochore I found to be a better captain for the backs. Whineray would play it very close to his chest. He'd allow you to drop the ball once but, if it happened again, he's say, 'Put it over the top' – and that was that. The forwards would do it all from there on in. But with Brian, he'd stick to the plan to run the ball no matter how many times the five-eighths dropped or mulled their passes because he was confident in his backs and in their ability ultimately to triumph.

SEVENTEEN

'RIGHT,' SAID FRED

'Put the little bastard on the ground and ruck shit out of him'

HAVING SET A standard with their play in Britain and France, the All Blacks toured Australia early in 1968 having dropped eight of their players from the British tour. Australia were coached by Des Connor, the former All Black and Auckland halfback during Fred Allen's era with the provincial side. He produced a combative side which was criticised by Allen for their spoiling tactics. Connor defended his strategy saying if they had attempted to play the running game Allen was advocating they would have suffered a heavy defeat that would have harmed the game in Australia. The same tactics were employed a week later in the second Test with a struggling All Blacks side only winning when a penalty try was awarded with two minutes remaining after both centre Bill Davis and wing Grahame Thorne had been obstructed. The result was a 19-18 win for the All Blacks.

Ian Kirkpatrick: We were in Adelaide and played a night game against the Junior Wallabies and some bastard kicked my thumb and broke it and they were going to send me home. I said to Fred I didn't want to go home. It was a clean break, nothing too complicated and I was meant to be in plaster for about two weeks. I had it X-rayed after about seven days and it looked like it was coming right. We were staying in Manly and someone told me to go and see this guy who was a shot putter in the Aussie Olympic team in 1964, and he gave it a massage and it seemed to come right. So they put me in the reserves for the first Test. It was the first game where they allowed replacements in a long time. So I'm sitting up in that old wooden stand at the Sydney Cricket Ground alongside Alistair Hopkinson, and BJ stopped one. He broke his thumb but he got it strapped up and he carried on, and I thought OK, I really didn't want to go on because I'd never come on as a replacement in my life. But then he pulled a hammy. So he started to come off and I said to Hoppy, 'Hell I might be on here.' My warm-up was walking down the stairs!

Brian Lochore: I broke my thumb and pulled my hamstring at the same time. I stayed on for a little while just because we weren't going too well, the Aussies were giving us a bit of stick and I thought I would stay until we settled it down a bit and then I would go off, which I did. And my replacement [Kirkpatrick] came on and scored three tries.

Ian Kirkpatrick: It was funny going on as a reserve, it must have been before half-time and somehow I fluked three tries. I was just Johnny on the spot really . . . Although I could have got a fourth one if Tom Lister had passed it to me! I was enjoying that tour before I broke my thumb, playing under Fred again was marvellous. You had a free rein pretty much. It was all about running into space so it really suited my game.

Opposite: A bloodied Fergie McCormick. *FotoSport/Photosport NZ*

Colin Meads: We weren't prepared for Des Connor's short lineouts in the 1968 Tests. It took us a while to cotton on but we were pretty shrewd with Tremain, Lochore and myself, and we soon sorted it out. We weren't panicked by it, more dumbfounded for a while.

Sid Going: When we toured Australia, really our accommodation was poor. We didn't eat in the hotels, we ate down around the corner half the time in a bar because they couldn't afford to pay the expenses. We were helping Australia to get to the point where they could afford to do things. They've certainly grown their game. They had some good backs, could run a backline very well, could bring in their wingers and slot them into a gap. Our forwards handled theirs with our scrummaging, but they had some pretty lively loosies. Ray Price was a hard nut Aussie. John Hipwell played pretty well. I played against Ken Catchpole in my first Test in 1967 and really rated him as a player. It never concerned me who was up against me, I would do what I could to get on top of them.

Colin Meads: I was blamed for hurting Ken Catchpole in a Test in Australia in 1968 when I tried to pull him out of a ruck while not knowing his leg was pinned. All sorts of stories grew up that I had ended his career. A few years later when rugby was getting pretty strong over there, they put on a testimonial dinner for Ken and I was invited. I had the press folks ringing me up and saying, 'Don't go. Please don't go, you'll get booed off the stage.' I said that was all the more reason why I should go. So I went across and it was bloody good. I told my side of the story. I blame Fred Allen for that. Graham Williams and them off the back of the lineout were cutting off the options and he [Catchpole] was ducking back into the forwards around the lineouts. The message came out at half-time with the baggageman, 'Put the little bastard on the ground and ruck shit out of him.' I reached in and grabbed one leg and put him on the ground. The other leg was pinned in there somewhere and he did the splits and a few other things and I was the dirtiest bastard in Australia. But as far as I was concerned I was doing exactly what Fred told us to do. I got on well with Catchy, and he did play again, people thought he was out for life but a year later several of us went to Tonga for a charity game over there. There were four or five Aussies, Fergie McCormick and I and a couple from other countries. We played over two weekends. Catchy was on that with us so we got to know him well.

Grahame Thorne: Towards the end of the second Test, Bill Davis was slashing through in our last desperate attempt to pull the chestnuts out of the fire and as I ran outside him, I found that Alan Cardy not only was holding my jersey but was also hitting me as I tried to wrestle clear. He had actually hit me the first time he had tackled me in the match. I have never in my life deliberately obstructed a player unless it was in self-preservation, but how do you make a guy let go of your jersey? There's only one way and by the time I'd hit Cardy back and forced him to let go, Davis was five or six yards away and I couldn't catch him. He was starting to angle out. There was only one covering player. Then Davis was trying to step inside. He had flashed me a quick look and had seen that I'd been obstructed, so he toed the ball ahead. Upon which, he too, was obstructed by a late tackle.

New Zealand were stone-cold certainties to have scored that try had it not been for the double obstruction and how the referee could be criticised for seeing this and doing what he had to do is well beyond my comprehension.

Back in New Zealand, the French were making their second tour. It was a bitter series with the first and second Tests niggly encounters. One try was scored in the first Test resulting from a chargedown of a French clearing kick for a 12-9 win and the second Test was all penalty goals as the All Blacks won 9-3. However, it was the French penalty goal that lingered longest in the memory. Pierre Villepreux placed the ball sixty metres from the goal at Athletic Park and received a chortling from the crowd. But when he hit the ball with his round-the-corner style it sailed between the posts for what is regarded as the longest penalty goal landed at the ground. The departure of the yappy French halfback Marcel Puget after the second Test resulted in a much better atmosphere in the third at Eden Park. The rugby was more in line with the Allen style and the French showed their own skills. The difference between the sides was the brilliant running of Sid Going who had come in for the third Test and he scored two tries in the All Blacks' 19-12 win.

Ian MacRae: I had suffered back trouble for a few years but I managed to keep playing but after the tour was when I chose to get it sorted. I was in a plaster cast around my chest and my spine was immobilised for eight weeks. I was fed up with the pain associated with it. I came back and played two Tests against France but missed the third Test. They were always a team to be wary of but were always fun after the game, even though you couldn't always understand what they were saying. Pierre Villepreux landed that incredible kick in Wellington. We didn't think he could kick it when he put the ball down for the shot. But he proved us wrong.

Brian Lochore: The second Test was a bitter Test. They decided they were going to kick everything above the ground that moved in case it was a ball. I remember Fred saying to us, 'You have got to forget about what they are doing, just get out there and play the game and play rugby.' The boys were coming to me and saying, 'BJ, we've got to do something. We are getting kicked to bits and we just can't be passive any longer.' So I thought the best thing to do was to go to the referee and tell him that if he wasn't going to tidy it up I was going to let my men go. He didn't take kindly to that comment obviously and I don't think he probably had a great deal of respect for me. But it had to be done. And he did sort it out.

The third Test was a magnificent game of rugby. Sid Going got a couple of tries around the short side. They always had good backs with the ability to run and play with the ball, and so were we, so you had two teams playing a similar style.

Colin Meads: Chris Laidlaw was a good player, he had a good brain. He'd talk around the scrums and I've never forgotten the try they jacked up against France in 1968 when Kirton scored. There was a chargedown, the ball rebounded off Thorne and hit Kel in the head and Kirton fell on the loose ball. Laidlaw got us to screw the scrum a bit further to give him half a length and I remember he had a lot to do with that try because Tremain said: 'Thanks Laid.' One of the tragedies of 1970 was that Sid Going was so brilliant too. You had two brilliant halfbacks, two different types and people still say to me, 'Who was the best?' and I say 'Whoever was first five-eighths. If Kirton was first five-eighths you played Laidlaw and if it was one of the others, [Blair] Furlong or Baker [Wayne] Cottrell, it was Sid.'

Sid Going: Against France in 1968, Fred told me to use my natural instincts. They were brilliant players with the likes of Jo Maso. I guess I played differently from the orthodox halfback and that just caught the opposition totally unaware. I almost scored another try but I dropped the ball just before the line. The French had the flair to counter-attack and that's what you always had to be aware of. If you kept pressure on them then you could take them down but if you eased up a little bit and let them run . . . their timing of the pass was superb and they had the ability to draw and pass and beat you in that way. They could be niggly and while I didn't get caught up in that some of my mates sure did in the forwards like Pinetree. They used a few hand movements that weren't nice. We were not aware that would be Fred's last Test. Ivan Vodanovich was a different coach without the eye that Fred had for helping you play to your best.

Brian Lochore: That was Fred's last Test and that was definitely a regret. It was Fred's team and we needed him to take us to South Africa.

Ian Kirkpatrick: Fred knew something was up during the Aussie tour, I remember him saying, 'I'm getting out of here before they kick me out.' We couldn't believe it.

Colin Meads: I always thought Fred over-played things a bit regarding his resignation. I'm quite sure he would have been selected again. He had all sorts of stories, like being asked not to pick Bruce McLeod, Ken Gray and myself for the 1967 tour. I honestly don't believe that because I knew Jack Sullivan [chairman] and I got on well with him, even though he had become chairman by then. But Fred always reckoned that's what he was told.

At the end of the series Allen controversially decided not to contest the election for the coaching job, a decision regretted by his players. While they had two Tests against Wales in 1969, they were looking further ahead to South Africa where they felt they needed Allen's guidance. But the job went to Ivan Vodanovich, a loyal servant of the game but with limited coaching experience. Wales arrived as the Five Nations and Triple Crown champions and with a young side who would become one of the great Welsh sides. But they happened to run into an All Blacks team, especially the pack, at the peak of its form and who achieved an outstanding 19-0 win in the first Test and a 33-12 win in the second Test where Fergie McCormick's 24 points broke the individual world record.

Ian MacRae: The Welsh in 1969 came with a well-regarded side with some emerging stars. Over the years they were the country who had beaten us as much as anyone else.

Fred Allen gives a team-talk with, from left, Kel Tremain, Ken Gray, Sid Going, Ian MacRae and Brian Lochore. *Peter Bush*

There was a lot of interest in them and we were looking forward to two good Tests. There was a lot of mud at Lancaster Park for the first Test but the forwards dominated there. Then in the second Test Fergie set the world record for most points in a game.

Ian Kirkpatrick: That was really just the team carrying on without Fred, it wasn't Ivan. He tried to emulate Fred, having been in on his team talks. He didn't have the background or the experience to be able to make it meaningful.

Brian Lochore: They were good Tests against Wales and we gave them a real pasting on Lancaster Park. I don't recall the second Test at Eden Park so much but I know we had a big win in Christchurch. We overpowered them and again, it was the forwards' ability to run with the ball that actually blew them away. I can clearly remember two or three occasions when we took off from quite a way out when it was the forwards who did the damage.

Sid Going: When Wales came out in 1969 there were enough of us who had played together and had cemented our places. We knew where our strengths were and I think our forwards and backs combined pretty well in that series.

EIGHTEEN

THE FALL

'every time I scored, or we scored, the coloured community
would go berserk with delight'

AFTER THE ALL-CONQUERING 1960s, the 1970s was a decade punctuated with defeat, controversy and some of the lower points in NZ rugby. Three series were lost, two to the Springboks and, for the first time, to the Lions. Six other Test matches were lost against France, England and Australia and three drawn, as well as defeats in eleven non-Test matches including, most gallingly, to a New Zealand Juniors side. And yet the decade began with great optimism.

Hopes were high that finally, a series could be won in South Africa. That there was a tour at all, was down to the Rugby Union finally showing some spine after decades of acquiescence, in which some of New Zealand's best players had been left at home. The message was simple: 'No Maoris, No Tour'. And so, the team featured three Maori players in Sid Going, Henare 'Buff' Milner and Blair Furlong, as well as the exciting teenage winger Bryan Williams, an Auckland-born Samoan, although the four were patronisingly classed by their hosts as 'honorary whites'.

One player who didn't tour was Ken Gray who was opposed to contact with South Africa. Rather than put his team-mates in a difficult spot, he kept his views to himself and retired. It was a big loss. A future All Black Bob Burgess had made himself unavailable for consideration.

Sid Going: I guess it was important for the whole country because there had been so much publicity about it but I was a person that was never into all that political thing. I was just glad to be available for the next tour and to be selected. There were no issues, they just bent over backwards to look after us. It was a great experience. It was a hugely complex country and it's a shame that it has not got any better.

Bryan Williams (1970-78, 38 Tests, 113 games): They were all my heroes. When I first made the team I was absolutely terrified of all of them. Was I going to call them Mr Meads, Mr Lochore? They were right up in there in my view of the world. That was daunting enough, but then we had the spectre of apartheid, which was something I had to deal with. I experienced a panic attack as the plane touched down in Johannesburg, when it suddenly hit me, that I had to not only prove I could be an All Black, but that I also had to face apartheid. I didn't know how that was going to unfold. So it was a very timid and panic-stricken Beegee that climbed off the plane. I was 19, it was very daunting. To be an 'honorary white' – that was the status they, with their warped system, felt they needed to give us, was a complete nonsense to me, I wasn't an honorary white, I was who I was. To be the first All Black of Samoan heritage since Frank Solomon in the 1930s, I was very

Opposite: Colin Meads prepares to hand off Frik du Preez during the fourth Test at Ellis Park in 1970. *NZ Herald*

proud of that, it was pretty special. The treatment of non-whites was quite something to behold. Coloured and black people were herded into the ends of the field, and the white South Africans were sitting in all the flash seats along the side and every time I scored, or we scored, the coloured community would go berserk with delight.

Williams was in dazzling form, shredding defences with his sidestep, speed and power. His try-scoring feats delighted the black and coloured fans, many of whom declared their support for the first genuinely mixed race team to tour the Republic. This riled some white South Africans and led to a nasty incident after the Griquas match. The other standout player in those early stages was Colin Meads. 'Pinetree' appeared to be in career-best form, his try in the opening match against Border a magnificent fifty-metre run complete with a couple of outrageous dummies. So it was a massive setback when, in the match against Eastern Transvaal at Springs, a stray boot thudded into Meads' forearm and broke it. He finished the game but missed the first two Tests. Still, the All Blacks went into the first international in Pretoria unbeaten, to be soon reminded why their predecessors had struggled so mightily.

Brian Lochore: Preparation was difficult for the 1970 tour to South Africa. When you're not supported by all the country (NZ) it always makes it a little more difficult. We played really well in the provincial games but we kept our bad games, unfortunately, for the Test matches.

Ian Kirkpatrick: Our first training run was down in East London. It was hot and the pitch was as hard as a rock and Ivan ran us for about an hour without stopping before we did any team work. Guys were falling over, or getting blisters. We were knackered. He was running us up sand dunes, carrying guys like Jazz Muller on your back, it was crazy stuff, very unscientific.

Bryan Williams: I was involved in a riot after the third game, against the Griquas, my second of the tour, and that was scary. I was hoisted onto the shoulders of some coloured people who were pretty delighted with what they'd seen. Suddenly, I was getting pulled down by a bunch of drunken white fellows who started beating up the coloured guys. Before I knew it, there were police running in with dogs and batons. I made a hasty retreat to the dressing room.

Earle Kirton: We'd have won with Fred and that's no disrespect to Ivan. Ivan was a hell of a good chap and you might say I am now damning him with faint praise but he wasn't a coach – he was a passionate man on rugby, a good and wonderful friend and a good bloke but he had nowhere the tactical, the needle, that you needed that Allen had. It was sad, really sad. BJ and Pinetree were half having to coach the side and it got hard as we were getting near the end of the road. We needed Needle to lift us and play a couple of big games. We would have won the series, we were too good and they just chopped us down in the middle with their own referees. It was diabolical.

Bryan Williams sears down the wing against Western Province. *NZ Herald*

Bryan Williams: We were playing a great style . . . and we had a lot of players at the peak of their game. Pinetree at the start of that tour was exceptional, he was running riot. The forwards were laying down a good platform, the grounds were hard and fast. I knew I could run and I knew I could step, and with the opportunities I was getting I was able to pull out the bag of tricks.

Colin Meads: When Brian Lochore broke his thumb in Perth on the way over I took over as captain. We were to play the second game against a country fifteen. They went away to a camp for a fortnight before the game, no papers, not a bloody thing were they allowed to see about the All Blacks. They probably didn't even know how we got on against Border. Well, I went out to toss the coin, and I've never forgotten the guy's name, Toy Dannhouser. I went to shake hands but he wouldn't. He was frothing at the mouth. I went back and I looked at my team, I had the Wednesday side. Alex Veysey [NZ journalist] had given me a dossier of all their players and what positions they played in the lineout and sure enough I'm marking this bastard. [Keith] Murdoch was playing, it was probably his first game. He was sitting in the corner, and I had told the team what they were like and that we were going to have to live with them for thirty or forty minutes and then we'd come right. I said to Murdoch, 'I could have a bit of a problem here, I'm captain and I might need you to help me out' and I said, 'but don't do anything until I tell you, I'll try him out first.' He'd played South African trials but he wasn't that good so I didn't worry. We'd been going about quarter of an hour and then all of a sudden, whack, Murdoch hits this poor bugger and I said to Murdoch, 'I told you not to do anything until I said to,' and he said, 'I couldn't be bothered waiting.' He set his seal for South Africa because the word goes through the system very quickly.

Ian Kirkpatrick: We were probably conned a bit by Danie Craven. He spoke after a few of the games as the chairman and was really talking us up saying we were the greatest team he had ever seen and so on. We didn't want to believe that but when you keep hearing it and the scores are indicating that, we needed someone to call us back into line and say, 'Listen you show ponies, it's not all about running around scoring tries.' Fred would have told us we would get a fright when we came to the first Test.

Having prepared for the Test behind locked doors, the Springboks came out into the thin air of Pretoria breathing fire, a thunderous tackle by centre Joggie Jansen on All Blacks fly-half Wayne Cottrell, serving notice of their intent. They harried the All Blacks into mistakes, and scored the opening try, through captain Dawie de Villiers after just a few minutes. Scrum-half Chris Laidlaw was left dazed after being castled by the great Springbok lock Frik du Preez. The Boks had a 12-nil lead at half-time. A brilliant try engineered for Williams by Laidlaw's replacement Sid Going, saw New Zealand close the gap to 12-6, but an intercept by winger Syd Nomis sealed a 17-6 victory, a crushing end to New Zealand's five-year unbeaten run.

Brian Lochore: In the first Test we had played against most of the South Africans in the provincial games and we weren't frightened of them. We didn't think they had played that well against us. What we forgot was when they put a green jersey on how much they changed. They hit us with everything in the first ten minutes or quarter of an hour and we really struggled to recover.

Ian MacRae: The first Test was unbelievable. The ferociousness they came at us with was incredible. I had never experienced the sort of fervour they had, or the speed. Their forwards were tearing around like mad things and they got plenty of help from the referees. Ian McCallum kicked everything that came their way, and he had plenty of opportunities.

Colin Meads: In the first Test they put Joggie Jansen in and he crunched Baker Cottrell. Frik du Preez dealt to Chris Laidlaw. I had my broken arm then and I had gone to their trials up in Rhodesia. Ivan sent me to have a look. When I went back I don't think the players believed me. I tried to tell them they needed to look out. I told them the South Africans were going to hit them with everything, which they did. They blew us out of the game. They were also fired up by the apartheid thing. The opposition was getting stronger to it and they were thinking if they didn't win they might never play again.

Bryan Williams: Going into the Tests there were two things – firstly we'd probably been lulled into a false sense of how good we were. The second was when Pinetree had his arm broken, that was a huge loss. The first Test was a big shock.

Ian Kirkpatrick: We knew it was going to be hard, I mean they're a tough team to beat, although they weren't such a big team in 1970, not like they were in '76, but we needed that pulling back into line and we never got it. They hit us with everything and we never tried to change our game plan. It was carry on the same, we'll just move it. Well, Joggie

Malcolm Dick looks to open up the Springbok defence during the first Test. *Getty Images*

Jansen just lined up Wayne Cottrell and poleaxed him, and that was probably the end of trying to run it. They did their homework, they came at us and we were a bit shell-shocked. That first Test set the standard.

In the sea air of Cape Town the All Blacks fought back well to level the series courtesy of a late penalty goal by Fergie McCormick, and with Meads due back, albeit wearing a protective leather guard on his still broken arm, hopes were revived of an elusive series victory.

Ian MacRae: The second Test was one we should have won more convincingly than the 9-8 margin. We were pretty much in control. There was a lot of blood and guts involved in the win. The dressing shed was like an ambulance ward. It was an important win. Overall in the series we always felt we had a chance.

Brian Lochore: We should have won by a whole lot more, we actually played quite well that day.

Colin Meads: Frik du Preez was an athletic lock. He was only 6ft 2in, he wasn't one of the huge monsters. He was spring-heeled and could jump and was quick and athletic. I can remember being in a World XV to celebrate England's centenary with players from several countries. We were standing around after training and these Frenchmen like Elie Cester were under the goalposts jumping up and touching the crossbar. Frik came along and clapped his hands above the crossbar. I saw that and I was gone – off to talk to the backs.

Hopes of a series win were dashed at Port Elizabeth. With the scores locked at 3-all into the second half, All Black prop Alistair Hopkinson needlessly obstructed the Springbok fullback McCallum, who put his team in the lead for the first time, and soon after winger Gert Muller made a scorching seventy-metre run to put the home team in control. A second try by Muller put the game and the series out of reach. However, after completing an unbeaten run through the provincial matches, the All Blacks still had a chance to level the rubber at Ellis Park.

Ian Kirkpatrick: Piet Greyling and Jan Ellis, the two flankers were good players, and I guess to use a modern day term, they got us behind the gain [advantage] line and we floundered. We clawed our way back into the series at Cape Town, but then we went to Port Elizabeth and we just couldn't put it together like we did in Cape Town. Our goal kicking wasn't great, but we didn't get a lot of penalties in the right places anyway.

Brian Lochore: In the third Test we had an awful second half, things did not go well for us and that was probably our worst performance of the tour.

Bryan Williams: There were some mysterious selections. I'd played wing except for one game against Western Province where I played at centre and suddenly I was in the Test team at centre and Grahame Thorne was on the wing, it lacked logic. We didn't fire too many shots at Port Elizabeth and were soundly beaten.

Vodanovich had shown a penchant for changing his line-up, even after the win at Newlands, and when he made another eight for the final Test it brought the number of players used in the four-match series to twenty-seven. Some were due to injury, and with Laidlaw needing an emergency appendectomy after Port Elizabeth, Going was forced to play the last four tour matches without backup at scrum-half. Also suffering from an appendix issue was prop Keith Murdoch who, according to his team-mates, played the final Test in severe pain. Another scintillating try by Williams, and the accurate kicking of Test debutant Gerald Kember, kept New Zealand in with a shot at squaring the series, but with the game in the balance another thumping Jansen tackle knocked the ball from Kember's grasp to be collected by the flying Muller who raced away for his third try of the series. The Test was South Africa's, and with it, a 3-1 series victory.

Brian Lochore: In the fourth Test we were as good as them and I think we were pretty unlucky not to have won that. McCallum fly-kicked three or four times when we had three or four on one and got out of trouble somehow. It was very frustrating because we hadn't been there since 1960 and it was an opportunity to win a series.

Ian MacRae: In the fourth Test again a penalty cost us the game. We leaked a try between my friend Blair Furlong and myself badly. Joggie Jansen was a great big brute of a centre. He was quick but a bit of a one-series wonder. When I went back there a few years ago and asked about him no one knew where he was. He went back up on the veldt to his farm.

Colin Meads: The referee blew us out of the fourth Test in 1960 and the same thing happened in 1970. We had the winning of that one but that little English fullback Ian

McCallum, even the Springboks didn't like him, there was a bit of that Afrikaans thing. He wasn't the most popular guy amongst them but he could kick goals. I was penalised one time, it was fifty-odd yards out and I told BJ not to worry because the little bugger couldn't kick that far and I said it loud enough for him to hear, but it went straight between the posts.

Brian Lochore: Bryan Williams was superb on that tour. I can't think of a game where he wasn't absolute perfection. Some of the tries he scored, and the breaks he made, were superb and he was only nineteen or twenty. And he was the star, on and off the field.

Sid Going: Bryan Williams was magnificent on those hard and fast grounds. He preferred it on the right wing, not because he could step out because he would always step in. I remember once in a game I broke around the short side and he was on his wing but his wing was hanging on him so I just put a little grubber kick through for him and it went out. He said: 'Just give it to me and I'll do the work, I'll beat him.' So that's what I did from then on.

Ian MacRae: Bryan was full of confidence. We roomed together a lot with an idea of the old dog looking after the young fellow. But I was the one who needed the help not him. He was so relaxed. He would sit around playing his guitar and all these visitors would come in before a Test match and he took everything in his stride. I tended to want to go off and be by myself somewhere quiet. When he started sidestepping people behind the goal-line we knew he was feeling confident.

Brian Lochore: I had been asked to captain a World XV for England's centennial after that tour and felt very comfortable with my form. But I came home after that and I didn't have the enthusiasm for another four Tests against the Lions. I kept thinking I could play. But unless you are going to absolutely put your body on the line in a Test match, you're not as good as you should be. I was walking around in the paddock one day, I could show you where it happened, and I just decided I was retiring. I went home and told Pam and I rang Alex Veysey, who was a respected journalist, and said to him, 'I just want to tell you I am retiring.'

Ian MacRae: At the end of the tour I retired. I had a mortgage and needed to work. I was also frustrated with the injuries. I'd had my share of pulled muscles and felt it was time to look after my family.

The All Blacks had played some sublime attacking rugby, but mostly in the provincial games. Vodanovich's coaching certainly raised eyebrows and prompted the burly Taranaki prop Brian 'Jazz' Muller to remark that he needed to play more games 'to get fit for all this training.' For whatever reason, a very strong All Black side was denied a history-making series victory. It was their first series defeat in a decade, and with a number of players retiring, a great era had ended.

NINETEEN

A PRIDE OF LIONS

'I was there, I gave what I had to give and I have no regrets.
I'm not worried about my reputation, I'm worried about my country.'

IT WAS SAID for decades after their departure that the finest rugby team to visit the Land of the Long White Cloud had been the 1937 Springboks. It is hard to judge teams from such vastly differing eras, but without question the 1971 Lions had every bit as profound an impact on NZ rugby. They struck the All Blacks at a vulnerable time, coming off the series defeat in South Africa and shorn of many of the great players of the 1960s. But the Lions not only became the first since 1937 to win a full Test series in New Zealand, they won every non-Test fixture, and were the first team since those legendary Springboks to force New Zealand to rethink the way they played the game. Like their predecessors, in 1959 in particular, the '71 Lions were spiced with star quality. The big difference was the coaching of Carwyn James, the supreme strategist, and architect of a style that gave licence to some brilliant backs, but was founded on forward power, particularly at scrum time. It speaks volumes for his team that they achieved a dominant platform despite the loss of front-line props Ray McLoughlin and Sandy Carmichael after an ugly match with Canterbury. But despite the superb performances of forwards like Willie-John McBride, Mervyn Davies and Derek Quinnell, it was the backline that lit up the tour. An early match against Wellington, a strong provincial combination, really made New Zealanders sit up and take notice, John Bevan and Mike Gibson standing out in a devastating 47-9 victory. The Lions swept through fourteen games ahead of the first Test, playing a wonderful attacking brand of rugby, although they were to tighten up noticeably for the internationals.

Bob Burgess: (1971-73, 7 Tests, 30 games): A couple of weeks before the first Test, the *NZ Truth* newspaper billboard declared 'Mr Hairy Gets The Nod'. On the Saturday the team was announced, I was driving back to Palmerston North from Feilding from a club rugby game and we had pulled into a local dairy to get something and it was on the radio. I was with my wife and a friend. It was very exciting. I had played in the first of the North Island trials, the 1.15pm game in Palmerston North, and I hadn't got into the final trials in Auckland so I was certainly an outsider.

Sid Going: The British press were just unreal, pathetic, and the same with the following tour. But it was a year when we didn't pick the best of the talent we had. I look at the backlines that we had in those Tests, they changed every game and we didn't get a flowing backline going at all. It was a shame, it wasn't the most enjoyable rugby I have played in my life.

Colin Meads: They should not have made me captain. I was a good captain for King Country but for the All Blacks I was more value not being a captain. You were restricted

Opposite: Bryan Williams and Lions wing Gerald Davies contest for the ball during the fourth Test. *Getty Images*

as a captain. Ian Kirkpatrick would have been ideal, he was a good guy and everyone liked him. It was an honour to be captain, don't worry about that, but I was getting to the end of my tether. And everyone pulled out after 1970 and they picked young fellows who I only met for the first time when the first Test team got together. Carwyn James was brilliant. He murdered Sid Going. He used to say it and he had all the press eating out of his hands. Jack Sullivan let us down as chairman because James got the referee he wanted in John Pring. He got him for every Test and the one referee we didn't want was Pring. Jack assured me after the third Test that Pring would not do the fourth Test but there he was. Carwyn James had him wrapped around his finger. He would penalise Sid when he was almost putting it under the Lions' feet. It put Sid off his game a fair bit. He was clever Carwyn, I had a lot to do with him after my rugby was finished. He was a religious, alternative lifestyle sort of guy but fanatical on rugby. He could sit down and talk to you for hours. He used his players well. Gareth Edwards picked his games, he didn't play a lot outside the Test matches. They said he had hamstring problems but Willie John didn't agree with that. Chico Hopkins played in the first Test and he was a good player, a good little fellow. Gareth was a good player and he made Barry John look good with his big pass. They were a good combination and they played together all their time at Cardiff. Mike Gibson was a brilliant player who was a first five-eighths who went to second, then they had John Dawes at centre and captain who was solid and a good player with JPR at fullback. We could have beaten them if we had had a front row. We got murdered in the front row. Fergie got sorted out in the first Test. He would always line up with me after games and I said to him not to worry, I would look after him. But he said when he didn't get back what a great mate I was. All we wanted was Alistair Hopkinson in the front row. Ivan and him fell out the year before in South Africa and he wasn't going to get back in. Richie Guy was a lovely guy but I would be butting heads all the time with their props.

Bryan Williams: They had players you would recognise as world greats, guys like JPR, Gareth Edwards, Barry John, Mike Gibson, Gerald Davies and David Duckham . . . .and a forward pack with guys like Willie John McBride, Mervyn Davies, Ray McLoughlin and so many others.

Ian Kirkpatrick: They were a top side, and British rugby from '71 to '75 was really strong. We had a few retirements [after South Africa in 1970] and in places that team was quite inexperienced. We lost a lot of cohesion and that real engine room ability to put teams away, to bury them up front. We had a lopsided front row, Richie Guy was about 13 stone wringing wet and on the other side Jazz Muller was about 19 stone, it was unbalanced and they had a very good scrum.

Bryan Williams: When we went into 1971, after being an absolute novice the year before, at twenty, still wet behind the ears, I was suddenly one of the more senior backs in the team. We were up against a top-notch outfit with a pretty inexperienced team. We did well to still be in it right to the very last minute, when we had a chance to draw the series.

In the first Test the Lions faced a New Zealand side featuring seven new caps, and did well to survive an early onslaught before prop Iain 'Mighty Mouse' McLauchlan charged down a clearing kick to score the first try of the series. New Zealand equalised by half-time but the second half belonged to the Lions and, in particular, Barry John. The Cardiff pivot had been part of a miserably unsuccessful Welsh team in 1969, but on this tour he was sublime. In the provincial games he'd played the running game, but it was his boot that won the day in Dunedin, slotting his goals and tormenting the All Black fullback Fergie McCormick with his tactical kicking, forcing the end of his career. Two second-half penalty goals gave the Lions a 9-3 win, and the series victory was on.

All Blacks captain Colin Meads on the burst against the Lions, Carisbrook, 1971. *Peter Bush*

Tane Norton (1971-77, 27 Tests, 61 games): The first Test team was picked the night after the Canterbury game. I'd played for the Maori team in front of the New Zealand selectors, and in the trials, and I thought I might get in as a reserve. Ron Urlich was the incumbent but after that Canterbury game I thought 'that's me shot' because I spent more of the game sitting on my backside than I did playing. It was a bit different, that game. You had two teams of similar ilk and neither would back down and there was only one result really. No one was going to lay off. I was in Ireland years later and ran into the flanker Mick Hipwell and someone said to him, 'Why did you come out fighting?' and he said, 'They weren't going to make a punching bag out of me.' He was a good bugger. I made a lot of friends in that Lions team.

Bob Burgess: When I joined the team for the first Test there was a welcome, and an acceptance, I didn't feel an outsider at all. We got together on the Wednesday afternoon so there wasn't much preparation. It was quite a new team – especially the backs. There must have been talk about moves and I remember there was one move I was involved with which was Sid running around the back of the lineout and my crossing with him – so there must have been some preparation of moves, some obvious ones that everyone knew about.

Tane Norton: Before the Test, Colin Meads was going out on the Friday just for a walk around town and he said to come with him. I thought walking around town with Colin, that's pretty good, but he said to me, 'The hardest thing coming up for the All Blacks will be South Africa in 1973.' And I said, 'Why?' and he said, '1972-73, they'll have played a season in New Zealand, then gone on a tour for four and a half months in the UK and that takes us into '73. We'll come back in February-March which will take us into the

New Zealand season again, and then the Springboks.' I mean we weren't a very good side, but we were tired [in 1973]. The Juniors beat us, England beat us, an England side that lost all their provincial games, the Springboks didn't come, but Colin was right.

Ian Kirkpatrick: The first Test was close but they probably deserved it. We had our chances but didn't take them, Alan Sutherland had a kick charged down and they scored from that and that gave them a bit of a sniff. Fergie missed a couple of shots and Barry John ran him around the paddock a fair bit. Fergie got ostracised for that, but he shouldn't have, Barry John was a great player. We didn't take our opportunities. I know I got close a couple of times. But I just don't know why we couldn't do that old All Black thing and grind them down. They were a good defensive side.

Bob Burgess: They were a classy side and the first Test was very close. I knew I was up against someone in marking Barry John. I don't know who the quote comes from but they said, 'He could run through a field of daffodils without crushing a petal.' Playing for NZ Universities against the Lions at Athletic Park he was lining up a dropped goal and I, and Alex Matheson, our flanker, raced at him to charge the ball down and suddenly he was behind the goalpost scoring a try. He just disappeared. He was very agile, had a fantastic boot, and he was a hell of a nice guy. I got to know most of those Lions players probably as well as I got to know the All Black players during that tour.

Tane Norton: Players weren't lasting. You go through the team around that time and the number of guys who were only in there for one game. They never gave people a go, there was no tolerance. If they didn't think they'd gone well they were straight out and a lot of good players were never seen again.

As so often happened, the All Blacks responded in the second Test in Christchurch. Bob Burgess, the 22-year-old All Blacks five-eighth, a new-age player with his long hair and academic background, set the All Blacks on the path to victory, wafting through the Lions defence for two tries. Sid Going also touched down and there was a penalty try for an early tackle on Bryan Williams, but the 'daddy' of them all was scored by Ian Kirkpatrick. Late in the game, the Poverty Bay farmer exploded out of a ruck on halfway, fending off Gareth Edwards and outstripping the cover defence to score one of the great All Black Test tries. It sealed a 22-12 win, and although the Lions had the last say when Gerald Davies scored the second of two fine tries, New Zealand fans started to believe normal service had been restored.

Bob Burgess: We felt we could come back after the first Test, it certainly wasn't a lost cause. But we knew they were a class side and Dawes and Carwyn James were very impressive people. I remember a brief conversation I had with Carwyn after that first Test in Dunedin and feeling that I was . . . not pulled apart but inspected and it wasn't just about rugby, it was about being a person. He was a very intelligent and decisive personality.

Bryan Williams: Sid Going set up lots of my tries . . . on that occasion he went to pass to me and had I been able to catch it I'm pretty sure I had the momentum to get over the line. But just before I caught it, suddenly Gerald Davies was pinning my arms to my sides, and so [referee] John Pring had no hesitation in going under the posts for a penalty try. Gerald and I have had the odd laugh about it since! Sid was a brilliant player, I loved playing with him and I loved watching him play, because he had a bag of tricks that no other halfback had, not even Gareth Edwards. Some people said his passing at times wasn't what it should be, but I thought he was a great player, one of the best I ever played with.

Bob Burgess: The second Test is rather blurred but I remember being over the tryline in the first half and thinking, 'How on Earth did I get here?' I recall running the blindside from a scrum with Bryan Williams outside me and a gap opening up with all of their side row and No.8 forwards rushing off to stop Bryan scoring a try. And it was exactly the same in the second half with my running with the ball on the blindside of a ruck, rather than a scrum, and again Bryan outside me and again a gap opening up. When Ian Kirkpatrick scored his try I remember trying to keep up with Ian and yelling. 'Pass it, I'm here.' And he just kept going. That was a great try.

Ian Kirkpatrick: Pinetree always says he had a hand in it. I mean Pinetree never gave the ball to any bastard, but we had a lineout and it turned into a sort of a maul. That's when Piney actually gave me the ball in a maul – so I was pretty lucky to get it! The maul swung around a bit, and, I can't really explain why I did what I did. I just went and they came at me. While I was running I don't think I heard the crowd or anything, you're too involved in what you're trying to do. I had to head for the corner flag because they were coming across at me. When I scored the try and got up the crowd was going bananas, I felt bloody embarrassed. It wasn't until I got back to halfway that Pinetree might have said, 'good try' or something. Nowadays they would probably be jumping all over you. I was walking back and I thought if there was a hole I could jump into I would.

Tane Norton: I always say to Kirky, 'I was a big help to you in that try because I pushed you out of the maul.' Mind you, I couldn't keep up with him. It was a fantastic try.

Ian Kirkpatrick sets out on the run for his try in the second Test against the Lions, Christchurch, 1971. *Peter Bush*

The Lions went off to the Bay of Islands for a week where they devised a strategy to deal with Kirkpatrick and Going, around whom so much of the All Black play revolved. Whilst the Lions arrived in Wellington in a state of great clarity, the All Blacks were in disarray. Keith Murdoch was selected to bolster a shaky front row, but as he had done ahead of the Otago tour match, withdrew without much of an explanation. Meads and Kirkpatrick were troubled by injuries, Bryan Williams succumbed to a groin strain and the All Blacks' excellent new lock Peter Whiting hurt his back in training. In a desperate move, former captain Brian Lochore, who'd been coaxed out of retirement to play the tour game in Masterton, now found himself back in Test rugby as Whiting's replacement. The Athletic Park crowd had barely taken their seats before the Lions had the match, and the series, by the scruff of the neck. A Barry John dropped goal and tries to Edwards and Davies saw them race out to a 13-nil lead after eighteen minutes, a lead they were able to ride home to the end. Whilst everything went according to the James masterplan, the Test was a nightmare for the All Blacks. They rallied in the second half and did manage a try by fullback Laurie Mains, but battled to find a way through the Lions defence, and on one of the rare occasions when they did, centre Howard Joseph tripped on a stray dog that had found its way onto the field.

It kind of summed things up.

Brian Lochore: I don't regret coming back for the third Test against the Lions. A lot of people have asked me why I did it because I had ruined my record or reputation. And I said to them, 'I'm a New Zealander.' They were in a very deep hole for a lot of reasons which were explained to me when they rang up at Friday lunchtime and had nobody in New Zealand never heard that story I wouldn't have played. But I knew damned well that people would find out that I had been asked to play and I turned my country down in a moment of need and that wasn't what I wanted to go to my deathbed on. Once I had made that decision I didn't have any problem. I played, I played OK, I was fit enough to play a Test match. I certainly didn't have any time to train with the team. It wasn't a good performance by the All Blacks at all. It was a poor performance and I was in that team and some people think I shouldn't have been there, but I didn't ask to be there. I was there, I gave what I had to give and I have no regrets. I'm not worried about my reputation, I'm worried about my country.

Ian Kirkpatrick: I didn't really want to be there. Poverty Bay-East Coast had played them in a midweek game and I'd popped my rib cartilage, and then I was on a young horse down at my brother's and it bucked me off. I caught my ribs on the saddle and reinjured myself. I actually rang Vodanovich on the Monday – we didn't assemble until Wednesday, and he told me to go to the doctor. My doctor was away so I went to Bill McKay, who was a Lion in 1950. He was the worst bugger I could have gone to because he told me there was nothing wrong. I knew there was something wrong all right. But I went down and I got through training. Vodanovich knew I wasn't comfortable so I had an injection. I'm sitting on the table there at Athletic Park and some bugger races in and says, 'You'd better hurry, the rest of them are out on the field,' and this needle is stuck halfway in my ribs and I'm jumping up to get out there on the field for the start of the game. We had a bad build-up. BJ Lochore had to come in for Peter Whiting. There was nothing wrong with that, we thought it was a good selection. It wasn't his fault none of us played any good.

Bob Burgess: There's that famous photo from the third Test that I see has been turned into a statue by a Welsh craftsman of Gareth [Edwards] pushing me in the face which was my attempt to tackle Gareth. He passed out to Barry John who scored a try under the posts. They took it to us but I don't really remember much of that game as I got knocked out. I was told it was in a ruck. JPR Williams probably saved my life. He was a med student and realised I was gagging, swallowing my tongue, and he did whatever it was that was necessary to stop me from choking. This story of course is second-hand – being knocked out at the time I can only pass on what I was told.

Gareth Edwards hands off Bob Burgess on the way to setting up Barry John for a crucial try in the third Test. *Getty Images*

The Lions still had to avoid defeat in Auckland to secure the series, and a win for the All Blacks was on the cards before a try by flanker Peter Dixon and an extraordinary forty-five-metre dropped goal by JPR Williams put the tourists in front. In the end the All Blacks rather meekly settled for a draw, milking a penalty for Mains to kick. And so the series was won, just as the Lions' popular manager Doug Smith had predicted, by two and a half Tests to one and a half. The result shook New Zealand rugby. It was, without doubt, a great Lions team but the result reflected a marked decline in the New Zealand game. The back play of the Lions in the provincial matches was superb, but the All Blacks had also been edged in much of the forward play and embarrassed at scrum time. When the Lions of 1971 departed, they took with them the spoils of an historic and deserved victory, and left a massive imprint on New Zealand rugby.

Ian Kirkpatrick: We went to Auckland and got that draw when JPR kicked that dropped goal from halfway which drew the game for them. We weren't a good side. It was a funny series and pretty disappointing, and it meant we had lost two in a row. It wasn't all great being an All Black around that time when you've lost two series in a row. It affects you a bit.

Tane Norton: We always underestimated the Englishmen in the forwards. We associated them with some of those flash clubs in London. It wasn't until we went over there in 1972

Gerald Davies and Bryan Williams in a foot-race for the ball. *Colorsport*

and played them in Workington. Well, we got a different kettle of fish there. They were tough, and that's where they were getting a lot of their power, from those guys in the northern area.

Bob Burgess: Gareth had a fantastic pass. My Test career was with Sid [Going] who didn't have a great length of pass and wasn't always quick with the pass. But Gareth had a pass, he could throw the ball halfway across the field. I played with him once when I was living in France in 1974 or 1975 in a team made up for a friendly game and I couldn't believe the length of his pass, I would stand halfway across the field. I never played with Chris Laidlaw (I played against him once) as the end of his career was 1970 before the start of my international career. He had a fantastic pass. I regret not playing outside a player who had a pass like that. Mike Gibson was incredibly skilled, a reader of the game, very intelligent. Dawes and Gibson in 1971 were a class act and they played together in that Barbarians game in 1973. Sublime.

Bryan Williams: The counter-attacking game the Lions brought to that tour was quickly adopted by a lot of New Zealand teams. They revolutionised the game. Their scrummaging was pretty special as well, so New Zealand rugby learned a fair amount from that team.

Two greats, Gareth Edwards and Sid Going, attended by two greats, Barry John (left) and Ian Kirkpatrick (right). *Peter Bush*

TWENTY

A NEW GENERATION

IF NEW ZEALAND needed a thumping series win to lift itself from the disappointments of '70 and '71, then the 'Awful Aussies' or 1972 Wallabies were just the ticket. New Zealand's problems were nothing compared to those across the Tasman, and a side that struggled even to beat some of the smaller provincial unions they met, was wiped out in three Test matches 29-6, 30-17 and 38-3. The All Blacks needed a new coach. An internal tour was undertaken under Jack Gleeson's guidance, while Bob Duff took the reins for the Wallaby series. Gleeson was something of a visionary, but as the man who'd led the All Blacks to their ground-breaking win over South Africa in 1956, Duff appealed to the traditional set at Rugby Union HQ, and the Canterbury man won a narrow vote. The Wallabies might have allowed a comfortable start to the rebuilding process, but a more formidable task lay ahead with a thirty-two-match tour of the Northern Hemisphere.

Ian Kirkpatrick: There were two of them [internal tours], the first one in 1972 before we played the Aussies. We played Tuesday, Thursday, Saturday, Tuesday, Thursday, Saturday and it was all over the country. We started the year with Jack Gleeson as coach. Then we played the Aussies. They were a pretty average team, but we played pretty well with Bob Duff as coach and then we went to the UK with Duff. I don't know why they had one coach for part of the year and another for the rest. Bloody bizarre.

Bob Burgess: I played the third Test in Auckland. I didn't play in the earlier Tests because I had glandular fever. This came back during the 1972-73 tour when I missed two Tests in the UK, against England and Scotland. I remember the coach saying, 'We'll say you have got a bad cold, we won't say you have got glandular fever.'

Bruce Robertson (1972-81, 34 Tests, 102 games): Being chosen to represent your country was an awesome thing, it might have been an internal tour but there was so much pride and it didn't matter who you were playing. You wanted to get out and do your best. Jack Gleeson got on well with all the players and got us working together. I missed the second Test through injury and came back in and made sure I did my job properly in the third. It is always good when you can do well and you get the ball running around in the backs.

Bryan Williams: In late 1971, I played in a North-South game alongside Bruce Robertson. He made an outside break and just took off. I'd never experienced anything like it, trying to keep up with that sort of pace, it blew my mind. I was at full throttle and left behind. We played together the next year against the Australians.

Opposite: A poignant shot of Keith Murdoch after being sent home from the All Blacks tour of 1972-73. *Peter Bush*

Whilst new talent emerged in players like Bruce Robertson, Grant Batty, Joe Karam, Ian Hurst, Andy Haden and Ken Stewart, the team was well short of both rugby and worldly experience, with nineteen of the touring thirty aged twenty-five or younger. After opening with an entertaining display against Western Counties in Gloucester, the All Blacks crossed into Wales to meet Llanelli. In their second tour match, three days after the first, they faced the powerful Welsh club in their centennial year, prepared by the master, Carwyn James. The Scarlets were roared on to a famous victory by a passionate crowd of 22,000 at Stradey Park, a merited win, celebrated to this day, and one that rocked the All Blacks. The tour became fraught with difficulty, with the Welsh media in particular, proving extremely hostile. To compound matters, it transpired the manager Ernie Todd had a terminal illness, and struggled to cope with pressure from the press, Home Unions officials, and from within his team. His running battle with Keith Murdoch came to a head in the early hours following the win over Wales. The lead-up to that first Test featured another defeat, to the English North-Western Counties at Workington, and a visit to Belfast, where despite the high tension in the troubled city, the All Blacks were greeted with great warmth by the 25,000 crowd at Ravenhill.

Joe Karam (1972-75, 10 Tests, 42 games): They still had All Black trials then, Batts [Grant Batty] and I were on opposing teams. He got the ball in the clear right in front of the old main stand [at Athletic Park] and I was the only one near him, no cover defence and he was flying. I knew exactly what he would do, but I still didn't have hope of laying a hand on him. He left me lying on the ground like a proper twit. Still, we both made the team. All I ever wanted to be was an All Black. It was everything to me. For a young guy from the King Country to pull on that jersey and walk out onto Cardiff Arms Park for my first Test and play a part in winning a Test many thought we would lose, you couldn't get much better than that.

Bruce Robertson: I had no issues with hamstrings in New Zealand. A group of us were doing sprint training and my boot fell off. I didn't put it back on and just ran with one boot on and one boot off and that was how the hamstring issues started. It was self-inflicted, through my stupidity. They didn't have any doctors with the team so wherever you went that had physios it was good. In London it was good because there were hospitals and soccer clubs. I broke my thumb against Cardiff when attempting to stop Gareth Edwards scoring a try and I got two hamstrings and it was either a case of go home or stay and play so I stayed and managed to get through but not as successfully as you wanted it to be.

Sid Going: The 'not feeding the ball straight to scrums' was something the Lions started here and when we got over there that was all they showed on TV. I got injured at our first training run in England. We didn't have doctors, so we went to their doctor and the first thing they wanted to do with my ankle was put it in plaster. 'You'll be out for the rest of the tour,' they said. I said, 'I will not put that in plaster, I'm going to be playing in a couple of weeks,' and I did. They just wanted me out of the tour. You couldn't say anything. We just closed in because the press would come in, and we had to stop the players because everything was so [uneasy] . . . We were riding in a taxi and a few of us were just talking quietly in the back, and the next thing we see things printed in the paper that we had been talking about in the taxi. It just made you careful which is such a shame because it could have been a really good tour.

Tane Norton: We didn't have a lot of experience. It's a good thing we had a back seat group. If one of the younger guys was stepping out of line, you'd give him a bit of a tune-up. Poor old Ernie Todd [manager] was dying and there was nobody to run the place. One man trying to run the tour and practically on his deathbed. Boy, the Rugby Union set him up badly, it was pretty sad. Ernie got a lot of blame he didn't deserve. It all turned sour and he took the brunt of it. The business with the hats, that was bullshit. In Vancouver there were a few of us, Grizz [Alex Wyllie], Sid [Going], myself and Alan Sutherland, we went for a walk and there's this shop selling these hats. Touring was all a new experience for me. Because I was a banker I got the job of looking after the team's finances, and they [the others] said, 'We want to buy those hats for a court session,' and I thought, 'That's a good idea, we'll buy them for the Sunday court session.' That's what they were for, but the trouble was you couldn't pack the things. They were too big so we wore them when we were moving around. I suppose I can understand what people must have thought, but there was nothing in it. I've still got mine, Grizz lost his and I think Sully might have given one to a girl overseas!

Ian Kirkpatrick: If they did it these days no one would take any notice. It was just the guys in the back seat wearing these hats and they had those moustaches – it was something that just got built up [in the media]. And when we started winning the Tests it just got worse. If the NZRFU had been half of what they should have been, they would have realised that things were getting pretty difficult for me as captain but there was no support at all for me from them, not one skerrick.

Joe Karam: Trevor Morris got hurt in his first game in New York, I played the next six in a row, including the loss at Llanelli. I guess everything went well for me, my goal-kicking was good, and Trevor lost his confidence. There were a few players on the tour like that, George Skudder was another one. He'd been playing amazingly well before the tour, but got an injury and by the time he got back playing . . . those guys were shadows of what they'd been before. It was tough for a lot of guys.

Andy Haden (1972-85, 41 Tests, 117 games): It would have been a trying tour for Kirky, he was a hell of a good player and he was a good skipper too. When I came back home I thought, 'If that is All Black rugby it wasn't what I was expecting.' I didn't have any problem at all about ditching out of there and going to France in 1974-76 because I thought it was not a big deal. It was a poor era because of a dearth of support for the captain, management support, overall leadership. It came right, because we saw how much better it could be.

Sid Going: Bob Duff was a really good guy and he had a hard row to hoe, with the extra load. Bob worked with me and Kirky really closely.

Llanelli's Delme Thomas celebrates as the Scarlets triumph over the touring All Blacks at Stradey Park. *Colorsport*

Bruce Robertson: Bob Duff was a forwards coach and we relied on Bryan Williams and Sid to help us [backs]. We either relied on those two or we generated our own stuff. It was a tough tour as they had come off the Lions tour and were wanting to show how much better than us they were. We were out there to show them that they may have won on their tour of New Zealand but we were there to beat them.

Andy Haden: I was quite disillusioned by the level of management we had, and saw it repeated over a number of years after that where it was a rotation sort of thing whereas today I see Steve Hansen has been fourteen years in the All Blacks [management]. I was fourteen years in the All Blacks and I had nine coaches. I don't think in four and a half months that Bob Duff said anything about rugby to me. Not once, and we were training most days. He made the odd comment about scrummaging which we were struggling with because of the success of the Lions and we knew the UK teams were concentrating on their scrummaging. We had to get up to speed because we weren't too flash at it at that stage. But apart from those scrummaging comments I never heard another thing from him. There was no coaching at all. I thought there would be, especially as a lock.

Ian Kirkpatrick: We started off down in Gloucester and they were right up there in the competition and we thrashed them. Then we went to Llanelli and I warned the guys that we were going into enemy territory, that it wasn't England that it was Wales. It was a niggly affair. It was a dark, gloomy day and they got into us.

Bryan Williams: The second game was on a Tuesday. As was the way back in those days, on a Sunday you had a few beers. Nothing changed, except we were coming up against a pretty committed bunch on the Tuesday. We had to travel down to Wales, get into a new hotel, and it was a case of minds not on the job. Psychologically, we were knocked back on our heels and never really recovered.

When you lose, as an All Black, it's a bit of a national tragedy, but there was a sequel forty years later. I was rung up by Derek Quinnell one night, and he said, 'Beegee, we're having a forty-year celebration of when we beat you fellows and we'd like you to come over and speak at the dinner.' I said, 'Certainly' . . . there's always a silver lining. It took forty years though! He's a lovely fellow Derek, exceptional.

Bruce Robertson: Llanelli was really interesting, just the passion they played with. They came out and really took it to us. In those days you didn't score that many tries. Sometimes you didn't see the ball that much. We knew they were going to be tough but perhaps we didn't prepare enough for them, they surprised us a bit.

Bob Burgess: The Llanelli game I could see seeping away. We had thought we could win all our midweek games – surely? I remember a kick, it may even have been one of my kicks, went deep into the in-goal area and Phil Bennett running back and catching the ball, on the full, right on the corner of the dead-ball line and the sideline. Two or three of us were bearing down on him. He just swivelled and kicked the ball out on the ten-metre mark. He was absolutely magic. He really came to his peak in that 1972-73 period. Barry [John] had retired and he replaced him. He replaced the King, but he was a King himself. They were both exceptionally skilful players.

Ian Kirkpatrick: Then we played Cardiff, another game where it was all on. They thought, 'If Llanelli can do it, we'll do it too.' They were a good team too with guys like Gareth Edwards, but in the end we beat them comfortably.

Andy Haden: It was a bit of a setback. It wasn't how I wanted to start my All Black career even though it was the second game I played. To get a Test on that tour you needed to start well and although I played nineteen or twenty games I wasn't playing in the Saturday team which is where you had to try and aim to be.

With the Llanelli victory to prime them, Wales, both team and nation, were confident of a first Test victory since 1953. It didn't look likely as the All Blacks, through a Murdoch try and some remarkable kicking under pressure from twenty-one-year-old debutant Joe Karam, took a 13-3 lead into the second half, but Wales came roaring back and in the end were denied a draw when Phil Bennett narrowly missed a late forty-metre penalty. Any boost to the spirits of Ian Kirkpatrick's men was short-lived. Early on the Sunday morning, amidst some boisterous post-match partying, Murdoch went to the kitchen of the Angel Hotel, where he became embroiled in an argument with a security guard. There'd already been one run-in with security earlier in the evening which had caused some resentment amongst the players, and this time the argument escalated. The All Black manager was called, and soon after Todd arrived Murdoch threw a punch that left the guard with a black eye. After deliberations, meetings and phone calls, Todd eventually decided to make good on his threat to send the prop home. Murdoch never arrived back in New Zealand, getting off the plane in Singapore, and eventually taking up a reclusive life in the Australian outback. His life story is one of mystery. Tales abound about his tremendous strength, he was clearly a player of great courage, but his reputation made him a media target, which he hated, and his demeanour did little to quiet the attention. Whilst he has made visits home, on one occasion performing life-saving mouth-to-mouth resuscitation on a drowning child, Murdoch has turned down numerous entreaties from old team-mates to attend reunions, and shunned approaches to tell his side of the story. His departure deeply upset his team-mates, many of whom lost respect for a manager they felt had buckled under pressure, and it was no surprise that they lost their next tour match against Midland Counties at Moseley.

Joe Karam: It was the first live TV broadcast of a Test back to New Zealand, and I knew with that, and Cardiff Arms Park with the Welsh crowd, my first kick at goal was going to be a nerve-wracking exercise.

Tane Norton: I've never forgotten sitting in the Cardiff Arms Park dressing room and hearing the singing and thinking, 'I'd rather be home watching this with my kids!' When you run out on the field and hear the crowd you wouldn't be in any other place, it's a great feeling – but those few moments in the dressing room . . . They were fired up. They were so passionate . . . I mean we think we are, but the Welshmen have got us whacked. Years later you'd walk down the street in Cardiff and someone would come up and talk and I'd be thinking, 'How the hell can you remember me?' But that's what they're like. I liked Wales, very generous, kind people. Great place to tour.

Andy Haden: They were desperate [in Wales] to get a win over the All Blacks. We were just as keen to make sure they didn't. It is still the same today.

Ian Kirkpatrick: Joe Karam was only young but he had plenty of confidence. He could handle kicking goals, it didn't worry him.

Joe Karam: It hosed down the three days leading up to the Test. We were training at some ground twenty kilometres out of Cardiff. I remember saying to Bob Duff the day before the Test that I'd like to stay behind and do some goal-kicking practice. He said, 'It's wet as hell and how will you get back?' He asked if he should leave someone with me and I said I'd rather be on my own. When you're standing over the ball with 60,000 Welshmen screaming at you, the rest of your team can't do much to help you and you've got to learn to keep yourself together. So Bob left a bag of about a dozen balls and I told him to send a taxi out in a couple of hours. I stayed there and tried to visualise what was going to happen the next day, just me, the ball and the goalposts. My answer to nervousness was that if you had your skill and your technique you could overcome the nerves.

Bob Burgess: Joe Karam earned the nickname 'Clock' after that Wales Test as he could kick them over like clockwork. He was very thorough, very methodical and was very much like he is now. He thought about things, he worked things out and he did things in a considered way.

Joe Karam: Phil Bennett missed a kick that could have drawn the Test with about five minutes to go. It was nearly dark by the time the game finished . . . all the lights were shining out on the scoreboard and I remember standing under the posts. He was kicking from about forty metres out and from where I was looking the scoreboard was right behind him. As the ball faded outside the uprights I looked up. They'd already changed the score to 19-all, and they had to take it back down.

Bryan Williams: Beating Wales was a pretty good achievement. They had a lot of great players. Barry John had retired but Phil Bennett had come along, so they were still in their greatest era with their greatest players so to win that game was hugely important for us.

Sid Going: Joe Karam was a steady player, never a brilliant player. He read the game and the things he could do well, he did well. If he kicked for touch, he found touch. He wasn't a great one for entering the backline but he did seem to come in when it was necessary and he was more of a link than one who forced his way through.

Bob Burgess: We weren't expected to win according to the Welsh press, and to the Welsh players. After the game, at the after-match function, one of their forwards puffed up his chest in front of Keith Murdoch, inches from Keith's face, saying: 'You're thick man, you're thick.' It was absolutely not expected that we would win and there was utter frustration and fury that Murdoch had scored the winning try. The frustration being that here was this front row prop, who certainly didn't have a reputation for being a thinker of the game, but who had done his job magnificently well. But it was this furious 'You're thick man.' Whether that was something that Keith remembered in the early hours of the morning when confronted by somebody telling him he wasn't allowed to make a sandwich caused that reaction and he decided, 'Stuff you, I'm going to do this.' I was surprised that he didn't hit our Welsh friend earlier in the evening.

Ian Kirkpatrick: I probably blame myself that he went home. After that Test the next morning – I hadn't been around when he had that kerfuffle with the security guy – Ernie Todd wanted to have a management meeting. By that time I had heard what happened and Ernie wanted to send Keith home come hell or high water. For some reason he had it in for Keith. When we first arrived in the UK from New York we went to some function put on by the four Home Unions. I said to Ernie we'd go but we didn't want to hang around too long because we were all pretty knackered. So we went for a while and then went back to the hotel leaving Ernie there with some alickadoos. When he got back to the hotel a couple of the guys, Keith, Grizz and one or two others were having a quiet beer in the hotel bar. And he went up to them and went ape shit at them, and threatened to send them home right then, so he had his digs into Keith from the start. Anyway, we got into this meeting and there was this Welshman sitting there, I don't know what he was doing. Todd said to me, 'I am sending him home' and I said to him, 'You're not sending him anywhere, we'll deal with this in-house.' So we went ahead and even picked him in the team to play Leicester. When we got there Todd must have spent the whole night on the phone talking to people in Wellington. He never said a thing to us and Keith was gone by half past seven the next morning. He [Todd] certainly had the power to do it under the tour agreement. As manager there were certain things he could do and one was that if he felt he had to he could send someone home. I guess I was too young. What I should have done, and I still think about it every time Keith Murdoch's name comes up, was to say, 'If he goes, we all go.' Keith hadn't misbehaved on that tour. The British media had it in for us.

Sid Going: I don't know why we didn't say, 'If he goes, we go.' I was vice-captain for that tour, and Kirky, myself and the manager and the coach had met and said, 'No, that wasn't an incident.' Those people brought it on themselves, you felt like smacking everybody. In the bars, the Welsh would just come up to you and get in your face. We had to pull Graham Whiting out of one bar when they came up to him and he just got sick of it and was going to head butt a guy. All they wanted to do was argue and pick on you. We had decided that Keith wouldn't go and that we would support him. But the next morning the press got onto our manager who said, 'OK he goes', and we didn't know that until we got in the bus to go to training and we were told. That was just diabolical. I absolutely regret that it happened. Keith was our bar manager. He would never put his mouth to a drink until he saw that everyone else had something. He always made sure I had an orange juice or a lemonade. He was a good guy and I've never seen him since which was a shame.

Bryan Williams: It was only when we climbed onto the bus on the Monday morning that we realised something was sadly amiss. What I've always understood is that Keith had gone down to the kitchen, he was hungry, and he'd been confronted by the security guard and it seems the initial tete-a-tete was supposedly over, but then Ernie Todd came into the kitchen saying, 'Right Murdoch, you're going home.' From what I can make of it, that's when Keith said, 'Well if I'm going home I'll make a job of it,' and that's when he waded into him (security guard Grant).

Joe Karam: Ernie was carrying fatal cancer, unbeknown to us, and he took it hard, he was almost useless by the end of the tour. He was a fellow Marist man and I had a few late nights in his room where he virtually cried his heart out that he'd bowed to pressure from the Home Unions and the New Zealand Union to send Keith home. He knew he shouldn't have done it, and he was in a terrible state about it.

Bob Burgess: We were told the next morning that there was an investigation, then we were told that everything was OK, there wasn't a problem. We were to go to practice and Keith didn't get on the bus. Then he came to the bus and said, 'This is it fellows, I'm off.' I remember the reaction of people like Grant Batty who was furious because we hadn't been informed of what was happening. Lindsay Colling who knew Murdoch well, looked after him extremely well, saw when he was about to get in a fury and would just calm him down and take him away. But Lindsay couldn't be there all the time and others of us didn't get that delegation from our management. We let Keith down. We didn't really stand up for him. It was a fait accompli and we were gutless I guess and we should have stood our ground. But it hadn't been a position that we had discussed. That would have been a spur of the moment thing which in hindsight we should have done and which may have delayed the decision and kept the discussion going.

Tane Norton: We were given the chance to go and see Keith and most of the guys did, and then he was gone. I haven't seen him since. Four of us, including myself and Kirky did a videotape and said things to him – that we'd love to see him, but he never replied. He was an unbelievable prop, God he was strong.

Bruce Robertson: A lot of the guys supported Keith and he was a really good guy. There was a movement within the group that if they send him home then we all go home but that changed a little bit so we stayed over there and decided to show them they could send one of our players home but we could still play good rugby. It was sad for Keith because he was a good team person and didn't deserve that treatment.

Joe Karam: It had a strange effect on the team. The core, the Test team, the top twenty group, it made us more determined than ever, but for those who didn't have much hope of playing a Test match, they just seemed to fold a bit, and we lost a few midweek games. Even though it was a young team we still had some tough guys in there, like Alan Sutherland, Grizz Wyllie, Kirky and Sid, they were uncompromising guys. Up until that first Test they'd seen young guys like Batty and myself as young prima donnas a bit, but after we came through and won that first Test . . . because Wales were favourites, they were probably the best team in the world at the time and had been the core of the Lions team that had thumped the All Blacks . . . there was some new found respect and Batty and I found ourselves sitting about three seats closer to the back of the bus!

Keith Murdoch, bags in hand, arriving at Euston Station en route to Heathrow after exiting the All Blacks tour. *Peter Bush*

Bob Burgess: I recall being nervous about going to Ulster during the Troubles but it wasn't really discussed. The NZRU had agreed to a tour and that was on the agenda, so everybody knew the game was on. What we didn't appreciate was what was illustrated in the letter I received before the Irish Test. And that was the level of antagonism by many people in Ireland to the English, Scots and Welsh rugby teams. It was something that was discussed but only in a minor way because I don't think we really appreciated the politics of what we were getting into. The team stayed in a hotel that was about half an hour north of Belfast, at Dunadry. We drove by bus to the game by what I understand was a rather circuitous route taking half an hour longer than we might have expected to take and I'm sure that was to do with secrecy. When we got to the ground, and right through the game, on the top of the stadium, which was like an amphitheatre, there were armed soldiers. We saw them at training on the Thursday before the game. We trained at Ballymena, north of Belfast, and it was snowing. God it was cold, snow on the ground and these British military forces were there all armed with machine-guns which they happily showed us. The reception we got on the day of the game was huge. When we ran onto the ground there was such a roar and hand clapping that just carried on and on and on, and the same at the end of the game. I think we knew that our presence had been appreciated. There was an uneasy feeling that what we were doing was political and that we were being used other than for it just being a game of football. The four Home Unions were wanting to make a point. England played in Dublin in 1973, but it was 1974 before Wales and Scotland went there, and neither team played Ireland at all in 1972.

The team dug deep to beat Scotland and England, and an unlikely Grand Slam was on before a last-minute try by Tom Grace earned Ireland a thrilling draw at Lansdowne Road, a draw that would have been a first defeat to Ireland had a wide angle conversion attempt by Barry McGann gone over.

Bryan Williams: Joe Karam and I always used to have competitions at training . . . drop-kicking and goal-kicking. That day at Twickenham I caught the ball and I could hear Joe yelling 'Give it here Beegee' and I thought, 'No.' I had a pot and hit it as well as any drop-kick I'd ever tried. It was a tight game too, only 9-nil.

Sid Going: That Test [Scotland] was the beginning of Kent Lambert making his mark. He was under a lot of pressure when he took Jeff Matheson's place but he handled it so well. It was the making of him. It was fantastic what he did. Kent was built right, he was as solid as a rock, short in the legs but solid in the shoulders and his body, and he was really determined with good ball skills. My try does pop up often in highlights. I just intercepted. I knew McHarg was going to pass the ball, I guess I sucked him into passing inside and I intercepted it and ran and scored, thank goodness.

Bruce Robertson: In the Scotland Test I wanted to be replaced at half-time but the duty doctor said I had gone on with both legs bandaged so they said I had the injuries before the game started. In spite of the obvious hamstring injury not long into the second half I slipped several players and kicked ahead to the in-goal area and Grant Batty got through to score.

Grim faces for a grim day, the All Blacks play Ulster under armed guard during troubled times in Belfast. *Peter Bush*

Joe Karam: Bruce Robertson set up an amazing try in that game against Scotland, and Sid got one too. I remember Sid in that game just going right through a ruck and coming out the other side with the ball. Sid was like Batts, he was a freak. He was a great fellow, a great team-mate. Bruce had a hamstring injury through that tour, even when he played he was affected by it, but he was still good.

Ian Kirkpatrick: We probably should have beaten Ireland by more than we beat the other teams. By the time we got to play Ireland it was late in the tour and we let it slip. It was one of those games where we just fell off the pace.

Bob Burgess: Before the Ireland Test I received a letter from the IRA. I wasn't aware of any other players receiving the letter. I didn't turn it into a point of discussion with the other players and I'm not aware of who the other players might have been who could well have received it. I do think I may have received it because my stance against South Africa was well known. That stance wasn't a topic that was brought up at all by other players during the tour and I didn't bring it up as an issue. It was simply something in the background as everyone was aware of my stance. They may have commented among themselves but not with me. There were others including Bruce Robertson and Sandy McNichol, who were opposed to the Springboks coming in 1973, but that was after the team came back to New Zealand.

What I remember about the Ireland game was the ball being kicked into the All Blacks' in-goal area and my turning and chasing after the ball and running alongside the Irish wing Tom Grace and thinking, 'I could knock his shoulder with my shoulder, barge him out of the way and then could probably beat him to the ball.' However, if he turned his shoulder so that I hit him either in the chest or the back then it would be a penalty try under the goalposts and they would certainly convert that try. This was going through my mind as I was trying to beat him to the ball. But he beat me to the touchdown – the photo shows it was by a head! However, Barry McGann wasn't able to convert it, so it was 10-10. During the Test there had been an explosion downtown, a bombing, that was audible from the ground and we were told afterwards what happened. I don't think it registered with any of the All Blacks but it certainly did with the Irish team and I think it affected their playing somewhat. It could have rattled them. I have often wondered if McGann, in attempting the conversion, was put off by a bomb?

The letter which Bob Burgess received in advance of the Ireland Test.
Written on Sinn Fein headed paper, it is signed by Mairin de Burca
and Tony Heffernan, recognised members of the IRA.

Joe Karam: They brought Tom Kiernan back, he'd retired a couple of years earlier and he was in his mid-thirties. We were winning 10-6 when Tom Grace scored with a minute to go. Just before the try they kicked it down and I got it inside our twenty-two, close to the sideline, and I really couldn't kick it out with much distance so I thought I'd just get the hell out of our half. I kicked it as far as I could down the touchline. Old Tom, he'd sat at the back and hadn't done much all game, and looked the least threatening player in the team. He got the ball back inside his twenty-two. Batts and I were following up . . . and blow me down if he doesn't sell us a dummy pretending to kick it out, and beats both of us. It might have been a Grand Slam if I'd just kicked the thing into touch. They missed a kick from right out on the sideline to beat us . . . Barry McGann, he was a good guy, too.

Bryan Williams: Ten minutes out from the end of the Ireland game the Grand Slam was ours, but inexplicably we allowed Tom Kiernan to counter-attack. He was getting pretty old by then and wasn't very quick, but he threw a dummy and went through a gap and managed to set up play further down the field. They had a ruck and from that they put a kick through. Tom Grace chased it through. Bats was running back from the left wing and I was coming across, but we weren't quite quick enough.

Sid Going: There was a lot of security, even at our trainings and I can vaguely remember a bomb going off during the Test in Dublin. We were well protected and they had police escorts everywhere we went. It didn't really affect us but we had to be aware of where we were all the time, and what we were doing.

Bruce Robertson: Ireland was one game we should have won. We probably didn't utilise the ball as much as we could have done and in the end we kicked it to them and they scored a counter-attack try and missed the kick that could have won the game. It was one of those games where you come off and say, 'That game was probably one of the easiest Test matches I've played but we drew.'

The tour ended on a high note with the traditional Barbarians game rated as one of the finest matches ever played, featuring a Baabaas try sparked by Phil Bennett and scored by Gareth Edwards that will assuredly feature in any debate about the greatest ever scored. The All Blacks performed a haka for the only time on tour and played their part in a stunning spectacle. The tour ended on a miserable note with defeat to France in Paris.

Bob Burgess: The Barbarians game, and their win, was an acknowledgment for their players who proved that they were a fantastic side in 1971 and it was confirmation of how good that team was and how well they had been coached, how intelligent their players were.

Bruce Robertson: The Barbarians game was the first time on tour we did the haka and while we wanted to win the game we were also determined to entertain as well. In those days you just talked about your defence patterns, you didn't really practice them at all. We didn't have a kick-chase pattern, you'd just chase it as a line. It was things you learn as you go. I always respected Mike Gibson as he was a gentleman off the field and a very good player on it. When you played against him you had to play at your best.

Ian Kirkpatrick: I know we didn't play a couple of our regular Test players because we didn't want it to be treated like it was a Test. I mean back in 1964 Ian Clarke had even played for the Barbarians against the All Blacks. It wasn't going to be treated too much like a Test match so we were pretty surprised at the way they came out. I thought I had Phil Bennett lined up when he made the break that led to their great try. But he had a great sidestep on him. We were a bit shell-shocked to start with and did pretty well to come back. We were pretty knackered after four months on tour, but they were good all right – British rugby was very strong at that time.

Bryan Williams: We spent most of the morning practising the haka. We'd decided we were going to do it for the first time on the tour, and it was an absolute shemozzle . . . we wasted all morning trying to practise it and in the end it was a pathetic effort. The try by Gareth Edwards was a special try, and whenever I'm speaking in public I give a bit of a commentary . . . 'Kirkpatrick has it, it comes out to Williams, down the right-hand side he goes, he puts in a brilliant centring kick, it's bounced in behind them, anything could happen here, but there's Phil Bennett, he's got it, one sidestep, two sidesteps . . . Beegee Williams misses with a high tackle, out to John Pullin, Tom David . . . and here comes Gareth Edwards and he's scored in the corner . . . what a score!' And then I say, 'Ladies and gentlemen, without me, that try wouldn't have been scored!' The greatest try of all time wouldn't have been scored without me. Every time I see it replayed I think it keeps my name up in lights . . . for all the wrong reasons.

Bob Burgess: As an aside about the Barbarians game in 1973, at the beginning of the tour when we caught up with Cliff Morgan he said: 'Would you like to play for the Barbarians against the All Blacks?' I was interested in the idea but it didn't come to anything. Carwyn James was pivotal in guiding the side again. I learned afterwards that he persuaded them to think of the game as the last match of their 1971 tour.

Bruce Robertson: After the Barbarians game I sat down with quite a few of their players and talked about how they worked their defence against us. They were using a drift defence and after that I thought, 'Yeah, we can use that' and we did, especially when Bill Osborne was in the All Blacks as he and I seemed to be able to do it quite well. You learned things in those days when you had a good talk with each other after games. People said it was an unhappy tour but I feel it was because the press and media were hassling us a bit. Within the team we really grew into one solid group and enjoyed each other's company. Mark Sayers and Ian Stevens, the Wellingtonians, were great and really made the tour enjoyable.

Ian Kirkpatrick: Touring was a different story in those days. You just turned up with your training gear. There was no meeting to talk about how difficult it was going to be being away for four months, difficulties at home, the financial problems guys were having to go through, there was none of that. Four and a half months is a long time to be away, guys were having hassles back home. Early in the tour Lin Colling met a guy from British Telecom and he set up this thing where you could get a few guys in a certain room each night, maybe four or five guys, and they could call and talk to home for nothing. We reckon it was about $40,000 worth of calls. The poor guy got caught out after the tour and he lost his job. Thank God that didn't hit the media. But it saved us, that's for sure, especially with what we were getting – about $1.50 a day!

Graham Short was the baggage man and a good bugger. In France right at the end he nearly died of meningitis. The guys felt so sorry for him that we had a whip round and managed to come up with enough money to bring him out to New Zealand for a holiday. It wasn't until about 1977 that he was able to make it, it took him so long to recover. He told me then that he knew Ernie Todd had cancer but had been sworn to secrecy and wouldn't tell us. I told him he should have, because we might have had some idea of what was going on.

Joe Karam: By the time we got to France we were over it basically. We were a hell of a happy team within ourselves, but the British media had been stuck into us and by the time we got to France it was like . . . 'Well we're in France, let's have a good time.' We didn't play very well against the French, it was a wet day and we were going through the motions. It all fell to bits in those last two weeks.

Bob Burgess: The French Test in Paris came after four months away. There was a different attitude in France towards the team. It was like the clouds being lifted. We were not under the sort of pressure we had been under from the British press. We were up against class teams and were beaten in the Test. I loved being in France. I couldn't speak a word of French but I made contact with a French rugby club in Lyon. Their president came along and talked to me in French and I talked to him in English while his son did the translation. And by the end of that quarter-hour conversation I had agreed to go back and play club rugby for Lyon Olympique Universitaire which I did for three seasons.

Joe Karam: It's hard to overestimate the effect of a tour of that length on players who were married, and who weren't farmers and didn't have enough money to manage things properly. There was some terrible homesickness when you've got no money, no support. Whatever our allowance was, it hardly bought you a pint of beer, and the pressure on players, I mean it was after the oil crisis, inflation had taken off and it really did have an affect on a lot of the players.

TWENTY-ONE

DOWN AND OUT, THEN UP AGAIN

'Batts was remarkable . . . pound for pound possibly the strongest man who's ever played for the All Blacks'

IF THINGS HAD been tough through 1972 they hardly improved in 1973. The NZRFU found itself staring at a void when forced by Prime Minister Norman Kirk to 'postpone' a visit by the Springboks. Kirk, who'd promised during the 1972 election campaign not to interfere, was prompted to change his mind after being warned by police that the tour would 'engender the greatest eruption of violence this country had ever known.' There was also the matter of averting a boycott of the Christchurch Commonwealth Games in 1974. Kirk directed the Rugby Union to put off the tour until South Africa agreed to pick their team from mixed race trials. The All Blacks, still weary from the UK trip, found themselves on a hastily-arranged internal tour, in which they lost a game to the NZ Juniors, an upstart bunch aged twenty-three and under, featuring eleven future All Blacks including Graham Mourie, Gary Seear and Brad Johnstone.

They split a two-game series with an International XV selected for Colin Meads' farewell tour, that ironically included Springboks Albie Bates and Tom Bedford, and beat NZ Maori, before losing their one and only international of the year against England. To compound the embarrassment, this was an England team that had lost all three of its lead-up provincial games, but led superbly by 1971 Lion John Pullin, took full toll of a bumbling All Black effort at Eden Park to record the first Test victory by any of the individual Home Unions in New Zealand.

Ian Kirkpatrick: In 1973 when South Africa couldn't come the NZRU put together another internal tour. It was bloody stupid, an absolute disaster. It was probably the low point. We had come back from the UK after being over there for four and a half months, and we were pretty tired. If we'd been playing the South Africans we would have got up for it. No one wanted to be there and the NZ Juniors beat us. It was pretty sad, there were guys who didn't want to pull on the All Black jersey because they were playing against their mates. The Juniors came at us big time. Then we played that President's XV at Athletic Park. It was a send-off for Pinetree. Sid Going wasn't available for that tour but he played against us for the President's XV. At one stage he took the ball off me and scored. He was a pretty good mate of mine but I could have killed them. Then we played the Maoris in Rotorua and the Maori guys in our team, Tane Norton and Kent Lambert, had to leave us and play for them. Then we lost to an England team that hadn't won a game against any of the three provincial sides they played.

Sid Going: I'd been away four and a half months, I didn't go on the internal tour. It was difficult to fit rugby in with my farming. It was terribly hard on my wife and when I look

Opposite: Sid Going, 1973. *Getty Images*

back on it I think, 'What a mongrel.' I honestly feel like that and I think, 'Why did I leave her to deal with all that?' And she did it. She brought up the kids, looked after and ran the farm, milked the cows, just did everything. She was a good sports girl herself and could have done her own thing but she didn't, she supported me 200 per cent. She has been my greatest strength. And still is.

I said I was unavailable and I ended up playing for Colin Meads' team. It was hard case because I knew the moves they were calling but it wasn't a game that I wanted to play. I didn't have to go down and train, we only assembled the day before and I said I guess I could spare a day to play. It was a game that we went out and played but we didn't really want to win. You almost barracked for your opposition instead of playing how we should have.

Bryan Williams: I didn't go on the internal tour in '73 because I had some legal exams, which was a blessing. I was all rugbyed out. We lost to England on Eden Park after they'd lost all their lead-up games, so '73 was not a great year at all. The team wasn't playing well.

Duncan Robertson (10 Tests, 30 games): I changed to first five-eighths in 1972 because I wasn't enjoying second five. In fact, I gave the game away as I had set up my own business and had a lot of guys working for me. Out of nowhere I was named in the President's XV to play the All Blacks in Colin Meads' farewell game at Athletic Park. We beat the All Blacks. When Colin came in and sat down afterwards, and some of the All Blacks came into the dressing room, we sat down and thought to ourselves: 'What have we done?' There was no celebrating at what we achieved. I don't think it occurred to anybody that we might win. Then there was another game the following weekend and there were several Kiwi boys in the side again but our hearts weren't in it. Grahame Thorne worked out there were six of us who had played for and against the All Blacks and who could claim a win. I went on to be named reserve for the England Test of that year.

The All Blacks had been coached through that unsuccessful 1973 campaign by JJ Stewart, something of a rugby intellectual. Stewart decided that change was needed, and there were shocks when he named his team for the 1974 tour of Australia. Gone were hard-nosed forwards Alex Wyllie and Alan Sutherland, Sid Going was not even invited to the trials, whilst Stewart also relieved Ian Kirkpatrick of the captaincy, handing it to Wellington's Andy Leslie, a twenty-nine-year-old veteran of the provincial scene. However he may have felt about losing the leadership, Kirkpatrick responded with some magnificent performances as a new-look team won twelve matches, taking the Test series 2-0 with the second in Brisbane drawn 16-all after a spirited Australian fightback. Having left Going out to try and ease the team's dependency on the North Aucklander, Stewart now had to persuade him to make himself available for a tricky end of year tour.

Duncan Robertson: In 1974 I had a good couple of trials and I think JJ Stewart wanted some hardened players and chose a team of guys who had played fifty, sixty or seventy games of provincial rugby and mixed them with some younger guys.

Ian Kirkpatrick: We had trials before we went to Australia. Missing was Sid Going, it was bizarre he didn't even come to the trials. The guy that made the blazers lived in Newtown, and he didn't have much time to get everything ready before the tour, so if you were one of the guys who had been around a while you got the call to go down and get measured up for a blazer on the Friday afternoon and you knew you were in. So I went down there and there were all these skeleton blazers on the hangers and I thought well, if we had had a Pick the Team competition I could have won it pretty easily. I saw Grizz's name on one of the blazers so I thought 'He's in.' So we get to the after-match where they named the team. I'd said to Grizz, 'You're in mate because I have seen your blazer.' They started reading the team out fullback first working through the backs then they got to the loosies. Mine was the last name read out, and I was starting to think I hadn't made it. And Grizz

Duncan Robertson in the big wet . . . the first Test against
Australia in Sydney in 1974. *FotoSport/Photosport NZ*

wasn't in. They left Sid out of the team to go to Australia, they did the dirty on him a bit, he was one of our greatest halfbacks and then they had to walk over broken glass to make him available for the team to go to Ireland.

Andy Leslie (1974-76, 10 Tests, 34 games): I heard no whispers at all before the trials. I had played in a lot of trials with free trips to Palmerston North or time in hotels in Wellington but I had always been in the early trial. I was used to hearing A.R., my initials, being called when Alan Sutherland's name was read out and my heart did a little beat when they said, 'A.R. Leslie.' I was sitting with Uppy [Petone and Wellington coach Ian Upston] and Nectar [All Blacks halfback Ian Stephens] and Nectar belted me on the back and said, 'You're in', then I missed the fact I was captain, and Nectar hit me and said, 'You're bloody captain too!' After Nectar had congratulated me, the next person up to me was Ian Kirkpatrick. It was funny, when I was away to South Africa with Petone earlier in the year I had written a letter home to [wife] Leslie and said that would be my last trip and once it was over it was time to put rugby aside and put some money together. I had always lived in hope that I might get a chance.

Ian Kirkpatrick: The captaincy thing didn't worry me too much. I didn't really want it in the first place, but when it's given to you of course you take it and give it 110 per cent. When they took the captaincy off me in 1974, I just carried on.

Andy Leslie: After the announcement we went back to the Grand Hotel for a meal. I knew there was disappointment among some older players that Kirky had not been told about losing the captaincy. It turned out the selectors hadn't made a decision until they chose the team, and I believe that. Leslie joined me at the Grand when she heard and we had dinner with Charlie Saxton. He took me through the whole gambit of captaincy – it was one of the most important meals I ever had. All his comments turned out to be correct. It was life-changing, something I didn't appreciate. It's not until you get away from it that you realise. You have to be a wee bit smarter and sharper in what you do.

When I got home the first telegram I received was from Kirky's mother wishing me all the best. That was the quality of the man. After being selected I spent a lot of time with JJ Stewart. He would be brilliant coaching the game now. He never said as much, and I'm not being big-headed in saying it, but I think he felt I was a ball player and he wanted me to develop that in myself as much as I could. He used to talk about the synthesis between the backs and forwards and saw me as his message carrier. He said we were going to Australia and would lay down the platform for years to come. We'd be training in warm conditions and would be able to practise and sit around in the sun talking about what we were going to do. I think it rained every training session on the tour.

Bryan Williams: There was a bit of a new broom, it was quite refreshing. I enjoyed playing under JJ Stewart. He'd a reputation for being a bit dour, not an attack-minded coach, but in the event we played an enterprising brand of rugby and training was enjoyable. That signalled a new dawn in All Black rugby.

Joe Karam: Dropping Sid, in a funny sort of way, had a positive outcome. Sid was the greatest player that I ever had anything to do with, but the team had, through the early 70s, come to almost revolve around him. It wasn't that JJ didn't love Sid, he just knew that we had to get a greater dimension to our game.

Andy Leslie: They called us 'Dad's Army' when we left. JJ hadn't coached at that level before but I think the big thing he achieved was getting the guys to think for themselves. The team chosen for Australia had fifteen of the twenty-five players as newcomers. We were all of a similar age around twenty-nine, thirty, and several of the players captained their provinces. There was a huge amount of experience. Captaining that team was the easiest of all the teams I led because they all knew what to do.

Bruce Robertson: JJ Stewart changed the philosophy of the side. He talked us all through it and where we were allowed to run the ball in our own half, and it was on to run the ball from there so long as we kept the ball. It meant we could start playing more attacking rugby, and there were some good players who were only too willing to have a go for it.

Joe Karam: Philosophically JJ was far and away the most outstanding student of rugby I've ever met. He loved the game to bits. If you're talking about coaches, administrators, he was the single greatest fellow in the game that I'd had anything to do with, streets ahead. I don't think he came in wanting to have a cleanout, but to have a team that followed his philosophy. It was a hell of a courageous thing to do to replace Kirky as captain with Andy Leslie. I don't think too many people would have gotten away with that. In fact, Kirky probably became JJ's greatest ally and Andy's as well. The siege mentality of the All Blacks disappeared under JJ.

Tane Norton: We were trying to improve our scrummaging, because the British were very good. We'd change our grips, our bindings and so on but most of it was in our heads. We hadn't put enough thought into it, but JJ was determined we were going to get that right. They were no more powerful than us, but we learned we had to keep everyone on the job at scrum time, no loosies hanging off, and we had to work at it over a long period. As a hooker your prime job was to get your own ball, and if you got one of theirs that was a bit of luck.

Andy Leslie: Probably the only time I felt out of my depth was in the first Test in Australia. The first forty minutes went so fast and come half-time I was still getting my breath. The message came out from JJ about how he wanted us to play the second half and at that stage Kirky and Beegee Williams stepped in and took over. They were a great support. It was a terrible day. The conditions were tougher than when we played the water polo Test against Scotland in 1975.

Duncan Robertson: During the first Test in Sydney it was snowing, hailing, blowing and raining. JJ sat down beside me when I was cleaning my boots. He said that wasn't a good look, but I told him that was what I had done all my career, to which he replied, 'Fair enough.' Then he said to me, 'I don't think I've ever seen the best of you,' and added,

'I'm counting on you. If you don't control it, we lose. Duncan, can you do it?' I told him I could and he said he would hold me to it. He said it wasn't just the All Blacks I was playing for but everyone back home who played the game from little kids right through. While it was my first Test, adrenaline takes over and lucky enough for me the weather was so bad it was like playing at Carisbrook in the mud, or any one of the other club grounds in Dunedin. When I scored my try I just decided to get the ball and go for it. I was a new kid on the block and the Aussies didn't know me. I can't recall the try now, but I can tell you about every game I ever played in that we lost.

Joe Karam: I was the only fullback on that tour and played every game, so I didn't have much time for fun! The Test in Sydney, and the one against Scotland a year later, they'd be the wettest conditions the All Blacks have ever played in.

Duncan Robertson: I roomed with Kirky [Ian Kirkpatrick] a lot on the tour and that was one of the most amazing experiences. In spite of being dropped as captain he never spoke a word of complaint. The night before the third Test I woke up and could smell fish and chips. I thought I was dreaming and went back to sleep. Then I thought again, I could smell fish and chips. I turned over and the light was on and Kirky was there. He said: 'I can't sleep. We've got to win, we can't lose to them.' He had gone downtown to get some fish and chips. I remember he said: 'Duncan, it is one thing to be an All Black, it is quite another thing to be accepted by the boys.' What he was meaning was never to wimp out, to go in and make the tackles, even if they take you off the field in a wheelchair. That one thing stuck with me. Kirky was one of those people, BJ Lochore was another, who when they speak you don't interject and you don't question them.

Andy Leslie: We met with the referee, Kevin Crowe, the night before the second Test and he said to me anything I wanted to know during the game to ask him. We got penalised for having too many in the first lineout and Paul McLean, their first-five, kicked the goal. Running back to halfway I said to Crowe, 'Why did we get penalised when it was our ball to the lineout?' and he told me, 'It's none of your fucking business.' We drew 16-16 but won the final Test. We went to Fiji after that game and only won in injury time which might have undone the lot.

Duncan Robertson: JJ taught me how to read people's body language. It was a very good skill and helped me in my coaching career. Not a lot of people know that JJ wrote a lot of [Prime Minister] Norman Kirk's speeches. He actually pulled out of the 1976 tour to South Africa two weeks before because he came under so much pressure from the Labour Party. But he told me he stayed on because he couldn't let the boys down. He was quite lonely and he and I often talked about coaching. We had a good tour, although we were lucky to get out of the last game against Fiji, the refereeing was abysmal. The ball flew through the middle of the goalposts but the referee waved it away.

Bruce Robertson: What happened in those days you would go on a tour with the aim of achieving something and games like that against Fiji were tagged on the end and perhaps we didn't prepare as well as we should have. You were thinking about home and not enough about rugby. I remember ankle-tapping someone in that game and he got up and was quite angry with me.

The All Blacks were to be a centrepiece of the Irish Rugby Union's Centennial, but dauntingly tacked onto the end of a six-game visit to the Emerald Isle were a midweek game against a 'Welsh XV' and a match against the Barbarians. Sid Going and older brother Ken were included in a twenty-seven-strong team that won all of the games in Ireland, including the Test in which Joe Karam scored all of New Zealand's 15 points. The last week of the tour was one of the most demanding ever undertaken by a New Zealand side. In the space of eight days they met Ireland, before the Wednesday clash in Cardiff against a full-strength Welsh Test side in everything but name, and then a powerful Barbarians line-up. Given the ill feeling that had laced their last visit to the Principality, the All Blacks were determined not to lose to the Welsh team, whatever it was called. Having had a fair shout for a try by Bryan Williams disallowed, they attacked relentlessly until the half-time 3-all deadlock was broken by a storming Kirkpatrick try. The game was eventually won 12-3, and was regarded by the All Black players as a Test win, even if they didn't receive Test caps. Virtually the same XV then attempted to overcome a Baabaas side featuring the entire pack and many of the backline stars of the successful 1974 Lions tour of South Africa. In a match as tight and tense as the 1973 game was free and spectacular, the All Blacks led at half-time but the Barbarians came back and scored a late try by Mervyn Davies to level the match at 13-all. Whilst they might have been disappointed not to end the year with a win, 1974 saw a resurgence in fortunes. Nineteen of twenty-one matches had been won with two drawn. There was some flair returning to the back play and, in particular, signs that the All Blacks were starting to cope with the power scrummaging that now dominated Northern Hemisphere thinking.

Andy Leslie: Before we went to Ireland we did a lot of scrummaging. Prof. Jim Stewart from Canterbury worked with us at several sessions around the country. I still joke with Tane Norton about the shape of his nose being caused by us getting so low in the scrums. We were so low it was impossible to hook the ball.

Sid Going: I had been dropped from the Aussie tour earlier in the year and listened to the games while I was working – I probably never worked so hard in my life while they were touring Australia – and then the coaches wanted me to prepare to go to Ireland. I was very reluctant but they talked me into it. I talked my wife into letting me go, but she never, ever stopped me. She was supportive.

Bryan Williams: In 1972-73 I think some of the behaviour was not acceptable for an All Black team and I'd decided I was never going to be part of an All Black team like that again, starting to grow up I guess, and taking a leadership role. The senior players decided to set a new standard.

Andy Leslie: When we arrived for the tour Noel [manager Stanley], JJ and I attended a press conference and we felt the British press were ready to fire some bullets. JJ explained that he was new to the role and didn't know who everyone was and would they mind introducing themselves when they asked a question? That contained their aggression a bit and by answering their questions honestly we ended up with the tag, 'The Smiling All Blacks.' John Reason, who was one of the toughest critics, and JJ Stewart were good friends by the end of it all. I think they were two intellectuals on the same wavelength. Sid Going was back and behind a forward pack that never really dominated was still the star of most games. There was a lot of criticism about his passing but the first five-eighths always ended up with the ball and time to do something.

Ian Kirkpatrick: We played well through Ireland, we beat them pretty comfortably in the Test – not by a big score – and got on a roll. We didn't think too much about backing up, Saturday, Wednesday, Saturday was pretty normal.

Andy Leslie: We embraced the challenge of playing Ireland, a Wales XV and the Barbarians within eight days. We stayed at Porthcawl. I had never been to Cardiff Arms Park so the day before the game Kirky, myself, Tane Norton and Sid got a taxi and headed in to look at the ground. We got out and were having a walk around when blokes came running out telling us we weren't allowed on the ground because there was a big game the next day. We said we were playing in the game and they said that didn't matter.

Duncan Robertson: I was standing by Kirky during the anthems and when the Welsh starting singing he said to me, 'Don't listen to the bastards. The only way to shut them up is to score points.' And we did that. The last week of that tour was tough. I don't think the guys today would really understand that. It was huge. It was more mentally tiring than physically.

Ian Kirkpatrick: They called it the Welsh XV, and we never got Test caps for it, but it was a Test team all right, and we played pretty well. We kept putting pressure on them and they ran out of gas. I got a hard time about the try I scored . . . Phil Bennett didn't really want to tackle me and they were all giving me hell afterwards saying it was the easiest try I ever scored.

Bruce Robertson: We played more adventurous rugby against Wales in 1974 and it paid off. We tried some different moves around that time which was good, but the referee wouldn't award a try to Beegee after Joe Karam kicked across field because he thought Beegee was in front of the kicker. Batts was awesome, a good team man, he set standards and was growly if you weren't adhering to them. He always said how he thought things should be.

Bryan Williams: Joe Karam cross-kicked for me from a quick tap penalty. He was only about five to seven metres from the goal-line when he kicked it and I was way out on the other side. I raced up as the ball was in flight but the referee hadn't been watching, and when he turned around and saw me picking the ball up to score he said I was offside. I'd honestly come from about twenty metres back. We'd been practising that move. JJ gave us licence to try things, and so we did it again in the Barbarians game, only this time it was Batts who cross-kicked it. It was all pre-planned, we knew where the space was, and he executed it perfectly.

Joe Karam: Beegee and Batts and I, I suppose it was the start of the term, 'the back three'. The fullback was often some joker who just stood at the back and waited for things to come his way. But the three of us were pretty onto it, and we'd often practice those things at training. Whenever there was a penalty towards one side of the field they'd be on the lookout for me to do something like that. The only reason Bryan was called offside was the ref got such a shock at what I did. I never said anything to him, and by the time he looked up, the ball was landing and Beegee was about to pick it up. He was never offside, he'd come from miles back.

Sid Going: It was a tough week, but it was good. We had to rise to the occasion and we were determined. It was tough physically but we were ready to go out and last. Our attitude was, 'Let's go and do this boys and then we're home.'

Andy Leslie: The Barbarians were supposed to be a Lions team but I think they were even stronger because they picked some players who had been unavailable to tour South Africa. We drew 13-13 and afterwards Grant Batty was in one of those big baths at Twickenham shaving off his moustache. Someone asked what he was doing and he said he had decided to shave it off after we beat the Barbarians. He didn't realise it was only a draw and was a bit upset.

Joe Karam: The crowds loved Grant Batty, they couldn't believe he was such a dynamo. Batts was remarkable . . . pound for pound possibly the strongest man who's ever played for the All Blacks. He was a super physical person, with amazing speed, balance and instincts. Before he got picked for the All Blacks, he was almost an unfettered maniac. He'd get the ball and take off beating people, but he didn't have many other skills. He'd run around people, over them, under them, through them, whatever it took, but he realised he needed more to fit in at the highest level. A halfback at school and then a second-five, he'd only played on the wing for a year before the '72 tour. By the end of the tour he'd become an absolute master at throwing into the lineout. He could hardly kick a ball when he got out of school. He and I used to go up to Athletic Park at lunchtime, I'd do my goal-kicking and he practised kicking – he learned to kick with both feet. He was just one out of the box, we've never seen another one like him.

Ian Kirkpatrick: In the first scrum of that Barbarians game – they got so low that Tane could hardly hook the ball. There was so much pressure on the scrum it was quivering and Tane's nose was just about on the ground. He pretty much hooked the ball with his nose. But it was about then our scrum started to come of age. Those Barbarians had pushed the Springboks around earlier in the year. They treated that game like it was a Test match, they didn't try to run the ball.

Andy Leslie: The Irish tour was a super one to be on. Hamish MacDonald said to me on the way home, 'If we could just keep playing rugby no one would ever beat this team.' And he was right. Sadly the next year we played only one Test and it slowed the momentum down after all the work we had done.

TWENTY-TWO

ONE LAST TIME

'Boys it's all right for you, you can go home now, I have to live here!'

THE SOLITARY TEST in 1975 will never be forgotten. Torrential rain in Auckland flooded the playing surface to the point where consideration was given to calling the game off. In what became known as 'the waterpolo Test', the players crashed, bashed and splashed about in massive puddles of surface water. The All Blacks were too good, scoring four tries. Karam converted all four in what proved to be his final Test. He stunned fans in early 1976 by signing to play rugby league. The professional code was making inroads into Australian rugby stocks, and casting nets into New Zealand, although Karam accepted an offer not from one of the glamour Sydney clubs, but Auckland's Glenora Bears. The defection was lucrative for Karam, but costly for the All Blacks. He was a solid figure at fullback, but brought his intense focus and level temperament to bear on his goal-kicking, and had often been the difference between winning and losing.

Andy Leslie: There was huge discussion going on before the [Scotland] game. JJ and I were involved. The Scots wanted it called off until the Sunday but we weren't worried. We never took any of that back into the dressing room. Scotland had half their team out there and they didn't have a great mindset. They were unlucky because their fullback Brucie Hay had to come off with a broken arm early in the game and Andy Irvine had to go back to fullback. Andy was a beautiful runner but he couldn't catch the kicks. We tried to play an error-free game under the conditions, although I can remember Bob Scott saying to me that I dropped the ball twice. It was sad when you consider that they play fourteen or fifteen Tests a year now that we only played once in 1975.

Duncan Robertson: Before the Scottish Test at Eden Park we walked out onto the ground on duckboards and JJ looked at me and said, 'It's not a good day.' I said to him, 'We should be excited about it,' and he asked, 'Why?' I said, 'Because they'll be pissed off.' 'So you're going to give them a few up and unders?' And I said, 'Too right.' I used to be able to make them hang in the air and our forwards would get there at the same time as the ball. In Auckland we had to remember it was a Test match so it was no good moaning about the weather. We just kicked it high, and put it down their end and waited for the points.

Ian Kirkpatrick: We didn't want the Test called off. We had gone to the ground about 10am just to get out of the hotel. It was OK then but when we came back later we could hardly get into the dressing rooms there was so much water around. There were some big pools of water on the ground. I thought Sid was going to drown at one ruck. We played well. Scotland weren't a bad side either.

Opposite: Morne du Plessis gathers a high kick under pressure despite the attentions of Joe Morgan, during the fourth Test. *Peter Bush*

Scotland and the All Blacks (in white) take to
the waterlogged Eden Park in 1975. *Ron Cooke*

Bryan Williams: That Scotland Test was one for the ages. The rain was torrential, it just never let up. No pun intended but I'd had a bit of a try-scoring drought so it was good to get a couple in that game. But one Test in a year? That was a pretty good Scottish team – Mighty Mouse McLauchlan, Sandy Carmichael, Andy Irvine, Ian McGeechan – but we played largely mistake-free rugby in conditions that weren't conducive to that, and were proud of that performance.

Tane Norton: That Test was unbelievable – all night and all morning it pelted down – there was water inside the dressing room. It was wet, not cold. Sandy Carmichael got a bleeding nose and went down in the water. The water around him got redder and redder. Kerry Tanner said, 'I hope there's no sharks around.'

Joe Karam: Our forwards blew them off the field and everything we did in the backs came off. Duncan Robertson had a really good game and I think JJ's team might have hit its peak.

Bryan Williams: That was Joe's last Test. I still have great regrets about that. We'd been starting to play pretty well, we'd brought in some new blood in the likes of Billy Osborne, and were heading off to South Africa with a real chance of turning around the results . . . with a good goal-kicker.

Joe Karam: I got married in 1975 two weeks after that Test against Scotland. The whole issue of payments, going on tour, the whole setup was a topical thing, and there was a lot of discontent amongst the players over the way the game was being run. There was zero respect for the Rugby Union, both the individuals and as a body. I'd seen the writing on the wall. I'd had some very big offers to play league in Australia during the '74 tour, and from Wigan in England, money right up in the stratosphere. I mean a couple of hundred thousand dollars in those days was like $2-3million today. I'd never thought about taking it but I got married, and I'd opened a business out in Porirua. I remember talking to one of the guys on the NZRFU during the summer of 1975-76. We had the South African tour coming up and I asked him how I was supposed to keep my business going for three or four months while I was away? He said, 'Joe, don't worry about your business or your wife, that South African tour's the greatest one of all, just go there and get stuck in.' That was the NZRU attitude to player welfare. Out of the blue I got a call from the Glenora Rugby League Club and that's how it happened. None of my team-mates knew what I was doing but I discussed it with my family. I could see that I wasn't going to be playing rugby until I was in my thirties. If I look back now I should have gone to South Africa first and then changed, it would have completed the career. I got a $20,000 signing-on fee, I didn't have to leave New Zealand and I was able to buy a house on a big section near the water in Mission Bay for $36,000. I went from being penniless with a lot of glory behind my name, to giving myself and my family a good start in life.

Andy Leslie: The 1976 one-off Test against Ireland was the only Test I ever played in Wellington. A lot of guys played thinking that if they got injured in that game they wouldn't get to South Africa. In that Test we were not as robust as we could have been.

New Zealand's attempts to win a rugby series in South Africa had been hampered by bad luck, odd selections, costly errors, demanding schedules, conflicting refereeing interpretations and ultimate disappointment. That's not to take anything away from the Springboks, who could always be guaranteed to play with tremendous pride, effective strategy, great power and athleticism, and above all a bloody-minded refusal to lose in front of their passionate fans. From a New Zealand perspective, the tour in 1976 embodied all of those factors, but the greatest of all was an abject frustration and unbreakable belief that they had been short-changed out of at least a share of the series by the officiating. Blaming the referee is an all too common excuse for losing in sport, and there have been plenty of teams visiting New Zealand over the years who have left feeling hard done by. There is no question the All Blacks made a rod for their own backs with mistakes; errant selection, costly fumbles, missed opportunities, poor goal-kicking, and lapses in discipline. For all that, they might well have returned home with a 2-all share, if not an historic series win, were in not for refereeing that was, by the latter stages of the tour, bordering on corrupt. What made it all the more galling was that in their efforts to persuade the All Blacks to tour in the face of mounting opposition, the South African union offered 'neutral' referees for the series, an offer bewilderingly declined by the NZRFU.

The team departed under a cloud, with large scale protest at home, and the threat of a boycott of the upcoming Montreal Olympics not enough to sway the Union and its glib determination that 'sport and politics should not mix'. One match was lost ahead of the first Test, against Western Province, a sad way to mark the great Ian Kirkpatrick's 100th game for his country, and it was soon obvious the loss of Karam and his goal-kicking was going to hurt. Neither of the chosen fullbacks, Kit Fawcett nor Laurie Mains had shown compelling form, but it was still a shock when Otago five-eighth Duncan Robertson was given the job for the first Test in Durban.

Things started promisingly at Kings Park. A cruel bounce in the in-goal denied Andy Leslie, but the All Blacks still got the first try straight after half-time to lead 7-3. The Springboks hit back with brilliant tries to wingers Gerrie Germishuys and Edrich Kranz, and a dropped goal by fullback Ian Robertson, the final score a sobering 16-7.

Tane Norton: Bill Bush and I met one morning for morning tea to discuss whether we should go to South Africa. We'd been told since we were little fellows that South Africa was the country we had to beat. I remember my father saying it, not that he thought I was going to be an All Black, but that's the way we talked at the dinner table. I thought back to what my father had said and I had to go. Later, in 2005, I had the pleasure of sitting for a whole afternoon with Nelson Mandela, and I said to him how I always wanted to play South Africa. He was a lovely man, an unbelievable man. I was president of the NZRU and was in the President's Room at Newlands and they said the President had arrived and they wanted me to meet him. As soon as he arrived everyone swarmed towards him. I stood back against the wall. He pushed through all these people, walked over, put out his hand and said, 'Welcome to South Africa.' We went out on the field to meet the teams. We hung around out there and someone said, 'Excuse me Mr President, we need to clear the field now,' and he said, 'I am not leaving the field until I have seen the haka.' When that was finished I said to him, 'We'd better go now or you'll be catching the kickoff!' When we were sitting there I said to him I had to come to South Africa in 1976 because of what my father had told me and he said, 'No problem.'

Bruce Robertson: I had just finished Teachers' College by the time of the South African tour. I talked to a lecturer there about it and he said the best way to learn about South Africa was to go over and experience it and make my own decisions on what I saw. I felt that was good advice and so I was available to go. Some of us went to places on the tour where no Europeans had been and the impression I got was that there were some very capable people over there who hadn't been given opportunities because of their colour.

While we didn't agree with all the rulings their referees came up with we had to live with them. I found when we played the first Test that they played a similar sort of game to us. They were strong in contact and played a very physical style of rugby. They were good all-round and that was what made it so difficult to win against them.

Andy Leslie: The whole South African thing, when you look at it in hindsight was hard to grasp. One of the things that struck us was that Mauritius was one of the countries who led the protest walkout from the Olympics [in Montreal] yet they had a volleyball or a hockey team touring South Africa while we were there. There was not one player in that side who was pro-apartheid. We thought we were building the bridge.

Bruce Robertson: It was always going to be difficult to win a Test series over there because they had lost to the Lions in 1974. There were some interesting stories. When we arrived they gave us some balls to practise our kicking and goal-kicking and we couldn't even get the ball over the goal in the twenty-two metre area. Laurie Mains went to a session and some of their kickers were there. He borrowed some of their balls and found he could kick them further than the ones they had given us.

Gary Seear (1976-79, 12 Tests, 34 games): I went as a lock and I think the main reason for that was that Andy Haden was still not well liked by the Rugby Union and hadn't quite got back from France. He should have gone to South Africa. It was a tough tour in that there was still a lot of politics behind it. JJ Stewart didn't really want to go, but had to go as coach. He had a great rugby brain but I think politics sometimes got in his way a bit. Andy Leslie as captain did a good job, but as a No.8 he was 6ft 2in and 14.5st and up against Morne du Plessis at 6ft 5in and 16st. My philosophy later was that nothing had changed since the tour in 1976 and that was why I wouldn't play against South Africa for Otago in 1981.

Ian Kirkpatrick: We went to South Africa without a really good goal-kicker after Joe transferred to league. I think there was some sort of a trade-off in the selection. I think JJ wanted Bob Barrell and Eric Watson wanted Laurie Mains. Barrell was clearly our best kicker, even Greg Rowlands should have gone as a goal-kicking first five-eighths or fullback. By the time of the fourth Test it was bloody near my turn to have a kick at goal. Beegee, Sid, they all had goes.

Tane Norton: It was a great country to be touring in, but boy it was a hard place to play. They had big men and top players everywhere you went. It was the same old, same old. We were short of a prop and at one stage Kent Lambert and Bill Bush played nine games in a row. Brad Johnstone got his ribs done and we went out to play Northern Transvaal. Brad's ribs weren't right and we didn't have a spare prop. Frank Oliver, he always called me Maori, said, 'Hey Maori, I played prop with you in a North v South game,' which he had, so he told JJ and they put him in the reserves. Well the game started and Brad came onto the field and after one scrum said, 'I'm not going to make it.' They had this prop Kressence Swanepoel, best prop I've ever seen. He didn't play in the Tests thank goodness. Brad had to go off and Bill said he would go on Brad's side and mark him. I said, 'No don't do that. Stay there and at least we'll only bugger up one side.' But Frank, good as he was, he couldn't handle that fellow. So I said, 'All right, Bill, next scrum you have a go on that side and put Frank on the tighthead.' The same thing happened to Bill and at the next scrum they were both standing on the same side. I was looking at this big bloke and I said, 'Well, I'm not marking him!'

Duncan Robertson: Max Baise, who had refereed no big games since the 1974 tour by the Lions, said to Lin Jaffray and I, 'You boys may as well go home, you haven't got a dog's show. You're never going to win.' I went and coached with the Sharks for a year and became friendly with Ian MacIntosh, who was one of the selectors in 1976, and he told me there was no way the Springboks were going to lose to us.

Ian Kirkpatrick: We should have won that first Test, the bloody ball curving around the goalposts just as Andy Leslie was about to dive on it.

Bryan Williams: They weren't such a great team, but we weren't either. I was asked to play fullback in one of the Test matches and refused. I hadn't played fullback at that stage and I sure as hell wasn't going to go into a Test match not having played the position, and in the end Duncan Robertson played fullback for two of the Tests.

Duncan Robertson: If I had played first five-eighths against South Africa in the first Test, it would have been my seventh successive game there, and that would have been a New Zealand record. But on the Thursday at practice I was told I would be at fullback. I had never played there before. Of course, they said I had played there in the past but the truth was I hadn't. It was doomed to fail.

Sid Going: I wasn't surprised Duncan was named at fullback in South Africa for the first Test because the fullbacks we had weren't playing that well and Duncan was very versatile.

The series was levelled at Bloemfontein, a gritty performance featuring a scorching solo try by Northlander Joe Morgan, an outrageous between the legs pass by Sid Going to set Doug Bruce up for a dropped goal, and a heroic tackle by lock Peter Whiting, who hurled himself at Springbok flanker Boland Coetzee, to deny the Boks a match-winning try at the death. In their next match the All Blacks staged a miraculous comeback from 31-9 down to beat the Quagga-Barbarians in front of 60,000 at Ellis Park, but from there the tour descended into rancour. The following match was lost to Northern Transvaal when the Blue Bulls captain Thys Lourens advised the referee Piet Robbertse in Afrikaans of their plans to reduce their numbers at the next lineout, resulting in a match-winning penalty.

Tane Norton: We went to Bloemfontein for the second Test. You always knew if you were going to be in the team by the way they read out the rooming arrangements, and when they said Norton and Fawcett, I thought, 'I'm a goner.' I just thought I had to take it on the chin. When I got on the bus I thought, 'Here it comes,' and JJ said, 'We've decided to put Fawcett in the team and I want you to keep an eye on him.' I wasn't really listening because all I could think of was I was still in the team.

Sid Going: Joe Morgan played well on tour. It was hard to get balance right through. There was a backline that stood out and said, 'Pick me', in a couple of positions. Fullback was one area we struggled.

Andy Leslie: I remember Peter Whiting tackling Boland Coetzee in the last stages of the second Test to give us a win. Pole was about the only guy who could match them for size. He was big and aggressive too.

Tane Norton: Coetzee was going for the corner and Peter dived full horizontal to put him out. He just cleaned him out. Peter was a good player . . . they got into him in Cape Town and it was pretty brutal. Kirky could handle himself, he gave Morne du Plessis two black eyes.

Duncan Robertson: When we played the Quaggas-Barbarians we were down 9-31. There were nine provincial captains of New Zealand teams playing in that side and we were standing behind the posts and I said, 'Let's run it.' But Andy Leslie said, 'No' because he was scared if we did they would score more points. However, we did run it, and we ran them off their feet to win 32-31. Ian MacIntosh told me that when they saw us run the ball like that their greatest fear was that would be what we did in the remaining Tests. They said we had the best backline ever to come to South Africa and MacIntosh said they chose Klippies Kritzinger, who was an 18-stone flanker, to deny us the ball and to slow the game right down.

The series hinged on the Cape Town Test, and for two members of the team, Ian Kirkpatrick and Bryan Williams, there was an unnerving prequel, when they became trapped in the middle of a street battle between police and coloured protesters. New Zealand also had a crisis at prop and were forced to rush replacement Perry Harris into the team. Springbok prop Johan Strauss pulverised the All Black scrum, while too many handling mistakes and missed shots at goal allowed the Springboks to edge it 15-10. The Boks were better at taking their chances, but the match featured some bizarre refereeing. Going was denied an easy shot at goal after the ball fell over three times, referee Gert Bezuidenhout ruling that forty-two seconds was enough time to complete the kick. Bezuidenhout was less vigilant when the Springbok lock Moaner van Heerden repeatedly raked the head of the trapped Peter Whiting, and there was considerable doubt as to whether the dropped goal by fullback Dawie Snyman went over.

Bryan Williams: Kirky and I, Bob Howitt [journalist] and Ross Wiggins [photographer] went downtown into Cape Town to promote a book that Bob had written called *Rugby Greats*. As we were leaving the bookstore we could sense there was a kerfuffle happening outside. Suddenly someone shouted from behind us 'Run to the right' and for some reason, instead of just heading back into the safety of the store, we ran. Something brushed past my head. It was a rock someone had thrown. It shattered a shop window . . . if it had hit me I don't think I'd be here today. We ran to the right, and found ourselves running into this wall of tear gas . . . our eyes were streaming, we couldn't breathe. Eventually we came across this police van and we started beating on the door . . . 'What do you want?' they yelled at us, 'You can't come in here, we are working.' We told them we were with the All Blacks so they let us in . . . Ross could hardly breathe and his eyes were streaming, but he kept taking photos. We got out eventually but got separated. I ended up in a shop for half an hour, until the shop owner said, 'Look, this fellow here will take you back to your hotel.' I had to get back for training . . . it was the Thursday before the third Test . . . a vital Test, it was one-all in the series. I climbed into a van with this guy and he said to me 'Don't you worry, any trouble I've got this' . . . and he pulled out a pistol! After all that I had to train and try and get ready for a Test match . . . I was pretty shaken up.

Andy Leslie: In the third Test we were terribly unlucky. There was a dropped goal awarded that definitely missed.

Bryan Williams: That third Test was when Moaner van Heerden did his stuff. What he did to Peter Whiting was shocking. Peter was a big influence on the lineouts, he was our main ball winner so if they could knobble him they were going to take out a big part of our game.

Ian Kirkpatrick: In the third Test Morne du Plessis kicked Sid fair in the back. That was blatant dirty play and dangerous. When we went to Johannesburg for the last Test it was going to be all on. We had a lineout ploy where I was a dummy jumper. Du Plessis pushed me and normally you warn them, but not this time, I just went and whacked him and got him in the temple. He went down in a heap and for a minute I thought I'd killed him. The referee never saw which was just as well. Then there was that Moaner van Heerden. We played him about five times on the tour. He would hit you from behind and then run on. He did it to me every time we played against him, and in the fourth Test we ended up in a scuffle. I called him something he wouldn't understand being an Afrikaner, and he tried to give me a Liverpool kiss. He missed, but I thought, 'Right.' He tried to run away but I went after him. And that's when Grant Batty came right across the ground. De Klerk came at me and I looked around and thought, 'A man's in a spot of bother here.' But Kent Lambert stepped in and got him fair in the jaw. It all happened pretty quickly but sorted a few things out. The third Test was a bit like 1970, it just didn't happen for us. Sid was having a shot at goal, and the ball kept falling over so the ref told him he had had enough time and called up a scrum.

In between the third and fourth Tests another tour match was lost, to Orange Free State, and only a series-levelling win at Ellis Park could save the tour from failure.

That finale at Ellis Park was a torrid affair, featuring an all-in brawl after the All Blacks decided they'd had enough of van Heerden. In their desperate attempts to square the ledger the All Blacks twice had strong claims for a penalty try turned down, and in the end the Springboks held on to win by one point, and take a brutal, highly controversial series 3-1. There is no question that there were serious deficiencies with this All Black team, most notably their lack of a dependable goal-kicker. But they also suffered some outrageous fortune, to the point where even some South African observers regarded the fourth Test victory in particular, as a hollow one. The tour sparked a ruinous boycott by African nations of the Olympic Games, and many New Zealanders who had stood firm in their support for the tour were left wondering if it had been worth it.

Bryan Williams: In the fourth Test there were two incidents involving Bruce Robertson that under normal circumstances you'd award a penalty try, certainly one of them, and then the last penalty when Billy Bush was moving about but had no influence on what was happening with the lineout . . . he was penalised and Gerald Bosch kicked the goal.

Bruce Robertson: The penalties in the fourth Test were frustrating. One of them should

Kevin Everleigh looks to outflank Klippies Kritzinger during the fourth Test in 1976, while Joe Morgan trails in support. *Peter Bush*

have been a penalty try at least and you were left with the feeling if he wasn't going to worry about that what was he going to worry about?

Ian Kirkpatrick: That bloody referee. I reckon we were 15 points better than them on the day, but there were two penalty tries he didn't give us. South Africa had offered us neutral referees but the NZRU said no. Mind you, if they got someone over there they would probably have gotten into him anyway. We heard a story from one of the players on the 1968 Lions tour of South Africa where Danie Craven had been sighted coming out of the referee's room and was followed by the referee looking white as a sheet because Craven had got stuck into him. We were a better side but we just couldn't beat them. We got the odd penalty but we never got them over.

Duncan Robertson: The refereeing was the worst I've ever seen. When you played a Wednesday game and went to ground, you curled yourself up in the foetal position and put your hands over your head to try and protect yourself. They were quite brutal in their approach and they saw it as their job to try and keep players out of the Test matches.

Tane Norton: We didn't get the selections right, especially in the front row where it's imperative you get the right guys. After Brad Johnstone went home they buggered around. They couldn't get Greg Denholm from Auckland, he should have come. John Ashworth should have come but in the end they got Perry Harris from Manawatu, and when Perry came in, it was hard work, they got into him.

Sid Going: Beegee and Batts were important to us. It was a shame Batts got hurt on that tour because that combination was brilliant. Batts looked for work and he could be all over the paddock. It didn't matter what the size of the opposition was, he would make his presence felt. And Beegee was the guy you could give the ball with a bit of space and you knew he could score a try.

Tane Norton: Sid was an amazing man. His knees were as wobbly as all hell on that tour and I don't know how he got through. He was always a hard person to mark. I played against him in a Northern Maoris v Southern Maoris game in Whangarei. I actually went and stayed with Sid for the game. Going into Whangarei for the game I said to him, 'Don't come around the front of the lineout.' Well, halfway through the game he tried to whizz round the front of the lineout and I stuck out a hand and got him right across the mouth and gave him a big fat lip. We went home and Colleen, his wife, said to me, 'You dirty so and so,' and she put out dinner for Sid and all the kids, but none for me.'

Bryan Williams: Unbelievably the referee, Gert Bezuidenhout, decided to come to the airport and farewell us at the end of the tour. The boys surrounded him and were demanding to know why he'd not awarded us a penalty try in the last Test. He said, 'Boys it's all right for you, you can go home now, I have to live here!' It was terribly frustrating, especially for Sid, Kirky and I who'd been there in 1970, to have those decisions cost you the chance of at least tying the series.

As one All Black team arrived home, another was preparing to leave.

A nine-match tour of Argentina was to prove an invaluable building block for an All Black resurgence. Coached by Jack Gleeson, and captained by Graham Mourie, the team featured only four players with international experience and the tour, which culminated in two unofficial 'Test' matches, earmarked players such as Mourie, Stu Wilson, Doug Rollerson and Mark Taylor for future reference as well as relaunching Andy Haden's career. It proved a rugged challenge, with some hair-raising experiences on and off the field, but both 'Test' matches were won and some optimism restored after the lows of South Africa.

Graham Mourie (1976-82, 21 Tests, 61 games): I think Argentina was a bit of a voyage of exploration. At that stage very little was known about them. I think the English team had picked up 'bajada' off them three or four years before. They had run Wales pretty close in a Test at Cardiff Arms. Because it was a young team, Jack Gleeson and Ron Don ran a pretty good ship in the sense that it was enjoyable and challenging, but at the same time it was a lot of fun.

Andy Haden: We had a fantastic tour to Argentina, it was like light and dark in comparison to 1972-73. I had just come back from France when the team went to South Africa and we were 'the others' if you like. One of the things I was disappointed about at the time was that we were playing the best Argentina had to offer as players, but New Zealand (Rugby Union) didn't feel they were worthy of Test status. That always rankled with me. We were playing clubs that had been in existence for up to 100 years. We felt we were undervaluing their efforts and being asked to look down on them. We were representing our country and they were playing for theirs. Not making them Tests was very condescending.

Stuart Wilson (1976-83, 34 Tests, 85 games): It started the relationship between Mourie and Gleeson, captain and coach. We only had two All Blacks – Andy Haden and Ian Stevens who had been on the 1972-73 tour. We had a lot of new guys who hadn't toured so a lot of eyes were opened. We won all the games, won a couple of Tests against the Pumas, but came back thinking a lot of the guys who had been in South Africa would be ahead of us the following year. But that wasn't the case because Jack Gleeson got the coaching nod and that was crucial for a lot of those guys who'd gone to Argentina.

Graham Mourie: The quality of some of the Argentinian players impressed. Hugo Porta, the midfield with Alejandro Travaglini and Daniel Beccar Varela and there were some fantastic scrummagers and they were very good at tight play. We could see there was some talent there. The first 'Test' match was a bit of a battle and in the second we had seen how they played and were fairly dominant in the second international. The first French I ever learned was in Argentina when I asked Andy Haden what the words were to speak to the referee and say 'Excuse me sir, he is dropping his shoulder in the scrum?' It worked because after I said it we got a penalty at the next scrum.

Andy Haden: We played the team that had gone to South Africa in a 'friendly' in March the following year and we whipped them. There was quite a bit on the game. We had far more enthusiasm and energy and lots of players with better skills. The 1976 South African team didn't seem to have the momentum that we were able to generate in Argentina and we appeared to have something of a joy for rugby. It was the energy, enthusiasm of it, a lot of skilled players that were enjoying their rugby. We weren't trying to grind away as we were in 1972 where the enjoyment level just wasn't there.

Graham Mourie: I'd had very little to do with Jack [Gleeson]. Obviously he had control of the 1972-73 internal tours and was overlooked for the tour to Britain between. I got to know him very well and had a huge admiration for him as a manager of men. He was a very good back coach, a good selector and on top of that he was good with people. He was logical, consistent and talked things through with people and was very much what I would see as a good coach with a sound tactical knowledge and an ability to talk through and get the best out of the players.

TWENTY-THREE

DESPERATE MEASURES

'I wake up every morning and can't believe I've ever been an All Black'

IT'S UNLIKELY ANY New Zealand team had performed an act as desperate as packing a three-man scrum in a Test match. But that's what it came down to, as the All Blacks fought to save the Lions series of 1977. The Lions had their own problems with unfavourable media coverage, an over-reliance on forward power and the misfortune to strike one of the wettest winters in New Zealand history.

Game after game was played in mud, occasionally so bad the players became unrecognisable. It didn't help the morale of a team that never gelled in the way the great side of 1971 had done. Yet they nearly stole a share of the series.

The All Blacks were under immense pressure, having lost three major series in seven years. They had a strong core of players, hardened by the South African experience, although Andy Leslie had retired, passing the captaincy onto the durable Canterbury hooker Tane Norton. They had a new coach, well, almost new. JJ Stewart was never going to survive the defeat of 1976 and whilst retained as convener of selectors, Jack Gleeson stepped back into the job he briefly held in 1972. His ability to think outside the square was going to be needed. The Lions suffered a shock defeat to an unfancied NZ Universities team in the days preceding the first Test. Otherwise they appeared solid if not spectacular. Andy Irvine harnessed the Wellington wind to kick a fifty-two-metre penalty to open the scoring in the Test series, but the All Blacks hit back through a typical Sid Going try in which he appeared to contemplate every possible option before powering through the close Lions defence. After the Lions failed to gather a missed penalty attempt by Bryan Williams, prop Brad Johnstone pounced for the All Blacks' second, but three penalty goals by skipper Phil Bennett had the tourists in front nearing half-time. Then came a defining moment of the series. The Lions attacked and looked set to score before a pass was intercepted by Grant Batty, the little All Black winger scampering away as fast as his ailing legs would allow, with prop Graham Price, of all people, threatening, but never quite managing to haul him in. It was Batty's last act in Test rugby, as his knees cried enough. But it proved to be a match-winner, with the second half dour and scoreless. The All Blacks had first blood, and the pressure went back on the Lions.

Tane Norton: I wake up every morning and can't believe I've ever been an All Black. Maybe four million people back then thought the same thing. But to be made captain of the side to play the Lions was something special. I hadn't been captain of Canterbury and yet they made me captain of the All Blacks. You felt the world was on your shoulders, especially when we lost the second Test. You walk down the street, and while it was probably in your imagination, you were thinking to yourself, 'That fellow is looking at me.' Winning that series was so important, especially after being beaten in South Africa. And the Lions were a good side, another good side.

Opposite: Tane Norton leads his side out against Phil Bennett's British and Irish Lions in 1977. *InphoPhotography*

Andy Haden: The 1977 Lions ignored a great backline. Guys like Mike Gibson, Phil Bennett and Andy Irvine were just appendages. They lost the series by not using them. If they had approached that tour like the 1971 tour they would probably have had a good chance.

Bryan Williams: They were forward-oriented. I got the impression Phil Bennett felt the pressure of being captain. He wasn't the most outgoing sort of person. Possibly they got a bit introverted as a result and that reflected in the way they played. I was goal-kicker in those first two Tests. My goal-kicking was erratic at the best of times. I could take the long ones, and frequently I'd put them over, but when you're having to land those clutch kicks from twenty metres to the right of the posts it does weigh on you. One of my kicks hit the upright and Brad [Johnstone] picked it up and scored, so you're allowed to miss a kick like that! Later in the first Test the Lions had the lead and they had a clear overlap on the right. It became very apparent that if they'd drawn and passed the ball it would have been a try. But Batts anticipated what they were doing and went in and intercepted it and just made it to the goal-line with his dicky knee. At that point the game had been in the balance. That was it for Batts, he retired straight after that Test.

Ian Kirkpatrick: For his size Batts was outstanding, so competitive. He had that attitude, and talk about upper body strength. You never wanted to get in a headlock with him either, he could break your neck. It was touch and go in the first Test until he got that intercept. He just made it to the goal-line.

Duncan Robertson: I didn't play for Otago against the Lions but played in the first Test with my ribs strapped up, and I played like that the whole season. My ribs still stick out because they were never fixed. The All Blacks won that Test but in the conditions in Wellington the forwards kept telling me not to run the ball. Then at the post-match discussion we were criticised for not running the ball but no one said anything about that being what the forwards had wanted. I was dropped but later JJ Stewart came up and put his arm around me and said, 'Dunc, we dropped the wrong guy.' But I had had enough and I retired.

The Lions fought back to level the series in an ill-tempered second Test in Christchurch, although the All Blacks almost stole it at the death when Lyn Jaffray couldn't quite gather a loose ball by the posts. That narrow defeat prompted significant changes in the All Black line-up.

Bryan Williams: I missed a penalty from virtually straight in front of the posts in Christchurch. I got too far around on the ball and it just about hit the left-hand corner flag. The week before the Test I'd kicked eight out of nine from all over the place for Ponsonby in a club game.

Sid Going: I knew I would get dropped after the second Test in Christchurch because they blamed me for that. The Christchurch press were onto me because they wanted Lyn Davis at halfback and I guess I was very, very aware of that and I know that I could have scored a try if I had held the ball and run but I passed it and it got mucked up out at second-five. We

Ian Kirkpatrick on the charge against the Lions. *InphoPhotography*

could have won but we didn't and I knew that was my swansong. It was not because of the coaches saying anything to me but because they just didn't even look at me after that. The next game I played was for the Maoris in Auckland. I scored two tries and we just got beaten 19-22. The coach wouldn't look at me, so I knew I wasn't going to be picked.

Bryan Williams: It was a shock to see Sid dropped for the third Test, very sad. I always admired his play, he was amazing, very competitive. He could have played most positions, even in the forwards. He was abrasive, tough, he was skilled, he could run, he could do it all. Colin Farrell had played the first two Tests, which hadn't been a great success, and along with my goal-kicking it made it important to pick a proper goal-kicker and that became Bevan Wilson.

Sid Going: It was a disappointing way to finish, I would sooner have finished on a winning note because I was going to retire at the end of the series and it would have been OK if the replacement was someone who was better than me but for ten years he was my understudy or not even in the hunt. Not that I'm saying anything derogatory against Lyn, we got on well together and were good mates but I still knew I was a better player. And I knew we were going to win that next game no matter who was playing.

Changes in the All Black line-up were made. Sid Going was dropped. In his place came Canterbury's Lyn Davis, whose long, accurate pass would allow the sort of back play Gleeson was demanding, whilst other notable debutants were goal-kicking Otago fullback Bevan Wilson, and at last, flanker Graham Mourie. Gleeson put his stamp on the team. At Carisbrook the response was emphatic. Within a minute Kirkpatrick had scored, and although Willie Duggan had the Lions back on level terms soon after, the All Blacks took control through an Andy Haden try, and pulled away via the boot of Wilson. A coolly taken Bruce Robertson dropped goal iced a 19-7 win.

Bruce Robertson: We were trying to build our attacking play by getting everyone involved. We scored within the first minute in the third Test. We should have thrashed them but we didn't finish our opportunities.

Graham Mourie: I had a fairly long apprenticeship – a year in the NZ Under-21s, three years in the NZ Under-23s. I missed the 1976 All Blacks trials because I had a small operation for a rib problem. Talking to JJ Stewart afterwards he said I probably would have made the tour to South Africa because they could have done with someone like me there as they had quite a few big guys. I was pretty nervous for my first Test. I grew up watching Ian Kirkpatrick and to finish up playing with Ian, who I have had a little bit to do with, not a huge amount, but I certainly had huge respect for him as a player and now have huge respect for him as a man. I wasn't awestruck but I was pretty determined and didn't want to let the team down when I finally pulled the black jersey on.

Bryan Williams: In the third Test we pulled a move early on, and scored from it. We had a drifter move where the centre would drift wide and the winger would come in and take a short pass from the second-five. We'd pulled that move several times in the series and they were expecting it, so this time I came in supposedly to get the ball, but instead we'd decided to move it past me to Bruce [Robertson] and he put in a chip that Kirky scored from. Steve Fenwick was down and ready, all braced to tackle me and got a heck of a shock when the ball never came to me.

Graham Mourie: Ian Kirkpatrick scored in the 54th second. It was a record. The Lions were a bloody good forward pack and we were relatively young and inexperienced. We did have an edge in the backs with Bill Osborne and Bruce Robertson in the midfield, Beegee on the wing, and Brian Ford from the third Test and Bevan Wilson at fullback.

The final Test was played on a rare fine day for that winter, in front of a sell-out crowd at Eden Park. A try, conversion and penalty goal to Scotland scrum-half Doug Morgan had the Lions in front at half-time 9-3. Their forwards troubled the All Blacks at scrum time. Finally, in desperation, during a period when prop John McEldowney was being replaced, a three-man scrum was called, as a means of getting the ball in and out as quickly as possible. Wilson closed the gap with a penalty goal, and five minutes from time the series was decided. Having almost been sawn in half by one Bill Osborne tackle, Phil Bennett then failed to find touch at a crucial moment. His kick was fielded by Osborne who pumped it high into the sunshine and then made a perfectly-timed crash tackle as Steve Fenwick fielded the kick. Fenwick threw a hospital pass to Morgan who was duly hit by Mourie, the ball jolting free and into the arms of All Black No.8 Lawrie Knight, who ran fifteen metres to the corner. There was time for one last charge from a scrum by Duggan and it took strong arms and indomitable will to prevent the powerful Irishman from denying the All Blacks their series victory. It was not the most convincing win, but it was hard earned against a team that was immensely strong up front but lacking the all-round quality of the 1971 and '74 teams. The Lions had not appeared a happy team. Many of the Welsh players were homesick, their coaching parameters were far too limited and players like evergreen Mike Gibson were strangely overlooked.

Tane Norton: The fourth Test is always remembered for the three-man scrum we had. John McEldowney had a crook back and he had to go off. I had no problem with what we did, I'd do it again tomorrow and it'd still work. When McEldowney went off and we had to wait for two or three scrums, there was no way I was going to put Lawrie Knight into the front row against Fran Cotton. I was getting involved in rugby spinal injuries at the time and there was no way. So we put down three men, and the silly buggers put down eight against us and we still won the ball. You just hooked it and it was gone. We packed straight down, the ball went in, and it was out before you knew. It was an embarrassment for the New Zealand public for the All Blacks to be humbled that way, but I wouldn't change what I did.

Ian Kirkpatrick: There had been some talk about a three-man scrum because they were giving us a bit of a hard time in the scrums. JJ Stewart had suggested that if we ever got in the cart at scrum time we should try putting down a three-man scrum. When John McEldowney went off the doctor had to say he wasn't well enough to carry on. That sometimes took a while and while that was happening there was a scrum and Tane looked at me. He said for me to go to prop and I said, 'No way' and pointed to Frank Oliver who had played at prop, but then Lawrie said, 'I'll do it.' We packed a regular scrum and Lawrie's feet just shot up off the ground and Fran Cotton said to him, 'Laddie, it might help if you keep your feet on the ground!' It was after that that we called the three-man scrum.

Bryan Williams: I don't think you could call it a great game. When the All Blacks are forced to put down a three-man scrum something is drastically wrong, but we hung in right to the end and Lawrie Knight got that try so we managed to sneak out of it. Having lost to them in 1971 it was a relief to win the series, some consolation, although again we didn't play particularly well. It wasn't great rugby, but we did what we had to do.

Graham Mourie: My memory was making the tackle that led to Lawrie Knight's try. Bill Osborne had nailed Steve Fenwick when he took a kick just out from the Lions line. He fed Peter Wheeler and I tackled him. The ball popped up to Lawrie who ran the ten metres to score. It was nice to have a role in that try because it was a pretty tight game.

Tane Norton: I'll never forget the end of the fourth Test. To get out of it the way we did with Lawrie Knight scoring that try. But the Lions came back at us. Willie Duggan drove at the line and I'll tell you what, my nose was just about where the ball was and he was that close to scoring. He didn't score, but he was very close. The referee Dave Millar saw it, and then blew full-time. Jeez, I was glad that game was over. It was a great series.

Ian Kirkpatrick: He was a good player, Willie Duggan. There wasn't much in it at the end. But it had got to the point where we couldn't afford to lose another series.

TWENTY-FOUR

GRAND SLAM AT LAST

'It's your responsibility to carry the mantle. There is an enormous
expectation every time the All Blacks take the field to uphold that legacy'

THE ALL BLACKS next headed for France, but not before Jack Gleeson dropped perhaps his biggest bombshell. After 113 matches for his country, 39 Tests, and a New Zealand record sixteen Test tries, Ian Kirkpatrick learned of his non-selection on a bus with his Poverty Bay team-mates. It was an unworthy end to the career of one of New Zealand's finest forwards, a man who had borne the captaincy through one of his team's most difficult periods. Also gone was Tane Norton, who'd at least been able to end his notable career on his own terms. Sid Going hadn't been so lucky.

A team, featuring several new players, saw off a succession of the notorious 'French Selection' XVs, usually stacked with a mix of internationals and up-to-no-gooders, before succumbing to France in a brutal first Test in Toulouse. The All Blacks battled on without prop Gary Knight, a victim of eye gouging, while late in the game Bryan Williams suffered a hip injury that almost proved catastrophic. The All Blacks' response to that defeat was a masterpiece of planning. Gleeson, Mourie, and Kevin Eveleigh devised a strategy to take the game away from the ruthless French forwards, and run them off their feet. The rapid-fire strategy worked a treat in Paris, a 15-3 win highlighted by a superb try by Stu Wilson in his second Test, a long range penalty goal by the Otago No.8 Gary Seear, and a dropped goal by rookie fullback Brian McKechnie, who would go on to feature in more infamous moments as both a rugby and cricket international.

Jack Gleeson: I came back to New Zealand at the end of the Argentinian tour – and, of course, we didn't get the credit where credit was due, because no one knew anything about Argentinian rugby and everyone thought it was just a bloody picnic – I said there and then at a press conference that Mourie would be one of the great New Zealand captains.

Graham Mourie: When I was named captain of the team to France I first saw it on television. They left Kirky out of that side and someone told me later it was to give me a free rein as a young captain. But it would have been good to have him on that tour as he was the sort of guy I would have loved to play with more.

Ian Kirkpatrick: I wanted to go because France was where it had started for me, and I always liked France. I'd hurt my shoulder and probably wasn't playing very well, but I had no inkling they were going to drop me. If I'd gone on that tour I would have called it quits at the end of it. We were playing Counties and there was always a delay before they named the team at about 5pm. The Counties guys were all hoping Andy Dalton was going to make it. I was captain of the Poverty Bay team and was saying a few farewells

Opposite: Bryan Williams breaks down the wing against South West Counties during the 1972 tour of Great Britain. *FotoSport/Photosport NZ*

to the locals. Between the rest of the team getting on the bus and me joining them they named the team. I was the last man on the bus. I walked on and I thought, 'Jeez, these blokes are quiet.' I went down the back of the bus where my brother Colin was sitting and he said, 'By the way, you're not in the team to go to France.' That's how I found out.

Andy Dalton (1977-87, 35 Tests, 58 games): There was a bit of a new broom put through the selection. The team was announced after a game at Counties and Kirky's name was missing. In the excitement of the moment I didn't pick that up. It was a pretty sobering moment. He could have given so much to help Graham. It was a very young, inexperienced side.

Graham Mourie: It was the first dedicated tour to France – games had usually been added onto the tail of longer tours – and it was interesting as the French were reasonably smart about how they organised the trip with plenty of travelling.

Andy Dalton: Early on I learnt an important reason for All Black success. On the bus to the airport I was called down the back, and faced Bryan Williams, Andy Haden, Bruce Robertson, Brad Johnstone and Doug Bruce. I was asked what it meant to me to be an All Black and what I was going to do to help the team? That had an overpowering effect on me. It was that sense of responsibility, that we had this record to protect. Guys like Bryan were very proud of what had been achieved. That lost its way a bit in the '90s, but it's part of it again now, that understanding the history and what it means to a lot of people. It's your responsibility to carry the mantle. There is an enormous expectation every time the All Blacks take the field to uphold that legacy.

Brian McKechnie (10 Tests, 26 games): It was interesting to learn from Jack Gleeson that it had been my game for Southland against the Lions which won me selection in the All Blacks. He had originally come down to see Steven Pokere. Italy proved an interesting opener for the tour. The game was against a President's XV but for all intents and purposes it was Italy. From a playing, and goal-kicking point of view, it was also significant because it was the first time several of us came up against the Adidas rugby balls. I found great difficulty in kicking them. They were directly attributable to the injury suffered by Bevan Wilson. Unfortunately, we were given older balls to practise with. This led to Bevan suffering his thigh injury that had such an effect on his, and ultimately, my tour.

Graham Mourie: In the first Test we were physically well beaten. We had a pretty inexperienced forward pack. Gary Knight made his Test debut, as did hooker John Black and No.8 Gary Seear while in the backs Mark Donaldson, Stu Wilson and Brian McKechnie also played their first Tests. And we lost Beegee with a dislocated hip which didn't help. We had a good look at them and there was a bit of shock therapy because in those days you couldn't get the television coverage and knowledge of the players you were up against. On those tours the first Test was often a voyage into the unknown.

Gary Seear: I'd been to South Africa and had experienced a fair bit of physicality, so

I knew about that side of it, but standing in the tunnel waiting to go out for my first Test against France . . . we were there for about five minutes and here's Gerard Cholley punching the walls. I thought, 'Jeez, so this is Test rugby!'

But the brutality we came across against Wales the following year was worse than what we encountered in France. We could have beaten them in that first Test if we'd kicked our goals.

Andy Haden: The first Test was rough. Gary Knight's eyebrow and eyelash were separated so he couldn't open his eye and the piece of skin with his eyelash was over his eye and he simply couldn't see. They were illegal in so many ways. They probably thought we were on drugs in the second Test there was so much difference between the two. They weren't too worried about the rugby side of it, it was more thuggery than rugby.

Brian McKechnie: The first inkling I had [that he would play fullback] was at training at Bayonne just before the Test team for Toulouse was named. Graham Mourie came up to me and said: 'I think you will be fullback.' The team was named and sure enough I was. The story was spread among French journalists that I played fullback quite regularly for my club. In fact my only other game was a social game. Bevan Wilson discussed positional play with me and while I felt confident enough, I was still unsure. Landing an early penalty goal made me feel that things were not too bad. But I was awakened soon after. Two easy shots from penalties, one from straight in front of the posts and the second, just to the left, missed. I was probably too tense, too nervous. Meanwhile French fly-half Jean-Pierre Romeu was doing to me what Barry John did to Fergie McCormick at Carisbrook in 1971.

Ian Kirkpatrick dives to score under the posts against Australia in 1972. *FotoSport/Photosport NZ*

Stuart Wilson: The French smashed us, manhandled us out of the game, with a lot of illegal tactics too, eye gouging. In the final move of the day Bryan Williams dislocated his hip trying to go over in the corner.

Bryan Williams: I dislocated my hip, which has had quite an effect on my life since. We were down at the time and putting on a lot of pressure to try and get back in front. Bruce Robertson passed me the ball and I took off for the corner. One of the French players dived and hand-tripped me. I ended up with my legs and arms flying all over the place while trying to get to the goal-line. My left knee pounded into the turf pushing the femur out of the socket. The medical staff weren't certain I'd be able to play again, and had I not got the treatment I did at the time it's quite possible I wouldn't have been able to. It affects the blood supply to your leg and your bone.

Brian McKechnie: I was perhaps fortunate that Bevan Wilson was out of the tour and Bryan Williams was injured, because there was no one else to play fullback in the second Test. Had it been in New Zealand, I would no doubt have been replaced.

Graham Mourie: The second Test was a landmark game. We made a decision to play a very fast game and to have them run rather than engage physically with the French pack. Kevin Eveleigh had an idea for short lineouts. We made sure we opened the lineout up and their hooker stepped across in the middle. Once we'd set the gap that removed a lot of interference. It wasn't something that was unknown. It was built around their size and lack of fitness and their desire to engage and beat the shit out of you.

Andy Haden: The main one who came up with the tactical plan was Kevin Eveleigh, and he wasn't even in the Test team. Lawrie Knight and I and hooker Andy Dalton went to a little park with no room at all, on a petanque rink, and worked out how, between Lawrie and I, we would cover Frank Oliver's situation [he played with broken ribs] with lineouts that sped the game up. We said to the other forwards, 'When there is a lineout, you're not in it.' We were dying for them to kick it out so we could use another lineout ploy. It was pretty innovative at that stage.

Andy Dalton: We just kept the ball away from them because we weren't too happy getting into rucks with them. We kept the ball moving and ran them off their feet. We practised those quick lineouts out in the park opposite the hotel. We were chased around by the gendarmes because you're not allowed to kick balls around their parks. The tactics certainly upset their rhythm and they never really got into the game. It was a good win.

Andy Haden: The French said we should never have been allowed to get away with it. The referee [John West] supported our tactic. I could hear what they were saying to him: 'Stop them, it's illegal, it's unfair.' They went in delegations to John West early in the game. When Stu Wilson scored, they were so befuddled by what was happening. Stu ran an angle and no one wanted to chase him.

Stu Wilson: The key thing was the forward pack had to admit we got smashed in the first Test, and it took a bit for guys like Frank Oliver to admit that. We had a week to turn it around, and in that week the brains trust got together and came up with the hit-and-run tactics, everything at speed, move that big French pack around. At half-time we knew we had them beaten because the French boys were blowing like sails in the wind. We'd run them off their feet, with quick lineouts, short lineouts, we didn't piss around in the scrums. As soon as they went down, the ball was in and bang it was out and off again. I thought 'Hell, you can play this way at the top level, and you can change your game completely in seven days.'

Brian McKechnie: I was more relaxed. We knew they would kick, especially when this tactic was used so well in the first Test. Early in the game Roland Bertranne, one of their three-quarters, kicked for touch from the goal-line. I was running across behind the play. Catching the ball, I managed to stop myself sliding over the sideline. On the spur of the moment I decided to drop-kick for goal. Even now, I don't know why I did. It was a great feeling however to see the kick go over. The whole team seemed to lift. It was the best tactically-planned Test I ever played in. It worked perfectly. That was Gleeson at his best. Frank Oliver said to me, 'You will get home and find that everyone will remember that dropped goal and have forgotten about the missed kicks of the first Test.'

Gary Seear: We've always been fitter than the opposition since then. We knew after about twenty minutes we had them. Andy Haden was fluent in French and he told us they were buggered! I had kicked goals before. Bevan Wilson had been injured against Italy and D-Day for him proving his fitness was in the game at Agen. While he played I ended up being the designated kicker and landed two conversions and a penalty goal. My first penalty attempt went astray. The second kick was a conversion right out in front that I missed! Bevan came up and said, 'Hit it like you're kicking from halfway.' The last two were conversions right out in the right-hand corner and I kicked them both. I was a kicker at school and I'd won a few bets for a jug in South Africa at training so kicking wasn't really foreign to me. But in the Test it was on the ten-metre mark so I took it. I didn't feel under too much pressure – when it's a one-off. If you get it, it's a bonus and, of course, the adrenaline was firing!

There was a point during the 1970s when rugby on the other side of the Tasman Sea was in critical care. The tour of the 'Awful Aussies' in 1972 was followed by a humiliating defeat to Tonga the following year, and one outstanding rugby player after another joined the professional ranks of Sydney rugby league. The future looked bleak, but in 1978 came the first signs of an Australian rugby resurgence. The All Blacks won the first two of three Tests in Wellington and Christchurch, before being torn apart at Eden Park in a match famous for the four tries scored by the bearded Wallaby flanker Greg Cornelsen.

Stu Wilson: Australia was starting to flex its muscles, and we knew that if they picked the right guys, picked the right coach, they had enough talent to trouble anyone.

Bryan Williams: I managed to score a try in the first Test. It was a great relief just to be able to run back on the field again, let alone for the All Blacks. I wasn't anywhere near as fit as I needed to be but Jack Gleeson took a punt on me and gave me the opportunity and we won the game.

Gary Seear: The first Test was tight. Ken Wright missed a penalty that could have won the game for them. While we were lining up for it I heard Haden say if this goes over we'll see the selectorial axe! The second Test was at Christchurch. It was wet but we played well. We went to Auckland for the third Test and the team to tour the UK was being named the next day. We were probably thinking a bit more about the tour than the Australians – not to be unfair to the Aussies – it was just one of those golden days for them. Cornelsen had never scored a try for Australia before and never got one again. Had they not won that game it would have been a disastrous tour. So it all hinged on that game for them, more so than it did for us.

Bruce Robertson: In the third Test we relaxed a tad too much and we suffered the consequences. They had good backs, Tony Melrose at first five, Kenny Wright at second and Bill McKid at centre.

Andy Dalton: It was a good wake-up call. We got sat on our backsides. The Aussies wanted it more than us, and everything we tried turned to custard, me included. I remember a long throw over the back of a lineout that turned into another try for Cornelsen. On paper we were stronger but what happened in that game was probably a big factor in setting us up for the Grand Slam.

Bryan Williams: A number of players weren't available. Graham Mourie couldn't play and a couple were rested. Others got an opportunity, like Dick Myers. They played very well that day though. Greg Cornelsen's a bit of a character. He and Grant Batty became very good mates over on the Gold Coast. We were having a beer one night and Batts was having him on, '27 Tests, four tries, all in the one game.' To which I added, 'Yes, and I was in every photo.' It's true, you look at any photo of one of those tries and there I am, in various poses!

Stu Wilson: Cornelsen's four tries were all down my wing. I kept saying to him during the game, 'Mate, what the hell are you doing out here making me look a Charlie on my own deck?' There was quite a good moment in the shed afterwards. Frank Oliver was captain, Mourie missed that series, and Frank said, 'Might be the last time some of us guys are sharing a shower for a while.'

Brian McKechnie: Australia ran the ball from everywhere. Their support play was first-rate. It was one of those days when everything they did had a golden touch. Coming off the field I was bitterly disappointed. My immediate thought was 'there goes the British Isles.' Three of us, John Ashworth, Dick Myers and I missed out [McKechnie and Ashworth subsequently made the team as late replacements]. The non-selection felt like we were blamed individually for the Test loss yet very few had played well.

The Australian hiding was hardly an ideal springboard to an end of year tour that would give the All Blacks another shot at the elusive Grand Slam. Seventy-four years without a Grand Slam was an anomaly. The Springboks had done it three times during the same period. Wales had denied the All Blacks three times, 1905, 1935 and 1953. Scotland twice, in 1924 when they resented the finances of the 1905 visit and England's flouting of the agreed method of issuing an invitation and in 1964 when they drew 0-0, and Ireland due to a foot and mouth outbreak in England in 1967, and a draw in 1973 also upset them. Relations between New Zealand and Wales had always been testy. The increasing desperation of the Welsh to repeat the great feats of their ancestors and New Zealand's equal determination not to let them, led to a fraying of the traditional respect between these two rugby-obsessed nations. If the Murdoch affair of 1972 had been the low point, another came in November of 1978, when the All Blacks stood accused of cheating to win the Test at Cardiff. They'd gone into the Welsh international on course for the Grand Slam, but not unbeaten.

Andy Haden: Bryan Williams, Bruce Robertson and I wanted the [1978] tour to be more enjoyable than what we experienced in 1972-73. Jack Gleeson continued with the mobile game that we had in Argentina in 1976. We won a lot of our games in the last quarter of an hour so we were fitter and we had a completely different mindset to 1972-73 when we were trying to grind out wins. In 1978 we were trying to play attractive rugby.

Brian McKechnie: The balls used in the British Isles were the best I had encountered for my straight-through style of goal-kicking. They held their shape better than those used in New Zealand. Also the same type of ball was used throughout the tour unlike New Zealand where different unions use different types of balls. The first six kicks I struck at Grange Road were probably the best I ever hit. Clive Currie played at fullback against Cardiff. It was while he was lining up his kicks at goal that I first noticed the crowd reaction. Clive took quite some time over his kicks and the crowd became restless and noisy. I made a mental note then of remembering not to linger too long over preparing to kick for goal.

Stu Wilson: We'd started out pretty well, won the first few games and we were travelling really well, getting some unbelievable press. We'd been told the UK media would get into us, but when we started out throwing the ball around, playing a flowing game of rugby, we could still ruck and drive and scrum, but we were playing a brand of rugby that had the UK press and fans thinking, 'This is a bit different, it's not that old dour stuff, it's quite breathtaking' . . . until we got to Munster.

Four days out from the opening Test against Ireland, they fell to a famous defeat by Munster, the first Irish team to beat the All Blacks, a performance engineered by coach Tom Kiernan. The All Blacks were knocked so far off their game they failed to trouble the scoreboard. The leadership used that defeat as a yardstick for what was needed to beat the four Home Unions at a time when rugby in Britain and Ireland was strong. Whilst they were an attacking team, their defence would prove crucial, going through the next ten games without giving up a try. They performed a great escape against the Irish, who'd threatened to at least repeat the draw of 1973, if not the Munster heroics of earlier in the

A great day in Munster rugby, the All Blacks are beaten and fans show their delight to Moss Keane. *Peter Bush*

week. With time up and the score locked at 6-all, scrum-half Mark Donaldson darted around the front of a lineout to put Andy Dalton over for a last-minute winner.

Graham Mourie: The 1978 side had a hell of a lot of good players in it and probably the strength was in the backs. We'd played some good open rugby but were vulnerable. Munster tackled us out of the game. We learnt that we didn't have the complete set of backs able to control the game from first five-eighths.

Andy Dalton: There was a function on the Sunday night at Bunratty Castle where we all got totalled drinking their honey mead! That was before the Munster game on the Tuesday, so our preparation wasn't the best. They got into us, tackled their hearts out. It was fantastic to watch the commitment they had. It didn't matter what we tried, they kept knocking us down.

Andy Haden: We got a similar reception at Munster as we had in Llanelli [in 1972] and we weren't terribly prepared for either. The research that had been done on Munster was that they hadn't beaten anyone that season. Someone sent us a whole dossier on them saying they'd just been to England and played Harlequins and got beaten by 30-odd points and it was along the lines of 'they're not up to much, keep your powder dry for the Test match' which was at the end of that week.

Brian McKechnie: When we arrived at Thomond Park about forty-five minutes before the game, Munster were already changed and ready to play. There was a confident atmosphere in our team of 'we'll win'; it did not feel as it should have done. Even if we had played them for another eighty minutes I still doubt we would have beaten them. Their game was based on marvellous defence. I have never seen a team tackle as they did. The inability to change our tactics proved fatal. They had obviously studied our approach and their plan was to stop us scoring tries. Munster's first try came when first five-eighth Tony Ward cross-kicked perfectly for winger Jimmy Bowen to pick up. I had no angle on him as he ran straight at me. He feinted out, and then cut back infield, beating me easily. Close to the line he passed to flanker Christie Cantillon, who scored. About five minutes later Tony Ward attempted a penalty goal. It was a bad kick. It floated towards the posts. I attempted to take the ball but I was unable to hold it, and lost it forward. From the scrum Ward drop-kicked a goal. Ward drop-kicked another goal in the second half. Their crowd was delirious when the game was finished. Munster didn't miss a crucial tackle. I received a fair share of the blame. Eddie Dunn did too. I know I felt pretty disappointed.

Stu Wilson: Up until Munster I had four or five tries . . . when we got beaten by Munster the whole thing changed. They completely blocked us and our free-flowing style out. They put a wall of men across the park and said, 'try and get through this' . . . and we couldn't.

Jack Gleeson: We learnt at Munster that we were starting to encounter a style of rugby that was to prevent us from running the ball, because, it was obvious from the previous four matches and the video tape which is easily now obtainable, the opposition were able to say 'we've got to stop them in the three-quarters' and so that became their style of rugby. Their rugby became a little predictable, I thought, and every side that we played against seemed to hoist whatever ball they won into the box; and they were kicking away ball they could have been passing. Munster, for instance, never passed the ball once past the fly-half.

Graham Mourie: After Munster we sat down and changed the game plan to become much harder to beat. I always had a philosophy that there's two ways you beat the opposition. In the first four games we operated on scoring more points than the opposition. But from Munster we operated on them scoring less than us. It was just a change in attitude that seemed to work because I don't think we gave away another try until the Scottish Test. We went ten or eleven games without conceding a try.

Bruce Robertson: We said after the Munster game that we were lucky to get zero, and we were. We didn't front on the day. They got stuck into us and we couldn't respond. It made us realise we weren't the perfect team and we had some hard work to do.

Graham Mourie: I think we were a little bit lucky that half the Munster team were in the Test side and they were turned loose for the next twenty-four hours but I think there was a lot of experience in that side and it was a wake-up call for us.

Andy Haden: I think if we had beaten Munster we would have lost the Test. The Test was very close, and they had a decent international side and were playing well. They were quite an experienced side. They were a major threat. The added intensity the loss to Munster gave us was probably the difference.

Andy Dalton: That Ireland Test was one of the toughest I ever played and we were lucky to come away with a win – a draw would not have been an unfair result. But we had a knack of winning in the last minute. I was concerned the ref wouldn't have seen it, because I went over in a pile of bodies in the corner, and there was a bit of controversy as to whether it had been scored. But he was in a very good position to see it. I was confident in my own mind that I had got it down, and the photographs that Bushy [Peter Bush] took, as only he could, proved it. Mark Donaldson ducked round the front of a lineout, and as he was passing it to Brad Johnstone I reached out and took the ball. It might have helped because Brad had a couple of defenders on him. I only had to go about two metres to score, but it felt like fifty.

Gary Seear: The Irish were always terrifically hard, very competitive. I marked Willie Duggan, he was a handful.

Then came the Test in Cardiff and all hell broke loose. The match was played in a feverish atmosphere, Stu Wilson setting the tone with an audacious run back off the opening kick-off. Wales did the early scoring, piling on pressure and earning a succession of penalties for a 9-0 lead, before the All Blacks responded with the game's only try, courtesy of a deft chip by centre Bill Osborne, and the searing pace of Wilson. Into the second half and both sides spent concerted periods on attack, but the All Black defence held firm and Wales' lead was whittled down to two points through Brian McKechnie's boot, an early substitute when fullback Clive Currie retired with a broken jaw.

With a few minutes left the All Blacks forced a lineout near the Welsh twenty-two.

What happened will be fumed over, berated, debated, and in some cases defended as long as there is rugby. The short of it was a penalty against the Welsh lock Geoff Wheel for pushing off the shoulder of his All Black opposite Frank Oliver. The long of it was that Oliver had fallen just a little too easily for a man renowned for standing his ground, whilst a couple of rows back in the theatre, Andy Haden had foregone any sense of subtlety, throwing himself to the turf. Even if he wasn't involved in the penalty, it was Haden's action that detonated anger in the Principality. For Haden, it was 'whatever it takes'. For Wales, it was cheating.

McKechnie stepped up, and kicked the match-winning penalty goal. Three years later McKechnie, in an incredible twist, would be at the centre of another infamous sporting incident, as the NZ cricketer who faced the notorious 'underarm' at the Melbourne Cricket Ground. Like Kiwis with that Chappell brothers stunt, the Welsh have never been able to let that lineout dive go.

Brian McKechnie: On the Thursday before the [Wales] Test Mark Donaldson was hurt and on Friday morning Dave Loveridge came into the Test team. Donaldson then went back into the reserves. I thought to myself then that I could be the next most logical reserve but I did not worry about it because no one said anything to me. The night before the Test, Graham Mourie came up to me in the bar and said: 'You might be in the reserves tomorrow.' After 10am on Saturday, Jack Gleeson finally came to me and said that Mark Donaldson was not going to be risked in the reserves. I was to take his place.

Dave Loveridge (1978-85, 24 Tests, 54 games): Mark pulled out on the Thursday afternoon. I was sitting halfway down the bus on my own [going to the game] and Jack came back and sat down with me. I had a great deal of respect for him, as did all of the players. He was very good at man management and tactically wise. He was a calming influence. I was fortunate that my first game in the All Blacks jersey, and on the tour, was against Cardiff at Cardiff Arms, so that wasn't too bad, but the Test match, and it still happens when you go and watch a Test there now, it sends chills up your back. A lot of people I have been with sitting in the stand say, 'Wasn't the singing awesome?' and I say to them, 'You [should] get out in the middle and having it coming at you from every angle.' It could be quite frightening.

Bryan Williams: The Welsh, in the lead-up to that game were all telling us, 'We're going to beat you.' They really give you stick, but I've always found, once they get over the disappointment, they're great people, but during the game they're pretty keen to take you down.

Andy Haden: All the way through that tour, teams were getting away with using illegal lineout tactics against us. We played three Welsh teams before we played the Test and they were all doing it. I was our main ball winner and most of each game was spent with a Welsh lock draped over my shoulders at lineout time and nobody seemed to get penalised. It was while sitting down waiting for Dave Loveridge to come from the other ground to replace Mark Donaldson on the Thursday before the Test match that we talked about ways to keep them from draping themselves over me. If I got a clear jump at the ball I could probably get it. But, if they obstructed me, it was going to be a battle. That was when Mourie said there had been a game when Ian Eliason marked Colin Meads, Taranaki v King Country, and on three occasions in the game Meads was penalised after Eliason jumped out of the lineout. I had never heard that story. I knew 'Legs' Eliason and Pinetree, and I could picture how that would have unfolded. I sat there thinking about this and then Loveridge turned up and we went on with training. We didn't say, 'That's a good idea' and then go and practise it.

Stuart Wilson: We knew they'd kick deep to start the Test, so we'd put it out and they'd get a lineout on the twenty-two. I was down in that deep corner by the goal-line and I said to Dave Loveridge, 'If it comes to me, just get out of the way,' and he said, 'Just kick it mate', and I said, 'No I'm going to have a crack, just back me up.' I thought, they never chase, they won't be expecting me to run so I just took off, and got to halfway before I got smacked. We only got one try. Billy Osborne put a kick across to the corner. We'd won some quick rucks and their backs were coming up offside. Steve Fenwick might as well have been in a black jersey half the time, and Billy got the ball and was checked. He knew there was room out there. I was waiting out wide and he put this lovely little kick across to the corner. It meant their backs had to turn and I was able to outsprint my marker and the fullback to score. It was a great kick, but it was the forwards who got us going. At the time the Welsh had probably the best pack in the world, and we had to be really good just to get our own ball.

Dave Loveridge: Steve Fenwick took Clive Currie in a legal tackle but it broke his jaw and it brought Brian McKechnie on and we all know what happened in the end. Clive was a good steady fullback and they put a Garryowen up and he got poleaxed in the tackle.

Brian McKechnie: Up 6-0, Wales made it back into All Black territory and Gareth Davies put up the bomb everyone had been expecting from the outset. It arrived at Clive Currie at the same time as Steve Fenwick. Clive took the kick well, but I am not sure if it was Fenwick's tackle, or when Paul Ringer slid in afterwards, that broke his jaw. I do know that all of a sudden up in the stand I was getting out of my tracksuit. I just wanted to get out there quickly.

Gary Seear: The Welsh players were kicking more than the French. It was brutal. It's a funny feeling, playing in a game you sort of know whether you're going to win or lose. Prior to the Test we'd been staying out at Porthcawl. At our team talk, Russ Thomas, the manager spoke, then Jack spoke for a couple of minutes. He looked around the room and said, 'I can see you guys are focused, I've got nothing more to say.' Well 9-0 down after twenty minutes he must have been thinking something a bit different.

Dave Loveridge: I pulled a hamstring just before half-time. I told Graham Mourie and he said I couldn't go off because we had no reserve halfback with all due respect to Eddie Dunn, he was filling in for us. I got it strapped by Brian McKenzie our physio and I played on.

Brian McKechnie: A penalty chance came from a lineout infringement about thirty-one metres out and fifteen metres in. I hit it straight and that made the score 12-10 with twenty minutes still to go. I remember thinking that the final result could rest on a kick at goal as we did not appear likely to score a try.

Andy Dalton: It was just a typical, tight Test match, there was nothing in it. The call was for the ball to go to Frank, but he flew out of the lineout. I mean nobody did that to Frank Oliver. I couldn't believe it. I had no knowledge of what was going on. They say they'd discussed it but I wasn't party to that. I couldn't believe what I was seeing. I stood there thinking, 'Shit, what happened there?'

Andy Haden: The next time I thought about the Ian Eliason trick was when there were one or two minutes remaining and the scoreboard said 12-10. We hadn't been down their end for quite a long time. But there was the chance we were going to get another go at it when we had that lineout. If we couldn't do something there and then we were probably going to lose that game. Doug Bruce was down just outside our twenty-two getting some attention. I went over to Mourie and I said, 'I'm going to do that dive.' He shrugged his shoulders and didn't say 'Don't do it.' There was no pre-meditation other than that discussion at training. I went back to the lineout, went over to Frank and said, 'Frank, this is it mate, we've got to do this now otherwise we are going to go back to our dressing room seats and say, "What more could we have done to win that game?"'

Quittenton [the referee] was on the front of the lineout on our side. He walked along the lineout, round the back and down to the front on the other side while we were lining up to get the ball back in play. When he was on the other side, at the front of the lineout, I was behind the Welsh lineout so he couldn't see me. There were not the big gaps that there are today so that's why I went quite early. When I went out, I heard the whistle before the ball had left Dalton's hand. If you get the pictures and slow it down, you'll find that I was already on the way out of the lineout. I heard the whistle exactly at the time I went.

Dave Loveridge: Andy landed beside me but I didn't even notice him coming out because I was watching the ball at the front. I remember the referee saying, 'Jumping off the shoulder.' He penalised Geoff Wheel. The crowd got quite emotional and booed and I thought, 'What are they going on about?' Andy sat down in the changing room afterwards and said, 'Did you see that?' and I said, 'What?' and he said, 'Me coming out of the lineout.' I said, 'No,' I was just concentrated on the top of the lineout. Then I realised what it was all about.

Graham Mourie: I guess the disappointing thing from the historical perspective is I saw a video later on that was taken directly behind where the referee was standing and he didn't see Andy come out of the lineout. His arm was up for Geoff Wheel jumping off Frank Oliver's shoulder well before he would even have been aware that Andy had moved. It's an historical quirk I guess. It wouldn't be something I would encourage if I was coaching. These things happen on the spur of the moment and on the day Andy said to me as he was wandering to the lineout, 'I'm going to do it.' I didn't have a clue what he was talking about. It had slipped my mind. As I said, I don't think it was the reason for the penalty. But in terms of the ethics and the sportsmanship I suppose it goes back to the 1905 Deans incident doesn't it? It probably squares it off.

Brian McKechnie: I did not see what happened. All I remember was the lineout being re-taken. Then the referee blew his whistle at the second throw-in and ran out to the fifteen-metre line to give us a penalty. My immediate thought was: 'The best thing to do is get up there and take the kick as quickly as possible.' When I arrived at the mark the ball was not there. I told myself to relax. I remember getting my mark ready and willing myself to do as well as I could. I was confident I could land it because I had struck every other kick well. As soon as I hit it, I knew from the way it felt on my boot that I had kicked the goal. I started running back before the touch judges had raised their flags. I had a great feeling of relief.

Dave Loveridge: I stood straight behind the Colt [McKechnie] when he took the kick and he didn't take any longer, he didn't seem too fussed about it. He went through his normal routine which didn't take long in those days. As soon as he kicked it, he turned with his fist in the air, and I started running back too before the ball even got halfway, you knew it was there. But we still had a few minutes to go in the Test so we hadn't won it at that stage. I think we still believed we could win the game and like all All Black teams, you never give up.

Jack Gleeson: Brian did magnificently. A lot of other men might have panicked. But he's a Test [sic] cricketer and I felt confident when he stepped up to take that kick that it was going to decide the game. I watched McKechnie rather than the ball and knew from his reaction that his kick had gone over. I think he was commendably cool.

Brian McKechnie: When Graham Mourie disclosed in his book that he had suggested a diving tactic used once by Taranaki lock Ian Eliason to Andy Haden before the Test, it came as a complete surprise to me. I'm glad I did not know about it at the time. To me, putting that kick over was one of the highlights of my career, but knowing Graham planted the idea for the lineout controversy in Andy's mind has detracted somewhat from my memories.

Andy Haden: I said in the dressing shed that it mightn't be a bad idea if I took Clive Currie back down to our hotel at Porthcawl and missed the dinner. Russ [manager Russ Thomas] agreed. At that stage not a lot of people knew what had happened. I went back with Clive. In reception there was one of those old-fashioned switchboards with about ten lines plugged in. There were about ten lights all lit up across the board and the girl behind reception said, 'Oh Mr Haden, all those calls are for you.' I swung my backside up onto the counter and leant over, pulled them out and said, 'They're going to be asking the same question in fifty years, don't worry about it.' I think Gareth Edwards summed it up that the worst thing about it was that they didn't think of it. He used to run from the base of the scrum pretending that he had the ball up his jersey or behind his camouflage to try and draw a loose forward offside and got quite numerous penalties doing it. He said he didn't see a lot of difference between what he used to do and what I did.

Andy Haden: In those years not a lot of thought went into the lineouts. There was a little bit of strategy but not much. It was very unsophisticated. I felt that with some study it could be an area where we could gain some advantage. It was happening with scrummaging so why not lineouts? Most of the coaches I had had five words for the lineout, 'Go and do your lineouts.' They left it to us to sort out.

It became an area of expertise for me and I wanted to perfect it as much as I could. Since then there have only been four lineouts that have been talked about by people in the same way that they might remember tries or tackles or scrums. Interestingly, I had an involvement in each.

They were the second Test against France in 1977, the Wales Test in 1978, the 2011 World Cup final, and the 2015 Test against South Africa at Johannesburg. The last two came about after a tongue-in-cheek comment I made about Steve Hansen not being a forward coach at a stage when the All Blacks forwards were not going well. When he talked with Joe Stanley about my comments, Joe, who knew how fastidious I had been about lineout play for Ponsonby, Auckland and the All Blacks, said he should talk to me. So we met and Steve asked if I had any ideas about improving the forwards?

I said to him that an idea I had for an attacking lineout had about a dozen variations that could be used. I used to think about lineouts all the time. There weren't many others doing that, and what I said to Hansen was that if you come up with innovative tactics you can exploit the circumstance that surrounds the lineout.

I explained the move that saw Tony Woodcock score in the 2011 World Cup. But I said there were three key things about it: He shouldn't use it until it was absolutely necessary, he shouldn't practise it because if he did it would get out and, thirdly, once it was done, pretend it was a mistake because it could be used again.

And I was delighted that when times were desperate at Ellis Park in 2015 they used a variation of it which saw Richie McCaw score the try.

Laurie Mains had also called me to have a look at the lineout before the third Test against the Lions in 1993. The All Blacks had been hammered in the second Test and he asked me if I had any thoughts. I went to training and at the end Laurie asked what I thought and I said, 'Don't kick the ball out, make them kick it out and at least you will be able to have the throw-in.'

Leaving the Welsh to fume, the All Blacks headed back to England, for more tour matches and a messy win over a below-par England at Twickenham, before heading to Edinburgh to try and secure the coveted Grand Slam. The Test at Murrayfield was a pulsating encounter in which Scotland threatened to thwart the All Blacks. It was already gloomy when play kicked off at 2.10 (when concerns were raised about the visibility the Scotland Union's response was to bring the kick-off forward by five minutes!), and the match ended in near darkness. Those who could see the action witnessed a tremendous finish. Scotland took an early lead through a try by Bruce Hay, the first conceded since the Munster game, but a Gary Seear try and the boot of McKechnie had the All Blacks in front by three with full-time approaching. Scotland launched a defiant bid, and with time almost up, Ian McGeechan set himself for a dropped goal to tie the scores and deny the All Blacks their prize. Doug Bruce raced up to block the kick. Bruce Robertson, the All Black centre, toed the ball into the darkness then outsprinted his Scottish opposite Jim Renwick to make the touchdown. New Zealand, at last, had its Grand Slam. The job wasn't quite done, although it might have been better for all concerned had the tour ended there. Two more games remained in Wales, the first against Bridgend captained by JPR Williams. Williams had his cheek opened up by the sprigs of All Black prop John Ashworth. Ashworth claimed he was going for the ball, Williams was adamant he'd been deliberately stamped on. Also in no doubt was the great Welsh fullback's father, Dr Peter Williams, who made his feelings known at the after-match function, prompting a walkout by players from both teams. It was not what the tour needed. The lineout saga in the Cardiff Test aside, the tour had been relatively free of controversy. The tour ended with the traditional Barbarians game at the Arms Park, in which the All Blacks faced an international-laden side including the great French flankers Jean Pierre Rives and Jean Claude Skrela. The match was a cracking spectacle, featuring the 66th and final try in the great All Black career of Bryan Williams, a try that saw the All Blacks out to a 15-7 lead, before the Barbarians came back to snatch the lead through a Phil Bennett penalty goal. But this All Black team had an uncanny ability to win in the dying seconds. They had done it against Ireland and Wales, they had only sealed their win over Scotland right on full-time and against the Barbarians, they did it again, this time through a dropped goal by their young fly-half Eddie Dunn. Despite the controversies of the Wales and Bridgend games, and the loss to Munster, it had been a highly-successful tour.

Jack Gleeson: We sensed England selected their side wrongly. We worked on their selection weakness and it paid off. We concentrated on the scrum; we knew we must beat them at the lineout because in our mind, [John] Scott wasn't a middle of the lineout man and Billy's [Beaumont] only a number three. So, they were beaten at the lineout, and at the scrum because you can't switch a loosehead to a tighthead – they are specialist positions, more so in international rugby – and we were then able to scrummage them into the ground, dominate possession, and, as our chaps have said, that was the easiest of the internationals up front. That enabled our men to run around and be mobile because their energy was not sapped.

Brian McKechnie: We thought England would have the toughest forward pack but our forwards held control throughout. It was one of those matches you felt you could win by 25-30 points. Our defence was now so strong that the fact we were not conceding tries was becoming a talking point. Our defence was based on pride. 'Pressure and tackle' were Jack Gleeson's favourite words. There are not many players who respond well under pressure and you cannot play well when you are tackled. We had the players to apply pressure. In our team, forwards were pulling off tackles. There is nothing more demoralising for a back than to be caught and tackled by a tight forward. It gave our team extra strength.

Gary Seear: I remember talking to the England winger Mike Slemen . . . he was a terrific winger and he said, 'I'd love to play a game for the All Blacks, because I'd get the ball.' Playing for England he never got it.

Graham Mourie: Against Scotland the weather was the pressure. The Scots weren't a bad team, they had some pretty good players. There was pressure on in the game and I think the chargedown relieved that. If they had kicked that dropped goal it would probably have made it a draw. But it was charged down and we scored at the other end. I guess there's always pressure but we had been away about ten or eleven weeks at that stage and we were a pretty together bunch, united in desire, and I think it was shown right through that tour that we had the ability.

Gary Seear: I remember going up the main street the day before about kick-off time and the lights were on. It was getting dark but I didn't think much about it. Scotland were the only team that really tried to run the ball at us on the tour. I got a try but really it was a pushover. That's all I remember about it. They had a chance at the end to draw the game – McGeechan had a dropped goal attempt and it would have gone straight down the middle, but someone blocked it and we scored down the other end.

Bruce Robertson: It was dark, but I don't think it was as bad as it appeared. You kept your eye on the ball and while you knew it wasn't as bright as if the sun was shining, you could still see. We made sure of the win after Doug Bruce's chargedown and we toed the ball ahead. It was dark enough for Graham to say to Beegee Williams, 'Good try', but it was me who scored.

Brian McKechnie: Bruce Hay ruined our defensive record when, after eight minutes, Ian McGeechan kicked the ball through, and behind, our backs. It should have been kicked out but Doug Bruce's fly-kick failed and the ball was eventually picked up for Hay to go over and score. I kicked one of my longest-ever goals, with the straight-through style, from well over forty metres out. It put us out to 12-6. It was dark for the last thirty minutes. I could only see the ball properly when it was kicked high. I had to rely on the directions the players were running to have any idea where the ball was.

Bryan Williams: I had a bad game; there's been lots of good times, but I take some humour from the bad stories, and in that game I dropped everything that came my way.

It got down to the end of the game and Ian McGeechan had a chance for a dropped goal to draw the match and I had this terrible dread that I was going to cost the team a Grand Slam, but in the end his kick was charged down and we took off.

Bruce Robertson and I and whoever else were chasing and we scored at the other end of the field. It was so dark, Graham Mourie came up to me and he said, 'Beegee, great try, all is forgiven!' and I said, 'Goss, I didn't score it, Bruce did!'

I didn't know it was going to be my last Test. Leslie had given birth to our first child and when I bade them farewell at the airport, when I kissed the baby, I nearly cracked up, and I thought, 'I can't do this anymore.' I'd also gone into a new legal partnership, and so there were a number of factors and I decided it was time to call it a day.

Andy Haden: The manner in which we achieved the Grand Slam was great because we played a lot of good rugby. That was attributable to Gleeson – that was his signature piece, he was very much the architect. We had some very good players but he was very important.

Stu Wilson: There was a bit of an ugly mess when we played Bridgend just before the end of the tour. JPR Williams got stomped on by one of our boys and there were some fairly heated moments at the after-match dinner. JPR's father made a few remarks about us and we decided to quietly get up and leave. Half of the Bridgend team came with us. They came to our bus and apologised.

Andy Dalton: There were a couple of real characters in the Wellington team in the '70s – Twig Sayers and Ian Stephens, and I think Stu Wilson might have picked up a few of his antics from those guys because he certainly blossomed when he came into the All Blacks. He and Dave Loveridge were the entertainment for the team and very, very funny when they got their show together. Those guys were brilliant on tour.

Stu Wilson: Mourie and Gleeson were like father and son. Always on the same level, they never argued. You'd see them sitting together at breakfast but you didn't join them. They would be planning – how to win the next game or who would be playing? You just left them to it.

TWENTY-FIVE

A FRENCH CONNECTION

'I could walk down the main street of any town in New Zealand and pick an All Black forward pack to do the same job I want you guys to do'

SADLY, THE GRAND Slam tour was Jack Gleeson's last. The Feilding taverner with the old-fashioned exterior but progressive mind was struck with cancer, and died in late 1979. Otago's Eric Watson took over. He'd enjoyed success with the NZ Juniors, most notably the side that beat the All Blacks in 1973. France toured New Zealand and the first Test was won comfortably, 23-9 in Christchurch, and after losing midweek to Southland, France were not expected to be up to much in the second Test. But the Eden Park match was played on Bastille Day. The All Blacks had to man the barricades as the French turned on an electrifying performance. Graham Mourie's late try closed it to 24-19, but France were able to celebrate their national day in style, a wonderful Test match.

Graham Mourie: They [France] certainly played very well in the second Test. They turned up on Bastille Day with their backs to the wall. They were inspired in the first half and we clawed our way back into it in the second half. They were a very good side when you look at the quality of players in that team and we know how well the French can play when they are focused.

Andy Haden: We more or less kicked off the French ability to believe that they could do that. We'd beaten them in the first Test and we hadn't prepared well and we didn't apply ourselves well.

Bruce Robertson: The French turned the ball over in midfield and took it to us. When that happens you are still trying to play your best and sticking to what you have trained because if you change in mid-stream then no one knows what you are doing and you get in worse trouble. They had something to play for and we weren't quite as sharp as we should have been and we got a lesson.

Stu Wilson: Half the All Blacks didn't know what Bastille Day was. We mentally just weren't there. We weren't ready for them and we got smashed.

Gary Seear: Try not to play France on Bastille Day. We had a few new players, which certainly didn't help, although we still could have won.

The Bledisloe Cup now holds such a significant place in trans-Tasman rugby that it might be difficult to believe that before 1979, two generations of players never knew what it was. The All Blacks hadn't lost a Test in Australia since 1934 and had last lost a series to

Opposite: Murray Mexted makes a break against the South and South-West during the 1979 tour to England, Scotland and Italy. *Getty Images*

them in 1949 when a 'third XV' were beaten while the All Blacks were in South Africa. When the All Blacks travelled to Sydney in 1979 they were favoured to win. However, a mistake-riddled performance saw the Wallabies cash in. The sight of the massive Bledisloe Cup on a victory lap in front of 33,000 delighted fans signalled a new era in Australian and All Blacks rugby. After forty-seven years, the Bledisloe Cup finally meant something.

Stu Wilson: Australia had come close to bailing out altogether in the mid '70s. That was when we started playing them more regularly. We started having the three-Test series and they started beating us a bit. They brought the crowds back and suddenly you're playing in Sydney in front of full houses.

Andy Dalton: We were watching the Aussies with the Bledisloe Cup – most of us had never even seen it before – and the effort they made in taking the Cup around the field was never forgotten. It was great to see the Cup that we were supposedly playing for, but I don't think any of us ever forgot how much it meant to the Aussies to have it. They stuck it right up us.

Gary Seear: We didn't even know we were playing for the Bledisloe Cup, and then they started doing a lap of honour and we said, 'What's this about?' I can't remember the ref's name [Dick Byers] but he was either a cheat or he just didn't know the laws of the game.

Dave Loveridge: The policy from the Rugby Union was that the XV who played against France couldn't be selected against Argentina. So there were basically two All Black teams although the Tests against Argentina were not official Tests because they weren't members of the IRB. At the time it was a second XV All Black team. I was a reserve for the one-off Test in Australia – the first time I saw the Bledisloe Cup. We thought, 'Hell, that's a big cup' but we didn't know where it had been hiding. I remember thinking it was probably something worth playing for with the size of it.

Graham Mourie: In 1979, having watched Murray Mexted play in France I came back to New Zealand and was pretty convinced he had what was needed. I tried to convince Eric Watson to select him for that Australian tour. But Eric wouldn't. We played a curtain-raiser against Queensland B which might have been about our level, before Wellington v Queensland. I remember sitting next to Eric and saying to him, 'Let's go and watch Mexted.' We got halfway through the game and he turned to me and said: 'You don't think we could bring him into the Test team this week do you?' I said he might have left it a bit late.

Murray Mexted (1979-85, 34 Tests, 72 games): After the 1977 tour of France, Graham stayed behind and played for the Paris University Club. He had some friends who lived in Auch which wasn't far from where I was playing and they invited me over for the weekend. We discussed the lines of running of an openside flanker and a No.8. In those days the traditional No.8 line was running behind the backline in the Brian Lochore-style. We discussed getting numbers to the breakdown and the logic was fairly simplistic, if you get two guys to the breakdown quicker you will win the breakdown area so there was just as much emphasis at that stage as there is today. That narrowed my margins and influenced my style of game from that moment on. I ran harder towards the ball than I had in the past and we decided it was someone else's job to cover any mistakes behind the backline. Mourie wanted me as close to him as possible so that if he got to the breakdown and cleared the ball I could carry it on.

Graham Mourie: I had played in a seven-a-side tournament in France in 1974 with Terry Morrison when I was twenty-one or twenty-two and finished up in a team with Jo Maso, Benoit Dauga, Andy Ripley and Morne du Plessis and all of the stars of world rugby and it was a bit of an experience for me. There was a guy in that team called Jean Le Droff who was a well-known French lock from Auch in the south of France. When I went back to play club rugby there, we had a couple of weeks off and the club officials asked me if I wanted to go and spend a couple of weeks with Jean on his farm. So I went down and he said there was a Kiwi boy playing in a little village a few miles away. I hadn't met Mex at that stage. He turned up and we had a long discussion about loose forward play.

Dave Loveridge: Murray Mexted appeared in that Argentine series and I went on to play the rest of my career with him at No.8. Murray was a great athlete. While he didn't drop goals like Zinzan Brooke, he was more that type of No.8. He was good with the ball in hand and running into spaces but he still did the hard yards and was obviously a good asset in the lineouts too. He was good at the back of the scrum and we built a really good rapport.

Murray Mexted: I had to mark a guy called Gabriel Travaglini, who was an outstanding footballer. He was about 6ft 6in. There was another loose forward called Ernesto Ure who was about the same size and a couple of locks, the Iachetti brothers, who were 6ft 10in. They were big men and then this mercurial No.10, [Hugo Porta] probably one of the best rugby players the world has ever seen, certainly at that stage, and they were the unknown quantity.

At the end of the year the All Blacks had a short tour of England, Scotland and Italy, a side that featured newcomers Murray Mexted, Bernie Fraser and Allan Hewson, a trio of Wellingtonians who were to have a profound effect on New Zealand's play. They lost one game, beaten by a powerful North of England side led by Bill Beaumont at Otley, but the Test against Scotland was comfortably won, and England were edged 10-9 at Twickenham.

Dave Loveridge: Eric took the team to England and Scotland at the end of the year and most of the guys who played Argentina went on the tour.

Graham Mourie: Eric had a style of play built on the Vic Cavanagh forward effort and he pretty much picked his team, and coached them, to play that game. It wasn't a style especially loved by the Aucklanders but I was comfortable that All Black teams could play that type of game pretty well.

Andy Haden: Eric would say, 'I could walk down the main street of any town in New Zealand and pick an All Black forward pack to do the same job I want you guys to do,' and if you thought about it a little bit he wasn't a long way off the mark. That sort of stuff kept our feet on the ground. He wanted a direct approach from the forwards, run and ruck and keep running and rucking and deliver quick ball to the backs. Eric said, 'I don't really want any of you touching the ball, we'll do all the touching of the ball we need out in the backline.' It was very effective. When we did it well there wasn't a team in the world that could match us.

Dave Loveridge: We found out Jack [Gleeson] had died the night before we played in Leicester against Midlands. It was very emotional for all the players who had played under Jack. We went out the next day and played some good football and I remember someone saying, 'We're going to go out and play for Jack today and do him proud' and we came away with a 33-7 win.

Andy Haden: Murray Mexted gave us more lineout options which was good. Having other options, more height and a little bit more athleticism helped a lot. We were struggling a bit, against Scotland. When things weren't going so well we thought 'Right, time to mix it up a bit.'

Dave Loveridge: Murray scored an individual try against Scotland and had to run a few metres for it too, he would probably say fifty metres but it was more like twenty or twenty-five and it showed what good ball-running capabilities he had.

Murray Mexted: My first official Test was at Murrayfield. It was extremely cold. I had trouble getting ball in the lineout. We were very short of ball in the first half. They had some tall players. Andy was our main ball winner but was having trouble. At half-time Andy said, 'Let's try some short lineouts,' which we had never even trained. Between Andy, Andy Dalton and myself we would have two men and Andy [Dalton] would throw

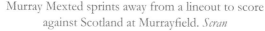

Murray Mexted sprints away from a lineout to score against Scotland at Murrayfield. *Scran*

Eddie Dunn is brought down by Clive Woodward during the 1979
tour match against the Midlands at Leicester's Welford Road. *John Griffiths*

it to the guy that winked at him. Having made up that plan we implemented it. And I scored a try from a short lineout. Andy Haden stepped into the front of the lineout and I was behind. It was called on me. I stepped back and the guy marking me stepped back then I jumped forward, took the ball and ran through and sidestepped [Bruce] Hay, and scored beside the sticks. Stu Wilson scored a good try in that game as well.

Andy Haden: North of England beat us, and that was very similar to Munster, handicapping the Ireland team by making us look at ourselves really quickly after a loss midweek before the Test. You are quite vulnerable playing a lot of guys who are lining up for a Test and in those days we weren't quite as fit and were probably saving ourselves a bit subconsciously and thinking a game ahead, instead of dealing with what was in front of us.

Graham Mourie: In 1979 they [England] picked John Scott instead of Roger Uttley and that would have been a stronger team but whether it would have made any difference to the result I'm not sure.

Dave Loveridge: North Division beat us 21-9 at Otley. Their first five Alan Old had a big hand in that win by nudging the ball around for their big forward pack to beat us up up front. But then in the Test match a week later they played Les Cusworth, who was more of a running first five, and didn't suit them on the day. We were quite happy with that.

Whilst finishing on a strong note, by All Black standards it had not been a vintage decade, their winning per centage in Test matches dropping severely from the eighty-five per cent of the 1960s to sixty per cent in the 1970s.

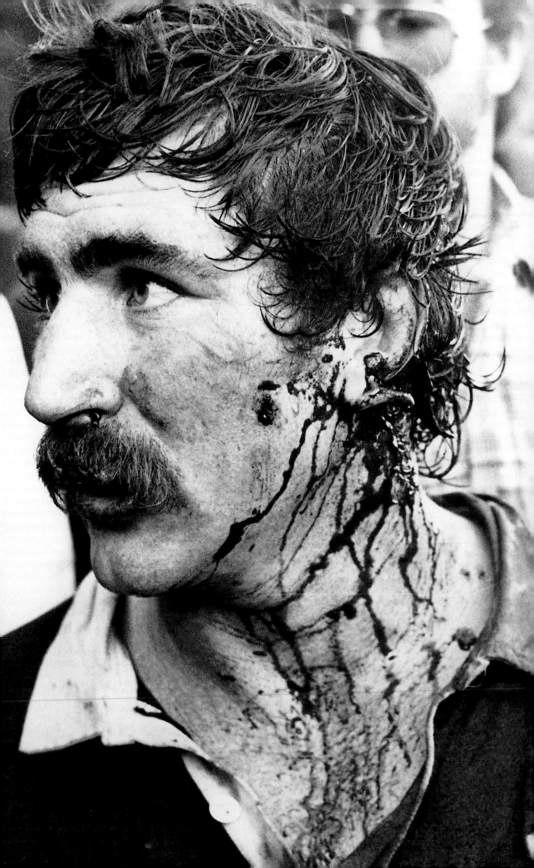

TWENTY-SIX

REACHING A PEAK

'Would Frank Oliver mind diving up here to get the pepper
and could Andy Haden dive up and get the salt after?'

WHEN AUSTRALIAN RUGBY hit hard times in the 1970s, the NZRFU recognised the need for the game to survive and flourish across the Tasman Sea. Early season games between the provincial and state teams of the two countries became common, and Test matches, scheduled with increasing regularity, aided a resuscitation of Australia's fortunes. By 1980 a tour of Australia had become a challenging assignment, the first of the new decade made even more difficult by the unavailability of several leading players through work commitments and injuries. Captain Graham Mourie missed the tour, while for some unfathomable reason, centre Bruce Robertson was left out. Dave Loveridge took over the captaincy. The All Blacks were tipped up in the first Test by the extraordinary Mark Ella. Injuries meant a recall for Robertson before the second Test in Brisbane, the folly of his initial exclusion shown up as he played a lead hand in a spectacular All Black try featuring seven passes between backs and forwards and ending with hooker Hika Reid sprinting up in support to score. That try proved vital in a series-levelling 12-9 win. At a gathering the night before the third Test, several players had a run in with a dodgy plate of oysters, and needed medical intervention to play. It didn't help the New Zealand performance. A 26-10 win meant the Bledisloe Cup stayed in Australia. The team then played for three matches in Fiji. The first, in Lautoka, was called off early as spectators ran onto the pitch to join in a players' brawl. The unofficial Test in Suva was won 30-6, with a hat-trick by Bernie Fraser, the All Blacks' Fijian-born wing. Coach Eric Watson contemplated stepping down but opted to stay on for a notable end of year assignment.

Graham Mourie: We had a tour of Australia in 1980 that I and Andy Dalton didn't go on and which Bruce Robertson wasn't picked for. Andy and I were both farming. Around that time rugby was becoming more of an entertainment and tours were more regular. I'd bought a farm the year before and was told by my bank manager that I couldn't afford to spend over three months away from the farm that tours to Australia and Fiji, and then Wales later, would involve.

Dave Loveridge: All of a sudden we were off to Australia and Eric said to me, 'You're captain.' Obviously the results didn't go that well but it was a great learning curve. It was one of those tours where we were lacking Graham and Andy but it was also the resurgence of Australian rugby. They aren't given enough credit for that. Their forward pack was much better although we matched them. They had some great backs. They've always had good backs but at that time they had some amazing players. There were the Ella brothers, Michael Hawker, Andrew Slack, Brendan Moon and Roger Gould. Mark

Opposite: Bledisloe Cup rugby was becoming a much tougher affair by 1980 as John Ashworth would attest after this ear injury needed stitching. *Peter Bush*

Ella was Australia's version of Nicky Allen. He had great hands and was a great runner. In those days you spent a lot of time with them after games and you got to know them pretty well. They went through a great era starting in the third Test in 1978. We lost the series 2-1 and got smashed in the last Test when we suffered some food poisoning with several of the guys getting injections in their backside on the morning of the game so they could play. It wasn't an excuse but it certainly had an effect. We played pretty well for twenty or thirty minutes then ran out of steam. But you can't take away how well the Aussies played.

Bruce Robertson: I was disappointed I didn't get picked initially for the Australian tour in 1980. Eric Watson was critical of my defence. But then they called me over there as a replacement and when you get that sort of chance it is a case of proving you can do what they think you can't.

Dave Loveridge: Having lost the first Test 9-13 there was heaps of satisfaction when winning the second 12-9, especially with the quality of the try we scored. Hika Reid actually started what was one of the most memorable long-range tries scored by the All Blacks. He gave the ball to me. I luckily got a pass over about two Aussies and Brucie Robertson caught it. He had been called over when Stu Wilson broke his hand, and away he went ghosting his way for about twenty metres before several other guys handled it with Hika taking the final pass to score. You do take satisfaction from tries like that where it's not all just over in a click of a finger, there're a number of passes that have got to be made, guys supporting one another.

Bruce Robertson: What I remember about that try in Brisbane was that we attacked from our own twenty-two and several players handled the ball before Hika scored. It showed we were capable of playing that sort of game.

Dave Loveridge: Most of the team suffered food poisoning in the third Test and they did well to be able to play at all. Sometimes you would make a run and guys couldn't keep up. I wasn't too bad but on the way to the ground some of the guys wanted to be sick, or to go to the toilet. It wasn't great. Then we flew to Fiji for some more games. The game against Nadroga was played at a beautiful ground. It was quite frightening the way it ended with the whole crowd making it onto the ground. We finally got off the ground and hopped onto the bus and away. They ordered us straight onto the bus and said someone else would get our gear and not to worry about it. We went straight back to the hotel but it was sad in a way because we had a wonderful ten days there.

The All Blacks were centre stage for another Home Unions centenary – their great rival Wales. It was a success, both on and off the field, as both nations put the tensions of the 1970s behind them. The All Blacks took on the four clubs who had beaten New Zealand; Cardiff, Llanelli, Swansea and Newport. All four were beaten, Swansea spectacularly 32-0, but the most significant moment came late in the Llanelli game. Lock Graeme Higginson was called out for over-vigorous rucking, and appeared to get his marching orders from referee Alan Hosie. Immediately, Llanelli's Phil Bennett and captain Ray Gravell began to

Referee Alan Hosie sends off Graeme Higginson at Stradey Park,
Llanelli in 1980, Graham Mourie watches on. *Peter Bush*

plead with the referee, knowing that a banishment would reignite all the old controversy.
The referee relented, and the captains, Mourie and Gravell, colluded in their post-match
interviews, saying it had all been a misunderstanding. Maybe it was, but more than likely
the tour was saved by an extraordinary act by the two Welsh players. The Test at Cardiff
turned into an exhibition by an All Black team in irrepressible form. Four superb tries
were scored, the first by Mourie who'd allowed Bruce Robertson to lead the side out in his
100th match for New Zealand. The brilliant young fly-half Nicky Allen was awarded the
second, despite appearing to drop the ball over the line, and Fraser and Reid completed
the rout. But for some average goal-kicking by fullback Doug Rollerson the score would
have blown out beyond 23-3. It was the last match in charge for coach Eric Watson, and
sadly the last for Nicky Allen, who became something of a rugby nomad until his tragic
death following a club match in Australia in 1984.

Graham Mourie: I think the team to America and Wales for the Welsh Centenary would
be the best All Black team I played with. Everyone was available and Nicky Allen, who
had gone over to Australia as a replacement, had done well enough to be picked. Dave

Loveridge, Nicky Allen, Bill Osborne, Bruce Robertson, Bernie Fraser, Stu Wilson and Doug Rollerson were probably as good as any backline. Perhaps Doug wasn't a regular fullback but he was steady. It wasn't a bad forward pack either with Cowboy [Mark Shaw], myself and Mex [Murray Mexted], Andy Haden and Graeme Higginson and Gary Knight, Andy Dalton and John Ashworth. It was probably the first time a number of experienced All Blacks didn't make the Test team.

Dave Loveridge: We played in San Diego and Vancouver before heading to Wales. It wasn't just the centenary Test, it was playing the four earlier games knowing the history was there and they had beaten the All Blacks in the past.

Graham Mourie: There was the small matter of an incident in Llanelli when Graeme Higginson looked like he had been sent off.

Stu Wilson: The referee was going to send him off but Phil Bennett came in and said, 'Don't do that.'

Graham Mourie: Ray Gravell, the captain of Llanelli talked to the ref and I think if you talk to any of the players afterwards they would have confirmed that Graeme Higginson hadn't made contact with any of the Welsh players, he'd actually stumbled over one of the New Zealand players.

Stu Wilson: Of all the places you want to stand and listen to the national anthem you want to do that in Wales. There's 60,000 of them and they can all sing. It still sends shivers down my spine. I used to love going to the Arms Park. It was always a great surface to play on. The two grounds I used to love playing on were Cardiff Arms and Eden Park.

Graham Mourie: From my perspective you always play the game to be in the best team you can be in, and to play the best rugby you can. I think there was probably a bit of a sea change in that Test of how All Blacks teams played the game because it was very much a day where the team had no thought of losing. It was a case of 'Let's get out there guys and be the best we can be. We know we're better than these guys so let's just play some really good rugby.' It was a pleasure and privilege to play in that team because it was a good team showing how well they could play the game.

Murray Mexted: Our win in Wales' Centenary Test was the beginning of Wales going down the levels a bit. At that stage they were recognised as probably being one of the top three teams in the world and their Centennial was a big deal. The Welsh crowd was very optimistic of course and our objective at Cardiff Arms Park was to stop the crowd singing by half-time. We achieved that with what was a wonderful, wonderful performance. We dominated them in all areas but particularly when we started moving the ball. We had some good ball players. Nicky Allen was a fluid player and very clever at making a half-break and with good loose forwards supporting breaks of the advantage line it became quite easy. We beat them 23-3 and in those days that was a hiding. It was a significant victory.

Andy Haden: They gave each of the Welsh teams who had beaten the All Blacks the opportunity for one of them to get another scalp. Five pressure games against Swansea, Llanelli, Cardiff and Newport, plus a Test match, was pretty tough going. In each of those games there was a lot of desperation and when we came to the Test match none of them had managed it.

Dave Loveridge: We ended up playing some pretty good football and had a good win. That backline was a really good attacking backline and very good defensively too. Bill Osborne was really steady in the midfield and had an attacking prowess.

Stu Wilson: Mourie got a great try. I took a couple of defenders with me by cutting back infield and left him with a run to the corner. He never thanked me for it! Typical loose forward!

Graham Mourie: My try was satisfying because we had spent ten, fifteen or twenty minutes attacking and we hadn't quite managed to crack them open. There's a point in any game when you know you're a lot better than the opposition. You know you need to score because if you don't the game could turn. So it was pretty important that we scored at that point. It was disappointing for the Welsh given it was their centenary but they were fortunate that Dougie couldn't convert a goal that day as it would have been a score in the 40s which would have been unprecedented in those days.

Andy Haden: That Centenary Test was one of the best All Black displays I have been involved with. I think the headline in the paper the next day was that the only time Wales looked safe was when New Zealand were kicking for goal. We didn't get many goal kicks but we got a lot of tries. The Welsh were pretty good to me on that tour. They had sort of accepted that what had happened, had happened. The players were much more accepting of it. Alan Martin and Geoff Wheel knew what had happened. They wished they had thought of it. There was a dinner early in the tour where Geoff was speaking and he said in his short post-game speech, 'Would Frank Oliver mind diving up here to get the pepper and could Andy Haden dive up and get the salt after?' They were treating it with a bit of humour.

Murray Mexted: By this time Mark Shaw had come in to join us and we developed a very good combination. You have to have complementary roles in the loose forwards and players have to have different attributes at six, seven and eight – they are very different positions. With Mourie wanting me within two or three metres, Mark, the blindside flanker, who didn't have as much opportunity, needed to make a big impact with less opportunity and that was a thing he was really good at. There wasn't so much ball in hand, but when he had it he had to be destructive, his defence had to be abrasive and he was the perfect man for the job.

TWENTY-SEVEN

THE TOUR FROM HELL

'It was like a war zone . . . wrecked cars, rubble, stones . . . unbelievable.'

SLEEPING DOGS, THE 1977 New Zealand movie that marked the big screen debut of actor Sam Neill, featured scenes that very few Kiwis thought would ever come to pass. Set in the not-too-distant future, the movie featured police in riot gear sent in by a far right-wing Government to deal violently with protestors. The movie was a success, but many Kiwis scoffed at the notion that visored helmets, perspex shields and long batons would ever be needed in their peaceful country. It took only four years to become a reality. In 1981 the NZRFU's determination to continue playing South Africa, and the New Zealand Government's refusal to stop them, finally blew up in the country's face. The National Party Government of Robert Muldoon had promised not to interfere as their predecessors had done in 1973, when the tour cancellation was a factor in the subsequent demise of the Labour administration. On one hand Muldoon urged the NZRFU to cancel the tour, saying he could see, 'Nothing but trouble coming from this . . .' but on the other he would not deny the Springboks entry visas, and claimed to be upholding New Zealanders' rights to make their own choices about where they travelled and who they played sport with. He also saw that support for the tour was high in several marginal electoral seats and that if the tour descended into an issue of law and order they could be crucial in deciding the general election later in the year.

Two notable All Blacks Graham Mourie and Bruce Robertson refused to play the Springboks. After captaining the team to a 2-0 series win over Scotland in June, Mourie announced his unavailability, while Bruce Robertson retired rather than face the South Africans. Thus Robertson's try that sealed a crushing 40-15 win over the Scots at Eden Park was the last act of his magnificent career.

From the moment the Springboks landed in Auckland, the tour was the subject of widespread, sometimes violent, protest. This came to a head with the abandonment of the second match, against Waikato after a group of around 300 protestors stormed Rugby Park to occupy the playing area and instigate a standoff with police wearing their recently acquired riot gear. Then came word of a stolen light plane, and a threat to crash it into the grandstand. The game was called off and Hamilton became a battleground as enraged rugby followers sought retribution on protestors and the media they believed had stirred up the issue. The tour caused unprecedented division throughout the country over whether it should continue. It divided families, communities, and even rugby clubs. Former All Blacks Ken Gray and Bob Burgess marched against the tour, as did future NZ Rugby chief executive Steve Tew. But continue it did. The Springboks sometimes slept in rugby club rooms, and on the odd occasion, at the stadium before games. That they managed to stay competitive to the bitter end was remarkable.

Opposite: A Cessna aircraft is flown low over Eden Park in an attempt to stop the third Test in the 1981 Springbok series. *Colorsport*

In between the first and second Tests a second game was called off, in Timaru, because security at the ground could not be guaranteed. The match in Napier against NZ Maori ended in a 12-all draw thanks to a late dropped goal awarded to Springbok centre Colin Beck that most observers felt had missed.

Graham Mourie: We had two Tests against Scotland, and it was a carry-on from the Welsh tour as both were pretty heavy thumpings. When I made my stand not to play South Africa, one or two players who I could name but I won't, sympathised with me and said they would have liked to have done it themselves but were a little frightened they might not get selected again. There was no flak from the players. I was told by Peter Burke [coach] afterwards that the senior players wanted me back as captain so that was heartening. I had done a lot of research and talked to a lot of people prior to making a decision and my view was that what happened, was what was going to happen. I think Muldoon pretty cynically used the tour as a way to ensure he was re-elected and I think the off-field activities, when you look at what happened in 1969 in Britain and Australia in 1971, it obviously wasn't going to be any better in New Zealand. I was friendly with a number of my ex-University team-mates, and you have got to remember Steve Tew [NZR chief executive] was out there protesting in those days too, so it wasn't people who were anti-rugby. It was something that was deep in the heart of New Zealand's political psyche in those days and I wasn't surprised, just bitterly disappointed, we had to go through it really.

Andy Haden: I remember that the Springboks were exactly what we expected them to be. We knew they were the benchmark for us. It wasn't the Wallabies, it wasn't the Welsh or any of the UK teams, or the French. Unless we could beat them, we couldn't lay claim to being the best. I had protestors painting slogans on my driveway, chanting outside the house, we had police down at the farm sleeping in the woolsheds and haysheds, all the sort of stuff. Largely as a result of being selected for the All Blacks I inherited all that. It was distracting but I doubt if it was any more distracting than sleeping in squash courts in Christchurch or under the stand at Athletic Park. They had their difficulties to overcome and we had ours. After the early game against Waikato was called off, it became a pitched battle on and off the field. The Springboks didn't want to go through all this and go home defeated and we didn't want to fight a rearguard action against the Springboks and lose after all the disruption as well.

Murray Mexted: I knew the Springboks captain Wynand Claasen from my time in France before either of us played international rugby. At one game they made it known to me that the opposing No.8 was a South African so I thought it would be good to chat after the game, but he was an Afrikaner so it was a bit of a struggle. We had a few drinks and a social night but the next time I saw him was in the first Test in 1981 when he was No.8 for the Springboks and I was No.8 for the All Blacks. It was incredible. And we are still friendly. We haven't really discussed the effect of the tour on him and South Africa, perhaps we should have. He was very much a broad-minded and liberal man.

Dave Loveridge: The big thing for the players, and it was the only thing, was that it was South Africa. We'd listened on the radio or watched on TV over the years and I remember going to the game in New Plymouth when they came out in 1965. I think that is still the record crowd at Rugby Park of 37,000. We had toured there in 1970 and 1976 and the competitiveness involved in playing the Springboks was ingrained in a lot of the players. From a rugby point of view it was a huge challenge but in light of what else was going on off-the-field it wasn't one of the most enjoyable tours because of the restrictions.

Andy Dalton: It was a bloody difficult time. There was disappointment that Graham and Bruce weren't available but everyone respected their decision. From my upbringing, the South Africans had always been the ultimate foe to play against, the ultimate test of your ability. The fact my father had played against them [in 1949] had a lot to do with it. I'd always wanted to be an All Black. I wanted to play against South Africa and beat them in a series, ideally in South Africa, because nobody had ever done it before. The protest became as much anti-establishment in my view as it was anti-Springbok. A lot of people in the front-line were there to have a crack at the police. I felt so sorry for the police, some of the things they had to put up with were appalling.

Murray Mexted: The reaction in 1981 was a shock to the system, it definitely split families and friendships. The thing for us players at the time was that it was a huge challenge to play a Springbok team in New Zealand because the All Blacks at that stage and, in fact, for 100 years have wanted to be successful and it's outstanding that we continue to have that same attitude and a lot of other countries don't. Beating the Springboks was going to be a hell of a challenge. We were trying to work out what they were like, what their style was like, where their strengths were, where their weaknesses were. I can truly say the apartheid demonstration factor was removed from my focus, it was going on in the background, we were very, very aware of it. But our prime objective and focus was on the games and that was a wonderful Test series. Some classic things happened during those three matches. But it wasn't good for the country.

Dave Loveridge: I didn't know what real physicality was until I played against them. I'd never played against such huge men. They were big men right through. Flippie van der Merwe was a prop, about 6ft 5in and over 20 stone and he was massive. They were just very, very hard and uncompromising players and that was the biggest shock. When I first got hit by a few of them in tackles, and in rucks, I had never been hit so hard in all my playing days.

Stu Wilson: We saw what happened in Hamilton, I was watching on television in Wellington and I thought, 'Jeez this is trouble.' I knew Muldoon wouldn't cancel the tour . . . it was in too deep. It split the country, and took a long time to heal. It split my family. There was no middle ground, you were either for or against and it was pretty hard for me because I was playing and I had a wife who was anti.

In Christchurch for the first Test, a group of thirty protestors attempted to storm the playing area before the game started on a puggy surface. After twice coming close, the All Blacks had the first try, Mexted and Loveridge working the blindside for Doug Rollerson to score, and then came a second through Stu Wilson, playing at centre and running a brilliant line to slice through for Rollerson to convert and give them a 10-3 lead at the turn around. When Shaw scored a third after more good work by Mexted, the All Blacks looked in control, but a try by Springbok lock Hennie Bekker made for a tense finish, the All Blacks winning 14-9.

Andy Dalton: It was critical to win in Christchurch. With what the country was going through it was a huge driver for us to be successful, and the team was fully committed to doing that. We had to go down to the Burnham Military Camp to train, and then the game was delayed because people threw fish hooks on the ground. Then, to run onto the ground with police all round us, and all that barbed wire, it was totally foreign to what we were used to.

Brian McKechnie: Rooming with winger Bernie Fraser for the first Test I remember him waking up on the windy and wet morning of the game and looking out of the window. 'You might as well prepare yourself to play. Hewie [Allan Hewson] doesn't like this sort of weather.'

Andy Dalton: The thing I remember most was the fact they blew a couple of opportunities which, had they scored, would have made it very difficult for us. We'd all heard about how big these South Africans were. Mark Donaldson had played against them for Manawatu and he said, 'You just don't realise how big these guys are.' Graeme Higginson was jumping at the front of the lineout, and when the first lineout was called to him, he looked over at Hennie Bekker, who was marking him and this guy was about 6ft 9in. Higgy looked at me and shook his head – change the throw.

Stu Wilson: We had three great Test matches. We won in Christchurch. They beat us in Wellington and we lined up in Auckland one apiece. In those days if you could hang up your boots at the end of your career and say I was in the team that beat the Springboks then you'd done pretty well. They were physically of a bigger build than us. They had this prop Flippie van der Merwe – he was about 135 kgs. He sat on Allan Hewson and I thought 'He's going to squash him, Hewie's going to pop.' Gary Knight was our big front rower. We thought he was big at 115kgs, but no he wasn't, not next to them! We knew we'd be fitter than them and a lot of it came down to technique. They were used to playing on hard grounds and when you got them onto a puggy pitch at Lancaster Park you knew they were going to be struggling a bit. But it was still very tough.

Murray Mexted: It was certainly the most physical encounter I'd ever experienced. They were so much bigger than us. It was a confrontation against a team of rugby players who were very physical but it wasn't only their size, it was their attitude towards the game. They are confrontational and they like to confront and to win that encounter. And we do too, so it was a good clash. I think we out-manoeuvred them in that first Test. I think we had a pretty sound game plan on that day, we needed to move them around and we did.

Brian McKechnie: Fortunately the Springboks hardly ran the ball at all because I could see some big holes in our back-line. The South Africans were twice as dangerous running the ball as they were kicking it, in that game. [Naas] Botha did not use his judgment very well in the first Test; the policy seemed to be kick first, regardless of the opportunities available. It was only late in the game when the Springboks ran the ball that they looked dangerous.

Stu Wilson: I got that try and I guess it changed the game. We got our noses in front and got that bit of self-belief. There had been a bit of self-doubt in our boys before that game. We knew we weren't going to win all three games. But we knew if we could get up early and win that first game then they would be chasing us. If we could be even with them going to Eden Park that would be good for us. There was a big fight, everyone knew it was going to happen, but after that it settled down and there was some good football. After that game we took two of their best players, Rob Louw, he was a great player, and Hempies du Toit, out on the town with us.

Rival captains, Wynand Claasen (left) and Andy Dalton (right) run onto Eden Park to decide the controversial 1981 series. *Peter Bush*

We just said, 'Don't bring any Springbok gear with you!' So we took them out and they got back late. I think there was a bus waiting to go to the West Coast. So they both got dropped for the second Test which they won. It backfired on us!

The Springboks roared back into the Test series in Wellington. All Black captain Andy Dalton gave South Africa first use of the wind, a move that backfired as the Boks raced to a 15-0 lead, and while the All Blacks staged a second-half rally, penalties allowed the Springboks to keep them at bay and score a morale-boosting 24-12 victory.

Andy Dalton: We had a terrible build-up to the Wellington Test. Gary Knight had to pull out because he couldn't get anyone to milk his cows. Graeme Higginson did his ankle at training and was out for a few weeks. Because of the security we had to go to the ground at eight or nine in the morning. I've never been so cold in all my life, stuck in those dungeons underneath Athletic Park – a terrible place. They dealt to us. They beat us quite comprehensively. I won the toss and decided to play into the wind. I copped a fair bit from my Wellington team-mates for that.

Murray Mexted: In the second Test they bounced back and there was only one team in that and it wasn't us. They didn't catch us napping, they lifted the bar and what we were doing wasn't satisfactory. The best Test series are those where you get better and better and you learn from the opposition or learn what you have to be able to do to beat the opposition and it's the same today. That's why Test series are so great.

Brian McKechnie: They rocked the All Blacks early, with what was a simple try. Gysie Pienaar provided the extra man from fullback for Gerry Germishuys to score. Botha also had one of those days when he did not miss with a kick. I felt we made a mistake by using short lineouts too soon in the game. Players like Frank Oliver thrive on the hard stuff but with short lineouts they were not getting involved in the physical contact.

As long as rugby is played there will surely never be another Test match like that of 12 September 1981. The decider in Auckland was played amidst the worst scenes of violence in New Zealand since the Queen Street riots during the Great Depression, with pitched battles in the streets, and a small aircraft flying low over Eden Park dropping leaflets, flares and famously, flour bombs, one of which flattened All Black prop Gary Knight. Outside police fought with a protest movement that had been joined by a faction simply there to fight with the law.

The match was an epic. The All Blacks made changes, giving a debut to both lock Gary Whetton and the nimble Southland centre Steven Pokere. Knowing they had to win to emerge from the saga with any credibility, the All Blacks started strongly, fullback Allan Hewson knifing through to set up fellow Wellingtonian Stu Wilson, and when Knight crashed over for New Zealand's second, they had a handy 16-3 lead at the break. But the Springboks again showed unbelievable resilience. Winger Ray Mordt had two tries to close it to 19-18, and then a third, unconverted from out wide by Botha, tied the scores at 22-all. The series looked headed for stalemate, until referee Clive Norling free-kicked the Springbok hooker Cockrell for an early strike at a scrum. In a flash, replacement halfback Mark Donaldson tapped and ran, passing to Rollerson who charged into the back-pedalling Springboks. Another whistle, much to the anger of the Springboks, as Norling deemed they had not been back ten, this time a full penalty. Up stepped Allan Hewson. The slightly-built Wellington man was not everyone's favourite. For all his attacking brilliance he was not the soundest of defenders, and had erred for at least one of the Mordt tries, but this was his moment. From thirty-six metres, and with time almost up, he landed one of the most important goals in New Zealand rugby history, and the series went to the All Blacks. Under unimaginable pressure, the Springboks had done remarkably well to force such a late conclusion. Some of them still bristle over Norling's penalty call, and they were a touch unlucky, but the All Blacks and their hard core fans were happy with the result. Pretty much everyone was happy it was over.

Gary Whetton (1981-91, 58 Tests, 101 games): I was down with Auckland in Invercargill to play Southland and Bryan Craies came along and got the guys together and said, 'Look, just to let you know that I have been told that Gary here is to be in the All Blacks for the second Test, we're just waiting on the press release.' They were chasing hard for 'Filth' [Frank Oliver] to come back from Australia and they brought him into the second Test instead. Greg Burgess got pulled in from the Auckland team at the same time and he played there. They lost so then they called me in for the third Test. It was very strange joining the All Blacks team. I came from nowhere. One and a half years playing for Auckland, 1981 was my first full season. Playing with Andy Haden helped I suppose. It was strange because I hadn't had my blazer game for Auckland and was twenty-one. Some of them were my heroes. They didn't know me. Andy Haden told them to give me a go, I'd be all right. We had the Red Squad surrounding the hotel the whole time because protestors were there 24/7. It was different but I didn't know anything else. All I wanted to do was get through the training runs to get to the Test.

Stu Wilson: We had to get to Eden Park for the third Test about ten o'clock in the morning, maybe earlier. The cops wanted us there early. It was worse for the Boks. Once we got onto the field there was that guy dropping flour bombs out of a plane. At one stage Andy Dalton called us together . . . there was a breakdown or something, and he was talking tactics and all I could think about was that plane. It was getting lower and lower and he's going 'Don't think about the plane, take the plane out of the equation, and I'm thinking 'Don't think about the plane? I could see the colour of the guy's eyes.' And then I started thinking my brother and my mum and dad were in the crowd. This thing was coming in just over the goalposts and it only takes one mistake, or a malfunction, and it's into the crowd. There were also a lot of tennis balls being thrown out of the crowd by protesters. They had sellotape around them and when they landed they burst open and fish hooks flew out. One time I slid to grab the ball and I came up with a fish hook in my leg. The first flour bomb was on my side of the field. I went to pick it up to get rid of it and there was a guy in blue overalls with a big shovel. He was a copper and he just said, 'Leave it', or words to that effect. I said, 'I'm just trying to get it off the field.' And he said, 'Leave it we don't know what it is.' We always knew Hewie was a bit frail on defence but even if he let one in, we knew we'd get two from him. He broke through and gave me the perfect pass, a great pass. He was never greedy. Hewie, Bernie and I reckoned between sixty and eighty per cent of our tries for Wellington came from passes by Hewie.

Andy Dalton: The comment was made, 'It's all right for you forwards, you've got your heads stuck in the ruck, we're looking at this bloody thing coming at us.' It was frightening. I didn't think anyone would get hurt in the process. Other than getting to the ground, that was the biggest drama,

Flour, protest pamphlets and stink bombs were dropped in an effort to disrupt the third Test. *APN Presspix* and this plane flying overhead dropping flour bombs. They were only little things and I thought they weren't going to bother anyone. I just told them: 'Focus.' It was only when one of them hit Gary Knight and felled him – I didn't think a little bag of flour could knock someone over like that. It was while he was lying there covered in flour that I started to realise that this was getting pretty serious. The referee asked us if we wanted to carry on. I was facing the scoreboard and we were leading. So I said, 'If you want to call it off, we're winning,' but Wynand Claassen quite rightly said, 'No, we'd better carry on.' So there's Gary Knight lying there covered in flour and there's water getting poured over him. Clive Norling came over and said, 'Don't put too much water on him, he'll turn to pastry!' Eventually Gary shook his head and came right, but we were all watching the plane after that.

Brian McKechnie: Between the second and third Tests Norling refereed Southland's game against Manawatu in which [Steven] Pokere scored a magnificent try. Norling commented to me as I set up the conversion, 'If he's not in the third Test then there is something wrong.' He was. The team performed well up to half-time, then started to make mistakes. We gave them a couple of tries.

Gary Whetton: Luckily I had some very good players around me who indirectly looked after me. The Springboks targeted me for a start but then they looked at Haden. I marked Louis Moolman, he was into me straight away, smacking and bashing and punching. I did nothing. I just kept on going. Our pack was going well in that first half. Moolman was a hard, physical Afrikaner. He had a big orange beard, orange eyes, like a lion. He was a hard man, didn't really speak English much. The second half dragged because they realised if they were going to hit us they might as well hit us out wide. You had Ray Mordt and Danie Gerber running hard at our 10-stone fullback and so they got on a roll. They were coming back at us, we were hanging in. They scored that try which was when Trapper Loveridge got knocked out so there was a bit of a wait while he got carted off. And then I thought, 'This is my career gone, you play one Test and you lose to the Springboks, you don't come back.' I was standing under the posts waiting for the conversion. I was on that post and it just went to the side. Naas Botha didn't miss too many. It was 22-all and at that stage I would have settled for a draw. Then we got back into it again.

Stu Wilson: Bullet [Mark Donaldson] came on as a replacement and was fresh. We were tired. We got that tap penalty and he took off, it was good, and in the end he managed to crib an extra ten metres and got us well over the halfway line. In fact, he probably cribbed about fifteen metres by the time the ball was put down for the kick. I mean it was a legit penalty – they didn't get back the required ten metres.

Andy Dalton: Hewie was taking the kicks from the right side with his left foot, and Doug from the left side with his right foot. They figured that out themselves and told me it was what they wanted to do. The penalty Hewie put over near the end was pretty near the middle so I wasn't sure who was going to take it. Hewie came up and grabbed the ball, with the confidence that only Hewie could have.

Stu Wilson: It was on that right-hand side, perfect for Hewie's left foot. I knew he'd get it. Andy Haden lined up next to me and said, 'Are you going to chase this Stu?' I said, 'I won't need to.' The only two guys who didn't chase it were Bernie [Fraser] and me . . . it went right down the middle.

Gary Whetton: I never thought Hewie was going to get it. He hit it really well and it went over and I thought, 'Great, we've won – fulltime.' But no, it was play on, the pressure went on again.

Andy Dalton: Hewie slotted it. I couldn't sleep for days after that Test with the adrenaline that was flowing and all the other things that were happening.

It was more relief we had won than anything else. My mindset was that we absolutely had to win because a lot of people had put up with a hell of a lot. You wouldn't want to see the country go through that again.

Murray Mexted: The third Test was probably my most memorable match. It was a huge occasion and we won it in controversial circumstances and Hewie [Allan Hewson] nailed that kick at the end. I've always thought, but I've always had debates with South Africans on this, we deserved to win that game. They scored some great tries but you feel whether you have an edge and I felt we had an edge up front in that game.

Dave Loveridge: If we had lost the third Test, and even though we only won with that late penalty goal, it would have put a whole different perspective on the tour from a players' point of view.

Gary Whetton: Afterwards, I didn't know what it was about, it was a relief, we were all jumping up and down. It wasn't because it was a fantastic win. It was relief. You could feel for the Springboks – it went beyond a game of rugby because of what was hanging on it. Justification that the All Blacks played the Springboks, the Springboks wanted to prove something – 'We are still the best even though all the world hates us.' This only came into my mind later on, I didn't come to all these conclusions then. We sat down in the changing room and it felt great we had won, I felt like I had arrived. I got my jersey, another jersey and guys were swapping some with the Boks. I went to swap with Louis Moolman but he didn't want to. 'No, you guys are cheats, go away.' Some of them took it very hard. They were a really aloof team. There was a north and south to that team.

Stu Wilson: We had to wait in the stadium two or three hours before we were allowed out. Then we could see what had been going on. It was like a war zone . . . wrecked cars, rubble, stones . . . unbelievable. It was an ugly tour. What happened to the country was unimaginable. I didn't think something like that would ever happen. It was horrible. If some of us had known about that before it all started who knows, maybe we'd have been like Mourie and Bruce Robertson and just backed away from it. But once we were in, we couldn't bail out . . . that would have been worse. We thought if we won the series it might help heal the country but it didn't. It didn't heal for years.

TWENTY-EIGHT

BACK IN THE MAINSTREAM

'His job was to soften you up, beat you up, break you up or whatever'

WITHIN A FEW weeks, a reduced All Blacks team were off to France without some leading players who had work commitments. The tour opened with two games in Romania, the second of which was an unofficial Test, won 14-6 in Bucharest. Once again the All Blacks were to face a string of French Selection teams and failed to win two of them, a loss in Grenoble, and a draw in Perpignan, but the Tests were won 13-9 and 18-6 a good finish to a difficult year.

In the early '80s, moves towards professional rugby gathered momentum. Australia led the way as more and more rugby players defected to league and, as in New Zealand, it became harder to get time off work. The 1982 Wallabies arrived without a number of leading players who'd refused selection in protest at the meagre daily allowance. However, they had a wily coach in Bob Dwyer, a brilliant captain in Mark Ella, and unveiled a startling talent in wing David Campese. The All Blacks lured Bill Osborne out of retirement, recalled Wayne Smith, and were expected to be too strong. They were in the first Test, although a late Campese try closed the final score line to a respectable 23-16. Campese again showed off his remarkable talent as the second Test, in Wellington, was won by the Australians 19-16, leaving the series to be decided at Eden Park. Once again New Zealand's biggest stadium became a stage for Allan Hewson. In conditions tailor-made for his running game, the fullback eclipsed the world record for points in a Test, set on the same ground by Fergie McCormick thirteen years earlier. Hewson scored a brilliant try, kicked two conversions, five penalty goals and a dropped goal, his 26 points dominating the 33-18 score line.

Graham Mourie: I injured my hamstring between the end of the rep season and leaving for France. I was sprinting down hills which I did occasionally to try and make myself a little bit quicker than my normal slow pace. I did a little tear in the sheath of my hamstring and got it right again then pulled it in the first training run after a long, long journey to get to Bucharest and down to Constanza. I missed the first two or three games which made it difficult because the team wasn't going well, the game plan wasn't right. I had a difference of opinion with Peter Burke [coach] over how the game should be played. With the support of the senior players we got that sorted out and got some confidence in what we were trying to do. I think on every tour there is always a turning point where the team has to front up. I scored a couple of tries in my first provincial game in France and then, probably not totally recovered, played in the first Test.

Dave Loveridge: Touring France was great. The Selection teams were tough. They would pick a forward-oriented team for one game and then a back-oriented team. We lost a game

Opposite: Andy Haden. *FotoSport/Photosport NZ*

to an Alpes Selection in Grenoble and drew with another Selection side in Perpignan before the first Test. But we won both Test matches, 13-9 and 18-6. It was great to tour in a different environment and for country boys from New Zealand, it was great to see another country and culture.

Gary Whetton: In France in 1981 we left a lot of the old school at home. Mourie came back into the squad. I've had two fantastic captains, Mourie and Dalton, different but similar – lived for the jersey, very methodical, great team people who could get out what was needed. The food was so different. You'd ask for chips and you'd get a bag of crisps, some couldn't eat the food, guys just sat at the hotel. I was lucky. It was Haden again, been there, lived there, knows everyone, so we'd be out on the town and go places, going to restaurants. He would always say, 'Come on GW, come with me.' And away we went, and he knew everyone. He translated for everyone. It was a hard tour – my hardest tours have been France. You play a French Selection team every other game and you might play someone three or four times. His job was to soften you up, beat you up, break you up or whatever. They were hard, physical, sometimes brutal, games. That toughened me up more than anything else. You had to fight back, you fight fire with fire and we pride ourselves on that.

On that tour I realised I had arrived. We used to have a saying in the All Blacks that it was one thing to be an All Black, anyone could do that, it was something else to be a good All Black. And who defines that and who makes that decision? There was a big Manawatu connection in those days and they would have their 'shed meetings'. They were strong, hard men, hard of mind – Mark Donaldson, a hard man in any position, he could have played anywhere, you think of Frank Oliver and he didn't give it away easily and nor did those guys the Shaws, the Knights. We had a big game, it might have been the French Barbarians. We had lost the game before and we had to win. It was a physical game and I got stuck in. There were all sorts of things going on – fights and all, but we needed to win leading into the Test. Back at the hotel I got a tap to go into the Manawatu shed meeting. The boys called me in to their room to have a beer with them, there was about four of them, 'We just want to let you know that you're all right, you're an All Black now.' They had accepted me. Things got a little bit easier. It was a good feeling walking out of there. The first Test in Toulouse was really hard, we got through by one or two points. Typical of the French they panicked. It was a good physical team but they changed it and it was to our advantage. We blew them away in the backs in the second Test, Stuey and the boys ran well.

Graham Mourie: The 1982 Australian team were a team-in-waiting to an extent. In one sense I think it was an All Blacks team that rolled over. We scored four tries winning the first Test and then didn't turn up for the second. I think the instruction to the team prior to the game playing into the wind was, 'Don't pass the ball beyond second five-eighths,' because we knew they were pretty handy out wide. The game plan was for the ball to go to the second five-eighths and then to take it in and come back blind, and just play the blindside – good Wellington windy weather rugby which we were pretty capable of playing. We passed the ball twice from second five-eighths, against the game plan, and believe it or not Australia scored twice. We couldn't come back. While they scored in the first minute of the third Test in Auckland I don't think they got a look-in after that and it was about a 40-pointer.

Gary Whetton: I came back and got dropped. Graeme Higginson had been injured the year before and they said they were playing him. I took that very hard. The All Blacks won the first Test then they lost the second in Wellington with Campese going wild and then they brought me in for the third Test in Auckland when Hewie scored all those points. We played really well.

Murray Mexted: In 1982 it was an opportunity to pick new players who went on for years and years. There were two or three Ella brothers, Mick Martin, their backs were very, very good. It was a changing of the guard, more of an evolution.

Stu Wilson: The Aussies came back in 1982 and taught us a few tricks. The Ella brothers could mesmerise and their passing made us think that we could do that sort of thing with cut out passes and missing guys out. We'd done it with Jack Gleeson and we did it in club rugby but after Jack we had a few coaches who wouldn't allow us to do it. Campo . . . he could run from his own twenty-two and take us on and beat four or five guys. You had to sit back as opposition sometimes and marvel at some of that stuff they were doing. David Campese was not everyone's favourite as a person, but as a rugby player he was gifted. You've got to respect that. He was beating great defenders. He did his goose step – he scorched us. He wouldn't beat one man, he'd beat four. There was some competition in the New Zealand backs too. Robbie Deans was coming through, but Hewie would always get the nod. I felt quite sad that time we ran out onto Lancaster Park and the Christchurch crowd booed Hewie. The guy won a Test series for us, he was a hero, and he was wearing the black jersey. In the final Test at Eden Park he claimed the world record for points in a Test. Hewie loved Eden Park, it was perfect for him, the way the ball just sat up. He could run on it, kick on it.

Dave Loveridge: In 1982 we got the Bledisloe Cup back from Australia. We won the first Test when David Campese made his first appearance against us but they knocked us over at Athletic Park in the second Test 19-16. Then in the third Test I think we kicked the ball out on the full to start the game. There was a scrum, Australia ran it and Roger Gould scored in the first minute. But that was Hewie's day, he scored a try and kicked eight goals for 26 points which broke Fergie McCormick's record of most points in a Test match. That was payback for 1980.

It was the last Test of the year for the All Blacks, and despite the temptation of a Lions visit in 1983, Graham Mourie and Bill Osborne called time on their careers. Osborne had been an outstanding member of an All Black backline seeking a more open game, while Mourie had been a ground-breaking captain, the combination of his strong and skilful all-round game welded to a deep-thinking approach made him an ideal leader for this transitional period in the game. Most importantly he had the respect of a group of experienced, headstrong personalities.

TWENTY-NINE

NEARING A PEAK

'You've got two choices, you can either be here for a weekend and think you've arrived, or you can be here ten years and think you've never arrived'

ANDY DALTON STEPPED up as captain for the Lions tour of 1983, the last four-Test series to be played in NZ. There was minimal change from the previous year, with Ian Dunn and Warwick Taylor following brothers Eddie and Murray into the All Black ranks, and Canterbury flanker Jock Hobbs replacing Mourie. The Lions played six games before the first Test, losing to Auckland, courtesy of a late dropped goal by a young Grant Fox, but their three weeks together gave them an advantage in preparation and the opening international in Christchurch was expected to be close. Ollie Campbell's boot had the Lions in front 9-6 at the break. New Zealand upped the tempo in the second half, going ahead with a try by Mark Shaw, and when Hewson, who'd had the Canterbury crowd on his case for much of the game, landed a forty-five-metre dropped goal near full-time, they were home 16-12. The second Test was notable for a masterful performance by Dave Loveridge. The Taranaki man had developed into one of the finest all-round scrum-halves New Zealand had produced, and all of his skills and acumen were needed as New Zealand defended a nine-nil half-time lead. Loveridge scored the only try in that half, and with the All Blacks facing a strong southerly wind in the second, his ability to direct play, and link with his loose trio, proved the winning of the game. The third Test was played in dreadful conditions in Dunedin. The Lions made a valiant effort on the sodden Carisbrook surface, and tries by winger Roger Baird and centre John Rutherford had them 8-6 up midway through the second half. However, a concerted All Black attack prised an opening for Stu Wilson, who splashed down after a powerful, angled run for his sixteenth Test try, equalling the New Zealand record held by Ian Kirkpatrick. A Hewson penalty goal sealed a 15-8 win, remarkable that for the second straight Test, the All Blacks had not allowed Campbell a penalty shot at goal. The fourth Test was a landslide as the Lions were shorn of confidence, some of their better players, and were powerless against a team firing on all cylinders. Chief beneficiary of the rampant display was Wilson, who scored three of the six tries to take his personal haul in Test rugby to 19, while Hewson added 18 points. The Lions made constant changes, but the All Blacks used only seventeen players and, as in 1966, an unchanged pack in the four Tests. A month later they put a cherry on top of their Lions cake by recording their first win against Australia on the Sydney Cricket Ground in nine years. New Zealand won 18-8.

Andy Dalton: That 1983 team was a side definitely near its peak. A very strong front five, and some real skills out wide, with Stu and Co., and a very confident team coming up against a Lions team that may not have been as well selected as it might have. They

Opposite: Dave Loveridge dive passes against the British and Irish Lions at Eden Park in 1983 as Murray Mexted, Graham Price and Jock Hobbs look on. *InphoPhotography*

had some very good players. Colin Deans is a classic example. He wasn't going to get in ahead of Ciaran Fitzgerald, but he was a tigerish forward, probably a better footballer. John Rutherford was another one who didn't get as much game as I felt he could have. It's a problem with some of those Lions teams, they struggle with selection at times.

Stu Wilson: We were a good team in good nick. We had a lot of older guys, but some good young guys coming through. It's a bit special playing the Lions, because you don't see them that often. To be honest they probably weren't the strongest Lions team ever to come to New Zealand, and by the time they got to Eden Park when we were starting to cut loose, they had nothing left. They had a few internal issues. Ciaran Fitzgerald was the captain, but as a hooker, Colin Deans was probably a better player. And there's always going to be a few issues getting those four countries together.

Warwick Taylor (1983-88, 24 Tests, 40 games): We'd had a trial a couple of weeks before and had some fitness tests and Smithy [Wayne Smith] put his back out, so Ian Dunn got in. He and I were new boys at first and second five-eighths, and Jock Hobbs was run-on flanker for the first time. I got engaged the morning before the first Test. Tracy and I had been going out about five years. I asked the management if it was OK, I got up early, grabbed a taxi and went home. Her Dad was there, he'd come down to see the Test, so I asked his permission, and then asked Tracy. As for the game, I just wanted to defend well, and pass, just do the core jobs. My brother [All Black Murray Taylor] told me the higher you went, the easier it would become because you had such good players around you. I had been pretty damned nervous and was very relieved afterwards as we sneaked a win out of it. At the end of the game I got a tap on the shoulder, it was my brother Ross and he said, 'There's an old bugger up the stand wants to see you' so I went up and saw Dad. Just seeing the look on his face, I was in tears, he was that proud. I remembered that when my son Tom played for the All Blacks, I knew how my Dad felt.

Gary Whetton: They [1983 Lions] never got an opportunity to come to light if I can be blunt. They came over with a lot of expectations and were very up themselves in belief and everything else, what they could do and what they were about, and where New Zealand rugby was. They played Auckland second game, in midweek, and we beat them 10-9, Foxy got a dropped goal which surprised them. Haden and I played and we dominated the lineouts big time. Andy and I played five times against the Lions and were on the winning side each time. They had a hard tour. They weren't a bad side, they had some great players. You didn't win Tests by much in those days. The first Test is always a hard one because we were rusty. The second Test was awesome, that was ten-man, eleven-man rugby when we played in that wind in the second half. We won 9-0. They had Ollie Campbell who could kick goals from anywhere but Trapper Loveridge just ran round the blindside.

Murray Mexted: It was a great series against the British and Irish Lions. They were a good team when they arrived but there's an example of our team getting better progressively throughout that tour. When we started in the first Test we were probably fairly even and we grew more than them by the end of the series.

In rugby the best confrontations are against good teams so there's a very old expression that a good team will always beat a team of good players so I think that even though they are picking from four countries it was the team that came together best that would go on and prevail. I know the two No.8s that I marked, John Beattie and Iain Paxton were outstanding rugby players, they were big men and big athletes, good in the lineout as well as around the field and that was a challenge for me, but what came through in that Test series was that our team was a better team.

Andy Dalton: The description of our front row of myself, John Ashworth and Gary Knight as 'the Geriatics' came in during this series. John Brooks, a reporter from Christchurch, threw that one at us. I was pissed off when he said it. I didn't say anything at the time, but I went back to Gary and John and said, 'These bastards are saying we're over the hill.' We were all pretty fired up, and I might have had a word to John about it after the game, but it stuck, and it probably didn't do us any harm. Those guys were at the top of their game. We had a common background, all coming from farming families, we were similar characters. We totally respected each other and I'll tell you, if you were ever in trouble those would be the first two guys to be at your shoulder to help you out. They were good mates and we were pretty close.

Warwick Taylor: The week before that second Test Canterbury had gone up and played

Andy Dalton throws the ball in during the second Test
at Athletic Park in Wellington. *Getty Images*

Marlborough and I got the 'flu. It was the worst 'flu I'd ever had. I went through about three sheets during the night I was sweating that much, and I couldn't play against Marlborough. I went over to Wellington for the Test and there were about four guys who had the same 'flu, and a couple more the next day, so as well as the wind, we had to deal with quite a few of us who'd been pretty bad. Dave Loveridge had one of those games. He completely dictated how we played into the wind, and again, the forwards played really well.

Murray Mexted: Athletic Park, was open to the southerly and Dave Loveridge had a bit of experience playing there but I had spent my whole life playing into strong winds at Athletic Park and you learn how to play into a wind and to use the short side. Throughout that game I was feeding Trapper on the short side, putting him into a little gap or he would kick it ahead. He was an outstanding rugby player, probably the most balanced No.9 the world had seen at that stage, he didn't have a weakness. He was very quick when he ran with the ball, his pass was beautiful and he was an instinctive player. He had a magnificent game, he was outstanding.

Stu Wilson: The Wellington boys in the team said to Andy Dalton, 'If you win the toss, take the wind. That way you get as many points as you can, and in the second half you just hold on.' You never gave the wind away at Athletic Park, because it could change, and you ended up playing into it both halves. I mean you're going to get every lineout in the second half because the ball's going to blow onto your side, and then it doesn't go further out than nine or ten. It was clinical . . . Mex took it up, Trapper Loveridge controlled it, left to right, right to left, forwards got involved, just moving it two feet at a time and how many points did the Lions get in the second half? None.

Dave Loveridge: It was a real gale. I can remember Allan Hewson marking the ball under the goalposts at the southern end, and in those days you could kick wherever you liked, and he kicked it dead at the other end of the Park. Suddenly the Lions were back on their 22m kicking off into the wind. That's how strong it was, unbelievable. It was all about ball retention or just playing the sidelines. You would kick the ball along the ground and put it out. Then it was difficult for them to throw the ball in straight. Ollie Campbell was their first five and a great goal-kicker but I don't think he had a shot at goal in the second half. That's how we won it, by starving them of the ball and guys not giving penalties away. Murray and I had a huge day, we had to keep it tight, and if the ball went out to first-five I don't think it went much further. We kept it within a very small perimeter and kept the pressure on them. It was nice to score a try but it was a great team effort, one of the great ones, especially in the forwards to lock them out of it.

Andy Dalton: Dave Loveridge was absolutely outstanding – the best halfback game I've ever seen, darting around the rucks he just had the ball on a piece of string. It was fantastic.

Gary Whetton: Jock Hobbs came in after some outstanding seasons for Canterbury. They were holders of the Ranfurly Shield and Jock was a different player to what we'd had at seven with Mourie. He never had Mourie's skill set but he was a worker. He just knew one way and fitted in with a very good pack. Jock was a great team man, and great thinker and talker. The last Test was the only one that blew out, they were demoralised by then but those first three Tests were hard and tough.

Dave Loveridge: The third Test was the diving suit Test. We trained out at Outram on the Thursday and it snowed. Back in town Stu Wilson, Steve Pokere and Hewie and myself walked into this shop and saw these wetsuits so we took them back to the hotel, cut the sleeves off them and wore them. It was just as well we did. After the game we got into the showers and couldn't take our clothes off or undo our boots. We had to get someone to yank our jerseys off and undo our boots. I've played a few games over in England in cold conditions, but that was the coldest I ever played in. John Rutherford played well for the Lions that day and they out-scored us two tries to one.

Warwick Taylor: I remember our first training for the third Test. It was snowing and freezing. I'd lived in Dunedin but had never experienced it that cold. Someone organised for us to get these wet suit vests . . . not thin ones like the ones they developed later, quite thick, and they were fantastic, kept the chill out. I think Hewie wore gloves.

Andy Dalton: Stu Wilson equalled New Zealand's Test-try scoring record in the third Test. He came right back against the run of play as Stu did. I mean it was just incredible how he did it in those conditions it was a great try.

Warwick Taylor: We had a dinner after that Test, my first experience of this in the All Blacks. We were seated, Lion, All Black, Lion, All Black and so on. We were waiting for dinner and they brought out these buns. We didn't touch them for a bit and then all of a sudden a bun got thrown at a group on the other side and then it was all on – a bun fight! And it wasn't All Blacks against Lions, it was mates trying to hit each other with them. Guys were ducking under tables, buns were being thrown at this official dinner and I'm thinking 'What do you do?' Nothing like that ever happened again in my career. Funnily enough it actually brought us together as a group of players, friendships came out of it. There were some really nice guys in that Lions' team and a few I got to know really well. Robbie Ackermann was one and Roger Baird was another.

Andy Dalton: The fourth Test was the first, in fact, the only Test I ever went into knowing we were going to win. It was just the feeling within the team and the way we were going, we were full of confidence. It was very satisfying.

Warwick Taylor: They'd had a pretty hard tour. The weather hadn't been that good for the previous two Tests, and it was much better in Auckland. We had good training, we were playing with a bit more freedom, and just had more confidence in what we were doing. We clicked. We hit them early, put some points on them. They started to come back towards the end and showed their worth but there'd just been a patch where they didn't turn up.

The captains: Ciaran Fitzgerald and Andy Dalton after the fourth Lions Test. *Getty Images*

Dave Loveridge: In Auckland we had a superb surface, a great day and we played some good rugby to not really give them a look-in.

Despite Mourie's retirement there was strong leadership, with senior players having a huge influence on tactics and preparation, perhaps even overshadowing coach Bryce Rope's influence, who nonetheless had five wins from five games in his first year. But things got more difficult for Rope and the All Blacks at the end of the year. A tour to Argentina was called off due to logistical issues in the aftermath of the Falklands War. An eight-match visit to England and Scotland was hastily arranged, only for a raft of top players, including the entire tight five from the Lions series, to declare their unavailability. Stu Wilson captained a side featuring twelve newcomers, including a future captain in David Kirk and Canterbury fan favourite Robbie Deans. Although the first three games were won by reasonable margins, it became clear this under-strength team was going to struggle. London Division was edged 18-15 before a loss to Midland Division in the final game before the opening Test against Scotland. New Zealand had two brilliant tries by Bernie Fraser and one from Jock Hobbs, but with another try and a kickable penalty both reversed after touch judge intervention, Scotland were able to stay in the hunt through the boots of John Rutherford and Peter Dods. In the final moments, after winger Jim Pollock had won the race to a loose ball in the in-goal, Dods had a shot at history, but his wide-angle conversion missed and it ended in a 25-all draw. A very good Scotland team would go on to win the Five Nations that winter. England then saw their chance for a first win over the All Blacks in ten years. A try by lock Maurice Colclough and the unerring boot of Dusty Hare put England in a winning position, and although the All Blacks got one back through prop Murray Davie, England's superior pack held on for a 15-9 victory. For the first time a New

Zealand team returned from a tour to the North without a Test victory. The team bemoaned high penalty counts in almost every game, which they felt stifled attacking rugby. Wilson's appointment as captain had not been a success and, with his retirement, it was hardly a fitting end to the career of such a popular and brilliant player.

David Kirk (1983-87, 17 Tests, 34 games): Being first selected for the All Blacks is one of the highlights of my life. I remember the season in the lead-up to it because there was quite a lot of competition. Dave Loveridge was injured and wasn't going on the tour to Scotland and England at the end so those of us in the next rank were all competing. There was a feeling of joy at being selected, I didn't find it unbelievable, I just found it, 'Wow' and overwhelmed really. It was quite an unusual tour. The All Blacks had won against the British and Irish Lions but then just about all of the forward pack was unable to tour – all of the tight five didn't go. Murray Mexted, Mark Shaw and Jock Hobbs were the incumbent Test players who were there and there were a number of missing people in the backs as well. So it was a very young team with a lot of players playing their first or second Tests and making their first tour. It had quite a different flavour from many of the All Black teams I played in later. We were incredibly excited and enthusiastic when we set off.

We knew England was going to be the most difficult game. Not much has changed when you play England. They have still got a very big forward pack. If you play them on Twickenham you are playing against a team who slow the game down, the grass is long, there is quite a tense crowd atmosphere so they are difficult to beat and they are very much occupying the space. And that was an All Blacks team that wasn't very big and didn't have much experience in the tight five so it was always going to be relatively hard work for us. If you dialled ahead two years we played a brand of rugby that didn't need dominance in the forwards, but in those days we were coming to the end of an era when we were always dominant in the forwards.

I think the midweek team was fantastic for the players. You built a camaraderie with that midweek team because they played together. You had your own goal, and your own 'we-will-not-be-beaten' attitude even though we weren't the Test team. For me, it sharpened my ambition. What it does is balance that sharpening of your ambition to be in the Test team with the cultural imperative of the All Blacks to support the players who are playing, because everyone wants the team to win. We are all part of that All Blacks touring team regardless of whether we are in the Saturday team or the midweek team. But at the same time you want to replace the guy that is playing in that team. That's a pretty good balance to develop and it leads, I think, to a maturity of attitude by players.

Warwick Taylor: I missed the England Test. Scott Crichton landed on my leg in the Scotland Test and I blew out my medial ligament. It happened about twenty minutes into the game and you couldn't go off unless you'd had a doctor's examination. I knew exactly what I'd done, but the physio strapped it up and said, 'Just see how long you can carry on.' I lasted until half-time. It was OK if I was running straight but as soon as I moved to the right my leg would flop out. I think back now . . . if I'd taken a tackle it could have ended my career. Because I had to be seen by a doctor, and that usually took five minutes, I kept going until half-time. When I started to run off, Andy Dalton said, 'Don't run, they'll say you can carry on.'

A new star winger was ready to step in. John Kirwan, a nineteen-year-old Auckland butcher's apprentice had been plucked out of lower grade rugby by Auckland coach John Hart, and was to become the prototype winger for the looming professional era. Like most good wings he was quick and good on his feet. He was also 1.9m (six foot three) and 93kgs (14 stone 9). Kirwan made his debut in 1984 in a two-Test series against France, runners-up to Scotland in the recent Five Nations. The first in Christchurch should have gone the way of the French. Trailing by one point they fluffed a great try scoring opportunity and then saw four late dropped goal attempts by their fly-half Jean Patrick Lescarboura sail wide, and the All Blacks scraped home 10-9. The selectors didn't panic, and an unchanged side had an altogether more comfortable 31-18 win in Auckland. The All Blacks headed for Australia and a tremendous series between arguably the best two teams in the world. The Wallabies, with their massive pack and skilful backs took the first Test 19-9 in front of 40,000 in Sydney, only for the All Blacks to square the series in Brisbane, thanks largely to five penalty goals by Robbie Deans. To the delight of Canterbury fans who'd long campaigned for his inclusion, Deans had replaced Allan Hewson at fullback, thereby ending the Wellington man's colourful Test career, although Deans' stay was not a long one. He kicked another five penalty goals in the third and deciding Test, and converted one of the All Blacks two tries in a thrilling 25-24 victory that ensured the Bledisloe Cup would stay in New Zealand. Such tightly-contested series between the Tasman neighbours were now commonplace, and with the Springboks no longer welcome in either country, the Bledisloe Cup rivalry became paramount.

John Kirwan (1984-94, 63 Tests, 96 games): I went down to Christchurch ahead of my first Test, [against France] I was nineteen, and I walked into the room and one of the old All Blacks said, 'Who are you?' I said, 'I'm John Kirwan, I'm from Auckland.' And he said, 'Well who picked you?' And I said, 'The coaches.' He said, 'Well, we didn't.' Then he said, 'And another thing, if we lose on Saturday, it's your fault.' So I went from a cocky young Aucklander to someone who wasn't quite so sure of myself. The next morning, the same person was there when I opened the door to go to breakfast, and I thought, 'Ah shit, here we go again.' I hadn't slept all night because of what he'd said the day before and he said, 'Everything I said to you last night was true. It's not the jersey, it's the man in the jersey. And when I said if we lose on Saturday it's your fault, if you can look in the mirror and you've done everything you can and played an outstanding game then you can come and criticise me.' And to finish he said, 'You've got two choices, you can either be here for a weekend and think you've arrived, or you can be here ten years and think you've never arrived.' That formed my attitude to the All Blacks very early.

David Kirk: It was a great learning environment but in terms of formalised specific coaching on position skills or even tactical plans I found throughout my All Black career we were mainly all very experienced players who were playing for all the top provinces. All those provinces had established game plans which were pretty similar so we just transferred that into the All Black environment because the skills levels and athletics levels were even greater, and we played even better. You learnt it from other players. I learnt about putting the ball into the scrum from the hookers and the way they wanted it put in. Grant Fox was a real technician when it came to kicking so he and I would be talking about technique for kicking into the box. You'd always be training in small units so I'd be practising my kicking into the box. JK would be practising his timing off my kicking and Foxy and Warwick Taylor would be practising Foxy putting the ball up under the sticks and Warwick doing the wipers kicks. You'd always be talking together, working together getting your timing and your rhythm and practising together.

John Kirwan: Two things happened in my first game. We won 10-9 and Lescaboura missed five drop-kicks in the last ten minutes. It was the first time I'd seen a man cry after a game of rugby. He cried in the tunnel and I was shocked. I also realised that the amateur game was wrong. We could only get together on the Wednesday while they were on tour. That forced me to make a decision that if I wanted to be the world's best I had to change everything. And I did. I got a personal trainer, changed my diet and decided to go pro without being paid. Pro is attitude.

Warwick Taylor: In Aussie we got beaten in the first Test. It was the only Test I played in that we lost. I never wanted to have that feeling again, and thankfully I didn't. We drew a couple, but the Aussies had a pretty good team starting to build then. Robbie Deans came on strong towards the end of that series.

Gary Whetton: Australia was starting to emerge and in my position in 1984, Haden didn't come across, there was a guy called Steve Cutler – the hardest guy I ever marked. He was about 6ft 10in with arms that were even longer. There was no lifting. They had another guy called Campbell who was just about as big. We lost that first Test and that was a hard one to swallow. I was really disappointed in my game, Cutler dominated me.

Murray Pierce (1984-90, 26 Tests, 54 games): It was those midweek games where I learnt what being an All Black was all about. All you had to do was worry about your role. I soon learned how specialised my role was and how I had to get fitter. We won the Test series and the midweek games. That sowed the seed.

Gary Whetton: We worked hard, did some homework, we called up Andy and worked on it, talking to each other about what we needed to do – short lineouts, options. He was a great thinker on lineouts. He was the maestro. So we went through it all and in the second Test in Queensland, at Ballymore, it was a great Test. They scored first and we came back at them hard and held on. We got through that and the last Test was a real nail-biter. We got home by one point in Sydney. They were a hard, physical team. Tony Shaw was a hard man, he would have fitted in any All Black team. They had a good front row, hooker Tom Lawton and Enrique Rodriguez from Argentina.

THIRTY

PLAYING BY A DIFFERENT LAW BOOK

'You don't agree with apartheid but you've got someone outside
your room telling you they want to blow up your family.'

SOUTH AFRICA WAS still a burning issue, with the All Blacks due to tour the Republic in 1985. In 1984, the Labour Party, under David Lange, swept to power, and urged the Rugby Union not to undertake the tour. The impending visit threatened to re-open the wounds of 1981, and protesters used the visit by England in June 1985 as a stage for their opposition. Two Test matches, one won narrowly by the All Blacks, the other comfortably, as well as half a dozen tour matches were targeted, although for various reasons, not the least being an unwillingness to see a repeat of the 1981 violence, the protests were comparatively peaceful.

It took two rugby people to scupper the tour. Lawyers Paddy Finnigan and Philip Recordon, both members of Auckland's University Rugby Club, gained an interim injunction from New Zealand's High Court to stop the tour, arguing that the Rugby Union was in breach of a constitutional obligation to 'promote, foster and develop' rugby. The timing of the injunction was critical, coming a few days before the team was due to leave, and the NZRFU had no option but to call it off. Fleeting thought was given amongst the team to going anyway, but though they opted not to defy the court order, senior players immediately started brewing plans for a rebel tour. The 'consolation' meantime, was a tour of Argentina featuring two official, at last, Test matches in Buenos Aires, the first of which was won 33-20. The second was a near sensation. Four penalty goals and three dropped goals by the great Pumas flyhalf Hugo Porta threatened to cause a boilover, the All Blacks managing to scramble a 21-all draw. The bright spots of the year came outside the Test arena. Auckland took the Ranfurly Shield off Canterbury in what is regarded as one of the greatest games of rugby played in New Zealand, an epic battle between two All Black-laden teams who provided the sort of spectacle rugby badly needed. And at last, the New Zealand and Australia Unions managed to win enough support from the Northern Hemisphere to get the green light to stage rugby's first World Cup tournament. They had barely two years to organise it from scratch, with scant resources and little financial backing. If other nations were sceptical, there was great excitement in the two host nations, although New Zealand still had shark-infested waters to navigate.

David Kirk: The court case in 1985 did hang over you. We had a couple of meetings in Wellington and everything was explained to us. They told us it was very serious and the NZRU's legal advisors explained there was no guarantee the tour would go ahead. That became a bit deflating because people didn't know what to expect. The reality was you just got on with what you had to do and focused on the next Test. You didn't worry about what you couldn't control.

Opposite: Frano Botica lines up against the French Barbarians in 1986. *Getty Images*

Gary Whetton: The 1985 season was hard for everybody. It was the ultimate, people wanted to tour, the All Black pack was getting older and that was their last hurrah. It was very disappointing, soul-destroying for a lot of guys. Not knowing [whether it was off or on] took a lot more out of the older guys. We had farmers trying to work out what they were doing, were they going or were they not? We had a lot of friends who were going on supporters' tours asking us whether we were going or not.

Warwick Taylor: I'd always wanted to go to South Africa. It had been a childhood dream. All of a sudden I had that opportunity and it was gone. It hurt.

Murray Pierce: Being a policeman was a complicating factor. Every All Blacks' dream was to play against South Africa. But, politically, it just wasn't on. In 1985 a lot of players, the Knights, the Ashworths, the Daltons, the Hadens, the Mexteds, the Wilsons, Bernie Fraser, were hanging around for that 1985 tour and rightly so, they had earned the right to tour South Africa but unfortunately the lawyers succeeded and the tour was off. It was beyond our control and we had to put up with it. Then the undercurrents started with the Cavaliers tour in 1986. I think a lot of the older All Blacks could possibly see that it was going to happen in 1986 so they extended their careers by another year.

David Kirk: I had been the starting halfback in the two Tests against England. It had always been a great goal of mine to go and play South Africa in South Africa and beat them. It was the kind of Everest for players of many generations. It was a difficult decision and there was a lot of angst about it but I definitely made the positive decision to go on the basis that at that time I could separate the political issues from the sporting issues.

John Kirwan: Before the tour was cancelled I hadn't really thought about it. It was always a dream to play in South Africa and to go on a Grand Slam tour. I felt if we were going as the official All Blacks then no problem, you are going to represent your country but as soon as that was cancelled then it was something we shouldn't be doing.

Dave Loveridge: It was a dream for most players to go over and beat the Springboks on their own soil but realistically I think a lot of the players knew it wouldn't eventuate, the odds were slim. In the end it was as big a disappointment as it could have been.

Gary Whetton: England were England. I hadn't had very much experience of that side of it. You have to go over there to learn to dislike them. Once you go there once that's how you learn what it is all about.

David Kirk: We played very poorly in the first Test against England. It was one of those very rusty Tests. We hadn't played for ages and we made bad mistakes all the time. We never had any accuracy or rhythm so we were lucky to get through. They weren't dominant but we weren't able to put them away. They spent a lot of time on attack and gave away a lot of penalties which is why we kicked all those penalty goals. For the second Test we had to leave our hotel at something like 9.00 a.m. to beat the protesters and we sat at Athletic

Park waiting for the game. There were barriers around the ground to stop the protests we had seen in 1981 so it was back to that environment – people were divided.

Murray Pierce: It was my second Test. The first had gone in a blur, it was so fast but in the second a lot of us newbies started to adjust and we had to front that day and luckily came out with a victory.

David Kirk: BJ [Lochore] did his team talk in the function room and it was very clear. The team had played poorly the previous week and if the team played poorly again, let alone lost, there was little doubt that some All Blacks' careers would end. I took it as being directed at the older guys who hadn't fired up, particularly in the forward pack. We were talking about the front row of Gary Knight, Andy Dalton and John Ashworth, who had brought out a book called, *The Geriatrics*, already and Andy Haden, Mark Shaw, Murray Mexted. BJ put the hard word on them and they played really well, and the backs played well too.

Grant Fox (1984-93, 46 Tests, 78 games): When Auckland and Canterbury were strong that helped create an exceptionally strong All Black team in that late-1980s. But in the All Black situation there was none of that rivalry. The whole thing went into the melting pot and guys were always putting ideas in. We had a lot of input in those days, because the management team consisted of five people, a manager, a coach, an assistant coach a doctor and a physio, nobody else.

Murray Mexted: The NZRU was very decent and arranged a replacement tour to Argentina at the eleventh hour which was quite fantastic. That was a new experience because all of us but Andy Haden had never been there. It was a new world. We played some really tough matches, and the Test series was tough. In the second Test Hugo Porta scored 21 points from seven goals, penalties and dropped goals, and we scored two tries, one of them to me. That was my last official Test.

Gary Whetton: Argentina was a hard tour. We had a lot of guys who were disappointed they weren't in South Africa so they were going to Argentina to make the most of it, play hard, socialise hard and it was pretty disruptive. I pride myself on not having lost in Argentina, I had two tours there, and to get through those tours is hard work.

Warwick Taylor: We drew the second Test and I was the guy who should have passed the ball to Craig Green and he would have had an easy try . . . the ball just fell out of my hands . . . I beat myself up for years over that!

*

There is nothing in sport quite as iconic as the All Black haka. It is powerful, symbolic, enthralling, controversial, and often misunderstood. Haka has been part of New Zealand culture since the arrival of Maori en masse around the 13th century, and whilst it is generally perceived as a challenge, or a display of aggressive intent before conflict, it can equally be a show of respect, of identity, and a gesture of welcome or celebration.

The first New Zealand teams did not so much perform a haka as a mass movement, but as a simple but powerful chant :

Ake Ake Kia Kaha   *For ever and ever, be strong*

This chant, later to be indelibly linked with the famous Maori Battalion of World War Two, was in evidence when the first representative New Zealand side toured New South Wales in 1884. The 1888 Native team performed the haka Ka Mate, the story of Te Rauparaha, the great leader of the Ngati Toa iwi [tribe] who, under pursuit by his enemies, was faced with the choice of life and death:

Ka Mate Ka Mate . . .   *Do I live, do I live?*
Ka Ora Ka Ora   *Do I die, do I die?*

Te Rauparaha took refuge in the kumara pit of his cousin Te Wharerangi, later to emerge into the sunlight, to live and to fight again.

Whiti te Ra, Hi!   *The sun shines!*

Despite some lingering indifference from the descendants of the victims of Te Rauparaha, Ka Mate stood the test of time, being performed at varying levels of authenticity over the years, although at times, not at all.

The 1924 Invincibles performed their own haka, composed by accompanying supporter Wiremi Rangi or Gisborne and Judge Acheson of the New Zealand Land Court

Kia whakangawari au i a hau.   *Let us prepare ourselves for the pray.*
Au! Au! Au-e ha! Hei!

Ko Niu Tireni e haruru nei.   *The New Zealand storm is about to break.*
Au! Au! Au-e ha! Hei!

It was not deemed appropriate to perform the haka in apartheid era South Africa, and before the 1987 World Cup it was never done at home, indeed the use of the haka dwindled somewhat in the 1970s before re-emerging on the Grand Slam tour of 1978. It was at that time that Wayne 'Buck' Shelford was asked to teach and lead his team-mates in the haka. Shelford, of the Ngapuhi iwi, said he would, but only if it was done properly. 'They came to Hika [Reid] and I to teach them, and I said to Hika, "Unless they're going to do it properly, we won't do it," and he agreed,' Shelford said. 'If they didn't do it properly, well, they were just disrespecting someone's culture. Once they bought into it, the team and the management, we could spend a bit of time learning it properly. We taught them a little about the origins of it. We talked about the story of Te Rauparaha, but it was mainly about getting the actions right. A lot of white boys don't have a lot of rhythm, they can't keep time when they stamp their feet. If you're into music then you seem to have a better sense of the rhythm, but a lot of our guys weren't – some of them were real gumboots, really awkward. They found it hard to get their feet moving when they were in a low position. But we got round that, and they were trying their hardest so as not to disrespect the Maori culture. Come the World Cup in 1987, this old kaumatua [elder] came up to me and asked if we were going to do the haka at the World Cup. I said to him, "But it's never been done here before, only overseas," and he said, "But it's ours, it belongs to us, why not?" I said, "Well you go get it cleared with all the people you know and we'll do it." He came back and said, "Do it," so we did.'

From there the haka became more akin to its true origins, no longer the shambolic effort typified before the great Barbarians game of 1973. Gradually, as the All Blacks delved into their legacy, the haka became as much a statement of their identity, as it was a challenge, culminating in the composition of a new haka, unique to the All Blacks in 2005.

Kapo O Pango was composed by Derek Lardelli, who described it as a ceremonial rather than pre-battle haka building 'spiritual, physical and intellectual capacity' before an important event. It also reflected the All Blacks' desire for a haka demonstrating their contemporary make-up. It was first performed against the Springboks in 2005, coming as a complete surprise to all but the players themselves.

Hi Aue hi! Ko Aotearoa e ngunguru nei!	*This is our land that rumbles*
Au, Au, aue ha!	*It is my time, my moment*
Ko Kapo O Pango e ngunguru nei!	*This defines us as the All Blacks*
Au, Au, aue ha!	*It is my time, my moment*

While the Carisbrook crowd and New Zealand fans were excited by the new haka, there was an immediate adverse reaction to the final act, in which some players could be seen drawing their thumbs across their neck in what was perceived as a 'throat slitting' gesture, whereas Lardelli intended for the movement to be across the chest, a symbolic drawing on the vital organs for a gathering of strength.

There is no question the haka has become a compelling part of All Black rugby, but it also has drawn widespread criticism. Detractors say it gives the All Blacks an unfair psychological advantage, that it has become over-dramatic and overplayed, and that a sense of entitlement has grown around the All Blacks, especially in relation to how teams respond to it. However, it is not unfair to suggest that some of the criticism bears more than a hint of colonialism, and a lack of understanding of, and respect for, indigenous culture. It is a sacred Maori ritual and therefore has to be performed in accordance with its true traditions.

There has also been some irritation, and this is shared by New Zealanders, at a World Rugby (IRB) edict that teams should stand back and not walk towards the haka.

Reponses to the haka have been many and varied. The English and South African crowds will often try and drown it out, the French more likely to watch in silence. Two notable responses came in Dublin. In 1989 Willie Anderson led the Irish team, arms linked right into the face of the All Blacks, in what became known as 'Paddy O'Haka'. In '91 David Campese left his team mates to face the haka, preferring to practice some handling drills in the Lansdowne Road in-goal before his match-winning performance in the World Cup semi-final.

Perhaps encouraged by that, the 1996 Wallabies turned their backs on the haka in Wellington and proceeded to be torn apart . . . ignoring it doesn't necessarily work. The French have never been afraid to stand their ground, and before the 2011 final, marched in an arrowhead formation at the All Blacks, only to be fined by the IRB. But the most infamous clashes over the haka have come in Wales, perhaps fittingly, as it was in Cardiff in 1905 that the Welsh first heard their national anthem before a rugby Test, and it was in response to the haka.

To mark the 100th anniversary of that great day, the Welsh Union proposed that the haka be performed before the Welsh anthem, the All Blacks agreeing on condition that it was a one-off. When Wales tried to repeat the order a year later, the All Blacks pointed out the agreement of the previous encounter, and an impasse resulted with the All Blacks performing the haka in their own dressing room. Two years later came the famous stand-off. For all the criticism it has aroused over the years, the haka (as are the challenges of Fiji, Tonga and Samoa) is something that sets rugby apart from other sports. It would, surely, not be the same without it.

*

John Kirwan: The tour to Argentina was a changing of the guard. I really enjoyed that tour. The coaches probably saw it as an opportunity to try a few things and they mixed things up a bit. Off the field there was probably too much of a good time because people were disappointed.

Grant Fox: Hugo Porta was still playing and was at his imperious best. The first Test we won 33-20. I'm pretty sure Dave Loveridge was crook or injured and so Kirky had to play, and Wayne Smith might have been under the weather as well and that gave Kirky and I an opportunity. It took us a long time to crack them. They were big, tough and abrasive up front, they could be mercurial in the backline too but they had a five-eighth who tended to look for field position a lot . . . which might sound ironic coming from me, given my style of play . . . but Porta was very experienced, incredibly talented, strong of mind, their leader and goalkicker and it was tough. We drew the second Test, Hugo kicked three dropped goals, so the first Test was tough, the second was even tougher.

Wayne Shelford (1985-90, 22 Tests, 48 games): We should have lost that second Test. Argentina had a chance for a pushover scrum but Ure, the No.8 fumbled the ball and dropped it going over the line. I didn't play a Test, but getting on the tour and becoming an All Black was good enough for me.

The game was again thrown into turmoil in 1986, when nearly all of the All Black side that had been picked to tour South Africa in 1985, left on an unauthorised tour of South Africa. Calling themselves the Cavaliers, the rebel team was managed by Ian Kirkpatrick, coached by Colin Meads, and captained by Andy Dalton. The only All Blacks chosen the previous year not to tour were David Kirk, who made public his opposition to the tour on moral grounds, and John Kirwan, who cited family reasons and the need for a break after back-to-back seasons in Europe as his reasons for staying at home. The players left the country in groups, gathering in Sydney as outrage erupted at home. There was no live TV or radio coverage of the games. The Cavaliers were beaten 3-1 in the series, and left seething over the refereeing. Anger over the tour was not constrained to the anti-apartheid movement. John Graham, a former All Black captain and headmaster of Auckland Grammar, the school that has produced the most All Blacks, called for the players to be banned for life. In the end, they were given two matches. It meant an entirely new team had to be picked for a Test against a strong French team coming off a joint share of the Five Nations Championship. For the Test in Christchurch, only four players, Kirk, Kirwan, Arthur Stone and Brian McGrattan had any previous Test experience, many of them did not even know each other, and they had but a few days to prepare. What they achieved was quite extraordinary. They cleverly took the game away from the powerful French pack, grabbing points any way they could, scoring the only try of the game through No. 8 Mike Brewer, with extras coming from the steady boot of fullback Greg Cooper and two dropped goals by Frano Botica. It was a performance that gained instant entry into New Zealand rugby folklore, the team forever to be known as 'The Baby Blacks'.

Murray Pierce: Personally it [the Cavaliers tour] wasn't hard to live through. Either people were too gutless or never fronted me one-on-one with their objections. It got a bit tough at home though as anti-apartheid black wreaths were being put at the front door of the house. That was a bit scary for my wife at home while I was doing shift work, or maybe away on an All Black tour. That sent a bit of a chill down the spine. My wife had to shift out as it was too dangerous. That was the worst. The Police Department was very supportive. I went on the Cavaliers tour and then came back to my day job with the police. I was grateful for that.

Warwick Taylor: For me going it meant I could lose my job, but I wanted to go. I remember thinking, wrongly, that somehow if we went over there and beat them we could prove to them that their apartheid system was wrong, some sort of silly way of thinking along those lines, that we could show them the apartheid system was crap.

Grant Fox: It wasn't an easy decision to make but I was just a young guy who loved my footy and South Africa was, and still is, our greatest foe, and to tour there was every young player's dream. We were rugby players, not politicians. As a young guy you're going to look at the senior statesmen in the team and what they're going to do. I wanted the rugby experience and we got a hell of a rugby experience. Tough place to tour, tough footy but very enjoyable too, they weren't official Tests but I learned stuff that put me in good stead for the rest of my career.

Sean Fitzpatrick (1986-1997, 92 Tests, 128 games): In 1985 I wasn't in the Auckland team. Harty got rid of me, but then the following year they had a few injuries and I was back on the fringe. I was a reserve when Auckland went down to play Canterbury and after the game, and I was walking back to the changing room in my tracksuit and Gary Whetton ran past me, Andy Haden ran past me, and by the time I got to the changing room they were out the door. We didn't know what was going on . . . they were off to London to assemble to go to South Africa. We got back to Auckland and John Minto and all the protestors were there at the airport, spitting at us as we were taking our bags off the carousel, and I was thinking, 'It's not us!'

John Kirwan: It was frightening in 1985. You don't agree with apartheid but you've got someone outside your room telling you they want to blow up your family. Then the Cavaliers challenged the first test of my character when I had to stand up and say, 'I'm not going.' That was a very, very difficult time but also a moment in my life when I had to stand up for myself and say to my peers that I wasn't going. I did that in Wellington at a meeting organised by the NZRFU in the boardroom. I came under pressure but there was never any backlash. I remember Andy Haden having a bit of a go at me and I had a bit of a go back at him but that was what that era was like, it was confrontational but not personal.

David Kirk: I had made the choice very early about not going on the Cavaliers tour and it was a whole range of different things. It was the fact it wasn't a sanctioned All Black tour. The year before I could get myself over the line because I was representing my country and doing something worthwhile. That was very different from going in a rebel team which for me undermined that rationale which had been strong the previous year. Also, money was offered to the players and I didn't want that. It was still in the amateur era and if it did end up that people took money then they would have to lie about it because you would be kicked out of the game if you didn't. I talked with friends and family and they didn't think New Zealanders would support a rebel team and they didn't think it was the right thing to do. Then I did come under quite a lot of pressure from my team-mates, the people who were going, not to let them down by being the person who didn't go. They felt like they were losing some of the solidarity and the reason for going, if others didn't go. It was harder to justify going if everyone didn't go. Briefly I wavered, and talked to the travel agent who was arranging everything in secret, but a week later I said I definitely wasn't going. It was a brief period of soul-searching but in a way it hardened my view and made me more certain that it was the wrong thing to do. I knew by not going what I was getting into in terms of my relationships with those players thereafter.

Wayne Shelford: It wasn't hard for me. After that Argentinian tour I was twenty-eight so I was an older guy. I knew what I wanted, and for me it wasn't a hard decision, you have to take your opportunities. The dream for all of us in those days was to play against South Africa. I think having that tour taken away from us in '85, really hacked a lot of us players off. There was a rebel tour going in '85 but it got called off. But the next one went. We learned a hell of a lot on that tour, the young guys like Steve McDowell, Warwick

Taylor, they'd never experienced anything like that before. A lot of them hadn't played in 1981. We lost the series but we took a lot from the experience. I ended up captaining the midweek team and that helped me get a bit of respect. We were up against it . . . we certainly didn't have too many people following us. Half the country wanted us to be there, half didn't. We came home and got slapped on the wrist, and got stood down for a couple of Tests. When that ended I was picked to play against Australia in the third Test but I had to pull out because I'd broken my hand in a club game. They lost that Test and the Bledisloe Cup but I got back in from playing NPC for the tour to France.

Warwick Taylor: There was an aborted trip early on. Canterbury were playing Wairarapa Bush and we were going to be travelling that week. A group of us in Christchurch decided we were going with the Cavaliers, so we told Grizz [Wyllie] we wouldn't be available for Wairarapa Bush game. We wondered how we were going to get up to Wellington without being noticed. Vic Simpson rented a van. He didn't want to use his driver's licence so he used his flatmate's, but it wasn't valid, so he had to use his own in the end. We jumped in the van and were going to pick Robbie up on the way. Craig Green didn't come with us . . . he went to the airport. He waited and waited before he got on the plane because he didn't want to be seen by people . . . and in the end they called his name over the loudspeaker, so everyone knew! The whole thing was about avoiding the media seeing us and figuring something was up. We drove late at night to Picton to get the ferry over to Wellington. We were in the car and Jock [Hobbs] kept looking back and saying, 'I'm sure that car's following us.' We were all on edge. We got up to Picton, to the ferry terminal and we decided we'd go in one at a time, one every five minutes, so there was less chance we'd be noticed. Albert Anderson got onto the ferry and suddenly he hears, 'Alby what are you doing here?' It was one of his old farming mates, and Alby said something about doing a bit of a promo. And the guy said, 'Oh yeah, I just saw Jock here too!' So this guy had spotted us. Anyway we got to Wellington, everyone was ducking and diving, and our physio came to pick us up in a Mini. There were seven of us so he had to do about three trips. We got to his place, and all the curtains were pulled so no one could see us, and then we got a phone call to say it was off . . . so it was out with the beers. An hour later I rang Tracy and got her to ring Alex Wyllie to see if he wanted us to play for Canterbury against Wairarapa Bush after all, because it had cost us a fair bit and he said yes. In the end Vic Simpson was the only one who played, the rest of us were in the reserves, and Wairarapa Bush beat us.

Gary Whetton: The Cavaliers tour in 1986 was disruptive. There was the secrecy of it and whether or not we were going. It was: 'Yes, no, can't say anything.' How do you talk to your employer about it, is he on your side or is he not? It was very hard on us with our provincial teams. A lot of people put a lot on the line to go on that trip. We wanted to play rugby and we had been stopped by a court. And we had an opportunity. It was hard work, the Springboks were only going to justify us being there if they won. They had to win no matter what. I didn't work that out until a bit later on. The teams they set us up with were hard work. As far as they were concerned we were the All Blacks. Sometimes doing our best wasn't enough. Burger Geldenhuys' punch on Andy Dalton was completely terrible. It ruined the tour. The older boys said, 'Well, fuck this, let's just go home.' The South Africans were panicking. Geldenhuys got lambasted by everyone who realised what a cheap shot it was. It really put the tour up in arms and gave us a bit more fortitude. It was hard to see Andy come back to the team with his jaw wired up and not playing, he was a great leader. I had no qualms about going there, or having played them in 1981, none whatsoever. Were we blindsided? Yes we were. So was the world, so were governments. Would it have made a difference? I don't know. The country's still a mess now, even moreso. We weren't discriminatory. We treated people as we saw people. I'm a dark complexion, Maoris, islanders, whatever, we're all the same and that's the way we do things in New Zealand.

Murray Mexted: We had a lot of halfbacks then so we didn't miss David so much but we did miss John because he was big and fast and a star and he would have been outstanding on those hard pitches in South Africa. It was a frustrating tour because we were encouraged by the New Zealand Rugby Union off the record, then the moment we went we were black-listed. It was a great tour because for an amateur rugby player it was a challenge to play against the best. We were an All Blacks side that was recognised as being the No.1 team in the world, and thankfully still is. You want to play those players who are your greatest opponents because that's a natural thing. We weren't making any political statement, it was purely a rugby statement. It was tough, the refereeing was crooked, there were no international referees. We used a Welsh referee who was supposed to be impartial but wasn't and he refereed all four 'Tests'. We were good at scoring tries from five-metre scrums in those days, we had good space awareness from the scrum and the creation of space and creation of an overlap, but we were only allowed to execute two five-metre scrums in the whole series. Every time we put the ball into the scrum the whistle went for an infringement. I'm not complaining about the refereeing, I'm stating a fact.

Andy Haden: The Geldenhuys incident was frustrating. We were disappointed to not be able to carry out our wish to go to South Africa and play that side, the benchmark side, the best or the next best in the world for us. We made every effort to go and when we ended up going as the Cavaliers, after the court injunction, we thought we had made a major effort to get there and then the bugger king hit Dalton from behind . . . The thought that went through your mind was that they didn't deserve the opportunity to play us – they were in isolation, we weren't.

Dave Loveridge: Losing Andy that early on that tour was huge. If that had happened now that guy probably wouldn't have played for a year. I'm not singling that instance out because there were some nasty incidents through the years but it was quite blatant. We weren't too happy with that but as a team we couldn't dwell on it or effect how we were playing.

Warwick Taylor: I had taken over an All Black track suit. Before the last Test I wanted something extra to get me going so I put on the track suit. It was then I realised it did not give me the lift it usually gave me when playing for the All Blacks because it didn't have the support of all the New Zealanders back home. It is the New Zealand people and their support that is a big part of what makes the All Blacks what they are.

Murray Pierce: It was a long tour with hard, midweek games played at altitude, the refereeing was still biased but a great experience and quite a good grounding for me because I was still a young All Black and learning the ropes. I learnt a lot on that trip.

Warwick Taylor: I almost lost my job for going AWOL from the school I was teaching at. It went to court to get sorted out. I'd asked for the time off and they'd said, 'No', then I left before I could get hold of them. We went to South Africa thinking it could cost us our All Black careers. There were a number of people high up who knew what we were doing, but when we came back it was like they hadn't known. We were banned for the first Test against Australia, then I got picked for the second Test in Dunedin. I had my court case up until the Wednesday – I could have lost my job but in the end the judge gave me a slap over the hand and as I was walking out he said, 'Good luck on Saturday.'

Sean Fitzpatrick: The Cavaliers came back and were banned. Out of the blue Brian Lochore got me into the All Black trials. He'd had me in the Colts. Iain Abercrombie was the Auckland hooker then, and I think I actually marked him in the trials. I was at Wellington Airport on our way back to Auckland and someone came up and said to me, 'You're in the All Black team.' I said, 'Nah . . .' and he said, 'You are, you're in the twenty-one, you're the reserve hooker.' It was a bit awkward . . . Abo was there, and I wasn't even in the Auckland team.

John Gallagher (1986-89, 18 Tests, 41 games): The Cavaliers went away and they needed to pick an All Black team to play France. I thought to myself if ever I was going to make it, this would be it. When I missed out I thought. 'That's it, I'll never make the All Blacks.'

Sean Fitzpatrick: We went down to Christchurch for the Test. I was rooming with Joe Leota, he was a reserve also, and he said to me, 'Gidday mate, what's your name?' We went to lunch . . . and there was Andy Earl sitting there and Joe said, 'Andy this is . . . sorry, what was your name again?' I mean luckily Kirky was there. He was captain of the University team in Auckland, but there were guys who'd never met each other before, guys like Brian McGratten, Brent Harvey, Gordon McPherson. We had a live scrummaging session on the Thursday . . . full-on live scrummaging and Bruce Hemara hurt his ribs, and on the Friday BJ Lochore came into my room and said, 'Sean you're starting, Bruce is out.' I couldn't believe it.

John Kirwan: One of my memories of the game involved Sean Fitzpatrick, we were great mates and we roomed together. He had been named on the bench and Bruce Hemara was starting at that stage. I got up on Thursday morning and Fitzy was really happy and I asked him why he was so happy. He said: 'I'm playing on Saturday.' And I said, 'No you're not, you're on the bench you idiot.' And he said, 'No, we've got live scrums today and I'm playing on Saturday.' And he broke Bruce Hemara's ribs at training. I don't know whether he did it on purpose or if it was just a coincidence but if I know Fitzy . . . he played and never looked back. I think he played ninety-two Tests in a row.

Greg Cooper (1986-92, 7 Tests): I got a call from a reporter in Wellington, I don't know how they knew I was at Wellington Airport . . . it was something like, 'Mr Cooper can you come to counter five,' then finding out from him I was in the All Blacks. Every youngster wants to be an All Black, but it became an even greater focus for me when I got sick. I was diagnosed with Ewings Sarcoma which is a rare form of bone cancer, when I was fifteen. It was in the first rib. The years '81 to '83 were extremely tough with the treatment, but part of my way of dealing with it was this burning desire to be an All Black. We had a barn at home, and when the treatments ended, as soon as I could get some food into me, I'd go out there and try to put on all the weight I'd lost, and while I was doing that I'd be thinking about pulling on that jersey, singing the national anthem. I had a messed up shoulder because of the radiotherapy and one lung was compromised, but I was just so determined to make it. It was my one focus. It was a way of telling the world that I was now cured. You can't be sick if you're an All Black, that sort of thing. So to ring my parents and tell them that I'd made it was a bit like giving them back something, just a bit, for the way they'd supported me through my illness.

David Kirk: The Baby Blacks were a significant moment in All Blacks history, and a lot of New Zealanders think that. They certainly did at the time. There was a buzz, an excitement. I recall some scepticism from all the old heads that there was no way 'these young guys' could win. They were a great French team and they would crush us in the set pieces. There was a nice old guy, Norm Wilson, who was the pundit on TVNZ, who played for the All Blacks at hooker. I was interviewed on TV and saw it after, when I was asked what sort of tactics we could expect to play against this big French forward pack? I said we were going to play a fast game with a lot of fluidity and were going to make sure we didn't make ourselves targets and get bogged down. They went back to Norm, and the guy sitting next to him said, 'Well what do you make of that?' and he said, 'I'm not sure what the hell he is talking about when he says 'fluidity'. So there was a lot of scepticism about whether we could do it.

John Kirwan: We never doubted we could win. We had a simple game plan about putting them on their arses, making them go backwards and hurting them, and we picked the team accordingly. New Zealanders are great when they've got their backs to the wall and it was a moment in time where the boys had chosen to go to Africa and the boys who stayed behind said, 'You're not going to get your All Blacks jersey back.' A lot of us went into the game with that sort of attitude. I had played nine Test matches. We knew this could be an historic win in All Blacks rugby and nobody would be able to take that away from those who played. BJ Lochore did a great job in bringing us all together. My job was to play the best that I could and to play with confidence and be confident all week. I tried to show I had no fear and we were going to win.

Greg Cooper: We only had four days to introduce ourselves, get outfitted and get ready for the game. BJ Lochore was so calm. He did a superb job of making the guys feel like they were good enough to be there, that we were the All Blacks. You could feel it building during the week . . . not to the point where we thought we were going to absolutely win, but by the time the game came around we were comfortable with what we were doing and feeling pretty confident that we could go out and do it. The French had been in Argentina and there'd been a bit of turmoil over there and, as we know, turmoil can either turn the French into a beast or it can tear them apart. But you look at who they had, it was one of the better French teams, I was marking Serge Blanco. But Kirky was very composed, JK was confident, and there was never a feeling of not deserving to be there.

Sean Fitzpatrick: Just before we'd gone out onto the field, Kirky got us into a circle for one last motivational talk . . . the door was open and out of the corner of my eye I saw the French walking past. I found myself looking at Laurent Rodriguez and he was like . . . 'Grrrrrrrrrr.' I thought, 'Effing hell, what are we doing here?' But, somehow, we beat them, I still don't know how. I remember the ball being kicked off by Greg Cooper. It was like 'I'm finally an All Black' because my feeling was I wasn't really an All Black until the ball was kicked off. Every scrum was like being in a washing machine. We got absolutely pummelled but Boro [Kevin Boroevich] and Gratts [Brian McGrattan] would get back up and we'd go again . . . I was thinking, 'How did we ever survive that?'

John Kirwan: In the game we were on fire. Joe Stanley was on fire. The boys were full of energy and we were getting them behind the advantage line. The goal was to get them there, knock them backwards so the forwards could get there and we tried to hurt their backs so they couldn't get those little passes away. When you play for the All Blacks you

New Zealand captain David Kirk passes the ball during the Test against France in Christchurch, 28th June 1986. *Getty Images*

never go on the field doubting that you are going to win. We have a fear of losing but never an inferiority complex. I was really pleased for a lot of the guys who played that day. It's a moment in history we shouldn't forget because of what we came through. Rugby was in real trouble in those years and the Baby Blacks were very important for the country.

David Kirk: I knew after about twenty or thirty minutes they weren't playing well. When you're playing against a team that is fired up and playing well you start to realise, 'Wow, this is going to be a hard game, we've got to really hang in here. When their surges come we've got to do everything we can to keep them out and we've got to take our opportunities.' But it didn't feel like that. It didn't feel like they were playing at their most aggressive, or most effective, which was a little bit of a relief. It did feel like we were able to play the sort of game we talked about. Our set pieces were a bit of a struggle throughout, particularly the scrum, so we did have problems there but we had players who could deal with that. We had Mike Brewer who was a great athlete at No.8. We had Frano Botica who was able to make space, there was the unpredictable Arthur Stone and we had finishers with JK and others so we had talent but we didn't have size. We hung in there and took our opportunities and scored a good try. In a way it was opportunist with a chip ahead, a regather and a couple of passes and a try. It was a good try from not a lot out of the mid-field but they didn't look like scoring.

Greg Cooper: With the dropped goal, in those days you could stand right by the halfback, I got as close as I could, Kirky tapped it and I got the ball in my hands as fast as I could and was ready to kick. When I hit it, I knew . . . it was one of the better drop kicks I'd ever done. I think I only missed one shot at goal and that was one from fifty metres that I hit really well. Lagisquet got into a bit of space and he could go but I managed to catch him. It was just one of those days where everything seemed to go right. The crowd started to get behind us, we got some momentum going, they got frustrated and even though you're thinking. 'This is the French, anything could happen' you knew it wasn't going to be their day. It was an incredible experience.

John Kirwan: One of the happiest days of my life was when Joe Stanley got selected for the All Blacks. When I had him inside me I knew I could run all different sorts of lines. He was the last of the distributing centres and after Joe I think the centre became more the attacking weapon than the wings. He was a great distributor and to run off him was a joy because he could straighten the line and pass at the last minute.

The heroic performance served to fuel contempt for the Cavaliers, some of whom would end their careers after the South African tour, but many of whom soon became eligible again for Test rugby. Much the same 'Baby Blacks' team took to the field for the first of three Tests against Australia in Wellington, narrowly losing by 13-12, but with the Cavaliers' ban ending, changes were made for the second in Dunedin. Of the forward pack, all but Brewer were replaced, whilst two changes were made in the backline, changes that didn't meet with unanimous approval. Only the contentious ruling out of a late try by loose forward Steve Tuynman denied the Wallabies a series-clinching victory. In the decider at Eden Park the All Blacks were no match for a superb Wallaby team, their lack of match fitness and combinations exposed in a 22-9 thumping that saw the Bledisloe Cup heading west again, and a jolt delivered to New Zealand's World Cup expectations.

Sean Fitzpatrick: A week later pretty much the same team went to Athletic Park and really, we should have beaten Australia too. I remember going round to Mum and Dad's on the Sunday morning after that Test, sitting around the table listening for the announcement of the team for the second Test, and with that they said there were eight changes for the second Test in Dunedin, the whole forward pack's been changed. I was still in the reserves.

David Kirk: We played reasonably well against Australia in the first Test but they probably played below their best because that was a pretty talented Australian team. We lost by one point and weren't far away from closing the gap. We didn't have that many opportunities but we did have field position in the second half that meant we could have won with a bit of luck. There wasn't much in it but David Campese scored what was a pretty talented try. Nick Farr-Jones made a little break, got tackled and the ball spilled free. Campese was quick enough, and skilful enough, to toe it forward, chase it, and then fall on it and it was again, a bit of good luck for them.

Greg Cooper: The first Test against Australia . . . it was a very windy day in Wellington and I missed a couple of shots I probably should have got. And there was a defensive error, JK and I got something wrong, and it was probably more my fault. It could have gone either way, we were not quite there on the day. Still, we were good enough to win it and didn't and then in the second Test we won it and probably shouldn't have . . . Steve Tuynman was unlucky not to be given a try.

Murray Pierce: I think that loss to Australia in their second Test by the Baby Blacks helped us to get back into the side after our suspensions. There was no trouble coming back together. That was the unique thing about All Blacks rugby when I played. Auckland was dominating and the coaches hardly had to mention it. They said we were all in the one team and to forget our provincial alliances. Personally it was never an issue combining. We all knew we had to combine otherwise we wouldn't be in the team.

Greg Cooper: When the Cavaliers guys came back there was as bit of a different dynamic I suppose, there was so much experience coming back into the team. I never got the sense of, 'He's a senior All Black and he's not talking to me,' or anything like that and it wasn't a bad feeling at all, but it was different.

John Kirwan: It was uncomfortable when the Cavaliers came back. The changing of the guard was forced on us. We'd moved on very quickly and there was a new breed, and when there's a new breed there's new attitudes and new styles and new ways of doing things. Most of us didn't feel the team should have changed.

David Kirk: This was the beginning of some of the difficulties that subsequently transpired with the players who had gone to South Africa. For one, they had gone away hoping and believing that the New Zealand public, once they got there, would be behind them, and that didn't happen. The games weren't televised because TVNZ decided that wasn't appropriate. So they felt quite abandoned over there – that was my take on it. When they came back they felt unfairly abandoned and pilloried, so they were in a sense of grievance from the get-go and then this team that had replaced them played really well and won so they had the personal anguish of thinking, 'Maybe my All Black career is over,' or, if they were young players, 'Someone else is going to take my place.' They saw the celebration and I think it was hard for them in the sense that they were on the outer. To some extent because I was the spokesperson for that team, and captain, I was interviewed often and they saw me having a higher profile, being praised publicly and they saw me in many ways as the lightning rod for that uncomfortableness and unhappiness. That barrier never broke down with some players. It would only be a very few. Because of the uncomfortableness of the team it was hard to get away from that, it was hard to un-say things. Attitudes and the way you behave towards people – they are what they are. As much as people want to move on and never refer to them again and never in a way hold them against people, you can't forget them. You can't pretend they didn't happen. For some players it wasn't an issue anyway. They never got into that, they didn't care. That was probably the majority. By 1987 it had rolled into quite a different team. A lot of those players had gone. One more tour was probably a step too far for some of them which was why they lost over there and they retired and disappeared.

Warwick Taylor: I went to Dunedin and played in the Test, then was dropped for the third Test. It was a turbulent time. I wasn't selected for the end of year tour to France either which made me realise I had some work to do. In South Africa I'd played some of the best attacking rugby I'd ever played. Missing out on the tour to France made me think about things a bit. I spent the summer doing weights and working hard to get myself back in.

David Kirk: If Steve Tuynman's try had been scored in Dunedin who is to say that we wouldn't have scored from the next play? The thing that was shocking in a way was that the selectors made such a massive change to the team. There were ten changes with only myself, Greg Cooper, Joe Stanley, John Kirwan and Frano Botica retained, although it became six when Mike Brewer had to replace Wayne Shelford who had broken a bone in his hand. It was a totally new team and they left me as captain.

Sean Fitzpatrick: To me it was a very steep learning curve, those three games watching the older guys. I learned a lot sitting on the outside watching Dalton, Jock, Gary Whetton, Ashworth, how they went about things.

Grant Fox: The Wallabies beat us in New Zealand. The players who'd been on the Cavaliers tour got sanctioned and it wasn't until the second Test that we could re-engage. It wasn't planned but it gave them a chance to blood a lot of players. I think that was one of the key ingredients of the success in 1987 and a few years after that. The whole thing was superbly led by Brian Lochore. He had the two leading provincial coaches, John Hart and Grizz Wyllie so you had a real, brains trust there. I think you learn more from adversity than success, and 1986 was adversity, and it was the platform for the success that followed.

Murray Pierce: The Australian connection was great around that time. You had the Kirwan-Campese battle which was always great. Australia were probably the most terrifying of the Tests I played because I had the joy of marking Steve 'Skylab' Cutler. I'm 6ft 6in and he's at least 6ft 8in with arms to match and we all had to jump by ourselves in the lineouts back then. I used to like getting up and competing and I like to think we came out 50-50 in those Test matches and I can recall only losing once to Australia in my Tests.

John Kirwan: We were gutted to lose the Bledisloe Cup. It was horrible. The environment was uncomfortable. Kiwis are kiwis you just get on with it and it was a natural changing of the guard. What they should have done was cut a lot of those older guys and moved on.

David Kirk: It was in the third Test that the lack of coherence and preparation rubber hit the road because we came out wanting to acquit ourselves well playing hard and fast, but making mistakes in the first twenty minutes. We had opportunities to score tries but balls got dropped and passes went astray because of the anxiety and stress in the team. Australia played well and their last try, to David Campese, which stretched the margin was based on us trying to run the ball from on our own line. I don't think they ever didn't deserve to win the Bledisloe Cup and take it home.

Murray Mexted: The World Cup had been mooted for the following year and I had played against all the teams who were coming so it didn't seem such a big deal. When we were banned for two games that was a tough pill to swallow because at that stage I had played every Test match for the best part of eight years. That was something I was proud of and to be denied on a technicality I thought was disappointing and a lot of other players felt it was a disappointing way to go out after good careers. Buck Shelford asked me if I was going back to New Zealand to play because he had been made an offer in South Africa and he would have stayed and played. I said I was retiring and he said, 'Thanks,' and came back and missed his two games and then became the All Blacks No.8.

The combined forces of the Cavaliers and the Baby Blacks were merged for an eight-game tour of France, as well as two newcomers in Auckland prop John Drake and English-born Wellington utility back John Gallagher. Six regional teams were accounted for and the French beaten with reasonable comfort in the first international, but the second Test was a different matter. In what became known as 'The Battle of Nantes', the All Blacks were beaten in brutal fashion by a French team so fired up as to arouse suspicions that there was more than sugar in their pre-match coffee. Worst affected was All Black No.8 Buck Shelford, who was badly concussed and had his scrotum ripped open by a well-aimed boot. Shelford later accused the French forwards of being on drugs, a claim given credence by a French investigative journalist who quoted a France team doctor as saying the players 'were loaded' with amphetamines. The result had two repercussions. A post-match drinking session saw members of the Cavaliers faction round on Kirk over his stance on their tour, highlighting a potentially destructive rift, whilst the game itself, and in particular the thuggish French behaviour, stuck in the craw of the All Blacks as they set their sights on Rugby's first World Cup.

John Gallagher: After the loss to Australia and with the World Cup in mind, the selectors obviously wanted an injection of new players [for the tour to France] . . . The tour really hit home to me the need to concentrate for eighty minutes, even more so than for representative rugby. The only way to learn is by playing top-class rugby to that level.

Wayne Shelford: In the early-mid-1980s I was in that Auckland team that really changed the way we were playing. It was all about a fast game with high skills, and that eventually was brought into the All Blacks. You had to be fit to play it. We won the provincial championship in 1982, lost it in '83 and won it back in '84, and through that time it was virtually the same team. Canterbury were playing a similar sort of game, although with perhaps a bit more emphasis on what was happening up front. We'd win the ball and play through the backs, they tended to play a bit more through the forwards but it was very good dynamic rugby. We had a thing we called SAPS – Simplicity, Accuracy, Pressure, Skill. I believe that changed the way we play rugby in New Zealand, because come '87 the two coaches of those teams, John Hart and Grizz Wyllie were assistants to BJ Lochore. They must have discussed how they wanted to play and a lot of it was the blueprint from that stuff we'd been playing with Auckland. We felt if we could play at that tempo the rest of the world would be caught napping.

John Gallagher: I came to New Zealand at the start of 1984 and I didn't play for Wellington as a fullback until 1986 when Allan Hewson retired. After about three months in Wellington I was loving it. I didn't want to come back [to London] at that stage. I went to see Don Bond the chairman at Ories and said, 'I love it here, do I have to go home?' He said, 'Come and see me Monday morning.' I had this address, walked into this big building and said I had an appointment to see Mr Bond. They pointed me to his office and there's this big door with a sign on it saying, 'Donald David Bond, Director of Immigration'! He had a list of twenty occupations and professions they were after, number one was brain surgeons and number twenty was chartered accountants. I looked at him and said, 'You're having me on.' He said, 'Look further down the page.' I did and it said, 'Other.' I said, 'Other?' And he said, 'Yeah, other.' He said if you make the Wellington team we can make a case for you. I got citizenship after five years. I had some good games for Wellington, I think I was man of the match against Auckland and Canterbury and later in the year they picked me as a utility in the team to go to France.

Gary Whetton: In France there were still a few players who were divided. I was lucky I wasn't finishing or near the end but it was quite a difficult tour to try and get the guys together. There was resentment from some players right through until the end.

John Gallagher runs down the touchline against France in 1986. *FotoSport/Photosport NZ*

John Kirwan: David Kirk and I roomed together a lot in France. There was a little bit of animosity towards him. I couldn't think of a better man to have done what he did putting up with all that pressure, and then taking on the captaincy during the World Cup. I love Kirky, he's a special individual and really different. I think what he achieved, under the pressure, was outstanding and I don't think many men could have done it, but he did. At times I think it hurt him, but in the end he held up that World Cup in 1987 and it was a real tribute to the man.

Wayne Shelford: Touring France is pretty hard, you're being set up all the time. They're all tough games and by the time we got to that second Test, of a twenty-six-man party, we had about fourteen or fifteen injured. We didn't want to go to the bench in that game because all the reserves were carrying injuries. I reckon they [France] were drugged up to their eyeballs in that game. It's come out recently that they were. A doctor wrote about it, but I remember looking at them in the tunnel. You look your opponent in the eye, and I could tell something was up. I mean normally you can see they're pretty focused, but I looked at these guys and their eyes were all red. They had guys like Carminatti, Erbani, Rodriguez, they played in a way that was pretty hard to contain. In the end I had to go off. I wasn't worried about what happened 'down there'. I was more worried about the concussion. I got concussed badly, knocked out cold and didn't know where I was, but Jock wouldn't let me go off. You wouldn't do that today. I got knocked out in the twentieth minute and I didn't go off until twenty minutes into the second half and in the meantime everything else happened, getting kicked down there, in the nuts, kicked in the face, losing teeth. It was a brutal game. I've never seen so much blood. Guys were bleeding

Wayne Shelford tackles Dominic Erbani during
the 'Battle of Nantes', 15 November 1986. *FotoSport/Photosport NZ*

round the eyes, cut heads. But it was a huge thing that came out of that game. We'd lost our mana, and I felt the only way we were going to get it back was to beat France in the final of the World Cup.

Gary Whetton: We played really well in France. We won every game up until that last game. They played extraordinarily, but the French can do that. We're not talking about drugs, or whatever, they can play that way. And when it clicks, it clicks, that's the French. They always play physical and they were determined. I came off just after half-time, my ankle was playing up. I played nearly every game and I needed a rest and BJ wouldn't rest me. So I came off about five minutes before Buck came off. It was 3-3 then. There were instances in the game where it was brutal but every French game is brutal.

John Kirwan: Nantes was filthy. We were out-muscled that day, we played poorly, they played really well and it was a shit fight. The game should never be played like that. On that tour I think Fitzy got 186 stitches in the head, in the end I was stitching him – the doctor had had enough. That type of rugby was old school and you can't do that anymore. That was the last time I saw it, thank God.

David Kirk: We played pretty well in the first Test in Toulouse. They went to Nantes having been beaten and I think Jacques Fouroux made a statement, probably in a far more emphatically Gallic way than Brian Lochore had made a couple of years before to the older players before the English Test and players were going to get the chop if they didn't play well in Nantes. They came out incredibly aggressive. And good luck to them, that's probably what other people have been on the end of from the All Blacks. But there's no question it was a very dirty game and the dirtiness came from them. It was punching, kicking and stomping and we suffered. Players were concussed, had cuts in their head. It remains the most physical and physically aggressive off-the-ball, or in circumstances where players have an opportunity to physically attack another player, game I've ever played in.

Murray Pierce: France was a hard country to tour. They'll give you an interpreter who hardly speaks any English, the bus driver gets lost, a real hard country to tour but enjoyable. By Nantes we were pretty exhausted. It had been a really long season and a lot of us were pretty stuffed at that stage, carrying injuries. We said after if ever there was a team high on drugs it was those jokers. They came out and the French props had blood running down their foreheads where they had been head-butting the wall of the changing room we found out afterwards. They kicked-off to us and all the All Black forwards got around to take the kick and I reckon all eight of us got smashed out of the way by this French forward pack who came and bulldozed us apart. We looked at each other and thought, 'Shit, we've got a game on here.' One of the few Test match losses I suffered was that game but it turned out to be a blessing in 1987.

Sean Fitzpatrick: That trip to France I think was a turning point for that team. We got rid of a lot of the older dead wood, and guys like Kipper [John Gallagher], then Michael Jones came in.

John Gallagher: After being selected I was driving with a colleague in a police car around Oriental Bay [Wellington] and he said, 'John do you know the haka?' I just went, 'Oh no!' I had some intensive training, and the night before my first game against a French Selection in Strasbourg, at the end of a team meeting, Buck [Shelford] said, 'Right all those boys who are making their debut stay behind', and we had a practice. I knew the words and I could do the actions OK, but just not the words and the actions together, so Buck looked at me, and he told the rest to go and for me to stay. He was really patient. You couldn't learn the haka, and the meaning of it, from anyone better than Buck. It was a real honour for me, but in the end it was getting painful and he said, 'Tomorrow night I'll be in the middle of the crescent, you just stand right behind me and do what I do.' In the end Maori people were saying I was doing a good job of the haka, so I put that down to Buck.

THIRTY-ONE

A RUGBY WORLD CUP

*'We all got fitness programmes, but I chucked mine away,
I thought it was too easy'*

THE RUGBY WORLD Cup has become the pinnacle of the game, reaching a stratospheric level few could have envisaged on a showery May afternoon in Auckland, 1987. Eden Park was not even half-full for the opening match between the All Blacks and Italy, a game preceded by a modest 'ceremony' consisting of the great Waka Nathan running through the rain with the Webb Ellis Cup and a group of school children. It had to start somewhere. The All Blacks were not the favourites. That tag was bestowed upon the Australians, having claimed the Bledisloe Cup the year before. But this was an All Black team well-primed for the challenge. Coach Brian Lochore had enlisted the help of the country's two leading provincial coaches John Hart and Alex Wyllie, polar opposites, but whose attributes were cleverly harnessed. They picked a team to play an expansive, high-tempo game, and employed the Scottish-born Auckland fitness guru Jim Blair to ensure they were in the best possible shape to be able to play it. With the addition of the extraordinary young Auckland flanker Michael Jones, an excellent team was put together. The only glitch was a training injury suffered by captain Andy Dalton, and it was David Kirk who would lead the team in all of their matches. Italy were put to the sword in the opening game, an encounter that began with a penalty try, followed by the first individual touchdown of the tournament scored on debut by Jones. The most memorable moments however, were an astonishing end-to-end solo try by Kirwan, and a post-match interview by the Italian captain Marzio Innocente, who tearfully bemoaned the fact that 'they have ALWAYS the ball.' They ran up a second twelve-try, 70-point score against Fiji, and despite fielding several newcomers, including Zinzan Brooke, comfortably accounted for Argentina 46-15.

John Kirwan: We played a game down south after the Ranfurly Shield challenge against Canterbury in 1986 and Michael Jones was just unbelievable. At the beginning of 1987 we went on a Baabaas trip to Britain with John Hart and he was just unbelievable. It was again a change in eras. I was the first big wing, he was the first loose forward who should have been a wing. This guy came into the game and he was an incredible athlete – fast, agile, tough. And it was also the beginning of the Polynesian athlete era.

David Kirk: I think the coaching strategy worked really well in the World Cup. Brian had been around for three years. The other two had only come in that year as selectors and it was a great move by the NZRU to put Alex and John in because they were coaching the two best teams in the country and possibly two of the best provincial teams we've ever had. The players had a lot of confidence in them. They selected a team that was dominated

Opposite: David Kirk, with team-mates behind, accepts the Webb Ellis Trophy Peter Bush

by those two teams with the honourable mention of Wellington who had a few good players in the team as well.

Andy Dalton: The World Cup was probably a year too late for me in some respects but it was exciting to be around and to be involved. The injury was frustrating and that's what I have to live with, more because it was self-imposed. I'd tried to run on a strained hamstring which was bloody stupid in hindsight. I pulled it so badly that I was out for the next three weeks. Brian told me I needed to play against Argentina if I wanted to be considered for the semis and final.

Wayne Shelford: We all got fitness programmes, but I chucked mine away, I thought it was too easy. I used to run huge miles every day, and I'd do speed work between the power poles on the way to work, sprint, jog, sprint, and then I'd do 400m sprints in my lunch hour, running for sixty seconds as fast as I could. I'd seen Michael Jones playing since he was in the Auckland Colts, Zinzan Brooke too, and you could see these guys were special. With that, blended in with the guys who'd come through that French game, it made for a pretty good team. They kept Andy in there because they wanted a leader, even though he got hurt, Andy was still there, talking to the guys, like a mentor.

Gary Whetton: We were unsure of what to expect with the World Cup. We had the last trial up in Whangarei and I was on the bench. The selectors told me I was fine, they had me marked. And then at training we threw the ball around and I fell over a machine and split my eye wide open. Then, all of a sudden it started to build. If they hadn't brought John Hart and Grizz Wyllie in as selectors it wouldn't have happened. It was massive. They had the nous to look at it and ask, 'How are we going to beat the world? Are we the best at lineouts, scrums whatever and with what we've got?' And they selected the guys to play to their game plan.

John Gallagher: Before the trial BJ said to me: 'Just play a safe normal game, don't do anything stupid like taking on the whole team like you usually do. It was also great having John Hart there, he got it into my head about running the right lines. He completed my tuition in the position. Clive Currie, Earle Kirton and John Hart have been the biggest influences on my game. Kirton wanted my running style of play for Wellington, and Hart refined it.

David Kirk: On one level we knew what the World Cup meant but on another level we didn't. No one could realise what an extravaganza, a kind of world festival and how much money it would generate, or how much the television viewership would be but that's a consequence of the world and what's changed, and how sport has become such a huge commercial enterprise globally. We couldn't have foreseen that but we definitely understood from the first moment that this was our opportunity and, in our case, it was the first opportunity to prove we were the best in the world. When it comes down to the crunch, when it is team against team, you've got to beat that team and that team, and you've got to win the final – that is the ultimate challenge in world rugby. That is the only time you can truly call yourself world champions. That hasn't changed.

Sean Fitzpatrick: I was in awe of Andy Dalton, he was a legend. We checked into our hotel a few days before the start of the tournament. BJ didn't make it to our first meeting because he'd got snowed in on his farm, and that's when Froggy [Dalton] took us for a run. He said, 'Right, we'll do some fitness work' and he led us on these Hennie Mullers. We were running around the track and he was fifty yards in front of me and I was thinking, 'He's as fit as a buck rat.' And then he pulled his hamstring. And that was it for him.

Warwick Taylor: Normally when you got selected for the All Blacks in those days you just heard about it on the radio. In 1987 they had trials up in Whangarei and then they got all the players from the trials together and announced the team. I found that was the worst thing I have ever encountered. I mean directly opposite me was Arthur Stone, we were good mates and I made the World Cup team and he missed out. It was terrible. I'd made my way back into the team which was a great feeling, but Arthur had missed out and that was his goal as well. It was a really funny night, they never did it like that again.

John Kirwan: Brian Lochore summed up our attitude to the World Cup. He said, 'We are world champions. We've got 100 years of history to back that and we don't need a World Cup to say we are world champions. But if we lose the first one then we've ruined 100 years of tradition.' We couldn't care who we played. I think in 1987 it was really important for New Zealand that we confirmed we were the world's best rugby team because we were that without a World Cup.

David Kirk: There were fourteen Aucklanders in the squad, and ten played in the final and the style Auckland played came through, and it was the same style that Canterbury played. I think Auckland had somewhat more athletic and skilful players so they could play that same style to a slightly higher level, but it was still the same style. It was based on continuity and this was really the first time the All Blacks started to develop that. We had wings who would run when we moved the ball, double-miss passes, fullbacks in the line all the time, sometimes going to the fullback, sometimes missing him out, wings would stretch the opposition and they were big and stood in tackles and looked for passes inside. Think of the number of times of John Kirwan giving it to Alan Whetton and Craig Green getting it to Michael Jones. It was always about continuity and getting the ball away in the tackle.

Warwick Taylor: We were a step ahead of the rest for fitness, which made the game a lot easier; to think about things, make decisions under pressure, everything gelled. We were more professional. We were still amateurs but what we did, training and so on, was really professional. That was the difference.

John Kirwan: I wasn't allowed to go to Italy that year, no one was allowed to go overseas. We got put on a Jim Blair fitness regime. I also had a personal trainer and we knew if there were bankers and people who owned bars coming down to play this game, we were going to beat them up physically. We trained really hard and were all in great shape. My job was to have a go but never die with the ball.

It was a Friday afternoon, 15,000 people at Eden Park and we started on this thing called a World Cup. The only reference we had was the soccer World Cup and we didn't know what we were getting ourselves in for. It just grew. From that day it took off. By the end we realised this was pretty special and was the way the game was going. It was a combination of things that made people sit up and take notice.

Sean Fitzpatrick: We didn't have any superstars, but everyone did their job. My job was to throw the ball in straight, Foxy to kick the goals, Drakey to keep the right side of the scrum up, others to carry the ball and everyone did their jobs well and made very few mistakes. We had guys like Zinny and Foxy who were such students of the game and always looking at ways to break down a side's defences. We were very hard on each other.

Warwick Taylor: In a way the [Cavaliers] tour to South Africa helped because we'd played four Tests week after week, and at the World Cup we were playing Test after Test. You needed back-up players because they could be needed down the track. Playing between Grant Fox and Joe Stanley was a dream ride. Foxy knew how to get us down the right end of the field and Joe had great ball-handling skills. He could crunch it up but he could put his outsides away . . . Joe and I used to love that the wingers scored most of the tries. We felt we had done our job if we could give them space and they could score. We had some great times.

John Kirwan: Joe Stanley made both John Gallagher and I. He would pass the ball thirty yards and it would stay on the same line so Kipper [Gallagher] and I could pick and choose. Sometimes John would look like he could get at it and he would leave it alone and it would come to me and I would change my angle. He was an outstanding timer of running lines so we became a double threat. The defences in those days played a lot of man on man, the French were the only ones who would drift. So when you had the pass from Joe and a double threat coming into your attacking line, we could cause a lot of problems for defences. John might hit a line and I would bounce late. My winger would be looking to take me while also keeping an eye on John, so I would bounce and the ball would come so I could beat them, or I would cut late which was something I learned off Craig Green. He was a great angle runner and I learnt a lot from him about running angles and working off the ball.

John Gallagher: I don't think it could have gone any better. The Cavaliers thing split the nation in 1986, as it had in '81, but I hadn't been part of the Cavaliers and I hadn't been an All Black so I could go in fresh. Andy Dalton was a great leader, even though he didn't take the field, he still did a great job, but from the media side, having David Kirk there as captain was quite a good thing. Foxy at ten and Joe at 13, they were the pivots of that backline. I run straight, I see space, and I could time a run . . . that was my big advantage . . . and having Joe there, forget about his defensive abilities, which were huge, but for someone like me, taking a twenty-five-yard run from the back to hit a spot after the balls been taken off the top of a lineout, I could just pick a spot and hit it, anywhere, because Foxy and Joe were the constants. Joe had this peripheral vision, soft hands, and if I'm running off his shoulder and I'm covered, then he had the ability to read it, and miss me and hit JK with a pass, or TJ [Wright] or Craig [Green]. Joe's contribution to the team, and to me, was immeasurable.

David Kirk: JK had been around and had been a star for two or three years. But Michael Jones just exploded at the World Cup. It's quite cool for me that the three guys who scored tries in the final were Michael Jones, myself and JK, they being two of my favourite players to play with. Michael's level of anticipation, his ball skills and his ability to be in the right place at the right time, was uncanny. Because he had such explosiveness off the mark he got more chargedowns, made more tackles behind the advantage line and more intercepts . . . he was quicker, he had thinking in his anticipation and his athleticism put him in the right position and that's what the very great athletes had, the Michael Jordans of this world. He was freakish and as the challenge went up, the scale went up and he got even better players around him, he got better and through that year and into the next year and beyond he was an uncannily good player.

Michael Jones (1987-98, 55 Tests, 74 games): That was a dream ride for me, and I suppose at the same time an armchair ride. All of a sudden as a 22-year-old I was playing alongside some of the best All Blacks that were ever to grace the field. Not only that, they were all playing at the top of their game. It couldn't have been better. What the 1987 All Blacks did was take the game to a new plane. It was a wonderful time to be involved . . . You can't ask for a better way to start your career.

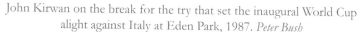

John Kirwan on the break for the try that set the inaugural World Cup alight against Italy at Eden Park, 1987. *Peter Bush*

Grant Fox: None of us really knew Michael Jones, but John Hart had had his eye on him and he excelled in the trial in Whangarei. You get a sense when you see someone about how special, how good they're going to be. You could see it with this guy, his grace and his balance, his silky skills, his anticipation. He was a freak. I believe if you'd said to Michael we want you to play centre, just give him a few games, he'd have done it . . . notwithstanding we had the great Joe Stanley. I have this enduring memory of Michael. It was when we played Fiji in the World Cup and we did one of our very simple moves . . . a miss two and Joe carted it up to set up a ruck, but he actually breached and Michael got on his shoulder. I've seen the replay, he just accelerates, and the ease and the grace with which he did it, and I can't remember if it was Kipper or Greeno, but he just ran it up, drew the fullback and put him away. It spoke volumes about this incredible athlete.

John Gallagher: We were arguably third favourites for that World Cup, having been beaten by the Aussies the year before and drawn the series in France . . . and we had a much-changed team. It wasn't just the New Zealand public, there was also pressure from the world media, so when the final whistle went it was relief. It's only when you look back you realise how fantastic the achievement was.

Warwick Taylor: Brian Lochore knew how to mould a team and he brought us together. During the tournament he took us down to Wairarapa and we were billeted out for two nights on farms, it was great. We went into a big hall and our names were called out . . . I was with JK, and the Whetton boys were on the next property. It took me back to my school days. It was a real good grounding, reality, and it rammed it home that these were the people we were playing for, real New Zealanders. It was a real connection, and I don't know anyone else who would have thought of doing that, other than Brian.

Scotland were expected to provide sterner resistance in the quarter-final in Christchurch, but they too succumbed to the All Blacks' running game 30-3, and when Wales, the last survivors of the Home Unions, were laid to waste by 49-6 in the Brisbane semi-final, the All Blacks had booked a place at Eden Park for the final. The only sharp intake of breath came when Buck Shelford took exception to a flurry of punches thrown by Welsh lock Huw Richards and meted out his own justice with a single blow that left Richards prone. Once he came to, Richards was sent off by Australian referee Kerry Fitzgerald, Shelford altogether fortunate not to join him. Retaliation then was not the cardinal sin it is today.

Gary Whetton: The hardest game mentally was the Scottish game. We rated them. They drew with the French earlier on and we all realised that if we lose this game we go home. We were playing well but hadn't really tested ourselves. We went out and executed our game plan. We wanted to scrum well because they were a very good scrummaging team, we wanted to be dominating at the breakdown and we wanted to use the ball wide and with good pace. Everyone talks about their hardest day of training. Grizz said, 'Right you're mine for the day,' and bang we were into it. We easily did more than 100 scrums. Drakey fell out first. He said, 'I've had enough of this.' It was hard work, and the Canterbury boys said, 'Get used to it.' We could be physical, but it made us mentally harder and tougher and demanding of each other. It was a big, big thing. You couldn't do that every week. It was a very good call, and Harty took the backs. We did our job and we won. We didn't realise how good we were.

Wayne Shelford: In the quarter-final, the papers were writing up that Scotland were going to take our front row apart, and the heat was on Drakey, Steve McDowall and Fitzy. We went to training in Christchurch and Grizz took the forwards and we were on that scrum machine for an hour, hour and a half. Then it was on the bags. Every time someone dropped a ball we'd have to go back and start again. He really flogged us. We went out and pretty much crushed them.

John Kirwan: I remember BJ Lochore coming into the changing room, because it was sudden death and we'd never had sudden death. He had two lots of tickets in his hands and he said, 'Lose on Saturday, here's your tickets home, and in this hand are tickets to Brisbane – 100 years of tradition' and threw them both in the air. There was silence and Buck Shelford said: 'Well, I'm not f . . . ing losing,' and walked out onto the training field so we all got up and followed. We were never going to lose. There was a determination among all of us that was fantastically palatable and great to be part of.

Sean Fitzpatrick: Andy was available for the quarter-final, but there were discussions and they said, 'We'll stick with the team that's been playing.' Kirky did a great job as captain but Andy was outstanding. If I'd been in that position I don't know whether I could have dealt with it the way he did . . . the guidance he gave me, he was like a father-figure. I always felt a little bit guilty about him not getting on, but in those days you couldn't fake an injury. I've always felt it would have been nice in that final if I'd said, 'I've got a sore leg,' and let Froggy on . . . but in those days it wasn't in my nature.

Andy Dalton: Fitzy went down several times during the semi and final but he never came off, the bastard, and neither would have I if it had been me! But it was still great to be part of a very good team. It was very technical and three outstanding coaches, although Brian's greatest achievement was probably managing Grizz and Harty, both of whom wanted a part of the action.

John Gallagher: The pressure was always on not to make mistakes. You could score three or four tries in a game, but the selectors were not looking at that, they were watching the number of mistakes.

Gary Whetton: We went to Brisbane against the Welsh. We weren't as nervous against them – only in the sense we realised we weren't going to work the next day, because there was a play-off, not that we wanted that, but our motivation was we don't want to go to Rotorua. We just wanted to get out there and keep executing our game plan. We were humming then.

Grant Fox: Australia were perceived as the biggest threat so that result was a bit surprising, but, as history has told us, never under-estimate France. That semi-final was one of the greatest games of rugby ever played, the ebb and flow, the skills involved, a lot of points for a Test at that time, it was spectacular. We didn't think about it until after the event, but I'm sure that was France's final. They expended a lot of emotional energy to get up that day. It's not easy to replicate that level of intensity whether it's a World Cup final or not . . . the All Blacks of 2011 had some trouble replicating the level of intensity of playing Australia the week before the final.

Wayne Shelford: We sat in our team room in Brisbane on the Saturday and watched the Aussie-France game, and every time the Aussies scored we'd go, 'Oh ****,' and when the French scored it was, 'YES' . . . we were all thinking about '86. We knew we had to get through the Welsh and then we'd have our shot at the French. We were so fired up for that game against Wales because we knew we would get our chance.

Gary Whetton: [Huw] Richards was retaliating for something I did, but no one saw that. That's what he was complaining about. He got me off balance and hit me, that was fine but then Buck stepped in big time and AJ tried to do something to someone else and the late Kerry Fitzgerald woke Richards up and asked him if he was all right and then to get off. That's all he saw. I was worried for Buck, we all were.

Wayne Shelford: Kerry Fitzgerald came up to me later and said, 'You're lucky I didn't see you hit him or you'd have gone as well.' He didn't see it, the touch judge didn't. We didn't have so many replays in those days, so I was quite lucky. Huw Richards, every time I see him says, 'Why did you hit me?' and I say, 'Well what were you doing to Gary Whetton?' and he'll say, 'But he deserved it,' and I say, 'Yes I know he did but he was my mate, he's on my side.'

Murray Pierce: Every now and then when you go on tour you are living with the same people you sometimes get a bit pissed off, and now and then alcohol would provide us with a great release. I remember we had a really good session three or four days before that semi-final in Australia and it released a lot of tension. Every Test match in that '87 campaign we just wanted to improve.

David Kirk: The captaincy was easy. I had captained the All Blacks the previous year. A lot of the team had changed so it was predominantly a team of younger players who I knew and had played with and who had confidence in me, and respected me, so I felt very much at home. It was really rotten luck for Andy [Dalton] but he was injured right from the beginning and didn't take part in any of the training runs before the first match so by the time we got to the final team run before that match he did try to slot in but he didn't have to do much to know that he couldn't do it. Brian was very quick to say, 'David you'll captain the team.'

John Kirwan: We always thought we would play Australia [in the final] but we knew that France were totally unpredictable. When France beat Australia it was brilliant and for me that was fantastic and I thought, 'Great, here we go.'

Warwick Taylor: When France scored that last try everyone, to a T, went up, cheering for France. You could hear it echoing down the hallway, because we knew how good Australia were. It was a kind of feeling that we knew France had played a fantastic game, but could they peak twice? If it had been Aussie . . . we would have been a bit more worried.

The All Blacks expected to meet Australia in the final, and had watched the first semi-final the previous day as the Wallabies unravelled against an inspired French team in Sydney. In one of the greatest of all World Cup matches, the French stormed home to win through a late try by fullback Serge Blanco. Not only were the pre-tournament favourites out, the All Blacks would get the chance to avenge their bloody defeat in Nantes. In front of a heaving Eden Park crowd there would be no repeat of Nantes, and little of the brilliance that had swept France to victory against Australia. The All Blacks took control early when Jones crossed following a miscued dropped goal attempt by Grant Fox. It was not until the middle of the second half that the resistance was truly broken. A period of pressure finally produced a second try when Jones ran strongly off a Fox inside-ball and offloaded to Kirk who darted over, thumping the ground in the knowledge that the game was, in all likelihood, New Zealand's. Moments later Kirk ducked around the side of a ruck that had formed from the restart, and shot off upfield, a brilliant pick up and pass by Shelford then putting Kirwan in for the clincher. The French got a late consolation try through skipper Pierre Berbizier.

Gary Whetton: The country had come alive, it was amazing. The drive to the game, the people, the horns and the crowd, it was fantastic. The only time we had had that before was in 1981 with planes, helicopters, containers and barbed wire. We got there, the pressure was on, we were anxious, there's no doubt about that. We weren't afraid, we just needed to execute and to do the job.

Grant Fox: I think the key to success is what you do Monday to Friday, that determines what happens on Saturday. The week leading up to the final was intense, focused, accurate, and actually very quiet. It was as if everyone understood what their job was. The captain's run was at King's College and we trained short and sharp, there wasn't a ball dropped, not much was said.

Warwick Taylor: I wasn't that confident but there was a thought that if we start well and get on top of them they weren't going to do two in a row – and we started well. [Philippe] Sella was the best player I played against at international level, just incredible. If there was a try scored against France he'd be the person there putting the tackle in trying to stop them, or he'd be making the pass to put someone in for a try. We knew we had to be on top of our game to contain him.

Murray Pierce: Our levels of confidence were pretty good ahead of the final. We were humming nicely without any injury concerns, apart from Andy Dalton. A lot of us had played in Nantes. This was the chance for revenge. When we saw the hundreds of people at the hotel to farewell us ahead of the final we thought, 'Wow, this is big.' I can never forget the bus trip. That can be one of the most nervous times because your mind is free to think about the game – the butterflies are flying and the adrenaline is pumping and there were people all along the road waving to us, cars tooting horns, supporting us. We were all buzzing before the kick-off and it was almost a case of settle down boys don't peak too early.

Gary Whetton: Did we think we would win the World Cup? No. Did we think we were a good team? Yes. You have to remember that all these teams didn't play each other too often and so we just thought, 'Right the next game is against France, keep to our team, keep to our patterns.' The coaches had more of an idea of what we could do than we did. We didn't quite know what we could do. I think they did but they weren't going to tell us that. BJ was the figurehead, he was a great motivator, he has a great aura about him and is still a fantastic guy. He could see players and pick players and he had these two guys who could see differences and subtleties and suggestions so that they worked very well as a team. We had all matured, arrived, hardened up. There were no primadonnas, we weren't conceited. JK was a superstar but then the fourteen guys made him.

John Kirwan: I thought I was going to score the first try when it deflected but the Iceman [Michael Jones] scored it.

David Kirk: I honestly felt, and that's why I thumped the ground with my fist, we'd won the World Cup when I scored my try. You know in games when you are getting on top and you feel when you are playing well and executing and being accurate and strong enough to stay on top. But we didn't quite have enough points and then we scored that try and that felt like enough and with two converted tries that was when I felt, 'Yes, that's it.'

John Kirwan: Kirky and I used to have a move called 'merde' where he would pass it to me and loop around me. We used it against the Aussies a few times and it worked. He would pass to me and I would try to hit between the loose forward and the halfback and jam those guys and try to bring my wing in, then give it to him on the outside. In the final I called the blindside, he looked up, sold a dummy and took off. I remember him getting hammered as he went down and Buck picked it up. I eased back a bit on the pace, then reaccelerated and Buck gave it to me. Pierre Berbizier came at me. I had been practising my fend a lot. I pushed him off and got this overspeed where you have to be careful to keep your feet.

David Kirk: We would always talk, saying, 'We'll do this move, we'll do that move.' We rehearsed things and were always ready for stuff and it was always a little bit made-up. You did what worked for the circumstance. But we had the skills and capability to make it work. I ducked under the tackle and then took off and JK couldn't keep up. I was looking for someone to pass to because I knew I was going to run into someone sooner or later. Then about thirty or forty metres later there was still no one there to pass to and he was supposed to be the guy. I hit the ground, placed the ball and Wayne Shelford picked it up and then JK arrived. He timed it well because he hit the pass pretty much at full gas, and went all the way.

John Kirwan: In those sorts of matches you have to stay in the moment. We knew the French can come back at any time but that try was a pretty important one to get. It broke their back. Running back to halfway the boys were saying we had to really smash them now and put the game out of contention, shut them out and not give them an inch.

Gary Whetton: There was no let-up, it wasn't until the last five minutes we knew we had it. We wanted to keep on doing it. That last try we went, 'Wow,' but got stuck in again until it was over.

Murray Pierce: I don't remember too much about the final, but I do recall France scored a try a few minutes from the end. I raised my fist to the crowd to say, 'We've won' and the crowd just erupted in unison. Going up the steps in the Eden Park grandstand to receive the Cup was a great buzz. But a real sense of relief as well.

The crowd poured onto the field at the end to watch Kirk hold the trophy aloft, and then call on Dalton to share the moment. It might be viewed in hindsight as a symbolic gesture, bringing together once and for all the leaders of the Baby Blacks and the Cavaliers. By today's standards the first Rugby World Cup was a modest affair . . . only 20,000 had attended the opening ceremony, a meagre 17,000 the fantastic semi-final in Sydney. But enough good had been done to ensure the tournament had a future. Almost immediately the Northern Hemisphere nations, amongst whose number had been many staunchly resistant to the concept, began to realise its potential. The biggest concern amongst traditionalists remained that it would set rugby on the path to professionalism, and whilst they would fight tooth and nail, they would, in a relatively short space of time, lose that

John Kirwan scores in the final. *InphoPhotography*

battle too. As for the All Blacks, no one would have considered it would be another twenty-four years before they held the trophy again.

Gary Whetton: With time the win means so much more than it did. It hadn't sunk in. We have great pride now and I'm, sure ninety per cent of the team think the same that we were the first, we did it well and are proud of it. It's not easy to win it. We always have the players but it's how we react under pressure. That's when you find out about people. I grew and grew and found out more about myself, good, bad, indifferent, reflection, better person, worse person, would have done that differently. It's not easy, you learn things. Leadership, when you are leading either directly, or indirectly, is a hard thing.

David Kirk: The Cup helped New Zealand rugby heal. It brought us all together and we all got focused again on seeing New Zealand win. But I do think you can't under-estimate the transition in players. New Zealand crowds were supporting new people, not people who had gone to South Africa so I think that was a big part of it. New Zealand rugby had moved on.

John Kirwan: A lot of people say the South Africans weren't there. But that first World Cup was so important for the history of our game. We had to win so that we were the world champions. We had an historical pressure on us that we had to win. And no one can take that away from you.

Wayne Shelford: The World Cup wasn't all that well supported by the Home Nations, even the IRB, not until after it had been completed and they could see what the repercussions could be, the potential for the thing to grow into something really big. It's a monster, but it's a good monster. I think it's great. The South Africans would say, Louis Luyt said it, that it wasn't a proper World Cup because South Africa wasn't there, but hey, they weren't there. If they'd sorted their politics out a bit sooner they might have been. Just because they weren't there, doesn't mean they would have won.

Andy Dalton: We were in the changing room and it was exciting that we had won, but I was quite happy to stay there and let them go and get the Cup, the job had been done and I was happy to go and have a shower but BJ pushed me out there and it was a nice touch. I don't think any of us realized how big the World Cup was going to become. It was a tournament that was great to win but certainly not the big deal that it is now. There's a whole four-year cycle that revolves around the Cup.

Warwick Taylor: At the end of the game the crowd was still allowed to run on the field, it took a long time to get off. Then when we got into the changing room, Andy Dalton was there and I think he was shedding a tear. Then we all went up those stairs to get presented, we were all looking around thinking 'Wow – what is this?' I went out the back of the stands to the car park to show my medal off to my wife and my parents, but when I got out there . . . I guess I just thought they'd put it round our necks but they hadn't and it wasn't on me, and I thought, 'God I've lost it already!' We were looking around, under cars, and I thought it was gone, but when I went back inside it was there in the dressing room.

John Kirwan: The World Cup established rugby as a money-making game and I think they [the IRB] put £10 million in an account in the Channel Islands which I was pretty pissed off about because we got nothing. But then marketing started coming into the game, crowds were turning up when ten years earlier in Australia no one was turning up and then the Bledisloe Cup became pretty important and we were playing pretty good footy.

David Kirk: The Test at Concord Oval was a very important Test for me. I had been the captain the year before when we had lost the Bledisloe Cup which wasn't something I was proud of, and it was my last Test. We hadn't played Australia in the World Cup so just to put the final icing on the cake by beating the team who the previous year had been the favourites to win the World Cup, on their home ground, there was a lot riding on it. It was a tough game and I made a bad mistake in the second half. I ran the blindside just after we had scored and got ahead and instead of passing to John Gallagher, who was in the gap and who would probably have taken us right down, or potentially even scored, I decided to play it safe and kick for the corner. If I had kicked it properly it would have been a pretty good outcome but I didn't. I kicked it into Brett Papworth's legs and it bounced way down the field. Because John Gallagher was in the line Papworth could just keep running and gathered the ball and scored at the other end. So that put us behind again. That was about 10-15 minutes into the second half. I felt pretty bad but no one blinked an eyelid. It was just like, 'Let's get back to halfway and get the ball and win the game.' And we did. We became dominant in the last twenty minutes and scored three tries after that.

Gary Whetton: We looked forward to the Aussies at Concord. We were ready for them. We really wanted to play this game. And they wanted us. We just put them to the sword. They were a good team, mind you, we had most of New Zealand at the game.

John Kirwan: We played well that day, it was a great game of football. The motivation there was that if they beat us they would talk about being world champions and so it was important we won.

Murray Pierce: We knew if we had lost that game who would have been crowing that they should have been world champions. So there was no way we were going to lose.

Warwick Taylor: In a way that game was even more important than the final of the World Cup. They got an early try and I thought, 'Jeez, here we go', but we came back and beat them pretty well.

Wayne Shelford: The Aussies were getting tougher. A lot of that was because we were playing them more often. In that period there was a home and away three-Test series every second year, and it really improved their rugby. Simon Poidevin will tell you if it wasn't for them playing so much against the All Blacks they wouldn't have got to where they were by 1991.

THIRTY-TWO

RUGBY SUBLIME

*'I don't think it was the declining of Buck Shelford,
I just think it was the arriving of Zinzan Brooke'*

THERE WAS NEVER any doubt that Lochore's replacement would come from his two World Cup assistants, but the choice between Hart and Wyllie rekindled an age old North-South divide. Wyllie's Canterbury team had been superseded, both in terms of success and method, by Hart's Auckland. Hart was given charge of an experimental All Blacks side that toured Japan in late-1987, but when time came to make the full appointment, it was Wyllie, backed by a heavy Southern influence on the NZRFU board, who came through. Wyllie's team made a seamless progression into 1988, despite David Kirk taking up a Rhodes Scholarship at Oxford University, and John Drake, the cornerstone of the All Blacks 1987 scrum, surprisingly opting to retire. Wales visited in May and June, and were ruthlessly dispatched in two Tests, the 52-3 and 54-9 score lines taking the total of points conceded to the old rival in three Tests to 155. An unbeaten thirteen-match tour of Australia followed for the All Blacks with one hiccup. After the All Blacks won the first Test 32-7, the Australians fought back to draw the second Test 19-all. However, any thoughts of a shared series disappeared in a 30-9 thumping in Sydney.

Warwick Taylor: After the World Cup I went to Italy and played for eight months, missing a tour to Japan. John Hart took that team and I saw on TV how he'd let the cameras in for his pre-match talk, and I thought, 'You don't do that.' It grated a bit. About a week before the team to play Wales was picked I got an injury and rang Grizz, who had been appointed coach ahead of Hart, to say it might be best to pick someone else, but he said they'd just announced it and I was in. John Schuster was around and he was a good player and I guess if I hadn't played it would have given him the chance. But the leg came right and we had that two-Test series against Wales where everything came right. We scored lots of tries. During the World Cup I had an auntie who was dying of cancer and I'd rung her up and told her I'd get a try for her. Well I hadn't got a try and she died at the end of that year, and in that second Test, the last thing I ever did as an All Black, I got a ball on the blindside and scored a try, and wrote JR in the air in her memory. A mate said he thought it was me signing off. When we went to Aussie after that I broke my hand and never got back into the Test side, so it was signing off really. To be an All Black is the ultimate . . . and you have to be the best you can possibly be.

Murray Pierce: We had a core group of players that had come through in 1986-87 and from 1988-1990 we had a really good run. It was that draw in Brisbane that really fired us up for the third and final Test in 1988. When you make an All Blacks team you want to be part of a successful era and that's where players of that stature who had tremendous careers all came together at the same time.

Opposite: Michael Jones is felled by Wade Dooley at Twickenham. *InphoPhotography*

Gary Whetton: In Australia you have to motivate yourself because in between the hard matches you get some easy ones. We drew the second Test at Ballymore when we shouldn't have. We didn't start well, they did. We came back. Foxy missed a kick as I remind him all the time. He should have got it. In the third Test we knuckled down. We were pissed off from the second Test.

Sean Fitzpatrick: Our best years were probably 1988 and 1989. In 1988 we were 40 points better than anyone else – apart from when we drew that second Test against Australia. The disappointment because we'd become a little bit casual, maybe a bit arrogant, took our foot off the pedal and they drew – although Foxy missed a late kick that would have won the game. There was a real sense of devastation, guys ripping shreds off each other. But then on the Sunday Grizz took us to the club where we were going to train and said, 'Bugger that' and we were given ten bucks each and spent the next three hours having a few drinks and getting stuff off our chests. Two weeks later we beat them by 30 points.

John Kirwan: In 1988 it was good football. I scored one of my favourite tries to make it 19-all in Brisbane. It was very satisfying for me that Campo changed wings after that series because I rated him as the best wing in the world. To play well against him, and we were two very different players, I changed my game, and my training. I knew I had to get very close to him because if I didn't he'd have the pace to cover me and be a nuisance. I changed by stepping a lot later so that he had to make contact with me and I had to leave him on the ground, otherwise he liked to drift off and he was very good at that. When you marked him you knew that he was an outstanding stepper, had great pace, invented the goose step. I loved Campo as a player. He was a much better player than me and it was a big challenge to play him. I also brought a lot of anger because he was a pretty free spirit and not very aggressive so I had to try and intimidate him.

Bloodied captain Wayne Shelford with the Bledisloe Cup, 1988. *Peter Bush*

John Gallagher: New Zealand was in a really good place, Australia was always good, France was good, but the rest of them were way off the pace. In three matches, the semi-final of the World Cup and then two Tests the next year, we averaged about 50 points a game against Wales . . . and in 1988 they'd been the Five Nations champions. The Home Unions were really off the pace, and what they needed was professional rugby. Rugby in the Home Nations was still very much a middle-class game, a public school game, with the odd farmer chucked in from Cornwall. It was more a pastime than a serious sport. Ironically, the one place where rugby really was the number one sport was Wales, and they'd had these great sides in the 1970s, but by the late-1980s they were struggling when they played us. They had some great players, Jonathan Davies, John Devereaux, Paul Moriarty, but collectively when they played us, they battled.

John Kirwan: Wales came out in 1988 and we were all on our game, we were at the right age, we were the right combination of experience and youth and we were on fire through 1988 and 1989. I think I lost only one game of football in three years – Marist lost to Varsity in the Gallaher Shield final. Confidence is an amazing thing. And when you are on fire, and you back it up with experience and ability, there's nothing better. We had a great time. We'd have a few beers and a few laughs afterwards.

Grant Fox: You get periods in a team where there's a coming together of a whole lot of things, a group of world-class players in one period, and I think we had that coming together. Success in 1987 helped breed the confidence. At that time if you picked a World XV more than half would be All Blacks. Grizz had a great footy brain. He wasn't the most articulate, he was pretty direct, but he was very smart. It started to come apart a bit in 1990, but 1987 through to 1989 we were undefeated in twenty-three Tests. Just that one draw against Australia, when some mug missed a conversion that might have made the difference! But we were fifty games undefeated when you include tour matches, so that's a pretty successful period.

John Gallagher: The Australian tour was hard, especially playing in eleven of the thirteen games. But I improved all the way through. The things you could do from fullback were unlimited. If the backs spun the ball twenty times, there were fifteen or sixteen of them when you could get into the line.

The All Blacks' schedule swelled. In 1989, there were seven Test matches and a tour of Canada, Wales, Ireland and England. For the five home Tests, two each against France and Argentina and one against Australia, the All Blacks used the same starting XV with one exception. During the second Test against the Pumas, Michael Jones took a fly-hack at a loose ball just as Bertranou, the Pumas flanker, tried to claim it. Jones suffered a dreadful knee injury some feared would end his career. The All Blacks won the five matches scoring an average of five tries a match, fifteen in all to the back three of Kirwan, Gallagher and Terry Wright, with Fox averaging, as he had done at the World Cup, almost 20 points a game. They were undefeated in seventeen Tests since Nantes in 1986, and were to add to that sequence on their tour of Wales, Ireland and England. The All Blacks struck Welsh rugby in decline, at war with itself over poor international results, accusations of mismanagement, and club inspired parochialism. They met angry teams on the field, and angry supporters off it, particularly after the Neath game where English referee Fred Howard needed a police escort to get off the ground. The match at the Gnoll proved a tougher task than the Test in Cardiff comfortably won by the All Blacks 34-9. The second international of the tour will forever be known for the response of the Irish team to the pre-match haka. As the Lansdowne Road crowd roared their approval, the Irish captain Willie Anderson led his team forward, arms linked, to meet the challenge face to face. It was dubbed 'Paddy O'Haka' by some media, but the All Blacks took no issue with it, and it set the tone for a fast and furious encounter. The All Blacks had to work hard against a fired-up Irish side, before emerging with a 23-6 victory including a marvellous long range try by Gallagher, playing what turned out to be his final Test match. Grant Fox was denied his first Test try. Fox scampered across in the right-hand corner, only to find assistant-referee Jim Fleming still had his flag up for an incorrect throw-in by Sean Fitzpatrick on the far side some minutes earlier. Still, Fox kicked his goals and went past 600 points in his forty-first match for the All Blacks. The tour ended a week later in London, where a strong Barbarians side was beaten 21-10, bringing the curtain down on the most remarkable decade of New Zealand rugby.

Gary Whetton: 1989 was a great year for us, the team had really arrived. It was a great tour we had to Ireland and England. We played in Canada first and went across. We won every game and it was a great bonding tour again. It was a great tour for everyone – players, coaches. John Sturgeon, the manager, came into his own.

John Kirwan: It was disappointing how the Achilles injury happened. I had an acute Achilles going into the Pontypool game and Grizz gave me the choice of whether I should play or not. But I had Inga Tuigamala and Craig Innes who were good players chasing me and I didn't want to give anyone a sniff, especially Inga. You have moments in your life when you just have to knuckle down and that's what I did, I was really determined to get back. I don't think I was ever the explosive player that I was previously. I had to change my game.

Ian Jones (1989-99, 79 Tests, 105 games): My first tour was in 1989, fourteen matches in ten weeks, Canada, Wales and Ireland. I played six midweek games, but it was wonderful to be part of that squad. I didn't know anyone in the team. I hadn't been involved in any other New Zealand teams. It was quite a bold move by Grizz Wyllie to pick me . . . I'd only played about twelve games for North Auckland at that stage. It was most of the World Cup-winning side, with Buck Shelford as skip. My first game was at Cardiff Arms Park against the Cardiff club – that was amazing. I was involved in the Neath game. We had a big squad, twenty-six players, and grounds like the Gnoll, really it was a tiny club ground with an old grandstand and only room for about ten people in the changing room, so we got changed before we left the hotel and turned up in our match kit. We got there and the changing room door was locked, and no–one came to open it. Grizz was getting pretty fired-up, he had his game face on and in the end he booted the door open . . . just as the little man with the key arrived. Poor guy, he then had to stand guard over the changing room for the duration of the game.

Sean Fitzpatrick: I remember that tour of Wales in 1989, going around the provincial or club teams. That game against Neath, it was unbelievable, they were fanatical.

Ian Jones: We were playing teams that had beaten the All Blacks: Cardiff, Llanelli and the like, and for the whole week before the game the papers would be full of the occasion, the memories, the old games. You knew where you were, where you stood and it was great to be part of it, and be part of that team.

Socially it was great too. We'd have Sundays off in those days so we'd have a bit of fun, and for a young kid it was awesome, and made you think, 'This is what I want to be part of.' Seeing the awe that the All Blacks were held in . . . well you'd read about it, seen it on TV, but to feel it first hand was pretty bloody special. And as All Blacks you get treated pretty well, get taken to places, see things that other people might not get the opportunity to see.

Wayne Shelford: In 1989 they decided to go to co-captains. Gary Whetton was a co-captain. Grizz never said why. I was the captain, but they wanted to create a co-captain in case I got hurt. They were probably doing it for succession planning, and if I didn't play any of the games they had another captain. They had three or four provincial captains in the team as well, guys like Mike Brewer, who was captain of Otago. I found out, about 1994, that there'd been meetings behind closed doors to try and get rid of me – Aucklanders mainly. Mike Brewer told me, they'd asked him to be part of it. They wanted Gary to take over as captain and Zinny Brooke to be No.8. Before we left to go on the 1989 tour we had a dinner, and Zinny came and said, 'Buck can I see you?' I said, 'What's up?' Thinking he was going to tell me he'd signed for rugby league. That's why they were trying to get him in, to try and stop him going to rugby league. What he said was, 'Mate I've been told I'm going to be playing No.8 in the Tests.' I said, 'Where'd you get that from, who told you?' He said, 'Harty.' That was Harty's influence in the background, trying to get rid of me through the power of the senior players. I said, 'Zinny I love you, I like the way you play your footy. If you're playing better than me I'll stand down for you, but I'm not going to give it up for you.'

John Gallagher: Most of the places we played at weren't far away, so we had a lot of time in Cardiff, and we'd be walking around the shopping centre. There was this guy, a bit of a vagrant, sitting on a park bench with a bottle in a brown paper bag. We'd walk past each day in our branded jumpers and shorts. It wasn't hard to figure out who we were, and this guy said to us, 'You're the All Blacks aren't you?' We said, 'Yes,' and he asked us, 'Who are you playing this week lads?' We said, 'Cardiff, at the Arms Park', and he said, 'Oh Cardiff, they'll beat you.' We beat them and a couple days later we walked by and the same thing, 'Llanelli, the Scarlets, they'll beat you.' And it was the same for every club side, Newport, Swansea, 'They'll beat you, they'll beat you.' But then the day before the Test when we told him we were playing Wales he said, 'Oh they're crap, you'll beat them.' It kind of summed up how things were in Wales at the time. The club sides gave us a harder time than the national team. They were so partisan in terms of their club sides, they just couldn't gel as a national side.

Sean Fitzpatrick: I wanted to do well in the Test with Wales. Dad played in the team that got beaten there in 1953 and I always wanted to play a Test in Cardiff. I'd grown up with the singing and the history of it all. But twenty minutes into the game we were up by 20 points and the singing stopped. I was almost disappointed! Mum was in the crowd but Dad wouldn't go, he'd had to live with the fact that he'd lost there, and wouldn't go. When he died a few years ago, I'd gone back to New Zealand for the funeral. When I got back to England I went into the pub on the Sunday and a fellow came up to me, very smartly dressed, and gave me his condolences for the loss of my father. He told me he'd been trying to get a hold of me through Jonathan Davies. He said, 'I've got a box at the Arms Park and in it is your father's old jersey from the 1953 game . . . and I'd like to give it to you.' It was amazing. Well, I could almost imagine my Dad upstairs saying, 'Don't bloody take it, son,' but I did and the chap and I have become great friends.

Wayne Shelford: Playing against the black jersey meant a lot to those Welsh clubs. That's what rugby is about – going to those clubs, playing against them, because they would always rise to the occasion. But at that time on the British scene they were miles behind. I went over there and played in 1990 and couldn't believe the way they kept kicking the ball away. The Welsh tried to use their backs a bit more, but not the English. It took me two years at Northampton to convince them to use their backs and we started getting our wings into the England team because we were giving them the ball and they could run.

Gary Whetton: I remember seeing the Irish advance at the haka and thinking 'Look at that captain, he's a madman.' I thought, 'You're staring down Buck, be careful.' And Buck just bringing us all up anyway. It was good the haka came into it more. Buck was the right man to deliver it. Hopefully the Poms keep complaining about the advantage the haka gives the All Blacks. It's great, it's just fodder. The Poms have always got to look for those things. They don't make it difficult not to like them. There're some good guys in the team as individuals but they don't know what it's all about, that's their problem as a country about rugby, and how to win it.

John Gallagher: I went to a Barbarians lunch recently in the company of Willie Anderson, who was the Ireland captain that day, and Dr Dave Irwin, the Irish centre. We ended up in a pub late at night where we re-enacted the haka from that day in 1989 at Lansdowne Road. It was hilarious. Willie had to get the Irish crowd going, he had to do something just to try and rattle us, and I'm sure Buck has said it, we didn't find it at all disrespectful, we enjoyed it. It was brilliant of them to throw the challenge back at us, it set up a great Test match.

Grant Fox: In the Ireland Test the incident where Fitzy put his foot over the line when he was throwing the ball in was a whole set phase earlier. We'd gone to a lineout on the far side of the field. The touchie Jim Fleming had his flag out, and it was in the law book I guess, but how often have you seen it refereed? Never. None of us knew about it until the ball kid ran on and delivered the message to Sandy McNeill, after I'd scored, that the flag was still up. The funniest thing about that was after the game, Fitzy was very embarrassed, and I was not to leave his side that night, as in, 'You're not paying for a beer.' We were downstairs in the

Ireland captain Willie Anderson faces up to Wayne Shelford as the
All Blacks perform the Haka at Lansdowne Road. *InphoPhotography*

bar before we went up to the official dinner, and were the last to leave. We went to get into
the lift and there was Jim Fleming! Fitzy sort of glared at him and then smiled and stuck out
a hand. Jim looked a bit horrified when he first saw me but that all changed pretty quickly.
I did score one Test try, in the next Test we played, the following year against Scotland, but
no one remembers that, they just remember the one that got ruled out!

John Gallagher: My try against Ireland came when we called a double miss, the simple
moves are always the best. I was coming up, keeping my line, and their winger tried to
shoot in on me. So I went on the outside. Terry [Wright] came in, drew the winger, and
I looped around Terry like we'd done in training so many times. He drew and passed to
put me away. Terry was another one of those guys, he had great peripheral vision with
people running off him. From there it was just a sprint to the line and then a step to beat
the cover defence coming across. It was a brilliant team try, and I couldn't have chosen
a better place to score what was probably my best try for the All Blacks, in front of my
parents, and my Irish family . . . my grandmothers in the stands, as well as a load of my
school mates who'd come over. It was a great way to finish my Test career as it turned out.
And then to cap it off with a win over the Barbarians, a team based around the Lions side
that had won in Australia, it was like I'd come full circle.

Murray Pierce: I had no inkling that John Gallagher was going to league. From a
monetary point of view I could understand why. He obviously wanted to do it, tried it
and it didn't quite work out but back then, let's face it, we were all amateur players and all
trying to scratch around for a living. If someone comes up to you from a different code

with an offer and some money attached to it, it would have been an interesting decision to make. John was a real, genuine good Pom. He wasn't a big physical specimen but he was an intelligent player, he made very few mistakes and he could run.

John Gallagher: There were a number of variables in my decision to go to league, the elephant in the room being the money. Playing for the All Blacks left me $2000 in debt every month. Things were going well, but I didn't have any security. I'd been away from south-east London from my friends and family and seeing them again affected me as well. All of a sudden I got an offer from rugby league that was a lot more than I expected. There was no sign of rugby going professional at the time. With hindsight I would have stayed around until the 1991 World Cup, and then gone after that. At the time, not one person I knew in rugby circles thought I was making the wrong decision. Ridgey had gone the week before me, Johnny Schuster, he was an amazing player, Frano Botica, Darryl Halligan, Brett Iti went, and after the 1991 World Cup Craig Innes and later Inga Tuigamala. The system was broken. I think after the 1987 World Cup players started to realise that there was a lot of money in rugby and they were getting none of it. Growing up I would have thought there was a better chance of my playing football for Brazil than rugby for the All Blacks. It was life changing, because when you're an All Black you're a bit out of the ordinary. You are aware you are the custodian of the jersey and you have to do your darnedest not to embarrass yourself in it. Outside of my wife and family it's probably the single-most important thing that's happened in my life.

Ian Jones: I made my Test debut against Scotland. I have Scottish roots on my father's side so I was very proud of that. Murray Pierce had left and gone off to play in South Africa. Back then the IRB had a rule you could only assemble on a Wednesday leading up to a Saturday Test match. Grizz, always trying to bend the rules a bit, decided we had to be down there on the Tuesday for a gear issue, because it was the first Test of the year. So we flew into town late on the Tuesday night, all cloak and dagger, there was a gear issue, we all got given some kit which was fantastic and then about 9.00 p.m. all the forwards, got loaded on to a bus and taken to Carisbrook for a scrum session under the grandstand on the sawdust with the Otago NPC team. They were all fired up, guys like Steve Hotton, Richard Knight, Gordon McPherson, and we scrummed for about forty-five minutes late on a Tuesday night. Test match rugby was unlike anything I'd experienced, even those All Black midweek games, it was so much quicker. It was over in a flash, but I did manage to score, sneaking over in the bottom right-hand corner with my family watching in the stand, it was pretty special.

Wayne Shelford: We played pretty well in the first Test against Scotland down in Dunedin and we struggled a little bit in the second Test at Eden Park, we needed Foxy to kick a penalty for us to win just out from full-time.

Ian Jones: In between the second Scotland Test and the first against Australia, North Harbour came up to Whangarei to play Northland. During the after-match function the All Black team was named and Buck Shelford, who played that day, wasn't named because he was allegedly injured. He came up to me in the after-match fuming. I'll remember it forever. He said, 'You've got to play every Test match like it's your last.' I didn't join the debate about him not being in the team, it wasn't my place. I was only twenty-two at the time and keeping my head down. There was shock around the country, but, hell, he was replaced by a pretty good player.

Wayne Shelford: In 1990 you started to see the selfishness come in on the field. It was there in my last Test match. They started to go against some of the things I was saying. They'd want to run the ball and I wanted them to kick the bloody thing out and have shots at goal. I had a talk with Foxy after the game. I told him that as the general, when my head was buried in a ruck he had to take control of the team and carry out the game plan. He wasn't doing that. He probably got his back up a bit about that but I said what needed to be said. When the guys went against me on the field it was totally unexpected. I was very surprised. I knew there was stuff going on in the background. But this was the first time they'd done it on the field. They said I had a hammy but it was just a bit of sciatica. I said to Grizz, 'If you want to drop me, that's your prerogative, you're the coach.' We talked by phone before he named Zinny to play the next game against Australia.

Gary Whetton: We were all in decline, call it complacency, call it age. And Buck was a man whose leadership was 'Follow me' and we weren't playing well. I suppose the selectors looked at positions who weren't playing well. It's as simple as that. I think we all thought that but for the grace of God it could have been us. Yes, they had an amazing player who came through who isn't a Buck Shelford but Zinzan was Zinzan, unproven in some things but with very good skill sets and a different player altogether. It did two things, whether it was Buck or anyone else. It made us all jump up and get ready because if they could do it to him they could do it to anyone. And I suppose when you are together and successful for a long time that's what happens. The pressure goes on everyone. Then you get appointed to the captaincy – it should be a highlight and there was controversy. So it's hard work. It was very difficult to deal with and I had to start dealing with it more than anyone else.

Grant Fox: We don't select the team, the selectors do. There was all sorts of things going around, nearly all of them not true . . . you know, never let the truth get in the way of a good story. What gets lost in it all is that there was a young guy by the name of Zinzan Brooke, supremely-talented, in a different mould to Buck and it gets forgotten that this was the start of the great career of Zinzan Brooke. It was all a bit sad; sad for Buck, he was the captain, a fearless leader, he'd never lost a Test match. The reason? Well they were different players and maybe that's what the selectors were looking for, something a bit different, just to change things up a bit but, really, I still don't know. The other thing is that Gary became captain, it's a great honour, and that got lost as well. So there were three people involved in it and in a way it was a bit sad for all of them.

John Kirwan: Buck had so much mana but I don't think he could be in the football team and go from captain to something else. I don't think it was the declining of Buck Shelford, I just think it was the arriving of Zinzan Brooke. It's sad when you get dropped, I got dropped, and it was a sad time for Buck. The country felt he still had a lot to offer and the selectors didn't.

Sean Fitzpatrick: If I was Buck I'd be a bit bitter too. He should never have been dropped. It wasn't his fault we almost lost to Scotland. He was the most inspirational player I'd played with. Admittedly, Zinny was on fire at the time and if you were picking the best No.8 just purely as a player, it would probably be Zinny, but we weren't helping Buck the way we were playing.

Ian Jones: You talk to the Australians and that one win for them, that one loss for the All Blacks, was the trigger, it made them feel they were good enough to beat us. I don't think their belief was there before that. We hadn't lost in twenty-two Test matches, fifty games, it was a remarkable streak broken only by that draw in Brisbane in 1988. We were two-nil up in the series, it was a shitty week, weather wise, we had other things going on, wives, girlfriends coming down for the Test. Whether that had any impact I don't know, but we never got into that Test at all.

One thing that did happen . . . and I have always been big on omens . . . in the changing shed, in the dungeons at Athletic Park, before the game, we walked in about an hour before kick-off, into this changing room that was lit by one forty watt light bulb, and that light went out on us. I put my kit bag down in the darkness and thought, 'Uh oh, that's not good.' A crucial moment came early in the second half. It came from a lineout, bottom left-hand corner, we threw it to Gary Whetton, but we missed it and Kearns went through and scored a try. I remember thinking late into that game, that the All Blacks don't lose games, that we'd find a way, that we'd get down there and Foxy would kick a goal, something like that, and we'd win. I thought that through until about the seventy-eighth minute. I couldn't believe we'd lost it, was dumbfounded, and I guess it was a wakeup call to all of us that you can lose games. All of a sudden, the Aussies thought, 'Yep, we can beat these guys,' and the next year, 1991, they did.

Grant Fox: The third Test in Wellington was the end of the unbeaten run. I think we were a team starting to struggle. Sometimes when you're in the forest you can't see the wood for the trees. There were guys trying their arses off and it wasn't working. Australia had started investing in this team two years before, and were allowed to get away with it . . . they lost a few Tests, we're not allowed to do that. With hindsight we were on the wane, but we didn't realise it.

Ian Jones: There were still quite a few guys left that had lost in Nantes in 1986. Guys remember losses like that vividly, it haunts them and redemption was often a big thing in those days. So when we went to Nantes for the first Test we had to win for a lot of these guys. We took on a side that was pretty fired-up. I was pushing behind Stevie McDowall that day and there was a fair bit of biffo going on in the front row and Laurent Seigne, who's become a friend of mine since then, wore a punch from Steve McDowall that only travelled six inches, but was probably the most explosive thing I ever saw and that's how Laurent got his nose bent. We won the game.

Grant Fox: We toured Argentina before the World Cup and, again with hindsight, perhaps we'd have been better staying at home. It's a tough place to tour. I injured my pelvis which led to me not being where I needed to be for the World Cup, but stubborn enough not to want to give my place up. I tried to fight through but I'd have been better off standing back and saying, 'This is an injury that takes twelve months to heal.' In the end I didn't play very well. I guess you're waiting for someone else to make the call and they didn't.

Sean Fitzpatrick: We went to Argentina and that's when the wheels really fell off. JK and 'Colt' Crowley went to Grizz and said, 'Look, we're not going to win the World Cup if we continue in this vein,' and they were quite right.

Ian Jones: We played two Tests against Australia before the 1991 World Cup. We lost over there, and then won by a penalty goal at Eden Park. Michael Lynagh had a shot to draw the game. To this day I'll debate whether it was me or Sean Fitzpatrick who gave away the penalty. Lynagh lined it up to win the series and the Bledisloe Cup on the ten-metre line, fifteen metres in. I wished with all my heart that he'd miss and he did. We won 6-3, but that was a Wallaby side on the rise.

The 1991 Rugby World Cup was held in England, Scotland, Wales, Ireland and France. The All Blacks arrived as defending champions but they were a team in transition, a shadow of the side that had lifted the inaugural trophy four years earlier. Wayne Shelford had retired and Michael Jones was unavailable for three of the fixtures as they fell on Sundays (he refused to play on the Sabbath).

The tournament started well when they defeated the England 18-12 at Twickenham and they then went on to defeat the United States 46-6 and Italy 31-21 in their pool before beating Canada 29-13 in the quarter-final. They were hardly thunderous statements of intent, but there seemed little reason for them to fear the Wallabies when they faced them in the semi-final in Dublin. However, Australia were in irresistible form and knocked the holders out with a stunning 16-6 victory.

John Kirwan: The 1991 World Cup was a disaster. There were some weak decisions from the leadership and the coaches. They needed to have a clean out to put everyone on notice and it didn't happen. I was pretty upset about it and took my thoughts to the coaches on a couple of occasions. They listened but nothing changed. I wouldn't have been able to sleep at night if I hadn't done that. I was in the lucky group because I was treated as an All Black but there were guys coming through who should probably have gone on that trip. And then we had a set of injuries. Colty [Kieran Crowley] was milking cows ten days before he played in the semi-final. It was probably one of the best second halves I played in the All Blacks jersey against the Australians the day we lost. It was the first time I cried after the game. I was also going through a lot personally and I think I was on anti-depressants during the 1991 World Cup and I needed, desperately, to play well. Grizz was probably suffering from the pressure a wee bit and it was not a very nice time. An unhappy football team. I think it was one year too long. We tried to fix it by bringing Harty in and a few things like that but it was a disaster.

Gary Whetton: I could understand why the [NZ] Rugby Union did it because we needed a little bit more help – whether Harty was the right person for it, I don't know. He had the skill set but those two, because they both wanted the job, had got on very well under BJ but then it changed. They were both strong characters with different skill sets and knowledge of what they wanted and expected. I knew Grizz really well, he was my coach and I was his captain for three years and I was vice-captain for two years before that. If it could have worked it would have been great but it was very difficult.

Grant Fox: We'd played Canada in a quarter-final in Lille. We'd struggled throughout the tournament, we just couldn't get anything going, and I guess we thought that because of where we'd been in previous years we'd been able to find another gear, we could do it again but the Aussies were ahead of us.

Ian Jones: When I look back and think about the decision and the coaching styles of the guys, you keep hearing the mixed messages. There was the same tactics, same passion, same desire to win, but coming from two different voices. Therefore, you interpret it differently and you start to display that out on the paddock. One thing that summed up the contrasting styles was training at Blackrock College in the lead-up to the semi-final against Australia. Blackrock College has two fields . . . a beautiful No.1 field with clubrooms and a track down to a No.2 field. On the Tuesday we trained on that No.2 field and Grizz Wyllie took that session. It was a great session and we were into it, very physical and did everything we needed to do, which was fantastic. The next day we all headed down to that bottom field, but then all the Williments' Tours buses turned up. There were lots of spectators, and John Hart whistled to us and turned us around and we trained up on the No.1 ground. John conducted the session and it was a brilliant session . . . tactics, movement and all the rest of it, but it was a real contrast from the earlier session . . . you know one was all physical, really tough, and the John Hart one was in front of an audience. They were quite different sessions and there were quite mixed messages about how we were going to play.

Grant Fox: We were a little bit brash as a team, whereas the Aussies went on a charm offensive that worked wonderfully for them in Ireland, we weren't so well thought of. I would agree with some of the things said about us, but at the time we didn't realise it. They played well. They'd had a big fright the week before in the quarter-final against Ireland. They were basically dead and buried and Michael Lynagh scored with just a few minutes to play. I think that was a wake-up call for them.

Gary Whetton: We weren't a settled team, one person was saying something and one the other. It was hard and I felt sorry for the coaches too because it was thrown onto them. We played well in the first game against England and won, and then we had a few easy games which isn't good for a team like us. We always knew Australia was going to be our hardest game. They had evolved, we were stagnant in a way. We had a lot of injuries and Foxy will say to this day that maybe he shouldn't have played but it wasn't because of him. The pack played very well if you watch the tape again but they just played extraordinary rugby. Campese's overhead pass, different things here and there – they were a team full of confidence. Our coaches took it hard, we all took it hard. It was my 100th game.

Ian Jones: We had played poorly all year against the Australians and that game was probably the best we'd played against them. But we weren't good enough on the day and tactically we weren't in sync. It didn't work even though we put in a hell of an effort and to lose was a blow. To lose a semi-final in a World Cup when we'd played as well as we could, but we just weren't good enough to win.

Grant Fox: Simon Poidevin was everywhere and now I know why . . . he'd worked out our calling codes so he knew where the ball was going to be. They're nowhere near as intricate as they are today and much easier to decipher and he was a step ahead of us all the way, and a pretty major disruption. They got out to a lead, 13-3. Today that would not be a problem, but then that was a pretty good lead. We chased it hard but ultimately they were better than us.

Ian Jones: There were a couple of great moments from Campo and they pushed up really hard on us. I think they knew what our backline was trying to do . . . funny old sport though, the week before we were about five seconds away from playing Ireland, and who knows what might have happened if they hadn't got out of that game?

Wayne Shelford: They [Hart and Wyllie] were clashing all the time. I never saw it come out until the World Cup in 1991. They [the All Blacks] were terrible, not just on the field but off the field, completely split camp, the Aucklanders with Harty, all the rest with Grizz. And when they came into that last function – I was over there with the media – they came in, some of them were pissed, they hadn't ironed their shirts, they were straight out of the packet, they looked like shit. They might have been disappointed but you can still hold some respect. What had happened was that Auckland had gone from strength to strength to strength, but when Auckland started failing, the All Blacks started failing. Auckland were uncoachable, some of those guys thought they could do it all themselves.

John Kirwan: You felt you'd let yourself down, you'd let your country down, you'd let your team-mates down. Losing at that level is indescribable at times. I think we were arrogant, but we weren't good enough either. The Aussies were a better football team than us, more complete, more energy, more want.

Grant Fox: No one likes criticism, it's easy to dish out but when you're on the end of it it's not easy to take. It has more of an effect on those around you, your wife and your kids and your Mum and Dad than it does on you. They were tough times but I think you learn more from adversity than success and I guess we started again from there.

THIRTY-THREE

REBUILDING

'You're too fat and too slow and you're bloody arrogant'

NEW ZEALAND'S RUGBY Union celebrated its centennial in 1992. A commemorative series against a World XV, a visit by Ireland, a tour of Australia, and the biggest candle on the birthday cake, a trip to South Africa, all lay ahead. Grizz Wyllie was done as coach, and the bosses opted for a new broom. In stepped Laurie Mains, a four-Test All Black fullback, who had overseen a turnaround of Otago's rugby fortunes through the 1980s, culminating in the Provincial Championship title. Mains recognised the need for a more positive image after the scathing coverage of their World Cup conduct. Mains and fellow selectors Earle Kirton and Peter Thorburn, set about deconstructing the old regime, dropping skipper Gary Whetton, putting others on notice, and introducing several new players, including Frank Bunce, the Auckland-born centre who'd played for Samoa at the World Cup.

Sean Fitzpatrick was given the captaincy, although Mains was said to have been leaning towards his Otago charge Mike Brewer before he was injured. The new era got off to the worst possible start with a loss in Christchurch to a star-studded International selection led by Scotland's David Sole, despite a thundering try by winger Inga Tuigamala and another for debutant No.8 Richard Turner. The tables were turned midweek in Wellington, the All Blacks' heavy win helped in no small way by the ordering off of the World XV's French lock Olivier Roumat, for kicking Fitzpatrick. There was plenty of intrigue about the third match of the series, with Grant Fox dropped, and the recently-sacked Gary Whetton turning out for an injury hit World XV, who were beaten 26-15.

Then came two Tests against an Ireland side who pushed the All Blacks to 24-21 in the first Test. Mains responded with six changes, dropping fullback Greg Cooper for his brother Matthew, who helped himself to 23 points, a world record for a player on debut as the All Blacks scored a crushing 59-6 win. Olo Brown and Robin Brooke were two other notable arrivals. A 16-match tour of Australia and South Africa followed. The three-Test series in Australia was as good as any ever played, an Australian team at the peak of its powers coming out 2-1 series winners, after matches decided by one, two and three points respectively. The only other defeat was an embarrassing 40-17 loss to Sydney, but Mains' rebuilding was to pay dividends in South Africa.

Sean Fitzpatrick: I went home having lost the World Cup thinking I was going to retire at twenty-seven but then to see Phil Kearns on the back page of the *Sydney Morning Herald* . . . he had the America's Cup in one hand and the Rugby World Cup in the other, and the headline was, 'The World's best hooker becomes the world's best sailor', and I was thinking, 'Hang on, aren't I supposed to be the best hooker?' It finally dawned

Opposite: Va'aiga (Inga) Tuigamala makes a break against a World XV in 1992. *FotoSport/ Photosport NZ*

on me, in fact [wife] Bronny said, 'No you're not, he's much better than you,' and I said, 'Well I can't retire like that,' and she said, 'No you can't.' Laurie Mains rang early in 1992 and said, 'Do you want to be an All Black again?' I said, 'Laurie I'd love to be an All Black again,' and he said, 'Well you're probably not going to be.' He said, 'You're too fat and too slow and you're bloody arrogant.' But the thing that really hurt was when he said I'd lost respect for the All Black jersey. He said, 'If you think you can change all that in the next six weeks, and I can see that change, I might give you a chance at the All Black trials.' Half the guys didn't change. I don't think he even rang Gary [Whetton]. He should have.

Grant Fox: I was a bit disappointed that a lot was being conducted through a public forum instead of engaging the players. I recall comments being made in the media, some of it by Peter Thorburn, which I wasn't happy about, because he never spoke to me, and I presume it was the same for other players who were in the firing line. There was a suggestion we weren't as committed to the All Black jersey as we should have been. That we were arrogant – there might have been a bit of accuracy in that – but to have your commitment to the All Black jersey questioned, that hurt and I went and confronted Peter and we had a fairly robust discussion, but I won't download that. They were also talking about what they wanted from their five-eighth. I was the incumbent and they didn't come to me and say, 'This is what we're looking for, so if you want to be in consideration this is what you have to do.' Instead, I was the one who had to demand a meeting before the trial in Napier to say, 'Look I've been part of this group for a long time, I desperately want to be part of it again, but I need to know what you want, you need to tell me and I'll work as hard as I can to see if I can do it.' It happened to Gary, and I implored Gary to make a phone call, because he didn't get beyond 1991. He was the incumbent captain, and they never spoke to him, and he never spoke to them. He can be a bit stubborn sometimes, but he wasn't going to do it. He thought they should be calling him and he was right. They should have done him that courtesy as a long-serving All Black and the current captain.

Gary Whetton: That was a bitter pill to swallow, I took it very hard in the way it was done. With Laurie, and Peter Thorburn, in particular, there was a lot of dislike of Auckland, through what we did and how we did things. You were a product of your own success. The All Blacks had failed – yes, but then all of a sudden you've been there for ten years, been the captain and then not even know that you're not in the trials when he's picked ten locks, so I thought it was pretty poorly done. I must admit in my day if I ever thought Laurie Mains or Peter Thorburn would be All Black coach I might have done things a bit differently and be careful what you say and do. It wasn't a professional game. In the end I found it too hard, that's why I left New Zealand. I played for Auckland for another year and that was great and then I needed to get out and had two-and-a-half years in France, won everything. It became a second home to me. Time is a great healer.

Sean Fitzpatrick: Steve [McDowall] got a chance but he hadn't changed enough. They needed a new captain, and it might have been Mike Brewer but he got injured. Earle

Kirton told me they talked for over an hour after the trial. They had the team picked but it took an hour and a half to decide who was going to be captain. Earle liked me, but Laurie wasn't going to have a bar of me because I was an Aucklander.

Ian Jones: It was a clean slate and Laurie came in and was so . . . black is black. A lot of things had happened off the field in 1991. Kevin Roberts, who was then the CEO of Lion Nathan [sponsors] came in and told us bluntly where he, and some of the New Zealand public, saw where the All Blacks were at. We were unfriendly, bad ambassadors for the country, needed to be a lot more accessible, approachable, and to give something back . . . .those sorts of messages and I have to say they were bloody true, spot on. He said, 'I'm the major sponsor with Steinlager and I can pull it today and you guys can be left with nothing, or you can change your ways and I can make things happen for you.' He was such a straight shooter it made us think. We could go with him or stay as the unsmiling, unfriendly All Blacks. We chose that other path and changed our attitudes. Laurie was a great coach. He actually coached the team. He knew the techniques he wanted his players to have. It was our [NZ Rugby] centenary in 1992. We had a new skipper in Sean Fitzpatrick and we had a new attitude. It was great.

Frank Bunce (1992-97, 55 Tests, 69 games): I got a phone call, out of the blue, from Laurie. He said he'd give me an opportunity if I wanted it. I was nearly thirty by then but he said, 'I don't care how old you are, if you're good enough and you want to be there I'll give you an opportunity.' Much as I owed Samoa for giving me a hand, I was only ever going to do one thing. Born here, grew up playing rugby here, I wanted to be an All Black, that's it. I knew I wanted to give it a go. I made my debut against the World XV during New Zealand's Rugby Centennial.

Matthew Cooper (1987-96, 8 Tests): Greg [older brother Greg Cooper] played those World XV games and he played the first Test against Ireland which was a tough battle and that's when they made the replacement.

I did get an indication that I'd made the team, but Greg was the first person to ring me. He said he was disappointed but if he was ever to lose his spot in the All Blacks he could think of no person better to replace him than his younger brother.

We called a miss two move off a lineout, just a wide pass, and I came off an angled run and Frank Bunce slipped me a short pass and I went through under the posts, and that's when I really felt it.

I managed to get another off a really great run by John Kirwan and when I came off that's when I learned it was a world record number of points for a player on debut

Grant Fox: Notwithstanding all of the issues, when I was involved with Laurie I loved it. He picked me, then he didn't pick me. And he was dead right in doing that. Then he picked me again and I had a couple more years playing for the All Blacks. I wasn't sure after 1991 I was going to play again, I had to fight through some adversity and I think I learned a lot about myself through that, and then got to the point where I was able to make the decision on my own career and not have someone else end it for me.

Sean Fitzpatrick: We had a couple of really tough years, and we copped a bit. I remember Wynne Gray [*NZ Herald*] stirring the pot. There was a billboard in Auckland saying we needed a coach, not a Laurie [lorry]. Andy Haden was driving things a fair bit behind the scenes and a lot of my mates, guys I'd played with were scathing. Laurie believed the Auckland mafia had taken over the team, and when we went to Australia in 1992 he said, 'If I see any two Aucklanders together alone they'll be sent home.' It was the training, I'd never trained like that. We did down and ups, we were hitting ruck machines. We thought we didn't need to. We thought, 'What's all this about?' We knew the Otago team had done it but we didn't think it was the way All Blacks should train. It was the best thing we could have done and it took me a long time to realise that.

Ian Jones: We lost the series in Australia 2-1 but when you added everything up, tries, goals, points scored, it was almost identical. We had a chance in Brisbane to level it and maybe win the series . . . there was a dropped goal that went just wide. It was a long tour, we had a big squad, we were playing in fantastic conditions against a very good Wallabies side and both teams played with a great attitude. It was a blueprint for how the game was played through to 1995. Of course, we had the carrot at the end of that tour of being the first All Black team to go to South Africa in sixteen years, which for all of us was a dream.

Frank Bunce: While the World XV series was my introduction to Test rugby, it wasn't until the Irish Tests – I managed to score two tries in both Tests – that I started to feel comfortable. All through those World XV Tests I'd felt nervous, full of doubt. I started settling down a bit in those Irish Tests, but the first one, we just about lost, I don't know why, we weren't playing that well and Ireland came out firing. In the Australian series they were pretty close to the best Test matches I played. They were close, exciting, the whole series was so even, played in the afternoon when it was nice and warm, top quality players, it was really good to be part of. Tim Horan and Jason Little were good guys. I still talk to them, we're friends now, they were a stable pairing, as me and Walter [Little] were. We didn't play England often back then, we did against the Springboks but they always had different guys, but with Horan and Little we clicked and it became a good rivalry.

Grant Fox: It was a great series against Australia in 1992. We were dead even in tries, penalties, points scored, and they just happened to win it 2-1. We got on well with that Australian side, a lot of them have gone on to do well in business, some of them have been involved in commentary, and we've caught up a lot over the years.

Sean Fitzpatrick: There were a lot of disruptions on that tour in Australia, a lot of injuries, guys coming and going, a few bombs being thrown in. In saying that, I thought that series was one of the best Bledisloe Cup series I ever played in. Going to Africa, winning there? Well it was hard to tell because we didn't know where the Africans were at after being out for so long, but I think we started to realise we could be a world-class team.

After South Africa released Nelson Mandela and dropped its apartheid policy the first official New Zealand team in sixteen years arrived in Johannesburg to an incredible welcome, the All Blacks winning four tour games before tackling the Boks at Ellis Park. In front of a 72,000 crowd the All Blacks scored their first Test win at the great fortress in 64 years, surviving an early onslaught, and controlling the middle stages before exhaustion, and a late Springbok fightback, closed the gap to 27-24.

It was a successful end to a year of great change.

Ian Jones: We flew into Johannesburg and I've never seen scenes ever like it, ever. Thousands of people were at the airport at midnight, chanting for the All Blacks and holding photos of the players, it was amazing. People followed us around in their cars, camped outside our hotel. None of us had experienced that sort of fanfare before . . . amazing but also daunting. We started off with Natal, they had Rudi Visagie. We'd all heard the stories about South Africa, about these huge men and how tough they were going to be, how physical, and you never know until you experience it first hand, but I thought that day, 'Wow, these are giants.' They were big, but they never intimidated me, or us.

Frank Bunce: Arriving at the airport was like a step back in time as well as a step into the unknown. A couple of the older guys like Laurie and Pinetree had been there but none of the players. We'd watched them on TV and were in awe of the rivalry. It was awesome. You got there and there were thousands of people, hanging off the rafters, comments coming at you thick and fast and you're thinking, 'Holy hell what have we let ourselves in for?' They love you, but they wanna kill you, they tell you that!

John Kirwan: In 1992 it was important that we won but my attitude was always that it was not our fault they weren't there. I didn't think going to South Africa would happen in my lifetime. It was unbelievable. We had fourteen guards looking after us and all were carrying pistols. They always put a mirror under the bus, and we weren't allowed to go out without protection. We had a barbecue two miles down in a mine and Mandela, de Klerk and Bolger [NZ Prime Minister] were there with teams. I lasted about twenty minutes and said, 'I'm not staying down here', having the odd panic attack being down that far.

Sean Fitzpatrick: It was fantastic to be in South Africa after everything that had gone on. Playing against Natal and teams like that, it was great. Laurie was such a dictator! Even as captain I never said anything. I'd go to a meeting thinking, 'I've got to say something here', and he'd finish what he was saying and it was, 'Right, on the bus', never, 'Sean would you like to say something?' The sad thing is it took him until 1995 to really hit the peak of his powers. In 1996 he would have had a dream run, because that's the team he created. He had to learn a lot too, especially with the media. Ric [Salizzo] came in in 1992. We'd had no media liaison officer before that. Laurie was getting in the shit with Wynne [Gray], he was flying off the handle about media stuff, so Ric came in and we took him to South Africa. Someone had leaked a story saying that Laurie didn't like South Africans or something like that. It was an agency story so there was no name on the article. This story came out just before one of our first training runs, and Laurie was due to have a press conference. So Ric was all excited because there were about thirty media there and he came over and said, 'Laurie they're ready for you,' and Laurie said, 'I'm not doing it. Until the person who wrote that story owns up I'm not talking to them.' Ric managed to persuade him to go over to the journalists, but all Laurie would say was, 'I'm not dealing with you guys until the person who wrote that article owns up,' and eventually someone did.

Frank Bunce: I'd been a fan of Bruce Roberston, Phillippe Sella and Danie Gerber, those guys were heroes, and to get there and have the opportunity to play against Gerber was awesome. He'd been around for years, he was thirty-four by then, but he was still good, he scored two tries against us. The night before the Test I was watching TV with John Timu, and they were showing a lot of highlights, and he was coming up all the time – running round people, through people, over people, under them, smashing them in tackles, and we were just sitting there looking an each other going ****ing hell!

Grant Fox: You aspire to be an All Black and you want to be tested on the biggest stage. We were denied the opportunity in 1985 but it came around in 1992. We were there at the same time as Australia, and it was amazing to be there for their reintroduction to world footy after being isolated for so long. We came out of a nine-game tour of Aussie, a tough tour so in all it was a 16-game tour in nine weeks. I know some of the older All Blacks will scoff at that, they were away for three months, but nine weeks was a lot at that time, and we were battle-hardened. It was just a great time, great memories. It was only short, five games but a hell of a lot of fun. We won the Test match, and more comfortably than the scoreline showed. They came roaring home at us. We were up 27-10 with not long to go and it ended up 27-24 so pretty tight in the end. But I have very fond memories of that time.

Ian Jones: You play under beautiful clear blue skies in big stadiums and you run out into this amazing atmosphere in conditions that are made for rugby, playing against a team of people who are made to play rugby, supported by people who love rugby, what could you not love about it? Playing at altitude for the first time, we'd heard about it, people telling us we were going to get nose bleeds, dry mouth and a headache, and we were going to be tired and all that and we did because our minds were telling us we were. I've been there subsequently and never had any of those problems! The Test was our sixteenth game on tour. Without disrespecting the South Africans, I think that game was won by us over sixty minutes and we were guilty of starting to think about getting on the plane – and whether some of that started to happen, maybe fatigue setting in, we allowed them to come back. Danie Gerber got two tries and it was tight towards the end.

John Kirwan: It was an amazing time and important that we won. I was struggling with the new coaching so there were some important games I had to play. The most pleasing thing for me about the Test match, I've got a photo somewhere, of me running off Frank Bunce as he took his man, came wide, and I came back on an angle. We did that at training three days in a row and it came off in the game so it was a nice one to score because we had trained it so hard. It was interesting when we ran out. There was total silence which was incredible. The other thing was the anger the boys felt about Louis Luyt who wasn't into there not being apartheid. We had to drag Robin Brooke out of the after-match. They shouldn't have played the anthem and they did. We were aware when that was happening because it is about respect so when you say you are going to do something you do it and if you don't do it you lose respect. And that really riled, especially Robin, and a couple of things happened during the week. We had to go to a party at Louis Luyt's place where he treated some people who were serving us with contempt.

Jon Preston (1991-97, 10 Tests, 27 games): Ant Strahan had suffered the same injury I'd had in Australia – a shoulder injury – and I ended up playing three-quarters of the game. It went well and we had a good victory although the South Africans came back at us. Ellis Park is a cauldron and the South Africans were so pleased to have the All Blacks back in town. It's that South African attitude of being very determined and very confident in their own team's ability to beat anyone. There were 72,000 people at the ground – it was amazing and one of the greatest experiences.

Eric Rush (1992-96, 9 Tests, 29 games): Touring South Africa gave me an idea about how tough it had always been for the All Blacks to win over there. The Test guys were all right, they had neutral refs, but for the midweek team, we had the local guys and it was a stand down, fall over, scratch your eyes out battle every single game. Even the ones when we put big points on them, they got their pound of flesh first and those refs did not help at all. I'm not saying they were cheating, just that they had totally different interpretations. And, like teams touring New Zealand, those provincial games might be a local guy's only shot at an international game. It was tough rugby, but we loved it. Uli Schmidt stood up at one of the after-matches, he was the captain, and spoke. He thanked the All Blacks for coming and said, 'There are two kinds of Springboks, those who have played against the All Blacks and those who haven't, so thank you for making us real Springboks.' Some of the guys said they weren't happy that the Test team kept to it itself, but those midweek games . . . if someone offered me one even today I'd be over the moon. I mean you were still the All Blacks, and if you lost it was still the All Blacks losing, not a 'B' team.

THIRTY-FOUR

A LIONS' SHARE

'If the attitude is right, and you have got fourteen other guys around you with the same attitude, you're unstoppable'

BRITISH AND IRISH Lions tours come fewer and further between now for New Zealand fans, and are always regarded with great anticipation. The 1993 Lions team, coached by Ian McGeechan, captained by Gavin Hastings and built around a strong England presence, laid down some early markers, losing one match, against Otago, before the first Test. They came within a whisker of a shock first Test win in Christchurch, six Gavin Hastings penalties having the Lions ahead 18-17 with time almost up before Australian referee Brian Kinsey penalised Lions No.8 Dean Richards at a ruck, and Grant Fox nailed the winning goal from near halfway. It was a fortunate win for the All Blacks, the penalty was debatable, and the Lions disputed Frank Bunce's opening try as well. They soon got their own back, squaring the series in Wellington through a tearaway try by Rory Underwood and lineout play by Martin Bayfield that was so good, the All Blacks were forced to fudge an injury to get Ian Jones on at half-time. That loss sent the Mains critics into a tailspin, and the pressure was immense going into the decider at Eden Park. The Lions shot out to a 10-0 lead, but the All Blacks responded with their best performance of the series, tries by Bunce, Fitzpatrick and Jon Preston and some pin-point kicking by Fox seeing them to a decisive 30-13 victory.

The All Blacks bounced off that into a one-off Bledisloe Cup Test in Dunedin, which they won, and an historic Test win over Samoa at Eden Park. Grant Fox then called time on his career. He had been an All Black since 1984, the first player to top 1000 points in the famous jersey, and one of the most influential players of the modern era. There was no standout successor, and for the end of year tour the selectors, at the urging of Earle Kirton, took a gamble on switching Marc Ellis, the flamboyant Otago wing/centre into a flyhalf. It worked a treat against Scotland, a match notable for a hat-trick on debut for the prodigiously-talented Southland wing Jeff Wilson, the All Blacks cutting loose to win 51-15. England was a different matter however, and with the reliable Matthew Cooper out with injury, it was left to Wilson, barely 20, to do both goal and general kicking. It was too much of a burden. A 15-9 defeat also ended the Ellis experiment. The Barbarians were beaten in Cardiff but the loss to England would burn in the players' minds until 1995.

Craig Dowd (1993-2000, 60 Tests, 67 games): At the time I didn't realise how important a Lions series was. Getting my debut against the Lions, as a twenty-three-year-old, was incredible. Leaving Lancaster Park after my first Test which was also Sean Fitzpatrick's fiftieth I promised myself I would get over fifty Tests as well.

Opposite: Sean Fitzpatrick lifts the Lions series trophy. *InphoPhotography*

Frank Bunce: I played the Lions for North Harbour early in the tour. They played Northland and then came down and we played them. I think they made a stand. They were a lot more physical. They were trying to ruck, but teams up north never really knew how to ruck. They always confused rucking with stamping on people. We'd ruck the shit out of people but it wasn't malicious, it wasn't stomping . . . but the crowds up there would always boo you because they thought you were kicking or stamping the guy. That's what the Lions tried to do but their technique wasn't quite right, hence Dean Richards ripping my ear in half! It had been physical and niggly the whole time, but when that started . . . I think it was Pod [Richard Turner] who took exception to it . . . I was lying on the ground and the Doc was tending to my ear and I said, 'What's happening?' and he said, 'They're trying to knock the shit out of each other, just stay there!'

Grant Fox: Part of the reason I wanted to stay on after 1991 was the challenge of a Lions series. It was immense and I desperately wanted to be part of it, and am grateful for the opportunity I was given. The Lions are a rare brand, you see them only once every twelve years in New Zealand now, and that's the great beauty of them, their scarcity. If you clutch at straws, the Lions might think that [last minute penalty in Christchurch] cost them the series, because they disputed the penalty decision against Dean Richards. It's easy to look back and think that's the case, but if we'd lost that game, maybe we would have won the second Test, you don't know. But I do know what All Black teams are like off a loss. We lost the second Test in Wellington, we were heavily beaten and got up to win the third in Auckland 31-13. We were down 10-0 inside ten minutes and came back and scored 31 unanswered points.

Frank Bunce: I scored a try in the first Test from a kick and it was a bit controversial. I was pretty sure I'd got it down but they were saying Ieuan Evans had the ball. In the end

Frank Bunce crosses the line for a crucial, albeit controversial, score. *Getty Images*

Foxy kicked the winning penalty from about halfway which wasn't the norm back then. Then they gave us a hell of a hiding in Wellington.

Ian Jones: I was dropped and bitterly disappointed. I'd gone from playing club rugby up north one Saturday to playing a Test against the Lions the following Saturday in Christchurch – no pre-season games, no Super Rugby, North Auckland weren't part of the Super Ten and so all of a sudden I'm taking on Martin Bayfield and I didn't have a great game. Sunday night I got the call from Laurie Mains – he'd never rung me before – and he said, 'Kamo you're not playing next Saturday, you're on the bench.' The game wasn't going great for us in the first half and I think Laurie might have said to Doc Mayhew, 'Tell Rigger [Mark Cooksley] he's got a hamstring injury.' I walked out to the huddle at half-time and Doc went up to Rigger and said, 'You've got a hamstring injury, you're off', and Rig goes, 'No I haven't,' and Doc said, 'Yes you have,' and that might have been the first tactical substitution. It made no difference, we lost.

Craig Dowd: I marked Paul Burnell, who was the Scottish tighthead, and I had a pretty good debut so he got dropped and a week later I had Jason Leonard in the second Test. That loss was horrible. They were fired up that day with Martin Bayfield, Martin Johnson and Dean Richards and gave us a hell of a battle. Grounds back then were a little boggy, heavy underfoot and Athletic Park was pretty unforgiving and a bit of a wind was blowing. For a lot of reasons, a lot of players didn't fire and the aftermath was something I wasn't prepared for. Just feeling the heat, from inside the camp and from outside where basically the knives were out for everyone in the team.

Frank Bunce: In Auckland we had a pretty horrendous week. We were under pressure from the whole country, Laurie was under pressure, the team was under pressure, the

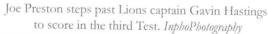

Joe Preston steps past Lions captain Gavin Hastings to score in the third Test. *InphoPhotography*

media were getting stuck in – and then there was the pressure from within. Things got pretty niggly at training, players standing up to each other, the forwards, never us backs, but there was a bit of blood spilt. It wasn't unusual.

Craig Dowd: Laurie had three famous words on occasions like that, 'On the line.' We were staying at the Poenamo Hotel on the North Shore and the training sessions were brutal. It was a welcome to the All Blacks environment, 'You're going to train harder than anyone else and because you're an All Black you have to.' He put us through the ringer. It was the finger pointed at you and the attitude and the bluntness and the way he delivered which meant, 'Get out there and do your job.' The big thing in that series was their lineout because you couldn't lift back then and they had this giant Martin Bayfield and Martin Johnson was there as well and to nullify them we had to come up with different ploys around getting some ball, winning our own even. We came up with things, like Robin Brooke would go up and we would nudge his back with our hands as he was going up to give him support. It was the beginning of lifting in lineouts. It was about subtle variations and how we could get an edge, or at least some parity.

Ian Jones: A remarkable thing happened the day before the third Test. Laurie is quite an intense guy and very passionate. On the captain's run bus ride from the Poenamo Hotel to Eden Park on the Friday afternoon there was dead silence on the bus. Laurie was sitting up the front and it was all very tense, no one wanted to say anything, we were all so desperate to win. Suddenly, Laurie got up and walked down to the back of the bus and started cracking jokes, making light of the situation and just trying to relax everyone. At first it made everyone a bit suspicious, sort of, 'What's happening here?' It was his way of trying to break some tension, and we ended up having a bit of fun at the captain's run, which was unheard of, played a bit of touch, loosened up, and on the bus ride back we were playing cards and so on. On the morning of the match everything was much more relaxed and we went out and played well to win the deciding Test. Foxy spent the week practicing those high kicks that were coming down outside the twenty-two, and we played a fast game.

Craig Dowd: Running out onto Eden Park for the third Test of the series you knew there was only going to be one result and sure enough, it was a good, solid win. That was a defining moment for me and one of the Test matches I will never forget, probably one of my highlights. If the attitude is right, and you have got fourteen other guys around you with the same attitude, you're unstoppable. I had played with Martin Johnson a couple of years earlier in the NZ Under-21s and there he was playing for the Lions. We came through together, made our Test debuts together and retired the same day when Wasps beat Leicester in the club final.

Frank Bunce: Lee Stensness came into the side. I think Laurie felt he offered a bit of variety because between me and Eroni [Clarke] there was no tactical kicker. Lee put through a grubber kick and I was able to score off it. During the game Lee found a $20 note on the field after he'd been tackled. He rolled over and there was $20, so he grabbed it and tucked it into his sock. We looked at him and he said, 'Hey, I'm a student!.' We were under no illusions, it was expected of us to win. The Lions are probably the best thing that happens in rugby. It's something special. The streets are empty when there's a Lions Test, even when they're in Australia or South Africa.

Jon Preston: I think that's when the real All Black mentality kicked in for us that 'You don't get beaten in an All Black jersey, you do anything you can possibly do to make sure you come out victorious.' There was massive pressure on during the week. I was probably as nervous as I ever was in my life, and for the entire week. It was a bit of a do-or-die not only for the team but also in terms of your own career. If you end up in an All Black side that loses two in a row, you lose a series, that can't be good for you. So there was a lot of motivation. As it turned out we put in a pretty good performance and ended up winning comfortably so it was satisfying. We identified a weakness in the way they defended the blindside. So we had a scrum inside their twenty-two with quite a big right-hand blindside. The move, I think it was a dummy cut with JK. They didn't defend with too many numbers and it opened up like the seas parting. I don't think I had a hand laid on me. I managed to score the try. It was a key moment and a memorable one for me.

Ian Jones: That was a good Lions side. Nick Poppelwell was an outstanding prop, Ben Clarke a tremendous flanker and they played an expansive style I think the New Zealand public appreciated. To play against the Lions was a highlight.

Grant Fox: We had two more home Tests to play, against Manu Samoa and Australia. When I ran out at Eden Park against Samoa I knew it would be my last Test there and against Australia at Carisbrook I knew it would be my last Test. It was good to get the Bledisloe Cup back. They were starting to rebuild a bit, Pat Howard was their No.10, but they were a good side and pretty confident. We were very determined to get that Bledisloe Cup back. Tactically we were pretty sound, and we didn't let Australia get their game going. It wasn't all that pretty but we got the result we wanted. I wanted to be absolutely certain so I waited until January just to be sure before going public with my retirement.

Jeff Wilson (1993-01, 60 Tests, 71 matches): I'd never dreamed of being an All Black. Starting off with Southland in the second division, there wasn't too much pressure. I went to Dunedin to do some study and play a bit of footy and Gordon Hunter gave me a chance with Otago. In 1993 a lot of things fell into place – firstly with the cricket, then later on rugby with Otago. I count myself fortunate I played with an Otago team trying to change the game. It was not like an old Otago team, there were a lot of guys who'd come down from Hawke's Bay, like John Timu and Stu Forster, Jamie Joseph from Marlborough, Marc Ellis from Wellington, playing with those guys allowed me to showcase what I could do. Laurie was prepared to take a chance on me. The Otago manager, Gerry Simmons took me aside and said, 'You're going to be named in the All Blacks.' I said, 'You're kidding me.' Otago had played that afternoon and I was in the stands, I wasn't even playing. He said, 'You're in but don't celebrate too much because there are some of your team-mates that haven't made it.' Not that I didn't love my experiences with the Black Caps [NZ cricket team], but once you've been an All Black it's not a hard decision to make.

Ian Jones: The Test against Scotland at the end of 1993, we had Marc Ellis at first-five and we had Jeff Wilson making his debut – we played pretty well, but not so well against England the following week.

Craig Dowd: It was my first tour, a nine-week tour. We were still playing midweek games and being a prop who could play both sides of the scrum I would have to cover midweek games. I would be playing on Saturdays and backing up in the midweek so in that sense it was a long tour.

Jeff Wilson: I made my debut on the week of my twentieth birthday against a South East Division team, and then my Test debut against Scotland a couple of weeks later. It was only a small squad so I was playing every three or four days, either playing or off the bench. Laurie was trying to build on what he'd started in 1992, getting his head around what he had and what he needed to do, looking towards 1995. I'm not sure it was a particularly strong Scotland team, and we were really excited about playing our first Test after being on tour for quite some time. We were all over them. Stu Forster was playing well at halfback, and Buncey set me up for my first Test try. I was on the outside with no defence marking me, so I didn't have to beat anyone, just run fast. My perfect sort of try really! It was bitterly cold and the new stadium at Murrayfield was only half built. We changed in a marquee out the back. It was so cold that whole day, that's something that I really remember.

I kicked a conversion at the end of the Scotland game and because of that Laurie thought I'd be fine to kick in the England game and I had to, because Matthew Cooper, who'd kicked beautifully against Scotland and had been playing really well, got injured.

Jeff Wilson enjoys a stunning debut against Scotland at Murrayfield in 1993. *Getty Images*

Frank Bunce: As a young fellow, Goldie [Wilson] had a lot of expectation on him, having come up through the schoolboy ranks, and he had a lot to deal with. In the Scotland Test everything went really well then we got to England, and with a bit more pressure things didn't really work.

Ian Jones: We had Marc Ellis at ten, Eroni Clarke at twelve and Frank Bunce at thirteen so we didn't have a [goal] kicker.

Jeff Wilson: England played well, they suffocated us. They gave away a lot of penalties, but none of them were 'gimmes'. I was zero for three by half-time and lost confidence. In the end I was three from nine. Fitzy kept pointing to the posts and I kept missing. We did enough to almost snatch it. John Timu went in at the corner but they ruled he put a foot in touch. But I would never have kicked the conversion from the sideline to win it, the way I was going. I went from the absolute high of Murrayfield to rock bottom, I was devastated. I'd grown up watching Grant Fox not miss – when you're goal-kicking for the All Blacks you know how important it is. There's one photo of me on one knee waiting for the sand to come out – we didn't have kicking tees then – and you can see from that photo I've got no idea where it's going to go. We had no one else in that team who could kick. I've often thanked Matt for getting injured and leaving me with all that responsibility!

Craig Dowd: Losing to England was horrible. It was all penalty goals, although John Timu scored a try but the referee said he didn't. There was no love lost. I've never seen the game replay but it was probably one of those dour, boring games that are a grind. Afterwards, the way the English acted was 'in-your-face' as if they thought they were the world champions. For a lot of them it was revenge for the third Lions Test earlier. It was a heavy defeat and the changing room after that game sucked it up and never forgot it. It was one of those games that moulded the dislike of losing. We didn't get our chance for revenge until 1995. We were all waiting for that one to come around. It was a pretty quiet night. I remember Neil Finn coming in and getting in the bus with the boys coming down the back and strumming the guitar and singing to us which was really cool.

Ian Jones: I was lying in the baths after the Test . . . Graeme Purvis was our team guitarist and I heard a Split Enz song, and I thought, 'Gee Purvy's getting good.' I got out, and walked through, ready to tell him how good he was going, and here was Neil Finn strumming away. That was pretty cool.

THIRTY-FIVE

FALTERING STEPS

'Fitzy could really wind them up, especially their forwards.
They hated him'

NEW ZEALAND RUGBY fans rubbed their hands together in 1994 at the prospect of the first Springbok visit since the dark days of 1981. First though, came a two-Test visit by France – a low point of the Mains tenure. Mains took a chance on Jonah Lomu, the colossal South Auckland teenager who a couple of months earlier shot the lights out at the Hong Kong Sevens. He had little experience on the wing, having played nearly all his rugby in the forwards, making his selection a calculated risk, even if the potential was there for something extraordinary. But this was a French team full of crafty schemers, in the mood to cause trouble. The first Test was a shock, France winning comfortably, 22-8 against an out-of-sync All Black team, who again felt the blow torch being applied as they headed to Eden Park. A better effort had them leading with moments remaining, but flyhalf Stephen Bachop failed to find touch, and from deep in their own territory, the French scored what became known as 'The try from the end of the world'. It was a wondrous, sweeping, end-to-end movement, with a bewildered Lomu tied in knots by Philippe St Andre and Emile N'Tamack, before fullback Jean-Luc Sadourney sailed over for one of the best ever scored. A rare loss at Eden Park, an even more rare home series defeat, and again Mains could hear the sound of knives being sharpened. Before the year was out he would have to survive an attempted coup.

Jeff Wilson: I was on the bench against France, JK had come back and Jonah Lomu got his first start. In those days with no tactical subs, you didn't get a chance from the bench! Laurie trained us hard, there were a lot of things he was working on, but it seemed like hard work, hard physically. He was creating a style of play through little pieces of the puzzle.

Eric Rush: When Jonah died there was a lot of talk about how he'd struggled when they first moved him to the wing – that was harsh. There're only two guys who've gone from the loose forwards to the wing, me and Jonah, and when I went out to the wing I made more mistakes than he did. I didn't get as much flak as he did, because he was Jonah Lomu. It's hard, you play a position all your life and you get to be instinctive, but then you get moved out to the wing where, if you have to stop and think about things, it's too late.

Jonah Lomu (1994-2002, 63 Tests): I made my debut four years after first playing union and I was the youngest All Black since the 1905 tour. And I lost my first two Tests, in the space of a week, against France. And to tell the truth I didn't play that well. It was tough because I found out then the deficiencies in my game. I learnt more out of those two losses than any other game. My positional play needed work, but the biggest lesson I

Opposite: The Tackle – Wallaby scrum-half George Gregan pulls off a matching-saving tackle on Jeff Wilson in the dying seconds of the 1994 Bledisloe Cup. *Getty Images*

Jonah Lomu makes his debut against France
during the first Test of the 1994 tour.
FotoSport/Photosport NZ

learnt was to listen to my instincts and not listen to anyone else, even the coach. The coach will teach you everything you need to know in terms of the game plan, but when you get out on the field it's your natural instincts that you have to get on board.

Ian Jones: Losing to the French still haunts me. We weren't playing great rugby, we were going through lots of players as Laurie tried to find the right formula for 1995. We didn't support each other well enough to win the game. And the French love taking us on. They scored that unbelievable try – we were powerless to stop it. People wanted to get rid of Laurie, wanted new players in the side. Laurie gave some new guys a chance, guys who'd played great rugby at provincial level, but they didn't take it, and as a consequence we suffered losses.

Craig Dowd: The reason I got my chance in 1993 was Richard Loe had been banned for an eye-gouging incident so he sat out the whole of 1993 and from that England Test there were a few casualties of which I was one. Laurie liked the cut of Loey's jib – he was the hard edge and experienced player that he wanted. Laurie got the best out of him. All the locks got injured against South Africa in Dunedin and Arran Pene went in to cover lock, then got injured so the only one left was myself. I was happy to put my hand up just to get onto the field. I wasn't on for long but I won a lineout.

Frank Bunce: Laurie had a plan from the beginning. We didn't know what it was, but he was prepared to try things. In 1992 things went pretty well, 1993, then in 1994 we had that French series. It was a poor year by All Black standards but he reminded us we were building towards a World Cup. Jonah Lomu was a schoolboy star, a phenomenon, then he got put into the All Blacks on the wing, out of position. One of the problems for Jonah was he was being told what to do by every single person he came into contact with. Everyone, no matter what position they'd played, was telling him what to do, and for a young player like that, with all that natural ability, he had so much on his plate, they should have left him alone to find his feet. We should have beaten the French in 1994 but they scored a try only the French could score, they were that sort of team.

Since their re-introduction the Springboks had been playing as often as possible, but were finding the game had moved on considerably during their exile. They were unbeaten going into the first Test in Dunedin, where they fought hard before going down 22-14. The second Test, in Wellington, became infamous for the biting of Sean Fitzpatrick by Springbok prop Johan le Roux. Fitzpatrick had quickly found a way under the skin of the South African players, and to le Roux, the All Black skipper was a red rag to a very angry bull. After a ruck, Fitzpatrick got up complaining he'd had his ear bitten, TV replays clearly showing the grubby deed. Le Roux played the match out, but was sent home, and banned for eighteen months. A tense 13-9 victory gave the All Blacks a shot at a first series sweep of the Boks at Eden Park, but they faltered, needing six penalty goals by fullback Shane Howarth for an 18-all draw. The 'failure' to close out the sweep meant more heat on both team and coach, and it only got worse two weeks later in Sydney.

Sean Fitzpatrick: We played the South Africans quite a bit in the early versions of Super Rugby so by the time they got to New Zealand in 1994 they were starting to get back into the swing of things. They weren't a great team but they were getting better. They were big men, hard men, and we had a battle on our hands because we still weren't the real deal either. We learned a lot in the Irish series in 1992, Robin Brooke and Olo Brown came into the team, and a couple of older guys dropped out. By 1994 we were starting to kick on.

Ian Jones: The public embraced the Springboks. They were so rapt to have them back in this country. It re-cemented this great rivalry between the All Blacks and Springboks, because by then a lot of us had grown up with them not being part of international rugby. These guys are our greatest foes. They think the game like us, they play the game like us. I remember talking to past All Blacks during that tour and they spelled it out to me. They try and intimidate you through physicality, and if they can do that, then they've won. If you don't front up to them, they don't respect you and they'll stand over you. You're not going to bully them because they're big and strong but you have to stand up to them, and take on the strong parts of their game. It wasn't like that with the Wallabies.

Zinzan Brooke celebrates the win against South Africa after the third Test in 1994. *FotoSport/Photosport NZ*

Sean Fitzpatrick: Before the first Test Loey and I identified Johan le Roux as the wild card. He was giving away penalties, putting in cheap shots. In the first scrum of the series Loey grabbed a hold of one of his fatty bits and that got him going. We won a penalty straight away, and we thought, 'Well, that was easy.' We'd wound him up and I couldn't believe they picked him again for the second Test because he'd given away about 12 points in Dunedin. In the Wellington Test he snapped. I pulled his jersey, held him back and he turned around and bit my ear. I thought, 'Jesus! What just happened?'

I still feel terrible about Stu Wilson, he was doing the post-match interview and I said to him, 'Don't ask me about the ear, I don't want to talk about it.' It was like 'What happens on the field stays on the field,' which was a bit stupid when you think about it. So I'm standing there with blood dripping on my collar, I could hear the producer yelling at Stu to ask me about the ear, and of course, he didn't because I'd asked him not to. I had a beer with le Roux afterwards, and then he got banned for eighteen months. I did see him in South Africa a year or so later, in Durban. A kid came over to me and said, 'Johan le Roux's in the car park, he wants to see you.' I was with Richard Fry and he said, 'Don't go over,' but this kid kept coming back. So I made the kid give me a hundred rand and I said, 'If he's not there I'm going to keep the hundred rand.' The kid gives me a hundred rand, so then I had to go over, and as I was walking over I could see him surrounded by these big Afrikaners and I thought, 'Jeez,' but I kept going, just went up, held out my hand and said, 'Hi Johan, nice to see you,' and he said, 'Nice to see you,' back and that was about it. Then blow me down if his first game back was Transvaal against Auckland at Ellis Park, and there was all this talk about what was going to happen at the first scrum. Standing in the tunnel he was on fire, glaring at me . . . Zinny was captain and I said, 'This is too much I'm going to have to go have a word with him,' and Zinny said, 'OK,' so I went over, held out my hand and said, 'Johan, I hope you had a good lunch!'

Frank Bunce: In the first Test they'd had a lot of personnel changes, and I marked Pieter Muller, who was quite early in his career. My game was to always try and intimidate your man a bit, put him off. I did something to him . . . I can't remember what it was, nothing much, but I was walking away and I heard these footsteps running towards me and it was him, coming back on the attack, I was like whoah! But we soon learned that a guy like Fitzy could really wind them up, especially their forwards. They hated him. I played against him and you just tried to let it go, not worry about what he was saying or doing, but they couldn't do it, they hated him so much and he wound them up so easily.

Ian Jones: I developed some wonderful relationships with some of those Springboks. Colin Meads, our manager played against some of their management and through him we socialised with them on a Sunday afternoon, spent some quality time with them and developed friendships. I've been lucky enough to play with a few of them in World XVs or Barbarians which helps cement those friendships. I was fortunate to play in an era when you could do that.

In the first Bledisloe Cup Test to be played under lights, Australia centre Jason Little scored a try fourteen seconds after kick-off. By half-time they had a commanding lead, but Mains urged the players to get out and 'play some rugby'. They did, storming back to 20-16 before Jeff Wilson broke through on the right and looked set to complete the comeback. In a flash, Wallaby scrum-half George Gregan made what will forever be known as 'the tackle', knocking the ball from a stunned Wilson's grasp to save an exhilarating Test match. The All Blacks' fast-paced attack in the second half had been a pointer, but the All Black coach faced a fight to stay in the job, a fight he only just won. Mains maintained he was building for the World Cup, and that was about to be put to the test.

Jeff Wilson: We'd beaten South Africa taking no risks at all, but when we went to Australia we fell behind so much we had nothing to lose and we just went for it – things like releasing Zinzan Brooke to do whatever he could. Inevitably, any talk about the Bledisloe Cup game that year brings up the Tackle. George Gregan hit me from behind and the ball was knocked loose. I don't know how many times I'd been able to score in that situation, reach out and score in a tackle and I'd never lost the ball, but he came up with a fantastic piece of play. It probably had an affect on the way I played for the rest of my career. I began to think about risk and reward. I became more conservative in what I did because of how much it meant to me, to the rest of the players. We didn't like losing. Losing with the All Blacks is a horrible, horrible thing.

Frank Bunce: It was a sign of things to come the way we played that second half. We had the personnel who could play that game, and we had nothing to lose. Before that incident with Goldie we'd already had a chance to win the game . . . someone made a break and didn't throw a last pass and the moment was lost. That was one of the classic Australian teams, Gregan, Eales, Little. The difference between playing the Australians and the Springboks was it wasn't so physical against the Australians, but you did a hell of a lot of running.

Ian Jones: That second half performance in Australia was a bit of a catalyst. It was a fifteen-man game with width. Everyone had to buy into what we were doing, including Laurie. It was a style that suited the players he had, and it was the way we thought the game should be played and Laurie said, 'Yes.'

THIRTY-SIX

WORLD CUP ANGUISH

'Give the ball to Jonah'

HAS THERE BEEN a year in rugby quite so monumental as 1995? In the space of a few weeks the game witnessed the greatest impact by a player in its history, a World Cup tournament that united a once divided country, and finally, the plunge into professionalism. There were times in 1995 when it looked like Jonah Lomu was not going to make the All Black team for the World Cup in South Africa. After his unsuccessful 1994 debut Lomu was jettisoned, and in early 1995 he failed to impress the All Black coach with his fitness levels, as he sought to condition the team for the high tempo game his players insisted on. Lomu was free to go to the Hong Kong Sevens, where he played a phenomenal hand in a New Zealand victory, and whilst Mains still had reservations, he relented. Lomu was back in. Notably, three other young players forced their way in, the impish Canterbury pivot Andrew Mehrtens, mobile Otago flanker Josh Kronfeld, and the elusive North Harbour fullback/wing Glen Osborne, and these players would have a big impact. The new boys showed their style in a hit-out against Canada at Eden Park, before heading off to a tournament with a massive unknown factor hanging over it. Was South Africa ready, were the Springboks ready, could Australia go back-to-back, were the All Blacks ready to claim back the trophy? After the Boks had upended the defending champions in a dramatic opener in Cape Town, the All Blacks were given the honour of the first match on Ellis Park, against Ireland. Ireland started well, but were soon pushed to one side as Lomu took centre stage, the young wing smashing through, over and around the Irish defence scoring two tries in an attention-grabbing 43-19 win. Wales managed to keep Lomu off the score sheet but not out of the action, Mehrtens bagged 19 points, Little, Ellis and Kronfield tries in a 34-9 victory. The final match of the pool was nothing more than an exhibition, the second string setting fire to the record books in a 145-17 win over Japan, scoring twenty-one tries, six by Ellis, and twenty of them converted by Simon Culhane, who added a try for a world record debut tally of 45 points.

Eric Rush: I take my hat off to Laurie. We had a camp in Queenstown at the end of 1994. There wasn't any rugby . . . we did some bungy jumping, jet boating and stuff, but one thing he did do was sit us down with a piece of paper and write down what we thought we needed to do to win the World Cup. The message was loud and clear. We didn't want to play programmed rugby, and he was a programmed rugby guy. What I put down was that I'd been picked for the All Blacks for a reason, and as soon as I got in it was coached out of me. The message was, 'We play it wide, man, let it have some air.' A lot of guys wrote that sort of thing, and credit to Laurie, Earl, Thorbs and Pinetree, they took it on board. At the next camp they said that was how they were going to do it, but if we were going

Opposite: Jonah Lomu exploded onto the world stage during the 1995 Rugby World Cup. *FotoSport/Photosport NZ*

to play that sort of game we had to be the fittest team there. He absolutely smashed us at every training camp. We were a notch above everyone else.

Craig Dowd: What Laurie Mains put us through to go to South Africa in the World Cup was one of the hardest things I ever experienced. The theory behind it was, 'You are going to have to play at altitude and to get over the altitude you are going to have to be that much fitter.' No matter how fit you are, you are going to feel it. The thinning of the air up there, the back of the throat you can taste the blood and it's horrible but fitness is the way of getting over it. But going beyond the levels that fitness will take you, right into the oxygen debt and pushing a little bit further, when you get fifteen guys all wanting to do that you will be unstoppable.

Jeff Wilson: The return of Graeme Bachop made a difference at halfback. He provided that link between forwards and backs. I think Laurie had found out the year before that it was very difficult to try and grind out wins in Test matches and in a World Cup. Those sorts of games can go either way. It was better if we could play at speed as a way of putting other teams under extreme pressure. We had the fitness and skill level that enabled us to do that. We had that balance of experience, and the youth and enthusiasm that a guy like Glen Osborne brought into the mix, that 'No fear' element. Mehrts [Andrew Mehrtens] had it as well. In the end it was the skill levels that made the difference, and the ability to let a guy like Zinzan Brooke play his game, let Josh [Kronfeld] do his thing. But we could only do it because we had a fantastic tight five – the ultimate balance.

Craig Dowd: At the end of 1994 I snapped my ankle. I had to get three pins in it so I was out for a couple of months. The first camp was in Queenstown and it was more of an organisational thing. At the second camp I had only just started jogging so I got to do quite a bit but not as much as everyone else and I think the way I got fit, showed Laurie that I was working hard to catch up. At the Rotorua camp we had the beep test and I had one of the top levels. Laurie was trying to pull me out because I was limping while I was running almost Igor-ish putting myself through it. I never pulled out and he saw how determined I was.

Eric Rush: We had these early camps and Jonah really bombed. We know why now, but we didn't then. He wouldn't say anything, and Jonah wasn't going to run a good three kilometre time trial as long as his arse was pointing to the ground! His attitude was, 'I don't care about running any three kilometre time trial, just give me the ball', but I said to him, 'Mate before you get the ball, you're going to have to put in some yards.' He put in the effort. Those training sessions must have killed him . . . I was a fit guy and I struggled so I can't imagine what they did to him. He loved the sevens, it made him sharp, and grew his confidence. He was outstanding up there that year in Hong Kong. When we got back there was another camp and he bombed again. They said he could go to Japan with the sevens team. That basically meant he wasn't in consideration . . . and that's when Jonah signed to go to the Canterbury Bulldogs.

Phil Kingsley Jones rang me up. It was our job to try and keep Jonah here, and the only thing I could say to Jonah was, 'Mate you do what you gotta do but just come and play one more game with the bros.' It was the North v South game in Dunedin, the last one they had. They roomed me with Jonah, with Frank, and Michael Jones and Walter Little in the next rooms, to try and talk him into staying. He absolutely smashed it in that game, he was killing everyone. So we talked him into another game. He kept getting better and better and Laurie knew then he had to pick him.

Sean Fitzpatrick: At the beginning of 1995 Jonah wasn't even in the picture. He'd failed at the training camps, but then Rushy pulled a hamstring and Jonah came back into the trials and scored five tries. We were the fittest and fastest team, that had always been the plan, play it as quickly as possible.

Craig Dowd: After the Christchurch camp I was sitting on the bus behind Laurie and Earle and Ross Cooper and they were saying: 'Who is it going to be – Norm Berryman or Lomu, what are we going to do?' I was sitting there and I couldn't believe I was listening to this but they were talking about which one was going to go and weighing the pros and cons of Norm vs Jonah. Norm Berryman was a pretty devastating ball carrier as well but they decided to give Lomu a crack because he needed to work on his fitness. Nobody knew about his kidney issues and we couldn't believe how he could be so unfit because one moment he could run the length of the rugby field and score the try and be absolutely fine. We all knew how good he was as a rugby player and we wanted him there. The rest is history but it was a fine line.

Sean Fitzpatrick: The game against Canada before we went to the World Cup, Mehrts and Josh [Kronfeld] came in and the impact they had was phenomenal. We hadn't had a regular ten since Foxy and Mehrts was so much better than anyone else we'd had. He was the new breed of guy who would stick up his hand and say, 'Why aren't we doing it this way?' He'd question things. Laurie was probably thinking, 'What have I done here? The older guys were being challenged by the younger guys. Instead of just sitting quietly in the corner, they questioned things. That's where that team started to develop.

Ian Jones: The new guys like Mehrts, Glen Osborne, Josh, brought something to the squad. We already had some good combinations, the front row, myself and Robin at lock, Bachop was playing a style that was new for an All Black halfback with the width of his pass. Mehrts came in, a guy who could read a game really well, the combination of Little and Bunce and power and speed out wide. Jonah was phenomenal. Something we'd never seen ever. We'd had Kirwan, Beegee Williams, Inga, big strong wingers in the past but never someone with the explosive power and pace of Jonah. Bunce could give Jonah twenty metres of space with a pass, or Kronfeld, who could keep up with Jonah and take an inside pass for a try. It was such an attractive style, one we loved playing, and were fit enough to play. I didn't think anyone could keep pace with us.

Craig Dowd: Being a Pacific Islander, all the blacks over there loved Jonah. In a country where apartheid had been around for so long to have this hero come out who was coloured

– the people just loved him. At every training session we had hordes who were there to see Jonah.

Eric Rush: Laurie was really strict on diet . . . we weren't allowed to eat any fried stuff, weren't allowed to eat too much. One morning at breakfast, the management guys had gone to the gym, and so we hooked into a lot. Well, Laurie came back early and walked into the breakfast room. I was eating corn flakes, but I had a plate of bacon and fried eggs there as well. When I saw Laurie come in I pushed the bacon and eggs over to where Walter Little was sitting . . . he was up getting his food. Laurie came straight to me – he and Jonah didn't talk, he decided it was better to communicate with Jonah through me – so he comes up to me because Jonah's over there eating a whole French stick stuffed with boiled eggs. I thought it was about sixteen eggs, Laurie said it was twenty-two. Walt had great peripheral vision. He was on his way back to the table and saw Laurie, and he saw the plate of bacon and eggs at his place. He pulled off the biggest sidestep of his career and went to another table. Laurie goes 'What the **** is he eating now?' So I went over to Jonah and told him to think about what he's eating and Jonah just said, 'Tell him to get stuffed,' so I went back to Laurie and said, 'He says he's just about finished!'

Craig Dowd: It was the World Cup when his ability really hit home to us. England was a fantastic game, but right through those pool games he was knocking guys over like he was a bowling ball. Guys were falling off him and to have someone in your team who could do that it was a case of 'Give the ball to Jonah.' The more he got told he couldn't do something the more he would go out of his way to prove he could. The worst thing you could say to Jonah was: 'You can't.' He would take that onto the rugby field and jam it up your arse. He was amazing.

The cards seemed to fall for the All Blacks. Moments before their quarter-final with Scotland, England had put Australia out, and with the Scots outdone 48-30 the All Blacks faced a much anticipated semi-final with England. By Sunday, Cape Town swarmed with English fans, some of whom had made a late dash and a high bid for a chance to see history. The England players were confident too, talking up their chances, playing down the threat of Lomu. Their bravado was quickly dashed. With but a few minutes gone Lomu collected a loose pass thirty metres out, fended off Tony Underwood, brushed through Will Carling and, in spite of being off balance, ran right over the top of Mike Catt. It set the tone, the powerful winger scoring four tries in an astonishing performance. With the eyes of the world on South Africa, Lomu had seized the moment and by the time the game ended, rugby had its first global superstar. It wasn't just about Lomu. Kronfield gave a masterclass of support play, Bachop, Mehrtens, Little and Osborne constantly wriggled through the England defence, and for good measure Zinzan Brooke lobbed in a dropped goal from near halfway. The All Blacks propelled themselves into favouritism for the final, South Africa having only just scraped past France the day before on a flooded Kings Park.

Jeff Wilson: Jonah was freakish, he was such a weapon. You think of the number of times

Jonah got the ball in games like that, it was nothing like the times a winger handles the ball in the All Blacks nowadays, but it seemed every time he touched the ball, when we made a bit of space for him, those guys, poor old Tony Underwood, Catt, Carling . . . they had no chance. I played against the guy and there were situations when he was undefendable. In that tournament, you put him on the outside and . . . game over. The only way people were able to stop him was to grab a hold of those loose fitting jerseys and somehow hold him back. We were playing at great speed. It wasn't perfect rugby, we made mistakes but we were able to keep going and going. I was never as fit as that again in my career. We had the perfect conditions over there to play our game, on top of the ground and we had the skill level to keep the ball alive.

Frank Bunce: Through all the camps, the trials and then a Test against Canada before we left, it was clear we were building. Fitness was building, the personnel was pretty much right, and when we got over there we were itching to get started. Teams like Wales and Ireland were starting with a hiss and a roar, and got stuck in, but we always felt in control, and we pulled away from them. We got to Cape Town and all the England fans, their press, we were hearing what they were saying, they were pretty bullish all right, saying what they were going to do. Guys like Tony Underwood saying Jonah had never faced anyone really experienced, or any good, or something like that, and that wound Jonah up a bit. People came up to us in the street, Simon Poidevin came up, and said, 'Just beat them will you.' And there was the fact that we'd lost to them in '93, the last time we'd played them. That still rankled.

Jeff Wilson: The 1993 loss played a big part in 1995, we don't like losing to England, and a lot of guys who'd played in '93 were there, guys who'd felt that loss. Jonah, for whatever reason, always got up for games against England.

Craig Dowd: After 1993 we were so fired up and even the young guys who were not there in 1993 we were telling them that this was payback. It was one of those games I could compare with the third Test against the Lions in 1993 there was no way we were going to lose. Although everyone was talking England up there was a feeling that we couldn't go through 1993 again. Jonah had a fantastic game but the platform was laid by the forwards. Laurie had us hunting as a pack and blowing things over. We'd trained for that moment. All those camps that we'd done over the summer, about how he wanted us lower than all the opposition, binding up, blowing over every breakdown and creating lightning quick ball – it all clicked. Jonah was the icing on the cake. He had good front foot ball but again he had that same attitude and poor old Mike Catt found out about it.

Andrew Mehrtens (1995-2004, 70 Tests, 72 games): The guys who'd lost to England in 1993, they were very bitten by that, they'd really been made to feel like colonial heathens and they were really wound up about England and for that semi final in '95.

Frank Bunce: We switched the kick off. We'd had success with that. We forced a couple of mistakes, made a bit of ground, and set the tone. After losing to them in 1993 they didn't come across as humble winners. Having said that, years later when you met the guys you played against you find they're pretty good guys. Will Carling for example, we thought he stood for everything we didn't like about English rugby and turns out he's a hell of a nice guy and when he came out with that '57 old farts' thing . . . you know he was forward thinking, he wanted England to play another sort of game. He was totally different to our perception of him.

Jonah Lomu: To tell the truth, if Catty had been two or three steps back, I would've fallen in front of his feet. He helped me get to the line because he kind of stabilised me. By me hitting him, he balanced me up. He stood me back up. I took two more steps and then I had to leap over the line or else I would have fallen head first.

I remember after the semi-final against England I went to buy some toothpaste and the whole mall followed me to the shop. So here I was stuck out the back in the storage cupboard and waiting for the security guys to clear a path so I could get back to my hotel. That's when I realised my life wasn't my own.

Did Tony Underwood wink at me during the haka? Yes he did, and I said I was going to wipe it off his face.

Ian Jones: England were bigger than us, so if it came down to an arm wrestle they might have won like they did in 1993, but we didn't let them settle into any rhythm. What we did at Cape Town had its origins in Warkworth, a little town just north of Auckland, in the days after the trials. Laurie had this plan for a split kick-off and this was how we were going to play England if we met them in a semi-final, so it had been in his mind, in our minds all that time. We'd practiced it at Mahurangi College on our way back to Auckland from Whangarei. We rehearsed that passage of play for an hour, so when it worked against England it was no surprise to us. After the game we got on a plane and went straight back to Johannesburg. The winning team, the team going to the final got to fly business class, and the beaten team had to sit at the back. Just by chance we got on the plane first. I was sitting there with Robin, not being able to touch the seats in front of us and poor old Martin Johnson and Martin Bayfield had to walk past us . . . if the shoe had been on the other foot, I know I'd have been gutted, would still be to this day!

Just over forty-eight hours before the final at Ellis Park, the All Blacks had lunch in their cordoned-off dining room at their hotel. By early next morning, most of the players and management were suffering from severe stomach cramps, vomiting and diarrhoea. At one point it became so bad, thought was given to requesting a postponement, but this was dismissed and the management opted to keep the illness quiet. That they were suffering from a severe gastric complaint, almost certainly food poisoning, is beyond debate. Having subsequently engaged a private detective to investigate, Mains has steadfastly maintained it was deliberately inflicted. Others are not so sure, including New Zealand journalists staying in the same hotel who did not eat with the All Blacks, but were also sick. It certainly impacted on their preparation for the final, and threatened to compromise their tremendous stamina.

Ian Jones: It was an energy-charged week. We were buzzing after the semi-final, although I wonder if some of us had put too much into winning in Cape Town. The week was going pretty well, until Thursday lunchtime. I was sick about 1am on Friday. I was rooming with Robin Brooke who had eaten out that day. He was sleeping like a baby and I was chundering my guts out, just a couple days out from the biggest game of my life. I went to the Doc's room and there were about eighteen other people in there. On Friday I was drained, wrecked. But come Friday night I was coming right. By then you're trying to convince yourself you're OK, you're fit, you're playing this big game and you'll be right. By Saturday breakfast I'd talked myself into feeling OK. I hadn't eaten too much but I'd managed to drink a bit. I don't want to use it as an excuse though. We did have our chances, we had opportunities and the South Africans played above themselves. They defended like their lives depended on it, they shut Jonah and our other backs down, we missed some opportunities, they took theirs and . . . I don't think about it every day but I think about it most days!

Frank Bunce: We were the high flyers, playing a great brand of rugby, and they were the underdogs under all the pressure. People asked how they were going to stop Jonah, they didn't have a running game, everything was against them, but as can happen, they got stuck in and South Africans are not going to give up to anyone. I wasn't as crook as a lot of the other guys. I did have the runs, one night. We were certainly disrupted, training and such, and some of the guys were really bad. We didn't know anything about the decision to keep it quiet. They would have had that meeting behind closed doors. My feeling was, 'We're sick, let's manage this the best we can, we've got a World Cup final to play.' I think it's OK the way it came out, it's only a theory. I get asked did I get sick? Well yes, but was I poisoned? I wouldn't have a clue. It would be nice to prove it one way or the other.

Zinzan Brooke (1987-97, 58 Tests, 100 games): We all felt we had plenty left to give in the final, but something was definitely done to us. Forty-eight hours before the big day and eighteen of us, plus management, go down with food poisoning. That may be coincidence, but I don't think so. For every game before then we had made a point of eating in public restaurants to avoid being targeted. But in the week of the final we isolated ourselves in a private room. We had asked for our chef [a New Zealander] in Cape Town to be brought to cook for us in Johannesburg, but the hotel management point blank refused. When we realised what had happened we thought about pulling out, getting the game postponed. But we decided to use it to motivate us even more. Unfortunately, things didn't work out as we had hoped.

Sean Fitzpatrick: Even as sick as some of the guys were, we should have won. We had opportunities to win, right up to the last minute of regular time when Mehrts missed that drop kick. We should have done a few things differently. Staying in Sandton was a mistake. On the Sunday after the Cape Town win instead of flying back to Jo'burg we should have gone somewhere else. We wanted to immerse ourselves in the atmosphere of the final, but once we made the final the whole town turned against us. They went from loving us to hating us and we'd have been better off out of it. It was a life-changing experience, a great thing to be part of. We nearly did it. But I'm not one of those who thought it was about more than just a game of rugby. We should have won.

The atmosphere at Ellis Park for the final was electrifying, the crowd enraptured by the appearance of President Nelson Mandela in a Springbok jersey, and enthralled by two low-flying passes by a South African Airways Jumbo. The match was an epic, tryless battle, decided in extra time by a dropped goal by Joel Stransky, a moment that will stand in South African history. The Springboks sensed a chance to achieve something that would resonate far beyond the playing surface. Defeat was a bitter pill for the All Blacks to swallow. Some have never been able to accept it, others have found some consolation in the knowledge that there was something bigger than a rugby match going on that day.

Frank Bunce: Playing in that final was the best experience of my rugby life. That's what you play the game for, the big occasion. By the time we got to the park I was feeling OK. Maybe some of the other guys who were sicker than me were still feeling crook, but it wasn't on my mind. I remember seeing those armed cops or soldiers ready to abseil down the stadium, hanging off the edge of the roof with their machine guns. It all added to the occasion. The game itself was awesome to play in, with the extra time, all the drama, both teams had opportunities – it was unreal. I had a chance, I took the ball reasonably close to the posts and I turned and Josh was right there. I remember thinking, 'Shall I give it to him?' If I'd popped it to him he could have taken it further . . . but I didn't, I took it to ground. I guess I was being conservative, it was probably the one time I thought of the bigger picture. Usually you'd just have a go without thinking about it. I don't think we quite realised the significance of what was happening that day . . . not until later, you started to think what it all meant. It took a while to get over the disappointment.

Ian Jones: At the time you're very much in the bubble and focused on what you have to do. I remember Mr Mandela walking down the tunnel to come on the field and the roar of the crowd as he came out, and saying to myself, and the guys around, that we had to feed on that.

Andrew Mehrtens: How much what happened on Thursday night affected us, well it comes down to pure speculation doesn't it?

Taking aside what happened to us in the buildup to the game, the predominant reason we lost was that we weren't able to play the game that had worked so successfully for us throughout the tournament. We got knocked over by a team that stood up to us physically, and made their tackles more than any other team that we'd played and we just weren't able to impose ourselves on them.

You had Japie Mulder making smashing tackles everywhere, James Small getting up in Jonah's face, and every time we got down into their area, they'd win a lineout under pressure and throw it back to Andre Joubert who'd just smash a massive punt, with no angle to work with and we'd be back inside our own half.

Jeff Wilson: The disappointing thing was we couldn't prepare properly because we didn't have enough people well enough. I was in no state to play a Rugby World Cup final. I had no strength, no endurance, nothing in the tank because I had not been able to fuel myself in the days leading up, and that's why I was done at half-time. A lot of it was a blur. Any time there was any physical exertion I would feel all hazy, just depleted. Mehrts put in a kick before half-time. I chased it and that was it, I was spent. At half-time I said, 'I don't want to be responsible for us losing . . . Macca's [Mark Ellis] here, he's fit, best get him out there.' I spent the rest of the game on the sideline, having a few dry retches watching us be not quite good enough. We had our chances . . . Mehrts missed that dropped goal . . . which I remind him about. He never showed any sympathy to me about the Gregan thing!

Andrew Mehrtens: I had a shot at a droppy just before the end of regular time. I've seen accounts that say it was just to the right of the posts . . . it was a mile off. We were right in the middle of the field on the twenty-two, and I don't know if he anticipated it, or just moved up really quickly off the ruck, but Joost van der Westhuizen got up and put real pressure on and it skewed off my boot.

Jonah Lomu: The final itself, well there was a bitter taste for about thirty seconds at the end at losing a close match but then I looked around at the crowd and listened to the roar when Francois received the trophy and it was obvious that something very big and good was happening to South Africa the country and it took all the disappointment out of the day.

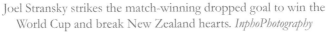

Joel Stransky strikes the match-winning dropped goal to win the World Cup and break New Zealand hearts. *InphoPhotography*

THIRTY-SEVEN

A BRAVE NEW WORLD

'He dragged the team, kicking and screaming at times, to new levels'

THE DAY BEFORE the World Cup final, the New Zealand, Australian and South African Rugby Unions made a ground-breaking declaration. Tired of losing players to other codes, tired of waiting for the International Rugby Board to take the lead, they put an end to the pretence. They were going professional. Immediately they became embroiled in what Sydney author Peter Fitzsimons dubbed 'The Rugby War', as a maverick group, the World Rugby Corporation, based in Sydney began to offer the players far more money and a radical global competition structure. The WRC proposal gained the approval of the majority of the players, and as the All Blacks and Wallabies met for a post-World Cup Bledisloe Cup series, a mass defection seemed imminent. Valiant efforts were made to sign up the next tier of players on NZRU contracts, but in the end it was a 'How much will it take?' offer from South Africa's autocratic rugby boss Louis Luyt that lured the strategically-crucial Springboks back to the establishment, much to the disgust of their Anzac counterparts. The WRC was history.

Sean Fitzpatrick: I didn't know anything about the WRC until the Sunday after the final. 'Bruiser' [Mike Brewer] had said something about it, he'd been approached by someone on the Friday. There was the announcement of the Sanzar deal on the Friday, we had the final on the Saturday and then on the Sunday Bruiser came to me and said, 'We'd better have a meeting.' That was the first I'd heard about it.

Eric Rush: It was the week of the semi-final, we were down in Cape Town, we started hearing about it [WRC]. At some point the senior guys went off and met a few of them, and the rest of us, we just got told a bit here and there. After we lost the final [NZRU chairman] Richie Guy came in and said, 'You're going to be professionals next year boys, this time next year you'll be getting paid $30,000 to be playing for the All Blacks.' And we were stoked, because $30,000 was $30,000 more than we'd been getting. Later that afternoon, the WRC guys said they were going to pay us $US800,000 each! Everybody said, 'We'd better look at this.' As the lawyer in the team, everybody was saying to me, 'What do we do, Rushie?' and I said, 'Sign nothing!'

Ian Jones: We started getting whispers of it the week of the World Cup final. One or two guys were getting calls. We were starting to hear something else might be up. I was too busy thinking about the game, but some of the non-players were getting word something was in the wind. After we got home things changed drastically. The NZRU outlined their plans for the professional game, and normally most of us would have been jumping at it

Opposite: A bloodied Sean Fitzpatrick during the 1995 Bledisloe Cup match. *Getty Images*

but Kerry Packer was on the other side with the WRC. Sanzar had signed up the Rugby Unions, but the Rugby Unions hadn't signed up the players, and that's when the WRC stepped in. The Rugby Union couldn't believe we weren't falling over ourselves to sign with them. We didn't know what we were worth, but the NZRU were offering us 'x' amount and then along came Kerry Packer and said we were worth 'y' . . . and they were poles apart. That's when the standoff started. I wasn't involved in the negotiating much but I was adamant, along with Sean and the other senior All Blacks, that nothing was ever going to happen unless it was global. I don't think it was anyone's intention for it to be a rogue, or rebel, competition, unsanctioned.

Sean Fitzpatrick: At the meeting we had I said, 'Right, there are two options on the table, and whatever happens we all go as one, and if there's a split then that's the end of it, because there can only be one competition, we can't have two factions.' We looked at both options and the best option was the Packer (WRC) deal. They were both the same money, but the WRC was the better setup and we tried to make it work. The thing that surprised me was that New Zealanders had been saying to us, 'You guys should be paid, you need a better deal', sort of thing, but as soon as it looked as though we were thinking about Packer the whole country turned on us. That was a stressful time. The whole history of the All Blacks was in the balance, where was it going to go? It was life-changing, to be dealing with those sorts of issues . . . it was Rushy, me and a couple of WRC guys and that was it. We had a video link set up with guys from the three countries. The South Africans were really driving it – they had all the signatures. We were going to sit at the table doing this link and go, 'Well here are our 250 signatures' but when it got around to the South Africans only Hennie le Roux was there, and I said, 'Hennie, where's Francois?' and he said, 'Oh he couldn't make it.' And that was it, really.

After that a few of the All Black guys started thinking, 'Oh shit', and a few of them went off and signed for the NZRU, and it started to splinter. It did make me very conscious about the loyalty of some guys. We'd said we'd stick together and suddenly everyone was looking after themselves. I appreciate some of the guys were very young and influenced by other people, but I'd have liked guys to be a bit more up front instead of going off doing their own deals and then us finding out about it later. Once two of three of them splintered that was the end of it. I don't think a lot changed when we went pro. We were getting paid and we didn't have to go to the office, but we were well and truly ready to go to the next level.

Craig Dowd: I was a carpenter, working on a building site. It was something you had always wished and hoped would happen but when it came about you looked to the senior guys and said, 'What are we going to do? How does this all work?' I had a WRC contract in front of me that added up to $750,000 a year. I couldn't comprehend that. Then there was a sign-on fee where you would get a $100,000 retainer just for signing. We got all sorts of advice. Rushy [Eric] got one of the partners from his office to speak to us and then it all started falling apart with Francois Pienaar pulling the pin, Louis Luyt obviously got to him but then chinks in the armour began to appear. It was a bit like a union where you were in a position of power with strength while you were all there but as soon as someone starts pulling chinks out and you take Pienaar out and the NZRU got Jeff Wilson and Josh Kronfeld and the cards all just crumbled. So I'm sitting there with my $750,000 contract saying: 'What do you mean?' We all thought in Australia that it would be the last game for the All Blacks. It was a very strange feeling.

Jeff Wilson: I loved being part of the All Blacks, they were a special bunch of guys, but Josh and I were part of another team too, down in Dunedin, mates we played with for the rest of the year, and we saw the game as being bigger than just what we were going to get. There was talk of there possibly being no All Blacks, how does that work? What would be the point of the game if there was no New Zealand team? The wider rugby fraternity believed in New Zealand rugby, our team-mates at provincial level certainly did, and we wanted to have a career in an All Blacks jersey. We were just young men facing this situation. I sat down and got some great advice from the likes of [lawyer] David Howman, and Richard Reid at Nike, from our families, and we decided what was important to us. We wanted to play our rugby in Dunedin with our team-mates and we wanted to be All Blacks, it was as simple as that.

Frank Bunce: Winning that Bledisloe Cup Test in Sydney was very satisfying. Given everything that was going on in the background and losing the World Cup final, we got quite a bit out of our system. It was the 100th match between New Zealand and Australia and as we ran out onto the field there were all these ex-All Blacks lined up on the field, and that's when I started thinking about the history of it all. Either way, rugby was never going to be the same, there was the WRC thing, there was Super Rugby all brewing up.

The team pose with the Bledisloe Cup after their 34-23 victory in Sydney. *Getty Images*

Ian Jones: It all came to a head when the time came to sign on the line, the WRC wanted a commitment, and because we were all in the one spot at the one time in Sydney it had to be then. We went out to a place in Watson's Bay on the way to the after-match . . . Colin Meads, who was part of the NZRU, stayed on the bus, so whilst he wasn't part of what we were doing, he didn't stop us either, and you have to respect that. We went through a process of due diligence . . . the players got an understanding of contracts and negotiating and what you were worth in the market and the Rugby Unions got an understanding that they were nothing without the players. What happened in the end was the best result for everyone. In New Zealand, the players signing for the national union put us ahead of the game 100 per cent. That was the greatest thing for the game in New Zealand, that the Rugby Union had control of the players, money, of the direction we were heading in, and also the unity we ended up with between the players and the union. Other countries missed out on that.

Frank Bunce: We got sick and tired of going to meetings and appointed Rushy to look after it, and told him, if it sounded good to him it was good enough for us. In the end Rushy was put off by the greed . . . the South Africans were the worst, they wanted all this money. The competition, the money, the concept it all sounded pretty good. We went off to someone's place, and they told us they had to have the All Blacks, that it wouldn't work without them. I mean $900,000 dollars over three years, back then sounded pretty good, a couple of guys would get over a million. They told us they'd put a million dollars into an account for the All Blacks just as an incentive to sign. Then Jock Hobbs started going around the country and signing guys up for the NZRU . . . in the end the whole thing fell apart. Was I happy about how it all ended up in the end? Yes. I think it's quite hard as a player to understand the enormity of it all, we didn't understand what it was going to mean for the All Blacks brand, the history, that it was going to change everything.

Jeff Wilson: We wanted to prove how good we were in those Tests against Australia. Losing the final in South Africa was a massive disappointment but it was time to go back to work. It was great to get the Bledisloe Cup back, but it didn't change what had happened earlier in the year.

Meanwhile, the All Blacks had taken back the Bledisloe Cup, winning in Auckland and Sydney, the second match again a stage for the incredible Lomu. Laurie Mains had one more job before stepping down, with an end of year tour to France.

A sloppy first Test performance resulted in a loss and an absolute bollocking from manager Colin Meads. It had the desired effect, the All Blacks came back to win the second in style, and provide an appropriate send off for a coach whom the players occasionally referred to as 'funeral face' but had developed great affection and respect for. He left a team primed for rugby's great leap into the professional era.

Craig Dowd: The end of year tour to France was enjoyable. Sean Fitzpatrick was uncompromising. He hated losing. He set high standards and expected high standards around him. Sean was a very strong hooker. Olo Brown, Fitzy and myself were packing down a couple of hundred scrums together every week and the combination was like putting your hand in a tailor-made glove. I guess that is why we became such a good front row. Fitzy would have a bit of chatter when things were going well, but even when they weren't, and you were under some pressure, he would talk it up. No matter how much pressure he was under he wasn't going to give in.

Eric Rush: We lost that first Test, it was windy and our inside backs got a lot of the blame. But, we got into that team room and Pinetree [manager Colin Meads] just ripped into the forwards, and some of the stuff he said, man it was beautiful. He said, 'You guys are always talking about 'blowing rucks', well you couldn't blow a hen off its nest!' He kicked out Tim Barry, the Lion Breweries rep, who'd been at all the meetings, he said, 'Since when has a breweries rep been in the team meeting?' and he added, 'That's my fault, he's a good boy, he's done a good job, but he's not an All Black and I shouldn't have let him in in the first place.' Then he ripped into Laurie. The French had put us in this pokey little change room and there was hardly enough room to stand up, let alone warm up . . . they [the French] had this big palatial room . . . so Laurie blocked off the entrance to the tunnel so we could warm up out there, but the Chief of Police and everyone else who needed to get onto the ground couldn't because we'd blocked if off. So Pinetree ripped Laurie anew over that, 'Who do you think you are, doing that, you just wrote them their team talk.' That's when we knew he was really angry, when he started getting into Laurie. He hooked into the forwards, he got into Jonah, the backs. He said, 'I hate talking like this but in my day we weren't half as skilled as you guys, we weren't half as fit, we didn't have half the ability and half the stuff you guys get, but I'll tell you what, we were scared of no bastard, and you bastards were scared of them . . . and that makes me sad.' If we'd played the next Test right then we would have won by 50. We went straight to one of the most brutal trainings we'd ever had. I knew then we wouldn't lose the second Test. It was Laurie's last. Before that the manager used to give you your jersey but for this one, Laurie did it. He went right around the room . . . he'd given Frank and Robin a roasting, they were two of the only players who'd played every Test under Laurie, and he'd roasted them all week. On the morning of the game he handed out the jerseys and had a word for every player, even the ones who weren't in the Test team. He went round, praised everyone, and said, 'Thank you.' We couldn't wait to get on the field. The French love it when they get on top, when they get up and get on top early, but if you get into them, they don't like it.

Craig Dowd: After we lost the first Test Colin Meads came in and gave us a good kick up the arse about the standards. They had dropped a little on that tour. We started to get a little slack after the Bledisloe series with all the WRC talk but that was all done and over and it was time to get the show back on the road, to pull our socks back up. We took that into the second Test in France. There was a lot of honesty and that is what we need sometimes. It was Laurie's last game, we'd been told off by the greatest All Black and we wanted to finish the season on a high. Simon Culhane kicked well and Jonah and Rushy played well.

Eric Rush: That tour, I loved it. It was the only one I went on where I was starting all the big games . . . Jonah was there, and Oz (Glen Osborne) and Jeff Wilson . . . and I played all three Tests. The thing about Test rugby is the more you play it the better you get, and that's what I love about the team today, is that the dirt tracker guys get a chance.

Justin Marshall (1995-05, 81 Tests, 88 games): Quite a few players had left post-World Cup, two of them were halfbacks, Graeme Bachop and Ant Strachan, so there was a vacancy there. We started that tour with a Test against Italy in Sicily. Zinzan Brooke really wound me up before we got there. He told me about the Mafia, that Sicily was still the stronghold and there were a lot of old Dons there. He fed me this line, which I swallowed, that if I saw any men in Sicily with a hat on I was not to look them in the eye, because they were Dons and to look them in the eye is a mark of disrespect. I saw nothing of Italy! Every second guy was wearing a hat and I spent the whole time looking at the ground. I was so naïve and young . . . straight from Mataura to Sicily, amongst all those experienced guys. He wound me up well.

Frank Bunce: We were getting to the end of Laurie's run. He never brought it up that he was going to finish. You've got to take your hat off to him. I don't think he's ever been given credit. He wasn't the coach when rugby went professional, but he'd already brought professional attitudes to the team. I don't think the All Blacks have ever trained as hard as they did when he was coach. He dragged the team, kicking and screaming at times, to new levels. As a rugby player I don't think you ever realise how much you can achieve unless you're really fit.

Michael Jones carries the ball against Italy. *Getty Images*

Justin Marshall: It was one of the last proper tours with midweek games, and the tour had gone swimmingly for us mid-week guys. Then we hit that first Test against France and the guys got smoked. Pinetree reckoned it was one of the worst All Black performances he'd ever seen. I couldn't believe the way he was speaking to some of those senior players. That week was the most amount of blood I've ever seen on a training field. It was opposed training and it was carnage, people were so wound up after what Pinetree had said. The mid-week team were heading off to Moet and Chandon but as I was about to hop off the bus to go into the Chateau, Laurie grabbed me and said, 'You're not drinking today, boy.' Nothing else, no explanation. I thought he was disciplining me for something I'd done wrong, too much alcohol maybe, but then he named me in the Test team the next day. It was a clinical performance. After getting such a serve from Pinetree the forwards really fronted so for me, it was a great ride. Jonah was fired-up too, he'd had an altercation with Laurie about eggs during the week. He was angry. That try he scored under the posts, no one was going to stop him. They had a big forward pack, with guys like Olivier Merle, but we annihilated them. That was the first paid tour. We got paid $30,000. I remember that figure because I'd worked three years at the freezing works before that, working five days a week, 6am-4pm, and I hadn't earned that much money in a year . . . and here I was going to earn that much in five or six weeks. The way I see it, paying the players on that tour was the NZRU getting the jump on everyone else in terms of what was about to start happening with the game going pro, paying the guys who were All Blacks was a way of showing they were on top of the way the game was evolving.

THIRTY-EIGHT

THE LAST FRONTIER

*'You'd look into the eyes of those guys, Fitzy, the Brookes,
Olo Brown, Kamo and you knew they'd find a way.'*

THE ARRIVAL OF professional rugby was more of an eruption than a landscape change. Super Rugby allowed the best 125 players in the country to be spread among five franchises, and the new, greatly-hyped competition took hold, with crowds queuing down the street for tickets to the inaugural final between the Graham Henry-coached Blues and the Sharks. Whilst players took time to grasp the realities of professional rugby, there was a massive buy-in over the concept of rugby as a form of entertainment. With the NZRU having contracted the players there was none of the club v country wrangling that caused so much difficulty elsewhere. With Laurie Mains stepping down, John Hart finally got his chance to coach the All Blacks and with his professional background and progressive views was seen as the ideal man to take the All Blacks into this brave new world.

Hart inherited a team already on the brink of greatness, with most of the 1995 group back, to be complemented by a new wunderkind, the young Hurricanes fullback Christian Cullen, fresh from wowing the crowds at the Hong Kong Sevens.

Cullen made a dazzling start, scoring three tries against Samoa and four in the first of two Tests against Scotland, both comfortably won to set the team up for a ground-breaking year. The new look Tri Nations Championship was the other major component of the Sanzar deal struck in Johannesburg the year before, bringing together the three Southern Hemisphere super powers on an annual home and away basis. As well, the All Blacks were due to tour South Africa, so in all faced two Tests each against Australia and South Africa as part of the Tri Nations and then a further three against the Springboks, as well as four midweek tour games, a daunting task, all within eight weeks.

Frank Bunce: Going pro was a real learning curve. It was fun. You travelled, you trained, and you got a pocket full of money . . . before that you'd get a pat on the back. My contract was $250,000 a year for three years. They offered me that and I thought, sweet! All right! So from one year you go from nothing to that, $30-40 grand in the bank every month. The biggest difference was the extra training we had to do. I was at the Chiefs and Brad Meurant was calling these extra trainings, and one of them was really for the forwards and I said to him, 'Why do we need to be there?' and he said, 'Hey, if I tell you to go and stand under that tree you'll do it because you're getting paid and I'm the boss.' The other new stuff was the night games, late starts, you had to get used to it as you went.

Sean Fitzpatrick: Everything seemed to work perfectly. A lot of us were playing our best rugby at that stage. We were very fit, very mature. That first win over Australia at Athletic Park was the most clinical game we played. Harty came in and managed the

Opposite: Josh Kronfeld carries the ball into the heart of the Springbok defence during the 1996 tour to the Republic. *FotoSport/Photosport NZ*

team perfectly. He hadn't coached for five years so he needed us to help him a bit, and we needed him in terms of the PR, someone who could press the right buttons. That game against Australia set us up nicely. We ended up playing about ten Tests in thirteen weeks, and we had a team at the peak of its powers. Cully [Christian Cullen] came in, Michael Jones came back and became the best No.6 in world rugby, having been the best No.7. We weren't a big team, and we'd learned in 1995 that we weren't the strongest team. We started doing serious weights and building ourselves up to take the Boks on physically.

Andrew Mehrtens: Cully coming along added a real new dimension. Amazing really, because only the year before we'd had Glen Osborne and he'd been astounding as an attacking fullback and then along came Cully. It's not like we hadn't had good attacking fullbacks before, thinking of John Gallagher for example, but Cully took it to a new level, before we'd even digested what Oz had brought to the table.

Eric Rush: There's no doubt Christian Cullen was a talent. Just like Jonah he was a quiet guy. They nearly took him to France at the end of 1995 but after what he did at the [1996] Hong Kong Sevens he was straight in. He got three tries in his first Test against Samoa and four in the next one against Scotland. But he wouldn't say 'boo.' He'd hang with me and Jonah because of the sevens. We were at a team meeting the morning after his second Test. He had exploded onto the scene and was an instant hero with the public. But at this meeting he was almost hiding behind me at the back. They went through the whole debrief; lineouts, scrums, defence, they mentioned the attack and said, 'Well done Christian' which made him all embarrassed. They said, 'Anyone got any questions?' I put my hand up and said, 'Christian wants to know when he's getting his new car!' Everyone cracked up but Cully was all red in the face and he was like, 'You . . .'

Their opening performance against Australia ranks amongst the finest in their history. They laid the Wallabies to waste 43-6 on a rain-drenched, windswept Athletic Park, a performance as close to perfection as could be imagined in such conditions. Michael Jones, who had reinvented himself after his terrible knee injury, scored the opening try. He became a power player in the No.6 jersey, complementing Kronfeld and the multi-skilled Brooke. It was a key combination. A much tighter game against the Springboks followed, the All Blacks needing five Mehrtens penalty goals for a 15-11 win. En route to South Africa, the return game against Australia was fought out in Brisbane, the match starting on an explosive note, with Wallaby flanker Michael Brial lucky to stay on the field after throwing a flurry of punches at Frank Bunce. Bunce had the last laugh as the All Blacks came from 22-9 down, scoring after a probing run by Mehrtens that was carried on to the goal-line by Cullen, where Bunce picked up to score.

Ian Jones: John Hart was the right man for the time. He knew how to organise, set up structures, plan the tours. That Test in Wellington, it just all went right from the start. We kicked deep, forced them into that right-hand corner and then worked a lineout move we'd been practising, throw to the back to Rob [Brooke], and Michael Jones driving over. It just went from there.

Jonah Lomu was at his devastating best against
Australia at Athletic Park in 1996. *FotoSport/Photosport* NZ

Jeff Wilson: On a perfect day Athletic Park was a wonderful place, but mostly it was tricky. It was either a southerly or a northerly. Usually you would wake up and know that at least half of the game you weren't going to enjoy. That day it was bucketing down, but the good thing is if you thought you didn't want to be there, well the Wallabies had no interest in those conditions. It was miserable and the pitch wasn't like the carpets you play on these days, it was heavy. It was wet and it was windy. We went out there, and while it wasn't perfect, some of the decision-making and execution in those conditions was phenomenal. They had no answers. Whenever we needed to make big plays we did. Guys were off-loading at the right time, making great decisions about what to do. Zinny was at his best, taking control of the game. It was a good Wallaby team, but the conditions didn't suit and we were all over them. We were building on what had started in 1995.

Frank Bunce: I don't know why everything fell into place for that game, it wasn't an extraordinary week training wise, preparation or anything. One thing we talked about was not letting the conditions dictate. We had some of the most skilled players ever, when you look at Zinny, Michael Jones, guys like that. We got a good start and carried on from there.

Craig Dowd: In 1996 Glen Osborne was the man, he was playing some fantastic rugby and it was a case of how could you not play Glen Osborne? And then Christian Cullen turns up and you thought, 'Oh my God!' You thought, 'This guy is incredible.' He glided across the ground, through gaps and scoring tries. He was so physically strong. His power for weight ratio was huge. Per kg for bodyweight he was stronger than all the All Blacks. He was class, just so silky smooth the way he ran. It's very rewarding to lay a platform down and you've got those guys on the outside, you know they are going to do something with it. David Campese did the team talk all week. He was talking up about what he was going to do and how he was going to do it, how he was going to treat the haka. He got a lot of media attention so nothing needed to be said. They didn't face up to the haka so we felt they were disrespecting us and when someone does that to you, you play as hard as you can. On the day it clicked. Justin Marshall was a spark, he had a good game on a platform laid by the forwards and whether it was wet or dry it didn't matter.

Frank Bunce: We beat South Africa in Christchurch, but not by much, and I remember one of their locks saying, 'We'll see you in South Africa, boys, we'll be waiting.' It was an exciting tour to be on. Four Tests in a row at all the great places to play. It was basically the team Laurie had built and Harty came in. One big thing Harty did, and I don't think we would have won the series otherwise, was negotiate with the Rugby Union to send two teams, because we also had mid-week games. Without that we'd never have made it. Even with the extra players it got to the stage where Harty would say, 'Who can train today?' and out of thirty people ten might put up their hand.

Craig Dowd: That game in Christchurch was the first time I marked Marius Hurter. He was a strong, tighthead prop and gave me a hard day at the office. That was something I didn't tend to forget. But in the Australian game in Brisbane there were a few incidents. I made a few mistakes and was aware it wasn't one of my best. So I did some extra training by myself, going to the gym and then getting into the sauna afterwards. Gordon Hunter came in and there was just the two of us. While we were chatting I said to Gordon, 'I know I didn't play well and I know that you guys as selectors will be looking at Bull Allen to give him a run', and I said to him, 'I promise you, if you give me a start I will make amends for previous performances.' I was serious, the team was named and I was in. There might have been an eyebrow or two raised but Gordon came up to me and said, 'Now you owe me one.' I went out onto Newlands in Cape Town and gave Marius Hurter a real hard time and scored the try that gave us the lead and got the MVP. I went up to Gordon after the game and said: 'There you go mate, I'll build on that now.' Having gained Gordon's trust there was no way I wasn't going to repay it.

Justin Marshall: That team had an ability to win Test matches on days when we were below our level of performance. Three or four times, through 1996 and 1997, playing big nations, I remember sitting in the changing room afterwards thinking, 'How the hell did we win that?' The closest we came to losing a Test was when we drew against England in '97 – and I was captain. That 1996 team was full of great All Blacks, guys who knew that no matter what situation we were in, we would find a way to win. As a young guy coming in, in situations where we might have been down ten or fifteen points, you'd look into the eyes of those guys, Fitzy, the Brookes, Olo Brown, Kamo [Ian Jones] and you knew they'd find a way. They were never rattled. I was a bit different to a lot of the older guys, because I'd grown up through the years when we weren't playing South Africa because of apartheid. To me it was more Australia, especially because I'd played them at age-group level. I hadn't been there in 1995, and didn't have that same appreciation of the history of it, and what we were attempting to do.

Frank Bunce: I'm not sure if it's the case because I've never spoken to him about it but when we toured Aussie in 1992 we played New South Wales and I flew into a ruck and broke his [Michael Brial's] ribs or something like that. There was a bit of fighting . . . it was quite a niggly game . . . two of our guys Arran Pene and Paul Henderson broke bones in their hands fighting, so a few people have said that what happened in Brisbane was a leftover from that, but I don't know. I started it, I elbowed him. He was put in the team as an enforcer, according to the papers, because the Aussie forward pack wasn't really up to it. It started with the haka, he was standing there a bit like Sam Scott-Young used to do, although not quite that bad, but he was really aggressive, and right from the start of the game he was into it. The ball spewed out of a ruck and when I bent down to pick it up he was coming at me and the look in his eyes . . . I thought I was going to get hammered so I just put my elbow up instinctively and it got him right in the face. He stepped back and then came at me, fists flying. It was only the first one that connected and straight away I could feel my eye go whiish! Then he just started throwing them so I covered up, held the ball . . . most of his shots were either hitting my arm or the ball so I wasn't getting hurt and then the ref stepped in and broke it up. The funniest thing that happened was someone got a photo of it, and here's Brial trying to bash me up, and there's Andrew Mehrtens just behind us and he's not even looking, he's just going the other way!

Christian Cullen (1996-02, 58 Tests, 60 games): I can't remember much about the game but I do remember the last try and Goldie giving me shit on the bus afterwards about the last try because he was unmarked outside me! Mehrts made that break . . . he reckoned he was the happiest man in the world when he looked up saw that Goldie and I had gone with him. I had visions of George Gregan . . . he was running across, corner flagging and when I went to step inside I took a bloody great chunk out of the grass and fell over. Luckily, Buncey was there to pick up and score. Afterwards Harty had a bit of a crack at me because Goldie was free, and Goldie had a dig too! I'd had a bet with Fitzy during the week. I was having a kick round with some of the guys, fielding a few bombs and I dropped a couple and he came over all serious and said, 'You'd better pull your head in because you don't want to be dropping those at the weekend.' I made a bet with him that I wouldn't drop one high ball in the game, and I didn't!

The South African series was an epic, as tradition demanded. Bizarrely, the first Test at Newlands didn't count as part of the tour series, but the All Blacks gained a massive upper hand by winning it, Mehrtens' kicking proving decisive in a come from behind 29-18 win. With the Springboks starting to falter, the All Blacks seized the chance to create history. Despite injuries keeping Mehrtens and Lomu out, the Durban Test was edged 23-19. Then followed the crunch point of the year and a landmark in New Zealand rugby history. With the final Test to be played at the oppressive Ellis Park, and wear and tear starting to take its toll, the All Blacks knew if they were to win the series, they had to do it at Pretoria. With the Springboks desperate to preserve their home record, it became one of the great chapters of this rivalry. To win, the All Blacks needed the ultimate team performance, but there were some remarkable individual contributions. Justin Marshall probed relentlessly, Jeff Wilson used his blistering pace to score two tries, and Jon Preston came on as a sub for the injured Simon Culhane and coolly kicked two long-range goals under immense pressure. But the player who stood above all was Zinzan Brooke. He scored a try, drop-kicked a goal to pad the All Blacks lead out to 33-26 and then led an incredible defensive stand as the Springboks went for the seven-pointer that would take the series to Johannesburg. At the final whistle the All Blacks slumped to the ground, exhausted yet jubilant. Fitzpatrick, who'd been the subject of some brutal attention both on the field and in the South African press, banged his fist on the ground in triumph. Sixty-eight years of disappointment, frustration and failure had ended. The campaign's end was anticlimactic, the unbeaten midweek team held to a dubious draw by Griqualand West, and an exhausted Test team overpowered 16-8 at Ellis Park, but it hardly mattered.

It was mission accomplished just in time for New Zealand, as it was the last time the two great rivals would meet in such a series.

Jeff Wilson: Going into that tour of South Africa I felt I hadn't been playing that well, Harty and I talked about it, and he showed faith in me. I got a try in the Cape Town Test, which helped my confidence. It was a funny series because the first Test in Cape Town was part of the Tri Nations, but not part of the tour and the Test series. That first Test was really important. Conditions weren't great. We knew it was going to take something monumental to win, so a good start was important. If we didn't win in Pretoria we'd struggle in Jo'burg. Mehrts was out injured, but Simon Culhane did a great job and Jon Preston was amazing.

Justin Marshall: When we hit South Africa, the mood changed, those senior guys became very serious, almost over serious. I'd played five or six Tests by then, and my objective was more to play well enough to stay in the team, whereas the older guys were driven to win the series, which made it great for me, playing behind a forward pack so powerfully motivated. Win that first Test and it would open the door to grab the series. We won reasonably comfortably, but it piled the pressure on the South Africans making them altogether more difficult.

Jeff Wilson: By the time we got to Jo'burg we were spent. Would it have been different if the series had still been on the line? Well, it would have been great drama, after the year before. It was a challenge, with in effect two separate teams, but the management did a superb job piecing it all together. The main focus was on the Test series, but the mid-week guys were just as determined to win their games, and there were no easy games. It was hugely satisfying after 1995, to go over there and create history. We showed two things; that we had a great team, but we had amazing depth in our squad.

Ian Jones: The key was Durban. That was the second Test match but it was the first of the actual series. If we were going to win, make history, we had to get that first Test of the three, go to Pretoria with a chance to win it there, because Ellis Park was always going to be tough.

Craig Dowd: In Durban, Simon Culhane kicked goals from everywhere and Goldie [Jeff Wilson] scored a couple of tries too. We did the job there. There were murmurings of repaying the debt for the 1949 team, who lost 4-0, but the greater feeling was we had lost the World Cup final to them a year earlier.

Frank Bunce: We scored some awesome tries in the first two Tests, and I remember looking at guys like Cully, Jeff Wilson, Oz, you marvelled at the speed at which they could play. I was slow compared to them . . . I mean I was fast enough, but their pace sticks in my mind. Zinny was the other guy that stood out. He was tough, he was competitive, and when the going got real tough, he was the guy who stood up. He'd go over to an injured Springbok and say, 'Get up, you're holding the game up,' and get into an argument with their physio, that sort of thing.

Jon Preston: Andrew Mehrtens had been injured earlier on and Simon Culhane started, and then I think he got a hand injury. I was only on for the last twenty minutes, but it turned out to be a fairly significant twenty minutes. It was a funny role I had in those days, with the ability to cover both nine and ten, and kick goals, I tended to be either playing or on the bench for every game on the tour. What came with that was that you were involved with every training session and so I had a lot of goal-kicking practice. South Africa is such a great place for goal-kicking. It all helped build my confidence. Everything happened so quickly. I had a few nerves for the first kick. It was the first time I'd touched the ball after coming on. I got that one, and the second one? Well on the high veldt I knew I'd get the distance because I'd been doing it at training. It was just a matter of trying to keep it straight. Those last few minutes really showed the determination in the side and the belief it could be done. It was desperate defence for quite a few minutes when South Africa were pounding away at our line. If we had relented then I don't think we'd have won at Ellis Park either because we were spent. Everyone focused on their own role that was about getting back up and trying to smash guys backwards. It was a full-on onslaught and you had to keep doing your job. There wasn't an opportunity to talk, just total focus on the job.

Craig Dowd dives over to score against the Springboks. *FotoSport/Photosport NZ*

Craig Dowd: We forgot about the next week's game, it was do-or-die and had to be done in Pretoria. Zinzan wanted to repeat what he did against England and have a dropped goal – he practised them at every training session. For me it came down to the last 10-15 minutes. We got the lead and we had to protect it. They were camped on our goal-line and hammering away. All I could think of was all those down-and-ups Laurie Mains had put in us for the World Cup, and the work John Hart had done. We knew we just had to dig deep and do it.

Justin Marshall: The week leading into that Test match in Pretoria was the most intense I experienced as an All Black, including World Cups. Michael Jones, Ice, was a quiet guy, but Fitzy, Zinny, even Frank Bunce, kept reinforcing to us, 'We win the Test series this week.' Here's me thinking, 'Oh well, we don't win this one, we can get them in the Ellis Park Test,' but they weren't thinking that at all.

Ian Jones: I had to go off about fifteen minutes from the end . . . I got my leg trapped under a South Africa player and damaged ligaments in my knee and ankle. It was the first time in 56 Tests I'd gone off injured, and in the most important Test you could ever play in. It was a damned sight harder watching than it was playing. It was a hell of a relief to win such an important victory.

Frank Bunce: In Pretoria, I took the ball up, got tackled, and placed the ball. As I did it I could see through Marshy's legs Zinny was setting himself and I thought, 'He's going to have a drop kick!' I saw the whole thing lying on the ground. I didn't see it go over, but I saw Zinny turn around and run back. That game at Pretoria was hard, especially being at altitude. At one stage after we scored as we ran back Zinny just fell over, collapsed.

Sean Fitzpatrick: What typified that effort in Pretoria for me was when Culhane got injured, we had a penalty on halfway, and Goldie was grabbing the ball and saying, 'I'll kick this', but JP had come on and I said to him, 'Are you happy for Goldie to take it?' and he said, 'No no, give it to me', and he nailed it. That for me typified the attitude in that team. Everyone was prepared to die for the cause. They had a lineout, the French ref said two minutes to go. In the last minute they had a driving maul . . . in those days you could stick it in the back and charge in a wedge . . . and Zinny, it was like he was in the starting blocks, ready to dive at Mark Andrews' ankles.

Craig Dowd: Jon Preston came on from the bench and kicked a couple of vital penalty goals, we called him 'The Cleaner' based on the Harvey Keitel character in Pulp Fiction who used to come in and clean up the mess. He did what needed to be done.

Michael Jones: We'd built a sizeable lead but expended a lot of energy and were close to exhaustion as the Springboks battered away at our line. It was one of the most physically sapping games I have ever been involved in. I doubt I could have picked myself up for another scrum. The referee's whistle for fulltime was the sweetest sound. It was a while before I could celebrate because Kobus Wiese, who I'm sure weighs a ton, was on top of me and most reluctant to get off. The qualities that brought us through were epitomised in the last five minutes at Pretoria – discipline, character, desire and pride. We were well coached and managed. Our success was a triumph for the management's strategic planning. As a team we were thirty-six dedicated individuals with a single-minded desire to obtain a common goal. We were driven by the challenge of beating South Africa in South Africa and making history.

Jon Preston: I looked around at some of the older heads and what it meant to them. It meant a massive amount to all of us but especially to those guys who had been there the year before and lost the battle. They led from the front providing a calming influence . . . they had the experience to know what to do at the right time. That had a significant influence on us winning. Without that it's very easy to make wrong decisions that can cost you the match. You can't go past Zinzan Brooke . . . that dropped goal. The confidence he exuded no matter what situation he was in. There's not many No.8s with that skill set and when he does something like that it lifts the whole side's confidence. Then you have Fitzy, who's been there and done that so many times and with that ruthless determination and an attitude of not giving anyone a chance to beat you. He led from the front but there were a number of players you could say that about.

Eric Rush: I was the oldest guy in that group watching in the stands. We had a good feeling that we were going to win and at half-time I said, 'Boys the only contribution we can make if they win today is to give them a haka when they come off, so get ready.' Everyone was up for it, and for the guys coming off the field, they said it just capped off the day.

Sean Fitzpatrick: Beating them in South Africa was a monumental thing. The reason I came back after 1995 was Kevin Roberts said to me, 'You have to come back here next year and beat them, be the first New Zealand captain to ever do that.' As I was walking off Don Clarke came up to me . . . he was living in South Africa and was in the tunnel. Tears were running down his face. He grabbed me and hugged me and said, 'Thank you for doing something that so many All Blacks had tried to do over the years but weren't able to do.' Some of the young guys didn't get that, but the older guys were brought up with it. We made a mistake in the last Test not playing some of the younger guys . . . a guy like Norm Hewitt could have been given a shot . . . and that followed through into 1997.

Christian Cullen: It means more to me now than it did then. I was aware of the history a bit, but not like the older guys. I look at it now, that shot of Fitzy banging his fist on the ground, and the one of Goldie running along the touchline giving it the fist pump . . . to me back then it was just another Test match, but now, it means a whole lot more. I loved playing in South Africa. They're passionate, knowledgeable about their rugby, awesome supporters. Hard grounds, great weather and they have rugby purpose-built grounds, Newland, Pretoria, Cape Town . . . those big stands, you feel like they're looking right down on top of you.

THIRTY-NINE

END OF AN ERA

'Too Old, Too Slow, Two Tries'

THE ALL BLACK machine powered on through 1997, but by year's end came the first hints of a decline. There was a shock at the start of the year when it was revealed Jonah Lomu had been battling nephrotic kidney syndrome for at least two years. He needed an indefinite break. It was also clear professional rugby's demands were taking a toll. Coaches hadn't acquired the art of managing player workloads, and chronic injuries started to impact. The year began with a rollicking 71-5 win over Fiji, with five tries for Wilson, two to Cullen and one on debut for Wellington wing Tana Umaga. Argentina were thrashed in two Tests, fourteen tries scored in a 93-8 bath in Wellington, whilst Carlos Spencer scored twenty points in a 62-10 win in Hamilton. Spencer's improved goal-kicking allowed him to hold his place in the starting XV, even with Andrew Mehrtens available, as Hart sought to further expand the attacking game. Australia lost a Bledisloe Cup Test in Christchurch, before a sensational win over the Springboks in the Tri Nations opener in Johannesburg. Frank Bunce turned back the years with two spectacular tries as the All Blacks fought back from 23-7, Spencer nailing a clutch penalty goal for a 35-32 win. Bunce continued his purple patch with another try in a win at the Melbourne Cricket Ground a week later, and then played his fiftieth Test at Eden Park where the Springboks had Andre Venter sent off soon after half-time and were beaten 55-35. A sweep of the Tri Nations was capped off in Dunedin, Cullen scoring an extraordinary try, swerving, stepping and speeding through the Wallaby defence on an eighty-metre run, as the All Blacks shot to a 36-0 lead at half-time. A flat second half, in which the Wallabies scored 24 unanswered points, may have been the first signs of a sea change.

Sean Fitzpatrick: A few of us played one year too many. Although we played well in 1997 a lot of us had had enough, and the game was moving on. We still went pretty well, didn't lose a game, there was just a draw against England right at the end, and we were still better than anyone else at that point. But for me it was a blessing in disguise that I got injured and had to call it a day. Zinny went too. In all about five guys retired at the same time which wasn't what the team needed, and there was no succession plan. They did have Taine Randell lined up to be captain but he never got a chance to captain a side in a Test match until he was there by himself.

Craig Dowd: In Dunedin against Australia, David Knox had come out with the statement that if he lost to the All Blacks he was going to run around Carisbrook naked. He had done a Campese and we got up 36-0 by half-time. We slacked off in the second while they scored 24 points.

Opposite: Christian Cullen in full, gliding flight against Ireland in Dublin in 1997.
InphoPhotography

Christian Cullen: That try in Dunedin. That's probably my favourite. Larkham kicked it and you can hear in the commentary Zinny calling out 'My ball,' and then catching and throwing it. Zinny had the vision . . . I can't recall calling for it, he sensed there was this space for me to run into and threw this massive twenty metre pass. I took off.

We lost this core group of senior players, either retired or injured. We didn't have that experience, that mental hardness, those guys had.

Frank Bunce: At Ellis Park we were 23-7 down. I'd made a couple of mistakes, lost a couple of balls in the tackle. The game had started at such a fast pace, but you develop this confidence that you can weather the storm. It might take seventy-nine minutes to win but there was no panic. We had guys who could crack the line, guys like Marshy, Cully, Lee Stensness, guys who had variations in their play, so you always knew something could happen and it was a matter of reacting to it.

I'd been criticised quite a bit. I was getting older by then, my Super Rugby form hadn't been great, they were saying I was too slow. Early in the second half, with us 19-23 down, I got through about forty-five metres out. I wasn't planning to run all that way to score, I was looking around but I had to keep going. I remember the headline after the game which we won 35-32 . . . 'Too Old, Too Slow, Two Tries'. That was a bloody good game.

A nine-match end-of-year tour highlighted difficulties the Home Unions were having in the new era. The team darted back and forth between Wales, Ireland and England, with a Wales Test at Wembley sandwiched between two against England. Llanelli and Wales A were soundly beaten and Ireland thrashed 63-15 before England put up a good fight at Old Trafford, losing 25-8 before embarking on a lap of the ground to thank the fans which was misinterpreted in New Zealand as a lap of honour for keeping the score down! Wales were then put to the sword 42-7 to leave the All Blacks on the verge of a 100 per cent winning record over eighteen matches in a year. England, under new coach Clive Woodward, made a flying start and led 20-3 after nineteen minutes. Slowly the All Blacks clawed their way back and when Walter Little scored they led 26-23 only for Paul Grayson's penalty goal ten minutes from the end to produce a 26-all draw that the All Blacks viewed as a defeat. Of more concern was the fact that the team was suffering breakages, and it was clear that plans for the core of the great 95-97 team to play through to the next World Cup were in trouble. A chronic knee injury took toll of Sean Fitzpatrick who'd been restricted to two games on tour as a sub, his late appearance in the Wales Test proving to be the last of a ninety-two-Test career, in which he had grown into one of the greatest All Black leaders. Within a year Frank Bunce, Zinzan Brooke, Michael Jones and Olo Brown would succumb to a combination of age, injury and a loss of competitive edge. Team fortunes would suffer as a consequence.

Justin Marshall: I got called into John Hart's room, I thought I was going to be disciplined about something. He'd named me as midweek captain against Llanelli and I'd gone out and had a few beers with the guys afterwards, nothing major, we weren't late and no one misbehaved, but one of the management saw me coming back to the hotel and I figured he'd told the coach. It took me completely by surprise when he said Fitzy wasn't right, wasn't going to come right, and how would I feel about captaining the team? I was a bit uncomfortable. I felt proud to be asked, but I didn't feel I could tell Zinzan Brooke and the like what to do, but he told me he'd already spoken to the senior guys and they were backing me. I said as long as I could talk to them and make sure they were behind me, then I'd do it. So I captained them in four Tests, Ireland, two against England and Wales.

Jeff Wilson: That was a great tour. It's worth remembering we were still getting used to the idea of playing a lot of high intensity games over an extended period of time. There wasn't rotation back then, the bench still wasn't being used that much, and guys weren't getting a rest. There was also that 'Don't change a winning team' adage. So even though we didn't play as well, and

Justin Marshall during the 1997 tour.
InphoPhotography

were held to a draw by England in that final Test, 1997 was still a phenomenal year. We were undefeated – eleven wins and a draw – and on the back of 1996, when we'd lost that last Test in South Africa, that's an incredible two-year period. It was a shame it turned out to be the end of an era. We'd lost core players, a lot of them forwards. Zinny used to make a lot of the calls. If you were in a certain part of the field he knew what play to run.

Justin Marshall: Ireland came out breathing fire but we got on top of them and had a really good win, Wales we won quite comfortably at Wembley, but the England game at Old Trafford was a bit of a blur because Martin Johnson knocked me out. It happened in the first twenty minutes. He king hit me as I was clearing the ball from a breakdown. I'd said something to him early in the match and it obviously wound him up! But we won it comfortably, and then went to Twickenham – a game where we, to be honest, got out of jail to get a draw. For a lot of people back home it was a poor performance and a lot of the criticism had to do with my captaincy in that Test. I never really got the chance to explain it at the time. John Hart wasn't happy with me. At one stage I got marched back about twenty, maybe thirty metres for back-chatting the referee Jim Fleming. We were trying to play a fast game, using our skills, but England did their homework and were trying to kill everything, slowing down our ball and we were struggling to build momentum. They were lying all over the ball, and our forwards were getting frustrated – remember we weren't allowed to ruck anymore. I went to Fleming and told him if he wasn't going to do anything about it then we'd have to deal with it ourselves, because it was stopping us from playing. He told me I couldn't speak to him like that. I said, 'But I'm the captain,' and with that he marched me ten metres. I told him I was just trying to explain our frustrations because he wasn't refereeing the breakdown . . . and I got another ten metres. He might have even marched me a third time. It cost us three points in the end. It did

Norm Hewitt and Richard Cockerill face off during the haka. *Getty Images*

not go down well in New Zealand because it looked like I was losing the plot, when really I was just trying to get him to police the ruck more effectively. I guess he took offence to the way I spoke to him. Maybe I could have worded things a bit better. England were comfortably ahead of us for much of the game and in the end we did pretty well to get a draw and stay unbeaten.

Andrew Mehrtens: Despite losing Fitzy at the end of '97 it was a good season. The Tri Nations had been fantastic, Carlos had come in and kicked a lot of goals and we had a great win at Ellis Park . . . I never did get to win a Test there, and so it was a shame to sully it with that draw at the end of it.

We'd beaten them reasonably comfortably at Old Trafford, but it was a bit ugly. We didn't play our best at Twickenham . . . you have to be really switched on for that last game of the year, because there's a danger of having one foot on the plane home . . . I don't want to make excuses, but we never seemed to perform that well with Jim Fleming on the whistle either . . . I don't think he helped us at all that day, in fact I think he had a real anti-New Zealand streak about him.

Sean Fitzpatrick: We're lucky people to be All Blacks. We belong to a special club. It means a lot. You see guys in later years and it's great straight away, because it's almost like you've been to war together. I love the legacy of the jersey. People are jealous that being an All Black

Andrew Mehrtens kicks for goal against Ireland. *InphoPhotography*

is so special. Sometimes I meet someone and you're introduced as a former rugby player and this person will say, 'Who did you play for?' and I love saying, 'the All Blacks.'

Craig Dowd: We played on three unusual grounds in 1997: the MCG against Australia where we were so far away from the crowd, against England at Old Trafford where there was the stand-off at the haka between Norm Hewitt and Richard Cockerill which fired us up, and then while the Millennium Stadium was being built we played Wales at Wembley. That was Fitzy's last game, he came off the bench because his knee was that bad. The 42-7 win was one of our highest wins against them in Britain. Wembley was a special place.

Frank Bunce: We started losing a few guys. Fitzy had that knee injury and Zinny. They're always difficult those northern tours. You don't play the rugby you play in the southern hemisphere on the harder, faster grounds. You always find it hard to hit any real heights. It didn't occur to me that that team was in any sort of trouble. I was aware Fitzy was injured but I never thought it would be the end of him. Never thought it would be the end of me. I was pretty confident at the end of 1997 that things were still going to be pretty good.

FORTY

STARTING AGAIN

'It must have been one of the worst years in All Black history'

TAINE RANDELL HAD been fast tracked into the captaincy, and under his leadership 1998 began well enough, with two heavy wins over an experimental and poor England side, games that featured the return of Jonah Lomu. But the wheels that had turned so smoothly through the previous two years began to fall off during the Tri Nations as, for the first time since 1949, the All Blacks suffered five consecutive defeats. It began with a 16-24 loss in Melbourne, Matt Burke scoring all the Wallaby points. Then came a 3-13 defeat to South Africa in Wellington in the fiftieth Test between the two. The Bledisloe Cup changed hands for the first time since 1995 after a 23-27 loss to Australia in Christchurch, before luck deserted them completely in Durban, Australian referee Peter Marshall awarding a winning try to Springbok hooker James Dalton, despite the ball clearly being dropped over the line. The Boks would go on to beat Australia and claim their first title. The All Blacks then went to Sydney for the dead Bledisloe Cup Test, hoping to salvage something, but to no avail, the rising Wallabies coming from 11-0 down at half-time to win 19-14.

Frank Bunce: I stuffed up the end of my career. Each year Harty and I would have a chat about the following season. He was saying, 'All you've got to do is get through Super Rugby and the trials and I'll pick you for the big games.' I'd work towards it. By the start of 1998 I was starting to lose interest, especially in the training, so I told him I didn't think I'd get through to 1999. He said we could manage my exit. Then I had an offer to go to France. I had to go over there to have a look. It fell in a week off between games, before the trials. I went up with Joe Stanley. I should have told him [Hart] what I was doing. What really stuffed things up was a pilot strike in France so I missed a couple of connecting flights to come home. It was in the press I wasn't there and Harty didn't know where I was. Joe kept telling me I had to ring him, and in the end I did. I was hoping his secretary would answer, but when I rang I heard, 'John Hart speaking.' I thought, 'Oh ****!' He was not happy. He told me I'd put him in a position where he'd had to lie to the media. When we got home he told me he couldn't put me in the trials on the weekend after I'd put him in that position. It was over. I was thirty-five when I retired.

Craig Dowd: After beating them at Old Trafford and drawing at Twickenham, England toured here in 1998. There was a lot of pressure on us in that home series because Australia had put 72 points on them before they got to New Zealand, and we only put 63 on them and in the third game the margin was only 30. That was the same England team that went through and won the 2003 World Cup. They were getting better and better. In 1998 there

Carlos Spencer makes a break against England in 1998. *FotoSport/Photosport NZ*

was increased emphasis on fitness levels and we were tested over a three kilometre run. I went from 118 kgs to 111kgs and did an 11min 45sec three kilometre run. The only forward who beat me was Josh Kronfeld so I was fit. But I lost all the bulk and I went into games wondering why I got so tired and struggled while being pushed around in scrums. I now realise it was dumb to expect everyone to be like a gazelle. As a prop you need your body mass. It was a disaster year, we lost five Tests in a row.

Jeff Wilson: It was tough in 1998 and sucked the life out of us. We'd lost some great players and a lot of leadership. The expectation was that the new guys would step into their shoes, but that doesn't just happen.

Justin Marshall: It must have been one of the worst years in All Black history. We weren't helped in Durban, we were leading right at the death. They needed a try to win and they went for the lineout drive. James Dalton clearly dropped the ball . . . I was right there I saw he hadn't grounded it, it was no try, but the ref gave it. When you're having a tough year, those things seem to happen. It was gutting.

I ruptured my Achilles tendon playing for the Crusaders. I was told I'd be out six to nine months, but I was back playing in just over three months. I was determined. I didn't want to let anyone else get an opportunity in that All Black jersey. People asked me if I came back too soon, but I actually came back quicker over 10m than I'd been before the injury. So I was fine, the injury didn't affect me, but things started to go a bit pear-shaped on me. The media, the public started having a go about my pass, and with the team not doing so well I guess I was one of the targets. I'd had a dream ride until that point, but suddenly the whole gravy train came to a bit of a halt, not just for me, but the team. Taine

The All Blacks try to regroup during their 19-14 defeat in the Bledisloe Cup at the Sydney Football Stadium in August 1998. *Getty Images*

Randell had taken over the captaincy and was copping it from everywhere. We were all under pressure. It was a tough old year.

Craig Dowd: It was a surprise when Taine Randell was named captain. He was a great guy and a good team man, but was still a boy. It wasn't fair to thrust that role on him. It was a mistake but the decision was made so you rallied around him and did your best. When your captain is twenty-one and he's fresh in the environment, he doesn't really know to pass on knowledge. We saw it with Richie McCaw, he grew into that role. It didn't happen when he was twenty-one or twenty-two.

Taine Randell (1995-02, 51 Tests, 61 games): Getting the captaincy so young was wrong. We had guys in that team like Robin Brooke and Ian Jones – guys who were genuine New Zealand greats – and we had this punk little kid stepping into the break. It was no good for me, it was no good for them. It was no good for the team. It was no good for anyone. When I look back, I realise how much I didn't know about captaining a side. I didn't do well for myself or the team. It was a team undergoing a lot of changes and I probably wasn't the right person for the job. I didn't know what I could have done to change things. I was trying my hardest but didn't know what to do. The biggest part is that as a player I didn't play well. As a captain that's not good enough. The captain really needs to be playing well and have that respect from everyone else. I thought I had to be a lot more serious. I thought I had to take things on more by myself. I didn't really have too many close confidants within the team, which every captain needs. I also wasn't as close to the management as I needed to be. Again, age was probably a factor, but it left me in a position where I felt isolated and didn't really have anywhere that I could turn. It was quite a lonely time.

FORTY-ONE

MILLENNIAL MISERY

'I don't think that I've ever felt so powerless out
on the rugby field as I did that day'

JOHN HART'S DETRACTORS came out of the woodwork, and speculation grew that he was losing friends in high places, before confirmation came that he would take the team again in 1999. Changes were made for World Cup year. Hart added successful Crusaders coach Wayne Smith to his staff in 1998 and there was much tinkering with the line-up. Jeff Wilson was switched to his preferred position of fullback, with Christian Cullen shunted onto the wing and later centre. Jonah Lomu was largely used as a sub during the Tri Nations, and the locking duo of Ian Jones and Robin Brooke was separated. The All Blacks also had a new look, the signing of a deal with Adidas prompting a rare change to the famous black jersey, the start of a commercial influence that got way out of hand when much to their embarrassment, the players found their images painted on the side of Air New Zealand jets. Early results raised hopes, with 71 points run up against Samoa, and a disinterested French team belted 54-7 in what was (to many, mercifully) the final Test to be played at Athletic Park. Then followed a morale-boosting Tri Nations title, with South Africa blanked 28-0 in Dunedin, and comfortably beaten in Pretoria, and Australia losing 34-15 at Eden Park. The return Bledisloe Test in Sydney was a different matter, Australia's comprehensive 28-7 win giving them a great springboard into the World Cup. The bid to win back the Webb Ellis Cup foundered spectacularly at Twickenham. The All Blacks beat England 30-18 in the group decider before a satisfactory win over Scotland in the quarter-final. Earlier in the year, French coach Jean Claude Skrela predicted the All Blacks would go through the year unbeaten, and at half-time in the semi-final his prophecy was still alive. The All Blacks' 17-10 lead at the break soon became 24-10 as Lomu thundered over for his second try. But from nowhere the French mounted the greatest comeback ever seen at a World Cup. A trickle that began with a Christophe Lamaison dropped goal soon became a torrent that a stunned All Black team could not stem. Everything the French tried came off, every All Black mistake was magnified, and in the end it was a crushing 43-31 defeat. France never looked like repeating that performance in the final, whilst the All Blacks' failure was compounded in a loss to South Africa in the playoff for third and fourth. The reaction, even by normal standards in rugby-obsessed New Zealand, was nasty. Hart bore the brunt. He was accused of playing key players out of position, of taking the French lightly, of putting too much faith in an inexperienced captain, and planning for the final before the semi had been played. Even one or two players suggested Hart's strong stance on discipline had stopped them from taking retaliatory action against some dubious French tactics. Hart had to deal with the loss of a clutch of influential players, and some of his senior men had not stepped up when needed, but that didn't stop vilification plumbing new depths when both Hart and the horse he owned were spat on

Opposite: Josh Kronfeld lies distraught at the final whistle of the 1999 Rugby World Cup semi-final. *InphoPhotography*

Jonah Lomu was once again at his brilliant – and destructive – best at
the 1999 World Cup. Here, in echoes of 1995, he is powering his
way past, through and over the English. *InphoPhotography*

at the New Zealand Trotting Cup in Christchurch. It was an unfitting end to a century in
which the All Blacks had achieved a degree of success second to none.

Jeff Wilson: I thought we were in good shape in 1999. We'd made positional changes. I
wanted to play fullback. I'd made no secret of that, it was where I'd played most of my
provincial rugby. We were in transition, trying to work out who was the best person to
play centre, and they settled on Cully playing at thirteen, Jonah and Tana on the wings
and me at fullback. They wanted all four of us on the field, we didn't have an obvious
thirteen and it was a matter of how to put all those skills together.

Christian Cullen: To be honest, I didn't care where I played, so long as I was in the team.
If I'd been a bit older, a bit more experienced, I'd have stood up and said, 'No I don't want
to play centre, I'd rather play wing or fullback. They're pretty similar, but centre . . . that's
a tough, tough position. I'd played it a bit at school but you can't just jump in there at that
level. Harty flew down to Wellington and we went out and played golf, and talked about
it. I know Goldie wanted to play fullback, but we had Tana, who ended up being one of
the best centres in the world, playing on the wing with me at centre.

Justin Marshall: We'd beaten the French earlier in the year at Athletic Park. We thrashed
them by about 50 points. There was no over-confidence, I don't think you ever do that
with the French. We'd had a good Tri Nations, even though we lost the game in Sydney.

Craig Dowd: I broke a bone spur off my ankle and needed to be operated on and I got back towards the end of the Tri Series but had lost my place in the starting XV. That carried through to the World Cup. Air New Zealand did me a big favour by putting a painting of the front row on one of their planes, Kees Meeuws, Anton Oliver and Carl Hoeft. Kees went down with a calf strain against Tonga so I got on the field and from that moment I wasn't going to get off it. I held my position while Kees had to recover. The England Test was my fiftieth. I didn't like playing England, so I got the MVP for that one as well.

Jeff Wilson: We weren't favourites, probably joint favourites with Australia. We were good enough to win it. We were a bit rough against Tonga but played well against Italy. We beat a good England team destined for bigger things at Twickenham. Looking back at Scotland maybe there were some danger signs. They came back at us late, when we should have blown them away. After dominating the first half we dropped off, let them back into the game. They played beautifully for forty minutes. We were struggling to put eighty minutes together.

Taine Randell: The tournament will always be remembered for the semi-final but, if you look at the thing as a whole, we'd played some pretty good rugby up until that point – and the team was united. Even in the semi-final, we had a good lead just after half-time. We got found out up front when it mattered. If you look at the forward pack we fielded that day, we had one senior guy in Robin Brooke. The next guys were all twenty-three and twenty-four-years-old. Once the French got on top, we didn't have the necessary experience to pull it back. Once they started going wild . . . I don't think that I've ever felt so powerless out on the rugby field as I did that day. It was a terrible feeling.

Philippe Bernat-Salles celebrates his try as France begin their extraordinary comeback. *InphoPhotography*

Craig Dowd: Up 17-10 up at half-time, things were on track. The team talk at half-time was to expect the unexpected but we needed to keep building on what we had been doing and to lift the intensity. The second half came around and I remember lying in a ruck with one French finger in my eye and my testicles being squeezed as hard as they could be. They were coming out to put a bit of filth in during the second half. The next thing there're a few up and unders and the bounce of the ball miraculously going into Dominici's hands when the ball bounced sideways and he had an open run to the line. It was bizarre the way it panned out. It was a different team from the first half. It wasn't just about the bounce of the ball, it was more their flair and their skill and they grew in confidence. It was like we had one hand on the Cup and it was slipping away. By the end of the game it was crushing because we had it then we lost it, and then we lost it badly. To this day I can't put my finger on why, or what we were doing that affected things. We weren't playing badly, but they were suddenly playing better.

Jeff Wilson: We were in control, playing well and Jonah was doing his thing. We made a couple of poor decisions, turned the ball over, let the ball bounce and they got some momentum. They beat us with a kicking game. A couple of dropped goals got them that little bit closer. We couldn't secure a kick-off, and they'd get the ball and put it back down our end. I lost the ball in contact, they turned it over, kicked it over Mehrts' head and scored. They scored from a five-metre scrum, I was defending out wide, trying to put some pressure on and there was no cover in behind.

Tana Umaga (1997-05, 74 Tests, 79 games): We took our foot off the pedal when we were going strongly. Once you yield that initiative against an opponent like that, it's so hard to win it back. We panicked when things started to go wrong and became desperate.

Andrew Mehrtens: The French had a much better team than they were given credit for. There was probably a bit too much put on the fact that we put 50 points on them in June.

We were up at half-time and I remember thinking they were looking a bit tired as they walked off, but then a couple of things changed after half-time, they started playing with more and more confidence, Lamaison had an amazing game, and every time they got up our end they scored.

In the end it just felt like we were chasing shadows.

Reuben Thorne (1999-07, 50 Tests, 51 games): Looking back at the 1999 World Cup it was difficult. Before the Cup I'd only played ten minutes of Test rugby in my debut, and then played all the games in Britain. When I compare it with other teams I've been in that have been successful, the whole atmosphere was very different. It was tense, and you couldn't be yourself too much. It was just . . . not very enjoyable really.

Christian Cullen: Was me playing centre the losing of that game? I don't know, I guess there was a lot of shit going down in that game, but it's a tough position and you can't just get thrown in there. I never watched that game until about 2011. I was at the gym and they were replaying old World Cup games on the TV, and I sat on the bike and watched the second half. The French played some pretty good rugby. They took penalties and dropped goals and knocked off that score, three points by three points. Then they got a lucky bounce and everything started to go their way. Sometimes that happens. Did we go to sleep? Did we rest on our laurels? I can't answer that question. I think there are times when you can't stop a team. France had a twenty to twenty-five minute period when it all went their way. The harder we tried the worse it got. It was weird. Standing under the posts after one of their tries everyone had a bit of a glazed look on their face, people staring into the stands, no one was listening to what was being said, we were in shock.

Jeff Wilson: In twenty minutes our World Cup disappeared. I don't know whether it was leadership, decision-making or what . . . I look back at that one and I can't explain it. We never managed to find that one big play that would swing things back our way. It got away from us. Before we knew it, it was gone.

Craig Dowd: In the dressing room half of us threw our boots in the rubbish in frustration. We were copping crap already when walking off the field from the crowd and by the time we got back to the hotel there were messages left on our answer phones from fans saying what a bunch of wankers we were for losing and we had ruined their plans of going to a World Cup final. It wasn't a nice time and in my career was the worst time collectively of what an All Black team had to go through, and what John Hart went through. We had a meeting at the hotel and John told the team he was resigning, stepping down as coach. It was a very emotional time. You could see it was devastating for someone who had such an influence on the All Blacks in the time he was there.

Tana Umaga: It's hard to pinpoint anything worse in my rugby career. I've experienced heaps of losses and disappointments but because of the significance of the occasion, it would probably be at the top of the heap. I felt especially sorry for guys like Jeff Wilson, Jonah Lomu, Andrew Mehrtens, Josh Kronfeld, Robin Brooke and Craig Dowd, who'd been through it all in 1995. At least they reached the final – we got blown away in the semi. I was quite distressed with my own performance that day.

Justin Marshall: For a fair while we'd played pretty well, Jonah scored a great try and we had a decent lead, so it wasn't like there was a lack of effort, as some people tried to suggest. The public reaction was embarrassing. As much as Harty and I had had a disagreement over my selection for the semi-final, I have to say the reaction was an embarrassment to the nation. Things like his horse being spat at at the races in Christchurch, the abuse he took, the fact that he virtually had to go into hiding, that was going way too far. It was too personal. It amounted to hatred. I didn't play in the semi-final, but when my bag came through on the carousel at the airport the baggage guys had written LOSER on my suitcase. I thought it was one of the blackest chapters in New Zealand rugby history.

Craig Dowd: The playoff for third and fourth place was hideous. It took a while to heal but you get back and get involved in your Super Rugby franchise and your family and friends and spend a bit of time at the beach and find the hunger again.

FORTY-TWO

NEW HORIZONS

'It was the biggest honour I could have on the sporting field, to play not just for your country, but for the best team that's ever played the game'

JOHN HART STEPPED down, and up stepped Wayne Smith. The seventeen Test fly-half had become a new-age coach, encouraging players to visualise key moments, and making heavy use of statistical data. He had taken the Crusaders from also-rans to back-to-back titles, and handed the captaincy to his Super Rugby leader Todd Blackadder. A regular season opener against Tonga with the gate shared, saw three tries on debut for lock Troy Flavell in a 100-point blanking, followed by two big wins over Scotland. Then came what must rank as one of the greatest, and most spectacular matches in Test rugby history. In front of a world record crowd of 109,874 at the new Sydney Olympic Stadium, the All Blacks powered out to an incredible 24-0 lead after eleven minutes, only for Australia to level the scores by half-time. When Jeremy Paul scored late in the match the Wallabies looked set for a great victory, but a brilliant offload by Taine Randell freed up Jonah Lomu, the big winger showing amazing balance to stay in play and run in the winner. That celebrated 39-35 victory gave the All Blacks the chance to reclaim the Bledisloe Cup in Wellington. An intricate set move, a Smith special, finished off by Cullen, had the target in sight, but a complete meltdown by the All Black lineout allowed the Wallabies to snatch it with a penalty goal by the remarkable John Eales deep in injury time. South Africa were beaten in Christchurch, but hopes of a Tri Nations title ended in an another high scoring blockbuster in Johannesburg, New Zealand coming from 33-27 down at half-time to lead before a Werner Swanepoel try got the Springboks home. The All Blacks were developing a reputation for making big mistakes late in games, or as their critics loved to call it, 'choking'. They also had an interesting new manager in Colonel Andrew Martin, a former Army man and provincial prop. Martin and Smith were behind a significant venture on the end of year tour in France, restoring an old All Black tradition of visiting the Belgium grave site of 1905 Originals captain Dave Gallaher. It planted the seeds of what would become, in time, a profound investment in the All Black legacy. When Smith picked up a handful of dirt and told the team 'there's New Zealand blood in this soil' it provided a powerful motivation for a hard-fought Armistice Day win in Paris, played for a new trophy in honour of Gallaher. A week later the tables were turned in Marseille, the French roaring out of the blocks, and roared on by a boisterous crowd to win 42-33. A 50-point win over Italy in Genoa ended a year of high scoring, but inconsistent results. Smith believed he had the foundations of a successful team, but would not see out 2001 in the job.

Jeff Wilson: I'd found 1999 tough. A big part of that was that my father passed away in late 1998. A lot of my sport was played in and around my Dad, there was no one I spoke

Opposite: Tana Umaga bursts past Joe Roff to score early in the Tri Nations match at Stadium Australia, Sydney in 2000. *Getty Images*

to more about sport than him. He was going to go to the World Cup with Mum. You've got to have a purpose for being out there, and I'd got to the point where I needed a break, to see whether I wanted to play again. I wasn't playing as well as I could, and probably didn't deserve to be in the All Blacks.

Craig Dowd: Wayne Smith came in and was very good, technically a great reader of the game with good ideas of how he wanted to play. He was good for the All Blacks. The one thing I struggled with was at the end of the Super Rugby campaign getting a letter to congratulate me on being selected for the All Blacks and advising that we were going into the Rugby Academy in Palmerston North for three months. The theory was that for all these domestic Test matches we could base ourselves in one place so we could train and eat, breathe and sleep rugby and fly from that one base to play our matches. For me, as a twenty-nine-year-old with a wife who was six months pregnant, it was very tough on my family. She was very supportive but I can't say it was one of my fondest memories of All Black rugby. We played South Africa in Christchurch and straight after the game I flew home to Auckland, my wife went into the hospital and was induced and had our daughter Georgia. A day later I had a ring from the manager Andrew Martin asking when I was coming back down to camp. I went back down and we headed over to South Africa. I ended up being a dirty-dirty [non-travelling reserve]. I played the last five minutes of the 'greatest Test'. We won that with Jonah Lomu tip-toeing down the sideline for the winning try after we had gone ballistic to lead 24-0 before the Aussies came back at us. It was unbelievable the way they never gave up.

Todd Blackadder (1995-00, 12 Tests, 25 games): We were pretty excited about the game. While there was speculation that we hadn't been tested, what mattered to us was that we had the chance to play the World Cup champions, and find out exactly where we were in our development. The first ten minutes were remarkable. I think there were only about two or three forwards who touched the ball. I remember standing at halfway thinking, 'I can't believe this is happening.' It was sheer brilliance from the backs. As the game went on, and as the Wallabies got back into it after our great start, there was a fighting spirit in our team. When the Australians got their last try, our guys were still attacking. If we'd lost, we could still have taken away the fact that the fighting spirit was back. I think New Zealanders in general when they get together and work bloody hard at things, is when they're probably at their best. There's nothing quite like hard work to bind guys. That's the glue behind your team spirit.

Justin Marshall: I'd never played in a Test quite like that one. In the first nineteen minutes everything stuck, it was clinical, and we were playing at real pace. They couldn't get the ball from the kick-off. We scored a try off a restart that didn't go ten metres . . . Maxy [Norm Maxwell] came forward and took it, even though he didn't have to, we built phases and we scored. The same thing happened at the next kick-off, and Maxy went for it again, but this time we lost it and they ended up scoring. We'd had all the ball for the first 12-13 minutes and we were 24 points up. If we hadn't given them that ball, who knows what might have happened? There were periods when it was hard to imagine us playing any better. Yet they kept coming back at us. Maybe a bit of anxiety crept in. We'd scored five or six tries and they were still right in it. It was an awesome game to play in. I never liked to leave the field during the game and I certainly didn't during that one, I was enjoying it so much. I kept enjoying it too, even though Byron [Kelleher] was on! For it to be won like that, with Jonah's try at the end, well that just took it into the realm of one of the greatest games of all time.

Christian Cullen: Three tries in six minutes thirty seconds. We were almost in shock ourselves. Every pass stuck, Jonah down the sideline to Alatini, Alama [Ieremia] makes a break, pops it to 'Ala' and I'm there on his shoulder, it was crazy stuff. Then, it was almost as if we switched off and the Aussies came storming back. I don't know what happens sometimes when you get up by a score like that, the mind can do strange things. You can beat a team by 30 points one week and they come back and beat you the next. Nowadays, mental strength is such a big part of a team. It's one of the great things about the recent All Black sides, what guys like Gilbert Enoka [who would later be the All Blacks assistant manager and mental skills coach] have done. Back then we had to rely on our own mental skills and they probably weren't as strong as they could have been. You look at that try by Jonah. I don't think anyone else could have scored that. Larkham's no slouch, and he had his chance to get the big guy. But Jonah was quick off the mark, those big strides, tip-toeing down the touch line. It looked easy but he still had to run it in, still had to beat Larkham. How cool was that?

Andrew Mehrtens: Sure it was a high scoring game, a close game with an amazing finish and so, yeah it was good, but compared to that Johannesburg Test between the All Blacks and South Africa in 2013, I think that was the most amazing game I'd ever seen.

It was good to win, because around that time we had a lot of tight games go against us in Sydney, so to get that win was great and for Jonah to get that last try, well, when you consider what's happened, then you appreciate that it was pretty cool to have played alongside him when he did that.

Justin Marshall: The return game was the first played at Wellington's Westpac Stadium and we scored off a really complicated move that Smithy had come up with. It involved lots of deception with Tana in the midfield and Cully scored it. It was a beauty.

Christian Cullen: You work out these moves, usually amongst the backs at training, but to have one like that, involving forwards and backs, I mean you had to get the lineout perfect just for starters. You had to get those forwards in the backline, the timing of the passes to Jonah and Mehrts, the switch with Tana coming back . . . I mean you dream of getting those things right, and they work on the practice pitch but to pull it off in a game like that, it was a bit different. Everything we talked about happened, 100 per cent. We only ever did it once, and it was probably one of my easiest tries, I just had to run, but it was one of my favourite tries because it was such a great team try.

Craig Dowd: I'll never forget the penalty I gave away in the dying seconds of the game.

Jonah Lomu shows his delight as Taine Randell puts him in for a late match-winning try in Sydney. *Getty Images*

I saw the ball was out of the back of the ruck and instinctively dived on it. Had I had the luxury of being on the field a lot longer, and having settled into the game, I would have realised it was a case of 'defend, defend' and run the clock down. But because I had come off the bench, I was operating at a higher level and saw the ball loose; it was a stupid act that cost us the game and the Bledisloe Cup. It was devastating and to see John Eales step up and kick the goal was a very, very dark moment in my career. It was my last act as an All Black. The headlines weren't kind, and even today I get people walking up to me in the street saying they will never forgive me giving that penalty away. That's the importance of the Bledisloe Cup. I still wake up in the middle of the night thinking, 'I wish I hadn't done that.'

Justin Marshall: It was heartbreaking to lose games like that. The Eales one, that's a famous one and rightly so. It was a hell of a kick.

Anton Oliver took over as captain from the deposed Todd Blackadder for a first-up win over Samoa. After big wins over Argentina and France, the All Blacks again made a good start to the Tri Nations, Tony Brown calmly slotting four penalty goals on a greasy Newlands for a 12-3 win over the Springboks. Much was made of the Carisbrook factor in the lead-up to the first Bledisloe Cup Test, the Wallabies having never won a Test there, and the All Blacks not having lost since 1971. The only milestone the All Blacks achieved in this game was to concede a penalty try for the first time in a Test match, when No.8 Ron Cribb hauled down Joe Roff without the ball. The walls of the southern fortress were breached, the Wallabies holding off a late fightback to win 23-15. A penalty try, this

John Eales lines up his kick for glory at Athletic Park, 5 August 2000. *FotoSport/Photosport NZ*

time in their favour, decisively swung the Eden Park Test against the Springboks, and the All Blacks went to Sydney knowing a win would secure the Tri Nations title, if not the coveted Bledisloe Cup. A strong second half performance had them in sight of a much-needed win, but at 26-19 the All Blacks suffered another capitulation. A penalty closed the gap, and right on full-time Toutai Kefu scored the match winner for the Wallabies. There was a suspicion of a knock-on by halfback George Gregan but referee Tappe Henning thought not, and another one had slipped through the All Blacks grasp. There was no serious thought of Smith losing his job but he did have to appear before a routine NZRU review committee, and in the morning session delivered what panel member John Graham described as an outstanding summary of where the team was at, and a strong vision of how to move forward. The panel went to lunch convinced he was still the man for the job. But it was a different Smith who returned for an afternoon interview session. His confidence had eroded to the point where he questioned whether he was the right man. Faced with this sudden display of self-doubt, the panel felt they had no choice but to recommend the job be re-advertised. Smith was invited to reapply, but the writing was on the wall. Finding a successor was not straightforward. One obvious contender was Robbie Deans, who had an outstanding record with the Crusaders, but appeared reluctant to give up a secure job for what was becoming a very insecure one. In the end it went to John Mitchell.

Jeff Wilson: I came back in 2001. We beat South Africa in Cape Town. I enjoyed playing under Smithy and Tony [Gilbert]. I felt the team was heading in the right direction, and to win down in Cape Town, with Brownie doing what he did, was incredibly satisfying. Then we played Australia at Carisbrook. We hadn't lost there in a long time, but Australia were motivated. We gave them a couple of soft tries, one a penalty try. At one point we were hard on attack and Brownie threw a pass which Joe Roff intercepted . . . we were down at that point and he had quite a start on me. I managed to mow him down and we got a penalty from the tackle to stay in it. I was pumped up and that's when I tried to get the crowd going. I was pumped up because it meant I wasn't slowing down! It was disappointing to lose, but they were better than us. I did my calf and missed the Test in Sydney. We lost that when Toutai Kefu scored, we'd overthrown a lineout.

Justin Marshall: The Kefu one was right on the line. I was right there, in fact I reached out and managed to get my arm under his. It's pretty hard to control the ball in that situation, but somehow he got it down. I almost saved it! They were tremendous Test matches. The Australians were having a great period, it was one of their best sides, a lot of Brumbies players, a great backline, with the hardness coming from guys like David Wilson and Kefu. You'd put a lot of those players into the greats of Wallaby history, and they were beating us consistently.

Jeff Wilson: I watched it in the box with Smithy and Tony and it was after that that Smithy came out and said he wasn't sure he wanted to be All Black coach any more. There was a change of the guard and I wasn't sure how things were going to work out.

Christian Cullen: Smithy, back then, was so passionate about the All Blacks. You take losses hard and he took them really hard, and he started questioning whether he was good enough for the job. It was sad.

The former midweek All Blacks captain John Mitchell had returned from five years in Britain, including time as an assistant to Clive Woodward with England, and had some success with Super Rugby underachievers the Chiefs. His appointment met with general approval, the public remembering him as a hard-nosed, popular captain of a successful Waikato team, his cause strengthened when Robbie Deans was appointed assistant without having to relinquish his plum Crusaders role.

    Their first task was a tour of Ireland, Scotland and Argentina. Despite initial shock over the omission of Christian Cullen, it was a success. Most notably, the Ireland Test marked the debut of twenty-year-old Richie McCaw. Early in the second half Ireland led 21-7, but the All Blacks mounted a strong recovery, and, with tries to Reuben Thorne, Lomu, and debutants Aaron Mauger and Dave Hewett, pulled away to win 40-19. Andrew Mehrtens kicked six penalty goals as Scotland were beaten 37-6, but it needed a late try by No.8 Scott Robertson, off a break by fullback Ben Blair, to get the All Blacks out of a hole against Argentina in Buenos Aires. Still, it was a successful start for Mitchell, and there was more to follow in 2002, although not without public consternation. When Ireland toured, they faced an All Black team made up of fourteen Cantabrians and Jonah Lomu, a team dubbed, not approvingly, as the 'Crusader Blacks'. Into the captaincy stepped Reuben Thorne, hard-working and under-rated, not a showy player with an almost shy exterior. In heavy Christchurch rain, the Wallabies were beaten 12-6 in the Tri Nations opener, followed a week later by a 41-20 win over the Springboks in Wellington, one that had the South African media in a ferment over the legitimacy of a try to hooker Mark

Hammett from a short lineout throw. The Bledisloe Cup was by now akin to the Greek legend of Sisyphus, who tried repeatedly to roll a stone to the top of a mountain only to slip with the summit in reach. In Sydney, a McCaw try and a Mehrtens penalty goal had the All Blacks 14-8 up with eight minutes left, but again they slipped, the game decided by a Matt Burke penalty, contentiously awarded on full-time by South African Andre Watson. The All Blacks still had a shot at the Tri Nations, and achieved it in an infamous match in Durban. Irish referee David McHugh had the Kings Park crowd boiling after awarding the All Blacks a penalty try and harshly ruling out a touchdown by Springboks winger Breyton Paulse. When he awarded a scrum feed to the All Blacks early in the second half, a weighty fan jumped the fence, ran past inattentive security and castled McHugh. The offender was restrained by players from both sides and escorted off. With McHugh nursing a dislocated shoulder England's Chris White took over the whistle and with full-time approaching, the All Blacks broke a 23-all deadlock when Aaron Mauger scored a try that decided the championship. With World Cup year approaching Mitchell opted to leave many front-line players out of the November tour to Britain and France, another decision that didn't sit well with fans. Despite missing a dozen first choice players the team acquitted itself well, losing to England by three points, splitting the France Test 21-all and beating Wales with ease. That tour turned out to be the last for two great All Blacks – Jonah Lomu and Christian Cullen. Sadly, Lomu's health deteriorated and he needed a kidney transplant. His career had done more to promote rugby across the globe than any player before or since. Cullen fell out of favour, while there was speculation that relations between Deans and Mehrtens had deteriorated providing a subplot to World Cup year.

Jeff Wilson: I got left out of the end of year tour, I got dropped. They left me, Anton Oliver and Cully out. That's when he [Mitchell] came out and said he didn't know anything about the previous All Blacks and so on. That was fine. You don't know what it means to be an All Black until you've done it. It was the biggest honour I could have had on the sporting field, to play not just for your country, but for the best team that's ever played the game.

Christian Cullen: From 2000-2002 I only played about seven or eight Tests, either through injury or not getting picked. You could sense the change when Mitchell and Deans came in, obviously trying to stamp their mark, do things their way, the John Mitchell way. It was a big change from Smithy. I didn't really get much from him [Mitchell], and what I did get I didn't understand, I mean talking gibberish. I read in the paper him talking about the fullbacks who were injured and so on. Seemed I was about fifth or sixth down the line. I had to work on basically everything; catching, passing, tackling, and I started to think, 'What am I doing playing rugby, when I apparently can't do all of these things?' I was one of a group of players who went to the UK to play for the Barbarians while the Crusaders were still going in Super Rugby finals. I came back, got named in the All Blacks, we had a camp in Gisborne and at the first day in training, Caleb Ralph, Jonah and myself had to do all this extra stuff. I mean we'd been playing and training, but we were the only guys that had to do extra. I thought it was a bit weird, like he was just trying to stamp his mark. For some reason Mitchell and I didn't see eye to eye. It seemed at times he'd pick anyone but me and Mehrts. What could you do, you just had to grin and bear it. I had a pretty good NPC with Wellington making the final, but I didn't see a future with the All Blacks if Deans and Mitchell were involved. I'd had enough and that's when I decided to go overseas. It was an honour to play for the All Blacks. I understand what's gone before, that the jersey's not really yours, that you just have it for a short time. I understand all that, but for me it was just a privilege to be able to pull on that jersey, play for your family, and for the people of New Zealand.

Aaron Mauger (2001-07, 45 Tests, 46 games): It's understandable people were uncomfortable [with the Canterbury dominance of the All Blacks during the Mitchell-Deans era] with it, because a lot of good players missed out, guys like Jonah and Cully at times, Doug Howlett, Anton Oliver, a lot of top players around that era. I suppose some of that came down to Robbie's influence, being coach of the Crusaders at the time. He had a bunch of men there he could trust to do the job, good combinations he felt could perform at that level.

Justin Marshall: I remember when Richie [McCaw] first came into the Crusaders set-up. I wasn't aware of his potential, I guess you're pretty much wound up in what you're doing, what the team's doing, to be looking at prospects from the academy, the development team. It was only when he came into the Crusaders set-up as part of the wider training group that I got an insight into how annoying he was. He was pretty quiet but once he got on the training field he was a pain in the arse. He was always part of the opposition, and I remember going to one of the coaching staff and saying, 'Who's this kid with the fluffy hair, the openside, what the hell's he doing?' He was always over the ball, disrupting our ball, playing every training session like it was a Test match. I got an insight into what he was all about. The coaches loved it because it made us work harder, made us react, so he was not only annoying me, he was getting praise for it. You don't get to know a player until you play with him. We had some good young flankers at the time, and for Richie to come into that mix, straight into the team, that was something.

Aaron Mauger: It was a bit of a shock to be named in the All Black team for the tour . . . both my brother and I were named which was pretty exciting for the family. I thought I would be going on the tour just to get some experience, to learn as much as I could. So it was quite a surprise to be named in the team for the first Test against Ireland, especially as Pita Alatini had been in such good form for the All Blacks for the couple of years before my arrival. I admired the way he'd been playing so to get that first Test was pretty surreal. I'd lived in Dublin for six months in 1997, so the last time the All Blacks had played in Dublin I was on the terraces . . . and when we turned up at Lansdowne Road in 2001 here were all my mates from the little club I'd played for, Suttonians, all lined up in jerseys with my number and my name on them. It was quite an emotional time. They put us under the pump, the crowd really got in behind them and they built a bit of a lead. At half-time I was thinking, 'We're going to lose this game and I'm going to be a one Test All Black!' But the biggest thing I learned was the

Richie McCaw makes his debut against Ireland at Lansdowne Road in 2001.
Here he celebrates with try-scorer Chris Jack. *InphoPhotography*

experience of guys like Mehrts and Tana. There was no panic, they reassured us and told us to just stick to our guns, and then in the second half we got a bit of roll on and took control. Jonah scored a great try to get us back into the game, and I was the lucky recipient of a Jonah offload and scored my first Test try to put us in front and after that it was one-way traffic and we came away with a good win.

Richie McCaw (2001-15, 148 Tests, 149 games): I think the Irish crowd saw their team was in with a shot of winning the game and it got pretty noisy. But as the game wore on, we got back in front and it quietened down a bit. It was a cool stadium, an old stadium but a pretty cool one.

Aaron Mauger: We ended that tour with a Test in Argentina which was one of the best rugby experiences of my life. We played at the River Plate Stadium. There must have been about 90,000 people there and as we ran out there were flares being set off and the atmosphere was amazing. It was about 9.30 at night when we kicked off, and I think some of our boys were half asleep . . . we played like that too. They went ahead . . . I think it was Lisandro Arbizu put a chip kick over the top and Mark Robinson dropped it right under our posts, and they were up 7-0 then they got a penalty, so we were really under the pump, they were playing like men possessed. In the last minute of that game, Benny Blair made a break to put Razor [Scott Robertson] in at the corner to win it . . . Razor tells me about it every time I see him.

Richie McCaw: In January – after the All Blacks experience but before the Super 12 –

I had a fear that I would be the guy that burst on the scene only to disappear again. I realised it was easy for me to stand out in 2001 because no one knew who I was. Now things were different. People knew me, they knew my game. It didn't help that after the tour there was a lot of hype around about me. I was apprehensive . . . and I played like it. The first couple of weeks of the Super 12 weren't great because I tried to be a hero and do something special every time. I had a yarn to the coaches because I ended up doing nothing properly. They told me to go out and do my job. They reminded me that an All Black is someone who does his job every week, not just some weeks.

Aaron Mauger: The 2002 Tri Nations was heartbreaking. We'd won the first Bledisloe Cup Test on a freezing cold night in Christchurch 12-6, all penalties. Then we beat South Africa in Wellington, so we were in good shape. Then we went to Sydney . . . we were up 14-13. Leon MacDonald got penalised for hands in the ruck, and Matt Burke kicked the goal ten metres in from touch to win the game. In my early days South Africa was quite a hostile place to tour . . . they've definitely become much friendlier. One time in Cape Town our fitness trainer Mike Anthony got hit in the face by an orange while we were warming up. The first time I'd gone there was with the Crusaders and I was on the bench in Jo'burg and we were getting heckled. I couldn't help myself and gave a bit back. I got abused and had things thrown at me for the rest of the game . . . when I got on the field I think I was more excited to be getting away from the crowd.

Justin Marshall: The crowd were pretty wound up. Every time McHugh blew his whistle there was a massive reaction. It was really intense. We were getting the rub of the green – sometimes you do, sometimes you don't.

Aaron Mauger: Then a guy ran out onto the field. AJ Venter grabbed him and started dealing to him, and I think Richie might have got him onto his back.

Justin Marshall: Richie might have grabbed him, but AJ Venter whacked him. It was bizarre, and then the ref was injured so he left the field and so you had a new ref coming on to try and take control of a game that's already beyond the limits of a normal Test match.

Aaron Mauger: It was quite a game, I was fortunate enough to get over the chalk right at the end for a bonus point try . . . but really most of the things that happened in the game were overshadowed by the guy running on.

Justin Marshall: The management decided to rest me and a load of other senior players for the end of year tour. I didn't like to not go on tours, I didn't like to not play for the All Blacks, I wanted to work hard to stop someone else having a go at the jersey. But they gave me reassurances, as they did with a number of other players and that eased my mind. They felt I would benefit from it the following year, and to be fair when I hit 2003 I was in the best condition I'd ever been in.

Aaron Mauger: They gave us the option of sitting out that end of year tour . . . we'd played quite a bit of footy in a short space of time, and some of us were advised to stay behind and freshen up for the World Cup. If I had my time again I probably would have gone on the tour. You look at how hard an All Black cap is to come by . . . it's one of my regrets, missing out on two or three caps on that tour.

Richie McCaw: Marty Holah was impressive. He really took his opportunity. In Paris . . . the way he tackled was awesome. He was right in there knocking their big guys over, and backwards, and creating turnovers. That impressed me. He had a real presence. Whoever is playing in the No.7 jersey, if you can have that presence and let the opposition know you are there, it has to be a good thing. He certainly did that on tour.

Ali Williams (2002-12, 77 Tests, 78 games): Every year, maybe every second year, we'd try to be up in the UK to see family, because of Mum and Dad. Getting that first Test match in London . . . the free tickets were for just in front of the Queen, where my grandmother, my aunty and someone else were. They held up a banner during the national anthem saying, 'Ali Williams, from Scotland to the All Blacks', but they held it so high it was covering the view of the Queen. I was standing there shaking with nerves, thinking about the haka coming up next and then this sign comes up . . . so it was pretty special. I cracked the navicular in my foot and there was huge doubt as to whether I'd be fit for the World Cup. Mitch stood by me, he had Maxy [Norm Maxwell] and Simon Maling available, but he went with me. I needed a few painkillers to get through, but it came good, to the stage where I couldn't feel it. Injuries and I became good friends.

If New Zealand needed a reality check as the World Cup approached, they got it first thing in 2003. England coach Clive Woodward gambled on sending a full-strength side down under to put down a marker, and it paid dividends when, despite being reduced to thirteen men at one stage, they beat the All Blacks 15-13 in Wellington, thanks to an amazing display of goal-kicking by Jonny Wilkinson.

Justin Marshall: We lost to England right at the start of the year . . . and in a way it was probably my fault. Two things stood out about that Test. Firstly, how good their defence was. We had seventy per cent of the ball and we just couldn't finish them off. And the other thing was their discipline, to hardly get any shots at their posts, says something. Of course they had a hell of a goal-kicker. Jonny Wilkinson had a shot at goal, just short of halfway, only five in from touch. Normally I'd stand behind the posts but I stood ten metres in front, where I thought it would land, and it cleared the bar with a bit to spare. When they were down to thirteen or fourteen I made a bust off the back of a lineout, I had Caleb Ralph looming up in support, a certain seven points . . . and I busted my hamstring. When you tear a hamstring it shocks you, and instead of composing myself I fell to the ground, and couldn't get the pass away.

Reuben Thorne: We had our chances but England didn't let us get any flow going. We certainly had enough ball but we either turned it over, or just got swallowed up by the England defence.

Tana Umaga: We were wary because England had composure under pressure – we didn't. And, to be honest, the performance we put in that night wasn't good enough for an All Blacks side. But we subsequently took a lot out of that game.

A week later Wales were thumped in Hamilton, a match that saw Tana Umaga accorded a citation for sportsmanship for attending to Welsh No.8 Colin Charvis after he'd been knocked out in a Jerry Collins tackle. France were also beaten, although history shows that in World Cup year that doesn't mean much. What did mean a lot was a clean sweep of the Tri Nations, achieved after a stunning away leg in which, within seven days, the All Blacks put 50 points on both the Springboks in Pretoria, and the Wallabies in Sydney. The return games were closer, the All Blacks having to battle hard to put away the Springboks 19-11 in Dunedin before at last laying claim to the Bledisloe Cup. On a night wracked with tension, the giant Cup was contested for the 100th time, the All Blacks holding their nerve to edge it 21-17. Rather than be dismayed, Australia's brains trust saw the outpouring of relief amongst the New Zealanders as reflecting a brittle confidence, and immediately began plotting for a World Cup semi-final showdown.

Aaron Mauger: We were in good form, were playing enjoyable rugby, Carlos [Spencer] was on top of his game at that time, and when he's like that any side he's playing in is going to score a lot of points. Joe Rokocoko had come on the scene and was scoring a lot of tries, Dan Carter and Ma'a Nonu were in their first Test years. They brought a lot of energy and some great skills. After those performances in Australia and South Africa we were feeling pretty confident, and then to come back to Auckland and win the Bledisloe Cup, finally, was very special.

Justin Marshall: South Africa in Pretoria was my first game back from injury. It was one of those games where we had everything go our way. George Gregan reckons they should have won the return game at Eden Park, when we won back the Bledisloe Cup. It was close but somehow we found a way to win. We'd already been to Sydney and destroyed them. They didn't pick Mehrts for the World Cup, or Cully, they were two big calls. They thought that Cully wasn't 100 per cent, and he wasn't, but I'd have taken an eighty per cent Christian Cullen myself, and it turned out we needed him. I would have had both Mehrts and Cully there.

Andrew Mehrtens: Don't get me wrong, I see a lot of Robbie Deans socially and I have respect for a lot of the attributes that he has, but I don't think we were ever on the same wavelength in the way I was with Wayne Smith, and that's not to say that he was wrong and I was right. I knew what he wanted and I probably wasn't the sort of player to deliver what Robbie wanted off the field, stuff like that. If you want to get in the team and you know what he wants, then you've got to go along with it as much as possible. I think he had much more of an influence on that team at the time than people gave credit for.

The All Blacks headed to Melbourne where they would remain, out of the spotlight, for much of the tournament. Their opening match against Italy, whilst won at a canter,

Joe Rokocoko flies in to score against South Africa in
Pretoria during the 2003 Tri Nations. *InphoPhotography*

came at a massive cost, with backline cornerstone Tana Umaga suffering a serious knee injury. Whilst unlikely to play again, Umaga stayed on, his condition the subject of daily enquiry. Other ailing players were sent home, to be replaced, it seemed, by anyone but Mehrtens or Cullen. Spencer was struggling with his goal-kicking, Dan Carter, in his first year of Test rugby, was battling a niggling injury, and in the end fullback Leon MacDonald was moved to centre to accommodate his goal-kicking. The All Blacks scored an impressive quarter-final win over a troubled Springbok team to set up a Sydney semi, the general consensus being that the Wallabies would not be good enough, given their unconvincing form. In fact their whole campaign had been aimed at this match. Coach Eddie Jones had come up with a brilliant strategy to defuse the All Blacks' reliance on turnover and counter-attack ball. He picked openside flankers George Smith and Phil Waugh to sew up the breakdown and negate McCaw's effect, and when the Wallabies put the ball out they put it deep into the stands to prevent the quick throws that had burnt them earlier in the year. The All Blacks started well and had fullback Mils Muliaina been able to force a ball down in the corner it might have been different. A lengthy injury break also stemmed their momentum, and in frustration they started throwing unnecessary passes, notably one from Spencer that ended up in the arms of Stirling Mortlock, who scored the game changer. Things got worse when Justin Marshall, the one player who might have got the All Blacks back into the game with a sniping run, was hit off the ball by Smith and suffered rib damage. As more and more mistakes crept into the All Black play, the Wallabies edged further ahead through Elton Flatley's boot, and another World Cup campaign was in tatters. France were beaten in the playoff for third and fourth, but few seemed to care. It was open season on Mitchell in particular. There was little sympathy for the coaching duo, who along the way had managed to upset key NZRU personnel, sponsors, unwanted players and in particular the media, exacerbated by Mitchell's curious turns of phrase. Many blamed the defeat on the refusal to play Umaga, despite him being only semi-fit, others pointed to the All Blacks being closeted in Melbourne, too far away from a spotlight that blinded them when the fat lady started singing in Sydney. As captain, Thorne was also singled out, although like Randell in '99, he lacked quality deputies, with players like Mehrtens and Anton Oliver seemingly discarded in part because of their strong personalities. The final words in the All Black story of 2003, will forever be credited to George Gregan, who taunted the All Blacks with: 'Four more years, boys, four more years.'

Aaron Mauger: For any All Black team going into the World Cup there's going to be a degree of confidence. Two things hindered us. We were based in Melbourne for almost the whole tournament, and there was very little hype down there. Some might say it's a good thing being away from all that, but on those occasions you have to embrace it. You see that with the Canadas, the Tongas, the Namibias, they get beaten by big scores between World Cups, but they rise to the occasion.

Ali Williams: Losing Tana was a massive blow. It definitely rattled us. Firstly because we were quite a young group of guys, and we started thinking, 'Whoa, we've lost Tana.' The crux of it was who would play centre, because we didn't have an out-and-out centre . . . he didn't want to put Ma'a in there. And then it became about the goal-kicking, because I'm not too sure if he wanted Carlos to kick. There was a momentum shift and we weren't mature enough to peg it back.

Wallaby centre Stirling Mortlock intercepts a pass from Carlos Spencer
and races in to score the decisive try in the World Cup semi-final. *Getty Images*

Justin Marshall: We had a few problems early on with injuries. Losing Tana was a huge setback. We ended up with Leon MacDonald playing centre. But we came right. We had a tough game with Wales in Brisbane which wasn't expected but then had an emphatic win over the Springboks. We played really well in that Test . . . it was Joost's [van der Westhuizen] last Test match, and then we had that bloody game against Aussie!

Aaron Mauger: We had a young group that had been fairly successful over a short period of time, and that might have hurt us when it came to the knockout stages. After putting South Africa away in the quarter-final we might have been a bit too confident. Australia were smarter than us. They had some tough games through the pool, and in the quarter-final, and were at a better intensity and had a more focused game plan, whereas we were playing ad lib rugby and scoring tries at will. Our mindset really wasn't where it needed to be and we were beaten as a consequence. We took them lighter than we should have. We'd put a few points on them earlier in the year and weren't respectful of the challenge coming.

Justin Marshall: Australia hadn't had a great tournament. Watching their quarter-final against Scotland they looked awful. It was one of those games where we started well, and got nothing out of it. Milsy [Muliaina] went over in the corner but couldn't get the ball down, then we went close from a lineout drive. Then they tried to clear, only got it as far as the twenty-two but then they got that Stirling Mortlock intercept. All of a sudden after dominating the first fifteen minutes of the game we were down 7-0 and that seemed to really galvanize them. We kicked off and while they only went about fifteen to twenty metres, they put thirteen or fourteen phases together and I thought, 'Oh shit,' because they were starting to find the rhythm they'd been missing all tournament. I got hit late by George Smith around the twenty-five to thirty minute mark. He cracked one of my ribs. I tried to play on . . . I went to a breakdown and I could see a gap where they weren't defending the fringe, the sort of thing normally I would take, but when I went to accelerate my rib went crunch, I couldn't run and I had to pass it. I did ask the doc [Mayhew] at half-time if he'd inject it to take the pain away but he said, 'I'm not doing that Justin,' . . . if it had been cracked I could have ended up with a punctured lung, could have died. I felt I'd been playing well, but I realised it would be selfish to stay on the field.

Reuben Thorne: We were well-prepared and did everything right, but to not get it right on just one occasion is heart-breaking. Those sort of things are really hard to take at the time but you move on. I guess it's one of those things that sometimes you have to go through those hard times and deal with it.

Justin Marshall: If I had one real criticism of that campaign it's that we'd seen a lot of England in the two weeks leading up to that Australia game, and I think to a degree we'd already got past Australia and were looking at England too early and we didn't hone in on Australia enough. We thought we were going to be playing England in the final. We weren't as focused on the 'now' as we should have been.

FORTY-THREE

LIONS AND WORLD CUP WOE

'What are we doing this for, do we want to be the best in the world or do we just want to be All Blacks?'

GIVEN THEY'D WON a creditable twenty-three of twenty-eight Tests in about two years, there was a case for the retention of Mitchell and Deans, but a late media campaign couldn't save them. The NZRU had a choice between Mitchell and a trio headed by Graham Henry, a choice they had little difficulty making. It was ironic, given the rather petulant response from New Zealand rugby officialdom when Henry left to coach Wales in 1998. Despite his record-breaking feats with Auckland and the Blues, the Auckland Rugby Union took his 'lifetime' Eden Park car park and grandstand tickets off him and the NZRU decreed that anyone coaching an overseas team would not be considered for the All Black job. That stance was quickly forgotten when presented with what the media dubbed the coaching 'Dream Team'. Henry had impressive running mates in Wayne Smith and Steve Hansen, although given his previous experience Smith had taken some convincing. Henry admitted having 'lost the plot' on the Lions tour of Australia in 2001, but had learned much, and was determined not to be driven by results, aiming to build a strong team culture and manage player workloads. He would ultimately guide New Zealand back to the summit of world rugby, but not without a few rockfalls along the way.

Aaron Mauger: The new coaches brought back the All Black trial, and I got injured playing in it. I hurt my knee just before half-time and was out for nine weeks missing that campaign. I came back as an injury replacement for the last game, against the Springboks in Johannesburg, where we were well beaten. I really enjoyed working under those guys, they did a great job and shaped a lot of my ideas and philosophies.

Ali Williams: It took more than one year to convince that old bugger [Henry]. He dropped me for Auckland against Canterbury in 2002, and I was pissed off! He dropped me in the Blues, and did it again in the All Blacks. He was straight up, he said, 'I don't think you deserve fourteen caps, I don't think you're good enough.' In a way that was the catalyst for a pretty honest relationship and how he was going to treat me for the years ahead, and how he wanted me to treat him. Getting dropped was the best thing, because it made me respect the jersey a lot more.

With a new captain in Tana Umaga, and a changed forward pack, Henry's All Blacks made a strong start, running up 36 points in both Tests against World Cup holders England, and 41 points against both Argentina and a combined Pacific Islands team before setting about their defence of the Bledisloe Cup and Tri Nations. The first of those targets was achieved

Opposite: Dan Carter delivered, throughout the course of the 2005 Test series against the Lions, what many pundits termed 'the greatest performance by a number ten ever'. *FotoSport*

in pouring rain in Wellington, Justin Marshall appearing in a record twentieth Tri Nations match, as Australia were beaten 16-7. The All Blacks came from 21-12 down to edge South Africa in Christchurch, the winning try by Doug Howlett a minute after the final hooter, following a prolonged build-up. Things went pear-shaped after that. The Wallabies hit back to win in Sydney 23-18, and then sparked by a Marius Joubert hat-trick the Springboks recorded a thumping 40-26 victory in Johannesburg. What happened after that Ellis Park Test brought matters to a head. A boozy post-match players' court session saw several players severely intoxicated, and it didn't stop there. Smith had seen enough, and told manager Darren Shand it was a dysfunctional team, and if things didn't change he was out.

Justin Marshall: We lost the Test in Johannesburg, it was the last Test of the Tri Nations and we'd been well beaten. Court sessions had been part of the game for as long as I'd been involved – a chance to get the team together, have a few laughs, a few beers. I feel that some things that happen in a team environment is where they should stay, not for publication, but Ted [Graham Henry] has felt the need to talk about it because there was something going on in the All Blacks he wasn't comfortable with. I don't necessarily concur there was a drinking culture – it was just a traditional end of campaign thing. What went wrong with that court session is, because it was the last one, a lot of the Polynesian players in the team wanted to be part of it. There was no compulsion to drink. You could drink water . . . and usually it was just beer and water. Some of the players who don't like beer, or don't normally drink very much, asked if they could have spirits and we [Carlos Spencer and I] said yes, which was the worst thing we could have said. Things normally done with beer, were done with rum and coke. They looked OK, everything looked fine, but obviously it hit a few players later. Some of the management were there too, and were drinking spirits. I don't regret the way Carlos and I ran that court session other than some of the players got really drunk, and later it got out of control. I realised things were going pear-shaped and stopped the spirits but by then it was too late.

Ali Williams: We'd lost the Tri Nations and we all jumped on the plane in Jo'burg as pissed as chooks. After that Smithy [Wayne Smith] stood up and said, 'I've been here. I've done this, and if this is the culture I don't want to do it again.' He was the one who made everyone think, 'What are we doing this for, do we want to be the best in the world or do we just want to be All Blacks?' We decided we could create a real legacy, but we had to change our mindset. The jersey had become a bit of a hand-me-down. There was no real buy-in about the history, and what sort of legacy you could create. Since the advent of professional rugby, guys were coming in and out more regularly – form was everything. But, if you look at what happened to our team, there was a lot more consistency in the selection, which allowed you to build a culture, and unbreakable beliefs in what you were doing. I think the result of that was the biggest shift in attitude.

Things did change. Players were put on notice, and more changes were made for an end of year tour that proved a turning point. Henry rotated his squad to build depth. Italy were dispatched 59-10 in Rome, but a young line-up, with Richie McCaw captain for the first time, had to fight tooth and nail to beat Wales. The All Blacks started to place more emphasis on the set piece, with the addition of scrum coach Mike Cron and the promotion of powerful props Carl Hayman and Tony Woodcock. That newfound determination was demonstrated in Paris, where a strong French pack was overpowered to the degree that, within five minutes of the second half, two of their props had left the field resulting, much to the disdain of the New Zealand players, in non-contested scrums. The result was a crushing 45-6 win, an emphatic statement to end the first Test campaign under new management, a romp against a Barbarians side featuring Justin Marshall providing a nice close to the year.

Justin Marshall: I didn't not want to go on that tour. They said they were looking at developing a few players and I wasn't the only one left behind. They said they wanted to give me a rest, but I showed I didn't need one by playing for the Barbarians against them. I thought it would be an amazing experience to captain the Barbarians, face the haka and play against a team I'd played for so many times. The fact I was allowed to play by the Rugby Union suggested things were starting to change, and maybe the end was approaching.

Jimmy Cowan (2004-11, 51 Tests, 53 games): I grew up in Mataura, same town as Justin Marshall, played the same position and our Dads worked at the freezing works together. I looked up to him right through my career. There were aspects of his game I tried to emulate. Then, after I made my debut in 2004, against Italy in Rome, I came off the bench against Scotland and started against the Barbarians at the end of that tour, I played against Marshy.

Aaron Mauger: The coaches and management put a focus on growing a leadership group, there was a paradigm shift around players becoming more professional and learning the legacy of the All Blacks. We learned a lot about All Black history and culture. Smithy being the passionate man that he is, with the help of Gilbert Enoka and Ted, those guys helped us understand what and who we were representing, and being proud to do that, and to acknowledge the responsibility and opportunity we were given every time we pulled the All Black jersey on. It was a pivotal moment in my career.

Keven Mealamu (2002-15, 132 Tests, 133 games): I got an email from either Ted or Shandy asking me to take part in a leadership meeting. It was kind of odd to see who was in the room, because in 2004 I was still a young All Black and I wasn't sure how to approach it. As we started to talk it became clear it was a great opportunity to play a part in how we were as a team, how we played, and how we conducted ourselves off the field, and to make sure those factors married up. It took a while for it to bed in, four or five years, but I can say by the time I finished I was really proud of the way the men conducted themselves on and off the field. BJ [Lochore] always used to say good people make good All Blacks, it gave us more balance.

Jerome Kaino (2004-15, 67 Tests, 68 games): That tour taught me a lot about being in that environment and around those professionals. It taught me how I needed to live my day-to-day rugby life. It was quite tough because I didn't really expect to be on that tour. I went from somebody happy to be in the NPC team to getting called up to play for the All Blacks. There was a lot of talk about that Test in France before they played, and the boys played really well. The word 'mettle' got introduced to me and I was impressed with how they put aside what had happened before and got out there and lived up to All Black expectations.

Ali Williams: In Paris, we walked all over them, put 40 points on them. Rodney So'oialo was outstanding. Maxy and Chris Jack started and they just dominated. I think it was one of Norm Maxwell's last real 'Maxy' moments, where he flew into everything. We smashed them.

Tana Umaga: We never wavered from what we were trying to achieve. Once they put the pressure on us, no one panicked, we just went about our jobs and focused on what we had to do next. They were on our line really threatening there, but we held strong and I think that was due to our commitment to each other. We just kept talking to each other, backing each other up and comparing that to what we had at the beginning of this year, I think that was better.

Keven Mealamu: It's hard to think of a better All Black front row performance than that one, Carl Hayman, Woody and Anton Oliver started. I think we knew if we started well, put a mark in the ground, got on top early we could win. Without being disrespectful, we felt there were two types of French team, the team that stays in the contest right to the

The 2005 Lions adopt a unique arrow-head line-up
in response to the All Blacks' haka. *FotoSport*

end if you let them or, if you get on top, the one that can fall away. We really did get on top of them in that game.

Great anticipation surrounded the first tour in twelve years by the British and Irish Lions. It was a tour of unprecedented grand scale, with coach Sir Clive Woodward operating on a seemingly limitless budget, bringing over seventy players and management, including political spin doctor Alastair Campbell, who instantly got up New Zealand noses. The Lions played six games before the first Test, losing only to New Zealand Maori in Hamilton. Tensions erupted with the first Test. A cold southerly front hit Christchurch just before kick-off and within two minutes the Lions had lost their captain. Brian O'Driscoll was upended at a ruck, landing heavily on his shoulder, an incident that would reverberate for the rest of the year. The All Blacks wasted little time taking a grip on the series, lock Ali Williams and winger Sitiveni Sivivatu scoring tries in a telling 21-3 win.

Justin Marshall: I've admitted times when I haven't played well, so I'm happy to say that I thought I played really well in Super Rugby that year and we won the title. Graham Henry came and saw me and said, 'We're going to have you involved but we don't think you're playing that well,' and yet I'd had few better campaigns. I'd rather he'd said to me, 'You're in your thirties, we want to develop someone else.' I'd have handled it. I said, 'Are you serious?' I was flabbergasted. I felt a sense of them wanting to move me on, but still have me as a back-up option.

Having told me I wasn't playing well, they picked me to start the first Test.

Aaron Mauger: I'd never seen so many supporters in New Zealand. It felt like about 100,000 Brits and Irish had turned up to support the Lions. You'd be in your hotel

Just minutes into the First Test, Brian O'Driscoll is injured out of the series. *FotoSport*

before a Test match and you'd hear them singing, the Welsh singing Bread of Heaven, the English singing Swing Low . . . it's about the only time the English and the Celts get along, I think. We knew we were going to come up against a good team whoever they picked, there was so much quality amongst those four nations, but it does sound like they might have been a bit distracted. They brought about 100 people out, the management was almost as big as the playing squad, and that can be distracting. It's always hard to keep a team tight when you've got so many people. They were splitting into different groups to travel to different places, they seemed to have a strategy of never picking all of their best players . . . all those things can affect the harmony of the group and if you don't have that, when you come under pressure playing against a good team you're going to fall short.

Ali Williams: Outside of winning the World Cup, the Lions tour was the best experience I had in an All Blacks jersey. I was on eggshells going into that series, I had been suspended for 'getting to know Richie better', so I hadn't played a lot of rugby. Also we knew about the experience Graham [Henry] had had with the Lions, it made us realise how big it all was, and it resonated with us. It was almost like the World Cup. It was probably the best rugby I played, over the three matches, in my career. Everything fell into place. Bit like Dan Carter. I think that Test in Wellington, you could say that five or six of our guys played their very best rugby, and Dan, well he was just out of this world. It started with our defence, and then we were on fire, especially after they scored the first try, we were like, 'Right, here we go.' It was pretty special.

Aaron Mauger: I think that first Test really rocked them, 21-3 in Christchurch on a freezing cold night. The injury to Brian O'Driscoll they used it as an excuse, a cop out really. We were just too good, too focused and they weren't.

Tana Umaga: While I played hard in all my games, I tried to play as fair as I could. That's just the way I am. It was an unfortunate incident [O'Driscoll] and these things happen. For the performance we put on, especially our tight five – they should have received the accolades they deserved. But instead all the focus was on that O'Driscoll injury.

Keven Mealamu: It happened so quickly. There was no intention to hurt anyone, I didn't mean to flip him. We didn't target Brian, it just happened to be him. I didn't even realise what had happened. It was a rugby action, and no harm intended at all, but even so, if I could take it back I would because I have so much respect for Brian. I reflect on it, and I guess things happen on the field; everything's happening so fast and sometimes things happen that you're not in control of. I still get heaps from Irish people about it.

Justin Marshall: The Lions accusing us of targeting Brian O'Driscoll, trying to take him out . . . that was so far from the truth it was ridiculous. Our focus was on attacking the inside channel where we felt their defence wasn't great. We never even discussed O'Driscoll, so for them to say we were targeting him was outlandish. At the time I didn't think the incident was too bad, but when I saw the replays later I thought, 'That's not good.' All it was, having seen it live, being right there, and having seen the replays was that

. . . it's just rugby. They got it wrong, and when you get it wrong in that situation, well it either has no impact or it has a really bad impact, and on that occasion it was terrible for Brian O'Driscoll. It's not possible to go out there with the intention of dropping a player on his neck. There's so many dynamics that come into it, including how the player reacts when he's falling. I saw that he was in a lot of trouble and so I went over to him and wished him well and gave him a pat on the chest as he was being stretchered off. That was it as far as the incident was concerned, the rest was about trying to stay warm. It was freezing. I came off the field with about twenty minutes to go and had soup. First time I'd ever had to do that.

Mils Muliaina (2003-11, 100 Tests, 102 games): There was no way we thought it would turn out like it did. The weather played a big part in Christchurch, and we played some outstanding rugby in the conditions to win 21-3. Our forwards took it to them and our backs played some classy stuff in really testing conditions. It even hailed, and was probably the one time you're quite glad you're on a bench because we kept ourselves pretty warm that evening. It was an awesome atmosphere and I think as a player you probably soak it up a bit more when you are on the bench.

Leon MacDonald (2000-08, 56 Tests, 56 games): Dougie [Howlett] and I couldn't even feel our fingers during the game. One time a kick went up and I was looking straight into hail going into my eyes, and couldn't see a thing.

Justin Marshall: When I made my Test debut ten years earlier in Paris, I played behind an absolutely dominant pack and in that Test a new set of forwards laid a fantastic platform. They made my job so much easier.

The lead-up to the Wellington Test was dominated by the O'Driscoll incident. Although there was no citing, the Lions believed O'Driscoll had been deliberately targeted, and turned attention on the two All Blacks involved, Keven Mealamu and Tana Umaga. A Campbell-orchestrated press campaign had the adverse effect of firing up the All Blacks who scored a landslide win, highlighted by a virtuoso performance from Daniel Carter. He scored two brilliant tries, the second from an exquisite chip and regather, added five penalty goals and converted four of the All Blacks five tries for an extraordinary haul of 33 points.

Tana Umaga: We talked about the Lions beginning with intensity and passion. They had been backed into a corner and had nothing to lose after being talked down between Tests. But they still caught us on the hop with their fighting opening and stretched us. We needed all our composure to come back. But we believed that we had it in us to play great rugby.

Mils Muliaina: That [O'Driscoll] incident was massive in the lead-up to the second Test moreso because of the way the Lions were whingeing about it in the media. The guys were a little bit annoyed about that whole incident and how much coverage it was getting.

And given the fact we'd played so well and outclassed them right across the park, and all the attention was focused on O'Driscoll, and how we dislocated his shoulder . . . Brian did have a case and was right to be annoyed about what happened and how it happened. But the whole hype surrounding the Lions' management's reaction got to our players. The series itself was ten times more intense in pressure and excitement than anyone had anticipated. We were determined to make sure that by the time the second Test finished everyone was talking about the way the All Blacks played.

Dan Carter (2003-15, 112 Tests, 112 games): I'm just happy I went out there, played the game the way I loved to play and it all just came off. And to clean up the series as well while doing that was fantastic. I think I'll always look back at it as one of those games where everything went right. For my first try I put the kick through and chased the ball and luckily I got to it before it went out. For the second I was probably a bit greedy. Some of the guys gave me a bit of stick afterwards for not passing, but I just put my head down and went for it and I made it to the line. The bounce of the ball pretty much went my way throughout the whole game. I never had another match like it . . . it was special.

Mils Muliaina: The physicality in the first few minutes of the game was second to none. They came out fizzing just as we had expected them to. They'd got rolled that first week and they were ready to make amends for that. And obviously Gareth Thomas, their replacement captain, scored first. I remember him stepping inside Kevvy and there was just him and myself left. I was probably a little bit too wide, and given the fact there were only twenty metres to go, he scored under the posts. It was the perfect start they needed for that game, but boys showed a lot of composure there. There were four elements of our game that we were really big on, and one of them was the 'now-focus'. That meant that

Leon MacDonald carves through the Lions' defence with
Richie McCaw in close support. *FotoSport*

you had to forget everything that had happened and just focus on the next job at hand. I do recall a lot of that being said, 'Don't worry, now-focus boys, now-focus.'

Aaron Mauger: We were under the pump early on in Wellington. They had a lead for about twenty-five minutes but then we just exploded. We were running the ball from deep in our own territory, I think Dan's first try might have come from an eighty metre breakout. The whole series was a pretty awesome experience, and it was great to be part of it.

Mils Muliaina: One person who did do things right in that game was Dan. He was just outstanding. He was brilliant. Those tries he scored and the way he kicked, he took his game to another level and really stamped his name on world rugby as an outstanding player and as a superstar. What he did was mind boggling. Having watched him develop, you always felt there was something special there but to bring it out against the Lions was unbelievable. The sheer strength he had to fend off the likes of Gavin Henson and go through and set Tana up for his try, and to then come back again and grubber through then have the ball bounce perfectly to score a try, and then sending the ball wide again and he was scoring out wide. I remember all those tries because you sit back and wonder how the heck he managed to score them.

The series sweep was completed in Auckland, where new cap Luke McAlister slotted in for an injured Carter. Umaga scored two of six tries and there might have been a seventh but for an indiscretion by Jerry Collins, who was in bristling form all series.

It ended 38-19, completing the rout of a Lions team that fell well short of the massive pre-tour hype. Justin Marshall came on and played the last thirty minutes of a notable All Black career. Woodward had one last shot when he told reporters the only thing he'd do differently would be to base the team in Melbourne and fly them over for games, a sour note on which to end a tour.

Tana Umaga: The coaches worked incredibly hard in ensuring that we were able to deliver our best rugby when it mattered. And the players around me in all the Tests withstood the pressure and expectation that built up as the series loomed. We became tighter as a unit and the new members who came in after selection decisions and injuries did not look out of place. We studied the Lions and combated their game plan. When I was in the sin-bin, the boys focused. A yellow can work two ways. You can leak points or react strongly to adversity. The boys scored fourteen points while I was on the touchline.

Justin Marshall: They came here expecting to control the scrum and lineout, but at the set piece we were a lot more physical than they would have planned for.

Mils Muliaina: Both Conrad [Smith], who scored a try, and Luke [McAlister] had big games. Tana scored twice and Ali Williams and Rico Gear scored one each in the 38-19 win. I recall after the game how proud we were at what we had achieved. It seemed like that was your whole rugby career, that you'd done everything you wanted to do. Apart from the World Cup, obviously.

The effort needed to beat the Lions might have taken the edge off the All Blacks in the Tri Nations. They lost in Cape Town, where the Springboks raced out to a 13-0 lead and went on to win 22-16, but the All Blacks regathered their strength and regained the title they'd lost to South Africa the previous year. Both Bledisloe Cup Tests were won, but the return Test against the Springboks in Dunedin was a gripping, bruising affair that got off to a sensational start. The All Blacks chose a match against their greatest foe to unveil a new haka, Kapa O Pango, composed for the All Blacks by Derek Lardelli a noted authority in Tikanga Maori (Maori ritual, custom and protocol) with input from the team. Few outside the team, certainly not the Springboks, knew it was coming, and both the Umaga-led haka and the response from the crowd were electrifying. The Springboks took up the challenge and led with five minutes to play, before a lineout drive produced a winning try for Keven Mealamu.

Ali Williams: We'd been training the new haka for a long time, and as a group we were saying, 'No, we're not ready,' and we'd held off. We had a session at the University Oval in Dunedin, and we did it over and over again. We were all red, belted ourselves. It was on the Friday I think, and Tana said, 'We're ready.' We knew that if we changed it, people would expect it to be monumental, that we were changing something that was part of the legacy. The reaction was amazing . . . a stunned silence that became a roar. That was a tough Test too, against the Springboks, and we won it with a lineout move we'd been practising, where I'd come across the line, give a little push on my opposite, and then as I stepped back into the line he'd throw it. And so I did it, against Victor Matfield! We drove it over, and Kevvy went over for the try. We looked at each other and went, 'You beauty!' People think you might have come up with that on the Monday or the Tuesday, but we'd been working on it for a long, long time.

Keven Mealamu: It was a huge game, it was the Springboks and the Tri Nations was on the line, so it seemed the perfect time to bring Kapo O Pango out. The response was amazing. It was so quiet at first as the crowd realised what was happening, and then they really fired up. It was done really well too, with good emotion, passion. Then it was such a tight game, it went back and forth, and to be able to come back and pull off that lineout move . . . to set it up, drive accurately, execute like that, and there was still a lot to do against such a good forward pack . . . in the end it comes down to all the effort you've put into it in preparation.

Ali Williams: Sometime in 2005 we started that thing with cleaning up the changing room. Shag [Hansen] was the big driver of it. He told us not to leave a changing room in a worse state than when we found it, so you had Tana and those guys on the broom sweeping up. At Twickenham one time, we'd had a session, and had tidied up and the cleaners walked in and it was all tidy and they were like, 'What the . . . ?'

Jerome Kaino: I had a lot of fluctuations after the 2004 tour and was in and out and it was largely down to me being a young man with things off-the-field distracting me. That man of the match performance against the Barbarians [in 2004] didn't really help. I thought I had arrived and that performance would carry me through to the next selection.

I worked hard but I didn't take it to the next level. So when I got dropped and my form fluctuated I knew it was just myself. I had to set out my stall to improve even further and get that jersey back. It was a journey.

To complete a momentous year the All Blacks then set their sights on the first Grand Slam in nearly three decades. Wales were crushed 41-3, and then, as Henry took his rotation policy to a new level, an all-changed XV ran up a similar score against Ireland. The crunch point was always going to be England, who'd bullied the Australian scrum en route to a 26-16 win the previous week, and there was huge anticipation over the clash of giant props Carl Hayman and Andrew Sheridan. An early England try raised hopes, hopes that grew when referee Alun Lewis yellow-carded three All Blacks in the second half. Despite being down to fourteen players for thirty minutes the All Blacks held their nerve to win a tense affair 23-19. With Scotland in no great shape, another much changed line-up cruised to a 29-10 win at Murrayfield, claiming the first All Black Grand Slam since Graham Mourie's team on the same ground twenty-seven years earlier.

Three other notable events took place during that tour. Firstly, the All Blacks made a pilgrimage to Ramelton in County Donegal, birthplace of Originals captain Dave Gallaher, a visit made via a bold initiative by the nearby Letterkenny club, and one reinforcing their connection with the past. In the week between the Irish and English Tests, the NZRU defied all predictions by winning the right to stage the 2011 Rugby World Cup, and finally, Tana Umaga chose the Scotland Test to be his last. The timing was right. It was evident the backlash to the O'Driscoll incident – apart from Donegal trip he'd barely left the hotel in Dublin – had taken its toll.

Aaron Mauger: Dan Carter talked about a group of us heading to London before the Wales Test in 2005 in his book. I'm ashamed to say I was part of it, not one of my better moments. I'd heard about the 'Church' [the famed Antipodean drinking spot on Sundays in London], but had never been to it, and never got there in the end. By the time we got to London, I thought it was best to round up the boys and head back. It was a bad judgment call. We managed to get back in time, and deal with the wrath but obviously for Leon [MacDonald] and myself, as part of the leadership group, it was embarrassing. We'd known we weren't going to be playing against Wales . . . we were pencilled in for the Ireland game the following week . . . so we had a bit of time up our sleeves, but Dan was playing at Cardiff and he was on edge for most of the week, especially when the media got hold of it. In the end he had a blinder, scored a couple of tries, got 20-odd points.

Keven Mealamu: It was a real challenge for us to get that Grand Slam. That last game can be really difficult, and it's usually the one you get remembered for. You lose it and it's like having a stone under your beach towel all summer. Part of you is already trying to go on holiday. But we felt we'd come that far, and to let it slip in that second to last game [England] would have been really disappointing. I think at times we got flustered. Our leadership group was still quite young, and we really hadn't started getting into how we would handle things in situations like that. We got out of it. It's amazing how much backbone you develop when you can come through a really difficult game like that.

Jimmy Cowan: Scotland in 2005 was Tana's last Test. He told the team after the game in the changing room. I had the utmost respect for him. I guess they were going into a transition phase and Richie was being groomed as the new leader – he'd captained the team against Ireland. There was a lot in the build-up to the England game about the meeting of the two colossuses in the front row, Carl Hayman and Andy Sheridan. Carl's a very quiet, humble guy, and there'd been a lot of media about the coming together of those two mammoth front row opponents, and who was going to get set piece domination. They were making a lot of how Sheridan had destroyed the Wallabies. Someone photo-copied the stories from the English papers, and pinned them all over the wall in the team room, on the doors, all through the hotel, Carl couldn't escape it. When the first scrum went down, you could feel the impact in the stand.

Aaron Mauger: In the early days Dan was pretty quiet, just playing his game. He had a lot of good leaders around, the likes of Tana and myself and we'd call a lot of the moves. We had good halfbacks, Marshy, Byron, and although he was wearing ten, had first touch of the ball, he had good people around him. Dan is pretty relaxed from a humble background, great parents, strong moral upbringing, he was never going to get ahead of himself.

Jimmy Cowan: The Test in Rustenburg was my first start. It was amazing staying in Sun City. The hotel was incredible, some of the rooms were $1,000 a night. We came off a big win in Pretoria the week before, bussed down to Sun City on the Sunday and stayed there the week. We were on an unbeaten run at that point, going back twelve months. We had one more game to go through the Tri Nations unbeaten, but it didn't end well. We lost by a penalty.

Richie McCaw took over as captain in 2006, a job he had been earmarked for. The All Blacks were building another winning streak, although they had to work extremely hard for wins over Ireland in Hamilton and Auckland, and then Argentina in Buenos Aires before an expanded Tri Nations, in which each team would play the others three times. It was tough. Mealamu scored two tries as Australia were beaten 32-12 in Christchurch, but the Tests in Brisbane and Auckland were won by single figure margins. The final two Tests against South Africa were played on the high veldt. Loosehead prop Neemia Tialata was an unlikely hero in Pretoria, scoring a try and switching sides of the scrum with great effect after an early injury to Greg Somerville, while Dan Carter kicked a sixty-two-metre penalty goal as the All Blacks won 45-26. With the title wrapped up, the All Blacks had won fifteen straight and were eyeing the record for consecutive Test wins, but their streak ended in remote Rustenburg as Andre Pretorius kicked a penalty goal two minutes from time for a 21-20 victory. The All Blacks quickly regained winning form in November, beating England, France twice and Wales by good margins to confirm their favouritism for the World Cup the following year.

The Three Rs had, in Kiwi vernacular, long been a reference to those old school staples, Reading, 'Riting and 'Rithmetic, but in New Zealand in 2007 they took on a new meaning as the All Blacks prepared for the Rugby World Cup in France. The Three Rs became Rest, Reconditioning and Rotation. Twenty-two players were pulled out of the first seven weeks of Super Rugby to heal tired bodies, before undergoing a conditioning programme to build muscle, core strength and fitness.

It prompted a mixed reaction from fans and media, didn't exactly thrill the broadcasters and frustrated Super Rugby coaches, but when the All Blacks came together the early signs were promising. A shambolic France was dispatched 42-11 and 61-10, and Canada thumped 64-13 before the All Blacks' new found fitness levels were evident in a comeback win over the Springboks in Cape Town.

They hit a speed bump on the way home, losing the first Bledisloe Cup Test 26-21 in Melbourne, before a below-strength Springbok team was well beaten in Christchurch. The Bledisloe was retained at Eden Park, Carter kicking seven penalty goals and new halfback Brendon Leonard scoring a cheeky try in a 26-12 win. The All Blacks headed for France as warm favourites to win their first World Cup in twenty years. Almost immediately they found themselves on course for a quarter-final with the host nation after France lost the tournament opener to Argentina. Italy were swept aside 76-14 in Marseille and 100 points were racked up against newcomers Portugal, before the All Blacks flew, incongruously, to Edinburgh for a farcical match with the Scots. The All Blacks, as required, turned out in their alternate grey strip, only to find it was ridiculously similar to what the Scots wore. Both jerseys had been approved by tournament officials who clearly hadn't put them side-by-side. The All Blacks were asked at half-time if they had their black jerseys with them, which they did not. Despite numerous cases of mistaken identity, the match was won 40-0, and Romania was swept aside 85-8 in Toulouse, before the All Blacks crossed the Channel again, this time for Cardiff and a French team in supposed crisis.

Not for the first time, France chose a match with the All Blacks to do something extraordinary. It didn't look that way after Luke McAlister scored off a Collins pass and Carter nudged the lead out to 13-nil, but soon after half-time McAlister was yellow-carded by referee Wayne Barnes and the game changed. France scored 13 unanswered points and although Rodney So'oialo got the All Blacks back in front, the French hit the lead again when Yannick Jauzion scored a converted try for a 20-18 lead. The All Blacks spent most of the remaining twelve minutes hammering away at the French line. They could neither score a try, nor eke a penalty out of Barnes, who found no fault with the French. It ended with a futile attempt at a long-range dropped goal by McAlister, and for the first time, a New Zealand side had failed to reach the semi-finals. Once again the Kiwi public went ballistic, pouring much of the scorn on the coaching staff and the Rest, Reconditioning and Rotation policy and blasting the team for not attempting a dropped goal when they had numerous chances from close range. After saying all the right things in the immediate aftermath, the coaches soon let it be known how dissatisfied they were with Barnes. The Jauzion try had come from a clear forward pass, they claimed that McAlister had been harshly sin-binned, and that over forty penalty offences by the French were ignored. They got little sympathy from neutral observers, and a pretty mixed bag from home, and straight away the calls went up for the axe to fall, again.

Aaron Mauger: We appreciated they were trying to rest players. But I loved playing footy, I loved playing for the Crusaders and to miss out on seven or eight games . . . I felt I always played my best Test rugby on the back of a good Crusaders campaign, so I was a bit apprehensive, and the comments I made at the time were probably made out of anxiety. It was a tough one. We were asked to back it, and commit to it, which we all did and probably wrongly one or two of us spoke out about it in public at the time because of our apprehensions. Jerry [Collins] didn't like it much but he was a bit different from me. He'd sneak along and get a club game, playing under someone else's name, wearing the No.24 jersey!

Keven Mealamu: JC [Collins] was a great friend. His loss [in a car crash in 2015] hit us all so hard. I have so many great memories of him, but one of my favourites was in 2006, when he was named as skipper for the Argentina Test in Buenos Aires. As a captain, JC was one that left his talking for the field, his demeanour as a player and a captain didn't change, but seeing him do his after-match speech in Spanish was a moment where my awe for the man went to another level; JC would amaze me throughout his career with so many moments on the field, but to be present at that after match will be something I will never forget.

As a leader his style was 'follow me'. He wasn't a man of words, but his actions on the rugby field always came across loud and clear, and because he would impose himself on the opposition he would always instil a confidence and excitement knowing he was on our side. He was hard working and was one of the brothers but also his own man, and I had a lot of respect for that – not being what others wanted him to be.

Mils Muliaina: The All Blacks had gone into the hunt for the Webb Ellis Trophy as overwhelming favourites. We had played a stimulating, positive brand of rugby. We felt good as a team, we were enjoying the way we were playing and we had a sense of ownership in our destiny. Our coaches had been innovative, supportive and determined in the face of some criticism. We breezed through our preliminary games. At half-time we were up 13–3 and felt like we had control of the game, although nothing is ever certain, especially against France. We gathered in our group just before going back out onto the field and the strangest thing happened. Out of nowhere, our halfback, Byron Kelleher, said: 'This feels like 1999!' You could have heard a pin drop in the changing room when he said that. It was like he had just tempted fate. Byron didn't say the brightest things at times, but I think everyone considered that to be one of the dumbest things he could ever have said. And then we went back out for the second half. We had started well: we were creating a lot of gaps and testing France's defences. Luke McAlister was breaking the line and getting close. But there was that middle part of the game where it just did not go our way.

Ali Williams: I think if we'd learnt how to take dropped goals no one would have said a thing about Rest, Rotation and Reconditioning, it would have been the most brilliant thing in the world. We always felt in control, so it wasn't obvious that things were falling to bits, it was just the scoreboard where we weren't in front. We were dominating every aspect of the game . . . although when they got a try we realised it was going to be tough to pull back. You don't like to say it but it's bullshit how the ref didn't award us any of those penalties. I don't want to grab a headline but . . . it was just bullshit. He's a far better ref than that and I just think it all got to him. It didn't feel like it was slipping away. We felt if we kept doing what we were doing the penalties would come, and that's how it's meant to work, but in that game it didn't happen. At the end we started thinking dropped goals, but by then people were thinking individually, not collectively.

Aaron Mauger: We had the team to do the job and, again, we took our eye off the ball . . . the French were up for it. It was a one off . . . I'm sure if we'd got through that game we'd have been OK, we'd have been better prepared to deal with the next game. It was tough not being involved. Sitting there watching it unfold and not able to do anything. It was my last time with the All Blacks, and I was hoping I might have got one more crack if we'd gone through to the semi-finals. I was really disappointed for the whole group; the players and the coaches had put so much effort into it. It was one of those days. If I'd been on the field I'd have maybe had a snap shot at goal and missed it and been the villain, you just don't know.

Richie McCaw: What you'd worked for for so long had come to an end, bang, like that. It was pretty tough. We were going home and hadn't quite done what we thought we were going to do. We hadn't played to our best and that was the tough part to take. On top of that, what was it going to be like when we got home? Obviously the whole country was disappointed, all the emotion, and you just thought, 'This shouldn't be happening,' but it was.

Aaron Mauger: I don't think we managed the game well. We should never have got into that position. We were a better side than the performance we put out there. Tactically we didn't get it right. We played into their hands by trying to go through the middle and when that didn't work we didn't adapt. Thierry Dusautoir played the game of his life, he made about forty-five tackles, chopped everything down. There was a bit of misfortune too, Jerry Collins got concussed, Dan hurt his calf and then Nick Evans came on and pulled a hamstring, and so two guys who might normally have been on at the end to kick a dropped goal weren't, and it was left to a couple of young guys, Luke McAlister and Isaia Toeava at ten and twelve . . . I mean you can't fault them, they were in great form at the time but they perhaps didn't have the experience or maturity to drive the team through that last ten minutes and get into a position where they could have won the game.

Dan Carter: It was the biggest game of my career and to have to watch the last twenty minutes from the sideline because of injury was tough. I wasn't feeling it beforehand but obviously with the lack of training leading up to that game, it fatigued and therefore 'went' so it was extremely frustrating. I would have been lucky to play that game [a semi-final]. So it was a tough time.

FORTY-FOUR

WORLD CUP BLISS

'You'd better get a hold of Ted, he wants to speak to you'

AGAINST A BACKDROP of wailing, gnashing of teeth and general bloodletting over the 2007 failure, few expected Henry to reapply for his job, let alone get it. But he did. Having first gained the consent of wife Raewyn and the support of Smith and Hansen, Henry faced the challenge of Robbie Deans who, with his glittering Crusaders CV, was also being hunted for the Wallaby job. Deans had plenty of public support, but too many detractors at Rugby Union HQ. Henry, Hansen and Smith were reappointed, and Deans signed for Australia. Henry was given two years to justify his continuation (his contract would be extended early in 2009). And so it was when, in their first Bledisloe Cup game under Deans, the Wallabies inflicted an embarrassing 34-19 defeat on an All Black side as poor as the Wallabies were good. The year had started with a win over Ireland in miserable conditions in Wellington, two over England and a 19-8 victory over the Springboks in more clement conditions in the capital. But the Springboks turned the tables with a dramatic late victory in Dunedin, their first in the southern city. Then came the defeat in Sydney, leaving both team and coaching staff under immense pressure as they headed for Auckland seven days later. The response was emphatic, a 39-10 win including two tries by prop Tony Woodcock. They still needed to beat South Africa at Newlands to stay in the Tri Nations hunt, and amidst great fanfare over the 100th Test for Springbok fullback Percy Montgomery, rained on the parade with an outstanding 19-0 win.

Richie McCaw: The tough part after Cardiff was knowing you hadn't played to your potential, knowing you could have played better . . . If you'd played to your potential and been beaten by a better team it might have been easier to take. When we got home there was a big crowd at the airport. It was almost embarrassing, but it showed that even though they were gutted, they understood we were hurting and that made it a bit better. When I got home I just went off to Raglan, and hung out there. I was twenty-six at the time, I was young enough to have another dig at it. It took a while to get to that point but I realised that we had to be the ones to move on first. Be the ones to stand up.

Wayne Smith: I didn't have to go to the interview . . . Ted did. The phone went that evening and it was Ted, and he said, 'We're buggered mate,' and I said, 'Oh well Ted, at least we've had a crack,' and he said, 'The interview didn't go well, I think we're buggered.'

Steve Hansen: If you want my honest opinion I don't think Robbie wanted it anyway. I think Robbie had already signed for Australia and he just went through the motions so he could be the martyr if he didn't get it . . . so he would win both sides of the table.

Opposite: From whitebait fishing to a World Cup final, Stephen Donald comes off the bench (in a too-small shirt) to ease twenty-four years of pain. *FotoSport*

Graham Henry: I didn't think it would happen, and when it did you could have knocked me down with a feather.

Richie McCaw: We were the ones who'd been out on the field and if we were going to get another crack at it, why not them? And we'd done such good stuff, I mean where that team was compared to where it had been a few years earlier, we'd taken huge strides forward in the way we were playing, the leadership. The disappointing part was we hadn't delivered when it counted, but if we were going to get a new bunch of coaches then we'd have had to start again. We needed to pick up where we'd been, and that was why I was keen to see those guys carry on.

Ali Williams: I was quite vocal about it. In the past every time we'd lost we'd changed coaches and the same thing kept happening, so keeping Ted was the best thing they could have done. The whole mindset changed, not as to what it was to be an All Black, but as to how you win a World Cup. We realised that World Cups aren't always going to be pretty. You're going to have shit games where you might need a few things to go your way . . . that was really the shift in thinking. Once we made that change in mindset everyone from the board down bought into it. From our perspective it was, 'Right, it's just us, no one is getting in the way.' It was awesome.

Keven Mealamu: There was a leadership group meeting in 2008, and I got a shock to see Wayne Bennett there because I'm a Brisbane Broncos fan. The Australian cricket coach was there as well. The thing that stood out for me was . . . he singled out Mils [Muliaina who had been switched to centre during the 2007 World Cup] and said to him, 'Do you want to be a world-class player?' 'Yes.' 'Are you a centre or a fullback?' 'Fullback.' 'So why weren't you playing fullback?' That was right in front of the coaches. It was quite different to hear it from someone like that, and amazing to hear it from a league man like him, you wouldn't think he'd even known what position Mils played, but he did.

Richard Kahui (2008-11, 17 Tests, 18 games): My debut was in the second Test against England in Christchurch, and the best possible thing happened. My first touch of the ball, Dan gave me a pass and put me under the posts for a try, and it just flowed from there. I felt I had one of my best Tests for the All Blacks in my first game. It helped me to believe that maybe I was good enough. The Tri Nations we struggled at times. We lost to the . . . I'll call them the 'Robbie Deans Wallabies' in Sydney, where we didn't play very well at all. Matt Dunning at the end of that game, just before the final whistle stood up and said to Woody, or Horey, 'We're going to beat you c***s 3-nil!' We were under a lot of pressure, people were saying we should have gone with Robbie Deans and not Ted. Coming back to Auckland was the first time I felt what it was like to be in an All Black camp in the pressure cooker. That's when All Black teams tend to be their best. We took them apart. I sat out on the wing and watched everything unfold, it was awesome.

Richie McCaw: The 2008 season was about getting respectability back. We wanted to remind New Zealanders that the All Blacks were going to compete at the highest level and hopefully win most of the Test matches, and by the end of the year we felt like we'd done that. We hadn't had any great thoughts about what we were going to do down the track.

Jimmy Cowan: I'd come off the bench in Sydney, broke my nose and strained the medial ligament in my knee, and I was in a pretty bad way . . . and the loss to go with it. I didn't train all week, but they picked me to start. I think Andy [Ellis] might have been a bit injured, but we're both competitive buggers and didn't want to give each other an inch. If I got through the captain's run they'd let me play. I was pretty sore but I didn't want to let on. They strapped me up and I played, it was probably one of my better games. I guess it says something about the team that we could come up with such a commanding performance a week later.

Richard Kahui: Smithy rang and asked if I wanted to play on the wing. Leon MacDonald had another head knock so they had to reshuffle a bit. I'd be marking Bryan Habana. I said, 'Of course Smithy I can do it,' but inside I was caking a bit. I mean I had the skills, but I didn't have the speed. However, it turned out well for me down the line. Being on tour gave me a chance to see how Richie and those guys prepare for a Test. The South Africans had distributed 60,000 drums, and while we were doing the haka they were all beating on them, it was an amazing atmosphere. Everything went right for us, all the guys put their hands up. Richie had come back from his ankle sprain, and Conrad played well. To win over there made me feel a connection to those past teams. Playing South Africa there's that fear that they're a team that can beat you, it's the way the stadiums are built, the fans, the team you're playing, so physical in nature, and a rivalry that dates back so long, it makes for really special Test rugby, and that Test at Cape Town would rate as one of my favourites.

After a fringe selection ran up a century against Samoa in New Plymouth, the All Blacks produced another fine effort to come from 7-17 down to beat Australia in Brisbane and secure the Bledisloe Cup. A fourth match was played against the Wallabies in Hong Kong ahead of the end of year tour. The All Blacks won a tight contest 19-14, and went on to the UK to try for a second Grand Slam in four years. Scotland were swept aside 32-6 before the All Blacks played for the first (and almost certainly only) time on the hallowed turf of Croke Park in Dublin, where Ireland were beaten 22-3, one of the tries scored by Brad Thorn who'd returned from rugby league. A rare midweek match followed against Munster to mark the thirtieth anniversary of the historic 1978 game. Against a team featuring four New Zealanders, including record All Blacks try scorer Doug Howlett, history threatened to repeat itself before Joe Rokocoko scored four minutes from time for a thrilling 18-16 win. That was the closest anyone got to the All Blacks on that tour, with Wales beaten 29-9 the following Saturday, and a challenging year ending on a high note, Mils Muliaina scoring twice in a 32-6 rout of England.

Cory Jane: I got a run in two Test matches and then Mils had come over and I figured I wouldn't get any more. Then the Munster game came up. We knew what had happened the last time the All Blacks had played Munster and we didn't want to let it slip, but we didn't know how big a deal it was going to be for them. The thing that struck me was how quiet it got when guys were kicking goals – 26,000 in the crowd and no one made a sound.

Richard Kahui: It was great. Before the game we did the haka, and then their Kiwi boys, Rua Tipoki, Jeremy Manning, Lifiemi Mafi and Dougie Howlett did a haka back which I thought was awesome. After twenty minutes we had dominance but we hadn't scored the tries. I thought they would come, but they didn't. Then we had a scrum on our five, didn't D up on the blindside and they scored. I love the photo of the winger scoring and the whole crowd going up behind him. It was great to get out of it when Roks [Joe Rokocoko] scored.

Stephen Donald: The night before the Munster game we went to the play about Munster beating the All Blacks in 1978. I don't know if it was great preparation for the game. For a time it was quite conceivable we were going to be part of another play, especially in that second half when things weren't going for us. It was amazing. The place was packed to the rafters and when you kicked at goal you could hear a pin drop. It was quite off-putting. It's something I'll never forget, that and the fact that they gave us the fright of our lives.

There were more dramatics around the haka in the Wales Test, following the All Blacks no show in 2005. This time the Welsh stood and eyeballed the All Blacks at the end of

Joe Rokokoko breaks away from the despairing tackle of Ian Dowling during the clash with Munster at Thomond Park. *InphoPhotography*

the challenge, having vowed not to be the first team to budge. As the crowd roared the two teams stood their ground. The impasse lasted a minute and twenty-three seconds as referee Jonathan Kaplan went between the two captains, first asking, and then demanding that they break off and start the game. In the end it was the All Blacks who stepped away, and they would go on to win handsomely after surviving an early Wales onslaught, but the over-riding memory of the day will be the spine-tingling standoff.

Richard Kahui: There was lots of talk about Wales doing something, but we didn't really expect that [haka stand-off]. They just decided they weren't going to take a backward step. I could see it was a bit of Warren Gatland flowing through their team. I wouldn't expect anything less of him, it's why I enjoyed having him as a coach, he knows how to motivate. Playing at the Millennium Stadium, it's probably my favourite stadium, and the crowd was just screaming, they were so geed up by the standoff, and so were the players. Jonathan Kaplan was running about trying to get everyone to get on with it, but they made their intentions clear, it was a memorable Test, and it was good to win it. It was a great tour, we were only the third All Blacks to win a Grand Slam.

Ali Williams: I was on the end of the haka. When I first started I used to hide at the back, but when we were discussing the new one Derek [Lardelli] spoke about the guys on the edge being there not to protect the younger ones, but the senior guys guarding them. So I liked to stand there. The standoff was brilliant, a lot of fun. It comes back to what the haka is about. You let them walk away before you do, like you win that battle, trying to win one before the game even starts. So Jonathan Kaplan comes up and says, 'OK, that's enough Ali,' and I didn't say anything, didn't move. Then he was trying to get Richie to get going. Richie turned and saw no one else was moving so he stayed

The post-haka stand-off at the Millennium Stadium. *FotoSport*

right there, and so then he tried the Welsh, saying, 'C'mon, c'mon!' and they weren't moving either. It was brilliant. I remember vividly, just standing there, Adam Jones and I eyeballing each other, and no one was taking a backward step. I never much cared how the opposition reacted, but you get a response like that and you're thinking, 'These guys are *up* for it.'

Things proved a lot more difficult in 2009 beginning with a loss to France in Dunedin, an All Black team without Dan Carter or Richie McCaw beaten more decisively than the 27-22 score suggests. A scrambled 14-10 win in Wellington couldn't prevent the Dave Gallaher Trophy heading to France. Carter had ruptured his Achilles playing in France whilst on a 'sabbatical' central to a deal keeping him in New Zealand through to 2011, and was out until late-August. However McCaw, who'd also recommitted, returned to lead the side to the first of four wins over Australia. South Africa was another matter. Coming off a series win over the Lions, the Springboks were all over the All Blacks in 2009, much to the delight of their coach Pieter de Villiers. They scored consecutive wins at Bloemfontein, Durban and, narrowly, in Hamilton, exposing the All Blacks with their kick-and-chase game and forcing errors they turned ruthlessly into points. It forced a major shift in thinking by the All Black coaching staff, who reshuffled their roles for the November tour. After a Tokyo stopover and a seventh straight win over the Wallabies, the All Blacks laboured to wins over Wales 19-12, a rather negative Italy 20-6 at Milan's San Siro, and England 19-6, before igniting in Marseille. With wingers Cory Jane and Sitiveni Sivivatu in sparkling form, the All Blacks crushed the French 39-12, a win that pointed the way ahead, although some of the gloss was taken off in a tour-ending defeat to the Barbarians at Twickenham.

Richie McCaw: There were quite a few senior players who were injured, and missed the two Tests against France and one against Italy [in 2009]. When we got those players back we meandered, thought it was just going to happen. The Springboks had come off a good series against the Lions and were playing pretty effective rugby and getting the results. At one point, especially when we lost at Hamilton, third time in a row by the Boks that year, you start to question yourself . . . are you the right man for the job? Although they say you shouldn't have those sort of thoughts, you really have to think, 'What am I going to do to sort this out?' or, 'Am I the right person?' It forced us at the end of that Tri Nations to really take a look at ourselves.

Jerome Kaino: I had a good year in 2008 in the full All Blacks season but 2009 was a tough year. We got beaten three times by the Springboks and my game in Hamilton against South Africa was probably one of my most disappointing performances. We were out-done physically and that was another crossroad, or a checkpoint, in my career where I had to ask, 'Am I happy to just be here or do I want to take it to the next level?' The team overall that year had to ask questions about themselves, the environment and what we were doing. I asked myself what I needed to do to improve. When you see the seniors asking questions of themselves you naturally do it too and all the guys, Richie, Kevvy, Brad Thorn were all questioning themselves about whether they were giving enough.

Conrad Smith: We had a lot of meetings, there was a leadership group that met for two years leading up to the World Cup. This time the thinking was that World Cups are different, let's confront the fact that we've been awful at winning World Cups, there's something different about them, they're not like Bledisloe Cups, they're not like Tri Nations series. We wanted to be very positive, to face the challenge, to look at the challenge and not be daunted by it.

Richie McCaw: The performance we had in Wellington against the Wallabies [in 2009] was a relief, and showed what we had to do every week, and I guess that's really where the build-up to 2011 really started. The end-of-year tour, culminating in the Marseille Test where we had a hell of a performance and won well, flowed into 2010. We had a bunch of guys who'd been beaten by the Springboks three in a row, and that was a huge motivating factor, it really kept guys on edge, and the performances we had, especially in the first two Tests against the Boks in New Zealand that year, they were huge for us, really built the belief. We started working on making sure we had systems in place to deal with what was going to come at the World Cup. It wasn't all about 2011, you know, it was as case of, 'We have to win today', but at the back of the mind were things that were going to serve us well down the track. Things like dealing with the pressure, having the tools in the box to deal with it when it came.

Cory Jane: We got to grips with how we wanted to play on the back end of that year [2009]. We had a tough Tri Nations, where the kicking came into it, the high balls, and we struggled a bit against South Africa in particular. We played those Tests in Africa, in Bloemfontein and Durban and lost both. I was on the bench for both but never got on. It just wasn't Roks' [Joe Rokocoko] and Siti's [Sitiveni Sivivatu] game to be catching those high balls and they were dropping a few, as everyone did at that time, and I was thinking, 'Any chance I could get out there and catch a couple?' But it didn't happen. I'd played a lot of my rugby at fullback. I knew how to catch a high ball. If you're willing to get up and put your body on the line that makes it easier. At the end of that series, against Australia I started to get a couple of chances, on the wing, and after that I couldn't get off the wing!

Jimmy Cowan: The game had evolved into a lot of kick-chase, and the Boks were very good at it, having halfback Fourie du Preez, a pin-point kicker of the ball, and wings like Bryan Habana who were prepared to chase it like there was no tomorrow. They really got one over us that year. At the same time we had coaches who believed in putting the ball into space, but at that time the plays weren't quite coming off for us, the wee kicks over the top . . . there was space but it was high risk stuff. It was a learning process. We started getting better at it, but at the time they were beating us to the punch. The amount of work guys like Cory, Richard Kahui put into catching those high balls after we'd lost those three Tests, I mean you look at what happened in 2010, 2011, those guys played a huge part in getting us to the World Cup.

Brad Thorn (2003-11, 59 Tests, 60 games): I liked scrumming when I was a six-year-old. It's just my make-up, I enjoy it, just like I enjoy having a wrestle, I enjoy making a tackle, I enjoy physical sorts of things and the scrum really suits me. I guess it's just my personality. There's nothing like it in league, I just enjoy the strength elements. That's something you can in do in rugby where you can really get in there and with a good technique use your strength and weight and really combine with other guys around you for the purpose of hopefully dominating the other team.

Stephen Donald: That Springbok team of 2009 was easily the best rugby team I'd played against. They were so clinical, obviously had built around a big pack that was at the peak of its power with Victor Matfield, Bakkies Botha and co. Pierre Spies was in great form and they were well led by John Smit. The Bloemfontein Test we probably let slip. We were hanging in, hanging in and with 10-15 minutes to go we felt like we were going to run over the top of them, but just as we were right back in it Jacques Fourie picked up a loose pass and scored eighty metres down the track. We ran into them at their very best in Durban a week later.

Cory Jane: We played France on the November tour and all week we talked about getting our game right, because you know how deadly France can be, and also how sloppy they can be. It was a week where everyone knew their roles, had the attitude right and we went out and took them, put something like 40 points on them. Against teams like France, Italy, Argentina, if you can kill the passion early then you're going to dominate the game, but if you don't it's going to be a tough eighty minutes.

Jimmy Cowan: We played Italy at that amazing stadium in Milan [San Siro] but it was frustrating. They were a niggly bunch, we couldn't get any flow going, they killed a lot of ball at the breakdown and the ref let them get away with it. It was Ben Smith's first Test. He dropped the first high ball – look where he is now. We had the captain's run at the stadium in Marseille, and seeing those high fences around the playing area and thinking 'Holy hell.' We'd heard the local fans were a bit nutty. First scrum of the game we went back about two metres at a great rate of knots and I thought, 'This is going to be a long night,' but from that scrum we were a different team. Something clicked and away we went.

As the World Cup came into focus, the All Blacks team began to take shape. Players like Kieran Read, Israel Dagg, Cory Jane and the Franks brothers had come into the side to make a significant impact. June was busy as New Zealand celebrated the 100th anniversary of the first NZ Maori side and hosted Tests against Ireland and Wales, the All Blacks maintaining their winning run against both. They then swept through the Tri Nations without defeat, including a 49-28 win over the Wallabies in Melbourne, but the most memorable match was the final game against the Springboks. The All Blacks had beaten the South Africans twice in New Zealand, helped in no small way by the yellow-carding in Auckland and subsequent ten-week suspension of the Boks' powerhouse lock Bakkies Botha, who'd responded to a jersey tug by Jimmy Cowan by chasing down and head-butting the All Black scrum-half. The All Blacks wanted to complete the reversal of their 2009 sweep by the Boks, but faced a fired-up South Africa team in front of nearly 98,000 fans at Soweto, the biggest crowd ever to watch a Test between the two. The Boks were inspired by the 100th Test appearance of their skipper John Smit, and led 22-14 midway through the second half before the All Blacks staged a tremendous finish. McCaw scored to level at 22-all, then with time almost up, Ma'a Nonu slipped the tackle of Smit and, despite losing a boot in the process, put a jubilant Dagg away for the winner. Dan Carter missed the Sydney Test against Australia, his place filled admirably by Aaron Cruden, the young Manawatu player who a couple of years earlier had beaten testicular cancer. A late Kieran Read try gave the All Blacks a narrow win, but the teams were to meet again in Hong Kong. Carter returned from injury, but with the All Blacks up 24-12, was taken off on the hour as a precaution and replaced by Stephen Donald. It proved to be a nightmare for the affable Waikato man, who started by missing a handy penalty and then, with time up, failed to find touch with a clearing kick, allowing the Wallabies to conjure up an equalising try for winger James O'Connor. O'Connor then nailed a touchline conversion, stranding the All Blacks at fifteen wins, two short of the record. That loss erased any complacency ahead of yet another Grand Slam bid, and once England had been overcome 26-16, it was never in any doubt, as Scotland, Ireland and Wales were seen off. The England Test marked the debut of high-profile league convert Sonny Bill Williams and was the last for Josevata Rokocoko, who since his debut as a twenty-year-old in 2003 had scored forty-six tries, four short of the Howlett record. It had been a highly-successful year with one loss, although it was the loss that stayed in the minds of the players over the summer as World Cup year approached.

Richie McCaw: Experiences like Soweto [in 2010], where we had to come from behind in a game we could easily have lost, but to believe and have a group that could find a way to win . . . that was gold. You look twelve months down the track when you're going to be in those sorts of situations again and know you have that experience in the bank. In Hong Kong, the game was there to be taken and we let it slip, and that was what annoyed me the most, rather than actually losing, it was the manner in which it happened. Having said that, losing that Test planted our feet back on the ground for that northern tour and leading into 2011. If we'd won we might have got carried away with things after getting out of jail a couple of times and might not have felt the need to address one or two things. We'd won the Tri Nations, kept the Bledisloe Cup and did a Grand Slam and if there was a Test to lose, that would be the one to lose because it didn't actually count for anything at that stage, although I look back and wish we hadn't, because we don't like to lose, especially to the Wallabies.

Jerome Kaino: I think 2010 was a good break-out year, I got some consistent rugby off a pretty solid Super Rugby season. We got our game going and as loose forwards Reado, Richie and I connected well. We didn't smash teams in the Tri Nations, but we got tested a lot and that taught us how to grind wins out.

Jimmy Cowan: By those first two Tests against South Africa in 2010 we had a pretty good brand of rugby going and were scoring some good tries. Regarding the Bakkies Botha incident, I didn't realise what had happened. I tried to put a kick through and he got a hand on it, and as he pushed through I held him back by the jersey. I went back, fell on it and tried to get the pass away. It felt like a clash of heads and I carried on, but I could hear all this booing. I looked up on the big screen and thought, 'Cheeky bugger, he got me there.' I didn't think much of it at the time. The guy I remember most from my early days playing against South Africa was AJ Venter, he was a hell of a good player, but next level with the niggle! I learned a bit from him. Later on that winter we played them in Soweto and that was phenomenal. There were close to 100,000 people there. We were under the cosh a bit and had a hell of a comeback to win it.

Cory Jane: That was the game where Ma'a lost his shoe and put Israel away. Playing South Africa over there they were up for it. It was a pretty cool game. It was close and then we fell behind. I remember Ma'a breaking through . . . John Smit it was . . . and sending Izzy away. We did our review on the Monday. Izzy, when he scored put his arm out and nearly went over the dead-ball line and Steve Hansen said, 'Great win, but Izzy, if you ever dive like that again you're out of the team.' Izzy turned to me and was like, 'It bloody won us the Test match, what's he talking about?' I jokingly said, 'Tell him, then,' but he wouldn't. It was a great way to finish. It showed we were figuring out how to win games right at the end and developing our mental toughness. The mental side of it really started to come in among the group. The coaches put pressure on us in training to try and replicate what could happen in game situations. Mental toughness training is a big part of rugby now, almost as much as doing your weights and your speed training. It brought us back in games that All Black teams in the past would have lost, and it helped us gain a bit of dominance in the years that followed.

Richard Kahui: I missed all of 2009, came back in 2010 and played the worst rugby I'd ever played. I spent a game or two trying not to get the ball. I talked a lot to Dave Galbraith [sports psychologist] and Gilbert Enoka [All Blacks assistant manager and mental skills coach] just to try and sort out my head. I thought there was no way I was going to make the All Blacks, but they decided to pick me. I didn't feel I deserved it. I sat down with Smithy and we went over a few things, along with Bert [Enoka]. Smithy's got the power to make you feel like the greatest player on Earth, and the ability to then bring you back to Earth. That conversation is something I'll never forget, it was career-changing. I still felt like more of a centre than a wing. I came off the bench against Wales in Dunedin and played on the wing, scored a try and felt good for the first time in a long time. Then I did my shoulder again playing against South Africa. I made a run down the touchline and Jacque Fourie tackled me and as I went down my arm slipped up. It didn't feel too bad at the time but I needed an operation and that's when I thought my All Black career would be finished. The good thing about the All Blacks is they kept the lines of communication open, kept saying they felt I was good enough, which was great, but deep down I thought it was over. Guys like Israel Dagg and Sonny Bill Williams were coming in.

Stephen Donald: Throughout my career I was backup to DC, but in 2010 everything had been flowing pretty well. I felt I'd been playing well in the ITM Cup and I was looking forward to expressing myself a bit more in the All Blacks' environment. Then

Hong Kong happened. It rankles with me to this day. I missed a kick that would have buried the game . . . fifteen metres in from touch around about the twenty-two. If I got that then everything else would have been a non-issue. What followed was pretty tough. I tried to block myself off from a lot of it but once we got back there were always reminders of it, one way or another whether it was directed at me across the street or sly remarks. Then, when Super Rugby started, whenever we weren't playing at Waikato Stadium it was pretty much open season from the crowd. You try to get used to it. It was probably one of the reasons I signed with Bath. I wanted to get out of the country and play some footy without always being abused over that one game.

Cory Jane: They can be tough games. It was the fourth game of the Bledisloe Cup series, we had the Cup, and games like that can be hard to get up for. We were into it, got in front and then James O'Connor scored right at the end and bloody converted it. It was frustrating. I guess it was the kick in the bum we needed. It made us realise that if we're not on our game, if we let key moments slip, we could be beaten.

Jimmy Cowan: It's never nice losing to the old foe from across the ditch. The way they carried on after they kicked that goal, you could see what it meant to them, but the way they acted . . . what Quade [Cooper] did to Richie – cheap shots, sledging. We didn't forget it.

No story of 2011 could fail to note the catastrophic events of 22 February when a massive earthquake hit Canterbury, claiming 185 lives and causing widespread destruction. It meant there would be no World Cup matches in rugby-mad Christchurch as the home stadium was rendered unsafe and unplayable. The Crusaders had to travel far and wide to fulfil their Super Rugby commitments. Care was taken to allow players time with their family, affecting the selection of All Black teams ahead of the World Cup. A Test against Fiji started the build-up, the last to be played at the famous old Carisbrook ground before the switch to a state of the art covered stadium.

A condensed Tri Nations followed and the All Blacks made the home games their priority. A below-strength Springboks were hammered 40-7 in Wellington, and a full-strength Wallaby side fared little better in Auckland. With the Crusaders having been to South Africa twice, and England once during Super Rugby, most of the Canterbury contingent were left out of the trip to Port Elizabeth, where in their first Test at the eastern city in forty-one years, the All Blacks kept the Boks tryless, but still lost 15-5. A much stronger combination took the field in Brisbane for the championship decider, but with Radike Samo scoring a spectacular try the Wallabies raced to a 20-3 half-time lead, and while the All Blacks fought back to level at 20-all, a late Kurtley Beale try gave Australia the win and the title.

To compound things, Kieran Read, a key weapon in the All Black arsenal, suffered an ankle injury, and there was an escalation of a feud between Richie McCaw and Wallaby fly-half Quade Cooper. Having given McCaw a shove and a verbal spray at the end of the Hong Kong game the previous year, Cooper appeared to knee McCaw in the head in Brisbane, guaranteeing a hostile welcome come World Cup time. The All Blacks would go into the World Cup on the back of two straight defeats.

Richie McCaw: I got back in training at the start of the year and ended up with a stress fracture in my foot. Now, you leave them and hope they come right, or you put a screw in them. Seeing as it was a World Cup year we decided to put a screw in. Having metalwork in your foot can cause stresses elsewhere which is why I was a bit fits and starts at the beginning of the year, but leading into the tournament it was fine.

Jerome Kaino: I still didn't feel like I was a safe bet to make that World Cup squad. In the 2011 season I got a lot of game time without Richie and Reado; Richie had head knock problems and Reado had a high ankle sprain in Brisbane. Leading up to, and in the early stages of the World Cup, I had a lot of games without them and had to initiate a lot of play. When they came back it felt natural.

Conrad Smith: We really targeted those two home Tests in 2011 against South Africa and Australia, we wanted to win them well because we knew they were coming back to the World Cup and if we could bury them at home then they'd have that burning in the back of their mind. There was a sense of fear about that Australian side, like, 'These guys could actually be better than us' . . . and All Blacks don't like admitting that. We had that feeling about Australia that they were slick, that their form meant we had to be on top of our game.

Kieran Read: It was our first chance to get the Eden Park crowd right behind us, we wanted to stamp our mark on it, say to these guys, 'If you're going to be coming back here later in the year it's going to be just as hard.'

Cory Jane scores against South Africa in Wellington. *InphoPhotography*

The players celebrate their victory over the Wallabies at Eden Park. *InphoPhotography*

Richard Kahui: They made it clear they weren't going to take guys like Richie and Dan to Port Elizabeth, but for guys like me, I was really desperate for that Test. Before the internationals I'd been at a Sevens camp with Titch [Sir Gordon Tietjens], it was really muddy. I slipped and did a hamstring. I'd never had a hammy before and that put me out for six or seven weeks – all of the home Tests ahead of the World Cup. So there was Port Elizabeth and Brisbane to put some pressure on, to earn a spot in the World Cup. In Port Elizabeth we lacked a bit of leadership, missed the calming influence of Richie and Dan, but I thought there was a lot of good stuff there as well.

The morning after the Port Elizabeth Test they named the team for the World Cup, and had to cut two guys. They were going to call you in your room before the meeting and let you know, before they announced the team, and unfortunately, it was Liam Messam and Hosea Gear who were cut, and it was a horrible feeling. We all got on the same plane and flew to Sydney. I can only imagine what it must have been like for them, to have to go home while we went up to Brisbane. Liam being a good mate of mine, I felt awful for him, still do. It didn't feel like losing in Australia was a bad thing for us just before the World Cup. It was a confidence boost for Australia, but we got more out of the loss than they got out of the win. It made us realise they were good enough to beat us. Before that we hadn't seen them as dangerous. They'd come over to Eden Park in the Tri Nations, talking it up that they were going to give it to us, and the boys dominated them. But when we lost in Brisbane they earned a bit more respect, flipped a little switch about what we were going to need to do. It was good for us.

Jimmy Cowan: We had that game in Port Elizabeth, I felt I was playing pretty well, and then they went and changed the whole team around for Brisbane. They were obviously trying to sort things out ahead of the World Cup but it did make it hard to get some flow into your game. Even though we lost in Port Elizabeth and Brisbane, they were hiccups, but they helped shape us going into the World Cup. We knew we had a good team.

Richie McCaw: Unfortunately, we lost away in South Africa and then we went to Brisbane and it was annoying to lose there, too. We could have had the Tri Nations in the cabinet as well, but to go there and lose with pretty much a full-strength team was hugely disappointing. When we played Australia at the World Cup that loss was pretty fresh in the memory. The thing that pleased me was that they started the match with everything they had. It was their big test, to beat the All Blacks and win the Tri Nations. We were in a hole at 20-3 down and it would have been easy to have let it get away on us, but we clawed our way back to 20-all. I had a feeling we were right on the verge of nailing the game, before a piece of brilliance from Will Genia took it away. That was all there was in it. You have to take the positives out of things like that, and if I had a choice between the Tri Nations and the World Cup I know which one I'd take.

As the World Cup finally kicked off, the All Blacks had to scrap for their opening night 41-10 win over Tonga. The second game, against Japan, was preceded by emotional scenes as tributes were paid to the victims of both the Christchurch earthquake and the tsunami in northern Japan, which haf occurred barely a fortnight apart. When Japan's most capped player, Hirotoki Onozawa, scored there was a great cheer, but the All Blacks, with Richard Kahui and Sonny Bill Williams scoring twice, won 83-7.

A day later, roared on by most of the 60,000 at Eden Park, Ireland upset the Wallabies. That put the Australians on collision course for a semi-final against the host nation.

New Zealand hit top gear in the pool decider against France, Dan Carter in commanding form as the All Blacks won 37-17, although even more memorable was a poignant post-game presentation of a commemorative cap to Richie McCaw to mark his 100th Test, by an ailing Jock Hobbs, the former All Blacks captain and NZRU chairman, who since playing a lead role in securing the tournament had been ravaged by leukaemia.

Then, at training before the final pool match against Canada, All Blacks rugby fans' worst nightmare occurred as Carter ripped a groin muscle, sending New Zealand into a state of shock. The trepidation levels rose further when it was revealed Richie McCaw was nursing a painful foot injury. Adding to the drama, an outbreak of stir craziness saw Cory Jane and Israel Dagg busted over a boozy night out, publicly berated by manager Darren Shand, and having to explain themselves to their team-mates. Colin Slade took over from Carter and Aaron Cruden was called into the squad, only for Slade to also suffer a tournament-ending injury in the quarter-final win over Argentina. For many, it looked as if the wheels were coming off another All Black World Cup campaign.

With the management not wanting to burden Cruden with too much responsibility, the man who really stepped up to steady the listing ship was halfback Piri Weepu, who became both general and goal-kicker, landing seven penalty goals against the Pumas. Dagg missed the quarter-final against the Pumas because of injury, allowing Mils Muiliana to play his 100th Test, the All Blacks walking off to learn they would be playing Australia in the semi-finals. The Wallabies had earlier in the day beaten the Springboks in a match controversially refereed by New Zealander Bryce Lawrence.

Australia had won their two previous World Cup encounters against New Zealand and were the reigning Tri Nations champions. The tension before the semi-final was palpable, losing to Australia seen by New Zealand fans as the worst possible scenario. After Quade Cooper, to the delight of the crowd, put the opening kick-off into touch on the full, the All Blacks took complete control, playing their best rugby of the tournament en route to a decisive 20-6 victory. There was one try, a thing of beauty laid on for Ma'a Nonu by Dagg, who atoned for his social misdemeanour with a brilliant performance. The only time Australia really threatened was when wing Digby Ioane made a searing break – only to be abruptly halted by Jerome Kaino.

Against all expectation, France made it through to the final, despite losing pool games to the All Blacks and, astonishingly, to Tonga. Their progress had been helped by the controversial red carding of Wales skipper Sam Warburton in the semi-final. They were at odds with their coach Marc Lievremont and under a barrage of fire from the French media. Tailor-made for them, some would say!

In front of a nervous crowd the All Blacks took an early lead when Tony Woodcock scored from a lineout move, but with Piri Weepu having strained a muscle in the warm-up, the All Blacks weren't landing their goals. Then Cruden went down in a heap, and on came Stephen Donald, who had been called in from a white-baiting expedition on the Waikato River following Slade's injury. Donald kicked a penalty goal from near halfway which proved crucial as the French stormed back with a try by their outstanding skipper Thierry Dusautoir. The rest of the match was pure trench warfare, and with France not able to cash in on a penalty and dropped goal attempts, the All Blacks held on to win, marshalled superbly by McCaw, playing at the height of his powers despite a broken bone in his foot. Craig Joubert's final whistle exorcised twenty-four years of frustration, disappointment and recrimination, and a country went wild with celebration before slumping back in its collective armchair, exhausted. George Gregan's 'four more years' took on a whole new meaning.

Conrad Smith: We had this amazing stretch of weather leading up to the tournament and everyone was in a real party atmosphere. The World Cup that everyone had talked about for so long had finally arrived. It was an amazing time to be part of the team.

Richie McCaw: It wasn't until the Tongans showed up and they showed the scenes on the news of what it was like at the airport with thousands of people turning out to meet them, I was like, 'Holy Smoke, if this is what it's going to be like it's going to be a hell of a six weeks.'

Conrad Smith: From the start we said, 'This is going to be fun, we need to enjoy this, and not try to hide from it.' When you try and hide away from it that's when the lingering doubts can start to come at you during a game and that's what we didn't want. We based ourselves in town, when the partying was going on right outside . . . some nights you couldn't sleep because of it. Sure there was pressure and there were times I remember thinking, 'Man we've gotta win this,' but it never got too overwhelming.

Jerome Kaino: It was exciting. I didn't feel the pressure so much because I hadn't been involved in earlier Cup campaigns but you could feel within that team there was an expectation to perform. It was in our favour that we were in our own environment, we were at home and where we were training and playing was familiar to us. We took that as a comfort. We knew anyone who came to play New Zealand was going to bring everything and the kitchen sink. The focus wasn't to win it, it was to perform each week and hopefully build and get to the knockout stages where we would have everything in place to perform.

Jimmy Cowan: I didn't play all that well against Tonga; we'd come up with a new dimension to our game and I didn't adjust to it. Andy Ellis got the next start against Japan and played extremely well, then Piri played against France and he played really well. Piri went up another gear when Dan was injured. Ted said we all had to give another per cent to make up for Dan not being there, but Piri grew two or three per cent, he really carried the nation with his goal-kicking. What he did in the quarter and semis was outstanding. He is a cool guy. It was his time.

Conrad Smith: I remember thinking when Ireland beat Australia, 'Wow this is going to change things a bit.' It was a reminder to everyone, to the public, that a World Cup is designed for these Northern Hemisphere sides . . . they can knock one of us over in these one-off games, even if they never beat us again. By that stage you're really into it, you're ready to play anyone and those sort of results showed we weren't going to be playing any easy games.

Richie McCaw: The French made the comment that they weren't going to beat New Zealand twice in New Zealand, so if they were going to win one it might as well be the final. And they were saying in the changing room after our qualifying game, 'We'll see you in the final.' At one point I remember thinking, 'It wouldn't surprise me.' But then they lost to Tonga the next week.

Cory Jane: At the World Cup we had groups within the team with a name. The outside backs were the Bomb Squad. That went back to the game against Wales in Cardiff 2009, when they kept putting up bombs and Zac [Guildford] and I kept defusing them. Part of our job was to catch the high ball, and if we did 100 per cent at that, we were going to be on the front foot, annoying the other team because they weren't getting those 50-50s.

Richie McCaw: The foot had got a bit sore after the French game. I thought it improved but it wasn't quite right, and we thought if it was going to get worse we'd leave it to the play-offs and not a game we expected to win. So I decided not to play against Canada, DC was named as captain and did the press conference, and bugger me, by that evening he was out too. I remember thinking, 'We're going to have to do this the hard way. Things that we didn't expect are going to happen and that probably won't be the only thing, there'll be others.' I wasn't wrong!

Dan Carter: I knew it was serious because of the pain and because it was so unusual. I've kicked thousands of balls, ever since I was a young fellow but I've never had this happen. After kicking a ball it felt like my groin had popped and I hit the ground in agony. I was just going through my usual routine. I was actually having a shorter session than usual. I normally kick a good fifteen to twenty balls at a captain's run but I was only having four that time around and it was my fourth kick. I honestly didn't know what happened.

Wayne Smith: He said to me after training, 'I'll just have four shots at goal . . .' He was captain for that game, against Canada, and it was going to be a massive occasion for him, something he'd earned and was really proud of. First kick went over, but he didn't hit it very well . . . next kick similar . . . next kick similar . . . and then his last kick . . .

Conrad Smith: I heard him scream and looked around . . . and he just kept rolling around on the ground. Wayne Smith's a man who finds it hard to hide his emotions, and his head had dropped, he looked worried.

Wayne Smith: I felt sick in the stomach . . . we had to get him out of there to reduce the impact it had on the team.

Richie McCaw: I was so gutted for him, he'd put so much effort into being ready to play in that tournament, and to see him gone like that, I didn't know what to say to the guy.

Conrad Smith: Ted pulled us into the changing rooms. It was a masterstroke. He pulled everyone in, because you look at the effect it could have on some of the young guys, and he said, 'We're going to deal with this.'

Graham Henry: I just said, 'Guys, we've had a major; the unexpected has happened but we are going to handle this.'

Jerome Kaino: That was one of the darkest weeks for us. The coaches had planned for 'What if?' situations and it happened. When Dan went down I didn't think it was too bad, just a little niggle then Ted took us into the changing room and said how bad it was. The boys rallied, we tried to put it behind us and Dan, although he was hobbling, was still amongst the group helping out with how we could do things. We still had his voice but it was tough knowing we had performed so well with Dan in the No.10 jersey and he gave us comfort when he was there to lead us but we didn't expect that. To Sladey's credit and Crudes', the boys just took charge.

Richie McCaw: You realise that every team is going to have their big day at some point and you have to make sure, especially when it comes to knockout rugby, there'll be a moment when it comes down to one or two decisions, one or two moments will be the difference between you going home and winning the thing.

Cory Jane: It wasn't good when Izzy and I had that night out. Part of it was not understanding the scrutiny we were going to be under at the World Cup, if you just go out for a night we didn't expect it was going to blow up that bad. I woke up on game day [Argentina] and it was in the paper and I thought, 'Oh my God,' and it was Milsy's 100th game. I felt like we'd done something stupid to take the limelight off him. We spoke to the team after the game. I apologised for letting the team down, making a bad decision. That was tough, but the boys acknowledged it, they knew it was a stupid thing to do but they said we had a job to do to win the World Cup and we needed everybody on board. Argentina was a refocus game for me . . . and I like playing big games, I enjoy a bit of pressure. I knew I had to deliver. Izzy got his chance the next week.

Richie McCaw: It was only towards the end of the tournament that my foot started to get niggly. But I thought, 'I'm just going to play.' I looked at poor old DC and he couldn't play and I thought, 'I'll just put up with it.' Yeah it was sore, but adrenaline's a great painkiller. If you're ever going to play with a bit of pain then a World Cup is the time you get out and do it. Everyone plays with a bit of pain at times. If it had got to the point where I couldn't have done my job properly I wouldn't have played. I couldn't train because I wanted to be as fit as I could for the games. Sometimes you've got to just grit your teeth, but that's what playing for the All Blacks is all about – although I'd rather not have had the pain.

Graham Henry: I looked at his foot and said, 'Hell, Rich, that bloody foot looks swollen mate, really swollen.' 'Yeah, Ted, it is.' His ability to lead and be inspirational to that group of people was immense. And because he couldn't even train, he got finer on the detail. He was outstanding, superb.

Jerome Kaino: I didn't realise how bad Richie's foot was. He was saying, 'I'm fine.' He hopped out of a few drills he didn't need to do. The way he performed I thought there was nothing wrong with his foot. But when you got into the changing room after the game there were a couple of packs of ice on it. It wasn't until the end of the tournament when a few people started talking about it, and the doctor said if it hadn't been a World Cup he wouldn't have been playing that we all realised how serious it was. He never spoke about his injury. He didn't want to affect the team.

Stephen Donald: In the quarter-final Colin Slade had gone down but I hadn't heard anything from the camp. I hadn't heard from anyone since Ted had called to say I wasn't in the World Cup squad. I had no right to think they were going to call me in. So I was out whitebaiting. I thought they would have been happy to have Piri covering ten.

Richie McCaw: We had plans if we needed a dropped goal, plans if things didn't go our way. We planned for the worst . . . and then you'd always have something to go to. Perhaps in '07 we didn't grasp that. We thought we did but we didn't quite grasp what it was going to be like when it really got tough.

Conrad Smith: When those two [Carter and Slade] went down, it became pretty lonely.

Aaron [Cruden] was coming into first five by that stage and we weren't going to burden him with a lot of the strategy.

Richie McCaw: From a team point of view we just had to say, 'We're not going to use any of this as an excuse, we just get on with it, every team has challenges, it's who deals with them the best will come through to win this thing.' We couldn't show any disappointment or let our heads drop.

Jerome Kaino: We didn't know the result of the Springboks-Australia quarter-final. We'd been preparing for our quarter against Argentina. At the end of our game Ted told us we were playing Australia in the semi-final. The first person who threw his jersey up in the air was Brad Thorn, he was yaa-hooing and everyone was happy. But I was like, 'Sheesh guys, I think I would prefer South Africa to Australia,' because the Aussies were building and playing well. But I think the leaders knew that it wouldn't take much for us to get up against Australia.

Conrad Smith: When I first started playing Australia we had a good interaction with the players and then, for whatever reason, it got a bit strained. I suppose particular individuals, like Richie's spat with Quade Cooper added to things. There was a lot of that behind the scenes.

Richie McCaw: The reason we played Australia was that they'd been tipped up by Ireland. In 2007 we'd been thinking about who we might play, if someone beat someone else and so on. The thing I learned from that is who cares who you play, you have to play the best teams eventually, be it in a quarter, a semi or a final, and you have to win all three, so whoever it is, just bring it on. We knew we were going to play Australia at some stage, it might as well be now. Because of what had happened in Brisbane the boys were right on edge and it was probably one of the best-prepared All Black teams I'd ever been involved in.

Jerome Kaino: That week there was a lot of tension and the guys were really focused. Usually the guys hop on the bus to go to the game quite early, and are relaxed, but the guys stayed in the hotel and were pacing back and forth.

Richard Kahui: When it got to the semi-final it felt like a really cold breeze coming through the hotel. It wasn't that people were scared but there was an edginess. I never had any doubts we were going to win because of the way we'd prepared. Everything was aimed towards that semi-final and when we got there, we ran out and I felt like I was running out with supermen. When Quade kicked that first ball out on the full, I knew it was going to be a long game for the Aussies.

Conrad Smith: There was this fear in the week leading up, like some of the plays that we'd come up with, 'Are they going to work?' Added to that you had an Australian team that had played so well and had beaten us the last time we'd played, and they were the last team we'd have wanted to lose to at that tournament. If anyone was going to spoil the party that was happening around the World Cup . . . it was almost too horrible to think of.

Richie McCaw: I remember waking up in the morning and thinking, 'World Cup semi-final, is there anything more we could have done to get ready?' And it was, 'No, we're ready.'

Conrad Smith: They kicked off, put it out on the full, scrum on halfway, and then Piri [Weepu], this move we'd practiced, put it right in the corner. Suddenly we're five metres out, the crowd was so loud, and even then . . . there was only a minute or two on the clock, but everything was working out, the feeling, the buzz. I mean we were *up* for that game. I remember them attacking, wave after wave, and we were getting up, fifteen guys up on their feet almost fighting each other over who was going to make the tackle . . . that's when you know you're playing really well. We were like men possessed, it was great to be part of.

Jerome Kaino: I thought they set the tone early on in the game and the important thing was not to go after their threats individually but to go as a pack and I thought our breakdown was immense.

Cory Jane: That Australia game was like the perfect game . . . not as in scoring five tries, but in that everything they threw at us we had an answer for and one-upped them. When we found out we were playing Aussie it was almost like a final to us. Israel was playing unreal,

Israel Dagg escapes the clutches of Quade Cooper before throwing a wonder pass inside to Ma'a Nonu to score. *FotoSport*

Kahui was a freak on the football field, he could do everything, anywhere on the field, and I tried to do my job and help us win, so we had a pretty tight back three in that World Cup.

Aaron Cruden (2010-15, 37 Tests, 37 games): You try and think about your role. That's the great thing with the All Blacks, everyone does their job and everything else falls into place. I put my head down and wanted to be really clear with what I wanted to do out there on the paddock and I think it worked pretty well. I got a bit of traffic running down my channel but I think the more you're involved in the game the more you're able to grow your confidence. I wanted to be effective in my decision-making and tackling and I was pleased with how I played.

Jerome Kaino: I didn't plan for the Digby Ioane tackle to happen that way. I was lucky he got slowed down by a couple of attempts from Kevvy and Izzy [Israel Dagg] but when I grabbed him I thought he was going to take me over the tryline so I put my foot down and the brake happened and I took him back. It wasn't planned or anything, just pure circumstance. As All Blacks we talk about 'No one crosses our line' and we do whatever it takes for them to go backwards – and that happened. Brad Thorn was always a big voice on the field and he said, 'Right! No one's crossing our line today boys.' And we grew. I think it lifted the team.

Richard Kahui: I didn't have to do much, but Cory Jane was amazing, Izzy Dagg was amazing, I could just stand out there watching these gold jumpers trying to bend or break our line and getting absolutely smashed backwards, time and time again. About sixty-five minutes was when I saw them break. They made a small break, Owen Franks tackled Pat McCabe and Piri pinched the ball, won a penalty and kicked the goal. And then the next scrum, our guys . . . I remember Jerome just getting up screaming, it was the first time in my whole career I saw a team broken. They had no answers. It was only 20-6 but it would have been the same feeling if it was 60. We hadn't had too many high testers so far and hadn't really dropped any, but they just kicked to CJ on the wrong day. He was something else. We'd done so much practice on the high balls because we knew if we played South Africa that's how they would come at us, so after every training we'd do twenty minutes of fielding high balls. We'd have bets, do it for drinks, for dinner. We'd have to catch it above our head, catch it with one arm, and so when it got to the game it was made to look easier, CJ was the best in the world at it. You'd think that after half time they might have changed tack, but they never did.

Richie McCaw: The intensity was the best it had been, and we nailed it. We were so on the job we weren't going to let it slip. At the end of that game it was like, 'That should be it . . . we're going to have to do it again.'

Conrad Smith: It's a tough thing to do, back-up a performance like that with another one, which we knew we had to do against a French team which, in a lot of ways, motivation-wise, had it all running for them.

Cory Jane: The week was difficult, we were tired, it was the end of our season, France were in the middle of theirs, and I kept saying to myself, 'C'mon Cory one more game, if we win it we'll be remembered forever.'

Stephen Donald: I was with a mate down the Waikato River all day. I got down there about 5.00 in the morning. My mate was all pumped up that I might get the call-up because there had been more injuries. He was on a stand across the river from me listening to the radio. He kept calling to see if I had heard anything. It was only later when we got into the area with better reception that I could see a few missed calls. It was actually Milsy [Muliaina] who got a hold of me which was pretty noble of him given that he had been ruled out, he said, 'You'd better get a hold of Ted, he wants to speak to you.'

Richie McCaw: The first time I remember watching the All Blacks on TV was the 1987 World Cup. Mum always tells the story I was outside, doing the haka, and only watched bits of it, and I remember pretending to be John Kirwan scoring that try and here I was, twenty-four years later, same place, playing the same game, same team . . . sometimes you just have to pinch yourself and realise how lucky you are.

Stephen Donald: When I walked into the camp I felt it was the most relaxed environment I'd ever been in as far as the All Blacks go. I'm not sure whether that was because of the state of mind I was in, but it was a great environment to walk into. Obviously there was some training and we had a few meetings where Gilbert Enoka talked about dealing with things that go wrong, but there was also a lot of downtime. By that stage they were nursing a lot of bodies. There was the feeling that with all the hype and excitement around town that we should just embrace it and enjoy it.

Jerome Kaino: I was happy for Beaver [Donald] when he got the call. We grew up together and I was pleased he would have the chance to make up for his disappointment from the year before. And I knew he would slot in well if he got a chance but I never imagined he would play the part he did.

Richie McCaw: We went out to do some lineouts at about three o'clock and already there were thousands of people around the hotel. I thought, 'Wow!' When we went to get on the bus to go to the game the whole street was chocka, I thought, 'I hope when we come back they've all got a smile on their face.'

Conrad Smith: It was all black, a massive amount of support, and I was lapping it up. It was special; Eden Park was a cauldron and it gave as a sense that it was just meant to be.

Richie McCaw: I tried not to get caught up in all the emotion . . . the one game that if you ever wanted to play in for the All Blacks that would be the one. The French had snuck through really, and I felt they still had a big one left in them, that's what made me nervous. You look through their forward pack, they were all good players, experienced guys and they knew what big Tests were all about.

Jerome Kaino: We knew something was going on within their environment between the coaches and the players but Richie said it was the World Cup final and they would bring something. The intensity they brought to that final was crazy. You see their performances in 1999 and 2007 where everything they did stuck and it seemed like that in the final. Every mistake we made they would pounce on it. It was one of the toughest games I ever played in in terms of the intensity. Things we had planned for didn't work out as a result of the pressure the French brought.

Richie McCaw: We didn't train too much early in the week. Ted had to give guys space to get their feet back on the ground. A lot of energy had gone into the previous game and there was no point trying to overtrain. The excitement of the final would take care of our energy levels, but we didn't want guys too much on edge. We needed to just build nicely, although not having done it before we didn't really know what the answer to that was. I think we did it as best we could but looking back now we didn't quite have the edge we'd had the week before.

Conrad Smith: I remember the anthem, almost choking up, thinking, 'This is massive, this is the day we've waited for.' We weren't getting the points we should have got early in the game, and they were hanging in there and you could see them get a lot of belief out of that. There were a few of us looking at each other thinking, 'Yeah this is what we've prepared for.'

Cory Jane: We knew that if we killed their passion we could win the game, and maybe if Piri had kicked a few of those goals we could have been up by as much as 13 or 14-0 at half-time and that would have been it. But we missed a couple, they stayed in it . . . and then the thirty minutes after half-time, honestly I thought we were going to lose. They just kept putting pressure on us, more and more pressure, we were going quiet, making mistakes, doing stupid stuff we'd never done before. A few of the boys were arguing with each other, guys were freezing, not saying the calls. But the last ten minutes, after they missed a kick, we started getting some momentum back, started putting some pressure on them. I knew in that last ten minutes we'd won the World Cup. We'd withheld the onslaught for thirty minutes and we hadn't buckled.

Richard Kahui: The game was much more difficult than it should have been. France played as good as they could possibly have played, but if Piri hadn't pulled his abductor in the warm-up, if he'd been able to land three of those kicks in the first half, we'd have been up by 14 at half-time we might have run away with it. Instead they scored and it turned into a grind.

Ali Williams: It wasn't pretty at times, and I'd say it wasn't necessarily the most enjoyable time of my life. There was a lot of stress, a lot of do-or-die moments.

You start thinking, 'What's Ted going to be remembered for, or Richie? What are we going to be remembered for, because in New Zealand now you only get remembered if you win a World Cup.' The pressure was huge, you couldn't enjoy it as much as the previous ones, and it was never going to be easy. It was perfect how it finished and the result was brilliant. The score, 8-7, reiterated how tough it was, it almost tamed the supporters as well, made them realise how hard it is to win a World Cup, made them respect the victory a bit more. When Andrew Hore and I came on it was like, 'C'mon buddy let's go and win this thing.' We'd done so much work we had to believe it was never going to go any other way.

It's one of those things you can appreciate more and more as you look back. At the time it was just about getting the job done and it wasn't about the accolades, or the trophy, it was about knowing you hadn't failed the jersey. At the end it was more about relief, and not so much about joy. We had such a huge array of characters and cultures in that team, and for us to come together with that ultimate desire to create a legacy on and off the field, it was pretty special.

Stephen Donald: I didn't know whether I was going to get on to the field or not. You don't think about injuries to other players so I certainly hadn't got my head around the thought of going out there for fifty minutes. I joked with Kaks [Richard Kahui] during the week and told him if I didn't get on with a few minutes to go he had to pull a hammy so I could get out there, and that was about the only thought I'd given it. I mean I was up to speed with everything so I was pretty relaxed. Obviously they had my size for the jersey, I guess I was probably carrying a bit more weight than normal because it was pretty tight!

Jerome Kaino: We practiced our lineout move in the week before the final. But we didn't do it out in the open. We trusted that we were at home and there wouldn't be too many spies. I don't think we did it on the field too many times, it was mainly in the gym. It came down to Steve [Hansen] and Kieran, he was our lineout master. They had studied that everywhere the French are, they always put two pods up so they said if I could step forward in front of their back pod and get the ball, and open the middle, then Woody [Tony Woodcock] would go right through. We thought he would get stopped because we had a plan after that but we didn't think the Red Sea would open as much as it did. When we practised it our timing was always off and Woody would say, 'They'll see me coming and they'll block it,' but Shag [Hansen] said, 'Just trust me, it will work if they get up. We've just got to make them jump.' And it did work, just like clockwork.

Richie McCaw: When we got to half-time we realised we could have been ahead more, but I thought, 'If we keep playing this way we'll create opportunities and we'll get the rewards.'

Stephen Donald: They told me at half-time, 'You're goal-kicking now.' I guess I had a wee chip on my shoulder about what had happened in Hong Kong and so when I got the opportunity to have a shot at goal, that was driving it a bit too. I wanted to make a point. I always aim just inside the right-hand upright. I don't curve it, it just goes naturally a metre to the left. So once I whacked it I had a quick look up, saw it was inside the upright and charged back like an idiot. It wasn't until later that night when I was having a beer with Mick Byrne that he told me the kick had actually taken off the other way, a fade which is not normally my thing. I'll just put it down to those shoddy balls they were using in the World Cup.

Tony Woodcock slides over to score in the final. *InphoPhotography*

Jerome Kaino: I thought it was going to miss but when he turned I had a look and the flags went up. I was so happy for him. It shows that the All Black environment does things for people.

Richie McCaw: He kicked it and it looked like it was going straight at the upright. He'd turned around and taken off back, run past me and I thought, 'Gee, he's certain it's going over.' As the game wore on, especially in the second half when they scored, all of a sudden you could see the belief in their eyes, that they could win it. Conversely, we started to think about making the mistakes that could cost us, and we started to take the conservative options, which is why it became a bit of an arm wrestle for the last twenty minutes. Neither side wanted to be the one to make the mistake so a lot of the game was played around the halfway mark.

Richard Kahui: I was happy for Beaver to be there. I'd always said to him that he'd kick the winning dropped goal in the World Cup, and told him to stay fit, something will happen. At the time it felt like just another kick in a way, but it turned out to be a big moment in the game. We made the decision to hang onto the ball, but near the end I was wide out on the wing, calling for a kick because there was masses of space, there was no one there defending they were all trying to get that ruck ball out, so it could have been a spectacular ending . . . I guess it was spectacular enough as it was.

Stephen Donald: When France scored the try to make it 8-7 it would have been easy to really hit the panic button, but there was the sense of calmness coming from Richie and the rest of the leaders that we weren't going to let bad things happen. I guess that came from all the preparation that had gone in, being prepared for any sort of situation.

Richie McCaw: We were under pressure because we were only leading by one point, but I kept thinking, 'They're under even more pressure because they're behind, they've got to score and the guy who's going to line-up the shots for them is going to feel it.' They missed a couple of shots and maybe that's the bit of luck you need, but then we'd missed a few in the first half. It's who deals with the pressure the best. My attitude was to be the guy who dealt with it the best.

Kieran Read: Definitely I can say that was the hardest game I'd played in my life.

Jerome Kaino: Thierry Dusautoir is an amazing man and I get along well with him off the field. I respected him as a player and the way he rallied his troops through the World Cup and to get that performance in the final was amazing. He led from the front, he always performed against the All Blacks. I hold him in the highest regard. He was uncompromising.

Richie McCaw: The big thing is to be calm, first of all me be calm, I had Conrad, and Andrew Hore was brilliant out there, Andy Ellis was brilliant as well, really calm. We didn't have the ball for a bit and Andy was great at directing the forwards around, staying onside, just leaving the ball. Having those guys, everyone else could keep doing their job. We had to defend and keep them outside of a dropped goal range, and we thought we'd get the ball back at some point. We had to keep thinking of the process, not what might happen at the end, it was what you have got to do right now that mattered. We got a penalty and put it out and then we had to win the lineout, and if there was ever a lineout in four years you wanted to win it was that one! Thorny got up and won it, we held it and got a penalty, and I thought, 'Jeepers let's not make any cock-ups, just get it out,' and Andy booted it out.

Stephen Donald: We would have loved to have scored tries. But I think it was something more to be proud of to be just tackling, tackling and getting up again and tackling. You knew there was always going to be somebody on your inside, and the fact we were able to do that made it even more special. We tried to get down their end but they just kept coming back at us. They were going from side to side which probably helped us defend them a bit.

Richie McCaw: My first emotion was, 'Thank Christ for that, it's all over.' Just huge relief thinking, 'I'm meant to be happy now,' but I was just that shattered. I was just happy it was over. It took every ounce of energy, mentally and physically, I was as shattered as I've ever been, but then that's what winning a World Cup should be like, it should take you right to that limit. We were the number one team in the world for a number of years, but everyone you talked to said, 'Yeah, but you haven't won the World Cup.' It was nice to get rid of that 'but'.

Stephen Donald: Most games in New Zealand the crowd leaves pretty quickly because they don't like getting caught in traffic, but this time they stayed for what seemed like an hour afterwards. It was my last game as an All Black and I was thinking, 'Do I really want to walk up the tunnel now?' I wanted to hang around and soak up as much as I could, I didn't want to leave the moment.

Conrad Smith: Once you're there in the middle, I think it's easier to play than it is to watch. All I was thinking about was the next little job. For us at the end it was about defending and trying to get the ball down the other end. That's all you try and focus on. You don't think about anything else until the whistle's gone.

Piri Weepu: You can't really express how amazing it felt. It was a great occasion and I'm glad we could share it with the people of New Zealand.

Richie McCaw: Stephen Donald a hell of a man and I'm just so pleased for him that he got an opportunity. He didn't dream he would be in a World Cup final and he got to play fifty minutes of it. He said he probably wouldn't have had fifty-one, he was at his limit. We probably didn't play our best, but we played good enough. I take my hat off to every single player who took to the field.

Israel Dagg: The team showed a lot of heart and put their bodies on the line for each other. The whole of New Zealand thought the final was going to be easy but I knew that wasn't the case. It was so hard out there and a lot of thoughts went through my head, but the boys dug deep to get over the line.

Richie McCaw: I don't know if it was the emotional stuff that had gone into that game but I don't think I've been as shattered as that. In the end I went to bed, not too early, but I was knackered. What made me happy, gave me great satisfaction, was the next day when we had the parade through Auckland and you saw how happy everyone was, that we'd been able to do something special. You understand the significance of rugby at a time like that, how huge it is to Kiwis . . . they'd all been part of it, going to the games, supporting us and topped off by us winning the trophy. It was pretty cool.

Cory Jane: It wasn't until I had some time alone that I started to think about how big it was as an individual, for your career. I grew up as a kid wanting to be an All Black, and to win a World Cup, it couldn't get any bigger than that. It was cool to reflect on what it meant to New Zealand, too.

FORTY-FIVE

A SPECIAL ERA

'You could bend him a little, but you could never break him, mentally or physically, and you were always in awe of that'

PLANNING FOR THE new cycle to build on their World Cup success began during the lead-up to 2011, with young players earmarked and, if not given game time, at least spending time in the All Black environment. With Graham Henry drifting into semi-retirement with a knighthood, Steve Hansen succeeded him in the top job. Wayne Smith also stepped down. Chiefs coach Ian Foster and former Canterbury coach Aussie McLean were appointed assistants and Grant Fox became a selector.

A strong playing core from 2011 were retained, including McCaw and Carter, through to the next World Cup in 2015. Rather than succumb to post-World Cup complacency, or planning for England four years on, the priority was on taking their game to a new level. The new players included Aaron Smith, Dane Coles, Beauden Barrett, Brodie Retallick, Sam Cane, Luke Romano, Charlie Faumuina and Julian Savea, who all made an impact. Savea scored three tries on debut against Ireland, the first of three Tests of which the first and third were won comfortably, the second in Christchurch by three points after a last-minute dropped goal by Dan Carter. The Bledisloe Cup was secured for the tenth year, the Sydney Test won 27-19 and the second at Eden Park 22-0, the first time in fifty years the Wallabies had been shut out by the All Blacks. The expanded Sanzar international series now included the Pumas, who were beaten 21-5 in Wellington before an explosive Test against the Springboks in Dunedin. Richie McCaw responded to some heavy treatment with one of his greatest performances while Aaron Smith scored a brilliant solo try in the 21-11 win. Argentina were beaten 54-15 in La Plata, before the Springbok rematch was played at Soweto seven days later. Given their two time-zone changes the All Blacks produced a fine performance to win 32-16 despite having Israel Dagg sin-binned and not being awarded a penalty by Irish referee Alain Rolland until the fifty-fourth minute. Having claimed the new-look Rugby Championship, the All Black streak was at sixteen wins, but once again they were denied at least a share of the world record, when held to an 18-all draw in Brisbane. In hooker Keven Mealamu's 100th Test, the All Blacks made a desperate bid to snatch the game, but Carter's late dropped goal attempt sailed wide. There was still a chance to complete an unbeaten year. Savea scored two tries in each of the big wins over Scotland and Italy and, with Aaron Cruden in great kicking form, Wales were beaten 33-10. Unfortunately, in Cardiff, the team was exposed to the norovirus stomach bug sweeping Britain. By Tuesday night most of the players and management were affected. Although it impacted on their final Test preparation it would be unfair to England to blame the Twickenham loss on the bug. Despite another two tries by Savea, Stuart Lancaster's team inflicted the first loss on the All Blacks in fifteen months.

Opposite: Kieran Read breaks into space against the Wallabies at Eden Park during the 2015 Bledisloe Cup match, supported by Ma'a Nonu and Nehe Milner-Skudder. *FotoSport*

Cory Jane: The coaches were always really good at coming up with different little focuses to get us back on the task at hand. At one point, Steve Hansen drew a circle on the whiteboard and we had to guess what it was. We were saying things like, a stone, a dot? He said, 'It's a full stop,' . . . a full stop on what had happened. He meant if we were going to stay where we were, other teams were going to get better and beat us. If we wanted to be the most dominant team in the world we had to keep winning the Bledisloe Cup, we had to get better every single game, because teams were going to come at us. Every year the rugby changes. You have to improve in little areas, and it can only be little areas, but those little areas make the difference. Teams get to know your style, so you have to keep making little changes to stay ahead of them.

Keven Mealamu: That Test against South Africa in Dunedin stands out for me for the way Richie kept getting up and getting back into it. From a playing point of view, Richie would empty the tank every time, every week. Everything was left out there. So when he asked it of the men around him, you knew he was prepared to go to that place every time. You could bend him a little, but you could never break him, mentally or physically, and you were always in awe of that. It was inspirational . . . this is what my captain can do. We're quite different people, he's a country boy from down south, but we get on really well. The thing I admire most about guys like him is their ability to make other players in the team better.

Ma'a Nonu (2003-15, 103 Tests, 104 games): What was great was that no one was ever able to rest on their laurels, there were always guys pushing us. Conrad and I set a world record for the number of Tests played as a centre partnership, but we were being pushed all the times by guys like Sonny Bill Williams and Ryan Crotty. I watched him Sonny when he played for the Bulldogs and thought he would never come to rugby. Then he switched and went to France and played for Toulon with Tana [Umaga]. I would speak to Tana and to Jerry [Collins] and they would talk about Sonny. Then he came here and I think we were in awe when we saw him. He's so big. But I like to think we pushed each other to the best of our abilities.

Sonny Bill Williams (2010-15, 33 Tests, 33 games): When I first came into the All Blacks squad I felt like I didn't belong, I didn't know anyone. I had come straight from ITM Cup and felt like I was out of my depth. I was still improving as a rugby player. Now that I understand rugby I have got the utmost respect for it.

Andrew Ellis (2006-15, 28 Tests, 28 games): He [SBW] genuinely loves the team and wants it to do well. When you get him away from the spotlight, he's a quiet, humble sort of a guy that loves a joke. He's got a good head on him and he knows very much it's about the team.

Keven Mealamu: You can't take anything away from England when they beat us – they played well . . . Manu [Tuilagi] played really well. It was our last game of the year. You think about all the big Test matches that have been played, guys have been on tour for a while, everyone's a bit tired, a bit on edge, they're tough games to win. And if you don't win then you have to wait until the next year to rectify it.

Cory Jane: We had a brilliant season in 2012. We got right to the end and then there was this bug flying around. Some players were losing it both ends. That's part of life, so no excuses. It was a game where we were flat early and England got up on us. Just after half-time we got the scores back but then we went tail up again and they scored a couple of tries. That's what happens in the All Blacks, teams are out to beat you, if they can beat you it's a good job, a big scalp and England were right there ready for that game. It was a disappointing way to end the year, it's always hard when it's your last game of the season because you have to wait months before you can change that feeling.

The chance to become the first team in the professional era to win every Test in a calendar year would come again in 2013, and this time the All Blacks would not let it pass. Another twelve players were introduced, and depth was building. After a tight first Test, the All Blacks completed a 3-0 sweep of France in June, before a second straight, and even more impressive unbeaten charge through the Rugby Championship. Ben Smith scored a hat-trick from the wing in a high-scoring win over Australia, consecutive wins were put up against Australia, Argentina and South Africa at home before a two-game road trip that would decide the title. Nonu and Conrad Smith played their fiftieth Test together and Ben Smith scored two more against Argentina, before Johannesburg and one of the greatest Tests ever played. The Springboks were motivated after a harsh red card to hooker Bismarck du Plessis had thwarted their hopes at Eden Park, and before a frenzied Ellis Park crowd got out to a 15-7 lead. Two tries by Liam Messam had the All Blacks back in front at the break, only for the Springboks to twice regain the lead in the second half and with two All Blacks yellow-carded by Nigel Owens, the game was within reach for the home team. However, sub Beauden Barrett's brilliant performance in which he scored a try, converted another by Read and cut down a try-bound Willie le Roux, saw the All Blacks emerge with a 38-27 win. Another Bledisloe Cup sweep was completed in a high-scoring game in Dunedin. A testing end of year tour started with a first official All Black Test in Tokyo, Japan beaten 54-5 before France were edged 26-19. England led briefly in the second half at Twickenham. Dan Carter left the field in his 100th Test, but another double by Savea denied England a repeat of 2012. The final match featured one of the most extraordinary finishes in Test history. From the third until the eighty-second minute at Lansdowne Road, Ireland led by as much as 22-7. Johnny Sexton missed a close range penalty that would have put it out of reach. Paul O'Connell and his men looked set to make glorious history. With seventy-nine minutes and thirty-two seconds gone, referee Nigel Owens awarded a ruck penalty to the All Blacks twelve metres inside their own half. One minute and forty-eight seconds, thirty-seven passes and ten phases of breath-taking teamwork later, Dane Coles slipped a miraculous pass for Ryan Crotty to score the equaliser. The drama wasn't over. Aaron Cruden missed a wide-angled conversion, but Ireland charged early. He was given another attempt and didn't miss. It was the All Blacks' greatest escape and they became the first team of the professional era to achieve a 100 per cent winning record in a calendar year.

Keven Mealamu: You go out to warm up at Ellis Park and you can feel the lungs burning. It's about trying to get yourself into second gear, get that second wind. The beginning of the warm-up is quite a struggle, and I remember that day just as I was starting to get my second wind a plane flew over, really low, and I thought, 'Yep, this is the home of South African rugby.' The way we started looking at challenges meant we went in thinking how awesome it would be to win there. Turning a burden into a challenge was what it was about.

Aaron Cruden: I was pretty stoked to get a second opportunity [at the conversion against Ireland]. My kicking style didn't change throughout the game so you would have thought they would be aware of that little stutter I do to calm myself. It was a shame they charged early but for us, it was great to have another chance and see it go over. You can sense runners coming as you line-up the kick but you're trying to stay focused. I suppose it was a reprieve, and I was pretty happy to see the flags go up after I'd kicked it. I would say that was the biggest kick of my life. I don't think it comes down to the kick: with thirty seconds to go we were able to get a penalty and launch an attack.

Keven Mealamu: I wasn't playing, I was bringing on the kicking tee for Aaron. You have to give it to the guys for the way they kept their composure, maintained clarity, and kept executing . . . It's important not to get caught up in the situation, not get too excited, aroused or emotional at the situation, just to stick to the task. It was the ability to keep that composure, keep working at it right to the very end that got us through.

Cory Jane: It was similar to 2012, where we'd played so well for so long, and then got to the last game of the year [Ireland]. If you're not all there, if the attitude's not there, teams are going to pip you. Ireland obviously didn't want to be the team that allowed us to have a perfect season. At the end I was sitting on the bench with Izzy, we'd been subbed off and were thinking, 'Oh no', and then they came up with 12-15 phases and built and built and built and [Ryan] Crotty became the national hero. It was one of those games where

Ryan Crotty goes over to break Irish hearts and end hopes of a first ever victory over New Zealand. InphoPhotography

Ireland deserved to win. They'd done everything in their power to beat the All Blacks, but in the end just the composure destroyed them. They were genuinely heartbroken, they played a hell of a game . . . the crowd were great, they deserved it, and you almost felt sorry for them. It was a huge way to end the year.

Steve Hansen: We've always felt that the All Blacks are at thier strongest when the forwards are running and catching and passing as well as doing the set piece. If you go back to the late-1960s and the great All Black team that really captured my imagination you had Kel Tremain, Brian Lochore, Colin Meads, Waka Nathan, Ken Gray, so many great forwards who could carry. It gives you so much versatility across the park when you've got forwards who can do that. It's a skill, so why not teach it? We've worked hard at trying to do that.

By 2014 the All Blacks turned extricating themselves from tight spots into an art form, although not as successfully as in 2013. They needed a seventy-seventh minute Conrad Smith try to win the first of three Tests against England in June, and survived a late England comeback in Dunedin to win by one point, before a more comfortable win in Hamilton. That took them to seventeen wins. Again their record bid stalled. A below-par showing against Australia resulted in a tryless 12-all draw. They rebounded to put 50 on the Wallabies at Eden Park, eased to a 28-9 win over Argentina in Napier and edged the Springboks 14-10 in a tense match in Wellington, Mealamu's 100th Test victory. After beating Argentina in la Plata to confirm another championship title, the All Blacks' run of twenty-two games without defeat ended at Ellis Park. Repeat showings on the stadium screen of an illegal challenge by All Black flanker Liam Messam persuaded referee Wayne Barnes to award a penalty two minutes from time, which was slotted from fifty-five metres by Pat Lambie – the Springboks' first win over the All Blacks since 2011. They kept their composure to win the third Bledisloe Cup Test in Brisbane by engineering a last-minute try for new centre Malakai Fekitoa. Colin Slade converted from a testing angle for a 29-28 win. New ground was broken at the famous Soldier Field in Chicago in the All Blacks' first official Test on American soil. The match gained rugby an unprecedented level of coverage in the United States, and drew a crowd of 62,000, three times bigger than the previous US record. The All Blacks put on a show for their new audience scoring twelve tries. Another tense encounter with England followed, the All Blacks winning 24-21 and becoming the first nation to record 400 Test victories, having played over 200 fewer games than their nearest rivals France. Scotland put up a fight losing 24-16, before two milestones in a 34-16 win over Wales – Richie McCaw's 100th Test as captain was at the stadium where he first led the side, and Keven Mealamu eclipsed the New Zealand record for first-class games, set at 361 by Colin Meads.

Cory Jane: We drew with Australia in Sydney in the wet in 2014. It was one of those games where you walk off the field knowing you should have won. Then you sit in the review on Monday and watch the number of opportunities you'd created only to throw a stupid pass or do something else wrong. If you can make the chances you create stick it's going to be a different ball game. We took that into the next week at Eden Park, where we managed to get most of it right.

Jerome Kaino: It was tough to come back from Japan, where I had been playing club rugby. In 2011 my role was just to get the ball and take it up, but when I came back things had changed and I really had to work hard at the skill set. It didn't happen straight away and I'm still trying to perfect it. It was a lot different but it was better because there was clarity on what we wanted to do.

Cory Jane: Chicago is a pretty cool place. You'd walk into shops, and they'd go, 'Are you the Noo Zealand rugby players?' They'd want to chat, ask what rugby is about. They'd talk about how physical rugby is. As for the game, it wasn't so much about the result. We wanted to play well, help build rugby in America, get people excited about the game. They're not one of the strongest teams in the world, but to have the crowd as packed as it was, and for them to come out and put in some big hits, put some pressure on us, it showed how big the occasion was for them.

Pinpointing a precise start to the build-up for 2015 is difficult. Great efforts had gone into enabling players to function in adversity, dealing with an unsympathetic referee, coping with having players in the sin-bin, playing in front of hostile crowds, and making the right decisions under duress. Although the All Blacks entered 2015 as World Cup favourites, they felt there were several teams likely to threaten their grip on the Webb Ellis Trophy. A long overdue match in Samoa was an ideal opportunity to take the team, in Hansen's words, 'outside their comfort zone' with a match in hot weather against a motivated Samoan team that pushed them to a 25-16 conclusion. The Rugby Championship was cut to four games, with the All Blacks having one home game against Argentina, and two away in Johannesburg and Sydney. The Pumas were seen off in Christchurch, and with Highlanders flyhalf Lima Sopoaga making a brilliant debut at Ellis Park, the Springboks were beaten 27-20. The series was decided in Sydney, and like four years earlier, the Wallabies claimed the title with a confidence-boosting 27-19 win, despite two sparkling tries by new All Black wing Nehe Milner-Skudder, a relative of 1970s All Blacks George Skudder and Henare Milner. That gave the Wallabies another shot at the Bledisloe Cup, but the All Blacks hit back to record a crushing 41-13 win at Eden Park.

The players celebrate another Bledisloe triumph. *FotoSport*

Keven Mealamu: Playing that Test in Samoa was very special. My Mum was born in New Zealand, her family comes from one of the other islands, but my Dad came from the same island (Upolu) where the Test was being played. He was so stoked to be able to see us play a Test in Samoa. You know how proud your Dad is when he comes from Samoa, but he's wearing his All Black jersey. He wore it the whole time! He had a smile one side of his face to the other. The day we went in the parade, the day before the Test, the whole road all the way to the parade was decorated. I was sitting with Woody in the back of the bus and he couldn't believe how the whole country had turned out to see us.

Jerome Kaino: Ellis Park is a special ground. They can get quite aggressive there, just like at Loftus Versfeld, but running out in an All Blacks jersey is really special. When the South Africans score points it is deafening. When we play in South Africa we prepare ways we can communicate with each other because there is a lot of noise. If you keep making mistakes the crowd get into you. I had been subbed by the time we got a lineout near their line, but I knew they were going to call a move to put Richie through the middle to score. We had practised it during the week but I didn't think it was going to come off as well as it did.

Brodie Retallick: (2012-15, 47 games, 47 Tests): It was our last roll of the dice, it was pretty special. Obviously you have got to be in the right place on the park to do it and it just worked out well that that was where we ended up and we were able to try it. The ball was lobbed into the space between two lifting pods and Rich took it from the scrum-half position and scored.

Richie McCaw: We hadn't been down their end for a long time and you have to feel what is happening during the game. We defended for a while then we got back down the other end and had this chance to pull a rabbit from the hat – and it worked and we won the game.

Lima Sopoaga (2015, 1 game, 1 Test): I was always confident about walking into that arena, at Ellis Park, I felt I had played well throughout the season; obviously, we won the Super Rugby title [with the Highlanders], and I had so much experience around me. I had my good mate Aaron Smith on my inside, I had the best mid-field pairing in the world on my outside, I had Richie McCaw as captain. You've got Ben Smith on the wing; it's just like 'how can I go wrong? All I have to do is my job' and that's exactly what I tried to do. I had a kick to win the game and I nailed it. It was a hell of a way to celebrate your first cap.

Richie McCaw: I got a standing ovation at Eden Park after we beat Australia. It's hard to explain but I didn't want that moment to stop. It's a memory I will always have and even talking about it now I feel a bit of a shiver down my spine. It was awesome.

Dan Carter: The crowd at Eden Park was amazing. The way they hung around afterwards to listen to Richie speak was awesome. There are so many great memories that I'll cherish forever from playing with him. He was just a machine and a real inspiration to play alongside; he deserves every accolade he gets. He was a special player and I was very fortunate to play alongside him. And above all that, he is a great man and a great friend.

FORTY-SIX

THE HISTORY MAKERS

'You realise that no person is bigger than the team.
Your job is to enhance and add to that legacy'

THE 2015 WORLD Cup was a massive success, played in excellent conditions promoting positive rugby – ideal for the defending champions. Their early form was questioned by a compulsively nervous sector of the New Zealand fan base, however. Their pool win was guaranteed after a hard-fought opening win against Argentina in front of a World Cup record crowd at Wembley, during which the All Blacks were reduced to thirteen men at one point. Namibia, Georgia and Tonga all put up stirring performances, the scores 58-14, 43-10 and 47-9 a far cry from the landslides of the past. But, for the All Blacks, the tournament was only just starting. Their plan was to hit their stride in the final three weeks. A quarter-final with France in Cardiff brought back bad memories for Kiwi fans, but their nerves were soon calmed as the All Blacks produced a stunning performance. From Brodie Retallick's chargedown of a clearing kick which he gathered and scored, the All Blacks cut the French to ribbons, scoring nine tries, three to an uncontainable Julian Savea including one that Jonah Lomu would have been proud of. Seven were converted by Carter, who played his best rugby in several years. That put the All Blacks into a semi-final with the Springboks. With heavy rain threatening at Twickenham, a different kind of strategy was needed. It was a tight contest, worthy of the best traditions of their rivalry. The All Blacks used their kicking game to great effect, but with Handre Pollard goal-kicking accurately, they were unable to put the Boks away. A crucial moment near the end, when Sam Whitelock won a crucial lineout steal, gave the All Blacks the field position they needed to close out a nerve-shredding 20-18 win to advance to their fourth final. The Wallabies won through the so-called 'Group of Death', beating Wales and the tournament's disappointment England, before a controversial escape from their quarter-final against Scotland and a more convincing win over the Pumas in their semi. Given their form, and their less arduous path through the pool phase, the All Blacks were heavily-backed to win the final, and were on course early in the second half. Milner Skudder's try before half-time, and a brilliant scything run by Nonu from a Williams' offload had them out to a 21-3 lead. But Ben Smith's sin-binning for a dangerous tackle changed things. The Wallabies roared back with two tries to close to 21-17, before a dropped goal from an ice-cool Carter and a blistering kick-chase by Beauden Barrett restored the advantage, the All Blacks taking a memorable match 34-17 – the highest scoring World Cup final – at the end of a memorable tournament. They became the first team to defend the Webb Ellis Trophy, and the first to win it three times.

Jerome Kaino: There was a lot of excitement as we headed off to the World Cup, the guys had put the challenge down in 2012 to do something no one had done before and to

Opposite: After a stellar career, Richie McCaw bows out of Test rugby at the conclusion to the 2015 Rugby World Cup. *InphoPhotography*

show that we could win a World Cup away from home. It was very different to preparing in 2011.

Keven Mealamu: When you come under pressure at the World Cup it's different, because you lose and there's no next week. You also know what it's going to be like back home, and all that starts to play on your mind. You have to understand pressure to be able to deal with it. When we started looking into it, one of the things we recognised was that you can't be looking too far ahead. It's about 'what does today look like, what do we have to do today?' We learned to break games down into segments . . . what does the next five minutes look like? Taking a breather when we needed it, taking control of the game so we could dictate the tempo not them, that sort of thing.

Dan Carter: Even though I was a part of the side in 2011 I didn't feel I had contributed as much as I would have liked, especially in those play-off games when I was watching from the sideline. So to be able to impact on the game and help my teammates gave me a lot of satisfaction. I had a lot of confidence in my body that had built up through playing Super Rugby . . . I played a lot of rugby there, and had a really good run, played a lot of eighty-minute games, and so I had confidence that even when I had a little problem with my knee in the quarter-final, it wasn't going to set me back to where I'd been two years before, that I'd done my rehab and I was going to be able to bounce back.

Aaron Smith (2012-15, 47 Tests): We trained quite hard leading up, then you have those little jitters like you're finally here, don't twist an ankle, don't go down the stairs funny, it was just a relief to hear the opening whistle. Getting to play at Wembley was special . . . you're walking through and you can see stuff from all the games that England have played there, the huge moments at that stadium. When I first run on I touch the ground, feel the ground, connect with the ground, show it some respect, then go for a bit of a run around the corner posts, check out the lines, and get into the warm-up. It's something I do, I'd be lost without it.

Dan Carter: During the pool stages we had a couple of eight-day turnarounds and we were training pretty hard. Steve Hansen explained it at the end of the pool stages, telling people not to worry, that we were about to freshen up for the play-off games. But those early trainings were really hard, very physical, and I guess it took a bit of an edge off our pool games. In saying that, we didn't have the hardest pool . . . you've always got to respect your opposition whoever they are, but to be honest a lot of us were really thinking about that quarter-final.

Steve Hansen: Early on there were a lot of nerves and that's usually when you get players doing dumb things, like Richie's foot trip in the Argentina game, which was so unlike him. It was just a matter of settling down and making sure the messages we sent them weren't going to unsettle them any more.

Aaron Smith: We started playing fast . . . I think I got a guy sent off . . . I wasn't trying to get him sent off I was trying to score. I took a quick tap and was trying to get away, but I ran into him, and got thrown by a big Argy fellow and he got sin-binned. We weren't able to capitalise enough. They were playing just as much footy as we were. We'd kick it to them, and they wouldn't kick it back, and so we were doing a lot of tackling. In the second half we wanted to pull the trigger, play our game, we were able to pressure them a lot and their fitness began to flag and they fell away a bit. They were a very good team, Argentina, so it was good to get a couple of late tries and get away.

Dan Carter: The Georgia game was frustrating. We started well, scored three or four tries but then we kind of just threw the ball around, expecting things to happen, and didn't execute. We waited for someone to spark something instead of building pressure, and credit to Georgia, they put us under a lot of pressure, and put us off our game for the middle part of the match.

Ben Smith: (2009-15, 48 Tests, 49 games): People have to give teams like Georgia, Namibia and Tonga a bit of credit for the way they played, the way they were able to put teams under pressure. It was awesome to have the game at Cardiff, the crowd got right in behind the Georgians, and they like to bring physicality to the game. It just shows at the World Cup that if a team plays well enough they can cause an upset. In the back of our minds we knew we hadn't been playing the best rugby. We wanted to put on a good performance to take into the playoffs. Things started to click in the Tongan game.

Samuel Whitelock (2010-15, 73 Tests): Any time in a game we could be behind. We could have players in the sin-bin, a number of different things might not be going our way, a high penalty count going against us, we talked about the next moment, taking that moment and being able to do the best thing you can. There's always going to be a tight moment. Rugby is a game where there's never an easy time to win, there's always a chance for a team to come back.

Aaron Smith: We were where we wanted to be. We'd talked about it, that we were getting four pool games and then a play-off game and we were going to treat it like a final. It was awesome to be part of that because that's when it really starts to count. It's not about the scores in pool games, it's not about bonus points, nothing else matters, as long as you have one more point than them.

Dan Carter: Cardiff 2007 didn't come up in our discussions really, there were only a couple of us, Richie and I, who'd been on the field in that game . . . there were a couple of others, Woody, Kevvy who'd been in the squad, but a lot of our guys were only thirteen or fourteen-years-old at the time and it didn't really have that feeling, or any sense of revenge. We were more concerned about how we'd been playing in the pool stages, because as much as Steve Hansen was telling everyone to keep calm, we knew we hadn't been playing as well as we could have, and if we didn't perform we were going home, so there was a little bit of an edge. Once we found out we were playing France again in Cardiff, well you could either get worried, let the demons come back from that game to get you, or you could embrace it. I couldn't think of a better team to play in a quarter-final.

Jerome Kaino: We planned for something similar to 2007 because we knew they would draw confidence from that, same ground, same game. Our preparation was similar leading into the Wallabies game at the 2011 World Cup, there was a lot of intensity. And our pool games worked in our favour because they didn't all go our way and we had to grind out wins. It all came down to how we were going to impact the French physically. We needed to set the tone early and we never thought the scoreline was going to blow out that much but the guys were focused on not being in their changing room again afterwards. There's always a focus that no matter what the scoreline is we stick to our processes and keep playing. While I was in Japan I noticed that whether the All Blacks were behind or ahead, attitudes didn't change and the Dublin result in 2013 reflected that. When I came in that was the message, 'Nothing changes, whether we're 20 behind or in front, just keep hammering away,' and in the quarter-final we didn't let off. Off-loading comes down to confidence and later in that French game the guys were pretty confident to throw them, and they stuck. With someone like Sonny Bill Williams you are always going to run off him because you know somehow he is going to get that arm free and get the ball away.

Aaron Smith: Play-off footy really changes the dynamic of your approach. To play the French . . . there was so much history but I don't think it got to me in terms of remembering 2007. In '07 I was eighteen and watching as a fan, pretty gutted about what happened. What better place to play than Cardiff? It's such a beautiful stadium, and it holds great memories for me because I'd been there in 2008 with the Under-20s. I always said I wanted to play in that stadium. It showed how much we wanted that game. I'd like to think it was all about the pressure we put on them, but when it got really tough . . . we

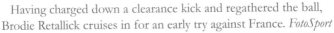

Having charged down a clearance kick and regathered the ball, Brodie Retallick cruises in for an early try against France. *FotoSport*

were playing good footy, not from set piece, it was just our counter-attack and turnover play was good and I think they might have given up a bit which was disappointing, and we weren't in a forgiving mood in a sense of easing up.

The second try . . . the catch from Bender [Ben Smith] was pretty amazing, to put your body on the line like that, I was yelling at him to slow down because if he missed it they could have breached us and I probably would have had to tackle Louis Picamoles! So I was yelling, 'Pull out,' but Bender got it, Richie and Reido did a wicked clean-out, I passed it away to Guzzler [Brodie Retallick] then magic happened really, Julian had his Jonah moment. As soon as he bumped the first guy off I was fist pumping because I knew they weren't going to stop him. The first guy missed him and the second and third guy it was just, 'Get out of the way mate because you're going to be on a highlight reel forever.'

But you need diversity. If you have two big power wingers it can restrict your play . . . Julian's a very good ball player mind, but Nehe [Milner-Skudder] can get in there and ball

Julian Savea brushes off Scott Spedding of France to score a spectacular try. *InphoPhotography*

play, he's very quick and he got some wicked tries because he can beat a guy clean. Julian may not need to step you because he can run straight over you or fend you. They're both dangerous because they've got pace but they have different weapons.

Ben Smith: [Carter and I] we might have been on the same wavelength. I might have given him a signal, just to chuck it up and I tried to chase it as good as I could. It was instinct really. The first thing is you've got to chase hard to get there and compete, and then it's trying to keep your eye on the ball, not worry where the French guy is. I remember getting up off the ground and Julian was bowling guys left, right and centre. It's always good see him with ball in hand, and it showed how destructive he can be. It was one of the moments that stuck out for me at the World Cup.

Dan Carter: It was a pretty special performance. We'd have been happy to win by one point to give ourselves another week, but to put 60 points on a French side in a play-off match, is almost unheard of . . . everything that day clicked. We got the balance right between wanting to enjoy that occasion after the game, so we did that, it was a game to be proud of, but we knew the following week against the Boks was going to be a completely different challenge. We couldn't just expect to roll through the week and have another performance like Cardiff.

Steve Hansen: We've got some pretty skilful guys who are comfortable on the ball under pressure and can create space for others. When you get that, you're a hard team to beat. You've got your set plays, but then you have the unstructured game where you can decide to do whatever you want. And we've chosen to say, 'Right, we've got eight forwards who can catch and pass' . . . you saw it in the French game with Joe Moody with a nice pass around the back, Charlie Faumuina's another who can do it. But we haven't forgotten their primary role is to win scrum, lineout and breakdown ball. And using our forwards the way we do, means our backs have to be good at the breakdown, because you can't be everywhere at once.

Aaron Smith: The good thing about the All Black game plan, Steve Hansen is always telling us that wingers are supposed to score tries, so the rest of us have to do our job to help them. That's why people are pretty humble about scoring, because they know it's a case of everyone doing their job that has created the space for them to get over the line.

Dan Carter: We're lucky enough to play the Springboks a couple of times a year, so you get a good understanding of how they like to play. They often fly up from the outside to put us under a lot of pressure. That means there's often a lot of space in behind them, often with just one fullback because their wingers are rushing up on the outside. If you look back at that game there were a lot of grubbers to the corners, a lot of up and unders. Their fullback was isolated because of the way their wingers like to defend. It wasn't a huge strategy that we took into the game with us, it was just a case of playing what we saw, and that was the picture we were seeing. They always feed well off mistakes and pressure, so controlling territory is a big part of playing the Springboks.

Richie McCaw leads the haka before the semi-final. *FotoSport*

Ben Smith: I remember getting to Twickenham, the rain was coming and I knew the South Africans would probably test us in the air, but I knew we could test them at the same time. The conditions meant it was better to put some contestables up and chase them.

Aaron Smith: It's the old foe, the South Africans. It's always a good game against them, it's always very physical, we respect them a lot and they respect us which is good and there's not much real dirtiness or anything like that, it's just, 'Let's play rugby as hard as we can and whoever's the better team will come out with the win.' That game felt like it took forever. There were a lot of mauls, a lot of scrums, and we struggled to get our game going. They had a really good plan about how they wanted to kick, using the high ball, using Bryan Habana in the air, and also with their maul. Once it gets going it's hard to stop, and the way Pollard was kicking it wasn't looking too grouse. But in the last twenty minutes we really stepped up our 'D' and they got a bit tired and their skills started dropping off. We were still pretty fresh and raring to go and really showed how much it meant, how much we wanted to make the final, and that last twenty minutes our defence was awesome.

Jerome Kaino: In the first half against South Africa we weren't playing the way we wanted. We were trying to beat them up the middle and were getting smashed. I got into a dark place getting a yellow card but at half-time the messages were quite clear that we had gone away from our game. If we played the edges and played into space we would make inroads. I thought Dan controlled the team really well but it was a typical All Blacks-Springboks game, they were always going to be abrasive and it was just a matter of us holding onto our own ball and hitting the spaces.

The players celebrate at the full-time whistle.
They were into a second consecutive World Cup final. *InphoPhotography*

Dan Carter: Teams like to shut us down from the outside, something that we hadn't always adjusted to, and so during the World Cup we worked on beating that, and we ran a lot of plays with that in mind, and to get a try [Jerome Kaino] from something you'd been practicing all tournament, for Richie to pop that ball over the top to Jerome like that, was pretty satisfying, especially in such an important game. There was a lot of self-belief that we were controlling the game. Even though the score was pretty close, in their favour at times, we still felt like we were controlling the game, it's just that we weren't getting any points.

It was a bit frustrating because they'd be in our half for just a few minutes and they'd get a penalty, a shot at goal and they kept the scoreboard ticking over. We were down to fourteen men, lacking a bit of momentum, under the pump a bit. We had a lineout and it turned into messy ball, and it was thrown to me. Obviously South Africa would have felt good about the lineout, and the fact we had only fourteen men, so to slot three points from a dropped goal like that, you could just see the body language in the opposition drop. I was really proud of how we played through the last ten minutes of that game, how we controlled the territory, controlled the game and were able to close it out. That's the unique thing about that All Black side, no matter what situation we were in, we backed ourselves to get out of it, to get the win.

Aaron Smith: Richie being able to pop that ball over the top to Jerome, that's the beauty of being able to play what you see, and not be restricted to a game plan. It was the same with Dan's dropped goal – he just hit it, that was pretty cool, because he was still moving. He just caught it and snapped a droppy . . . then he did the same thing a week later. Sam [Whitelock] and Reido are amazing at reading the lineouts, and they seemed pretty confident about it. We gave away a penalty I think and they had a lineout on the fifty which was pretty dangerous because if they had a maul and we stopped it, the way Pollard was kicking, it could have turned a bit hairy. I was thinking, 'Sam it would be good if you got this one.' It was really hosing down by that stage too, and he got up and tipped it back nicely, and I just dived on it, and we reset. That was a big moment in the game a real momentum shift for us, especially against Victor Matfield, knowing how good their lineout was. It was tough on him, he probably should have called it away from him.

Samuel Whitelock: The first thing we'd talked about, as a team, the lineout leaders, was to compete in the air. We'd done really well throughout most of the game, getting up, competing, getting a fingertip to balls, a couple of times we'd stolen their ball. Everyone knew if we gave them free ball we could be in trouble. Victor came on, and the lineout forward he is, we knew he was probably going to call to himself, and we'd planned for that, to get someone in the air around him. It was important to get someone high, to have good strong lifts. We knew if they won the ball they were going to drive it. They'd had some success against us in the game with that, if we'd given away a penalty they'd have been in front. So we had to get up and compete without giving away advantage or a penalty. It was critical for us. It was a really good lift from the guys. I got nice and high and managed to take the ball. You could feel a bit of relief amongst the guys, we only had a couple of minutes to go and we could close the game out.

Steve Hansen: There was a natural edge throughout the week before we played Australia because it was a final, and they'd beaten us earlier in the year. We don't like losing to Australia. During the week it was about making sure we didn't play the final on Thursday, or at the captain's run, just building the momentum so you have a full tank on Saturday ready to play right at kick-off, and not before, and our staff did a great job, our wellbeing staff, the medical team. We had every player bar one available for selection, which was incredible. The guys that weren't in the twenty-three did an amazing job. They did what they needed to do to prepare well for themselves, but they made sure the team was able to prepare well at training by doing the things we thought the Australians might do. We couldn't have had them any better than we had them. It was a case of 'let's make the most of the luck we get, and deal with the bad lack, because we'll get them in the same amount.'

Dan Carter: We knew the Australians were a quality side and if they could get the right platform they could score some amazing tries. They were a huge threat. It started up front, and our big boys, our forwards, really turned up in the final and made it tough for them to get their plays done. Set piece is where it all started. I guess we built as the World Cup went on . . . I'm not saying the Aussies didn't, they were deserving finalists, but it felt like we had good control of the match.

Keven Mealamu: Trying to go to sleep the night before the 2011 final, I couldn't, there was so much going through my mind . . . what ifs, things you can't control. The night before the 2015 final, I had an awesome sleep. In 2011 you could feel the tension in the team, 2015 we were excited about it, we wanted to go out and express ourselves, just show what we were all about. There were a few short breaths at one point. When I was told to warm up we were ahead by two tries. By the time I got to the sideline ready to go on, we were only up by three points. I guess the way we looked at it, it was an awesome challenge for us to try and finish well.

Steve Hansen: Ten minutes before half-time I felt Australia were starting to really get into their stride. I leaned over to Foz [Ian Foster] and said, 'I reckon we can put the big man [Sonny Bill Willaims] on, and he's going to hurt them.' He's a different kind of player to Conrad. Conrad had played really well up to that point and it might sound strange thinking to change your midfield up at that stage, but there was a big difference between the two of them and it was something I didn't think the Australians would expect. I think we caught them off guard. Sonny made a couple of good plays, got the ball away, stole some ball. I thought he was outstanding the whole World Cup Sonny, coming off the bench he made a massive difference in the Argentina game. He really lifted the whole bench. It's a twenty-three-man game – they wanted to make a difference and he led that. One of our big advantages at the World Cup was our bench.

Dan Carter: Nonu's try was pure genius from Sonny and Ma'a. It's not something you can train – it was just general play, Sonny managed to get an offload away and Ma'a ran through a hole. It had nothing to do with their defensive pattern or any strategy it was about backing your instincts, and for Ma'a to finish the try off like that was pretty special.

Having replaced Conrad Smith at half-time in the final, Sonny Bill Williams prepares to slip a game-changing off-load to Ma'a Nonu. *InphoPhotography*

That ten-minute period when Bender was in the sin-bin and they scored a couple of tries and we were defending for long periods of time, was pretty draining, and there was a time in that ten-minute period when the momentum of the game had completely shifted to Australia and we were under the pump. They were right on the comeback trail.

Aaron Smith: We knew the Australians always have points in them. Their maul is a very big weapon. As soon as Bender got binned, they put it out, mauled and scored, we knew we were in a bit of trouble off the bat. But then you saw the true spirit of our leaders. They were just so calm. 'Let's do this, trust the plan.' We'd talked a lot about what we'd do if this player or that got sent off, how we'd change the plan . . . but when your fullback gets sent off it can be interesting because he covers the back, the wingers the sides, so the wingers had to cover half the field. When Will Genia did that kick I was hoping it would go out, but no, it bounced, sat up and the scored a try. But then we got back to fifteen men we got going again, and we got through it. It would have been a bit hairy if we'd played the last ten minutes with fourteen men, but because he was sent off in the middle stages, I knew he'd come back on and make up for it, and he did that.

Ben Smith: We'd played Australia twice that year and they'd beaten us over in Australia and we beat them at Eden Park, so it was one-all for the year. They had a great team and they'd been playing really good rugby. They certainly deserved to be there. It was a long week and there were certainly a few nerves.

I'm sorry about the yellow card. I didn't mean to do it, I just got into a bad position technique-wise and I lifted him. As soon as I did it I thought, 'I'm in trouble here.' I had never had a yellow card before and I get one in the World Cup final. Once I found the seat . . . I couldn't find it at first, I spent the first two minutes thinking, 'You idiot.' Then I started thinking that I would have a chance to go back on and I needed to make an impact when I did. While I was on the bench they scored two tries and it got a whole lot closer. At one stage if the ball had gone out I would have been able to get back on with only seven points down, but it didn't go out and they got a second one. I was thinking, 'I'm going to have to shift my wife and daughter to live somewhere other than New Zealand.' The gap was really close when I came back on but we started to get a couple of opportunities, we started to get down in their half.

Aaron Smith: A big moment was DC's dropped goal. The play was more of a setup play to get to a drop-kick, but it didn't really work, we didn't get enough gainline. It was average . . . I couldn't hit the forwards because they'd get smashed so I threw it to Dan and he just hit it. I didn't look at the kick, but I can remember hearing him yelling at it.

Dan Carter: To kick that dropped goal and give ourselves a little bit of breathing space was an important part of the game. It was instinctive. But to secure that momentum back, to get that dropped goal and a penalty and get that seven-point buffer . . . Beauden's [Barrett] try was just icing on the cake. I wouldn't know how many dropped goals I've had in my career, a pretty small number probably. I do a lot of practice, a lot of work behind the scenes even if I don't go for many during games and to be able to pull them out at crucial stages in a couple

2015 Rugby World Cup champions lift the Webb Ellis Cup. *InphoPhotography*

of those big games, just to give us a buffer and also help change momentum, it was a pretty good feeling. I'd tried to set a dropped goal up a few plays before that. Ma'a was yelling at me to have a go. The dropped goals weren't planned, we were always encouraged to back our instincts, and that's what those dropped goals were about. With the last penalty I wasn't sure if I had the distance, it was a long way out. I was contemplating with Skip [McCaw], who was trying to tell me to put it in the corner and sort of wind down the clock. But I knew I had adrenaline going through my body and it was such a crucial part of the game, so I wanted to go for it.

Ben Smith: Getting that final try was a great way for us to finish the match. The ball spilled, I managed to get hold of it, and I saw some space at the back, so I kicked it. I had no idea Beaudy was steaming through after it. He did pretty well to control it, it's hard to do when it's bobbling around like that. He did a bit of hot dogging and that was it really. I was pretty buggered at the final whistle. It had been a tough week.

Dan Carter: I was on the other side of the field and missed Ben Smith stepping a couple of guys . . . I saw the ball being kicked ahead and Beauden chasing after it. To be honest

I was pretty buggered by that stage of the game . . . I was like every other Kiwi at that moment, yelling at him to run faster! Game guaranteed right there, with a minute and a half to play.

Aaron Smith: We call him [Barrett] Golden Balls because things just happen around him. I mean who can hack it like that and have it just sit up for him? I don't know how he does some of the things he does. We knew we'd won and I was just so happy to be part of something like that. Something that no one can ever take away from you. It was the best day of my life.

Samuel Whitelock: It was a different feeling for myself. The two or three minutes before the end when Beaudy scored, I was still in game mode, but some of the guys were jumping up and down, Dan must have been nice and relaxed because he kicked the conversion with his other foot. But I was just getting ready for the next kick-off, trying to keep everyone worried about the task, that was my focus, but then when the whistle went it was total joy. I had a real good friend out there in Aaron [Smith]; we'd talked about it when we were at school – we were in the same class at Feilding High School – that one day we'd love to play in a World Cup final and to do it, and see each other out there was pretty special.

Dan Carter: Liam Messam ran on with the kicking tee and said, 'Kick it with your right!' I'd been talking to Aaron Smith at the start of the World Cup and he'd asked if I'd ever kicked a conversion with my right foot. I told him, 'No, but that I'd love to before my Test

Dan Carter and Ma'a Nonu enjoy a well-deserved drink after their final appearance as All Blacks. *FotoSport*

Coach and captain enjoy the spoils after years of hard work and dedication. *InphoPhotography*

career finishes.' Aaron said, 'Imagine if we're more than seven points up at the end of the World Cup final, would you do it?' and I said, 'Yeah of course I would.' So Liam said to have a go, and I said, 'Right,' and then he went, 'No, no, no I don't want you to miss it,' but I said, 'Man I'm going to do it,' but I tried to do it quickly so no one would notice, which is a bit hard with all the TV cameras and 80,000 people watching the game. I was pretty happy when it went over.

Jerome Kaino: Dan worked hard to be at the World Cup and to play well after missing out in 2011. He had a lot of injuries ahead of 2015 but he put in a lot of work before the World Cup and was still the best in the world. He worked hard and produced the best. I was pleased with the way he came back and played in the quarter, semi and final. When I was in the sin-bin, the way he got the dropped goal against South Africa after the five-man lineout was perfect and just what the team needed. And his dropped goal against Australia was perfect timing. Throughout all those play-off games he was the man for us.

Steve Hansen: In 2011 it was definitely relief, we had such a big monkey to get off our back. The second time it felt more satisfying, because most of the things we wanted to do we did well, they worked. It was one of the best World Cup finals and we'd won it and we were pretty proud of that. You had so many guys who were finishing and to see them finishing on such a high was very satisfying.

Jerome Kaino: It's an era people will look back on and say how lucky we were to see guys like Dan and Richie play. It has been a huge honour to play alongside them. Richie did a lot around the team off the field, and after great performances it is easy for a team to relax a bit but that didn't happen with Richie at the helm. I think that leadership was perfect for how we performed. We can attribute a lot of what we achieved to his leadership.

Richie McCaw: Steve's [Hansen] led the way in terms of the attitude that the team aspired to. The standards that we kept were led from the top and it made it easy to follow along. In 2012, after the World Cup win, it would have been easy to roll into that year and live off what we had done previously, but the standard was set straight back up high again – we were going to play and have the world champion tag and deserve that each year. And that was the attitude right the way through.

When you become an All Black, that's the attitude that you inherit. You come into a team where a lot of good men have gone before you. The All Blacks, for over a hundred-plus years, have, more often than not, gone out and performed well on the field and I think that's what you feel – that responsibility. Straight away you realise that. Coming into the team you realise that no person is bigger than the team. Your job is to enhance and add to that legacy. You don't have to do anything more special than what gets you there but just doing it every week is the key.

And so, 110 years after first arriving in the UK, the All Blacks took their place again at the head of the rugby table. The win in the 2015 World Cup final was their 413th out of 538, a success percentage of almost seventy-nine per cent. Richie McCaw would retire after a record 148 Tests, 110 as captain and having played in 131 wins, Dan Carter would step away as the highest points scorer in Test rugby, and other notable players Keven Mealamu, Conrad Smith, Ma'a Nonu and Tony Woodcock (who'd been injured midway through the tournament) could end their careers on a high note. Almost as importantly to them and their fans, they'd been able to achieve the victory in style, playing the open, creative and yet still physical game that had, for much of a glorious history, been the hallmark of All Blacks rugby.

REFERENCES

PUBLICATIONS
New Zealand Rugby World
Rugby World
The New Zealand Footballer
The New Zealand Sportsman
New Zealand Listener
Sports Digest
The Evening Post
The Guardian
The New Zealand Herald
The Otago Daily Times
The Southland Times
The Dominion Sunday Times
New Zealand Truth
New Zealand Listener
The Referee (Sydney)
The Art of Rugby Football, Thomas Ellison
The Complete Rugby Footballer on the New Zealand System, Billy Stead and Dave Gallaher
All Blacks and Springboks, Graham Barrow
Haka! The All Blacks Story, Winston McCarthy
Rugby: A New Zealand History, Ron Palenski
Last Post: Rugby's Wartime Roll Call, Ron Palenski
Living the Dream, Mils Muliaina/Lynn McConnell
McKechnie, Double All Black, Brian McKechnie/Lynn McConnell
Something to Crow About, Lynn McConnell
History of South African Rugby Football, Ivor D. Difford
It's Me Tiger, Peter Jones and Norman Harris
Don Clarke Champion, Richard Becht
Owaka Jack: The Jack McNab Story – Shirley Deuchrass
Rugby on Attack, Ron Jarden
The Bob Scott Story, Bob Scott and Terry McLean
Pathway Among Men, Jim Burrows

TAONGA (NZ SOUND ARCHIVE)
Reid Masters (T 582)
Miscellaneous v Springboks (T1142)
Harold Abbott, George Nepia (T366)
Ron Dobson (T371)
Neville Thornton (T437)
Bob Stuart (T367)
Bob Duff, Ron Jarden (1146)
Denis Young (T497)
1905 All Black Reunion (D1167)
Miscellaneous v Lions (T582)

SKY TV
Weight of a Nation Documentary and interviews, 2012
Seven Games Documentary and interviews, 2016

OTHER
State Library of New South Wales
Mitchell Library

1: James Allan
2: Henry Braddon
3: George Carter
4: John Dumbell
5: George Helmore
6: John Lecky
7: William Millton
8: Timothy O'Connor
9: James O'Donnell
10: Henry Roberts
11: George Robertson
12: Thomas Ryan
13: John Taiaroa
14: Hart Udy
15: Peter Webb
16: Edward Millton
17: Joe Warbrick
18: Robert Wilson
19: Edwin Davy
20: Henry Butland
21: Sam Cockroft
22: Archibald D'Arcy
23: Thomas Ellison
24: David Gage
25: John Gardner
26: Francis Jervis
27: James Lambie
28: William McKenzie
29: Frederick Murray
30: Walter Pringle
31: Graham Shannon
32: Charles Speight
33: Hoeroa Tiopira
34: Tabby Wynyard
35: Alfred Bayly
36: Maurice Herrold
37: John Mowlem
38: Angus Stuart
39: Charles Macintosh
40: Henry Wilson
41: George Harper
42: Alan Good
43: Roderick Gray
44: Robert McKenzie
45: Robert Oliphant
46: Billy Watson
47: William Balch
48: Walter Bayly
49: Alfred Cooke
50: Hugh Good
51: Daniel Hughes
52: George Humphreys
53: George Maber
54: Dick Stewart
55: John Swindley
56: Lewis Allen
57: Harry Frost
58: Alec Kerr
59: Peter McDonnell
60: Nisbet McRobie
61: Sydney Orchard
62: Thomas Pauling
63: William Roberts
64: Frank Surman
65: Donald Watson
66: Francis Young
67: John Blair
68: Joseph Calnan
69: Jimmy Duncan
70: Robert Handcock
71: Bill Hardcastle
72: William Harris
73: Arthur Humphries
74: George William Smith
75: William Wells
76: Alexander Armit
77: Frank Brooker
78: Ernest Glennie
79: Alex Wilson
80: Hugh Mills
81: John Burt
82: Bill Cunningham
83: Ernie Dodd
84: William Hay-MacKenzie
85: John Jacob
86: Robert McGregor
87: John O'Brien
88: Bernard O'Dowda
89: Charles Purdue
90: Dan Udy
91: Morrie Wood
92: Tom Cross
93: Loftus Armstrong
94: Albert Asher
95: Reuben Cooke
96: Dave Gallaher
97: Frederick Given
98: Henry Kiernan
99: Henry Kiernan
100: Andrew Long
101: Duncan McGregor
102: Archie McMinn
103: George Nicholson
104: John Stalker
105: Billy Stead
106: George Tyler
107: Billy Wallace
108: Bernard Fanning
109: Harry Porteous
110: John Spencer
111: Billy Glenn
112: Eric Harper
113: Patrick Harvey
114: Paddy McMinn
115: Charlie Seeling
116: Steve Casey
117: Frank Glasgow
118: Jimmy Hunter
119: Mona Johnston
120: Simon Mynott
121: Fred Newton
122: James O'Sullivan
123: Fred Roberts
124: Hector Thomson
125: John Corbett
126: George Gillett
127: Ernest Booth
128: Alexander McDonald
129: Bob Deans
130: Harold Abbott
131: William Mackrell
132: Bob Bennet
133: George Burgess
134: Arthur Francis
135: Colin Gilray
136: Donald Macpherson
137: Pat Purdue
138: William Smith
139: Hubert Turtill
140: Eric Watkins
141: Edgar Wrigley
142: John Colman
143: Frank Fryer
144: Ned Hughes
145: Frank Mitchinson
146: George Spencer
147: Alfred Eckhold
148: Harry Paton
149: John Hogan
150: Donald Cameron
151: Ranji Wilson
152: Paddy Burns
153: George Gray
154: Donald Cameron Hamilton
155: Peter Murray
156: Alexander Paterson
157: William Reedy
158: Harold Hayward
159: Sam Bligh
160: Alf Budd
161: David Evans
162: William Fuller
163: Joe O'Leary
164: Jimmy Ridland
165: Jack Stohr
166: Frank Wilson
167: Gerald McKellar
168: James Maguire
169: James Ryan
170: Henry Avery
171: Billy Mitchell
172: Frederick Ivimey
173: Henry Atkinson
174: John Cuthill
175: Henry Dewar
176: Albert Downing
177: Tom Lynch
178: Dougie McGregor
179: Jock McKenzie
180: Toby Murray
181: Dick Roberts
182: George Sellars
183: Henry Taylor
184: Peter Williams
185: Jim Wylie
186: Alex Bruce
187: Mick Cain
188: James Douglas
189: James Graham
190: James Baird
191: James Barrett
192: Charles Brown
193: William Cummings
194: William Francis
195: Mac Geddes
196: Charles Gillespie
197: Edward Hasell
198: Victor Macky
199: James McNeece
200: Gus Spillane
201: James Stewart
202: Reginald Taylor
203: Eric Cockroft
204: Alfred Fanning
205: James Tilyard
206: George Loveridge
207: Edward Roberts
208: John Irvine
209: William Lindsay
210: Jack O'Brien
211: Bobby Black
212: Tom Fisher
213: Lyn Weston
214: Beethoven Algar
215: Ces Badeley
216: David Baird
217: Alphonsus Carroll
218: Jim Donald
219: William Duncan
220: Hohepa Jacob
221: Charles McLean
222: James Moffitt
223: Jack Steel
224: Percy Storey
225: Alfred West
226: Ernest Belliss
227: Vivian Wilson
228: Jack Shearer
229: George Aitken
230: Richard Fogarty
231: Charles Kingstone
232: Harry Nicholls
233: Marcus Nicholls
234: Johnstone Richardson
235: Andrew White
236: Les McLean
237: Laurie Brownlie
238: Phillippe Cabot
239: Cyril Edward Evans
240: Charles Fletcher
241: William Ford
242: Paul Markham
243: Lou Petersen
244: Edmond Ryan
245: Sydney Shearer
246: Jock Turnbull
247: Francis Ward
248: William Fea
249: Karl Ifwersen
250: Keith Siddells
251: Reginald Bell
252: Les Cupples
253: Charles Fitzgerald
254: Harold Masters
255: Robert Mathieson
256: Andrew O'Brien
257: Frank Smyth
258: Kenneth Svenson
259: Alexander Williams
260: Victor Badeley
261: Maurice Brownlie
262: Umberto Calcinai
263: George Dickinson
264: Percy Hickey
265: Sam Gemmell
266: David McMeeking
267: Jimmy Mill
268: Waate Potaka
269: Len Righton
270: Jimmy Sinclair
271: Frank Snodgrass
272: Peina Taituha
273: Fred Tilyard
274: Joseph Bell
275: Quentin Donald
276: Fred Lucas
277: Patrick McCarthy
278: Arnold Perry
279: Alexander Pringle
280: William Irvine
281: Read Masters
282: Herman Morgan
283: Harold Nicholls
284: Tiaki Ormond
285: Lui Paewai
286: Cliff Porter
287: Edward Stewart
288: Ron Stewart
289: Robert Tunnicliff
290: Handley Brown
291: Cyril Brownlie
292: Bert Cooke
293: Gus Hart
294: Henry Munro
295: George Nepia
296: Bill Dalley
297: Brian McCleary
298: Neil McGregor
299: Jim Parker
300: Alan Robilliard
301: Ian Harvey
302: James Archer
303: Jackie Blake
304: Bill Elvy
305: Innes Finlayson
306: Jack Harris
307: Lance Johnson
308: Alexander Kirkpatrick
309: Laurie Knight
310: Mick Lomas
311: Herman Mattson
312: John Walter
313: George Wise
314: Donald Wright
315: David Dickson
316: Jack McNab
317: Tommy Corkill
318: Davy Johnston
319: Arthur Law
320: Gordon Lawson
321: Arthur Thomas
322: Archie McCormick
323: Bill Hazlett
324: Arthur Knight
325: Toby Sheen
326: Don Stevenson
327: Geoff Alley
328: Bill Wright
329: Bert Grenside
330: Swinbourne Hadley
331: Herb Lilburne
332: George Scrimshaw
333: John Swain
334: Sydney Carleton
335: Edward Ward
336: James Burrows
337: Frank Kilby
338: David Lindsay
339: Ruben McWilliams
340: Charlie Rushbrook
341: Eric Snow
342: Archie Strang
343: John Hore
344: Walter Batty
345: Nicholas Bradanovich
346: Victor Butler
347: Frank Clark
348: Frank Freitas
349: Arthur Holden
350: Llewellyn Hook
351: William McClymont
352: Charlie Oliver
353: Bert Palmer
354: Dick Steere
355: Stanley Willoughby
356: George Mehrtens
357: Topi Robinson
358: James Howden
359: James Mackay
360: Craig Mackenzie
361: Curly Page
362: Anthony Cottrell
363: Rawi Candy
364: Wiremu Heke
365: Keith Reid
366: Charlie Sonntag
367: Alfred Waterman
368: Clinton Stringfellow
369: Bert Geddes
370: Atholstan Mahoney
371: Walter Reside
372: Robert Souter
373: Jack Tuck
374: Tiny Leys
375: Alfred Kivell
376: George Hart
377: Don Oliver
378: Merv Corner
379: Hubert McLean
380: Nelson Ball
381: Ronald Bush
382: Ted Jessep
383: Don Max
384: Thomas Metcalfe
385: Rusty Page
386: George Purdue
387: Frank Solomon
388: George Bullock-Douglas
389: Harcourt Caughey
390: Ray Clarke
391: Arthur Collins
392: Gordon Innes
393: Jack Manchester
394: Joe Procter
395: Raymond Williams
396: Harold Pollock
397: Ned Barry
398: Edward Holder
399: Jack Griffiths
400: Bill Hadley
401: Arthur Lambourn
402: Hawea Mataira
403: Rod MacKenzie
404: Ronald King
405: John Leeson
406: Charles Smith
407: Mike Gilbert
408: Tori Reid
409: George Adkins
410: Jack Best
411: Douglas Dalton
412: Neville Mitchell
413: Cyril Pepper
414: Joey Sadler
415: Dave Solomon
416: Bill Collins
417: Eric Tindill
418: Frederick Vorrath
419: Henry Brown
420: James Wynyard
421: Everard Jackson
422: Brian Killeen
423: Jack Rankin
424: Jim Watt
425: Jock Wells
426: Colin Gillies
427: Terry Lockington
428: Jack Sullivan
429: Ron Ward
430: Donald Cobden
431: John Dick
432: Jack Hooper
433: Allan Parkhill
434: Harold Simon
435: Jack Taylor
436: David Trevathan
437: Bill Phillips
438: Trevor Berghan
439: Les George
440: Harold Milliken
441: Tom Morrison
442: Charles Quaid
443: Charles Saxton
444: Claude Williams
445: Snow Bowman
446: Bill Carson
447: Arthur Wesney
448: Alan Wright
449: Fred Allen
450: Walter Argus
451: Has Catley
452: Jack Dunn
453: Ken Elliott
454: Ron Elvidge
455: Jack Finlay
456: Harry Frazer
457: Jimmy Haig
458: Morrie McHugh
459: Patrick Rhind
460: Bob Scott
461: Johnny Smith
462: Roy White
463: Charles Willocks
464: Jack McRae
465: Eric Boggs
466: Alf Budd
467: Morrie Goddard
468: Keith Arnold
469: Ben Couch
470: Ray Dalton
471: Lachie Grant
472: Fred Hobbs
473: Jack McLean
474: Johnny Simpson
475: Percy Tetzlaff
476: Neville Thornton
477: Jim Kearney
478: Tim Mason
479: Vincent Bevan
480: Leo Connolly
481: Jim McCormick
482: Peter Smith
483: Tom Webster
484: Arthur Hughes
485: Neville Black
486: Ian Botting
487: Pat Crowley
488: Peter Henderson
489: Jack McNab
490: Larry Savage
491: Kevin Skinner
492: Norman Wilson
493: Graham Delamore
494: Lester Harvey
495: Peter Johnstone
496: Bill Meates
497: Des Christian
498: Bill Conrad
499: Jack Goddard
500: Keith Gudsell
501: Alan Blake
502: Ronald Bryers
503: Ronald Dobson
504: Jack Kelly
505: William Lunn
506: Graham Moore
507: Bill Mumm
508: Thomas O'Callaghan
509: Rex Orr
510: Robert Stuart
511: Richard White
512: Hector Wilson
513: Garth Bond
514: Desmond O'Leary
515: Roy Roper
516: Harrison Rowley
517: George Beatty
518: Nau Cherrington
519: Laurie Haig
520: Graham Mexted
521: John Tanner
522: Maurice Goss
523: Bob Duff
524: Percy Erceg
525: Brian Fitzpatrick
526: Ian Hammond
527: Bill McCaw
528: Eddie Robinson
529: Brian Steele
530: Len Wilson
531: Ron Jarden
532: Tom Lynch
533: Ray Bell
534: Peter Burke
535: Alan Reid